This book creates a new framework for the political and intellectual relations between the British Isles and America in a momentous period which witnessed the formation of modern states on both sides of the Atlantic and the overthrow of an Anglican, aristocratic and monarchical order.

Jonathan Clark integrates evidence from law and religion to explain these events by revealing how the dynamics of early modern societies were essentially denominational. In a study of British and American political discourse, he shows how law and religion were profoundly related and how rival conceptions of liberty were expressed in the conflicts created by Protestant Dissent's hostility to an Anglican hegemony. The book argues that this model provides a key to collective acts of resistance to the established order throughout the period. Its final section focuses on the defining episode for British and American history, and shows the way in which the American Revolution can be understood as a war of religion.

The Language of Liberty stands as part of a project aimed at revising our map of early modern English-speaking societies, which includes Dr Clark's previous books *English Society 1688–1832* (1985) and *Revolution and Rebellion* (1986). This work has implications for both Britain's and the USA's understandings of their historical identities and present predicaments.

THE LANGUAGE OF LIBERTY

THE
LANGUAGE
OF LIBERTY
1660–1832

*Political discourse and social dynamics
in the Anglo-American world*

J. C. D. CLARK

CAMBRIDGE
UNIVERSITY PRESS

Published by the Press Syndicate of the University of Cambridge
The Pitt Building, Trumpington Street, Cambridge CB2 1RP
40 West 20th Street, New York, NY 10011-4211, USA
10 Stamford Road, Oakleigh, Melbourne 3166, Australia

© Cambridge University Press 1994

First published 1994

Printed in Great Britain at the University Press, Cambridge

A catalogue record for this book is available from the British Library

Library of Congress cataloguing in publication data

ISBN 0 521 44510 8 hardback
ISBN 0 521 44957 X paperback

WV

Contents

Preface   *Page* xi
Acknowledgements   xv
List of abbreviations   xvi

INTRODUCTION: THE STRUCTURE OF ANGLO-AMERICAN
POLITICAL DISCOURSE   I

I   Law, religion and sovereignty   I
II   Constitutional innovations and their English antecedents   6
III   The genesis of political discourse   10
IV   Transatlantic ties and their failure   13
V   The Commonwealth paradigm   20
VI   Denominational discourse   29
VII   The implications of theological conflict   35
VIII   Denominational dynamics and political rebellions   41

I THE CONFLICT BETWEEN LAWS: SOVEREIGNTY AND
STATE FORMATION IN THE UNITED KINGDOM AND THE
UNITED STATES   46
I   Law, nationality and nationalism: monarchical allegiance
       and identity   46
II   The creation of the United Kingdom, 1536–1801: religion
       and the origins of the common-law doctrine of sovereignty   62
III   Sovereignty in political theory from Justinian to the English
       jurists   75
IV   Natural law versus common law: the polarisation of a
       common idiom   93
V   Sovereignty, Dissent and the American rejection of the
       British state   111
VI   Sovereignty and the New Republic: the American
       constitution in transatlantic perspective   125

2   THE CONFLICT BETWEEN DENOMINATIONS:
THE RELIGIOUS IDENTITY OF EARLY-MODERN
SOCIETIES   141
I   Before redefinition: politics and religion in the old society   141
II   Anglicanism as an agency of state formation: the question
       of establishment   153
III   Canon law, heterodoxy and the American perception of
       tyranny   167
IV   The Anglican ascendancy as the hegemony of discourse   180
V   The Anglican dream: harmony and conflict in the English
       parish   190
VI   The Anglican nightmare: sectarian diversity in colonial
       America   203

3   PREDISPOSITIONS: REBELLION AND ITS SOCIAL
CONSTITUENCIES IN THE ENGLISH ATLANTIC EMPIRE,
1660–1832   218
I   Rebellions and their analysis in the Anglo-American tradition 218
II   Covenanters, Presbyterians and Whigs: resistance to the
       Stuarts in England and Scotland, 1660–1689   225
III   Colonial American rebellions 1660–1689 and transatlantic
       discourse   240
IV   The rights of Englishmen, the rhetoric of slavery, and
       rebellions in Britain and America, 1689–1760   249
V   The right of resistance and its sectarian preconditions in
       North America, 1760–1799   257
VI   The rhetoric of resistance and its social constituencies
       in England and Ireland, 1733–1832: some transatlantic
       analogies   282
VII   Denominations, social constituencies and their activation   290

4   POLITICAL MOBILISATION: THE AMERICAN REVOLUTION
AS A WAR OF RELIGION   296
I   The American Revolution as a civil war   296
II   Predispositions, accelerators and catalysts: the role of
       theology   303
III   Heterodox and orthodox in the Church of England   311
IV   The divisions and disruptions of English Dissent   317
V   Heterodoxy and rebellion in colonial America, 1760–1776   335

(A) The American Anglicans   339
(B) The American Presbyterians   351
(C) The American Congregationalists   363
(D) The American Baptists   372

CONCLUSION: 'DESOLATING DEVASTATION':
THE ORIGINS OF ANGLO-AMERICAN DIVERGENCE   382

Index   392

Preface

This book contributes to a small but growing genre: studies of the history of transatlantic links.[1] It is drawn to adopt this transatlantic perspective by the realisation that many problems in the domestic histories of both America and Britain are more accessible when so addressed. The transatlantic dimension provided a screen on to which the tightly-knit problems of its constituent societies were projected, a screen on which inconclusive local processes can be observed unfolding to a conclusion often absent in some parochial setting. The object of this book is not to provide a comprehensive or even an outline history of domestic events on either side of the Atlantic; it is, rather, to attempt a selective and thematic enquiry into the nature of transatlantic ties and the inner causes of their dissolution. It takes its standpoint on territory bounded by the historical disciplines of political theory, law and religion; it examines the aspirations for civil and religious liberty, legal government and moral regeneration that were expressed and pursued within the boundaries of those bodies of ideas. Its ambition is to add some insights drawn from colonial history to the history of Britain, and to contribute some insights from British scholarship to the history of America.

[1] I am particularly indebted to J. R. Pole, *Political Representation in England and the Origins of the American Republic* (London, 1966); Jack P. Greene, *Peripheries and Center: Constitutional Development in the Extended Polities of the British Empire and the United States, 1607–1788* (New York, 1986) and *Pursuits of Happiness: The Social Development of Early Modern British Colonies and the Formation of American Culture* (Chapel Hill, 1988); Bernard Bailyn, *The Peopling of British North America* (New York, 1986) and *Voyagers to the West* (New York, 1986); Edmund S. Morgan, *Inventing the People: The Rise of Popular Sovereignty in England and America* (New York, 1988); David Hackett Fischer, *Albion's Seed: Four British Folkways in America* (New York, 1989) and 'Albion and the Critics: Further Evidence and Reflection', *WMQ* 48 (1991), 260–308; for important analogies with the early seventeenth century, Avihu Zakai, *Exile and Kingdom: history and apocalypse in the Puritan migration to America* (Cambridge, 1992).

British and American history was long explained chiefly through the eyes of rival elites – the Founding Fathers and their aristocratic British opponents. Elites were certainly important in framing and sustaining public discourse, and the arguments of the elites are examined here; but this study attempts also to give due weight to the contributions on both sides of the Atlantic of the rank and file, the marginalised and the excluded. It recognises the leading role played by the various denominations of Protestant Dissenters, whose perspective on the Anglican ascendancy, its theology, its liturgy and its social forms, crucially shaped the theoretical formulations of liberty which triumphed or failed in the years between 1776 and 1787. It links this redressing of the intellectual balance with an awareness of the diversity of the English-speaking population of the North Atlantic world: the Scots and Scots Irish too have their story, and recognition of the combination of ethnicity and religion in the protest of such groups is a means by which the vehemence of their protests can be made intelligible to the modern liberal mind.

Without such a wider vision, surveys of this period have almost inevitably been drawn to explain the American Revolution as a grand, and presumably inevitable, climax. An event so momentous in its consequences is expected to have had causes which both dominated the history of previous decades, and were unique to it. So the American Revolution, by the very brightness of its example, has obscured the many other relevant conflicts of religion, law and ethnicity in the English Atlantic world, with which this book seeks to reintegrate it. In the absence of the theme of sectarian strife, the Revolution of 1776 has, similarly, rearranged many of the antecedent constitutional relations of Britain and America into a teleology, an unfolding logic moving naturally from the rise of the colonial assemblies through resistance to imperial taxation to a vindication of legislative autonomy and nationhood in 1776. This story has much to be said for it; its familiar components – the Stamp Act, the Townshend Duties, the Intolerable Acts – were undoubtedly subjects of daily political conflict in the transatlantic arena. This book seeks not to discard this too-familiar story but to supplement it, and so profoundly to modify it, by the addition of certain themes neglected by recent historiography but sufficiently prominent in eighteenth-century discourse.

It concerns, especially, the themes of religion and law, rights and duties. In Britain and in colonial America, debate about both was incessant: in no strong sense are secret or unconscious motives here being ascribed to historical actors who would have disavowed them (though some individuals, from Isaac Newton to Thomas Jefferson, undoubtedly concealed their theological heterodoxy from their contemporaries for prudential reasons). A study of political argument must be largely a study of public argument, often from published sources, and these are called on here. Nor is this a study which gives priority to conspiracy over catastrophe: a conspiracy is only a plan viewed from the outside, and if different denominations at times pursued plans for aggrandisement within the English-speaking world, which ended in mutual catastrophe, their actions are inherently no more resistant to historical explanation than those of the merchants and planters, politicians and administrators who usually fill the pages of works on the American Revolution.

The role of law and of religion in Britain or colonial America, each treated in relative isolation from the other, has been the theme of much fine scholarship: this is acknowledged extensively in footnotes rather than in a separate bibliography. The importance of religion in the American Revolution in particular has, of course, engaged a generation of colonial American scholars, and no discovery is claimed here: but this theme is seldom explored in the extended transatlantic setting proposed in this book, and seldom linked to the other developments in law and politics with which an Anglo-American study seeks to reintegrate it. One of the objects of this analysis is to draw together academic specialisms, and geographical areas, which have too often been discussed in that splendid intellectual isolation which successful rebellion created.

Studies which presume homogeneity or consensus in their subjects may appear to be complete. A survey of this nature, emphasising the political and religious diversities of societies on both sides of the Atlantic over a century and a half, can only be an introduction to a complex and ambiguous reality, selectively addressing certain themes, attempting to combine the broad sweep with the significant detail. I am very aware of how much more there is to be said even on the topics raised here, and hope to address those subjects and others more fully in a future book on Anglo-American relations in the seventeenth and eighteenth centuries. By focusing on religion and law, no mono- or even duo-causal explanation is being proposed: attention to some subjects does not exclude others.

The present work took its rise from my earlier research on England's relations with Scotland, Ireland and Wales. Since I am mindful of the importance of these distinctions, 'England' in this book means England and is not used as a thoughtless synonym for the rest of the British Isles; Wales, Ireland and Scotland, where intended, are specified. The English lacked a single term to cover England, Scotland, Ireland and Wales exactly because England's church and common law reached out with such considerable success to absorb its neighbouring societies: this study explores some aspects of that process. 'America' refers to all the British mainland colonies before 1783 and to the United States thereafter. The hegemonic role of the Church of England within the North Atlantic world justifies the term 'Dissent' in relation to other Protestant denominations, even in those colonies in which Anglicanism had not yet attained the position of a legal establishment. 'Civil law' today means private as opposed to criminal or military law; in the period covered by this book, the term referred to Roman law (as distinct from canon law) and generically to the Roman-law-influenced legal systems of continental European states, as contrasted with England's common law system. Finally, since this book is, in part, an attempt to draw evidence from the realms of religion and law on to the territory of the history of political ideas, I have felt it appropriate more often to quote than to paraphrase texts, and where possible to present evidence rather than merely allude to it.

Acknowledgements

In a work which trespasses so unrepentantly into the specialisms of so many scholars, it is a pleasure to record the encouragement and advice which I have received on both sides of the Atlantic. Jeremy Black, Ian Christie, Geoffrey Elton and John Kenyon have been exemplary critics of my work on British history, and have suggested sources for some of what follows. For references and suggestions I am indebted also to Grayson Ditchfield, Peter Doll, John Elliott, Madeleine Forey, James McConica, Richard Sharp, Guenter Treitel and Charles Webster. Colin Haydon kindly showed me, before publication, the text of his book *Anti-Catholicism in Eighteenth-Century England*; I am grateful also to Anthony Waterman for a copy of his forthcoming paper 'The Nexus between Theology and Political Doctrine in Church and Dissent', to Patricia Bonomi for her paper 'Religious Dissent and the Case for American Exceptionalism', and to Stephen A. Marini for a copy of his 'Political Theologies of the American Revolution'. During the past three years some of the ideas advanced here have been developed in seminars, at conferences, and in published form; they have been fundamentally revised for this book in the light of the criticisms of many audiences. Timothy Breen and Jack Pole have indulgently guided my first steps among the impressive but unfamiliar scholarship on colonial America, and John Pocock has graciously allowed me to operate within a field of enquiry which he has made his own. For detailed criticisms of drafts of this work, and other advice, I am particularly indebted to Gerald Aylmer, Richard Barlow, Patricia Bonomi, James E. Bradley, Daniel Walker Howe, Edmund S. Morgan, John Morrill, Jack Pole, Quentin Skinner, Harry S. Stout, John Walsh and Anthony Waterman. None of them are necessarily in agreement with the arguments of this book, however, responsibility for which must remain with its author.

Abbreviations

Adams, *Works*	C. F. Adams (ed.), *The Works of John Adams* (10 vols., Boston, 1850–6)
AHR	*American Historical Review*
Bailyn, *American Politics*	Bernard Bailyn, *The Origins of American Politics* (New York, 1968)
Bailyn, *Ideological Origins*	Bernard Bailyn, *The Ideological Origins of the American Revolution* (Cambridge, Mass., 1967)
Bailyn (ed.), *Pamphlets*	Bernard Bailyn (ed.), *Pamphlets of the American Revolution 1750–1776. Volume 1 1750–1765* (Cambridge, Mass., 1965)
Blackstone, *Commentaries*	Sir William Blackstone, *Commentaries on the Laws of England* (4 vols., Oxford, 1765–9)
Bonomi, *Cope of Heaven*	Patricia U. Bonomi, *Under the Cope of Heaven: Religion, Society, and Politics in Colonial America* (New York, 1986)
Bradley, *Religion*	James E. Bradley, *Religion, Revolution and English Radicalism: Nonconformity in Eighteenth-Century Politics and Society* (Cambridge, 1990)
Clark, *English Society 1688–1832*	J. C. D. Clark, *English Society 1688–1832: Ideology, Social Structure and Political Practice during the Ancien Regime* (Cambridge, 1985)
DAB	Allen Johnson and Dumas Malone (eds.), *Dictionary of American Biography* (20 vols., New York, 1928–44)

DNB	Leslie Stephen and Sidney Lee (eds.), *The Dictionary of National Biography* (63 vols., London, 1885–1900)
EHR	*English Historical Review*
Evans, *American Bibliography*	Charles Evans (ed.), *American Bibliography: A Chronological Dictionary of all Books, Pamphlets and Periodical Publications Printed in the United States of America from the Genesis of Printing in 1639 down to and including the Year 1820* (12 vols., Chicago, 1903–34)
Franklin, *Works*	Jared Sparks (ed.), *The Works of Benjamin Franklin* (10 vols., Boston, 1836–40)
Franklin, *Papers*	Leonard W. Labaree (et al., eds.), *The Papers of Benjamin Franklin* (New Haven, 1959–)
Greene, *Peripheries and Center*	Jack P. Greene, *Peripheries and Center: Constitutional Development in the Extended Polities of the British Empire and the United States, 1607–1788* (New York, 1986)
HJ	*Historical Journal*
HMPEC	*Historical Magazine of the Protestant Episcopal Church*
Madison, *Writings*	Gaillard Hunt (ed.), *The Writings of James Madison* (9 vols., New York, 1900–10)
Jefferson, *Papers*	Julian P. Boyd (ed.), *The Papers of Thomas Jefferson* (Princeton, 1950–)
Jefferson, *Writings* (Ford)	Paul Leicester Ford (ed.), *The Writings of Thomas Jefferson* (10 vols., New York, 1892–9)
Jefferson, *Writings*	Andrew A. Lipscomb and Albert Ellery Bergh (eds.), *The Writings of Thomas Jefferson* (20 vols., Washington, 1903–4)
Parl. Hist.	W. Cobbett (ed.), *The Parliamentary History of England, from the Earliest Period to the Year 1803* (36 vols., London, 1806–20)
P&P	*Past & Present*
Robbins, *Commonwealthman*	Caroline Robbins, *The Eighteenth-Century Commonwealthman: Studies in the Transmis-*

	sion, *Development and Circumstance of English Liberal Thought from the Restoration of Charles II until the War with the Thirteen Colonies* (Cambridge, Mass., 1959)
Stevens (ed.), *Facsimiles*	B. F. Stevens (ed.), *Facsimiles of Manuscripts in European Archives Relating to America 1773–1783* (25 vols., London, 1889–98)
TRHS	*Transactions of the Royal Historical Society*
Washington, *Writings*	Jared Sparks (ed.), *The Writings of George Washington* (12 vols., Boston, 1837)
WMQ	*William and Mary Quarterly*, Third Series

Introduction

The structure of Anglo-American political discourse

I. LAW, RELIGION AND SOVEREIGNTY

By the mid-eighteenth century, Englishmen on both sides of the Atlantic proclaimed their faith in liberty: they appealed to a common constitutional tradition even as they disputed its ownership and its application.[1] They claimed the 'rights of Englishmen' and revered the texts in which they believed them to be embodied, like Magna Carta and the Bill of Rights. They commemorated a similar Protestant calendar of momentous anniversaries, including the Spanish Armada, the Gunpowder Plot, the execution of Charles I, and the birthday of the reigning monarch.[2] They celebrated, and suspected a minority who were ambiguous about, the Restoration, the Glorious Revolution, the Act of Settlement, and the accession of the House of Hanover. They structured the political lives of their communities around representative institutions, and had the Westminster Parliament in mind as a model. As the Scots and Irish in the New World and the Old were progressively caught up in this hegemonic English myth, they too were drawn to subscribe to it and loudly profess it in order to exploit its libertarian implications: they were implications to which their very different sectarian and political traditions also pointed. Law and religion dominated men's understanding of the public realm.

Englishmen on both sides of the Atlantic received, and idealised, the

---

[1] For an exploration of these differences built around a regional and cultural interpretation of migration and settlement patterns, see David Hackett Fischer, *Albion's Seed: Four British Folkways in America* (New York, 1989), pp. 189–205, 398–418, 584–603, 765–82.

[2] David Cressy, *Bonfires and Bells: National Memory and the Protestant Calendar in Elizabethan and Stuart England* (London, 1989). For American membership of an Atlantic community and intellectual exchanges within it, see Daniel Walker Howe, 'European Sources of Political Ideas in Jeffersonian America', *Reviews in American History* 10 (1982), 28–44.

common law.[3] Law was, nevertheless, an area in which transatlantic discourse broke down, and this book explores, on a theoretical level, one of the pathways along which this process developed. On a practical level, much more might be said.[4] The success of English law in unifying England's possessions, especially in respect of what was later termed nationality law, was only partial. Colonial issues were not near the centre of attention of many of the law's practitioners in London. Since appeals from American colonial courts lay to the King in Council, not to the Court of King's Bench, few records of colonial cases were publicly available in England: common-law reports and commentaries, from Sir Edward Coke through Sir Matthew Hale to Sir William Blackstone, consequently said little or nothing about America,[5] and the problem of binding the colonies to the mother country by a single legal code was not effectively addressed. Even Blackstone's treatment of the question was brief, and indecisive.[6]

On a theoretical plane, it will be argued that the pathway by which the hold of the common law over America was weakened was by a growing polarisation of a shared legal tradition into antitheses of common law and natural law. Natural law, as Lord Bryce remarked, 'which had been for nearly two thousand years a harmless maxim, almost a commonplace of morality, became in the end of the eighteenth century a mass of dynamite, which shattered an ancient monarchy and shook the European Continent'.[7] He wrote of France, but his insight applies to the American Revolution also.

[3] For the dominance of common-law paradigms in English political debate, see Howard Nenner, *By Colour of Law: Legal Culture and Constitutional Politics in England, 1660–1689* (Chicago, 1977), a theme which could be traced throughout the eighteenth century; for colonial analogies, Zechariah Chaffee, Jr, 'Colonial Courts and the Common Law', in David H. Flaherty (ed.), *Essays in the History of Early American Law* (Chapel Hill, 1969), pp. 53–82.

[4] On the indeterminacy of transatlantic legal and constitutional relations, see especially Greene, *Peripheries and Center.* For other areas see especially Shannon C. Stimson, *The American Revolution in the Law* (London, 1990) and J. R. Pole, 'Reflections on American Law and the American Revolution', *WMQ* 50 (1993), 123–59.

[5] Wilcomb E. Washburn, 'Law and Authority in Colonial Virginia', in George Athan Billias (ed.), *Law and Authority in Colonial America* (Barre, Mass., 1965), pp. 116–35 at 118–19.

[6] Blackstone, *Commentaries,* vol. 1, pp. 104–6. For the restricted sense in which common-law writs ran in the American colonies, and the large degree to which colonists who claimed the heritage of the common law were seeking to appropriate a political symbol, see Max Radin, 'The Rivalry of Common Law and Civil Law Ideas in the American Colonies' in *Law: A Century of Progress 1835–1935* (3 vols., New York, 1937), vol. 2, pp. 404–31.

[7] James Bryce, *Studies in History and Jurisprudence* (Oxford, 1901), vol. 2, p. 163, cited in Francis Stephen Ruddy, *International Law in the Enlightenment: The Background of Emmerich de Vattel's Le Droit des Gens* (Dobbs Ferry, New York, 1975), p. 33. For a colonial use of Vattel to elevate 'the constitution' above amendment by metropolitan legislation, see Greene, *Peripheries and Center,* p. 120. For the 'explosion' which accompanied the 'sudden upsurge of importance of natural law for the civil law' in the seventeenth and eighteenth centuries, especially in Protestant countries, see Alan Watson, *The Making of the Civil Law* (Cambridge, Mass., 1981), pp. 83–98, at 88.

Natural law and common law were, it will be argued, closely related in the English-speaking world. The mythology of the common law contended that it had always existed as a self-contained system, uncontaminated by any other legal code, rugged and immemorial, resisting foreign intrusions. This myth had some foundation, but needs to be importantly qualified. From the earliest times, the system known as the common law embraced a delicate interplay of English custom and Roman law principle in which, though the first predominated, the second was never extinguished.[8] Daniel Dulany, Sr. assumed in 1728 that the 'Common Law, takes in the Law of Nature, the Law of Reason, and the revealed Law of God; which are equally binding, at All Times, in All Places, and to All Persons'.[9] Moreover, many of the jurists venerated as champions of the common law – Bracton, Coke, Blackstone – had a deep knowledge of Roman law, and their major works were attempts to systematise the common law in ways reminiscent of Justinian.[10] Reformers in England, as in America, could therefore sometimes emphasise the natural-law element within the common law tradition. Granville Sharp quoted with approval an Oxford civil lawyer:

> What use our ancestors have made of the civil law will readily appear to any one, that will take the trouble to compare the several works which compose that voluminous body, with some of the most ancient English lawyers, as Glanvil, Bracton, and others; who have adhered very closely to the rules and method of Justinian; have transcribed his Laws in their own proper language, and sometimes intire titles, as familiarly as if they were the original laws of England.[11]

This eclectic quality of the common law preserved a role for Roman law concepts within it,[12] and the tactical need to find arguments to limit the

---

[8] Thomas Edward Scrutton, *The Influence of the Roman Law on the Law of England* (Cambridge, 1885), opened an enquiry too seldom explored by later historians.

[9] [Daniel Dulany, Sr], *The Right of the Inhabitants of Maryland to the Benefit of the English Laws* (Annapolis, 1728), reprinted in St George Leakin Sioussat, *The English Statutes in Maryland* (Baltimore, 1903), pp. 79–104, at 82.

[10] Hans S. Pawlisch, *Sir John Davies and the Conquest of Ireland: A Study in Legal Imperialism* (Cambridge, 1985), pp. 161–75; Alan Watson, 'The Structure of Blackstone's Commentaries', *Yale Law Journal* 97 (1987–8), 795–812.

[11] Thomas Bever, *A Discourse on the Study of Jurisprudence and the Civil Law* (Oxford, 1766), p. 17, quoted in Granville Sharp, *A Declaration of the People's Natural Right to a Share in the Legislature* (London, 1774), p. vii. Sharp singled out Fortescue's quotation, 'Quod Principi placuit (juxta Leges Civiles) Legis habet vigorem' (see chapter 1, part III below), as the objectionable principle of civil law, and the source of the tyrannical features of modern French society: a standing army, the salt tax, secret trials and surreptitious executions. Reformers might seek to exploit what they saw as the other, more favourable, implications of civil law.

[12] [Richard Wooddeson], *Elements of Jurisprudence Treated of in the Preliminary Part of a Course of Lectures on the Laws of England* (London, 1783), pp. 85–7.

unified King-in-Parliament who was created in the 1530s and who more securely ruled after 1660 kept an Anglican version of natural law near the political centre of attention. In this sense American colonists were merely emphasising one strand in a common tradition; but they emphasised it to the point where 1776 may be understood as a revolution of natural law against common law. This constitutes the first of the main theses of the present book.[13]

The American Revolution was mainly 'about' law: that is, the legal aspect of political authority, taxation and trade was at the centre of political controversy and determined the timing of the outbreak of armed resistance. But it was 'about' religion too, not only because religion created intellectual and social preconditions of resistance, but also because religion shaped the way in which British and colonial legal thinking developed and came to define certain practical problems as non-negotiable, beyond that sphere of pragmatic adjustment in which, for much of British and American history, legal disagreements had been addressed.

A second thesis of this book therefore concerns religion. The English-speaking peoples of the North Atlantic world were, by a large numerical majority, Protestants; and they defined themselves against Rome at a time when Protestantism was loud in claiming that it alone promoted civil liberty. Yet Protestantism in the Anglophone world had from the outset been marked by its proliferating diversities, and even the Church of England had been torn by conflict and schism over the interpretation of its status and its theology. The denominations which had separated from it in turn – Congregationalist, Presbyterian, Baptist, Quaker and others – competed for members with each other as well as with their parent. The uneasy and insecure existence of the sects, as well as their need continually to justify their separation from a parent both powerful and attractive, acted as perpetual irritants which kept vivid the memories of ancient grievances and encouraged Dissenters to wage a guerilla war, sometimes desultory, sometimes militant, against the Church. In this war, they were often prepared to employ against Canterbury many of the charges that Canterbury itself still levelled against Rome. Within England, Wales and Ireland, the Church of England maintained an uneasy hegemony; but within the thirteen colonies these denominational problems, often exported versions of Anglican England's difficult relations

[13] The theme of the conflict of legal systems has sometimes been explored by lawyers in the area of private law, e.g. W. W. Buckland and Arnold D. McNair, *Roman & Common Law: A Comparison in Outline* (2nd edn, Cambridge, 1952). It has yet to attract historians of eighteenth-century political thought in the area of public law, though see H. F. Jolowicz, 'Political Implications of Roman Law', *Tulane Law Review* 22 (1947), 62–81.

with the religious traditions of Scotland and Ireland, grew in intensity; they lay behind many episodes of violent insurrection like those of 1689 in which James II's authority was overthrown in the colonies, and finally exploded in 1776.

The Church of England was not, itself, theologically homogeneous, any more than were the denominations which separated from it. With the decline in numbers and energy of 'Old Dissent' in the century after 1660, the most significant conflicts were increasingly played out within the Church rather than between the Church and the sects: High Churchmen and Low Churchmen, Trinitarians, Arians and Deists could all be found to assert that theirs was the authentic voice of Anglicanism. If Anglicans could increasingly win over Dissenters attracted to what was depicted as the immemorial and firmly established doctrinal orthodoxy of the Church, the opposite was also true: Low-Church Anglicans could be profoundly influenced by developments within Dissent, especially by the political mobilisation of libertarian Nonconformists, playing on the claim that the Church too embraced a right of private judgement and had been founded at the Reformation in protest at the same forces of 'Popery and arbitrary power' that eighteenth-century Nonconformists on both sides of the Atlantic came to imagine were threatening them also. In this study the American Revolution is analysed theologically, as a rebellion by groups within Protestant Dissent against an Anglican hegemony, a rebellion which played on divisions within the Anglican Church itself.[14]

Law and religion were profoundly related, however; the third main thesis of this book seeks to explain one of their points of contact. A rebellion of natural law against common law and a rebellion of Dissent against hegemonic Anglicanism were the same rebellion, since their target was the unified sovereign created by England's unique constitutional and ecclesiastical development: King, Lords and Commons, indivisible and irresistible, credited (according to Blackstone) with absolute power by the common law, dignified with divine authority by the Church. It is argued here that the English doctrine of sovereignty, classically but explosively expounded in Sir William Blackstone's *Commentaries on the Laws of England* of 1765–9, was neither his recent invention nor a legal doctrine only: it was and was seen to be quintessentially Anglican, worked out in the process of England's relations with Scotland, Ireland and Wales, and still asserted in a context that Dissenters in the British Isles

---

[14] For a developing debate on this issue, compare Clark, *English Society 1688–1832*; Bradley, *Religion*; A. M. C. Waterman, 'The Nexus between Theology and Political Doctrine in Church and Dissent', in Knud Haakonssen (ed.), *Enlightenment and Rational Dissent* (forthcoming), and the discussion below, which addresses the question in a transatlantic setting.

as well as America recognised as an ecclesiastical one. Appropriately, therefore, the Blackstonian conception of sovereignty has been described as 'the single most important abstraction of politics in the entire [American] Revolutionary era'.[15] Some principles traditionally ascribed to the natural law tradition might equally better be traced to the ecclesiastical polities of Protestant Dissenters. Granville Sharp admitted that his favourite maxim, 'Law, to bind all, must be assented to by all', had been explicitly excluded from the laws of nature by Pufendorf, and had to argue that Pufendorf was in error: *'the necessity of Assent'* was 'sufficiently proved to be a *Law of Nature* even by the learned Baron's own arguments'.[16] A central issue of legal conflict was whether metropolitan statutes had automatic validity in the American colonies; and despite some colonists' desire to deny this, denominational needs could override their scruples and create a double standard. In 1707 the Irish Presbyterian missionary Francis Makemie, arrested for preaching in New York without a licence, urged in his defence before the Anglican Governor, Lord Cornbury, that the Toleration Act automatically extended to the colonies even though they were not named in it.[17]

II. CONSTITUTIONAL INNOVATIONS AND THEIR ENGLISH ANTECEDENTS

It has been argued by some scholars that the conception of sovereignty most memorably expressed by Blackstone was new, either in 1688 or with the accession of George III, and that colonists reacted swiftly against this innovation in the 1760s because they perceived its incompatibility with their local, long-established and acknowledged conception of constitutional law as custom rather than as command.[18] In the 1760s and 1770s, there were both colonial and British observers who reacted in just this way. William Knox, one of the undersecretaries of state for the colonies, saw in c. 1779 how the 'Claim of unlimited unrestrained Jurisdiction in Parliament' had 'alarmed and terrified' the colonists, but had also

[15] Gordon S. Wood, *The Creation of the American Republic 1776–1787* (Chapel Hill, 1969), pp. 344–54; Bailyn, *Ideological Origins*, pp. 198–229; Greene, *Peripheries and Center*, passim. None of these fine studies locates the Blackstonian conception of sovereignty within the denominational context proposed for it here.

[16] Granville Sharp, *A Declaration of the People's Natural Right to a Share in the Legislature* (London, 1774), pp. v, xx.

[17] Francis Makemie, *A Narrative of a New and Unusual American Imprisonment Of Two Presbyterian Ministers . . .* ([Boston], 1707).

[18] Jack P. Greene, 'From the Perspective of Law: Context and Legitimacy in the Origins of the American Revolution', *South Atlantic Quarterly* 85 (1986), 56–77 at 64–5, 72, 74; idem, *Peripheries and Center*, pp. 144–50; H. G. Koenigsberger, 'Composite States, Representative Institutions and the American Revolution', *Historical Research* 62 (1989), 135–53, at 149–50.

contradicted the substantial self-government actually developing in America, so that 'while these high Claims of Prerogative were kept up in words, the real and substantial Authority of the British Government was suffered to be sapped, and at length overturned'.

The Declaratory Act of 1766 was an affront to this system, Knox continued: 'Was it to be expected that Assemblies which had garbled and abrogated Acts of Parliament without Control or Censure who had been often told they were the mere Creatures of Prerogative, belonged to the Crown, and were the King's Domain, should readily acquiesce in the claim of absolute uncontrolable Jurisdiction all at once set up by Parliament?'[19] Nevertheless, however novel the policies embodied in the Stamp Act or the Townshend duties, the dominant British definition of sovereignty had been evolving for a very much longer period.[20] Colonial resistance to metropolitan assertions of authority, too, was at least as old as New England's arguments against the regime of James II's Governor, Sir Edmund Andros.[21] Yet that same British definition of sovereignty had long been internalised by many colonial theorists, so far indeed that, under the pressure of tactical necessity in the 1760s, they found it almost impossible to frame an alternative despite the pressing need to do so. Why they finally did so, and why long-standing legal disagreements led at last to armed rebellion, is chiefly to be explained by new developments in the colonies.

The Revolution of 1776 was slow to happen partly because Englishmen on both sides of the Atlantic were locked into the belief that they were already living in a libertarian polity. The spheres of law and religion were not spheres of dictatorial power: in both the ideal of liberty was variously maintained, and in both the principles of consultation and representation were of long standing. Yet of all the transatlantic analogies the representative assembly was the most surprisingly ineffective and proved least able to evolve to resolve transatlantic problems.[22] Whig regimes in England after 1688 progressively destroyed adjacent assemblies in the name of

[19] William Knox, 'Considerations on the Great Question, What is to be Done with America', ed. Jack P. Greene, *WMQ* 30 (1973), 293–306, at 297, 302, 305. Knox's interpretation is central to that of Greene in *Peripheries and Center.*

[20] It is argued here that the Blackstonian position was less the herald of an evolving positivist theory of the modern state (Greene, 'From the Perspective of Law') than the end-point of a dynastic and religious process which began in the sixteenth century.

[21] J. R. Pole, *The Gift of Government: Political Responsibility from the English Restoration to American Independence* (Athens, Georgia, 1983), pp. 12–16. For the denominational predispositions and the theological catalysts which provoked a more virulent repudiation of the Blackstonian position in mid-century, see chapter 1, part V below.

[22] For the way in which the fictions of divine-right monarchy slid into the fictions of the sovereignty of the people, see Edmund S. Morgan, *Inventing the People: The Rise of Popular Sovereignty in England and America* (New York, 1988). Morgan reveals how theories of representation were unable to prevent this process.

unified authority: the Edinburgh Parliament with the Union of 1707; Convocation, the Church of England's representative assembly, in 1717; the Dublin Parliament in the Union of 1801. Even English parliamentary reformers, elaborating schemes for the renovation of the House of Commons, neglected to include plans for the incorporation of Members from the colonies, and the Scots and Irish allowed the Edinburgh and Dublin Parliaments to be snuffed out without producing alternative schemes for an imperial federal parliament.[23] Similarly, eighteenth-century colonial assemblies steadily strengthened their positions in a series of daily conflicts with governors and imperial authorities without extrapolating their aims into a persuasive theory of representative democracy or a goal of a presence in the House of Commons.[24] The demand of the 1760s for 'no taxation without representation' seemed to echo an ancient English constitutional principle; it was not a forward-looking blueprint for Jacksonian democracy or for seats in an imperial parliament.

Whatever the functions of colonial assemblies, these did not include the mobilisation and expression of public opinion: no debate of any colonial assembly was ever published in a colonial newspaper, and the assemblies in general retained rules and assumptions safeguarding the secrecy of their proceedings that characterised the Westminster House of Commons in an earlier age. However principled the conflicts between the assemblies and colonial governors or proprietors, those conflicts did not dictate that the assemblies developed a role as the democratically-mandated agents of colonial voters, and with the exception of Massachusetts', most of the assemblies played a strikingly reticent role in the process of mass political mobilisation which led to revolution in 1776.[25] The theory which grounded the legitimacy of government on the consent of the governed did not arise primarily as a comment on the practice of representation in the colonies: it drew its main force from the idea of covenant in colonial religion.[26]

On secular constitutional matters, the large areas of agreement between Britain and the colonies have been eclipsed by smaller but explosive disagreements. Even the Anglican loyalists of the 1770s could

---

[23] These themes are silently and naturally omitted from the standard works on this subject, e.g. G. S. Veitch, *The Genesis of Parliamentary Reform*, ed. Ian R. Christie (London, 1965); John Cannon, *Parliamentary Reform 1640–1832* (Cambridge, 1973).

[24] Jack P. Greene, *The Quest for Power: The Lower Houses of Assembly in the Southern Royal Colonies 1689–1776* (Chapel Hill, 1963).

[25] Pole, *The Gift of Government*, pp. 117–40, at 134. Even the proceedings of the Continental Congress, and the Philadelphia Convention of 1787 which framed the new Constitution, were secret; and this was not a matter of significant controversy.

[26] For which, see Michael J. Crawford, *Seasons of Grace: Colonial New England's Revival Tradition in its British Context* (New York, 1991), pp. 180–3; Perry Miller, *Errand into the Wilderness* (New York, 1964), pp. 159–61.

take their stand on what were easily and conventionally designated the principles of 1688. Jonathan Boucher happily stigmatised 'the ridiculous and damnable doctrines of passive obedience and non-resistance'.[27] Charles Inglis seconded him: 'I am none of your *passive obedience and non-resistance men*. The principles on which the glorious Revolution in 1688 was brought about, constitute the articles of my political creed; and were it necessary, I could clearly evince, that these are perfectly conformable to the doctrines of scripture.'[28] Turning the charge on the patriots, Samuel Seabury pointed out that their own use of intimidation and mob violence 'smells most confoundly strong of passive obedience and non-resistance'.[29]

Yet some colonists, and some men in Britain, saw things in a very different light. English visitors to the colonies could easily imagine that they were stepping back into a world still preoccupied with ancient quarrels. From an English perspective, colonial rhetoric often displayed three marked characteristics. It represented a throwback to political alignments which Englishmen thought had been settled, at least within the British Isles. It addressed those old fears in the idiom of conspiracy theory. Finally, conspiracy theory was given its strangely intense significance by the immense power of denominational phobias. All three were classically present in the jeremiad of Peter Whitney, Congregational minister of Northborough, Massachusetts:

> What are the leading springs and motives of the present measures of administration it is hard to say. We have reason to fear, at least, that a design is forming to dethrone his present majesty, King George the third, our rightful sovereign, and to introduce the Pretender, and with him the popish religion.

Popery was 'gaining ground in England', as Jonathan Mayhew had shown, 'the people being, as it is said, perverted by popish bishops, priests, jesuits &c. by hundreds and thousands, if not ten thousands, yearly'.[30]

Speculation about the origin of political authority still led colonists back to the dangerous controversies of the seventeenth century. Stephen

---

[27] [Jonathan Boucher], *A Letter from a Virginian to the Members of the Congress to be held at Philadelphia, on The First of September, 1774* (Boston; reprinted London, 1774), p. 15.

[28] [Charles Inglis], *The True Interest of America Impartially Stated, in Certain Strictures On a Pamphlet Intitled Common Sense* (2nd edn, Philadelphia, 1776), p. 31.

[29] [Samuel Seabury], *the Congress Canvassed: or, An Examination into The Conduct of the Delegates, at their Grand Convention, held in Philadelphia, Sept. 1, 1774 . . . By A.W. Farmer* ([New York], 1774), p. 19.

[30] Peter Whitney, *The Transgression of a Land punished by a multitude of Rulers. Considered in two Discourses, Delivered July 14, 1774 . . . a Day of Fasting and Prayer, On Account of the Dark Aspect of our Public Affairs* (Boston, 1774), pp. 61-2.

Hopkins, the elected Governor of Rhode Island, summarised the alternative accounts of the origin of government:

> Some have found it's origin in the divine appointment: Others have thought it took it's rise from power: Enthusiasts have dreamed that dominion was founded in grace. Leaving these points to be settled by the descendants of *Filmer*, *Cromwell*, and *Venner*, we will consider the *British* constitution, as it at present stands, on revolution principles . . .[31]

Hopkins sought to refute Parliament's claim of authority to tax America by recourse to the principles of 1688 alone.

This was not enough to calm those ancient hatreds, often sectarian, which still moved great masses of men in the colonies. The English Methodist itinerant Joseph Pilmore was surprised to encounter near New York 'a Gentleman, who appeared to have his heart full of bitterness against the Memory of *Charles the First*, though he allowed they went a little too far in cutting off his head. How strange', added Pilmore, 'that men should distress their minds now, about the character of that unfortunate Prince!'[32] Americans could make the opposite claim: according to Arthur Lee, the British proponents of a war to suppress the colonists were 'the Tories, Jacobites, and Scotch . . . *They* see it is the *old cause*, though *we* cannot'; but despite denying the analogy with 1642, Lee still wished to call on it to stigmatise his opponents. The 'doctrines lately promulgated, under great patronage, by Dr. Johnson and Mr. Wesley' were indistinguishable from 'those of Filmer, Manwaring, and Sacheverell, or those in support of ship-money'.[33] What it was that created agonised perceptions like his is a major problem addressed in this book. Englishmen in England and America were united in a shared political tradition, but it was not a sufficient bond of union to prevent breakdowns in 1688 and 1776, and it did not evolve to defend transatlantic ties against those other forces which threatened that tradition on both sides of the ocean.

III. THE GENESIS OF POLITICAL DISCOURSE

Constitutional challenges were articulated within the idioms of political discourse supported by the transatlantic English-speaking populations. Such idioms had no disembodied existence; they were generated and

---

[31] [Stephen Hopkins], *The Rights of Colonies Examined* (Providence, 1765), pp. 3–4. For Venner see below, pp. 225–6.

[32] Frederick E. Maser and Howard T. Maag (eds.), *The Journal of Joseph Pilmore Methodist Itinerant For The Years August 1, 1769 to January 2, 1774* (Philadelphia, 1969), p. 94 (17 July 1771).

[33] [Arthur Lee], *A Second Appeal to the Justice and Interests of the People, On the Measures Respecting America* (London, 1775), pp. 55–6.

sustained by specific groups of men engaged in practical, mundane and daily activities in the public arena.[34] Trade and war to a small degree produced such idioms; but commerce had its reward already,[35] and war was an intermittent activity which, for the English at least, increasingly took place elsewhere. The two dominant idioms of discourse, daily reiterated, practically applied and prominent partly by reason of being lastingly contested, were law and religion. Burke rightly emphasised that these two idioms were predominant in the American colonies. The first was religion:

> Religion, always a principle of energy, in this new people, is no way worn out or impaired; and their mode of professing it is also one main cause of this free spirit. The people are protestants; and of that kind, which is the most adverse to all implicit submission of mind and opinion.

The second was law:

> In no country perhaps in the world is the law so general a study. The profession itself is numerous and powerful; and in most provinces it takes the lead. The greater number of the Deputies sent to the Congress were Lawyers. But all who read, and most do read, endeavour to obtain some smattering in that science. I have been told by an eminent Bookseller, that in no branch of his business, after tracts of popular devotion, were so many books as those on the Law exported to the Plantations. The Colonists have now fallen into the way of printing them for their own use. I hear that they have sold nearly as many of Blackstone's Commentaries in America as in England.[36]

The Revolution was duly recognised as a challenge within each idiom: Samuel Curwen, émigré, justified his flight from 'a people licentious and enthousiastically mad and broke loose from all restraints of Law and religion'.[37]

Each idiom had its own dialects. The English common law spoke with a different accent from canon law or the civil law applied in admiralty and ecclesiastical courts; in religion, Anglicanism stood defined between

---

[34] This point is more evident from the perspective of political history. It does not emerge, for example, from the sophisticated and scholarly essays by students of political theory assembled by Antony Pagden (ed.), *The Languages of Political Theory in Early-Modern Europe* (Cambridge, 1987).

[35] For the political impotence of the American trading lobby in England, see Jacob M. Price, 'Who Cared about the Colonies? The Impact of the Thirteen Colonies on British Society and Politics, circa 1714–1775', in Bernard Bailyn and Philip D. Morgan (eds.), *Strangers within the Realm: Cultural Margins of the First British Empire* (Chapel Hill, 1991), pp. 395–436.

[36] *The Speech of Edmund Burke, Esq; on Moving his Resolutions for Conciliation with the Colonies, March 22, 1775* (London, 1775), pp. 17, 19.

[37] Andrew Oliver (ed.), *The Journal of Samuel Curwen Loyalist* (2 vols., Salem, Mass., 1972), vol. 1, p. 1.

Roman Catholicism and the harsh variety of Protestant Dissent. The conflicts and unities of these idioms are a major theme of this book. Not only was colonial religious discourse much more plural than its English counterpart; the colonial legal idiom similarly placed much more emphasis on the traditions that rivalled the common law. Since separate ecclesiastical courts did not exist in the colonies, their business was conducted in the common-law courts. Jeremiah Gridley, leader of the Boston bar, warned the young law student John Adams in 1758 that 'the difficulties of the profession are much greater here than in England' for in the colonies the student must study not only common law, but also 'civil law, and natural law, and admiralty law'. Nevertheless, insisted Gridley, 'the common law, to be sure, deserves your first and last attention; and he has conquered all the difficulties of this law, who is master of the Institutes. You must conquer the Institutes.'[38] The ghost of Sir Edward Coke, pursuing his crusade against early-seventeenth century Stuart monarchs, still walked in England's mainland colonies.

The dominance of these two idioms meant that the insurrections discussed in this book owed little to forces which later historiography has associated together as agents of 'modernisation', like individualism, radicalism or liberalism. The structure of the Anglo-American debate in the two decades before the Revolution heavily and increasingly emphasised the corporate and collective element in American life.[39] Colonists resisted British policy and finally demanded independence not as individuals but as parts of a collective voice in town meetings, colonial assemblies or supra-colonial gatherings like the Stamp Act Congress; they were mobilised not as individuals but in groups, whether local or denominational; the independence they seized was that of their colony corporately; the cosmic scenario in which their theology pictured them engaged was played out not by rebellious individuals but by a triumphant 'people', the children of God, the new Israel. The increasing use of the language of contract, and increasing claims that contracts had been broken, did not contradict the fact that one of the parties to the contract was assumed to be 'the people' of each colony collectively. Coke's doctrine of the God-given, perpetual allegiance of subject to sovereign was not broken up by the 'rise of the individual' but by the drafting of individuals into an atavistic crusade against what sectarian theology identified as a Godless monarch.[40]

---

[38] Adams, Diary, 25 Oct. 1758: *Works*, vol. 2, pp. 46–7.
[39] For New England in particular, see Fischer, *Albion's Seed*, pp. 199–205.
[40] James H. Kettner, *The Development of American Citizenship, 1608–1870* (Chapel Hill, 1978), pp. 173–5. For an argument that covenantal religion personalised religious faith rather than making it private or individualistic, see Timothy L. Smith, 'Religion and Ethnicity in America', *AHR* 83 (1978), 1155–85, at 1178.

Religion and law were, of course, not the only two influences on transatlantic consciousness. Encounters with the material world also prompted colonists, as they prompted Englishmen, to develop a sense of identity which made possible both alliances and antagonisms.[41] It is not clear, however, that such a process offers any easy guide to colonial risings or to English foreign policy orientations. In material respects, the colonies often sought to become more and more like their European homelands, and often succeeded. The Swiss missionary Michael Schlatter reacted in his journal to his first sight of Boston and New York in 1746:

> from my own experience, I can truly testify, that often, when contemplating the towns, the level country, the climate, and the sensible inhabitants, living in the same manner, enjoying the same culture, pursuing the same business, and differing but little from Europeans, I could scarcely realise that I was in reality in a different quarter of the world.[42]

It was not, in general, the material pattern of life which marked out different sectors of the colonial population from each other, or colonists from Europeans. Trade, population and consumption, though important in themselves, were matters too general and too slowly changing to account for the specific political crises on both sides of the Atlantic between 1660 and 1832 addressed in this book.[43] American exceptionalism, if it is to be a viable explanation, has to be relocated on the territory of American religious experience, and, especially, with regard to that profound shift in the composition of the colonial population which meant that while less than a tenth of Englishmen in 1776 were Dissenters, more than three quarters of Americans were enlisted in other denominations.[44]

IV. TRANSATLANTIC TIES AND THEIR FAILURE

Many other cultural sources of transatlantic union suffered from not being reified, turned from ideas and attitudes into things, concepts with capital

[41] J. E. Crowley, *This Sheba, Self: The Conceptualization of Economic Life in Eighteenth Century America* (Baltimore, 1974); T. H. Breen, *Tobacco Culture: The Mentality of the Great Tidewater Planters on the Eve of Revolution* (Princeton, 1985); idem, 'An Empire of Goods: the Anglicisation of Colonial America, 1690–1776', *Journal of British Studies* 25 (1986), 467–99; idem, ' 'Baubles of Britain': The American and Consumer Revolutions of the Eighteenth Century', *P&P* 119 (1988), 73–104; Jack P. Greene, *Pursuits of Happiness: The Social Development of Early Modern British Colonies and the Formation of American Culture* (Chapel Hill, 1988). The challenge of relating the mental worlds explored in such studies and in the present book remains to be addressed; it is not one of the goals of this enquiry.

[42] Henry Harbaugh, *The Life of Rev. Michael Schlatter* (Philadelphia, 1857), pp. 126–7.

[43] For a different argument see Greene, *Peripheries and Center*, pp. 167–8.

[44] Patricia Bonomi, 'Religious Dissent and the Case for American Exceptionalism', in Ronald Hoffman and Peter J. Albert (eds.), *Religion in the Revolutionary Age* (Charlottesville, Va., 1994, forthcoming). The internal developments which mobilised American Dissent, however, had close parallels within the British Isles: see chapter 4 below.

letters which could be commemorated, celebrated and exploited. Englishmen in England and America prided themselves on their modernity, on their rejection of ignorance, superstition and barbarism, their commitment to the values summed up in the phrase 'liberty and property' – the values of a polite and commercial society.[45] Yet this still had few political implications at odds with the existing order. No-one in the English-speaking world then referred to 'the Enlightenment'[46] or supposed that such a thing was shared on both sides of the Atlantic,[47] any more than they thought their world released from its technological parameters by an 'Industrial Revolution'. The Enlightenment is an explanatory device of historians; the men of the eighteenth century could not define it as antithetical to any political or social order, for 'it' had not yet been organised out of what were later to be its component parts.

Many studies of politics in Britain and America in the late eighteenth century have been premised on a view of the Enlightenment as a process of secularisation,[48] embracing as a necessary unity aristocratic scepticism, bourgeois materialism and proletarian emancipation from patriarchal social relations. Yet each of these component parts has been challenged separately, and finally the ensemble itself is progressively questioned. National differences, too, were more important than Europe-wide similarities. Whatever may have been the case in France, and however much the French intelligentsia was influenced by materialist atheism, the English and colonial American scenario conformed to a different pattern. The elite's support for religion in the form of the established church was strong, and periodically reasserted in political crises from the Restoration through the Revolution of 1688 to the French Revolutionary challenge of the 1790s and beyond. The middle ranks of society markedly failed to

[45] These phrases have rightly been taken as emblematic of eighteenth-century attitudes in works by H. T. Dickinson and Paul Langford.
[46] The earliest English usage of 'the Enlightenment' is traced by the *Oxford English Dictionary* to 1865. It is clearly a term of historical art in Henry F. May, *The Enlightenment in America* (New York, 1976), where the analytical category is refined into four component 'Enlightenments': 'Moderate', 'Skeptical', 'Revolutionary' and 'Didactic'.
[47] Similar preoccupations and tendencies in the history of ideas can of course be found among men of letters on both sides of the Atlantic: J. R. Pole, 'Enlightenment and the Politics of American Nature', in Roy Porter and Mikulas Teich (eds.), *The Enlightenment in National Context* (Cambridge, 1981), pp. 192–214, and work there reviewed. It will be argued here that such shared trends, partly because they were not reified into a single 'Enlightenment', were sources of schism and insurrection rather than consensus and co-operation.
[48] Classically in Peter Gay, *The Enlightenment: An Interpretation* (2 vols., London, 1967–70), corrected by J. G. A. Pocock, 'Clergy and Commerce: The Conservative Enlightenment in England', in R. Ajello et al. (eds.), *L'Età dei Lumi* (Napoli, 1985), pp. 523–68; idem, 'Conservative Enlightenment and Democratic Revolutions: The American and French Cases in British Perspective', *Government and Opposition* 24 (1989), 81–105.

develop a group consciousness, whether as a commercial bourgeoisie or a middle class, and their attachment to church or Dissent was even more evident than that of the elite. Finally, if rates of church attendance did decline among the populace after 1689, it is now clear that this cannot easily or simply be interpreted as emancipation into a new social order. Patriarchal forms were undoubtedly modified, but the structures of authority and order still engaged with a mental world very different from that of nineteenth-century utilitarianism. The writing conventionally assigned to the Enlightenment in England, far from being secular, was suffused with theological and ecclesiastical argument;[49] and heterodoxy was not a high road to secularisation.[50]

It was once conventional to associate the Enlightenment especially with Dissent, to take as the starting point Dissenters' exclusion from office by the Test and Corporation Acts, and to treat as consequences of this both Dissenters' sense of political alienation and their theological heterodoxy. These two, however, could plausibly be presented as consequences only on the premises that Dissenters pointed towards modernity; that the secular and the modern were synonymous. Heterodoxy was neglected as merely a short route to secular materialism; what mattered for the Dissenters was presented as the experience of exclusion and alienation, if not outright repression. Evidence against this reductionist interpretation is presented in this book. In particular, the irrelevance of Dissenting religion is implausible if Nonconformist denominations remained stubbornly divided from each other, and locked in internal conflict over issues of theology as well as ecclesiastical polity. Socinians and Deists, in the 1790s as in the 1690s, had difficulty in making common cause. In 1794 the Socinian Gilbert Wakefield mounted what he termed a 'defence of the religion of Jesus' in one such attack on Paine's Deistical *Age of Reason*. Heterodox Dissenters, he claimed, were true religion's best defenders: '*Christianity* CANNOT be vindicated adequately and consistently against *Deism* by any slave of *systems* and *establishments*.' But this did not endear him to the orthodox, since Wakefield also insisted that 'The sway of creeds and councils, of hierarchies and churches, whether Protestant or Popish, over the bodies and consciences of men, is diminishing apace:

---

[49] John Redwood, *Reason, Ridicule and Religion: The Age of Enlightenment in England 1660–1750* (London, 1976); Sheridan Gilley, 'Christianity and the Enlightenment: An Historical Survey', *History of European Ideas* 1 (1981), 103–21; John Gascoigne, *Cambridge in the Age of Enlightenment* (Cambridge, 1989); J. A. I. Champion, *The Pillars of Priestcraft Shaken: The Church of England and its Enemies, 1660–1730* (Cambridge, 1992).

[50] Roy Porter, 'The Enlightenment in England', in Porter and Teich (eds.), *The Enlightenment in National Context*, pp. 1–18 at 6–8, argues both that the English Enlightenment was not secular and that it had no orthodox religious establishment to combat. The present study offers evidence against the second argument.

and the temple of revelation, deprived of the mouldering props, which priestcraft, and tyranny, and superstition had framed for it's support, must repose solely on it's proper basis, the adamant of TRUTH.'[51] In the American colonies even more obviously than within Britain, Dissenters like Anglicans insisted on living in a mental world, an extension of the seventeenth century, in which theology still claimed to dictate conduct.

When the Enlightenment was construed as a process of secularisation it was conventional to dwell on its positive affirmations, its visions of a better society; the centrality to some sectors of eighteenth-century thought of their negations is now the more striking lesson. Prominent among those negations was the rejection of what were identified as feudal survivals, especially in the case of eighteenth-century France.[52] It may appear paradoxical that eighteenth-century English society, increasingly picturing itself in terms of religious toleration, politeness and commerce, should have been increasingly pictured by its own dissidents and by American colonists in terms of sinister feudal, monarchical and clerical anachronisms.[53] Part of that paradox is resolved by the discovery that the rebellions of the 1640s and 1688 did not constitute a revolutionary watershed, a complete break with the past; that many social forms and institutions of ancient lineage survived into a Whig present to be the targets of attack, or objects for revival.[54] Part of the paradox is resolved, too, by the recovery of religion as a central component both of daily, grassroots communal practice and of the various discourses of political theory in which transatlantic relations were discussed. Since the term 'feudalism' did not appear in English until the 1830s,[55] the hated phenomena had to be attributed as characteristics to other causes, especially religious; they could not be reified, and isolated, as a separate and secular historical force.

These continuities illuminate the survival also on both sides of the Atlantic of a powerful trope within legal and historical discourse, that of the ancient constitution. This retrospective idyll of a Gothic and prefeudal libertarian polity of robust yeomen or freeholders and law-giving, law-abiding patriot kings[56] was actively exploited and developed in seven-

---

[51] Gilbert Wakefield, *An Examination of the Age of Reason, or an Investigation of True and Fabulous Theology, by Thomas Paine* (London, 1794), dedication, pp. 2–3. Socinians and Deists were equally unitarians, but Socinians depended on revelation in a way that Deists did not.

[52] J. Q. C. Mackrell, *The Attack on 'Feudalism' in Eighteenth Century France* (London, 1973).

[53] Classically in John Adams, *Dissertation on the Canon and Feudal Law* (printed in the *Boston Gazette*, August 1765); see chapter 2, part III below.

[54] R. J. Smith, *The Gothic Bequest: Medieval Institutions in British Thought, 1688–1863* (Cambridge, 1987).

[55] Smith, *Gothic Bequest*, p. 7. By contrast, 'féodalité' had been accepted into French dictionaries in the 1750s: Mackrell, *Attack on 'Feudalism'*, p. 6.

[56] Samuel Kliger, *The Goths in England: A Study in Seventeenth and Eighteenth Century Thought* (Cambridge, Mass., 1952).

teenth-century England, survived the Restoration and, though weakened, was quickly adapted for use after the Glorious Revolution.[57] William III could be praised by analogy with William I, redefined by authors like Sir William Temple and Viscount Bolingbroke as a restorer of ancient Saxon liberties. George I was hailed by the Anglo-Saxon scholar Bishop Edmund Gibson as a living reaffirmation of shared Saxon origins. Montesquieu, a visitor in England from 1729 to 1731, traced its present freedoms to the German forests, as described by Tacitus.[58]

Robert, Viscount Molesworth's edition of a French Renaissance text had classically formulated, for an eighteenth-century audience, the idea of an ancient, pan-European, and libertarian constitution, 'so wisely restor'd and establish'd (if not introduced) by the *Goths* and *Franks*, whose descendants we are'. François Hotman, writing in 1574, made no use of a theory of the 'Norman Yoke'[59] and insisted that it was

> not yet a hundred Years compleat, since the Liberties of *Francogallia*, and the *Authority* of its *annual General Council*, flourished in full Vigor . . . So that we may easily perceive that our *Commonwealth*, which at first was *founded* and *establish'd* upon the *Principles of Liberty*, maintained it self in the same free and sacred State, (even by Force and Arms) against all the Power of Tyrants for more than Eleven Hundred Years.[60]

So Hotman was fitted into Molesworth's scenario: liberty was the invention of the ancient Germanic tribes. His attention had turned first to Denmark: 'The Ancient Form of Government here was the same which the *Goths* and *Vandals* established in most, if not all Parts of *Europe*, whither they carried their Conquests, and which in *England* is retained to this day for the most part.'[61] Other nations, however, progressively lost this precious inheritance as faction and corruption paved the way for monarchical absolutism.[62] The same happened in the France of Louis XI. Molesworth's Preface of 1721 to *Francogallia*, republished in London in 1775 as *The Principles of a Real Whig*, emphasised the same point to the generation of the American Revolution: it was Louis XIV's monarchical absolutism,

[57] J. G. A. Pocock, *The Ancient Constitution and the Feudal Law: A Study of English Historical Thought in the Seventeenth Century. A Reissue with a Retrospect* (Cambridge, 1987), pp. 229–51, 362–87.

[58] Hugh A. MacDougall, *Racial Myth in English History: Trojans, Teutons and Anglo-Saxons* (Montreal, 1982), pp. 73–86.

[59] Christopher Hill, 'The Norman Yoke', in *Puritanism and Revolution* (London, 1958), chapter 3.

[60] [Robert, Viscount Molesworth, ed. and trans.], Francis Hotoman (sic), *Franco-Gallia: or, An Account of the Ancient Free State of France, and Most other Parts of Europe, before the Loss of their Liberties* (London, 1711; 2nd edn, 1721), pp. i, vi, 122.

[61] [Robert, Viscount Molesworth], *An Account of Denmark, as It was in the Year 1692* (London, 1694), p. 42.

[62] Ibid., pp. 43, 73.

given its force and local application by orthodox and established religion, which was depicted as antithetical to the 'ancient constitution' rather than William I's feudal tenures.

Yet the idea of the ancient constitution became steadily less powerful than it had been in the seventeenth century. Under the impact of a strengthening doctrine of unitary sovereignty, and of the omnicompetence of that unitary sovereign, the fundamental law which was often held to underpin the English constitution came after 1688 to be identified more with natural law than with the ancient constitution as immemorial and inviolable custom.[63] The natural law tradition then steadily abolished itself in eighteenth-century England by its very success in producing an identity of religion between nation and monarch, so opening the way for the common law to modernise itself in the unhistorical idiom of Benthamite utilitarianism. The ancient constitution was increasingly unnecessary to those who took their stand on the principles of 1688 and 1714, and largely irrelevant after 1832. Reformers, however, could use that idea to appeal beyond the Revolution settlement to some pre-existing polity and what were supposed to be its original principles.

From the middle of the eighteenth century in both England and America, it began to be re-emphasised that William I had corrupted the Saxon constitution by imposing the 'Norman Yoke';[64] that its restoration had been the work alternatively of the barons who drafted Magna Carta; or of sixteenth-century Protestant reformers; or of Civil War heroes; or of Glorious Revolution patricians; or, most radical of all, that it remained to be accomplished. One who so argued was the Arian-educated, Deist-professing, Welsh Dissenting minister David Williams (1738–1816).[65] Friend of Benjamin Franklin, libertine and would-be liturgical reformer,[66] he reproached the limited aims of modern Dissenters: 'The general outline of the English constitution seems to have been brought by the Saxons from Germany; filled up and perfected by the astonishing genius of Alfred; almost totally defaced by the feudal alterations of William the Conqueror; and restored, in some parts, by various attempts, from the Reformation to the Revolution' of 1688. In those attempts the Dissenters' ancestors had borne a more distinguished part.[67] A group of religious reformers in

---

[63] Cf. Pocock, *The Ancient Constitution and the Feudal Law*, pp. 238–9, 367.

[64] This point, like the supremacy of natural law, could be found in Blackstone (*Commentaries*, vol. 4, p. 420); here too, a reforming position was created by giving far greater emphasis to one part of a common tradition.

[65] Whitney R. D. Jones, *David Williams: The Anvil and the Hammer* (Tuscaloosa, 1986), pp. 3, 5, 11, 24–5, 42, 46, 48.

[66] Williams reputedly simplified the Creed to one article: 'I believe in God. Amen': *DNB*.

[67] [David Williams], *A Letter to the Body of Protestant Dissenters; and to Protestant Dissenting Ministers, Of all Denominations* (London, 1777), p. 4. Williams's tract was a diatribe against

particular exploited the cry against feudal innovations on both sides of the Atlantic, since it was they who wished to argue that the Reformation, like the Glorious Revolution, had been incomplete. If this group of religious reformers were prominent in devising an image of English rule as a system of 'slavery and arbitrary power' (a thesis explored in more detail in chapter 4 below), they were prominent also in the denunciation of priestcraft and tyranny which was held to characterise contemporary Catholicism and, to an even greater degree, the European feudal monarchies. Such an idea offered a powerful set of negations, in the absence, as yet, of an equally powerful set of positive images.

If Englishmen in England and America were ignorant of the term 'Enlightenment', they had equally never heard the word 'nationalism'. Yet among the most powerful negations of eighteenth-century transatlantic discourse was its rejection of the foreigner and, especially, of the Roman Catholic religion. Nationalism, and the clash of clearly-formed national identities, do not however provide an easy answer to the problems of transatlantic relations. The old assumption that nationalism was a single, homogeneous phenomenon which, once established, contained a strong inner logic of development has been overset by the discovery that early-modern societies could sustain different, and varying, self-images; that these were often difficult to devise and preserve; and that they could be broken up rather than promoted by the advance of what is conventionally termed the Enlightenment.[68] The colonies were too diverse in composition, too dependent on Old World historic myths, early to evolve a clear sense of their necessary distinctness as individual colonies, still less a sense of the common identity of all colonies. The early formulations of many colonies as religious experiments led them to seek a revitalised, purified homeland, not to reject their origin; their later insistence on claiming 'the rights of Englishmen' locked them into the

---

his fellow Dissenters for their intolerance of theological heterodoxy, and a recommendation that they adopt '*Intellectual Liberty*' instead: 'Machiavel says, that the way to preserve a state tending to a decline is by recurring to its first principles. This must not be your method to recover the strength and credit of your body. Nothing would so effectually ruin you as recurring to your original principles' (pp. 24–5).

[68] Rosalind Mitchison (ed.), *The Roots of Nationalism: Studies in Northern Europe* (Edinburgh, 1980); Linda Colley, 'The Apotheosis of George III: Loyalty, Royalty and the British Nation 1760–1820', *P&P* 102 (1984), 94–129; Gerald Newman, *The Rise of English Nationalism: A Cultural History 1740–1830* (New York, 1987); Otto Dann and John Dinwiddy (eds.), *Nationalism in the Age of the French Revolution* (London, 1988); Raphael Samuel (ed.), *Patriotism: The Making and Unmaking of British National Identity* (3 vols., London, 1989). C. Kidd, 'The Ideological Significance of Scottish Jacobite Latinity', in Jeremy Black and Jeremy Gregory (eds.), *Culture, Politics and Society in Britain, 1660–1800* (Manchester, 1991), pp. 110–30 and 'Scottish Whig Historiography and the Creation of an Anglo-British Identity 1689-c. 1800' (Oxford D.Phil. thesis, 1991); Murray Pittock, *The Invention of Scotland: the Stuart Myth and the Scottish Identity, 1638 to the Present* (London, 1991).

historical scenario and national myth within which those rights were carried.

However much the symbols later vital to the nationalism of the United States were available in the colonial period,[69] they were not yet given their nineteenth-century significance and until the Revolution were never assembled under the pressure of tactical necessity into coherent wholes. In France, it took the cataclysmic events of regicide and revolution to weld together the symbols of liberty into a representation of national identity.[70] In colonial America similarly, the celebration of collective symbols of identity lacked a referent before 1776; it could only take the form of a stern and austere defence of the ancient constitution, the liberties of Englishmen. How a different sense of collective identity evolved to unite the thirteen colonies (and distinguish them from England's other colonies) after 1776 is explored in chapter 1. It was not, however, a development which colonists had long premeditated or metropolitan Englishmen anticipated.

Even before 1789, the most 'advanced' English reformers disavowed national exclusiveness and affirmed a principled cosmopolitanism. This they tended to derive from their sense of solidarity with co-religionists everywhere. As the Low Church Anglican Granville Sharp observed,

> under the glorious Dispensation of the Gospel, we are absolutely bound to consider ourselves as *Citizens of the World*; that every Man whatever, without any *partial distinction* of Nation, Distance, or Complexion, must necessarily be esteemed *our Neighbour*, and *our Brother*; and that we are absolutely bound in Christian Duty to entertain *a Disposition* towards *all Mankind* as charitable and benevolent, *at least*, as that which was required of the Jews, under the Law, towards their *national Brethren*.[71]

Such sentiments were much more powerful among the Dissenting denominations, united to their co-religionists in the thirteen colonies and elsewhere by shared theologies, ecclesiastical polities and historical myths.

V. THE COMMONWEALTH PARADIGM

If the Enlightenment, the 'ancient constitution' and nationalism offer only ambiguous clues to the nature of transatlantic links, a fourth option appears more promising. It has been maintained that Englishmen in England and America were united in a single idiom of political discourse,

[69] Richard L. Merritt, *Symbols of American Community 1735–1775* (New Haven, 1966).
[70] Lynn Hunt, *Politics, Culture, and Class in the French Revolution* (London, 1986).
[71] Granville Sharp, *The Law of Retribution; or, A Serious Warning to Great Britain and her Colonies, Founded on unquestionable Examples of God's Temporal Vengeance against Tyrants, Slave-holders, and Oppressors* (London, 1776), p. 6.

native in England but universally adopted in the American colonies. The history of the American Revolution in particular has been dominated by a paradigm established in the 1960s, 'the assertion that the effective, triggering convictions that lay behind the Revolution were derived not from common Lockean generalities but from the specific fears and formulations of the radical publicists and opposition politicians of early eighteenth-century England who carried forward into the age of Walpole the peculiar strain of anti-authoritarianism bred in the upheaval of the English Civil War':[72] by the unmodified application, that is, to colonial America of the tradition brilliantly evoked as that of the Commonwealthmen,[73] men writing in the idiom of John Milton and James Harrington, a tradition placed in a grander historical setting by the elucidation of its Florentine, civic humanist roots,[74] and extended, especially for the early years of the American state, into an historiographical paradigm based on the idea of republicanism.[75]

This study seeks to pluralise our map of political discourse by the addition of other, no less crucial, frameworks and political idioms. It has been suggested that Caroline Robbins's 'Commonwealthmen' are not to be understood as standing within a single tradition of thought,[76] given different expression by three clearly-related generations of authors; that their common feature lay in their theories of religion, even in their theology, rather than in any secular speculations on civic virtue or in Harringtonian enquiries into the basis of power in landownership and trade,

---

[72] Bailyn, *American Politics*, pp. ix–x; idem., *Ideological Origins*, pp. vii–x.

[73] Robbins, *Commonwealthman*.

[74] J. G. A. Pocock, *Politics, Language and Time* (London, 1971); idem, *The Machiavellian Moment: Florentine Political Thought and the Atlantic Republican Tradition* (Princeton, 1975); idem (ed.), *The Political Works of James Harrington* (Cambridge, 1977); idem, 'Between Gog and Magog: the Republican Thesis and the *Ideologia Americana*,' *Journal of the History of Ideas* 48 (1987), 325–46, especially for the way in which this paradigm eliminated the thesis of 'Lockeian' or 'bourgeois' liberalism. A not-exhaustive list of the languages of political discourse in the early-modern English-speaking world would include 'common law, republican civic humanism, Protestant apocalyptic and eschatology, natural jurisprudence, political economy, and the Enlightened assault on the concept of Christ's divinity': idem, 'The Language of Political Discourse and the British Rejection of the French Revolution', in E. Pii (ed.), *I Linguaggi Politici delle Rivoluzioni in Europa XVII–XIX Secolo* (Firenze, 1992), pp. 19–30, at 20.

[75] Daniel T. Rodgers, 'Republicanism: The Career of a Concept', *Journal of American History* 79 (1992), 11–38, traces the historiography and argues that a new synthesis is required. Cf. James T. Kloppenberg, 'The Virtues of Liberalism: Christiantity, Republicanism, and Ethics in Early American Political Discourse', ibid., 74 (1987), 9–33.

[76] Robbins's *Commonwealthman*, despite its meticulous scholarship, was less clear in explaining why the writings of the theorists it dealt with constituted a 'canon', and almost silent on the problem of why and how traditions or idioms of political discourse were created and sustained.

important though these things were.[77] Yet if a common theme can be found in the works conventionally ascribed to this idiom, this common theme did not unite its authors: their identity and polemical purposes become fully evident only when they are placed in the denominational traditions to which they consciously subscribed or from which they passionately dissented. As a corollary, this study argues that religion was a vital concern both of the political elite and of populations at large in this period as private practice, as public morality, and as political symbol. Political discourse in England's North Atlantic possessions in the 'long' eighteenth century was plural, not homogeneously 'Commonwealth', and this pluralism is here traced chiefly to the sectarian diversity of those possessions. In the rivalry and antagonism of religious sects is to be found a crucial component of imperial politics and a central theme in the history of political thought, hitherto largely the province of church historians,[78] but deserving of a more central place in the historical arena.

Our confidence in identifying an idiom of discourse should be qualified by the fact that eighteenth-century 'Commonwealthmen' were not, at the time, identified as a school, either by themselves or by others; the term was used, infrequently, to disparage individuals by an analogy with the 1640s rather than by asserting present membership of a recognisable group. It is now evident that these writers have been retrospectively assembled into a tradition by a distinguished work of history,[79] just as the religious revivals of eighteenth-century America were subsequently entitled, and thenceforth indelibly identified as, the Great Awakening.[80] 'Commonwealth' doctrine was not recognised as an idiom of political discourse in the late seventeenth and eighteenth centuries, and in order to be understood in its contemporary tactical setting it needs to be resolved into its component parts.

The most salient feature of the 1770s and 80s for the historian of ideas on both sides of the Atlantic is that opinion was profoundly divided; the

---

[77] Clark, *English Society 1688–1832*. This framework of explanation occasionally attended to non-secular issues but regarded these as secondary ones which arose when 'the logic of secular liberty' was 'applied' to 'the condition of religion and the churches': Bailyn, *Ideological Origins*, p. 265. For a defence of the secular nature of the 'Commonwealth' paradigm, see Bernard Bailyn, 'Religion and Revolution: Three Biographical Studies', *Perspectives in American History* 4 (1970), 85–169: although 'religious ideas in general and the views of specific denominational groups in particular provided significant reinforcement to the Revolutionary movement', nevertheless 'The effective determinants of revolution were political' (p. 85). The present study offers evidence against this defence.

[78] E.g. Sidney E. Mead, 'Denominationalism: The Shape of Protestantism in America', *Church History* 23 (1954), 291–320.

[79] Robbins, *Commonwealthman*.

[80] Joseph Tracy, *The Great Awakening: A History of the Revival of Religion in the Time of Edwards and Whitefield* (Boston, 1842).

conflict of ideas as of armed forces took the form of a civil war.[81] The revolutionaries won the war of independence; but they won it not in a comprehensive and decisive military conquest, like that achieved by the Northern over the Southern states in the 1860s, and much was owed to the professional army of the French monarchy. Among the colonists themselves, both sides in the conflict of 1776–83 scored notable successes; both could point to remarkable feats of arms, displays of courage and outrageous atrocities; the hold of both sides over the areas under their control was liable to collapse until a late stage. The military conflict between patriot and loyalist militias was bitter but indecisive. Americans achieved independence because they avoided defeat for long enough, despite widely varying degrees of enthusiasm and support for the war among the colonists, until the international conflict and French military and naval intervention made Britain's position impossible.[82] Yorktown did not symbolise the triumph of the American yeoman or prove his wholehearted consent to a single body of values; indeed it was the culmination of a campaign in which Catholic French regular forces (the navy included) outnumbered their colonial allies.

These features of the military conflict emphasise that the Revolution was not made by a previously-existing nation, united around a shared ideology, which threw off a foreign yoke in a decisive act; rather, the revolutionaries were left the victors in a fragmented civil war after their opponents had been compelled to give up the struggle. They were the survivors of an internecine conflict in which colonial opinion, like opinion in the British Isles, had been profoundly divided. This characteristic, emphasised by military historians, has been obscured for other disciplines by the dominance of successive unitary paradigms, especially the Commonwealth paradigm. Its dominance led one historian to omit opponents of the Revolution from his history on the grounds that 'the future lay not with them',[83] a decision which created the very homogeneity which the Commonwealth paradigm presumed. Yet even the position of the victors cannot be correctly recreated without reference to what they were arguing against,[84] and it is the reinstatement of these neg-

---

[81] For the Revolution as a civil war, see chapter 4, part I below.

[82] John Shy, *A People Numerous and Armed: Reflections on the Military Struggle for American Independence* (revised edn, Ann Arbor, Mich., 1990), pp. 17–22; Morgan, *Inventing the People*, pp. 161–5.

[83] Bailyn, *Ideological Origins*, p. x.

[84] Cf. Bailyn, *Ideological Origins*, p. 19: 'By 1763 the great landmarks of European life – the church and the idea of orthodoxy, the state and the idea of authority: much of the array of institutions and ideas that buttressed the society of the *ancien régime* – had faded in their exposure to the open, wilderness environment of America.' The present study takes as its point of departure the old order, outlined for England in Clark, *English Society 1688–1832*, and for colonial America by Gordon S. Wood, *The Radicalism of the American Revolution* (New York, 1991), pp. 11–92.

lected themes, first in the history of Britain, then in the history of colonial America, that has moved our understanding of the Revolution closer to contemporary perceptions of it.

Once the sectarian sources of division were overlooked, it could be assumed that eighteenth-century America was a 'relatively undifferentiated society' whose different intellectual traditions were 'harmonised into a single whole by the influence of one peculiar strain of thought, one distinctive tradition' – that of the Commonwealthmen. Yet this harmonising role has been only asserted, not demonstrated,[85] and the rich but conflicting diversity of transatlantic traditions of political and religious thought has been obscured by a process of historiographical homogenisation. It is suggested here that the history of the transatlantic English-speaking realm is a story of division rather than unity, conflict rather than harmony. Disaggregation rather than the search for consensus is, consequently, the keynote of recent enquiry.[86] If earlier scholarship on the 'Commonwealth' idiom was overwhelmingly secular, it was likewise confined by the related assumption that 'England' was synonymous with 'Britain'.[87] It could still be presumed therefore that the 'Commonwealthmen' had provided the single or the dominant idiom of political discourse for all 'Britons' and all 'Americans'. Yet widespread as denunciations of corruption and perceptions of conspiracies to impose tyranny were, their importance and their bearing on political events can only be fully discerned if these two homogeneous political actors, 'Britain' and 'America', are disaggregated into their component parts – English, Scots, Irish, Welsh, and, in the colonies, Germans, French and others. Once disaggregated, it can be appreciated why this political and social pluralism mattered: less because of ethnicity, more because of religious denomination and the traditions of identity and authority for which denominations were the vehicles.

The public ideologies widespread in the Anglophone world by the late eighteenth century warned against 'slavery', denounced 'tyranny', pointed out the ways in which men could be defrauded of their ancient liberties, recorded the threat posed by standing armies, and lamented the enervating effects of vice and luxury. All these themes were prominent in

[85] Bailyn, *Ideological Origins*, pp. 13, 23, 34, 43, 51, 54. For a contrary picture of profound and growing diversities in colonial societies as causes of repeated insurrections, and of the difficulty of mobilising colonial society for war in 1776, see Shy, *A People Numerous and Armed*, pp. 117–32. Cultural diversities are now beginning to be emphasised in, for example, Bailyn and Morgan (eds.), *Strangers Within the Realm: Cultural Margins of the First British Empire*.
[86] For law, see Pocock, *Ancient Constitution*, pp. 290 ff; idem, 'The Varieties of Whiggism from Exclusion to Reform', in *Virtue, Commerce and History* (Cambridge, 1985), pp. 215–310.
[87] E.g. Bailyn, *American Politics*, pp. 15, 53, 57, 150.

the rhetoric of American revolutionaries, but it was rare that they were greatly owed to a reading of authors like Henry Neville, Walter Moyle or Robert, Viscount Molesworth. Most were standard themes of the folk memories of Protestant denominations; they formed part of their myths or histories of their origins, of their reasons for dissent from the Church of England, and of their principled resistance to episcopacy or 'Popery'.[88] Moreover, the goals of the Revolutionaries of 1776, like the goals of other champions of insurrection in the English-speaking world, went far beyond the negative rejection of the threats that 'Commonwealthmen' identified. Some of the Americans who rebelled in 1776 sought to found a new and timeless social order, *novus ordo seclorum*, in which material prosperity would naturally attend moral and religious purity, in which peace and righteousness would be, without further exertion, the inheritance of their descendants, in which human nature would be freed from its ancient disease and released into a new age of creative fulfilment and innocent emancipation. The translation of this millenarian vision into worldly terms entailed not secularisation but a holy war. As an act of quasi-religious expiation, revolution was required for Britain also, for, as Patrick Henry warned, America would not be safe until Britain's

> ruin, or at least . . . her extreme humiliation, which has not happened, and cannot happen until she is deluged with blood, or thoroughly purged by a revolution, which shall wipe from existence the present king with his connexions, and the present system, with those who aid and abet it.[89]

Only if the divisions of denominational discourse were overlooked could a 'Commonwealth' school be created by the assembly of a list of able but diverse authors.[90] Their writings undoubtedly reached the colonies in imported English editions, though in very limited numbers and often, even then, donated to college libraries by active English propagandists like Thomas Hollis (1720–74); they were sometimes excerpted in newspapers; but more striking is the almost complete absence of

---

[88] J. G. A. Pocock has rightly emphasised that civic humanism was neither a secular nor a secularising idiom of political discourse. Such characteristics have, however, been imputed to it by others.

[89] Patrick Henry to Richard Henry Lee, 18 June 1778, in William Wirt Henry, *Patrick Henry: Life, Correspondence and Speeches* (3 vols., New York, 1891), vol. 1, p. 564.

[90] Robbins, *Commonwealthman*, gives particular prominence to the names of Richard Cumberland (1631–1718), Andrew Fletcher (1655–1716), Thomas Gordon (d. 1750), James Harrington (1611–77), Edmund Law (1703–87), John Locke (1632–1704), Edmund Ludlow (?1617–92), Andrew Marvell (1621–78), John Milton (1608–74), Robert, Viscount Molesworth (1656–1725), William Molyneux (1656–98), Walter Moyle (1672–1721), Marchamont Nedham (1620–78), Henry Neville (1620–94), Anthony Ashley Cooper, 3rd Earl of Shaftesbury (1671–1713), Algernon Sidney (1622–83), John Trenchard (1662–1723) and James Tyrrell (1642–1718).

colonial reprints of their works. Current bibliographic studies[91] suggest that, from 1660 to 1776 inclusive, the total number of colonial reprints of the works of Cumberland, Fletcher, Harrington, Law, Ludlow, Marvell, Molesworth, Molyneux, Moyle, Nedham, Shaftesbury, Sidney and Tyrrell was nil, despite, in many cases, continuing reprints of their works in London, Dublin, Edinburgh or Glasgow. Henry Neville was represented by just one colonial imprint, whose publisher, Marmaduke Johnson, was fined £5 in Cambridge, Massachusetts, for printing it without licence.[92]

John Locke was first honoured by a colonial press only in 1743 when some Yale seniors printed *A Letter Concerning Toleration* in protest against the manifest intolerance of the Congregational president and governors of Yale College in expelling two students who had joined a Separatist church, a move which almost cost the protesters their degrees.[93] Although the same work was reprinted in Wilmington in 1764, Locke's *Second Treatise on Government* had to wait until 1773 before it attracted a colonial reprint in Boston.[94] Even this did not release a long-frustrated enthusiasm: the next American edition of the *Second Treatise* waited until 1937.

John Milton's political writings, with one exception aimed at a denominational conflict,[95] inspired a similar indifference in colonial printers. The more relevant authors, from an American perspective, were undoubtedly Trenchard and Gordon: their periodical *The Independent Whig*, published in London in 1720–1, saw collected editions in Philadelphia in 1724 and 1740. Yet this appealed to denominational concerns, as its full title made clear: *The Independent Whig: or, a Defence of Primitive Christianity, And of Our Ecclesiastical Establishment, Against The Exorbitant Claims and Encroachments of*

---

[91] Evans, *American Bibliography*, vols. 1–5; *The Eighteenth Century Short-Title Catalogue*. The significance of the lack of colonial reprints of the Commonwealthmen, and the proliferation of unexamined politico-theological writings, are overlooked in Robbins, *Commonwealthman*, pp. 391, 393.

[92] Henry Neville, *The Isle of Pines, or a late Discovery of a Fourth Island in Terra Australis* (Cambridge, Mass., 1668).

[93] Benjamin Trumbull, *A Complete History of Connecticut* (2 vols., New Haven, 1818), vol. 2, pp. 179–83. In September 1742 the *Boston Weekly News-Letter* carried an advertisement for the reprinting by subscription of Locke's *Letter Concerning Toleration* 'as being very seasonable to check the Spirit of Persecution rising up among us' as a result of religious revivalism: it does not seem that the proposal was acted on. Edwin Scott Gaustad, *The Great Awakening in New England* (New York, 1957), p. 113.

[94] For colonists' ignorance of Locke's *Two Treatises*, see John Dunn, 'The Politics of Locke in England and America in the Eighteenth Century', in John W. Yolton (ed.), *John Locke: Problems and Perspectives* (Cambridge, 1969), pp. 45–80; Oscar Handlin, 'Learned Books and Revolutionary Action, 1776', *Harvard Library Bulletin* 34 (1986), 362–79.

[95] John Milton, *An Old Looking-Glass for the Laity and Clergy of All Denominations . . . being considerations touching the likeliest means to remove hirelings out of the Church of Christ* (London, 1659; Philadelphia, 1770; New Haven, 1774).

Fanatical and Disaffected Clergymen.[96] This work purported to defend the existing Anglican establishment, which it tendentiously identified as 'the Bishop of Bangor's Scheme', the extreme Low Church position controversially advanced in 1717 by Benjamin Hoadly, as the only alternative to '*Rome*'. In reality, it consisted almost entirely of a sustained and venomous denunciation of High Church Anglicanism for its claims to priestly authority and support for the doctrines of hereditary right and passive obedience: '*Orthodoxy* has made many Tyrants, and exceeded All.'[97] The ecclesiastical bearing of this periodical was well understood in America. In 1756 the 20-year-old John Adams confided to his diary:

> The Church of Rome has made it an article of faith that no man can be saved out of their church, and all other religious sects approach to this dreadful opinion in proportion to their ignorance, and the influence of ignorant or wicked priests. Still reading the Independent Whig.[98]

By contrast, Trenchard and Gordon's less explicitly denominational *Cato's Letters* was not reprinted in the American colonies.

The almost complete absence of reprints of the Commonwealthmen in America is not consistent with the thesis that their 'ideas acquired in the colonies an importance, a relevance in politics, they did not then have – and never would have – in England itself'.[99] Moreover, this neglect is even more telling evidence by comparison with the reprinting in the colonies of many other English works which clearly did engage closely with colonial concerns.[100] These included works defending the English parliamentary and legal tradition,[101] and the chief summary of Scots resistance theory;[102]

[96] Into the same genre fell Thomas Gordon's ironic *A Modest Apology for Parson Alberoni, Governor to King Philip, (A Minor,) and Universal Curate of the whole Spanish Monarchy: the whole being a short, but unanswerable defence of priestcraft and a new confutation of the Bishop of Bangor* (London, 1719; [Boston], 1724).

[97] *The Independent Whig* (7th edn, 2 vols., London, 1743), vol. 1, pp. v, xxxii, xl (this idiom retained its currency: a third volume was added in 1746 and a fourth in 1747).

[98] Diary, 16 Feb. 1756, in Adams, *Works*, vol. 2, p. 5; this work duly attracted an American reprint of a denominationally-oriented reply by the rector of Exford, Somerset: Francis Squire, *An Answer to some Late Papers, entitled, The Independent Whig; so far as they relate to the Church of England, as by law established* (London, 1723; New York, 1753).

[99] Bailyn, *Ideological Origins*, p. xi.

[100] For law texts, see Eldon Revare James, 'A List of Legal Treatises Printed in the British Colonies and the American States before 1801', *Harvard Legal Essays* (Cambridge, Mass., 1934), pp. 159–211.

[101] E.g. George Petyt, *Lex Parliamentaria: or, a Treatise of the Law and Custom of the Parliament of England* (London, 1690; New York, 1716); John Somers, *The Security of Englishmen's Lives; or, the Trust, Power and Duty of the Grand Jurys of England Explained* (London, 1681; Boston 1720; Philadelphia, 1773); Henry Care, *English Liberties, or the Free-Born Subject's Inheritance* (London, [1680]; Boston, 1721; Providence, R.I., 1774); John Somers, *The Judgement of Whole Kingdoms and Nations, concerning the Rights, Power and Prerogative of Kings, and the Rights, Privileges & Properties of the People* (London, 1710; Philadelphia, 1773; Newport, R.I., Boston and New York, 1774).

[102] George Buchanan, *De Jure Regni: or the due right of Government* . . . (Philadelphia, 1766), reprint of *De Iure Regni apud Scotos, dialogus* (Edinburgh, 1579).

they included also tracts denouncing the Jacobite menace to shared trans-atlantic freedoms.[103] Colonial memories were long: they extended to recollections of Catholic atrocities in Ireland[104] as well as the crimes of the Stuart family in England. They included theological works which spoke to growing colonial heterodoxy;[105] but they included also classic works of Anglican theology, moral teaching and polemic.[106] They naturally included works in which other denominations justified their separate status in the Old World, and did so, evidently, in ways relevant to their co-religionists in the New.[107] For such an audience, evidence which seemed to point to Anglican intolerance was avidly seized and quickly disseminated: minor issues could have an immense strategic significance for the relations of

[103] E.g. Benjamin Bird, *The Jacobites Catechism, that is to say, an Instruction to be learned of every person who either desires, or expects to be confirmed by the late Bishop of Ely to which is added, The Williamites Catechism, or, instructions to be learned of all those who are well-wishers to the Protestant Religion, and the English Liberties* (London, 1691; Boston, 1692); James Macpherson, *The History of the Present Rebellion in Scotland* (London, 1745; Boston, 1745); *A Discourse on Government and Religion, Calculated for the Meridian of the Thirtieth of January* (London, 1750; Boston, 1750).

[104] *Popish Cruelty Displayed: Being a True and full Account of the Bloody and Hellish Massacre in Ireland* (London, [1753]; Boston, 1753; Portsmouth, N.H., 1757).

[105] E.g. Giles Firmin (1617–97), *The Real Christian . . . To which is added . . . a few words concerning Socinianism* (London, 1670; Glasgow, 1744; Boston, 1745); Thomas Emlyn (1663–1743), *An Humble Inquiry into the Scripture-Account of Jesus Christ* ([London], 1702; Boston, 1756).

[106] E.g. Thomas Ken, *An Exposition on the Church-Catechism* (London, 1685; Boston, 1688); Charles Leslie, *The Religion of Jesus Christ the Only True Religion, or, A Short and Easie Method with the Deists* (London, 1698; Boston, 1719; Williamsburg, 1733; New York, 1745); Henry Scougal, *Vital Christianity: A Brief Essay on the Life of God, in the Soul of Man* (London, 1677; Philadelphia, 1725, 1730; Boston, 1741; Philadelphia, 1766; in German translation: Germantown, 1755; Philadelphia, 1756); Edmund Gibson, *The Bishop of London's Pastoral Letter to the People of his Diocese . . . occasioned by some late writings in favour of infidelity* (London, 1728; Boston, 1730); George Whitefield, *The Marks of the New Birth. A Sermon Preached at the Parish Church of St. Mary, White-Chapel* (London, 1739; New York, 1739); George Lavington, *The Enthusiasm of Methodists and Papists Considered* (London, 1749; Boston, 1750); Thomas Sherlock, *The Tryal of the Witnesses of the Resurrection of Jesus* (London, 1729; New London, 1754); John MacGowan, *The Arians and Socinians Monitor* (London, 1761; Boston, 1774; Norwich, 1775).

[107] E.g. William Chandler, *A Brief Apology in Behalf of the People in Derision call'd Quakers* (London, 1693; Philadelphia, 1719); Thomas Woolston, *A Free Gift to the Clergy* (London, 1722; Philadelphia, 1724); Charles Owen (sometimes attributed to John Withers), *Plain Reasons, I. For Dissenting from the Communion of the Church of England. II. Why Dissenters are not, nor can be guilty of schism, in . . . separating from . . . the Church of England. And III. Several Common Objections brought . . . against Dissenters, answer'd* (London, 1715; Boston, 1725); Micaiah Towgood, *The Dissenting Gentleman's Answer, to the Rev. Mr. White's Three Letters: in which a separation from the Establishment is fully justified* (London, 1746; New York, 1748; Boston, 1748); republished as *A Dissent from the Church of England fully justified* (Boston, 1768); Micaiah Towgood, *A Calm and Plain Answer to the Enquiry, Why are you a Dissenter from the Church of England? . . . By the Author of the Dissenting Gentleman's Letters to White. Being a Summary View of the Arguments contained in those Letters* (London, 1772; Boston, 1773; Philadelphia, 1774).

denominations.[108] Nor were all works in these idioms necessarily colonial reprints: colonial authors could articulate them equally clearly.[109] The 'Commonwealth' tradition, if a tradition it was, was native to England. American political discourse was preoccupied with its own issues, often denominational. The idea of the existence of a universal secular idiom of politics for colonial Americans by 1776 is difficult to reconcile with the richness, diversity and sectarian nature of colonial American publishing.[110]

The recovery of the plural nature of political discourse in the English-speaking world dovetails with the contemporary perception that the Revolution of 1776 was precipitated by small and distinct groups; it also rescues that perception from its overtones of conspiracy theory and relocates it within a body of evidence. Emigrés insisted that the Revolution had been incited by 'small numbers' of the disaffected, men 'of considerable abilities, and little fortune, – restless and ambitious spirits, – educated in republican principles, and of course destitute of those attachments which would have formed and fixed their loyalty'.[111] They were, as we can now see, loyal in very different attachments and educated to a high degree in very different principles.

VI. DENOMINATIONAL DISCOURSE

Americans derived their perceptions of England's corruption far less from any free-standing Commonwealth tradition than from denominational sources. These were the reverse of homogeneous.[112] It has been emphasised that there is no single American theological tradition, but rather a diversity within the sects, and secondly that American theology 'is far more *derivative* than is German, or French, or English theology': until the first quarter of the nineteenth century it derived from its European, especially British, sources. American theology consequently shared the three overriding preoccupations of reformed Protestantism: 'the depravity of man, the sovereignty of God, and the necessity of

---

[108] E.g. John MacGowan, *Priestcraft Defended. A Sermon Occasioned by the Expulsion of Six Young Gentlemen from the University of Oxford. For Praying, Reading, and Expounding the Scriptures* (London, 1768; Philadelphia, 1769; Boston, 1769; Newport, R.I., 1770; Boston, 1771; New Haven, 1771).

[109] E.g. *The Madness of the Jacobite Party, in attempting to set a Popish Pretender on the British Throne, demonstrated* (Boston, Mass., 1724) appears to lack a London imprint.

[110] Evans, *American Bibliography*; T. R. Adams, *American Independence: the Growth of an Idea* (Providence, 1965); idem, *The American Controversy* (2 vols., Providence, 1980).

[111] [Joseph Galloway], *An Account of the Rise and Progress of the American War* (4th edn., London, 1780), p. 8.

[112] The role of religion in the Revolution has conventionally been explored with reference to Congregationalists and, to a lesser degree, Presbyterians. For an important corrective see Stephen A. Marini, 'Political Theologies of the American Revolution' (forthcoming).

worshiping God and ordering the church strictly in accordance with Biblical prescription'.[113] In the early seventeenth century, it was different conceptions in the third area that split Protestants into Episcopalians, Presbyterians and Congregationalists; 'Apart from problems of church order, there was a remarkable degree of consensus between contending parties.'[114] All these components were carried together in the denominations' sense of their past, and given intensity by contemporaries' understanding of ecclesiastical history not as the private life of a sect but as the cosmic drama of God's dealings with man throughout time.[115] The fate of mankind in this divine scenario, not just the institutional fortunes of a sect, was the prize which subscribers to this discourse perceived to be at stake and which gave the fortunes of their sect its significance. These questions of ecclesiastical polity, fading in eighteenth-century England, remained vivid in Scotland and Ireland, intensified in the American colonies, and engaged with newly-developing controversy on key points of theology.

The religious denominations of the English-speaking North Atlantic world sustained their own idioms of political discourse; those denominations were explicitly conscious of, and acknowledged, transatlantic sources that reveal their importance only in denominational settings. It was to a denominational constituency that the Deist Tom Paine appealed with such spectacular success; *Common Sense* was partly censored on its first publication in France because, as the American envoy John Adams noted, that work 'undertakes to prove, that Monarchy is unlawful by the old Testament'.[116] Paine owed his remarkable impact to introducing into an American denominational setting theological catalysts which had been devised in England many decades earlier. This was true of others also. As late as 1775 the patriot and Presbyterian minister John Witherspoon was citing[117] as a reminder of divine sovereignty and evidence of impious

---

[113] Sydney E. Ahlstrom, 'Theology in America: A Historical Survey', in James Ward Smith and A. Leland Jamison (eds.), *The Shaping of American Religion* (4 vols. in 5, Princeton, 1961), vol. 1, pp. 232–321, at 234–5.

[114] Ibid., p. 239.

[115] For which, see especially Avihu Zakai, *Exile and Kingdom: History and Apocalypse in the Puritan Migration to America* (Cambridge, 1992), pp. 1–11.

[116] Adams, Diary, 11 Feb. 1779, in L. H. Butterfield (ed.), *Diary and Autobiography of John Adams* (4 vols., New York, 1964), vol. 2, p. 351. Within the 'Commonwealth' paradigm, by contrast, it has been held that the 'intellectual core' of *Common Sense* was its 'attack on the traditional conception of balance as a prerequisite for liberty': Bailyn, *Ideological Origins*, p. 285. For an alternative reading see Clark, *English Society 1688–1832*, pp. 324–30.

[117] John Witherspoon, *The Dominion of Providence over the Passions of Men. A Sermon, Preached at Princeton, May 17, 1775, being the General Fast Appointed by the Congress through the United Colonies* (Philadelphia, 1775; reprinted London, 1778), p. 27. It was a Dissenting diagnosis of English corruption which guaranteed to Witherspoon that 'the confederacy of the

English military pride a tract of 1746, *Britain's Remembrancer*, written by a fellow Scot and would-be Presbyterian minister James Burgh.[118] Many of the arguments of the Congregationalist publicist Jonathan Mayhew[119] were borrowed from the heterodox English bishop Benjamin Hoadly.[120] British authors now largely forgotten could be influential in the colonies if they engaged with colonial sensitivities on religion. In 1773 the youthful James Madison, still smarting at the persecution of Baptists in his native Virginia, wrote to a friend[121] to request a copy of the heterodox Newcastle Dissenting minister James Murray's[122] *Sermons to Doctors of Divinity*, published anonymously in London in 1771 but reprinted with the author's name in Philadelphia in 1773.[123] Practical grievances were articulated and dramatised in Biblical imagery: Hermon Husband, apologist of the Regulator movement in the North Carolina backcountry in the 1760s, borrowed the text, arguments and style of Murray's *Sermons to Asses* to incite the colonists against the perceived injustices of the administration of the tidewater elite.[124]

The structure of these Dissenting idioms was self-sufficient. James Burgh is often quoted to establish the secular understanding of 'corruption' contained within 'Commonwealth' mentality;[125] his starting-point was, however, profoundly denominational. He had taken as the occasion of his moralising tract the 'Dread of a general Ruin' and even 'a general Massacre' with which the Jacobite rebellion of 1745 had confronted his countrymen, a dire warning which Burgh claimed was the most auspicious moment for moral regeneration within 'these last 30 Years', that is, since the Jacobite rising of 1715. His analysis was heavily providentialist, appealing to a God 'who by his Providence over-rules the Revolutions and disposes the Fates of Nations', who used calamity to punish the

colonies has not been the effect of pride, resentment, or sedition, but of a deep and general conviction, that our civil and religious liberties, and consequently, in a great measure, the temporal and eternal happiness of us and our posterity, depend on the issue . . . We have sometimes taken the liberty to forbode the downfall of the British empire, from the corruption and degeneracy of the people' (pp. 28–9, 40).

[118] James Burgh (1714–75), born Perthshire, son of Presbyterian minister; studied for the ministry at St Andrews, but desisted officially through ill health; published *Political Disquisitions* (3 vols., London, 1774–5).

[119] See below, pp. 168–9, 364–70.

[120] Bailyn (ed.), *Pamphlets*, pp. 208, 697–8.

[121] James Madison to William Bradford, 28 April 1773, in Madison, *Writings*, vol. 1, p. 15.

[122] For Murray see below, pp. 267, 329–31.

[123] Evans, *American Bibliography*, vol. 4, p. 376. Murray's *Sermons to Asses* (1768) reached a fifth edition in Philadelphia (1770) and was reprinted in Boston the same year.

[124] [Hermon Husband], *An Impartial Relation of the First Rise and Cause of the Recent Differences, in Publick Affairs, In the Province of North-Carolina* (n.p., 1770), in William K. Boyd (ed.), *Some Eighteenth Century Tracts Concerning North Carolina* (Raleigh, 1927), pp. 247–333, at 312.

[125] E.g. Bailyn, *Ideological Origins*, pp. 86–7.

wicked and call the pious to repentance.[126] The major 'deliverances' of English history all revealed 'the immediate Hand of God': the Spanish Armadas of 1588 and 1596; the discovery of the Gunpowder Plot in 1605; the Glorious Revolution; the Battle of the Boyne; the frustration of invasion attempts in 1692 and 1696; the aversion of a Jacobite conspiracy by Queen Anne's hastened death in 1714; the defeat of the Fifteen; the wreck of another Stuart invasion flotilla in 1744; the defeat of the Forty-Five.[127]

Within this vision, it was plausible that the harvest-threatening bad weather of the previous summer, and the Stuart invasion, were equally intended by God as reproof of 'LUXURY and IRRELIGION . . . the characteristic Vices of the Age', but a mere point of entry for their accompanying vices of 'Venality, Perjury, Faction, Opposition to legal Authority, Idleness, Gluttony, Drunkenness, Leudness, excessive Gaming, Robberies, clandestine Marriages, Breach of Matrimonial Vows, Self-murders, and innumerable others'. These private practices were linked to Burgh's world-historical scenario because, he claimed, 'nothing in the World is so likely to open a Door to Popery as unbounded Luxury and Voluptuousness; it being a Religion calculated for the Indulgence and Gratification of the Lusts and Appetites of Men'. Indeed, it was difficult to see what social problem or political practice could not be brought under Burgh's general rubric, or how any of them could be explained in any other terms than personal vice and irreligion. Burgh duly offered a brief history of the world in which each of its great civilisations – Babylonian, Persian, Grecian, Roman – 'at last sink under Luxury and Vice'.[128] Irreligion was a still 'more certain Means of bringing Destruction upon a Nation'. How could any doubt the truth of Christianity 'in the very Age, in which a *Newton*, a *Clarke*, and a *Locke*, (a Triumvirate which no Age since the Appearance of Christianity can exceed) have declared their Belief, and exerted the utmost force of their Genius in demonstrating the Truth of it'?[129] He named three Arians;[130] and the significance of theological heterodoxies like theirs in triggering the most extreme forms of Dissenting political commitment is explored in more depth below.

James Burgh is better known to historians for his compendious survey, *Political Disquisitions* (London, 1774–5). When reprinted in Philadelphia in 1775, the work had an impressive list of 'the encouragers' including

---

[126] [James Burgh], *Britain's Remembrancer: or, The Danger not over* (London, 1746), pp. 1–2, 16; reprinted Philadelphia, 1747, 1748; Boston, 1759.

[127] Ibid., pp. 29–35.

[128] Ibid., pp. 3, 6–9, 36.

[129] Ibid., pp. 18, 22.

[130] John Locke has recently been claimed as a Socinian in the work of John Marshall; Clarke was widely perceived as an Arian, though his theology is open to dispute.

Francis Alison, Silas Deane, John Dickinson, Christopher Gadsden, John Hancock, Thomas Jefferson, Benjamin Rush, George Washington, James Wilson and John Joachim Zubley.[131] But the work's success was possible only because the Dissenting idiom within which Burgh stood, and to which he had contributed, was already current in America: so Burgh was able to conclude two lengthy volumes on English parliamentary reform and a third on moral decay with an otherwise wildly irrelevant invocation to the Deity to save 'this once favoured nation' from impending ruin, not merely from corruption but – again without previous discussion – that God should 'Save the protestant religion' from 'the infernal cloud of popish delusion'. 'Assert thy supreme dominion over those who impiously pretend to be thy vicegerents upon earth', Burgh encouraged the Almighty:

> Let the cause of civil and religious Liberty prove victorious . . . Arise, and come forth from thy sacred seat, clothed in all thy terrors. Let thy lightnings enlighten the world. Let thy thunders shake the mountains. Let dismay and horror overwhelm the courage of thine enemies.[132]

The schoolmasterly, mildly impractical corrector of malpractices in parliamentary elections stood revealed in stark clarity as the Dissenter militant, the prophet of a holy war.

It was not only contractarian or Dissenting books which had an influence in America: the Anglican tradition was well able to hold its own in the public arena. In 1722 the New England Congregational establishment was rocked by the conversion en masse to the Church of England of a group of ministers based around that Congregational stronghold, Yale College. The 'Yale Apostates' – the rector, four tutors and three others – were convinced of the necessity of episcopacy, episcopal ordination and the apostolic succession by books sent to the college library by Jeremiah Dummer, Connecticut's agent in England. The validity of episcopacy in the primitive apostolic church was convincingly established by works including John Pearson's *An Exposition of the Creed* (London, 1659); Simon Patrick's *The Devout Christian Instructed* (London, 1672); Peter, Lord King's Presbyterian study, *An Enquiry into the Constitution, Discipline, Unity and Worship of the Primitive Church* (London, 1691),[133] corrected by John Slater's *An Original Draught of the Primitive Church* (London, 1717); William King's *A Discourse Concerning the Inventions of Men in the Worship of God* (London, 1694); and John Potter's *A Discourse of Church-Government* (London, 1707).

---

[131] James Burgh, *Political Disquisitions; or, An Enquiry into public Errors, Defects, and Abuses* (3 vols., Philadelphia, 1775), vol. 3.

[132] Burgh, *Political Disquisitions* (edn. cit.), vol. 3, pp. 458–60.

[133] For which, see below, p. 312.

They were further persuaded of the importance of episcopal ordination and the sin of schism from the Church of England by the debate articulated in Edmund Calamy's *A Defence of Moderate Non-conformity* (London, 1703–5) and Benjamin Hoadly's *A Serious Admonition to Mr. Calamy* (London, 1705).[134] Under the influence of this sort of reading, there was a steady haemorrhage of Congregational students to the Anglican church in succeeding decades.[135] Such works retained their currency: in 1767, Thomas Bradbury Chandler cited Hooker's *Ecclesiastical Polity* and Archbishop Potter's *Church Government* in support of his defence of the apostolic succession and call for bishops to be sent to America.[136]

The two centuries before the 1830s were marked by the extreme longevity within England too of Anglican works of devotion and social teaching.[137] Richard Allestree's *The Whole Duty of Man* (1658), the spiritual best-seller of the period, was continually reprinted, and echoed by works with titles like *The Whole Duty of Woman* (1753) and *The Whole Concern of a Christian* (1703). Allestree's later titles, *The Ladies Calling* (1673) and *The Gentleman's Calling* (1660) were also long in demand, and different emphases were given to this teaching in the orthodox *New Whole Duty of Man* (1744) and the Evangelical Henry Venn's *The Compleat Whole Duty of Man* (1763). Equal currency was enjoyed by such texts as *A Week's Preparation towards a Worthy Receiving of the Lord's Supper* (1678; 52nd edn., 1764); Robert Nelson's *A Companion for the Festivals and Fasts of the Church of England* (1704; 36th edn., 1826); Jeremy Taylor's *Holy Living* (1650) and *Holy Dying* (1651; 30th combined edn., 1820); and William Law's *A Serious Call to a Devout and Holy Life* (1729; 20th edn., 1816). The long currency of Anglican social teaching marked the stability and success of a certain social order and its associated idioms of discourse. The polemics in which Restoration Anglicans like Isaac Barrow, Robert South, Edward Stillingfleet and John Tillotson engaged had a powerful influence into the early nineteenth century. They achieved a 'synthesis of scriptural revelation and human reason' which maintained their writings in print and which was relied on

---

[134] For which, see below, p. 161.

[135] Peter Doll, 'Imperial Anglicanism in North America, 1745–1795' (Oxford D.Phil. thesis, 1989), p. 169; Richard Warch, *School of the Prophets: Yale College, 1701–1740* (New Haven, 1973), pp. 96–125; Donald Geraldi, 'Samuel Johnson and the Yale 'Apostasy' of 1722: The Challenge of Anglican Sacramentalism to the New England Way', *HMPEC* 47 (1978), 153–75.

[136] Thomas Bradbury Chandler, *An Appeal to the Public, In Behalf of the Church of England in America* (New York, 1767), pp. 6, 18.

[137] On the long currency of devotional works, see J. Wickham Legg, *English Church Life from the Restoration to the Tractarian Movement* (London, 1914), chapter XI. The same conclusion emerges from the publication dates of the titles listed in the Bishop of Chester's bibliography: William Cleaver, *A List of Books Intended for the Use of the Younger Clergy, and other Students in Divinity, within the Diocese of Chester* (Oxford, 1791; 3rd edn., 1808).

as an established premise by large numbers of their coreligionists. If eighteenth-century Anglican preaching often limited itself to moral exhortation, it has been suggested, it was because a belief in the achievement of this generation of divines freed later generations from certain at least of the possible dogmatic challenges to their position.[138]

VII. THE IMPLICATIONS OF THEOLOGICAL CONFLICT

Religion meant many things in early-modern society; all must take their place in a map of political discourses. Otherworldly piety was not necessarily its most striking feature. The wide extent of Anglican practice, and the prevalence of anticlerical sentiments in the colonies, opened the Church to every secular as well as sacred motive. Commissary Johnston complained from South Carolina how 'among all those that have the Church continually in their Mouths, ffew of them have any concern either for it or Religion. More than as it Serves for a Cloak to carry on their Worldly Designs.'[139] Such men were however constrained in their tactical options by the nature of their chosen rhetoric, whatever the sincerity of its articulation. Religion meant, most obviously, formal public worship; but its extent at different periods in Britain and America is still a subject for quantification, and the significance of the figures available is still a matter for interpretation. It meant, secondly, informal meetings for worship where church buildings or ordained ministers were not available. It meant the practice of private piety and family observance. It meant the form taken by or the expression given to deep psychological needs and aspirations. It meant a set of doctrines concerning theology and ecclesiastical polity. It involved each denomination in patterns of daily life which, to greater or lesser degrees, distinguished them from other denominations. Religion thus acted as a definition and a symbol of group identity, often extrapolated from the denomination to the state. It embodied a society's or a sect's sense of its historic trajectory, both its past experience and its future expectations. Sometimes this forward-looking perspective included a vision which was covertly or overtly millennial. Often the remembered past sustained a negative image of rival denominations, bitterly resented for ancient crimes and denounced for these iniquities in a context which denominational conflict made apocalyptic.

[138] Gerard Reedy, S.J., *The Bible and Reason: Anglicans and Scripture in Late Seventeenth-Century England* (Philadelphia, 1985), pp. 142–3.

[139] Gideon Johnston to John Chamberlain, 28 May 1712, in Frank J. Klingberg (ed.), *Carolina Chronicle: The Papers of Gideon Johnston 1707–1716* (Berkeley, 1946), pp. 108–12, at 110.

The simultaneous presence of all these elements made early-modern societies far more theoretically articulate than the societies which succeeded them, and their social relations were expressed to a much larger degree in terms of grand theory.[140] Among ordinary men and women, the degree of religious awareness in the early-modern transatlantic world was high. It was a culture in which the laity 'sustained churches by adhering to theological and ecclesiastical principles, and . . . destroyed churches by overturning theological and ecclesiastical traditions'.[141] The ideological imperatives which drove men to overturn those traditions are therefore of some importance, and are one recurring theme of this book. Theological conflict could have the widest implications. The debate between evangelical New Lights and establishmentarian Old Lights, Calvinist revivalists and the moderate rationalism of the existing sects, was 'not so much a debate between theologians as a vital competition for the intellectual allegiance of the American people'.[142] Jonathan Edwards's tract *Some Thoughts Concerning the Present Revival of Religion in New-England* (Boston, 1742) was, it has been argued, 'like the Awakening he defended . . . in a vital respect an American declaration of independence from Europe, and the revival impulse was one toward intercolonial union'.[143] John Adams admitted and defended the religious enthusiasms of the first English settlers of America: 'I believe it will be found universally true, that no great enterprise for the honour or happiness of mankind was ever achieved without a large mixture of that noble infirmity';[144] he was clearly influenced by his perspective on the political dynamics of his own day. Anglican historians for their part frequently took up the loyalists' insistence on an identity between Dissent in religion and rebellion, or republicanism, in politics.[145] This simplistic equation nevertheless elided

---

[140] The contrast is sharp with recent societies which, lacking clear theoretical rationales, find difficulty in sustaining theoretical disciplines of self-presentation: Quentin Skinner (ed.), *The Return of Grand Theory in the Human Sciences* (Cambridge, 1985).

[141] Jon Butler, *Awash in a Sea of Faith: Christianising the American People* (Cambridge, Mass., 1990), p. 8.

[142] Alan Heimert, *Religion and the American Mind from the Great Awakening to the Revolution* (Cambridge, Mass., 1966), p. 11.

[143] Ibid, p. 14. Heimert argued for an association between revivalist religion and rebellion, and against any link between Arminianism or unitarianism and rebellion. This study accepts (with qualifications) the first thesis and presents evidence against the second. It may be suggested that Heimert's second category of 'Liberals', embracing Latitudinarians, rationalists, Arminians and unitarians, is too inclusive and obscures the theological dynamics which induced many men included in that category to countenance resistance.

[144] John Adams, *A Dissertation on the Canon and Feudal Law* (1765), in *Works*, vol. 3, p. 452.

[145] Mary Beth Norton, *The British Americans: The Loyalist Exiles in England 1774–1789* (London, 1974), pp. 130–54.

crucial links in the chain of connection. Dissenters did not easily or necessarily rise in rebellion, and the principled grounds of their separation from the Church of England did not necessarily make them republicans. Nevertheless, connections undoubtedly existed, and are a prominent theme of this study.

Its chosen period includes episodes of extreme theological ferment which may validly be set beside the 1530s or 1640s; indeed the 'long' eighteenth century witnessed extended contests over doctrinal issues which had not been central, and sometimes had been virtually overlooked, in those earlier episodes. The doctrine of the Trinity, in particular, was the source of labyrinthine and interminable dispute within each denomination: its meaning, its evidences, and the senses in which it could be subscribed, provided a network of traps for the unwary. Trinitarians were in danger of defending their position in a way which drove them towards tritheism; a rejection of the Trinity could take the form of Sabellianism (which accepted Christ's divinity but emphasised it to the point of rejecting any division of the Godhead) or Arianism (in which Christ was accepted as a divine being, but created by, and so subordinate to, the Father); Arians could be pushed down a path towards Socinianism (in which Christ was accepted as a divinely-chosen but human moral agent). These long-drawn-out controversies meant that the writings of former theologians remained at the centre of contemporary debate.[146] As a movement, Arianism[147] was given its impetus by the publication in 1712 of the Anglican Samuel Clarke's *The Scripture-Doctrine of the Trinity*, his preferred conceptualisation; it was given its hostile definition by Daniel Waterland's *The Case of Arian Subscription Considered* (Cambridge, 1721). Clarke had disavowed (Proposition XVI) the claim that Scripture proved that the Son was a being created in time, but this did not protect him from the charge of full Arianism, nor halt the progress of his followers to that doctrine.[148]

The correlation between theological heterodoxy and a preference for political reform was strong, but not exclusive. Exceptions stood out, however. One was Granville Sharp (1735–1813), son of an archdeacon, grandson of Archbishop John Sharp of York, a Trinitarian of whom John

---

[146] As late as 1813 the English Congregationalist minister Samuel Palmer (1741–1813) felt it necessary to rescue his long-dead co-religionist Dr. Isaac Watts (1674–1748) from such a charge: Samuel Palmer, *Dr. Watts No Socinian. A Refutation of the Testimony of Dr. Lardner, as brought forward in The Rev. T. Belsham's Memoirs of the late Rev. Theophilus Lindsey* (London, 1813). This was necessary, declared Palmer, since the Socinians would give the story 'full credit' and 'greatly triumph in having so eminent a man as Dr. WATTS, who had written so much on the opposite side, at last brought over to their own' (pp. 1–2).

[147] See especially J. Hay Colligan, *The Arian Movement in England* (Manchester, 1913).

[148] J. P. Ferguson, *An Eighteenth Century Heretic: Dr. Samuel Clarke* (Kineton, 1976).

Adams wrote, while American minister in London: 'very amiable & benevolent in his dispositions, and a voluminous writer, but as Zealously
attached to Episcopacy & the Athanasian Creed as he is to civil and
religious Liberty – a mixture which in this Country is not common'.[149]
Heterodox doctrines of the Trinity had wide implications, as Dissenters
were aware:

> When the Saviour is reduced from an equality with God to the condition
> of a creature, he is infinitely less powerful and compassionate. Hence as
> man has not so glorious a Saviour, his case is not so deplorable as the
> orthodox represent it to be; his guilt is neither so aggravated, nor his
> depravity so great. An atonement made by a creature will suffice for his
> forgiveness; and the grace of a creature, for such the Holy Ghost is said to
> be, will render him all the assistance of which he stands in need.[150]

So Arianism, a technical doctrine of theology, acted more widely to promote a profoundly modified view of human nature. It was left to the more
advanced position of Socinianism, however, to generate the most vivid
forms of political engagement in the late eighteenth century. To Socinians,
the doctrine of the Trinity was not merely false theology, unknown to the
Jews, to Christ himself and His apostles; it was, as Gilbert Wakefield
announced in 1794, 'a doctrine, which will happily prove a mill-stone of
destruction to all *political* establishments of Christianity'.[151]

Other forms of heterodoxy had their political impact also. Profoundly
influential in eighteenth-century Europe was 'the comprehensive moral
philosophy of deism, which concealed itself under the title of *ius naturale*
and, after first disregarding the eternal law, finally culminated in the
complete moral autonomy of reason (Kant)'.[152] The 'high degree of correlation in the early eighteenth century between neo-Harringtonian republicanism and deism' has rightly been observed;[153] the correlation between
Deism and anti-monarchical politics was to survive and indeed culminate
in 1776 in the most effective of all Deist political tracts, Paine's *Common
Sense*. Arianism and Socinianism shared with Deism one novel consequence. The more unnecessary the doctrine of the atonement, the more
it could be presumed that man was inherently benevolent; it followed

---

[149] John Adams to Marquis de Lafayette, 31 Jan. 1786: quoted in Colin Bonwick, *English
Radicals and the American Revolution* (Chapel Hill, 1977), p. 7.

[150] David Bogue and James Bennett, *History of Dissenters, from the Revolution in 1688, to the Year
1808* (4 vols., London, 1808–12), vol. 3, pp. 386–7.

[151] Wakefield, *An Examination of the Age of Reason*, p. 4. For a full analysis of the theological
and political implications of anti-Trinitarianism, see Waterman, 'The Nexus between
Theology and Political Doctrine', passim.

[152] Heinrich A. Rommen, *The Natural Law: A Study in Legal and Social History and Philosophy*
(trans. Thomas R. Hanley, St Louis, 1947), p. 80.

[153] Pocock, *Machiavellian Moment*, p. 476.

that he was corrupted, or enslaved, only by outside forces (that is, by other people). Nurture rather than nature was prioritised; and the more that the human condition or the workings of divine Providence were excused, the more the blame for society's ills had to be laid at the door of minorities of wicked individuals. The tyranny of sin was subtly transformed into the tyranny of kings and bishops. It was a trope of eighteenth-century historiography that detailed, inner knowledge of public affairs disclosed how great events were the result of small and personal causes;[154] the heterodox imagination seized on this insight and inflated it into self-sustaining conspiracy theories. As much as the 1640s, the late-eighteenth-century era of revolution was (in modern terms) an age of paranoia. Even in the absence of formal theological millenarianism, the discourse of late-eighteenth-century heterodox Dissent became increasingly preoccupied with threats of persecution in its perceptions of slavery and corruption, increasingly strident in its invective against civil and ecclesiastical tyrants. To interpret this construction of a social demonology as part of a process of the secularisation of politics[155] is to miss the doctrinal origins of these secular commitments and the theological context in which these social dramas were played out.

To an Anglican, the doctrine of original sin implied that natural liberty, the liberty enjoyed by man in a state of nature, meant for each person 'the uncontrouled Power of doing *as much Evil as he can*'; hence, by the social contract, man is 'necessarily restrained by particular *Obligations*'. A '*Law of Nature*' should therefore be understood not as a blueprint for frictionless perfection but as a regulatory law imposed by the Creator on an imperfect creation. This 'Law, call it of Nature or of God' was to be identified with Revelation. 'I insist so much upon the Rule given in the *divine* Law', explained one author, 'because many of the American Leaders have attempted to sanctify their Revolt by a specious Appearance of *Religion*.'[156] Emancipation from Calvinist doctrines of predestination, however, did not necessarily or easily release men from the consequences of the Anglican and orthodox Dissenting understanding of original sin. The progress within Anglicanism and Dissent of an Arminian doctrine of universally offered redemption did not of itself predispose men to rebellion: something different was needed to trigger that commitment. Nor was Providence banished

---

[154] J. C. D. Clark (ed.), *The Memoirs and Speeches of James, 2nd Earl Waldegrave, 1742–1763* (Cambridge, 1988), Introduction, pp. 18–21.

[155] Robert Hole, *Pulpits, Politics and Public Order in England 1760–1832* (Cambridge, 1989).

[156] [Ambrose Serle], *Americans against Liberty; or an Essay on the Nature and Principles of True Freedom, shewing that the Designs and Conduct of the Americans tend only to Tyranny and Slavery* (London, 1775), pp. 6–7, 10–12.

from human affairs; rather, politically mobilised Dissent redirected the
hitherto-confused Deity to become a warrior against kingly and episcopal authority. The role newly designed for God in punishing transgression actually assumed a far greater immediacy in the context of
just resistance, or impious rebellion, against the Anglican symbols of
Church and State. Far from being secularised, spiritual commitments,
zeal and hatreds were transferred to the political arena in the 1770s
to greater effect than at any time since 1688–9.

Two themes have recently dominated the study of the role of religion
in the American Revolution: the Great Awakening, and millennialism.
The Great Awakening is a term coined in the nineteenth century which
dignified with too great an appearance of cohesion a variety of Protestant religious revivals in the North American colonies, and the psychological or temperamental predispositions to liberation from ancient forms
in the name of personal experience that went with them. Millennialism,
often associated with 'revivalist' movements, was a much older theme
within Christian thought, referring to the expectation of the thousand-
year rule of the saints on earth, foretold in the Book of Revelation,
which would succeed (or, alternatively, precede) the Second Coming.[157]
Millennialism was an ancient component of New England public discourse. The idea that the ultimate purpose of the Puritan experiment
in the New World was to return to and transform the corrupt religion
of the Old was initially powerful, and though it receded after 1660 it
left echoes which resurfaced in many local religious revivals. Jonathan
Edwards made such a prediction of the world mission of New England
in 1742, for the ancient sense of sectarian destiny was preserved in
the theological doctrine of the millennium.

> 'Tis not unlikely that this Work of God's Spirit, that is so extraordinary
> and wonderful, is the dawning, or, at least, a Prelude of that glorious Work
> of God, so often foretold in Scripture, which in the Progress and Issue of
> it, shall renew the World of Mankind . . . And there are many Things that
> make it probable that this Work will begin in *America*.[158]

Millennial themes can indeed be found in colonial rhetoric, especially

---

[157] Millennialism was a minority position within English religion. For an argument that
'most Tudor Protestant thought was apocalyptic but not millenarian' see Richard Bauckham, *Tudor Apocalypse* (Abingdon, 1978), pp. 208, 227–8. Millennialism assumed a significantly larger role in the American colonies.

[158] Jonathan Edwards, *Some Thoughts Concerning the Present Revival of Religion in New-England*
(Boston, 1742), p. 96. Edwards was not expressing a sense of national separateness,
elsewhere justifying his outspokenness: 'I will take the Liberty of an Englishman, (that
speaks his Mind freely, concerning publick Affairs)' (p. 349). Cf. Christopher M. Beam,
'Millennialism and American Nationalism, 1740–1800', *Journal of Presbyterian History* 54
(1976), 182–99.

during the Seven Years' and Revolutionary wars, but were far less prominent, even 'moribund', in the decade 1765–75: it was not millennialism which first framed the colonial case against Britain or activated colonial ideas of a right of resistance.[159]

However valid these two themes, they were specialised, localised, occurred at different times or are otherwise difficult to link with the revolutionary outbreak of 1776: the Revolution has, as a result, remained securely within a secular framework of interpretation. A larger theme, explored here, illuminates the nature of the Revolution as a religious and civil war on both sides of the Atlantic. It is a major contention of this book that early-modern societies were essentially sectarian in their dynamics: traditions of political thought and action were carried within and articulated by the mosaic of religious denominations which made up the British Isles and, still more, the North American colonies. Those denominations – Anglicans, Presbyterians, Congregationalists, Baptists, Quakers, Catholics and a host of less numerous sects – were sometimes influenced by revivalism and millennialism, sometimes not; but at all times they necessarily brought to the public arena long-rehearsed and still keenly-debated doctrines about their origins, purposes and destinies, and about what these entailed for the kingdom or empire within which they found themselves.

VIII. DENOMINATIONAL DYNAMICS AND POLITICAL REBELLIONS

If eighteenth-century England was relatively free from profound political upheaval, this must be attributed to the increasing hegemonic efficiency of the regime of peer and bishop, squire and parson, rather than to the presence of a Lockeian consensus about the justice of the settlement of 1689 or a passively deferential submission to the rule of the elite. The turbulence and fierce passions of the populace have been inescapably reasserted by a generation of scholarship, results which need only be balanced by an understanding that the same populace nevertheless ultimately sustained elite hegemony and manned an astonishingly successful imperial naval and military machine. Some of the parochial challenges to Anglican hegemony in England are reviewed in chapter 2 below. In the thirteen colonies, however, the position was markedly different.

Rebellions were far from being occasional intrusions into an orderly daily routine of colonial political life: the colonies displayed a level of political conflict significantly higher even than that of the British Isles.

There was strife, first of all, between branches of government – between

[159] Harry S. Stout, *The New England Soul: Preaching and Religious Culture in Colonial New England* (New York, 1986), pp. 253, 306 n. 56.

the executives on the one hand and the legislatures on the other – strife so rampant as to be more noteworthy by its absence than its presence and so intense as to lead on occasions to a total paralysis of government . . . There was, besides this, a milling factionalism that transcended institutional boundaries and at times reduced the politics of certain colonies to an almost unchartable chaos of competing groups . . . The surface of public life at the level of provincial government was thin and easily broken through.[160]

This conflict was formerly explained on the assumption that the 'Commonwealth' paradigm was dominant, and political turmoil was ascribed to the powerful presence in the colonies of just those features which the 'Commonwealthmen' warned against: the prerogative powers remaining with the executive were greater in the colonies than in England (the governors' veto on colonial legislation, authority to prorogue and dissolve the lower houses of colonial assemblies, and to dismiss colonial judges), but were combined with the weakness in the colonies of those informal mechanisms of patronage and 'influence' by which the executive in England is supposed to have preserved political stability.[161] Yet, however true this picture, it was not normally within their assemblies that colonial rebellions took their rise, and the widespread social constituencies and highly principled nature of insurrections in the English Atlantic empire,[162] especially those of 1688–9 and 1776, gives reason to doubt whether the scarcity of patronage was a sufficient explanation for their outbreak.

In the daily exchange of politics, too, denominational dynamics provide an essential explanatory key, especially at those times of crisis when rebellion lifted the lid and allows a special access to the tensions and conflicts usually negotiated, or disguised, within the constitutional structures of representation and law. If a particular political discourse was a shared possession of Englishmen on both sides of the Atlantic, why did England increasingly avoid insurrection while America increasingly experienced it, with cataclysmic but still not final results in the 1770s? This book offers the outline of an answer by questioning the assumption that England *was* wholly immune from violent threats and by disaggregating the political discourse of England's possessions on both sides of the Atlantic. If the 'Commonwealthmen' were largely English, or operated within the English political arena, they had less to say to the Scots, Irish and Welsh, and less still to the even more resolutely diverse populations of the American seaboard. Moreover,

---

[160] Bailyn, *American Politics*, pp. 64–5 and passim.
[161] Ibid., pp. 66–88.
[162] See chapter 3 below.

ethnic unity was relatively weakly conceptualised in the early-modern world.[163] What counted was denominational diversity, since the identity, rationale, historical origins and future mission of religious denominations were as clearly articulated and repeatedly stressed as ethnic identity was vaguely presumed and seldom raised.

In the early-modern period it was religious sects which, more than any other social groups, possessed international networks of communication which both mobilised their supporters and kept them informed of the activities of friends and enemies on two continents;[164] by letters industriously written and sought, published journals, evangelical newspapers and magazines, and unwearied itinerancy, the degree of cultural contact surpassed anything yet available in a secular context. It was the ministers of these sects who were able to draw together popular audiences, sometimes of many thousands, and exhort them to a frenzy of collective commitment that secular politicians did not begin to approach until the Chartist mass movements of Victorian England.[165] Like Chartism, religious engagement spread by example. News of the special operation of divine grace quickly touched off interest and emulation in other countries or even other continents: the work of George Whitefield in England was quickly news in America, urged forward the revivals in the Connecticut valley in 1739–42, and these in turn were a deliberate model for Scots revivalists of the 1740s.[166] Groups with such a sharp and eloquent sense of self-identity, and with such sophisticated means of communication, could not be other than central in the process of political mobilisation.

Denominations were not equal in their political roles. The significance of the inner dynamics of Congregationalism was greatly enhanced by that denomination's numerical preponderance in the colonies: 'By 1776, Congregational ministers in New England were delivering over two thousand

---

[163] Despite its thesis, MacDougall, *Racial Myth in English History*, pp. 73–86, presents evidence for historic myths of origin as built around the shared possession of liberty and law rather than around the ethnic uniformity of Saxon or Gothic ancestors.

[164] For a transatlantic study of emigration and religious revival which reveals the links between sects in Germany, Austria, Switzerland and Holland, as well as the British Isles, with those in the American colonies see W. R. Ward, *The Protestant Evangelical Awakening* (Cambridge, 1992); for a study which focuses on the strength of Anglo-American links, see Crawford, *Seasons of Grace*.

[165] From a wide literature, see Leigh Eric Schmidt, *Holy Fairs: Scottish Communions and American Revivals in the Early Modern Period* (Princeton, 1989). Whitefield's open-air communions at Cambuslang near Glasgow in July and August 1742 attracted 20,000 and 30,000 attenders: Crawford, *Seasons of Grace*, p. 163. Among the Kingswood colliers he claimed a congregation of 10,000, and in Boston 8,000: Harry S. Stout, *The Divine Dramatist: George Whitefield and the Rise of Modern Evangelicalism* (Grand Rapids, Michigan, 1991), pp. 73, 119.

[166] Crawford, *Seasons of Grace*, pp. 151–79.

discourses a week and publishing them at an unprecedented rate that out-numbered secular pamphlets (from all the colonies) by a ratio of more than four to one.'[167] The contributions of these ministers were, moreover, well attuned to their hearers. For local New England audiences, their message was couched 'totally' in covenantal terms, 'nothing less than the preservation of Sola Scriptura and New England's privileged position at the center of redemptive history'. For those other colonies to which New England exhortation was massively exported, the message used the 'secular vocabulary of 'rights and property' that all colonists shared in common'.[168] One reason why the nature and purpose of the Revolution could be reinterpreted in merely secular terms was that the diverse sectarian composition of the colonies dictated the search for common denominators, indeed for a rhetoric which would disguise the ulterior motives of the Revolution's New England leaders. For those leaders, it has been well observed, 'Republican governments, like earlier half-way covenants, religious toleration, and revivals, were merely means to the end of maintaining pure churches and a virtuous people of the Word.'[169] It was this mission which was destined to disillusion in New England's denominational and theological transformation during the next half-century.

Observers who underestimated the role of religion were denied a crucial insight into events. Thomas Pownall advanced a stadial theory of territorial possession: first 'the power of the *sword* was the predominant spirit of the world'; next, 'the power of *religion* . . . did actually become the ruling spirit of the policy of Europe'; finally, 'the spirit of *commerce* will become that predominant power'. Such was the force of commercial integration that colonial rebellion was inconceivable, he insisted in 1768:

> nothing is further from their nature, their interest, their thoughts. If a defection from the alliance of the mother country be suggested, it ought to be, and can be truly said, that their spirit abhors the sense of such; their attachment to the protestant succession in the house of Hanover will ever stand unshaken; and nothing can eradicate from their hearts their natural, almost mechanical, affection to Great Britain, which they conceive under

---

[167] Stout, *New England Soul*, pp. 6; 260, n. 6; 277, n. 48.

[168] Ibid., p. 284. This may explain the weakness of the American sense of statehood and its pre-Revolutionary antecedents: the state 'was less an end in itself as an object of local patriotism than an instrument of deeper purposes': J. R. Pole, 'The Politics of the Word 'State' and its Relation to American Sovereignty', *Parliaments, Estates and Representation* 8 (1988), 1–10, at 9.

[169] Stout, *New England Soul*, p. 310: such elements gave to 'the transforming events of 1776 a familiar, atavistic quality'. For the unimportance of natural rights in British Calvinists' resistance theories, see Richard Tuck, *Natural Rights Theories: Their Origin and Development* (Cambridge, 1979), pp. 43–4.

no other sense, nor call by any other name, than that of *home*. Besides, the merchants are, and must ever be, in great measure allied with those of Great Britain; their very support consists in this alliance, and nothing but false policy *here* can break it.[170]

It was an unfortunate prediction. Pownall was right in thinking, as was indeed obvious, that the substance of Anglo-American disagreements, and the timing of their eruptions, had most to do with the issues of trade, taxation, customs duties, legal jurisdictions and the use of military power.[171] Yet these apparently self-evident explanations of the conflict of the 1770s, as of former conflicts, were seen at the time as strangely inadequate. Englishmen on both sides of the Atlantic shared a tragic sense that these ostensible causes of Anglo-American conflict were insufficient to explain the awesome scale of what actually happened.[172] Even in 1774, Joseph Priestley addressed the English Dissenters on the wickedness of the government:

> The *pretence* for such outrageous proceedings, conducted with such indecent and unjust precipitation, is much too slight to account for them. The *true cause* of such violent animosity must have existed much earlier, and deeper. In short, it can be nothing but the Americans (particularly those of New England) being chiefly *dissenters* and *whigs*.[173]

Americans did not, in the 1760s, suddenly adopt the ideas of John Locke; 1776 was not the outcome of an upsurge of what was later termed 'radical liberalism'. Denominational discourse had been familiar for more than a century in Britain and America; what principally changed was that it was reinterpreted in retrospect, following the Revolution, as secular natural rights discourse. 1776 was a 'Lockeian moment' chiefly in the sense in which Locke himself had been an anti-Trinitarian, preoccupied by the political menace (as he saw it) of orthodox religion, firmly located within a denominational and theological context. The American Revolution opened a new era; but its origins had little to do with visions of a hitherto-unrealised future, much to do with ancient divisions and hatreds. The Revolution of 1776 was, therefore, not unique: like many of the crises which had convulsed the early-modern world, it still retained many of the characteristics of a war of religion.

---

[170] Thomas Pownall, *The Administration of the Colonies. Wherein their Rights and Constitution Are discussed and stated* (4th edn, London, 1768), pp. 3–4, 40–1.

[171] J. R. Pole, *The Decision for American Independence* (London, 1977).

[172] Wood, *The Creation of the American Republic 1776–1787*, pp. 3–4.

[173] [Joseph Priestley], *An Address to Protestant Dissenters of all Denominations, On the Approaching Election of Members of Parliament, With respect to the State of Public Liberty in General, and of American Affairs in Particular* (London, 1774), p. 5.

I

The conflict between laws: sovereignty and state formation in the United Kingdom and the United States

I. LAW, NATIONALITY AND NATIONALISM: MONARCHICAL
ALLEGIANCE AND IDENTITY

Whatever the causes of the successive breakdowns in governments on both sides of the Atlantic between 1660 and 1832 examined in this book, it is important to establish from the outset that nationalism was not among them; and the evidence for this hypothesis throws much light on those real causes which will be discussed below. Early-modern societies sustained a variety of forms of collective self-consciousness, but these turned only to a small degree on the later preoccupations of ethnicity and language; here as elsewhere, a new term in the early nineteenth century accompanied a new phenomenon. Nationalism was a mentality which postdated, and (it will be argued) necessarily postdated, the profound redefinitions compelled by the events of 1776 and 1789. Its histories appropriately begin with the French Revolution and the Romantic reaction to it, less appropriately finding in early-modern states only 'proto-nationalism': 'roots' or obscurely-expressed 'origins' of what is wrongly assumed to be a single phenomenon, that nationalism which came to 'maturity' in the nineteenth century.[1]

National identity in the 'old society' was indeed a very different matter from its later forms, and the early phenomena were in no strong sense the 'origins' of the later ones. The Anglo-American experience suggests that national identity during the Anglican ascendancy had a legal and religious conceptual structure quite different from its conceptual structure

---

[1] Hans Kohn, *The Idea of Nationalism* (New York, 1945); A. D. Smith, *Theories of Nationalism* (London, 1971); John Breuilly, *Nationalism and the State* (Manchester, 1982); Ernest Gellner, *Nations and Nationalism* (Oxford, 1983); E. J. Hobsbawm, *Nations and Nationalism since 1780* (Cambridge, 1990); Liah Greenfeld, *Nationalism: Five Roads to Modernity* (Cambridge, Mass., 1992), and earlier work there cited.

in the era which followed, and that the denominational, monarchical formula of the Anglican ascendancy[2] occupied the relevant ideological territory so completely that it successfully inhibited the development of a nationalism built around culture and ethnicity, with all that such a notion entailed in implying progressive national self-awareness and political assertion. Nationalism, in other words, was impossible without the nation state, whose secular, republican framework demanded and was eventually given a different rationale.[3] Ethnicity had long been unable to generate such a nationalism, for ethnicity itself was an historical construct, not an objective fact. Ideas of ethnic integrity were mostly developed after 1789 in order to provide emotional content for some newly-emergent nation states; ethnicity did not form a foundation, long present, on which a nineteenth-century superstructure was finally and appropriately built. Early-modern national identity found its conceptual structure provided instead by two systems of ideas: law and religion.

They formed a common inheritance on both sides of the Atlantic. The Puritan sense of mission in New England was generically identical with the sense of divine mandate which fuelled a variety of degrees of churchmanship in Old England in the sixteenth and early seventeenth centuries.[4] Although many wrote in a similar idiom, attention focused on and reinterpreted one classic text. John Foxe's *Acts and Monuments of Matters Most Special and Memorable Happening in the Church with an Universal History of the Same* (first published in Latin in 1559, in English in 1563), though famous as *Foxe's Book of Martyrs*, contained far more than an account of the Marian persecutions: beginning with the early Church and the Christianisation of England, it grew in successive editions to include a world history of the Christian religion as the setting for the sufferings and mission of reformed religion in England. Continually augmented and reprinted, made more widely available in a condensed version,[5] Foxe's

---

[2] Clark, *English Society 1688–1832.*

[3] For the emergence of a modern meaning for the term 'the state' by the end of the sixteenth century see Quentin Skinner, *The Foundations of Modern Political Thought* (2 vols., Cambridge, 1978), vol. 1, pp. ix–x, vol. 2, pp. 349–58. It is argued in the present work that the sense of collective identity which existed within the framework of the monarchical state took a form importantly different from that to be found in the nineteenth-century nation state.

[4] Winthrop S. Hudson (ed.), *Nationalism and Religion in America: Concepts of American Identity and Mission* (New York, 1970), pp. 153–99, 'The English Heritage'; for the creation of a Protestant historiography of national identity, see Avihu Zakai, *Exile and Kingdom: history and apocalypse in the Puritan migration to America* (Cambridge, 1992), pp. 12–55. For the elaboration of a mythology, William S. Maltby, *The Black Legend in England: The Development of Anti-Spanish Sentiment, 1558–1660* (Durham, N.C., 1971).

[5] Timothy Bright (ed.), *An Abridgement of the Booke of Acts and Monvments of the Chvrch ...* (London, 1589), still devoted 504 pages to the years from the Crucifixion to 1526, and added another 288 pages on the story to 1572.

Book of Martyrs provided the central components for a subsequent vision
of the nation as an identity of church and kingdom: a myth of origins; a
scenario for the working out of Providence; a record of persecution; a
promise of deliverance; a world mission. Bright prefaced his abridgement
with 'A speciall note of England':

> England, the first Kingdome that vniuersallie embraced the Gospel.
>
> Constantine, the first christian Emperor (who vtterlie destroyed the
> idolatrie of the Gentiles, and planted the Gospel throughout the world) an
> Englishman.
>
> Iohn Wickliff, that first manifestly discouered the Pope, and mainteyned
> open disputation against him, an Englishman.
>
> The most noble Prince, king Henrie viii. the first king that renounced the
> Pope.
>
> The worthie Prince, king Edward vi the first king, that vtterlie abolished
> all popish superstition.
>
> Her Royall Maiestie, our most gratious Soueraigne, the verie Maul of the
> pope, and a Mother of Christian princes: whome the Almightie long pre-
> serue ouer vs.
>
> England, the first that embraced the Gospel: the onely establisher of it
> throughout the world: and the first reformed.

Foxe himself was not a proto-nationalist, exhorting with a convenient
apocalyptic rhetoric the 'elect nation', let alone the secular nation
state; rather, he urged that divine election to a special historical role
had been reserved for the true church, of which the reformed Church
of England was undoubtedly part. It was because the church national
was not identical with the church universal that the Church of England
had a world mission, to ally with Protestants everywhere in the cosmic
struggle against Rome and to reclaim the dark areas of the earth for
true religion.[6] Yet it was the identity of the church with the kingdom,
politically initiated by Henry VIII, consolidated by Elizabeth I, which
in the later sixteenth century mobilised the whole, not just a part, in
the pursuit of these goals. In Scotland, where an even more Calvinist
and anti-Erastian kirk had achieved a substantial independence from
the state, no such vision of a divine mandate for the Scots nation
became politically important.[7] Equally, collective self-identity was weak

---

[6] William Haller, *Foxe's Book of Martyrs and the Elect Nation* (London, 1963), corrected by:
V. Norskov Olsen, *John Foxe and the Elizabethan Church* (Berkeley, 1973), pp. 40–7; Paul
Christianson, *Reformers and Babylon: English Apocalyptic Visions from the Reformation to the Eve
of the Civil War* (Toronto, 1978), p. 41; Richard Bauckham (ed.), *Tudor Apocalypse*
(Abingdon, 1978) pp. 86, 177–80; Katherine Firth, *The Apocalyptic Tradition in Reformation
Britain, 1530–1645* (Oxford, 1979), pp. 106–9.
[7] Arthur H. Williamson, *Scottish National Consciousness in the Age of James VI* (Edinburgh,
1979), pp. 1–47.

in Ireland and Wales in the early-modern period; the English intellectual matrix was unique.[8]

For the southern kingdom, this identity of church and state fused the nexus of ideas memorably summed up in 1559 by the exile John Aylmer, destined to be Bishop of London (1577–94), in a laconic marginal note to a work of patriotic exhortation: 'God is English.' He established this proposition (perhaps a non-sequitur) by a eulogy of the Providential prosperity of a chosen land: 'Oh if thou knewest thou Englishe man in what welth thou liuest, and in how plentifull a Countrye: Thou wouldest vii times of the day fall flat on thy face before God, and geue him thanks, that thou wart born an English man, and not a french pezant, nor an Italyan, nor Almane.' In battle, 'you haue God, and al his army of angels on your side'; God would ensure victory, 'For you fight not only in the quarrel of your country: but also and chieflye in the defence of hys true religion, and of his deare sonne Christe, not against men of the same religion, whiche might make theuent doubtfull, but againste his ennemies.'[9] What Aylmer began as a tract arguing against the Roman Catholic, and Roman law, objection to a female ruler, Queen Elizabeth, proceeded by a demonstration that Scripture, interpreted in Protestant fashion, justified no such ban, and culminated in a xenophobic exhortation to Englishmen to do battle with irreligious foreigners. It was this shared tradition which fell into schism in 1776.

Medieval English law ruled no sharp line between subject and alien, Englishman and foreigner: it envisaged a spectrum of statuses with different privileges and disabilities. This diverse picture had been simplified by the early seventeenth century, though with residual echoes of the old diversity of ranks in the surviving distinctions between natural-born subjects, naturalised subjects and denizens. But if the distinction between subject and alien was clear by the reign of James I, the means by which and the principles on which subjectship might be acquired were not. It was these which the common law finally established on the basis of a personal, indefeasible relation between subject and sovereign, expressed simultaneously in terms of God-given natural law and of the patriarchal relations of parent and child. Hierarchical social order, monarchy and religion formed an interlocking matrix of national identity for British subjects into the nineteenth century.[10]

---

[8] By contrast, in the nineteenth and twentieth centuries, unreconstructed, monarchical England registered only weak signals on the gauges of ethnic and cultural nationalism; it was Scotland, Ireland and Wales, most resistant to English cultural hegemony and English religion, which then developed self-designated nationalist movements.

[9] John Aylmer, *An Harborowe for Faithfull and Trewe Subiectes* (Strasburg, 1559), sig. P4, r, v.

[10] James H. Kettner, *The Development of American Citizenship, 1608–1870* (Chapel Hill, 1978), pp. 3–61.

The classic formulation of the common-law doctrine of nationality was given in *Calvin's Case* (1608),[11] in which it was held by the English Court of Exchequer Chamber that English nationality was acquired, indelibly, by birth within the realm to parents who were themselves subjects: that is, that a person born in Scotland (and by analogy in any other of the king's territories) after the accession of James VI of Scotland to the throne of England as James I in 1603, was as much a subject of the King of England as a person born of English parents in England. In this judgement, delivered after a joint conference of the two Houses of the Westminster Parliament had resisted a similar solution, the English common law thus united the two populations in a single allegiance (or nationality) long before the union of crowns in 1707. The doctrine may even have implied that persons born in the Netherlands during the reign of William III, and those born in Hanover during the union of crowns (1714–1837), enjoyed the same status as pre-Union Scots. The early-modern conception of nationality-as-allegiance was inclusive; it extended far beyond the bounds of nineteenth-century ethnic nationalism.[12]

The grounds of the decision in *Calvin's Case* were explained by the Lord Chancellor, Lord Ellesmere.[13] He insisted that different legal systems in Scotland and England did not invalidate the unity and indivisibility of sovereignty and allegiance: 'for where there is but one souereigne, all his subiects borne in all his dominions bee borne *ad fidem regis*; and are bound to him by one bond of faith and allegeance . . . ' The contrary doctrine, that there were several allegiances due to the king in regard of his several kingdoms, was 'a daungerous distinction betweene the king and the crowne, and betweene the king and the kingdome'. It was maintained only by

> treasonable papists, as Harding[14] in his confutation of the apologie maintaineth, that kings have their authority by the positiue lawe of nations, and

---

[11] *The Seventh Part of the Reports of Sir Edward Coke Kt.* (In the Savoy, 1738), n.f.; William Cobbett (ed.), *State Trials*, vol. 2 (London, 1809), cols. 559–696. Robert Calvin was a minor, born in Scotland after James's accession, who had been wrongfully deprived of a freehold in England.

[12] Clive Parry, *British Nationality* (London, 1951), p. 7. The situation was unclear: William III was only Stadtholder in the Netherlands, and George I only Elector in Hanover. It appears that the national status of the Dutch during William's reign was never judicially decided; the subjectship of Hanoverians until 1837 was only confirmed by a judgement in 1886: Kettner, *American Citizenship*, p. 146.

[13] J. Mervyn Jones, *British Nationality Law* (Oxford, 1956), pp. 54–5; Louis A. Knafla, *Law and Politics in Jacobean England: The Tracts of Lord Chancellor Ellesmere* (Cambridge, 1977), pp. 65–76, 202–53.

[14] Thomas Harding (1516–72) a convert to Roman Catholicism under Queen Mary; in exile after accession of Elizabeth; engaged in lengthy controversies with Bishop John Jewel in 1560s, notably in Harding's *A Confutation of a Booke, intituled An Apologie of the Church of England* (Antwerp, 1565).

haue no more power, than the people hath, of whome they take their tem-
porall iurisdiction; and so Eiclerus Simanca,[15] and others of that crew. Or
by seditious Sectaries and Puritans, as Buchanan de Iure Regni apud
Scotos,[16] Penry,[17] Knox,[18] and such like.

Allegiance had a religious dimension, and was therefore denominationally
specific: 'This bond of allegeance, whereof wee dispute, is *vinculum fidei*; it
bindeth the soule and conscience of euery subject.' As the subject did not
have a 'politicke body' to choose differently from his 'naturall body', nor
did the king. 'As the king nor his heart cannot bee diuided, for he is one
entire king ouer all his subiectes, in which soeuer of his kingdoms or
dominions they were borne, so hee must not be serued nor obeyed by
halues; he must haue intire and perfect obedience of his subjects.'[19]

By the 1640s, denominational discourse (following Jeremiah 18, 7–10)
treated 'kingdom' and 'nation' as almost synonymous: Puritans like other
Anglicans by now assumed an identity of church and state. Edmund
Calamy (1600–66), even in the midst of the Great Rebellion, appealed to
Jeremiah's text as 'a Looking glasse . . . wherein God Almighty declares
what he can do with Nations and Kingdoms, and what he will do'. He
asserted 'four Doctrinal conclusions':

1   That God hath an absolute power over all Kingdoms and Nations,
    to pluck them up, pull them down, and destroy them as he pleaseth.
2   That though God hath this absolute Prerogative over Kingdoms
    and Nations, yet he seldome useth this power, but first he gives
    warning.
3   If that Kingdome against which God hath threatened destruction,
    repent and turn from their evill; God will not only not destroy that
    Kingdome, but build it, and plant it. Or thus, Nationall Repentence
    will divert Nationall judgements, and procure Nationall blessings.
4   That when God begins to build and plant a Nation, if that Nation

---

[15] Jacobus (also known as Didacus) Simancas (d. 1583), bp. of Zamora, author of *Iacobi
Simancae . . . de primogenitis Hispaniae libri quinque* (Salmanticae, 1566).
[16] George Buchanan (1506–82). Scots humanist, Calvinist, tutor of James VI, for whom he
composed *De Iure Regni apud Scotos* (Edinburgh, 1579), asserting the location of political
authority in the people and the legitimacy of resistance to tyrants.
[17] John Penry (1559–93), Puritan; wrongly presumed the author of the tracts pseudonym-
ously signed 'Martin Mar-Prelate', 1587–9, for which he was executed.
[18] John Knox (?1514–72), Calvinist, pioneer of the Scottish Reformation; author of *The First
Blast of the Trumpet against the Monstrous Regiment of Women* (1558), arguing that political
rule by a woman was contrary to natural law and divine ordinance.
[19] *State Trials*, vol. 2, cols. 684, 690–1; Ellesmere thus rejected the doctrine described by
Ernst H. Kantorowicz, *The King's Two Bodies: A Study in Mediaeval Political Theology*
(Princeton, 1957).

do evill in God's sight, God will repent of the good he intended to
do unto it.[20]

Such a framework left little scope for ethnicity, culture or language in
forming nations or guiding national destinies. It did, however, possess a
rich content of history and theology, which led it in turn to engage in
conflict with the continental monarchies the polities of which were held
to be among the political consequences of Roman law. The imperatives
which had driven it into that conflict were religious, the need to defend
or advance the Protestant Reformation and its princely exponents in
England.

Providential destiny as demonstrated from scripture and history, not
ethnicity, was the earliest matrix of English national identity. The
common law quickly joined in the creation of that identity, especially via
the process of state formation in the British Isles. That process, like the
independence of the American colonies, owed nothing to nationalism. The
concept of 'nationalism' could not emerge before that of 'nationality', and
nationality itself took a quite different form in common law. Before 1776,
for colonial Americans[21] as for the inhabitants of the British Isles, the
relation of an individual to the state was still as it had been legally defined
in *Calvin's Case* in terms of the subject's allegiance to a particular monarch.[22] While this monarchical tie remained in place, indeed unchallenged
except by denominational or dynastic rivalry, it was almost impossible
for a different sense of national identity to arise: it had no theoretical
framework into which to flow. By contrast, cultural stereotypes were
familiar, lovingly tended and satirically exploited in the old society; but
they existed for decades, even centuries, without generating 'nationalism'.[23] It was the permanent disruption of a monarchical tie, in America
in 1776–83 and France in 1789–93, which compelled the development of
an alternative framework of self-identity, built slowly, with difficulty and
immense effort around the presumed coherence of those with a common
language (ignoring their profound divisions of dialect, vocabulary and

[20] Edmund Calamy, *Englands Looking-Glasse, Presented in A Sermon, Preached before the Honorable House of Commons . . . December 22, 1641* (London, 1642), pp. 1, 3.
[21] The term 'nationalism' is absent from the earliest editions of the new Republic's standard dictionary: Noah Webster, *A Compendious Dictionary of the English Language* (Hartford, Conn., 1806); idem, *A Dictionary of the English Language* (2 vols., New York, 1828; repr. 3 vols., London, 1832). The latter includes the term 'nationality', but defines it as 'National character; also, the quality of being national, or strongly attached to one's own nation': only gradually did the term come to include a legal definition of the individual's allegiance to the state.
[22] Jones, *British Nationality Law*, pp. 1, 51–62.
[23] J. O. Bartley, *Teague, Shenkin and Sawney: Being an Historical Study of the Earliest Irish, Welsh and Scottish Characters in English Plays* (Cork, 1954).

accent), a common culture (ignoring even larger regional variations) or shared ethnicity (however hard this was to demonstrate empirically). In revolutionary regimes, nationality came to mean the duty of allegiance owed by the individual to the abstract state, secular and non-monarchical, and therefore to the common culture.[24] The active assertion of this relationship constituted nationalism.

Colonists had been effectively incorporated in allegiance to the crown, and the all-absorbing quality of the law had been even more evident in America than in England. Aliens suffered considerable disabilities in the early-modern period; until the Aliens Act of 1844, only a private Act of Parliament could confer the privilege of naturalisation.[25] In America the position had been far easier, since the Act of 1740 allowed all foreign Protestants to claim naturalisation who had resided in the colonies for seven years and took the oaths of allegiance, supremacy and abjuration.[26] It was this institutionalised and long-successful drive to incorporation that made the American Revolution so difficult to envisage and to initiate. When from the mid 1760s some colonists claimed that their incorporation in the empire was through a personal allegiance to the monarch only, and not to the King-in-Parliament, they professed no challenge to the unified national identity that *Calvin's Case* had created: their challenge was to the unified sovereign confirmed in 1660 and the Anglican sovereign confirmed in 1688.[27] It has been argued that they had already prepared the ground by rephrasing the formula of the widely-revered Sir Edward Coke. Successive waves of immigration, often of aliens requiring naturalisation, had encouraged even English colonists to redescribe the bond of allegiance itself by analogy with the means of acquiring it: not as personal, natural and indefeasible, but as contractual and revocable.[28]

---

[24] In nineteenth-century Europe, nationalist societies sometimes re-created their monarchies after the tide of the French Revolution had receded; but these monarchies were profoundly different from those of the world before 1789, however much they yearned to symbolise continuities.

[25] Jones, *British Nationality Law*, pp. 63–9.

[26] 13 George II, c. 7, in Danby Pickering (ed.), *The Statutes at Large*, vol. 17 (Cambridge, 1765), pp. 370–3, imposed a Protestant (not necessarily Anglican) sacramental test on all applicants except Quakers and Jews.

[27] *Calvin's Case* was frequently cited in the approach to 1776 to justify the colonial claim of a personal allegiance to the monarch rather than a political allegiance to the King in Parliament: e.g. by the Massachusetts House of Representatives, in John Phillip Reid (ed.), *The Briefs of the American Revolution* (New York, 1981), pp. 131–3. Thomas Hutchinson replied that the judgement in *Calvin's Case* meant that allegiance was not due to the king in his 'Politick Capacity *only*'; that the 'Natural Capacity' and 'Politick Capacity' invariably went together; that Massachusetts' first Charter accepted allegiance to Charles I, 'his Heirs and *Successors*', which covered allegiance to the sovereign power as redefined in 1660 and 1688: ibid., p. 152.

[28] Kettner, *American Citizenship*, pp. 131–72.

Allegiance, even if redefined as contractual, still contained no legal tendency to its own dissolution. Contracts, once made, were still generally assumed to be permanent. The idea that allegiance was 'volitional' – that the individual could choose and re-choose his own nationality – became a reality only after the Revolution: it was not a prior cause of the drive to independence.[29] No alternative matrix of group identity arose before 1776 to challenge the monarchical one. This was true even of a system of ideas which appears on the surface to be an obvious candidate for that role. If the eighteenth-century world was without 'nationalism', it possessed what appears to be a synonym but in reality operated less effectively and within a very different context: 'patriotism', a term coined in the 1720s[30] and given currency by Bolingbroke's *Letters on the Spirit of Patriotism* (the first dated 1736).[31] This was a reification of that 'LOVE *to one's Country*', described by Shaftesbury as 'Of all human Affections, the noblest and most becoming human Nature', inspired in the hearts of men 'enjoying the Happiness of a real Constitution and Polity, by which they are *Free and Independent*'.[32] This civic sense, built around a shared constitutional tradition, was in its own insistence libertarian: absolute power would destroy those moral and rational feelings of community on which love of country depended.[33] Patriotism, as a doctrine of universal libertarian benevolence, posed for its adherents the same problem as that faced by denominations of Protestant Dissenters contemplating the relations between their own church and the church universal. Trenchard and Gordon, Shaftesbury and Bolingbroke articulated a similar doctrine; but in so far as their 'love of country' was reformist, it was universalist rather than specific in its reference to the English or to the American colonists. From Shaftesbury in 1711 to Richard Price in 1790, this conceptualisation of national identity was never more than a minor tradition in English public discourse; in America a secular republic after 1783 provided the concept with its Arcadia.

The more familiar terminology itself post-dates the period under

---

[29] Ibid., pp. 173–209. Kettner does not consider the denominational reasons for the activation of contractarian and resistance doctrines by some colonists, instead positing the erosion of ideas of natural allegiance in eighteenth-century England as the result of a putative advance of the doctrines of John Locke.

[30] The *Oxford English Dictionary* cites as its earliest source Nathan Bailey, *Universal Etymological English Dictionary* (3rd edn., London, 1726).

[31] [Lord Bolingbroke], *Letters on the Spirit of Patriotism: on the Idea of a Patriot King: and On the State of Parties, At the Accession of King George the First* (London, 1749).

[32] Anthony Ashley Cooper, 3rd Earl of Shaftesbury, *Characteristicks of Men, Manners, Opinions, Times* (3 vols., [London], 1711), vol. 3, p. 143. The term 'patriotism' was evidently devised after the publication of this work.

[33] So love of country was not 'a Relation to mere Clay and Dust, exclusive of any thing *sensible, intelligent,* or *moral*': ibid., p. 144.

discussion: 'nationality' and 'nationalism' began to be widespread usages in England only after the 1830s.[34] Neither term was used in *Calvin's Case*, and subsequent law defined allegiance without recourse to nineteenth-century conceptualisations. National identity and national fortunes did, however, retain their reference to religion, for the Bible is full of instances of God's dealings with 'nations' (especially the 'nation' of Israel, with which Protestant Englishmen on both sides of the Atlantic found a special affinity). The sense of the nation as a moral person derived from an ancient tradition of Biblical exegesis, still fully in repair in the late eighteenth century. English sermons during the American Revolution are replete with theological reflection on the dealings of divine providence with the English nation, with the analogies between England and Israel, and with reflections on the moral economy of English society which divine retribution and purpose entailed.[35] The reforming cause taken up with most passion and unanimity in English society after the American war, anti-slavery, could exploit the same body of ideas. Granville Sharp urged that *'National* Wickedness, from the beginning of the World, has generally been visited with *National* Punishments ... The Histories of all Nations, indeed, afford tremendous examples of *God's Vengeance* against Tyrants' – a point which he established by the extensive quotation of Scripture.[36]

The term 'nationalism' was, as late as the 1830s, so lacking an exclusively statist meaning that it could be appropriated by one Anglican theologian[37] to define a theory of election: the three alternatives, he maintained, were Calvinism, Arminianism and Nationalism '(if, for want of a better name, I may so designate the System of Mr Locke)'. Where Calvinism and Arminianism postulated the election of individuals, though by different understandings of the workings of divine grace, Faber defined Nationalism as the doctrine of 'the Election of certain whole nations into the pale of the visible Church Catholic, which Election, however, relates purely to their privileged condition in this world, extending not to their collective eternal state in another

[34] *The Oxford English Dictionary* (2nd edn, Oxford, 1989) gives only an isolated instance of 'nationality' in 1691. Thus 'the common-law writers of the sixteenth and seventeenth centuries did not speak of nationality'; the formula was, rather, that of a 'subject of the King of England': Jones, *British Nationality Law*, p. 51.

[35] I am indebted here to James E. Bradley, whose research on this topic is forthcoming.

[36] Granville Sharp, *The Law of Retribution* (London, 1776), pp. 10–11.

[37] George Stanley Faber, *The Primitive Doctrine of Election: or an Historical Inquiry into the Ideality and Causation of Scriptural Election, as Received and Maintained in the Primitive Church of Christ* (London, 1836).

world'.[38] For George Faber, the Church of England's doctrine seemed to argue against too easy a reliance on God's providence for the nation; but few others had been so cautious.

Providence was a leading actor in the British Isles during the seventeenth century. The cosmic drama of the Civil War, the execution of Charles I and the restoration of Charles II encouraged all parties to perceive events in heavily providentialist terms, whether or not they entertained millenarian beliefs. The partisans of Cromwell and the loyal subjects of Charles II in turn pictured their hero as a David or a Moses, leading the new Israel, and upheld by the 'special providences' which God extended to nations.[39] The restoration of Charles II in 1660, wrote Clarendon, was 'such a prodigious act of providence, as God hath scarce vouchsafed to any nation, since he led his own chosen people through the Red Sea'.[40] If this typological idiom faded in the 1670s and 80s,[41] it was revitalised for particular denominational groups, especially in Ireland and Scotland, by Whig panegyrics on William III and George I as deliverers in and after 1688 and 1714; by Jacobite hopes, repeatedly played upon, for a second deliverance from an ungodly regime by another Stuart restoration; and finally by the rhetoric which canonised the Founding Fathers of the American republic. For theorists of divine-right monarchy and of the social contract, for millenarians and expounders of the ancient constitution alike, 'so great was the weight of Scripture in the period that it was seemingly impossible to theorise upon the nature of the state or the monarchy without casting their origins, existence and maintenance in

---

[38] Ibid., pp. 4, 20–9; drawn from Locke's *A Paraphrase and Notes on the Epistle of St. Paul to the Romans*, section viii: in *The Works of John Locke* (10 vols., London, 1823), vol. 8, pp. 336–7; cf. p. 361. Faber quoted Locke's argument that in Romans, chapter 9, 'what is said of God's exercising of an absolute power according to the good pleasure of his will, relates only to Nations or Bodies Politic of men incorporated in civil Societies, which feel the effects of it only in the prosperity or calamity they meet with in this world, but extends not to their eternal state in another world, considered as particular persons, wherein they stand each man by himself upon his own bottom, and shall so answer separately at the day of judgement'. Cf. [James Burgh], *Britain's Remembrancer* (London, 1746): 'National Guilt can only be punished in this present Life, the Punishments in the next being for personal Guilt' (p. 36).

[39] Gerard Reedy, S.J., *The Bible and Reason: Anglicans and Scripture in Late Seventeenth-Century England* (Philadelphia, 1985), p. 66.

[40] Edward Hyde, Earl of Clarendon, *The History of the Rebellion and Civil Wars in England* (3 vols. in 6, Oxford, 1807), vol. 6, p. 1048.

[41] Steven N. Zwicker, 'Politics and Panegyric: The Figural Mode from Marvell to Pope', in Earl Miner (ed.), *Literary Uses of Typology from the Late Middle Ages to the Present* (Princeton, 1977), pp. 115–46. Zwicker suggests (p. 136) that 'The Exclusion Crisis is the final moment when political intrigue could seriously be read as prophetic history.' This study extends that moment at least to the close of the eighteenth century.

scriptural terms'.[42] Law and religion co-operated to retain national identity within this dual framework.[43] Only its revolutionary overthrow would allow the new formulation of nationalism to emerge.

American nationalism has posed a problem for students of nationalist phenomena in nineteenth- and twentieth-century Europe. In so far as colonial Americans mirrored the ethnic and linguistic unity of the English, no nationalist explanation accounted for the schism of 1776. Yet, equally, if colonial Americans already displayed features of ethnic and, still more, religious diversity, this distinguished them from European nationalist models. Americans, too, lacked the sense of attachment to an ancient homeland which was crucial in Europe. What, then, was the essence of American nationalism? It could only be 'the English tradition of liberty as it developed from older roots in the two revolutions of the seventeenth century. John Locke is the representative philosopher of this tradition.'[44] The disaggregation and demythologising of that putative tradition[45] reopens the question of American nationalism in turn. It points also to the solution: nationalism was a consequence, not a cause, of the Revolution; rebellion in 1776 as at other times was a result not of a shared tradition of liberty but of the division of that shared tradition by forces among which illiberal sectarianism was inconveniently prominent.

Powerful barriers checked the development of an American nationalism before 1776.[46] None of its later symbols were peculiar to the colonies. Many common bonds united their inhabitants before Lexington and Concord challenged them to form a nation, but those bonds equally or more strongly bound the colonists to Britain or to sectors of British society. Images of civil liberty, the rule of law, the Civil War or the Glorious Revolution only tied the colonists more firmly into the English Whig myth, since those symbols were reverenced on both sides of the Atlantic. Denominational images of persecution in the Old World and escape to the New, of the iniquities of Archbishop Laud and the Marian persecutions or

---

[42] Reedy, *The Bible and Reason*, p. 66 and passim.

[43] For the way in which the cultural content of British life flowed into the intellectual matrix set by the old order of monarchy, aristocracy and Church, see Linda Colley, *Britons: Forging the Nation 1707–1837* (New Haven, 1992). For the nature and duration of that matrix, see Clark, *English Society 1688–1832*, passim.

[44] Hans Kohn, *American Nationalism: An Interpretative Essay* (New York, 1957), p. 9 and passim. Hence, 'undoubtedly the thirteen rebel colonies stood for a progressive principle, socially and politically, compared with the Britain of 1770' (ibid., p. 106), etc.

[45] J. C. D. Clark, *Revolution and Rebellion: State and Society in England in the Seventeenth and Eighteenth Centuries* (Cambridge, 1986), and work there cited.

[46] For an argument that 'at least until late in 1775, there was no significant split in the loyalties of the Americans', see Max Savelle, 'Nationalism and Other Loyalties in the American Revolution', *AHR* 67 (1961–2), 901–23, at 908. Savelle used the term 'nationalism' without discrimination to refer to all forms of collective self-consciousness.

the fanatical sectarianism of the 1640s were likewise common property. The accounts of their historical origins which colonial Congregationalists, Presbyterians, Baptists and Quakers nurtured were cherished by the same sects in Britain. With undiminished emphasis but with greater frequency and more pressing tactical relevance, colonial orators into the 1770s and 1780s insisted that 'America' was the New Israel;[47] yet the impossibility, in the colonies, of identifying one church with one civil government ensured that providentialist rhetoric was not in itself a stage on the road to the nation state. For this reason, colonial preaching, even in its most urgent and agitated accents in the approach to 1776, did not necessarily promote American unity. Especially was this true of the numerically dominant and rhetorically most strident group, the Congregationalists: by the new Israel, God's covenanted people, they still meant New England, not the American colonies collectively.[48]

If American identity was difficult to conceptualise, there was no pressure to express the same thing in other words. John Dickinson's hugely-popular *Farmer's Letters* of 1767–8, though addressed to 'My dear Countrymen', evidently understood these as Britons: his tracts were directed to 'the happiness of *British America*' in so far as they were not expressive of a generalised love of *'humanity* and *liberty'*. Dickinson warned against 'pretences of patriotism'; he wished to inspire his readers with 'a spirit, that shall so guide you, that it will be impossible to determine whether an *American's* character is most distinguishable, for his loyalty to his Sovereign, his duty to his mother country, his love of freedom, or his affection for his native soil'.[49] The absence of a previously-existing sense of American identity was admitted even by those who were to be most prominent in promoting independence. In 1760, Benjamin Franklin relied on the widespread nature of that belief when he claimed (perhaps disingenuously) that a union of the colonies against Britain was impossible: they already constituted

> *fourteen separate governments* , , . not only under different governors, but [they] have different forms of government, different laws, different interests, and some of them different religious persuasions, and different manners. Their jealousy of each other is so great, that, however necessary a union of the colonies has long been, for their common defence and security against their

[47] John F. Berens, *Providence & Patriotism in Early America 1640–1815* (Charlottesville, 1978), pp. 69–72, 81–5.

[48] For a similar situation in the 1740s, see Michael J. Crawford, *Seasons of Grace: Colonial New England's Revival Tradition in its British Context* (New York, 1991), p. 224. In this respect, New England had closer links with Scots evangelicals than with Virginian Anglicans.

[49] [John Dickinson], *Letters from a Farmer in Pennsylvania, to the Inhabitants of the British Colonies* (Philadelphia, 1768), pp. 3–4, 15 (letters I, III).

enemies, and how sensible soever each colony has been of that necessity; yet they have never been able to effect such a union among themselves, nor even to agree in requesting the mother country to establish it for them.

Only 'the most grievous tyranny and oppression', he claimed, could provoke colonial union.[50]

American unity was not an empirical fact, but predicted as a logical consequence of an appeal to natural law against a common-law sovereign. As Patrick Henry declared on the first day's meeting of the Continental Congress,

> Government is dissolved . . . Where are your landmarks, your boundaries of Colonies? We are in a state of nature, Sir . . . The distinctions between Virginians, Pennsylvanians, New Yorkers, and New Englanders, are no more. I am not a Virginian, but an American . . . I go upon the supposition that government is at an end. All distinctions are thrown down. All America is thrown into one mass.[51]

In a state of nature, men were emancipated from their status as subjects, their identities as Englishmen or Virginians; they became individuals. But as equal individuals, all men became brothers. Such, at least, was the theory.

Recalcitrant humanity lagged far behind. Nevertheless, although the military conflict began and continued as a civil war, its pressures acted to homogenise the rival parties at the level of discourse: collective action presumed a common identity. David Ramsay soon explained how

> A continental army, and Congress composed of men from all the States, by freely mixing together, were assimilated into one mass. Individuals of both, mingling with the citizens, disseminated principles of union among them. Local prejudices abated. By frequent collision asperities were worn off, and a foundation was laid for the establishment of a nation, out of discordant materials.[52]

Independence could only be fought for by 'continental' soldiers; if British troops opposed them, the enemy must be a unitary 'Britain'.

Newspaper evidence confirms that colonists' self-image as a nation did not crystallise while the tie with Britain remained. Popular usage as recorded in colonial newspapers of the mid eighteenth century treated 'America' as a geographical term, and when the emerging sense of a common cause had turned 'America' into a political actor by c. 1770, it

---

[50] [Benjamin Franklin], *The Interest of Great Britain Considered, with regard to her colonies and the acquisitions of Canada and Guadaloupe* (London, 1760), in Franklin, *Works*, vol. 4, pp. 41–2.

[51] John Adams, Diary, 5 Sept. 1774, in Adams, *Works*, vol. 2, pp. 366–8.

[52] David Ramsay, *History of the American Revolution* (1789); ed. Lester H. Cohen (2 vols., Indianapolis, 1990), vol. 2, p. 631.

was a category still without significant content: unity was compelled by the need to resist British policy, not spontaneously generated by any cultural homogeneity, and with the end of the revolutionary war this compulsion faded in the face of the parochial identities of individual states. Not until the Constitution of 1787 did the inhabitants of the thirteen states find a master symbol which rallied a national consciousness and encouraged the ascription of their culture to a prior Americanism; which created a context in which Washington could be hailed in 1790 as 'equal in dignity, and superior in worth and excellence, to any Sovereign in Europe'.[53] James Wilson believed with good reason that the constitution

> will at least make us a nation, and put it in the power of the Union to act as such . . . As we shall become a nation, I trust that we shall also form a national character; and that this character will be adapted to the principles and genius of our system of government; as yet we possess none – our language, manners, customs, habits and dress, depend too much upon those of other countries. Every nation in these respects should possess originality.[54]

Revolutionary France passed through a similar process. The Jacobin ideal of fraternity, like Bolingbroke's conception of 'patriotism', professed to be humanitarian, libertarian and universal: 'nationalism' as a conception has been dated in France to 1798, when it suggested, by contrast, an egotistical, assertive state of mind. The pre-revolutionary matrix of French identity was closer to the English pattern. The *cahiers des doléances* returned to the States General, that opinion poll out of its time, only occasionally dwelt on the geographic boundaries of France; spoke much of the French *nation* though without a sense of racial identity; presumed the importance of a common religion; appealed frequently to common traditions; and ignored the role of a common language. In those remarkably revealing texts, the monarchy and Catholicism were almost unanimously regarded as the essential constituents of the French.[55]

Even the experience of revolution was not sufficient to forge a unified, homogeneous American identity and discourse: the marks of outward diversity remained long after the Revolution. Tocqueville described the

---

[53] Joseph M. Torsella, 'American National Identity, 1750–1790: Samples from the Popular Press', *Pennsylvania Magazine of History and Biography* 112 (1988), 167–87 at 177; for a different interpretation see Michael Zuckerman, 'The Fabrication of Identity in Early America', *WMQ* 34 (1977), 183–214.

[54] J. B. McMaster and F. D. Stone, *Pennsylvania and the Federal Constitution, 1787–1788* (Philadelphia, 1888), pp. 415–18, quoted in Geoffrey Seed, *James Wilson* (Millwood, N.Y., 1978), p. 119.

[55] Beatrice Fry Hyslop, *French Nationalism in 1789 According to the General Cahiers* (New York, 1934), pp. 22, 29–32, 35, 38, 47, 59.

United States in 1831 as 'a society which comprises all the nations of the world', its people 'differing from one another in language, in beliefs, in opinions; in a word a society possessing no roots, no memories, no prejudices, no routine, no common ideas, no national character . . .'[56] The diversity of the ethnic, linguistic, cultural and religious composition of Britain's mainland American colonies was pronounced, and grew even more obvious with successive waves of immigration as 1776 approached. Whether the United States ever fully participated in the new European ideas of folkish nationalism so triumphantly affirmed in 1848 is open to doubt.[57] American identity's sectarian component, however, allowed the dynamics of burgeoning evangelicalism from the 1790s onwards to sustain an ecumenical sense of national moral purpose very different from the secular ideologies which swept continental Europe.[58] Even 'to this day', it has been argued, American patriotism 'retains some of the character of the Revolution . . . it possesses a confessional and creedal quality'[59] in which, it may be suggested, natural rights doctrines occupy the place of a creed and rival creeds like that of ethnicity are systematically denied. In national identity as in other respects, the American Revolution, by coming before 1789, acted to freeze certain public practices in their older forms at the same time as it acted to destroy the old order in England itself.

The dominance of Anglican, common law paradigms on both sides of the Atlantic leaves no room for an account of the American Revolution as a result either of nascent American nationalism or of American reaction to nascent English nationalism. Englishmen increasingly spoke of 'Americans' from the middle of the eighteenth century, but until 1783 the term had a geographical, not a national, meaning. The revolution of 1776 was unexpected in England partly because an evolving British (or English) national identity in the 1750s and 1760s had not compelled Englishmen to define Americans as 'the other'; nor did Americans so define Britons. The growth of British military power in the Seven Years' War, the bur-

---

[56] Tocqueville to Chabrol, quoted in J. P. Mayer, *Prophet of the Mass Age: A Study of Alexis de Tocqueville* (London, 1939), p. 30.

[57] Torsella, 'American National Identity', distinguishes the self-identity of 1790 from nineteenth-century nationalism. Cf. Yehoshua Arieli, *Individualism and Nationalism in American Ideology* (Cambridge, Mass., 1964), p. 24. It has been argued that even 'manifest destiny' – the ideology of American territorial expansion – was not, as late as the 1840s, fuelled by nationalism in the later sense: Frederick Merk, *Manifest Destiny and Mission in American History: A Reinterpretation* (New York, 1963), pp. 57–60, correcting Albert K. Weinberg, *Manifest Destiny: A Study of Nationalist Expansionism in American History* (Baltimore, 1935).

[58] Emphasised by Reinhold Niebuhr and Alan Heimert, *A Nation So Conceived: Reflections on the History of America from its Early Visions to Its Present Power* (London, 1963).

[59] William H. Nelson, 'The Revolutionary Character of the American Revolution', *AHR* 70 (1964–5), 998–1014, at 1014.

geoning prosperity of the middle orders, the proliferating consumer culture of the North Atlantic contained no seeds of its own dissolution.
British national awareness steadily enhanced its cultural content, with
powerful additions like 'God Save the King' and 'Rule, Britannia': most
of these additions were devised to reinforce the libertarian, Protestant,
Hanoverian matrix. It was this matrix from which American revolutionaries chose to fight to escape, and they chose to do so for reasons hardly
connected with a shared transatlantic sense of national identity. The
nature of those reasons, largely at their core sectarian ones, is the subject
of this book.

II. THE CREATION OF THE UNITED KINGDOM, 1536–1801: RELIGION AND THE ORIGINS OF THE COMMON-LAW DOCTRINE OF SOVEREIGNTY

In 1776, colonial Americans advocating a confederal interpretation of
empire confronted a metropolitan definition of sovereignty which
excluded such a possibility a priori. American patriots duly perceived
such a definition as an aspect of monarchical absolutism, and historians
too have explained the doctrine of the centre as 'a 'tory perspective'.[60]
Yet herein lay a central paradox of the Revolution, for the Westminster
Parliament defined the sovereign power in Britain as a tripartite federa-
tion of King, Lords and Commons, each checking and balancing the
other, and imagined that this unique political formation was uniquely the
achievement of English Whigs over the previous century and a half. How
this remarkable doctrine came to evolve in the practicalities of English
politics is the subject of part II; its expression in English jurisprudence
and political theory forms the subject of part III.

The characteristic English doctrine of sovereignty emerged within the
process of state formation. Such a process was not in itself unique to the
British Isles. Most of the political entities of western Europe have undergone clearly-defined and well-documented processes of state formation,
as the characteristic structures and ideologies first of the dynastic and
then of the nation state were devised and propagated.[61] Yet however

---

[60] Greene, *Peripheries and Center*, p. 150. From an English perspective, it may be suggested,
it was the colonial claim of direct and sole dependence on the monarch which appeared
to be a Tory doctrine.

[61] Karl W. Deutsch and William T. Foltz (eds.), *Nation-Building* (New York, 1966); J. H.
Shennan, *The Origins of the Modern European State 1450–1725* (London, 1974); Charles Tilly
(ed.), *The Formation of National States in Western Europe* (Princeton, 1975); Kenneth H. F.
Dyson, *The State Tradition in Western Europe: A Study of an Idea and Institution* (Oxford, 1980);
Leonard Tivey (ed.), *The Nation-State: The Formation of Modern Politics* (Oxford, 1981);
Richard Bonney, *The European Dynastic States 1494–1660* (Oxford, 1991).

similar across those states was the later rhetoric of nineteenth-century nationalism, these processes were often strikingly different from polity to polity in earlier centuries. One ancient source of distinction has been the way in which states were assembled from their component parts, and the divergent geographical components welded by doctrines of sovereignty into single entities. The doctrine of sovereignty worked out and applied in early-modern England proved uniquely powerful as an instrument of state formation not only because of the unitary conception of authority which it offered, but also because it associated England's imperial career both within the British Isles and overseas with the moral imperatives and chiliastic destiny of England's Church. By contrast, it has been rightly observed that the 'notion of a legislative power exercised conjointly by king, lords and commons is a notion of legislative sovereignty undeveloped in classical republican theory';[62] the English doctrine of the separation of powers is now revealed as a euphemism for a system in which the 'powers' were not only unified, but unified in the context of an overarching ecclesiastical polity.

The uniqueness of the dominant English doctrine of sovereignty was seen in sharper focus within an earlier conceptualisation of the issues. 'Constitutional history', stemming partly from a tradition of public law (Anson, Dicey and Maitland), partly from nineteenth century Whig–Liberal polemic (Lord John Russell, Erskine May), had to address the episodes in which the United Kingdom was assembled from its component parts – the unions with Wales in 1536, Scotland in 1707, Ireland in 1801, and the moves for Home Rule and devolution in the nineteenth and twentieth centuries which partly reversed these earlier achievements.[63] 'Church history' too had inevitably recognised the conflicts – indeed the armed clashes – which attempts to impose Anglicanism outside its homeland provoked; it was these conflicts which, in English-speaking societies, increasingly redefined 'ecclesiastical history' as the inner history of each church rather than the divine drama of God's dealings with mankind.[64] This theme of denominational conflict in particular emphasises that Eng-

---

[62] J. G. A. Pocock, *The Ancient Constitution and the Feudal Law* (2nd edn., Cambridge, 1987), p. 310.

[63] E.g. Albert V. Dicey, *England's Case against Home Rule* (London, 1887); Albert V. Dicey and Robert S. Rait, *Thoughts on the Union between England & Scotland* (London, 1920).

[64] Welsh history was for long organised around its chief framework, the fortunes of its component denominations. For Scotland, see W. Makey, *The Church of the Covenant* (Edinburgh, 1979); Julia Buckroyd, *Church and State in Scotland 1660–1681* (Edinburgh, 1980); I. B. Cowan, *The Scottish Covenanters* (London, 1976); A. L. Drummond and J. Bulloch, *The Scottish Church 1688–1843* (Edinburgh, 1973). For Ireland, W. A. Phillips, *History of the Church of Ireland from the Earliest Times to the Present Day* (3 vols., London, 1933).

land was not synonymous with Britain, indeed that England did not stand proxy for Britain.[65] Rather, the creation of 1801, the United Kingdom of Great Britain and Ireland, has been identified as a composite state achieved not by the homogenisation but by the negotiated political union of radically different societies. The principles which structured that composite state had powerful points of resemblance to those of the composite states of early modern continental Europe.[66] Like many of them, the United Kingdom was assembled around a principle which had little to do with the homogenising nineteenth-century doctrines of imperialism or nationalism, socialism or liberalism. Its principle of unity was dynastic.

Because of her dynastic and religious track record, eighteenth-century England was heir to a conception of sovereignty which contrasted with that of many of her continental neighbours. Until 1789 continental European composite states, most notably France and Spain, similarly stressed their monarchies as unifying principles; but their Roman law traditions, the entrenched local privileges which Roman law countenanced, and the ultramontane claims of the Roman Catholic Church[67] for long inhibited any development of an idea of a unified sovereignty that could not be shared, and when dynastic regimes were swept away after 1789, jurists henceforth attributed sovereignty not to an indivisible person or institution but to an abstraction, 'the republic'. The traditional English polemic which depicted Roman law and Roman Catholicism as uniquely conducive to centralising tyranny itself requires historical explanation.[68]

The ideology of continental monarchies is not the subject of the present study, but qualifications to the familiar and exaggerated image of absolutism are assumed.[69] Roman law was in some ways inimical to monarchical power: it was not taught at the University of Paris until 1679, 'lest recognition be given to the theory that laws made by the successors of Justinian

[65] J. C. D. Clark, 'English History's Forgotten Context: Scotland, Ireland, Wales', *HJ* 32 (1989), 211–28; idem, 'The History of Britain: A Composite State in a *Europe des Patries?*', in Clark (ed.), *Ideas and Politics in Modern Britain* (London, 1990), pp. 32–49; idem, 'National Identity, State Formation and Patriotism: The Role of History in the Public Mind', *History Workshop Journal* 29 (1990), 95–102.

[66] H. G. Koenigsberger, 'Composite States, Representative Institutions and the American Revolution', *Historical Research* 62 (1989), 135–53.

[67] Roland Mousnier, 'The Exponents and Critics of Absolutism', *The New Cambridge Modern History*, vol. 4 (Cambridge, 1970), pp. 104–31; J. P. Sommerville, *Politics and Ideology in England, 1603–1640* (London, 1986), pp. 195–9.

[68] For a corrective, Myron Piper Gilmore, *Argument from Roman Law in Political Thought 1200–1600* (Cambridge, Mass., 1941), pp. 131–2 and passim. A similar study for the eighteenth century is needed.

[69] François Dumont, 'French Kingship and Absolute Monarchy in the Seventeenth Century', reprinted in Ragnhild Hatton (ed.), *Louis XIV and Absolutism* (London, 1976), pp. 55–84; Nicholas Henshall, *The Myth of Absolutism: Change and Continuity in Early Modern European Monarchy* (London, 1992) and references.

were binding on territories which had once been Roman provinces'. Nevertheless, 'Under the influence of Roman law the conception of kingship became more and more of an abstraction: the power of the state existed of itself.' Even the political theorist Le Bret, who began to emphasise the indivisibility of sovereignty in France, accepted Bodin's moral restraints as defining limits to sovereignty which distinguished it from tyranny, a point emphasised by Cardinal de Retz and others.[70] 'Even the French monarchy, the quintessential *dominium regale* in the contemporary view, found it convenient to leave newly-acquired provinces, like Burgundy and Brittany, with their provincial assemblies intact.'[71] English theorists in the eighteenth century might seek to conflate Roman law and natural law in order to make usable the technical excellencies of the first; continental theorists might seek to divide the two in order to make natural law the rationale for enlightened despotisms, unchecked by local immunities and customs because universally applicable.[72] Roman law was nevertheless sufficiently influential to ensure that the continental states in which it predominated remained until 1789 a patchwork of local privileges and immunities.

Especially was this true of the Empire. The German language contained no word for sovereignty until the foreign term *Souveränität* was imported in the late eighteenth century, and only later still did the term take on its eighteenth-century English meaning; meanwhile

> it was because of the problem created by the previous history and the continued existence of the Empire that theories of limited sovereignty or of double majesty were prevalent in the German area, where they also acquired a special character on account of the relative backwardness of these territories. In Germany all these theories accepted that there was a double sovereignty in the political society, that of the Ruler and that of the People. But some of them further divided the ruler sovereignty between the Emperor and the territorial princes ... To deepen the confusion, the German theories came to grips with the implications of sovereignty to so small an extent that they all designated both the sovereignty of the Ruler and the sovereignty of the People as an absolute power ...[73]

[70] Dumont, 'French Kingship', pp. 59, 61, 66, 69, 75, 77. France was divided. One third, in the south, was the *pays de droit écrit*, where Roman law counted as customary law; the rest was the *pays de droit coutumier*, in which local custom dominated. So northern France was less of a Roman law system than Germany or Italy until Napoleon's *Code civil* of 1804. Alan Watson, *The Making of the Civil Law* (Cambridge, Mass., 1981), pp. 7–8.

[71] Koenigsberger, 'Composite States', p. 136. It might be suggested that this lack of a centralising drive is evidence against Fortescue's distinction (challenged below) between *dominium regale* and *dominium politicum et regale*.

[72] Heinrich A. Rommen, *The Natural Law: A Study in Legal and Social History and Philosophy* (trans. Thomas R. Hanley, St Louis, 1947), pp. 75–109.

[73] F. H. Hinsley, *Sovereignty* (2nd edn, Cambridge, 1986), pp. 136–7.

Germany's juristic tradition and political circumstances echoed each other. The Holy Roman Empire sustained a juridical division of authority, as well as a practical division of power, between the Emperor at Vienna, the Electors, the Diet at Regensburg, the Reichshofrat (Aulic Council) at Vienna and the Reichskammergericht (Imperial Cameral Tribunal) at Wetzlar.[74] Such a system proved the despair of political theorists who attempted to reduce it to order:

> Absolutism, like the system of estates, assumed numerous forms within the empire and the multiplicity of German states. If absolutism means the unlimited exercise of authority at will by a sovereign territorial lord, then absolutism did not exist in legal terms within the imperial community. But it also did not exist practically either, because the unlimited exercise of authority was restrained by local and estatist rights and by an inadequate administrative apparatus.[75]

Similarly France was an example of an 'absolute' monarchy subject to powerful moral restraints which meant that it was less 'uninhibited by the rules' than modern states.[76]

By contrast, the United Kingdom's progressive dynastic unification, crucially following the union of Church and State at the Reformation, endowed her with a unitary, absolutist doctrine of sovereignty, and a divinely sanctioned sense of the inviolability of unitary sovereignty, within which the federal concept of 'sharing sovereignty' became a contradiction in terms. Even the survival of a separate kingdom of Ireland was not allowed to challenge this juridical construct. Yet nineteenth-century nationalism in the British Isles drew little support from this powerful ideology. The fact that the United Kingdom was a state already assembled in a dynastic age had a particular relevance for its subsequent sense of national identity: no post-dynastic nationalist sentiment was the premise of national unification, and none therefore ever fully emerged.

The monarchy and the Church, not ethnic nationalism, dominated the early history of English state formation and of England's relations with Wales, Scotland and Ireland. It was Protestantism which gave modern England its associated sense of manifest destiny, a sense to which the United States was heir only in an attenuated form (in the early seven-

[74] John G. Gagliardo, *Reich and Nation: The Holy Roman Empire as Idea and Reality, 1763–1806* (Bloomington, 1980), pp. 16–46. 'The tendency of nearly all important limitations on the Emperor's authority was toward the strengthening of the concept and the reality of *Landeshoheit*, the essentially unhindered exercise of the attributes of sovereignty in both internal and external affairs by the immediate Estates' (p. 18). Cf. Karl Otmar Freiherr von Aretin, *Heiliges Römisches Reich 1776–1806: Reichsverfassung und Staatsouveränität* (2 vols., Wiesbaden, 1967).
[75] Rudolf Vierhaus, *Germany in the Age of Absolutism* (Cambridge, 1988), p. 88.
[76] Bertrand de Jouvenel, *Sovereignty* (Cambridge, 1959), pp. 90–1.

teenth century, Puritan colonies in New England had a weaker sense of the Providential assignment to them of a specific promised land than did the more orthodox Anglican projectors of the Virginia colony).[77] This sense of Providential mandate can be observed in England from the early sixteenth century, together with another source of a sense of growing differences between the English and continental experiences. The contrast of common law and Roman law began to be emphasised by Protestant reformers. John Aylmer insisted that 'our lawe muste direct vs' because

> it best agreeth with our country, we haue no further to do with the ciuil law than in arch matters, that is for testaments, marriages and such other, as for landes, and enheritance, pains for offences and many other poynts touching the law: ours doth meruelously iarre with the ciuill law . . .[78]

This sense of the alien nature of Roman law had been present from at least the fifteenth century, and can be traced in the works of Sir John Fortescue;[79] but with the Reformation it steadily grew. It became an unexamined conviction that the common law was essentially Protestant, Roman law was essentially Catholic; that the first led to liberty, the second was biassed towards slavery.

Law and religion therefore combined in the process of state formation. The Union with Wales of 1536 was a phase of the Protestant Reformation in England, initially prompted by the need to secure the new order against possible military intervention by Francis I of France or the Emperor Charles V; its success in Wales too finally depended on the successful export of Anglican Protestantism to the Principality. The vision of the unitary state, incorporating Wales, was held by the reformer Thomas Cromwell, not by Cardinal Wolsey. It was fortuitously dynastic as well as designedly religious. Out of the baronial conflicts of the Wars of the Roses had emerged – by chance rather than because of any peculiarly Welsh power-base – a Tudor king of England, but this evidently created no decisive inducement to Welsh loyalty throughout the sixteenth century.[80] Wales in the 1530s was widely regarded as on the verge of rebellion over threatened and actual ecclesiastical reforms. The religious imperative governed the hurried timing of the union. The Act of Supremacy of

---

[77] I place this interpretation on the evidence reviewed by Zakai, *Exile and Kingdom*, pp. 94–119.
[78] Aylmer, *An Harborowe for Faithfull and Trewe Subiectes*, sig. K4v.
[79] Skinner, *Foundations of Modern Political Thought*, vol. 2, pp. 54–5.
[80] The absence of a Welsh national consciousness at that time is evidenced by the failure of the Tudors to make propaganda use of their Welshness within Wales, and the acceptance of Welsh economic migrants in London in sharp contrast to the hostile reception accorded to Scots after 1603: G. R. Elton, 'English National Selfconsciousness and the Parliament in the Sixteenth Century', in Otto Dann (ed.), *Nationalismus in vorindustrieller Zeit* (München, 1986), p. 75.

1534 recognised Henry VIII as head of the Church of England, but Wales was already included within the Province of Canterbury: the creation of a state church entailed that ecclesiastical and civil boundaries should coincide.

Wales was not yet part of the realm of England: the common law, and the statutes of the Westminster Parliament, that engine of the Reformation, did not run there. Wales (like parts of the American colonies in a future era) had been conquered by private enterprise: Anglo-Norman barons who seized the lands of Welsh chieftains in the eleventh and twelfth centuries held by right of conquest, not royal grant, and even English royal conquests within Wales initially became personal possessions of the monarch, not parts of the realm of England. These 'marcher' lords exercised kingly rights within their lordships: law, administration and armed force were their own, essentially unmodified by acknowledged feudal obligations to the English king. Even lordships acquired by the king and combined in the Principality of Wales were not until 1536 subject to the common law and had no representation in the Westminster Parliament. The Acts of Union of 1536 and 1543 obscured this earlier relationship by their propagandistic claim that Wales had always been 'incorporated and annexed' to the realm of England. In fact, the Union was essential if Parliament were to extend the Reformation to Wales.[81]

Legislation had to be enforced. From the accession of the Tudors in 1485 into the 1530s, unrest in Wales continued: a dynastic union alone was not sufficient to eliminate the lawlessness which flourished under the aegis of the marcher lords. Major problems of public order were addressed via the Council in the Marches of Wales, which acquired judicial functions after the Union, and of which Rowland Lee was appointed Lord President on his elevation to the bishopric of Lichfield in 1534: trusted by Thomas Cromwell, he enforced the common law with zealous precision. This, and the institution of Justices of the Peace on the English model by an Act preceding the Union had an impact; but English ministers perceived them to be insufficient without that massive abolition of local jurisdiction and personal privilege in favour of royal authority that was entailed by the Union itself. Unified sovereignty was what was

---

[81] William Rees, 'The Union of England and Wales', *Transactions of the Honourable Society of Cymmrodorion* (1937), 27–100, at 30–2, 45, 49–50. The union nevertheless had important pre-modern features. The sweeping powers of legislation reserved to the Crown meant that the measure would have turned out very differently if the plan of 1541 to reconstitute Wales as a Principality in favour of Prince Edward had come to fruition: P. R. Roberts, 'The Union with England and the Identity of 'Anglican' Wales', *TRHS* 22 (1972), 49–70; idem, 'The 'Act of Union' in Welsh History', *Transactions of the Honourable Society of Cymmrodorion* (1974), 49–72.

sought; and it was unified sovereignty which was effective, affirmed by the Act of Union of 1536 and reinforced in 1543, legislation largely concerned in substance with legal jurisdictions. The 1536 Act (27 Henry VIII, c. 26) was indeed entitled 'An Act for Laws and Iustice to be ministered in Wales in Like Fourme as it is in this Realm', legislation which cancelled the remaining jurisdictions of the marcher lords in favour of the English system of shires and sheriffs.[82]

The need to protect the Reformation from the strategic threat now increasingly feared from Catholic Ireland similarly pointed towards unified sovereignty. Scotland, Ireland and Wales had of course always offered bases and allies to continental powers seeking to intervene militarily in England; but from the 1530s the European Reformation and Counter Reformation vastly added to the danger. That Wales never again posed such a strategic threat after the early sixteenth century reflects, among other things, its early religious uniformity with England. This contrasted sharply with the Irish case, for Roman Catholic clergy were not notably successful in arousing a Welsh response to the imposition of Protestantism.[83] Protestantism was not native to Wales: there were no Welsh universities, no native reformers; but equally there was no ecclesiastical infrastructure able to resist the impact of Cambridge and Canterbury. Part of the success of the Reformation in Wales must be attributed to individuals like William Barlow, Bishop of St Davids from 1536 to 1548; but the consolidation of the major religious changes came under Elizabeth. Appropriately, the triumph of the Elizabethan settlement was contemporary with the enunciation by Richard Hooker in *The Laws of Ecclesiastical Polity* of the full doctrine of the unity, indeed the necessary identity, of Church and State.

In the localities the supersession of feudal marcher lordships could be welcomed on a functional level as a move to a rational, centrally-administered jurisdiction; but the church settlement imposed was more than merely functional. It was determined in substance by the Elizabethan Acts of Supremacy and Uniformity, mediated through church services in Welsh, and finally capped by a monumental achievement of Welsh literature, William Morgan's translation of the whole Bible, published in 1588. It succeeded the 1567 translation of the New Testament

---

[82] For the way in which the introduction of the English institution of Justices of the Peace drew Welsh gentry into political involvement, see W. R. B. Robinson, 'The Tudor Revolution in Welsh Government 1536–1543: Its Effects on Gentry Participation', *EHR* 103 (1988), 1–20.

[83] For the acceptance by the Welsh elite of the legislation of 1536, and the Reformation, see Glanmor Williams, *Recovery, Reorientation and Reformation: Wales c. 1415–1642* (Oxford, 1987), pp. 275–6, 324–6.

and *Book of Common Prayer*, a translation ordered by the Act of 1563, in which Bishop Richard Davies's Preface argued that the Reformation in Wales merely restored the Church to its ancient Celtic purity. Legislation of the 1530s both for Wales and Ireland had envisaged the eradication of native languages and the substitution of English as a unifying medium; from the reign of Elizabeth this policy went into reverse.[84] Such devices generally prevented the emergence of a widespread sense that Protestantism was an English import. Catholic recusancy was initially at a low level, and the evidence for the 1580s suggests revival rather than survival;[85] but by then it may have been too late to offer any effective challenge to the Elizabethan settlement.

The dynastic union with Scotland in 1603 illustrated the weakness of dynastic allegiance to London when it ran counter to the imperatives of local and unreconstructed religious commitment. The Stuarts, like the Tudors, found their way to the English throne through genealogical good fortune rather than through any long-standing Scots attempt to build a union; but dynastic allegiance proved fragile when major religious differences placed it under strain. Even within Scotland before 1603, localism powerfully qualified the authority of the Crown: private jurisdictions in the Highlands contradicted Stuart absolutist rhetoric, and were not significantly overridden until the early eighteenth century under Hanoverian monarchs more effectively absolute than the Stuarts had ever been.

Before the Reformation, Henry VIII gave little attention to Wales and Ireland or to the conquest of Scotland: his diplomacy was directed to reversing the verdict of the Hundred Years' War by territorial gains in France.[86] In 1513 a campaign in northern France prevented the exploitation of the crushing Scots defeat at Flodden, which could otherwise have opened the northern kingdom to English conquest. With the progress of the Reformation a dynastic union with Scotland soon became an English goal, yet one which was impossible for Henry VIII to attain because of the northern kingdom's Catholicism; only the subsequent progress of Protestantism there made feasible the accession of James VI to the throne of England in 1603. He sought an Anglo-Scottish union on the Anglo-Welsh model, a merger of laws and parliaments rather than an English takeover;[87] it was not to be. Local ecclesiastical developments took the lead and, as with Ireland, prevented the complete success of that aggress-

---

[84] Roberts, 'The Union with England', pp. 61–70.

[85] Williams, *Recovery, Reorientation and Reformation*, pp. 329–30.

[86] J. J. Scarisbrick, *Henry VIII* (Harmondsworth, 1971), pp. 40–64.

[87] John Morrill, 'The National Covenant in its British Context', in idem (ed.), *The Scottish National Covenant in its British Context* (Edinburgh, 1990), pp. 1–30; Bruce Galloway, *The Union of England and Scotland, 1603–1608* (Edinburgh, 1986).

ive 'incorporating union' which the English sought and which some English civil lawyers hoped in 1604 could be brought about on the basis of a fusion of civil and common law.[88]

Failing a full union in 1603, the English common law, through the doctrine of allegiance affirmed in *Calvin's Case*, attempted with some success to reach out to absorb Scotland in one key respect; thereafter, progress towards legal union stalled.[89] A short-term tactical option[90] often appealing in London was to resist an incorporating union and keep Scotland and Ireland as separate and subordinate kingdoms, not fully participating in the 'rights of Englishmen'; but even when this political option was preferred, English law acted as a system threatening to impose itself on these neighbouring realms. The English Church made a similar, less successful, attempt. Laudianism, in the ascendant in England, was exported to Scotland via the episcopacy which James had restored there in 1612.[91] Yet Scots Protestantism, which had been a precondition of dynastic union, continued to develop in an extreme Genevan idiom to the point of threatening that very achievement. Under Charles I the imposition of an English Prayer Book led to resistance and the Scottish rebellion of 1638 which in turn triggered that war of three kingdoms inappropriately known as the English Civil War.[92]

From that era, the English and Scots churches grew steadily further apart. By contrast, political pressures to unification only grew with the Civil War: Charles I was crowned King of Scotland in 1633, but Charles II's coronation in that kingdom in 1651 after subscribing the Covenant was as King of Great Britain, a move which then triggered English conquest and an incorporating union on English terms.[93] Sanguinary conflict between Scots Episcopalians and Presbyterians resumed with the Restoration; but the exile of James II in 1689 meant that the Episcopalians north of the Border were hopelessly compromised. William III saw that his rule could only be defended by a Presbyterian settlement, and it was this, therefore, which he imposed on Scotland for English reasons.

[88] Brian P. Levack, *The Formation of the British State: England, Scotland and the Union 1603–1707* (Oxford, 1987), pp. 28, 82.
[89] Brian P. Levack, 'English Law, Scots Law and the Union, 1603–1707', in Alan Harding (ed.), *Law-Making and Law-Makers in British History* (London, 1980), pp. 105–19.
[90] Emphasised by Morrill, 'National Covenant', p. 6.
[91] D. G. Mullan, *Episcopacy in Scotland: The History of an Idea, 1560–1637* (Edinburgh, 1986).
[92] For a fuller exploration of this theme, see John Morrill, 'The Religious Context of the English Civil War', *TRHS* 34 (1984), 155–78, and 'Sir William Brereton and England's Wars of Religion', *Journal of British Studies* 24 (1985), 311–32; Conrad Russell, *The Causes of the English Civil War* (Oxford, 1990) and *The Fall of the British Monarchies 1637–1642* (Oxford, 1991).
[93] Morrill, 'National Covenant', p. 21; idem, *The Nature of the English Revolution* (Harlow, 1993), pp. 116–17.

Episcopalians were ejected from posts in the church, in schools and universities. By dynastic accident, the monarchy was deprived of its most committed supporters, and compelled to rely on those whose attachment to monarchy was at most pragmatic. Unassimilated Scots legal and ecclesiastical systems were the price of union in so profoundly divided a society. A representative assembly, which might articulate Scots grievances, became quickly unacceptable to England's rulers after 1689. Equally with Ireland in 1800, the threat of Scottish secession after the death of Anne meant that it could plausibly be argued that the Westminster Parliament abolished its Edinburgh rival, by the Union of 1707, in the name of unified sovereignty.

The English commissioners who negotiated the treaty in 1706 displayed a deep distrust of federal solutions: the Earl of Mar complained in that year that the English 'think all notions about federal unions and forms a mere jest and chimera'.[94] But the Scots commissioners similarly rejected federalism and sacrificed the Edinburgh Parliament since they too accepted that a union would necessarily contain a sovereign body, and that this would be the Westminster Parliament: the Scots too 'revealed that they were incapable of thinking in terms of divided sovereignty'.[95] Without an episcopalian or common-law foundation, however, the Union was subject to repeated political challenges from within Scotland. As a result of their defeat, Scots law was not as immune from revision as the Scots unionists of 1707 had hoped. Symbolic of English victory over the rebellion of 1745 was the legislative programme which followed, and, especially, the abolition of heritable jurisdictions in Scotland by the Act of 1747: unified sovereignty, again, was asserted. It is unlikely that these jurisdictions alone had been significant in allowing certain clans to be drafted into the rebellion; but the English conception of unitary sovereignty would now brook no challenge.

Ireland illustrated the difficulties of union when a long-established dynasty reneged in the 1820s on the religious premises of its title to power. Royal sovereignty was once more a Reformation creation, Henry VIII claiming headship of the separate Irish church when at the instigation of an Irish faction he accepted the title 'King of Ireland' in 1541. Once again, on the English side the first steps towards legislative incorporation had been planned in the mid 1530s by Thomas Cromwell.[96] Intended as

[94] Quoted in Levack, *Formation of the British State*, p. 50.
[95] Ibid., p. 51; John Robertson, 'Andrew Fletcher's Vision of Union', in Roger A. Mason (ed.), *Scotland and England 1286–1815* (Edinburgh, 1987), pp. 203–25.
[96] 'It had been argued in Ireland that the 'regal estate' rested in the papacy: the 'dominion' enjoyed by the king of England was 'but a governance under the obedience of the same'. So the decision of 1541 followed from the break with Rome': John Guy, *Tudor England* (Oxford, 1988), pp. 358–9.

a step towards unification, the assumption of the title of king only later had the opposite effect as the Irish began to claim the status of a kingdom equal with England.[97] Meanwhile, however, even more clearly than in the case of Wales, a unified or at least homogeneous legal and ecclesiastical jurisdiction was an English imposition. The pattern it replaced had much in common with that of Wales: the ancient unity of Ireland under a single monarch was a distant Celtic legend of weak modern relevance.[98] From the middle ages, Ireland was ruled by shifting alliances between warring clans or septs, within each of which the title to chiefdom was determined by Brehon law rather than primogeniture, each clan owing only a shifting and uncertain allegiance to the monarchy planted in Ireland by Henry II's conquest. It was this patchwork of lordships over which Henrician sovereignty sought to impose a single jurisdiction. Constitutional reform rather than military conquest was the Henrician keynote.[99]

The flourishing state of lordship, and the far greater resilience of local Brehon law,[100] meant that the Tudors were never able to win Ireland, like Wales, merely by breaking, and inheriting the power of, a feudal Anglo-Norman baronage. Irish lords lastingly resisted, often to the point of rebellion, successive Tudor viceroys' reformist programmes for introducing English land law and its attendant political structures. The progress of English religion then received a greater check than the progress of English law: Henry VIII's unified ecclesiastical jurisdiction soon shrank from inclusiveness to minority status when the re-enactment in Dublin of the Elizabethan Acts of Supremacy and Uniformity defined the new order as irreversibly Protestant and saw the 'Old English' settlers take sides with persecuted Catholicism.[101] The Reformation thus ensured that the power-base of English rule in Ireland soon became religious, not baronial, as the rebellion of 1594–1603 and the Catholic massacre of English and Scots settlers in 1641 demonstrated and successive traumatic episodes confirmed: the Cromwellian conquest, the Restoration land settlement, the civil war of 1689–93, the Penal Laws, the rebellion of 1798. The success of the episcopalian Church of Ireland was far less than that of her sister Church of England in Wales, and was offset by resilient Scots

---

[97] M. Perceval-Maxwell, 'Ireland and the Monarchy in the Early Stuart Multiple Kingdom', *HJ* 34 (1991), 279–95.

[98] F. J. Byrne, *Irish Kings and High-Kings* (2nd edn., London, 1987).

[99] Brendan Bradshaw, *The Irish Constitutional Revolution of the Sixteenth Century* (Cambridge, 1979), pp. 139–63, 231–8 and passim; Ciaran Brady, 'The Decline of the Irish Kingdom', in Mark Greengrass (ed.), *Conquest and Coalescence: The Shaping of the State in Early Modern Europe* (London, 1991), pp. 94–115.

[100] Hans S. Pawlisch, *Sir John Davies and the Conquest of Ireland: A Study in Legal Imperialism* (Cambridge, 1985). This study focuses on land law and commercial conflicts; it does not discuss the nature of the 'sovereignty' which the English common law extended to Ireland.

[101] H. Jefferies, 'The Irish Parliament of 1560: The Anglican Reforms Authorised', *Journal of Ecclesiastical History* 26 (1988), 128–41.

Presbyterianism in Ulster. Religion bound the Catholic Irish to the exiled Stuart dynasty as firmly as it bound Protestants to William, Anne and the Hanoverians: James II might have securely united Ireland to England and Scotland on the basis of monarchical federalism and religious toleration or a re-imposed Catholicism, but the uneasy hold of his successors on Ireland was intimately but unstably bound up with the narrowly-based ascendancy of the Church of Ireland.

By comparison with this chief pillar of English rule, the existence of a separate Dublin Parliament was at best an anomaly, at worst an affront, and there were few English protests about its abolition with the Union of 1801. Only the operation of Poyning's Law (1495), which required previous assent from the king to bills in the Dublin Parliament, saved the system from the contradictions of a dual monarchy. These sometimes threatened to return. Once the Restoration in 1660 undid the Cromwellian union of England, Ireland and Scotland, it could be argued that the system had reverted to what it had been; yet although the Westminster Parliament had legislated for Ireland, some Irish authorities continued to dispute its right to do so. As the English Attorney General explained in 1671, although 'an English act do in truth bind Ireland', nevertheless the Dublin Parliament also was 'endued with a legislative power', so that 'if a statute were made in England to forbid the transportation of wool out of Ireland; yet a statute in Ireland might make it lawful again there'.[102]

It took the Revolution of 1688 to clarify this relationship, since the Westminster Convention Parliament gave William and Mary the crowns of both England and Ireland without consulting the Dublin assembly. This, the Williamite conquest of Ireland, and the subsequent repression of Roman Catholicism, produced a situation of English domination so complete that formal union was for decades unattractive in London;[103] the Declaratory Act of 1720 was sufficient to establish the Westminster Parliament's supremacy over Dublin until the Renunciation Act of 1783 restored Irish legislative equality in a form so unacceptable as to lead swiftly to the Union of 1801. The religious basis of this settlement was not thereby revised. By the 1820s, those in Ireland who defended the Union, like Lord Redesdale, did so by defending their Protestant Constitution in language similar to that of its English champions like Lord Eldon. For them, the rise of Daniel O'Connell's militant Catholic movement, and the concession of Catholic 'Emancipation' which it extracted

---

[102] Thomas Carte, *The Life of James Duke of Ormonde* (2nd edn, 6 vols., Oxford, 1851), vol. 5, p. 123. It seems that only the political balance of the two kingdoms could resolve this ambiguity in their legal relations.

[103] James Kelly, 'The Origins of the Act of Union: An Examination of Unionist Opinion in Britain and Ireland, 1650–1800', *Irish Historical Studies* 25 (1987), 236–63.

from Westminster by the threat of civil war in 1829, signalled the beginning of the end of England's domination of their island[104] – as indeed they
did.

III. SOVEREIGNTY IN POLITICAL THEORY FROM JUSTINIAN TO THE ENGLISH JURISTS

The issues of parliamentary representation and the role of subordinate
legislatures which united, or divided, England's Atlantic empire become
fully intelligible only in their European dynastic and religious setting.[105]
That setting illuminates also the theoretical pathways along which early-
modern England devised, and the nineteenth-century United Kingdom
only partly modified, a characteristic doctrine of sovereignty: unitary,
absolutist and claiming a divine mandate. Such a study highlights the
fact that the term 'sovereignty' is an anachronism if applied to the Roman
law tradition: in this, Justinian's *Institutes* do not prefigure Blackstone.
But this is more than a contingent fact: rather, the English common law,
by its very success in distancing itself from its European civil law origins,
was able to become the foundation for a body of political theory which
set the British Isles (and, until 1776, mainland America) aside from European norms.

The Anglo-American tradition systematically repudiated Roman law
as tantamount to arbitrary power. Justinian, echoing earlier sources like
Ulpian and Gaius, had indeed maintained that 'A pronouncement of the
emperor also has legislative force', but this is 'because, by the Regal Act
relating to his sovereign power, the people conferred on him its whole
sovereignty and authority' ('Sed et quod principi placuit, legis habet vigorem, cum lege regia, quae de imperio eius lata est, populus ei et in eum
omne suum imperium et potestatem concessit').[106] This was conventionally translated 'What has pleased the Prince has the force of law . . .',
so perpetuating in the English-speaking world the image of Roman law
societies as wholly directed by the arbitrary whim of their rulers.
Although intending to interpret the increasing power of the emperor, this
passage was not a description of an arbitrary tyranny but a claim that
authority – sovereignty – was not the state's or the ruler's but the people's.

---

[104] See the correspondence of Redesdale and Eldon printed in Horace Twiss, *The Public and Private Life of Lord Chancellor Eldon* (2nd edn, 3 vols., London, 1844).

[105] For the historiographical isolation of English and American legal systems from the broad sweep of the Western legal tradition, see Harold J. Berman, *Law and Revolution: The Formation of the Western Legal Tradition* (Cambridge, Mass., 1983), pp. 17–18 and passim.

[106] Peter Birks and Grant McLeod (eds. and trans.), *Justinian's Institutes* (London, 1987), Book 1, title 2, sections 3, 6: pp. 36–7.

Indeed, imperial command was only one source of law, continued the *Institutes*: 'Written law includes acts, plebeian statutes, resolutions of the senate, imperial pronouncements, magistrates' edicts, and answers given by jurists.' Moreover, 'Law comes into being without writing when a rule is approved by use. Long-standing custom founded on the consent of those who follow it is just like legislation.'[107] Justinian's society was one dominated by custom, not by arbitrary executive action; and despite the splendour of the emperor, other bodies also made the law. So it remained in the Roman law societies of early-modern Europe.

In medieval Christendom, similarly, no unitary conception of sovereignty developed. Authority was held to be shared or divided, secular rulers possessing varying degrees of jurisdiction over the things that were Caesar's, the Pope ultimately claiming jurisdiction over the things that were God's. The role of kings was circumscribed by law – divine law, natural law, and the law of communities expressed in custom; subjects commonly held that a king was absolute only in executing the law, not in any ability to make new law by statute. This was a component of the medieval English constitution as expressed in *De Legibus et Consuetudinibus Angliae* (a compilation influenced by Justinian and supervised by Henry Bracton, d. 1268), which placed the king 'under God and under the law, because the law makes the king',[108] and in the writings of Sir John Fortescue (?1394–?1476). Both Bracton's text[109] and Fortescue's insisted that the King of England should only declare what the law was or levy taxation after consultation with his subjects. Fortescue, in stigmatising Justinian, was responsible for the misleading antithesis between *dominium politicum et regale* (like the English monarchy) and *dominium regale* (like the French),[110] but it was a distinction proposed for tactical purposes and considerably exaggerated.[111] Fortescue indeed had an elementary understanding of continental societies, offering as an explanation of why the French did not rebel against their royal tyranny: 'it is not pouerte that

---

[107] Justinian, *Institutes*, edn. cit., Book I, title 2, sections 3, 8; cf. Hinsley, *Sovereignty*, p. 44.

[108] *Bracton on the Laws and Customs of England*, trans. and ed. Samuel B. Thorne (4 vols., Cambridge, Mass., 1968–77), vol. 2, p. 33.

[109] Ibid., vol. 2, p. 305.

[110] Sir John Fortescue, *The Governance of England: otherwise called The Difference between an Absolute and a Limited Monarchy*, ed. Charles Plummer (Oxford, 1885), pp. 110–13. Fortescue cited the single famous sentence from Justinian, 'quod principi placuit, legis habet vigorem', to identify his category of 'Realmes dominium tantum regale'. Fortescue's misleading division of monarchies into two categories passed into English political mythology. For a different interpretation see H. G. Koenigsberger, '*Dominium regale* or *Dominium politicum et regale*: Monarchies and Parliaments in Early Modern Europe', reprinted in Koenigsberger, *Politicians and Virtuosi* (London, 1986), pp. 1–25.

[111] Cf. R. W. K. Hinton, 'English Constitutional Theories from Sir John Fortescue to Sir John Eliot', *EHR* 75 (1960), 410–25, at 412.

kepith Ffrenchmen ffro rysinge, but it is cowardisse and lakke off hartes and corage, wich no Ffrenchman hath like vnto a Englysh man'.[112] Charles Plummer observed[113] that Bracton[114] had used Justinian's passage but given to it 'a very different interpretation . . . whereby he almost makes it the foundation of constitutional government'; from Fortescue's day it was used as a symbol of arbitrary power. Increasing English disparagement from the Reformation of the arbitrary power which, it was assumed, accompanied French Popery obscured an understanding of the points of similarity between the two cases, but it also had the effect of highlighting the differences.

Many of the pressures which led men towards a unified doctrine of the state were nevertheless visible in both England and continental Europe. From the sixteenth century, more centralised formulations of political authority began to be advanced, chiefly in response to the wars of religion which devastated Europe and of which the 'English' Civil War was one instance. Searching for a solution to such breakdowns of government, Jean Bodin (1530–96) enunciated in *Six livres de la République* (Paris, 1576) the functional component of absolutism: that the essence of sovereignty was the right to impose laws, ultimately regardless of custom or consent. But since Bodin overtly rejected religious pluralism as an ideal, his sovereign was still constrained by natural and divine law, as interpreted by the Catholic Church, and though necessarily undivided and unaccountable to his subjects was obliged to work within a framework of constitutional law.[115] Constitutional law survived as a notion far more powerful in Roman law societies than in common law societies. Local and sectional privileges were to be far stronger in France than in England from Bodin's era to 1789.

Englishmen meanwhile, independently of continental thinkers like Bodin, had already evolved a heightened doctrine of royal absolutism and undivided sovereignty by the early seventeenth century. As John King, Bishop of London 1611–21, preached in 1606, it was 'no more possible there should be two authentic authorities within one kingdom, than that one and the same body can bear two heads'.[116] The English Parliament's victory in the Civil War did not mean the triumph of limited government, divided sovereignty or the ancient constitution: it meant that 'parliament-

---

[112] Fortescue, *Governance*, p. 141.
[113] Ibid., p. 185. For a profound discussion of this point, see Brian Tierney, 'Bracton on Government', *Speculum* 38 (1963), 295–317, and Ewart Lewis, 'King Above Law? 'Quod Principi Placuit' in Bracton', ibid., 39 (1964), 240–69.
[114] *Laws and Customs*, ed. Thorne, vol. 2, pp. 19, 305.
[115] Skinner, *Foundations of Modern Political Thought*, vol. 2, pp. 248–9, 253, 284–301; Nannerl O. Keohane, *Philosophy and the State in France: The Renaissance to the Enlightenment* (Princeton, 1980), pp. 67–73.
[116] Sommerville, *Politics and Ideology*, pp. 36–7, 203–4.

ary absolutism was victorious', that is, that Parliament could legislate subject only to the laws of God and nature.[117] The Restoration of 1660 re-established a constitutional theory of the tripartite sovereign and the Church of England as integral aspects of the state without upsetting this legal definition of absolutism. What distinguished the finally-prevalent English understanding of sovereignty was, first, the doctrine that sovereignty resided in 'The King in Parliament'[118] – that what Montesquieu was to misinterpret as a division of powers did not entail *divided* sovereignty – and, second, the doctrine that the monarch was also 'supreme head' of the Church. If the title to the Crown in English law came to be described like the title to a landed estate in fee simple, it was the headship of the Church which gave a peculiar sanctity to the monarchy and to the hereditary principle which governed the title to the Crown, a principle only haphazardly observed in pre-Conquest and medieval kingship, obviously breached in 1485 but tenaciously defended through the seventeenth and eighteenth centuries by royalist lawyers and divines alike.

It was this peculiar sanctity which proved ideologically effective against the right of rebellion which continued to threaten the Roman law monarchies of continental Europe and finally destroyed the most powerful of them.[119] Apart from assuming headship of the Church, Tudor monarchs did not escape from the limitations placed on their predecessors. The sovereign's ordinary prerogatives were still set by positive law, and this restricted his arbitrary power to the prerogative of dispensing with the law in emergencies: the law could only be changed by the King-in-Parliament. The formal difference in the status of Tudor monarchs stemmed from the ecclesiastical dimension: it was Henry VIII's Act in Restraint of Appeals (to Rome) of 1533 which contained the famous

---

[117] Mousnier, 'The Exponents and Critics of Absolutism', p. 104; Sommerville, *Politics and Ideology*, pp. 90–1, 100, 169.

[118] Elton, 'English National Selfconsciousness', p. 79, emphasises the Cromwellian vision that that 'From at least the 1530s the king was regarded as a member (the head) of the Parliament which structurally included him. He should not be seen standing outside and over against it.' This doctrine was lastingly reaffirmed in 1660 when it was necessary to condemn those who had tried Charles I by arguing that the Parliamentary authority which they claimed was invalid since it did not include one of Parliament's three components, the king.

[119] Similarly, the most rebellious part of the British Isles for a century after the Restoration was also the one most heavily influenced by Roman law: Scotland. See Peter Stein, 'The Influence of Roman Law on the Law of Scotland', *Juridical Review* 8 (1963), 205–45; idem, 'Law and Society in Eighteenth-Century Scottish Thought', in N. T. Phillipson and Rosalind Mitchison (eds.), *Scotland in the Age of Improvement* (Edinburgh, 1970), pp. 148–68; idem, 'The Legal Philosophy of the Scottish Enlightenment', in Reinhard Brandt (ed.), *Rechtsphilosophie der Aufklärung: Symposium Wolfenbüttel 1981* (Berlin, 1982), pp. 61–78; idem, 'From Pufendorf to Adam Smith: The Natural Law Tradition in Scotland', in Norbert Horn (ed.), *Europäisches Rechtsdenken in Geschichte und Gegenwart* (München, 1982), pp. 667–79.

phrase 'this realm of England is an Empire' – that is, a jurisdiction from which there was no appeal.[120] It was an empire within which statute law could now take precedence over all other forms of law, including custom and canon law: it was statute law which effected the Reformation, and it was Christian (but specifically Anglican) duty, defined by the Church of England's Canons (1604) and Book of Homilies (1547, 1571), which limited the rights of non-compliance of the subject to passive (dis)obedience.

Although Hooker did not argue like some early-Stuart clergy that the monarch's powers were derived directly from God, he defended the Church of England against Puritan criticism by defending its national character, that is, by endorsing the arguments of Henrician common lawyers like Christopher St German that Church and State were two aspects of a single body.[121] Whether the Church was henceforth ruled by a caesaropapist monarchy or by the King-in-Parliament, the sovereignty of the kingdom was sanctified by the Church; and whether Henry VIII's caesaropapist version of the monarchy was in the ascendant, as under the Stuarts, or Christopher St German's and Thomas Cromwell's model of the King-in-Parliament,[122] as after 1660, the Church of England equally credited the sovereign power with a divine (though differently limited) mandate. Hooker laid down that this applied whether kings received power 'immediately from God' or via human choice: 'By which of these means soever it happen that kings or governors be advanced unto their states, we must acknowledge both their lawful choice to be approved of God, and themselves to be God's lieutenants, and confess their power his.'[123] It followed that 'A king which hath not supreme power in the greatest things, is rather entitled a king, than invested with real sovereignty.'[124] Hooker continued:

> The parliament of England together with the convocation annexed thereunto, is that whereupon the very essence of all government within this

[120] Only subsequently was the term widely used in its second sense: a collection of kingdoms or principalities under a single monarch.

[121] Guy, *Tudor England*, pp. 374–8. 'St German did for English common law what, a generation or so later, John Jewel and Richard Hooker did for the Anglican church. Within St German's framework, the universal laws of God and Nature were shown to be both rationally antecedent to, and harmoniously co-existent with, English common law (the law of man) and good conscience (equity), despite the fact that conscience, as derived from natural reason and moral calculation, might sometimes speak directly contrary to general rules of common law in specific instances': J. A. Guy, *Christopher St. German on Chancery and Statute* (London, 1985), p. 19.

[122] Guy, *St. German*, p. 39; G. R. Elton, 'The Political Creed of Thomas Cromwell', in Elton, *Studies in Tudor and Stuart Politics and Government* (4 vols., Cambridge, 1974–92), vol. 2, pp. 215–35.

[123] Richard Hooker, *Of the Laws of Ecclesiastical Polity*, Book VIII, ch. ii, 5.

[124] Ibid., Book VIII, ch. ii, 12.

kingdom doth depend; it is even the body of the whole realm; it consisteth of the king, and of all that within the land are subject unto him: for they all are there present, either in person or by such as they voluntarily have derived their very personal right unto.

Nor could kings of England be excommunicated: since they are 'within their own dominions the most high, and can have no peer, how is it possible that any, either civil or ecclesiastical person under them should have over them coercive power, when such power would make that person so far forth his superior's superior, ruler, and judge?'[125]

Despite Henry VIII's and Hooker's striking contributions, the legal and ecclesiastical ideal of unified sovereignty was realised only by stages. The amalgamation of local representative assemblies was one contributory process, not completed until 1801. A second was the erosion of the medieval idea that the king, the two Houses of Parliament and the courts of law each held certain indefeasible powers defined by custom: for both monarch and Parliament, the civil war replaced this with the doctrine that the powers of institutions were defined and could be redefined by the sovereign body (whatever that was).[126] When, in the early seventeenth century, Sir Edward Coke sought to use common law against monarchical authority, he did so by quietly emphasising, within the common law, maxims derived from the Roman law tradition, and by identifying natural law with divine law:[127]

> The Law of Nature is that which God at the Time of Creation of the Nature of Man infused into his Heart, for his Preservation and Direction; and this is *Lex aeterna*, the Moral Law, called also the Law of Nature. And by this Law, written with the Finger of God in the Heart of Man, were the People of God a long Time governed, before the Law was written by *Moses*, who was the first Reporter or Writer of Law in the World.[128]

After 1660, it became clearer that limitations on this undivided tripartite sovereign were henceforth provided by natural and divine law rather than by institutional constraints. Thomas Hobbes's fully secularised ver-

---

[125] Ibid., ch. vi, 11; ch. ix, 6.

[126] This is the heart of the uniqueness of the English case after the Civil War, hinted at by J. P. Cooper, 'Differences between English and Continental Governments in the Early Seventeenth Century' (1960), reprinted in idem, *Land, Men and Beliefs*, ed. Gerald Aylmer and John Morrill (London, 1984).

[127] Edward S. Corwin, *The 'Higher Law' Background of American Constitutional Law* (Ithaca, 1955), pp. 41–8. For Coke's 'inaccuracy or disingenuousness' in wrongly citing an earlier authority to suggest in *Bonham's Case* 'that in many cases the common law will control Acts of Parliament and sometimes adjudge them to be utterly void', see Frederick Pollock, 'Sovereignty in English Law', *Harvard Law Review* 8 (1894), 233–51 at 245.

[128] *Calvin's Case* (1608) in *The Seventh Part of the Reports of Sir Edward Coke Kt.* (In the Savoy, 1738), p. 12b.

sion of this tradition shocked his contemporaries mainly because it subordinated morality to law and identified law with the command of the unitary sovereign, whose rights 'are indivisible': 'If there had not first been an opinion received of the greatest part of *England*, that these Powers were divided between the King, and the Lords, and the House of Commons, the people had never been divided, and fallen into this Civill Warre.'[129] Eighteenth-century French jurists, like Restoration Anglican divines, indignantly complained that Hobbes had conflated 'absolute' and 'arbitrary', and insisted that this was not true of their own monarchy.[130] Nevertheless, following the return of Charles II in 1660 the English henceforth generally agreed with Hobbes that sovereignty in England was indivisible and absolute, distinguished from arbitrary power by its accountability to natural (i.e. divine) law.

An object of the doctrine of the ancient constitution was to separate the English monarchy from its medieval, Roman law inheritance by appeal to an earlier native source. One commentator tried to excuse the Roman experience itself. Emperors, he admitted, had acquired tyrannical power through the surrender of the ancient liberties of the Roman people. Nevertheless, that power was not complete; it did not completely destroy liberty or property; it did not reduce the people to slavery; it 'was abolish'd together with the Roman Empire, which ended in the West with *Augustulus*'.[131] And whatever had happened in Rome, the kingdoms of northern and western Europe 'never own'd this Royal Law', as Caesar observed in his *Commentaries* and Tacitus confirmed. The power of western sovereigns was so limited

1. That they could make no Laws without the States General of the Kingdom.
2. That they could not levy any Mony on their Subjects without their Consents.
3. That they could not break the Laws according to their Will and Pleasure.
4. That in case of their violating the Fundamental Laws of the State, they were liable to be depriv'd of a Power which they abus'd.
5. That the States were free to chuse such a Form of Government, and such a Person to govern them as they thought most fit.

---

[129] Thomas Hobbes, *Leviathan* (1651), ed. Richard Tuck (Cambridge, 1991), p. 127.
[130] E.g. *Maximes du droit public français* (2nd edn., Amsterdam, 1775), vol. 1, pp. 141–2, quoted in Jouvenel, *Sovereignty*, p. 211.
[131] *Reflections upon the Opinions of some Modern Divines, concerning the Nature of Government in general, and that of England in particular*, in *A Collection of State Tracts, Publish'd on Occasion of the late Revolution in 1688. And during the Reign of King William III* (3 vols., London, 1705–7), vol. 1, pp. 492–4.

Even the French monarchy was 'limited in its Constitution', despite what Bodin had said of it.[132] This was, however, an unusual insight into Roman law; most English commentators took a less well informed, and less favourable, view. Roman law defined the people as the source of legislative authority; but it continued to be debated whether the lex regia produced a complete alienation (*translatio*) of legislative power to the Emperor, or whether it represented only a delegation (*concessio*), which would be revocable.[133] English commentators instinctively preferred the first interpretation.

Roman law was unjustly neglected, complained English academics: 'One very plausible ground of the disgust, so long conceived against the civil law in this country, was the intemperate bigotry of the popish clergy . . . Inspired likewise with a zeal for the supreme and universal authority of the pope, they had imposed upon the nation the yoke of the canon law.' Hence 'For many ages . . . the laity, when they had once found their way into the profession of the common law, treated the civil law with open contempt; they affected an ignorance of it; and held it almost unconstitutional even to read or quote its authors.'[134] By the American Revolution, colonists had collapsed Roman law and divine right monarchy into each other as an account of the full, Popish version of unitary, tyrannical sovereignty. James Wilson, one of the framers of the Constitution of 1787 and a Justice of the Supreme Court, made this assumption explicit; as an American editor explained Wilson's doctrine:

> While it is true that at the period of the American revolution the idea of the divine right of kings was not in terms advocated, the substitute therefore was the doctrine precisely like that of Justinian, which passed under the name of the original compact, and it consisted in nothing else, than the idea that the people vested in the sovereign body all their power by an irrevocable grant, the violation of which would destroy the whole social fabric.

In this vision, the usurped tyranny of the Roman Emperor and the checked and balanced English sovereign were indistinguishable.[135]

For patriotic reasons, English lawyers often claimed to reject civil law even when they borrowed from it: civil law was often blamed for what were to become characteristics of the common law itself. Despite Sir

---

[132] Ibid., pp. 498, 500–1.
[133] Otto von Gierke, *Political Theories of the Middle Age*, trans. F. W. Maitland (Cambridge, 1900), p. 43.
[134] Thomas Bever, *A Discourse on the Study of Jurisprudence and the Civil Law* (Oxford, 1766), pp. 14–15.
[135] Introduction, in James DeWitt Andrews (ed.), *The Works of James Wilson* (2 vols., Chicago, 1896), vol. 1, p. xxxvi. Other references in the present work are to the 1967 edition of Wilson's *Works*.

Edward Coke's idolisation of Magna Carta and his belief that it constituted fundamental law, he also (perhaps in contradiction) ascribed legislative authority to Parliament: 'Of the power and jurisdiction of the Parliament, for making of laws in proceeding by Bill, it is so transcendent
and absolute, as it cannot be confined either for causes or persons within
any bounds.'[136] The same conception of supreme unitary authority was
expressed, with greater rhetorical force, by Sir William Blackstone in the
1760s, and with the same potential contradiction by natural law;[137] but
whereas in Coke the enemy was the person of the monarch and his claims
to absolute power, in Blackstone sovereignty securely resided with the
King-in-Parliament, and the enemy was Dissent. Blackstone's *Commentaries* were therefore a sensational affront to colonial and English Dissenters
alike. Moreover, where early-eighteenth-century Whigs had employed a
false rhetoric to claim checks and balances as the characteristics of the
constitution, Blackstone candidly emphasised sovereignty, the unity of
King, Lords and Commons in Parliament. His account of the very extensive residual power of the monarch could easily raise alarms that the putative balance of King, Lords and Commons (or Montesquieu's rendition
of it into legislative, executive and judiciary) might be upset. Moreover,
Blackstone defined law as command, neglecting those Whig judicial
decisions which (in order to deny the independent validity of canon law)
had derived the binding force of an Act of Parliament from the idea of
representation and the consent of the people.[138] Blackstone evidently saw
no contradiction between deriving the authority of statute law from natural law and revelation, and insisting that the King-in-Parliament was
absolute and that its statutes must be obeyed even if they conflicted with
natural law. This was, however, no simple logical mistake.[139] What to
secular or Dissenting critics was an obvious problem was obscured by

[136] Sir Edward Coke, *The Fourth Part of the Institutes of the Lawes of England; Concerning the
Jurisdiction of Courts* (London, 1669), p. 36.
[137] Blackstone, *Commentaries*, vol. 1, pp. 156–7.
[138] E.g. Middleton v. Croft (1736), in *Reports of Cases Argued and Determined in the High Court
of Chancery . . . Collected by John Tracy Atkyns* (3 vols., London, 1765–8), vol. 2, pp. 650–
75, at 654, ruled that 'Every man may be said to be party to, and the consent of every
subject is included in an act of parliament; but in canons made in convocation, and
confirmed by the crown only, all these are wanting, except the royal assent.' Cf. Matthews
v. Burdett (1701), in William Salkeld, *Reports of Cases Adjudged in the Court of King's Bench*
(3 vols., In the Savoy, 1742–3), vol. 2, pp. 672–4, in which it was held that an unlicensed
schoolteacher was not bound by canon, 'Ratio est, because being a Lay-Man, he is not
represented, and therefore his Consent is not given, and a Man cannot be under the
Obligation of a Canon without his consent express or implied.'
[139] Michael Lobban, *The Common Law and English Jurisprudence 1760–1850* (Oxford, 1991),
p. 29, treats Blackstone's doctrine on this point as a 'confused' echo of Pufendorf which
had, in the last resort, 'Hobbesian premisses'. It might better be placed in the denominational context suggested here.

Blackstone's major premise: that the Anglican sovereign, as head of the Church, represented and articulated law-as-revelation.

These characteristics of the book were quickly appreciated by both English and colonial American Dissenters. If, as Burke rightly observed, religion and law were the two dominant idioms of transatlantic discourse, they were not unrelated. When Blackstone's *Commentaries* attracted a colonial edition (Philadelphia, 1771), it was quickly followed by an anthology[140] containing the main pamphlet exchanges between the Anglican lawyer and his English Dissenting critics: Joseph Priestley's *Remarks on some Paragraphs in the Fourth Volume of Dr. Blackstone's Commentaries on the Laws of England relating to the Dissenters*, Blackstone's *A Reply to Dr. Priestley's Remarks*, Priestley's *An Answer to Dr. Blackstone's Reply*, Blackstone's *The Case of the Late Election for the County of Middlesex* and Philip Furneaux's *Letters to the Honourable Mr. Justice Blackstone, concerning his exposition of the Act of Toleration*. Quickly and indelibly, Blackstone's Anglican framework of thought was established for a colonial audience. Blackstone was presented not merely as reducing the law to elegant order, but as restructuring it in the interest of the monarchy and the established Church.

The need to identify natural law with divine law, and so implicitly with Anglican Christianity, was pressing for all common lawyers. One civil lawyer in Blackstone's Anglican Oxford similarly sought to justify his subject by collapsing into each other Roman or civil law, jurisprudence, and divine law: mankind are 'induced, by an indefeasible certainty of good, both to make law their religion, and religion their law . . . Whatever then may be comprehended under the idea of ecclesiastical polity, or the government of the visible church, is a proper object of jurisprudence.'[141] William Paley in turn carefully distanced his most famous work from the writings of Grotius and Pufendorf: they were 'too much mixed up with the civil law, and with the jurisprudence of Germany, to answer precisely the design of a system of ethics'. Almost all English philosophers, objected Paley, 'divide too much the law of nature from the precepts of revelation'. He wrote what became an Anglican classic by uniting them, and could thereby offer an account of sovereignty which echoed Blackstone's:

> As a series of appeals must be finite, there necessarily exists in every government a power from which the constitution has provided no appeal; and which power, for that reason, may be termed absolute, omnipotent, uncontrollable, arbitrary, despotic; and is alike so in all countries.

[140] *An Interesting Appendix to Sir William Blackstone's Commentaries on the Laws of England* (Philadelphia, 1772; 2nd edn., Philadelphia, 1773; 3rd edn. as *The Palladium of Conscience*, Philadelphia, 1774).

[141] Bever, *A Discourse on the Study of Jurisprudence and the Civil Law*, pp. 2–5. For Bever's reproof of the intolerance of New England Puritans, p. 6.

The person, or assembly, in whom this power resides, is called the sovereign, or the supreme power of the state.

Since to the same power universally appertains the office of establishing public laws, it is called also the legislature of the state.[142]

Blackstone's next but one successor in the Vinerian chair similarly combined an account of how positive law and social institutions depended on 'the natural law of morality', with an account of law as the absolute command of a superior (ultimately, of God).[143]

The mutual influence of the two legal systems was made explicit even in the career of Blackstone, who had been trained in civil law and failed to obtain the Regius Professorship of Civil Law at Oxford in 1752 only because his Tory-Jacobite associations were anathema to the Secretary of State, the Duke of Newcastle. Blackstone nevertheless was an English patriot, concerned to use his systematisation of the common law to advance the process of state building.[144] To this, he had sacrificed an early loyalty. Many of the ambiguities in his text actually reflect a residual attachment to the early-eighteenth-century Tory party and its periodically-dubious loyalty to the regime in power. Nevertheless, in his lectures of the 1750s and in the *Commentaries*, Blackstone was careful to point out his acceptance of the Revolution of 1688 and the Hanoverian dynasty. His account of sovereignty was one to which 1688 had seemingly made little difference, because he echoed Richard Hooker's disclaimer:

> How the several forms of government we now see in the world at first actually began, is matter of great uncertainty, and has occasioned infinite disputes. It is not my business or intention to enter into any of them. However they began, or by what right so ever they subsist, there is and must be in all of them a supreme, irresistible, absolute, uncontrolled authority, in which the jura summi imperii, or the rights of sovereignty, reside . . . By the sovereign power . . . is meant the making of laws . . .'[145]

Partly this was a logical claim, advanced as a condition which must be satisfied for an association of men to count as being under a government

---

[142] William Paley, *The Principles of Moral and Political Philosophy* (London, 1785), pp. i, iii, 449.

[143] [Richard Wooddeson], *Elements of Jurisprudence treated of in the Preliminary Part of a Course of Lectures on the Laws of England* (London, 1783), pp. 4, 6, 27.

[144] John W. Cairns, 'Blackstone, an English Institutist: Legal Literature and the Rise of the Nation State', *Oxford Journal of Legal Studies* 4 (1984), 318–60; Klaus Luig, 'The Institutes of National Law in the Seventeenth and Eighteenth Centuries', *Juridical Review* 17 (1972), 193–226.

[145] Blackstone, *Commentaries*, vol. 1, pp. 48–9. This account emphasises the tactical political demands which shaped Blackstone's arguments. For a complementary reading, arguing for his failure to fit common law into a Roman law structure as the cause of Blackstone's contradictions, see Michael Lobban, 'Blackstone and the Science of Law', *HJ* 30 (1987), 311–35; idem, *The Common Law and English Jurisprudence 1760–1850*, pp. 17–46.

(Blackstone did not use the abstract and secular term 'state'; the current term, in law as in popular discourse, was 'kingdom'). Partly this was an empirical claim: that is what governments were like; in any government, *some* person or group would have final authority.[146]

In England, that group was Parliament, composed of the King, the Lords spiritual and temporal, and the Commons; or as it was elsewhere termed, the King in Parliament.

> The power and jurisdiction of parliament, says Sir Edward Coke, is so transcendent and absolute, that it cannot be confined, either for causes or persons, within any bounds . . . It hath sovereign and uncontrolable authority in making, confirming, enlarging, restraining, abrogating, repealing, reviving, and expounding of laws, concerning matters of all possible denominations, ecclesiastical, or temporal, civil, military, maritime, or criminal: this being the place where that absolute despotic power, which must in all governments reside somewhere, is entrusted by the constitution of these kingdoms.

Locke's claim that the people retained 'a supreme power to remove or alter the legislative, when they find the legislative act contrary to the trust reposed in them' could not be accepted, insisted Blackstone:

> For this devolution of power, to the people at large, includes in it a dissolution of the whole form of government established by that people, reduces all the members to their original state of equality, and by annihilating the sovereign power repeals all positive laws whatsoever before enacted . . . So long therefore as the English constitution lasts, we may venture to affirm, that the power of parliament is absolute and without control.[147]

Blackstone was aware of the problem which his definition of sovereignty posed for the composite state which the British Isles had become by 1765. 'The kingdom of England, over which our municipal laws have jurisdiction, includes not, by the common law, either Wales, Scotland, or Ireland, or any other part of the king's dominions, except the territory of England only',[148] he noted. Section IV of the Introduction, 'Of Countries Subject to the Laws of England', explored these problems at the very outset of the *Commentaries*. It resolved them in terms of conquest rather than of a

---

[146] Blackstone's account of statute law has encouraged modern scholars to see his argument for the natural- and divine-law basis of statute law as a 'pious afterthought' (Sir Carleton Kemp Allen, *Law in the Making*, 7th edn., London, 1964, p. 450); one claims that Blackstone's treatment of law has a 'Hobbesian character' and is 'a forerunner of Austinian jurisprudence': Paul Lucas, '*Ex parte* Sir William Blackstone, 'Plagiarist': A Note on Blackstone and the Natural Law', *American Journal of Legal History* 7 (1963), 142–58, at 149, 156. This overlooks the crucial role of natural-law limitations in distinguishing between 'absolute' and 'arbitrary' power.

[147] Blackstone, *Commentaries*, vol. 1, pp. 156–7.

[148] Ibid., p. 93.

federal division of sovereignty. Blackstone reviewed Welsh history to prove the point: 'Thus were this brave people gradually conquered into the enjoyment of true liberty.' England held Ireland by right of Henry II's conquest: 'as Ireland, thus conquered, planted, and governed, still continues in a state of dependence, it must necessarily conform to, and be obliged by such laws as the superior state thinks proper to prescribe'.[149] Where Ireland was specifically named in any Act of the Westminster Parliament, it was bound by that Act; 'For this follows from the very nature and constitution of a dependent state: dependence being very little else, but an obligation to conform to the will or law of that superior person or state, upon which the inferior depends. The original and true ground of this superiority is the right of conquest', a subordination reasserted in the Declaratory Act of 1720.[150]

Scotland was somewhat different. As a recent convert from early-eighteenth-century Toryism, Blackstone tactfully ignored the facts of Jacobite Scotland's military conquest in 1715 and 1745. Instead, he insisted on the myth that the two kingdoms had formerly been one; cited Sir Edward Coke to prove 'how marvellous a conformity' existed in their laws and institutions;[151] and passed over in silence the seamy political dimension of the Act of Union of 1707.[152] Although that Act contained the absolutist provision that Scots as well as English law was 'alterable by the Parliament of Great Britain',[153] there was an apparent limitation which appealed to Blackstone the Anglican more than it deterred Blackstone the absolutist. The Act of the Westminster Parliament ratifying the Treaty of Union incorporated and confirmed both an Act of the Parliament of Scotland, 'whereby the church of Scotland, and also the four universities of that kingdom, are established for ever, and all succeeding sovereigns are to take an oath inviolably to maintain the same', and also an English Act, confirming the Acts of Uniformity 'and all other acts then in force for the preservation of the Church of England', with the requirement of a monarchical oath to maintain them.

The Treaty of Union (Appendix II) prescribed the oath 'to maintain and preserve inviolably the said Settlement of the Church of England and the Doctrine Worship Discipline and Government thereof as by law established within the kingdoms of England and Ireland the Dominion of Wales and Town of Berwick upon Tweed and the Territories thereunto

---

[149] Ibid., pp. 94, 99.
[150] Ibid., p. 101.
[151] Ibid., p. 95.
[152] For which, see P. W. J. Riley, *The Union of England and Scotland* (Manchester, 1978).
[153] Treaty of Union, clause XVIII: in George S. Pryde (ed.), *The Treaty of Union of Scotland and England 1707* (London, 1950).

belonging'. By 1725, North American Anglicans were appealing to the last phrase to claim that Anglicanism, not Congregationalism, was the legally established religion in New England.[154] This controversy steadily grew in importance up to the outbreak of the American Revolution: Blackstone cannot have been unaware of the sanction which his account of the Union of 1707 gave to Anglican militancy in the colonies. The Union with Ireland Act (1800) similarly contained a provision that united the Churches of England and Ireland, announced the inviolability of their 'doctrine, worship, discipline and government . . . for ever', and affirmed that 'the continuance and preservation of the said united church, as the established Church of England and Ireland, shall be deemed and taken to be an essential and fundamental part of the union'.[155] The two Acts guaranteed by the 1707 Union which defined the religious settlement in the two societies Blackstone deemed 'fundamental and essential conditions of the union'. Blackstone seized on them as bulwarks of the Church of England as much as of the Church of Scotland. An infringement of these conditions would trigger an unspecific threat:

> whatever else may be deemed 'fundamental and essential conditions', the preservation of the two churches, of England and Scotland, in the same state that they were in at the time of the union, and the maintenance of the acts of uniformity which establish our common prayer, are expressly declared so to be . . . That therefore any alteration in the constitutions of either of those churches, or in the liturgy of the Church of England, would be an infringement of these 'fundamental and essential conditions', and greatly endanger the union.[156]

The conditions of the absolute sovereignty of the King-in-Parliament thus became: that its essential Anglicanism was indefeasible; and that it should not exercise that sovereignty to impose episcopalian Anglicanism on Scotland. Blackstone's inconsistencies conformed to the political realities of his age.

No such settlement as that of 1707, however, had limited the Anglican sovereign in colonial America. Until the publication of Blackstone's *Commentaries*, the legal position of the colonies was nowhere systematically stated in any easily-available source. The question 'has never been very clearly and fully handled by any modern writer, that I have had the good fortune to meet with', complained the widely-read James Otis in 1764; even the law dictionaries 'speak of the *British* plantations abroad as consisting chiefly of islands', presumably held, like Jamaica, by right of con-

---

[154] Thomas J. Curry, *The First Freedoms: Church and State in America to the Passage of the First Amendment* (Oxford, 1986), pp. 109–11.
[155] This provision was violated by the disestablishment of the Irish Church in 1869.
[156] Blackstone, *Commentaries*, vol. 1, pp. 95–8.

quest. The mainland colonies were acquired by settlement, claimed Otis; Ireland was different: it was 'a *conquered* country'.[157] This was the opposite of Blackstone's doctrine, however: he presented the common-law sovereign as making a direct claim to the colonies also by right of conquest.[158] Other English theorists similarly asserted the supremacy of the common law over colonial charters. The Massachusetts charter of 1629, wrote George Chalmers, although by 'the enthusiasm of those days considered as sacred, because supposed to be derived from the providence of heaven', was not intended to turn the colony into 'a province of the English empire, to be regularly governed by the acts of a provincial legislature'. Although the union of England and Scotland was 'formed by statute-law', and 'the coalition of Great-Britain and her dependencies is established by common-law . . . both are equally binding and equally effectual for knitting together the various regions of which the British empire is composed'.[159]

The Blackstonian doctrine of sovereignty was a legal commonplace: jurists with less firm Anglican convictions merely gave it a more positivist expression, with less deference to the law of nature.[160] It also had a certain vogue at court, and was echoed by those close to the throne.[161] The artist and man of letters Allan Ramsay (1713–84), appointed portrait painter to the king in 1767, published in 1769 a work, written by him in 1766, which argued from the inequality of man in a state of nature, the protection of the weak by the strong, and the consequent absurdity of an original contract to the conclusion that the power to tax was a necessary attribute of sovereignty; '*Sovereignty* admits of no degrees, it is always *supreme*, and to level it, is, in effect, to destroy it.' In Britain, argued Ramsay, that 'absolute', 'supreme', 'uncontroulable' authority was Parliament.[162] It was

---

[157] James Otis, *The Rights of the British Colonies Asserted and proved* (Boston, 1764), pp. 24, 43.

[158] Blackstone argued (*Commentaries*, vol. 1, pp. 104–5) that the American colonies were 'principally' not uninhabited places, occupied by Englishmen who would therefore carry their laws with them, but obtained 'either by right of conquest and driving out the natives (with what natural justice I shall not at present enquire) or by treaties. And therefore the common law of England, as such, has no allowance or authority there; they being no part of the mother country, but distinct (though dependent) dominions.'

[159] George Chalmers, *Political Annals of the Present United Colonies, from their Settlement to the Peace of 1763* (2 vols., London, 1780), vol. 1, pp. 139–40.

[160] For Blackstone's immediate successor as Vinerian Professor, see Sir Robert Chambers, *A Course of Lectures on the English Law Delivered at the University of Oxford 1767–1773*, ed. Thomas M. Curley (2 vols., Oxford, 1986), vol. 1, p. 140 (these lectures were not published until 1986). Chambers argued that divine laws, if violated, would 'find their vindication in another state', i.e. after death.

[161] For a review of similar opinions see Greene, *Peripheries and Center*, pp. 106–10.

[162] [Allan Ramsay], *Thoughts on the Origin and Nature of Government. Occasioned by The late Disputes between Great Britain and her American Colonies. Written in the Year 1766* (London, 1769), pp. 53, 55. Ramsay, like Blackstone, insisted that his absolute sovereign was absolute in making 'such laws only as are not repugnant to the laws of nature'; he merely denied that any natural rights had been violated in the American dispute (pp. 20–1, 26–7).

a pamphlet which appealed to colonial loyalist Thomas Hutchinson as 'the best thing I have ever seen on the subject'.[163]

For Jeremy Bentham, Blackstone's ideal cases – the state of nature, the sovereign state – were merely unrealistic: actually-existing states displayed various degrees of obedience. An individual might be in the status of subject in one relation, free in a second, a governor in a third.[164] Similarly, with states, sovereignty was not something which must of its nature be either wholly present or wholly absent:

> In the same manner we may understand, how the same man, who is *governor* with respect to one man or set of men, may be *subject* with respect to another: how among governors some may be in a *perfect* state of *nature*, with respect to each other: as the KINGS of FRANCE and SPAIN: others, again, in a state of *perfect subjection*, as the HOSPODARS of WALACHIA and MOLDAVIA with respect to the GRAND SIGNIOR: others, again, in a state of manifest but *imperfect subjection*, as the GERMAN States with respect to the EMPEROR: others, again, in such a state in which it may be difficult to determine whether they are in a state of *imperfect subjection* or in a *perfect* state of *nature*: as the KING of NAPLES with respect to the POPE.[165]

Blackstone had insisted juridically that all governments must contain 'an authority that is absolute'; Bentham retorted empirically:

> To say this, however, of *all* governments without exception; – to say that *no* assemblage of men can subsist in a state of government, without being subject to some *one* body whose authority stands unlimited so much as by convention; to say, in short, that not even by convention can any limitation be made to the power of that body in a state which in other respects is supreme, would be saying, I take it, rather too much: it would be saying that there is no such thing as government in the German Empire; nor in the Dutch Provinces; nor in the Swiss Cantons; nor was of old in the Achaean league.[166]

Political power, Bentham insisted, was established by 'a habit of, and disposition to obedience'.[167]

Yet this insight was quickly swamped by a more powerful strand within Benthamite jurisprudence. For what Bentham and his disciple John Austin (1790–1859) chiefly sought to do was to strip Blackstone's unre-

---

[163] Bernard Bailyn, *The Ordeal of Thomas Hutchinson* (London, 1974), p. 77, identifies Ramsay's pamphlet as 'a handbook of applied Hobbesianism', appealing to Hutchinson's 'essentially cold view of ordinary men'. Ramsay's position might better be placed in the context of English common law and Anglican writings on sovereignty.

[164] Jeremy Bentham, *A Fragment on Government* (London, 1776; ed. J. H. Burns and H. L. A. Hart, London, 1977), chapter 1, paras. 13–14, 17.

[165] Ibid., para. 15.

[166] Ibid., chapter 4, para. 34.

[167] Ibid., chapter 4, para. 35.

formed common-law sovereign of its Anglican and natural-law limitations. These were, they held, mere fictions, part of the rhetoric of the
Anglican Church-and-King ascendancy. That ascendancy broken, both
Austin and Bentham were content to accept Hobbes's absolutist precept
that law was whatever the sovereign commanded; they merely used an
empirical rather than a metaphysical yardstick to identify who the sovereign was. Every legal system must contain one supreme power: 'If a *determinate* human superior, *not* in a habit of obedience to a like superior,
receive *habitual* obedience from the *bulk* of a given society, that determinate
superior is sovereign in that society, and the society (including the
superior) is a society political and independent.'[168]

Austin chose to say that in limited monarchies 'a single individual
shares the sovereign powers with an aggregate or aggregates of individuals',[169] but did not envisage that this formulation might divide his
unitary sovereignty in a federal or confederal state, and claimed that nor
did it infringe 'that independence which is one of the essentials of sovereignty'.[170] Indeed, 'the name *limited monarchy* involves a contradiction in
terms. For a monarch properly so called is sovereign or supreme; and . . .
sovereign or supreme power is incapable of legal limitation, whether it
reside in an individual, or in a number of individuals.' International lawyers' notions of '*half sovereign states*' were misleading: they obscured 'the
essence of sovereignty and independent political society. It seems to
import that the governments marked with it are sovereign and subject at
once.'[171] Thus was Bentham's original insight abandoned.

Austin did not attend to continental European examples. 'It is inaccur-
ate to speak of his main doctrines as truisms', observed John Macdonell,
writing of his life in the *Dictionary of National Biography* in 1885; 'The best
proof of this is that they are still unknown to, or opposed by, the chief
jurists of Germany and France.' However sound Bentham's case, he too
wrote as a rationalist: his text contained only the two passages cited above
in which continental European examples were rehearsed, and this part of
his argument was soon overlooked. Benthamite jurisprudence argued
from what it claimed were first principles rather than from historical or
comparative data. Due mainly to their lasting critique of continental
Roman Catholicism, the English political elite had seldom achieved an
accurate understanding of contrasting attitudes to sovereignty within
other legal and political traditions. Anglican theorists had internalised the

---

[168] John Austin, *The Province of Jurisprudence Determined* (1832), ed. H. L. A. Hart (London,
   1954), p. 194; for the defence of Hobbes, pp. 276 ff.
[169] Ibid., p. 221.
[170] Ibid., p. 220.
[171] Ibid., pp. 223, 238.

common-law doctrine of sovereignty to such a degree by the late eighteenth century that they projected it onto all other political thought. Jonathan Boucher maintained:

> That no political society can subsist, unless there be an absolute supreme power lodged somewhere in the society, has been universally held as an uncontrolable maxim in theory, by all writers on government, from Aristotle down to Sidney and Locke, and has been as universally adopted in practice, from the despotism of Morocco, to the republic of St. Marino; as long as government subsists, subjects owe an implicit obedience to the Laws of the supreme power, from which there can be no appeal but to Heaven.[172]

Within this vision, rebellion and war (an 'appeal to Heaven') rather than the negotiation of federal structures seemed the only alternative to monarchical allegiance.

Thanks chiefly to Benthamite rationalism, nineteenth- and twentieth-century Englishmen were even less well informed about continental law or the evolution of sovereignty from Bodin through French absolutism to its embodiment in that sometimes vague Napoleonic abstraction, the state; in England, Great Britain or the United Kingdom, it was generally held that sovereignty was exercised not by an abstraction, 'the people', but by an institution, the Crown in Parliament; that its boundaries were not the secular 'state' or the ethnic 'nation' but the personified 'kingdom'. Blackstone's attempt to use the Union with Scotland to retain a limited role for fundamental law in the English constitution was a failure (the repeal of the Test and Corporation Acts in 1828 and Catholic 'Emancipation' in 1829 would otherwise have invalidated the treaty).

Bentham mocked Blackstone's attempt, indignant at its Anglican exclusiveness.[173] Yet although Anglican hegemony was broken in 1828–32, it remained lastingly influential; so too did its implications for the common law. Even the American Revolution and subsequent relations with colonies or overseas treaty organisations did not fundamentally modify England's understanding of its domestic sovereign status after 1776. Within England, things went on much as before: legal formulae, political theories and popular attitudes constituted an interlocking system of remarkable durability. The claim of doctrines to represent historical realities is more effective if those doctrines come to stand, like these, as codifications of the entrenched attitudes and dispositions of ancient nations. The history of the development of the English, British, and finally

---

[172] [Jonathan Boucher], *A Letter from a Virginian to the Members of the Congress to be held at Philadelphia, on the First of September, 1774* (Boston; reprinted London, 1774), pp. 19–20.

[173] Jeremy Bentham, *A Comment on the Commentaries*, ed. J. H. Burns and H. L. A. Hart (London, 1977), p. 112.

the United Kingdom's hegemonic doctrine of sovereignty illustrates the way in which a legal theory became a self-evident truth, part of English patriotism, English history and English religion. 'Nothing can be, more Interesting to the State, than maintaining its Sovereignty', wrote the barrister, MP and colonial agent James Abercromby (1707–75); 'the Moment, a State gives up Sovereignty, it becomes, *Felo de se*, as a State.' The American colonists had 'subverted' government by contending for 'a Divisibility of the King's Sovereignty'.[174] His analysis accurately identified the dominant English theory. Absolute sovereigns do not commonly relinquish their sovereignty, and in 1776 that absolute sovereign, the King-in-Parliament, went to war because it could not envisage a federal redefinition of its structure as anything other than the successful rebellion of part of its possessions.

IV. NATURAL LAW VERSUS COMMON LAW: THE POLARISATION OF A COMMON IDIOM

British and colonial loyalist observers of the American Revolution were best able to discern one of its novel and sensational features. American claims against Britain, and American ideals for the construction of a new social order, came increasingly to be expressed in that language of natural law and natural rights which was to have an equally explosive impact on the old order in Europe after 1789. From the perspective of the mid-1770s, James Abercromby saw that the colonists rejected the claim of the Declaratory Act to unitary sovereignty over America as 'a Law contrary to the Law of Nature, consequently, ab initio Void': James Otis, he believed, had argued for the right of the colonies to be independent, since men who separated themselves from their parent society were 'under the Law of Nature only' until they founded another; Richard Bland, Abercromby recorded, had argued that subjects had a natural right to withdraw from societies with which they were 'Dissatisfied', and by withdrawing recovered their 'Natural Freedom and independence'. Abercromby denied both arguments, appealing to Coke and to natural law correctly understood;[175] but Pandora's box had been opened, and neither British nor

---

[174] [James Abercromby], *De Jure et Gubernatione Coloniarum, or An Inquiry into the Nature, and the Rights of Colonies, Ancient and Modern* [c. 1774–5] (Huntington Library MS HM 513), ff. 1–2. For an edition of this tract see Jack P. Greene, Charles F. Mullett and Edward C. Papenfuse, Jr (eds.), *Magna Charta for America* (Philadelphia, 1986). It does not appear, from Abercromby's many sources, that he was merely echoing Blackstone.

[175] [Abercromby], *De Jure et Gubernatione Coloniarum*, ff. 3, 9. For Otis (1764) and Bland (1766), see below, pp. 116–8, 103.

loyalist theorists were able thereafter to close it. This outcome was, however, neither easy nor self-evident. Part IV attempts to identify and to date the process by which a shared legal idiom became polarised; in part V below it is argued that legal thought alone does not explain that process, which can only be understood in terms of the impact upon colonial law of adjacent developments in colonial religion.

England's legal tradition successfully established a shared transatlantic idiom in which natural law discourse was subordinate until a late date.[176] In the late seventeenth century, colonial assemblies defended or advanced their positions by appealing to the rights and liberties of Englishmen, denouncing uncongenial metropolitan policies as contrary to the Bill of Rights or Magna Carta. These rights were conceived principally as specific privileges, defined by common law; they were sometimes spoken of as fundamental law, but less often identified with natural law as anything distinct from the common law tradition.[177] Colonial assemblies continued to defend or advance their powers and privileges in the early eighteenth century; but, after 1689, they were compelled to do so by arguing from the 'rights of Englishmen' that those assemblies were instituted, authorised and summoned on the same basis as the Westminster Parliament, by the crown.[178] The commitment of Dissenters and Low Churchmen to the Protestant Succession therefore proved overriding: before the 1760s the daily frictions between governors and assemblies were generally expressed in practical terms and seldom generated systematic analysis of their consequences for the nature of metropolitan authority. Metropolitan institutions meanwhile consistently replied that the source of the authority of colonial assemblies in the crown meant that the crown could limit the authority of those assemblies.[179] Precedent, custom and statute still dominated debate.

[176] For different interpretations, see Max Radin, 'The Rivalry of Common-Law and Civil Law Ideas in the American Colonies', in *Law: A Century of Progress 1835–1935* (3 vols., New York, 1937), vol. 2, pp. 404–31; Lester H. Cohen, 'The American Revolution and Natural Law Theory', *Journal of the History of Ideas* 39 (1978), 491–502; John Philip Reid, 'The Irrelevance of Natural Law', part of idem, 'The Irrelevance of the Declaration', in Hendrik Hartog (ed.), *Law in the American Revolution and the Revolution in the Law* (New York, 1981), pp. 46–89; Martyn P. Thompson, 'The History of Fundamental Law in Political Thought from the French Wars of Religion to the American Revolution', *AHR* 91 (1986), 1103–28.

[177] Charles F. Mullett, *Fundamental Law and the American Revolution* (New York, 1933), pp. 70–8. For Coke's ambiguities and colonists' selective use of his arguments, see Charles F. Mullett, 'Coke and the American Revolution', *Economica* no. 38 (1932), 457–71.

[178] Greene, *Peripheries and Center*, pp. 31, 33.

[179] Ibid., pp. 28–42. Colonists' resort to their charters against such an argument only locked them more firmly into claiming the specific 'rights of Englishmen'. The evidence does not however suggest a 'continuing struggle between the center and the peripheries over their competing demands for control and autonomy' (ibid., pp. 42, 53), but rather intermittent minor friction over unresolved disagreements which might in certain circumstances ignite a surrounding nexus of ideas. Colonists' 'silence' on the nature of Parlia-

Early seventeenth-century colonial legal codes, especially in New England, similarly made frequent and emphatic reference to the supremacy of divine law, while making only rare mention of natural law;[180] the controversies surrounding Bacon's rebellion of 1676 and the Glorious Revolution in 1688–9 were equally without reliance on the second. As late as the Seven Years' War, colonial assemblies in their disputes with metropolitan authorities continued to invoke the rights of Englishmen.[181] Natural law was a minor theme as late as the protests and resolutions against the Stamp Act of colonial assemblies and the Stamp Act Congress: constitutional argument was still based chiefly on the ancient constitution and colonial charters.[182] It was chiefly these which colonists regarded as 'fundamental'. This reliance on specific provisions could be sustained because continental European doctrines of natural law had been given a distinctly different expression within the seventeenth-century English-speaking world. Thomas Hobbes (1588–1679) used natural law as the starting point for the creation of the absolute state and the state's positive law which, once established, eclipsed natural law. John Locke (1632–1704) used natural law to define inalienable rights for the individual which applied equally after the creation of political society by self-interested contracts between individuals; but Locke thereby 'substitutes for the traditional idea of the natural law as an order of human affairs, as a moral reflex of the metaphysical order of the universe revealed to human reason in the creation as God's will, the conception of natural law as a rather nominalistic symbol for a catalogue or bundle of individual rights that stem from individual self-interest'.[183]

A different tradition began to be imported into the colonies in the early eighteenth century with reference both to classical authors, especially Aristotle and Cicero, and to a continental tradition embracing Grotius and Pufendorf, Montesquieu and Burlamaqui.[184] In this process of absorption, specific colonial needs still dictated the uses to which European authors were put. The Congregationalist minister John Wise's *Vindication of the Government of New-England Churches* was notable for an early (but largely ignored) invocation of a figure from the continental pantheon – 'I shall Principally take Baron *Puffendorff* for my Chief Guide and Spokesman'; but the object of Wise's tract was to defend Congregational ecclesi-

---

ment's authority between 1688 and the 1760s (ibid., chapter 4) points in the same
direction.
[180] Benjamin Fletcher Wright, Jr, *American Interpretations of Natural Law* (Cambridge, Mass., 1931), pp. 13–35.
[181] Ibid., pp. 36–42.
[182] Mullett, *Fundamental Law*, pp. 87–8.
[183] Rommen, *Natural Law*, pp. 89–90.
[184] Wright, *Natural Law*, pp. 44–9.

astical polity against pressures to reform it on a Presbyterian model.[185] So the denominations began sometimes to appropriate natural law arguments to defend their privileges or local monopolies with a more exalted rhetoric; but only after the repeal of the Stamp Act did natural law become a prominent theme in colonial propaganda.[186]

It has been maintained that natural law arguments were urged earliest and with most zeal in New England, and that it is 'only after the passage of the Coercive Acts in 1774 that the doctrine is whole-heartedly accepted outside of the colonies in which the clergy had for generations been thundering their interpretation of its teachings from their pulpits'; this is certainly the appearance given by the role assigned to fundamental law in Calvinist theology.[187] By contrast, the reticence of non-Congregationalist propagandists in the middle and southern colonies in resorting to natural law is evidenced in the writings of Daniel Dulany of Maryland, author of one of the most influential tracts against the Stamp Act. Recognising the existence of natural law, and the possibility that Acts of Parliament might be void 'in Theory', he nevertheless preferred 'in Practice' to redress colonial grievances by resort to 'Positive Law', the British constitution.[188] John Dickinson likewise made some use of the concept of natural law during the Stamp Act controversy, but found that it was seldom taken up with enthusiasm. Dickinson's draft of the Resolutions of the Assembly of Pennsylvania, giving priority to natural rights, was revised by that body to relegate natural rights to the role of reinforcing the rights of Englishmen.[189] His subsequent draft of resolutions for the Stamp Act Congress made no attempt to ground the colonists' 'rights and liberties' in natural law.[190] For a wider audience, Dickinson preferred to phrase his understanding differently: the right of no taxation without consent was a 'sacred Right'.[191] To another audience, he made the source of his motivation explicit:

[185] John Wise, *A Vindication of the Government of New-England Churches. Drawn from Antiquity; the Light of Nature; Holy Scripture; its Noble Nature; and from the Dignity Divine Providence has put upon it* (Boston, 1717), p. 32.

[186] Wright, *Natural Law*, pp. 71–99; 'the more extreme the claim the more abstract the basis': Mullett, *Fundamental Law*, p. 80.

[187] Wright, *Natural Law*, p. 75.

[188] [Daniel Dulany], *Considerations on the Propriety of Imposing Taxes in the British Colonies, For the Purpose of raising a Revenue, by Act of Parliament* ([Annapolis], 1765; repr. London, 1766), Preface.

[189] 'Resolutions Adopted by the Assembly of Pennsylvania relative to the Stamp Act . . . September 21, 1765', in Paul Leicester Ford (ed.), *The Writings of John Dickinson* (Philadelphia, 1895), vol. 1, p. 169.

[190] 'The Declaration of Rights adopted by the Stamp Act Congress . . . October 19, 1765', ibid., p. 179.

[191] 'An Address to 'Friends and Countrymen' on the Stamp Act . . . November, 1765' (broadside), ibid., p. 197.

Kings or parliaments could not *give* the *rights essential to happiness*, as you confess those invaded by the Stamp Act to be. We claim them from a higher source – from the King of kings, and Lord of all the earth. They are not annexed to us by parchments and seals. They are created in us by the decrees of Providence, which establish the laws of our nature.[192]

But in his best-selling *Farmer's Letters*, attacking the Townshend duties and the suspension of the New York assembly, the natural law tradition was scarcely mentioned.[193]

Since it was no secret that the franchise in England had been confined to forty-shilling freeholders since the reign of Henry VI, colonists were indeed encouraged finally to found their claim that 'taxation and representation are constitutionally inseparable' on another basis: 'it is an eternal law of nature', urged Arthur Lee by 1776, that an individual's property was not to be taken without his consent or that of his representative, a principle which could be illustrated from Cicero, Tacitus, Hotman and Locke as well as from Magna Carta and Coke's *Reports*.[194] Yet this tactic had been perceived by colonists in the mid 1760s to be too weak to secure swift redress in the case of the Stamp Act. If an appeal to generalised natural-law limitations on the common-law sovereign was ineffective, colonists sometimes turned to a second device – a jurisdictional distinction between duties imposed to regulate trade and internal taxation, classically expounded in John Dickinson's *Farmer's Letters* of 1768. Yet this argument too might have a natural-law resonance, initially not emphasised. To Americans, the Blackstonian theory would be stigmatised as a 'modern doctrine'; prior wisdom showed that 'Whatever difficulty may occur in tracing the line, yet we contend, that by the laws of God, and by the laws of the constitution, a line there must be, beyond which her [Britain's] authority cannot extend.' If these were not to be found in law, Blackstone in his *Commentaries* 'has thought proper, when treating of this subject, to point out the '*precedent*' of the Revolution [of 1688], as fixing the line'. By 1774, John Dickinson had thrown aside his earlier caution and resorted to a string of authorities to derive that line from natural law, beginning with Grotius and Pufendorf, Virgil and Burlamaqui before turning Blackstone against himself and appealing to Hoadly to justify 'submission to the

---

[192] [John Dickinson], *An Address to The Committee of Correspondence in Barbados* (Philadelphia, 1766), ibid., pp. 251–76, at 262.

[193] [John Dickinson], *Letters from a Farmer in Pennsylvania, to the Inhabitants of the British Colonies* (Philadelphia, 1768), ibid., pp. 277–406.

[194] [Arthur Lee], *An Appeal to the Justice and Interests of the People of Great Britain, in the Present Disputes with America, by an Old Member of Parliament* (4th edn., London, 1776), pp. 5–7.

divine authority' rather than to 'the *assumed authority*' of unjust government.[195]

Thomas Hutchinson, Chief Justice of Massachusetts from 1760 to the Revolution, articulated a very different conception of law from that of the revolutionaries. He stressed the supremacy of statute law, strictly construed; held to custom (even if Massachusetts custom) over natural rights claims; and resisted the pressures to develop judicial review against politically unpopular legislation. Law, 'fixed, certain, and known', was the best safeguard of liberty, he wrote. Laws with which Hutchinson disagreed, including the Stamp Act, had to be enforced until repealed; to do otherwise would mean, he argued, that 'the will of the judge would be law'.[196] Hutchinson initially opposed the Sugar Act of 1764 as violating the hitherto tacitly-accepted 'distinction between duties on trade and internal taxes', asserted the sole right of colonial assemblies to levy colonial taxation, and denied the convenient distinction of principle between internal and external taxation. Yet these claims were, he argued, not natural rights but the specific provisions established by the British constitution, which Parliament therefore had the ultimate right to abrogate 'when the safety of the whole shall depend upon it'. Nevertheless, believed Hutchinson, in order to preserve the traditional restraints on which liberty depended, the sovereign had to be recognised as unitary and ultimately supreme: to invest the Massachusetts General Court, as the representative of the people, with sovereignty would be to surrender all traditional restraints.[197]

The doctrine of sovereignty, not representation or natural right, was therefore the basis of the British claim to legislative authority over the colonies. Indeed the idea of virtual representation – that colonists were as much represented as Englishmen in England who had no votes in elections, since the Westminster Parliament was the collective embodiment of that estate of the realm, the Commons – was essentially another way of expounding the English theory of sovereignty, according to which interests, ranks or estates were merged in a common allegiance. It was introduced by Thomas Whately, spokesman for George Grenville's ministry, in the debate on the Stamp Act; but it was too effective an argument for the colonists long to dispute. To deny that Acts of Parliament were binding on non-electors would nullify the effect of all Acts, not just Acts to tax the colonies. The British 'Privilege' of 'being taxed only with their

[195] [John Dickinson], *A New Essay [by the Pennsylvanian Farmer] on the Constitutional Power of Great Britain over the Colonies in America* ... (Philadelphia; reprinted London, 1774), pp. 33–4, 39, 42–7, 104–5.
[196] Quoted in William Pencak, *America's Burke: The Mind of Thomas Hutchinson* (Washington, 1982), pp. 39–58, at 42–3, 45.
[197] Ibid., pp. 105–10.

own Consent, given by their Representatives' therefore still held, argued Whately: 'May this sacred Pledge of Liberty be preserved inviolate, to the utmost Verge of our Dominions, and to the latest Page of our History!'[198] Since this was obviously true of all legislatures, including colonial assemblies, the colonists' bluff was called: they were not acting on the ideology of universal suffrage, and representation was not centrally at issue in 1776. Colonists defending the legality of the Stamp Act Congress of 1765 and the Continental Congress of 1774 fell back on the claim that 'the only Representatives of the People of these Colonies, are Persons chosen therein by themselves';[199] but this echoed a Dissenting attitude to the communication of spiritual authority[200] rather than a new attitude to individual representation which would have swept up women and blacks in the new society promised by the English doctrine of universal suffrage as a natural right.[201]

American patriots initially found it impossible to break out of the grip of the common-law conception of sovereignty.[202] Their first tactic was professedly to accept the ultimate superiority of metropolitan legislation but to emphasise the natural- or divine-law restraints which Blackstone's sovereign, like Filmer's, acknowledged in order to distinguish 'absolute' from 'arbitrary' power. This tactic seemed a powerful one to colonists since American constitutional and legal thought still echoed early-seventeenth-century English models. In England the Restoration of 1660 had confirmed Thomas Cromwell's interpretation and decisively fused the warring factions into that composite sovereign the King in Parliament, an Anglican Trinity of monarch, lords and commons; in colonial America commentators could still appeal to early Stuart precedents for the status of colonial charters as royal, not parliamentary, documents to prove the dependence of the colonies on the Crown alone, not on the Lords and Commons of the Westminster Parliament.[203] Natural-law restraints on the

---

[198] [Thomas Whately], *The Regulations Lately Made concerning the Colonies, and the Taxes Imposed upon Them, considered* (London, 1765), pp. 104–14, at 104; Edmund S. and Helen M. Morgan, *The Stamp Act Crisis: Prologue to Revolution* (2nd edn., New York, 1962), 104–9.

[199] Edmund S. Morgan, *Inventing the People: The Rise of Popular Sovereignty in England and America* (New York, 1988), pp. 240–5, at 241.

[200] By contrast the relations between Westminster MPs and their constituents, it may be suggested, echoed to some degree the relations between Anglican incumbents and their parishioners.

[201] For the theological origins of this doctrine in English Dissent, see Clark, *English Society 1688–1832*, pp. 330–46. For the importance, by contrast, of colonial claims of corporate rights, see Greene, *Peripheries and Center*, pp. 83–4.

[202] For the difficulties of colonists in framing clear ideas of statehood, see J. R. Pole, 'The Politics of the Word 'State' and its Relation to American Sovereignty', *Parliaments, Estates and Representation* 8 (1988), 1–10.

[203] R. G. Adams, *Political Ideas of the American Revolution* (3rd edn, New York, 1958), pp. 118 ff.

Crown had, therefore, a greater significance in the colonies. In England the confirming of the inevitably Anglican character of the monarch by the Glorious Revolution muted the common law's earlier efforts to check statute law; late-colonial Americans appealed beyond Blackstone's common-law sovereign to Sir Edward Coke's doctrine in *Bonham's Case* that 'it appears in our Books, that in many Cases, the Common Law will controll the Acts of Parliament, and some times adjudge them to be utterly void', that is, 'when an Act of Parliament is against Common Right and Reason, or repugnant, or impossible to be performed'.[204]

Coke's doctrine in *Bonham's Case* was an attempt to devise an extensive natural-law check to the unified sovereign which the Reformation had created and the early Stuarts sought to exploit; by 1660, in England, that attempt had failed, being reduced to the procedural provision that legislation, admittedly binding, was to be construed in the light of its common-sense meaning. In the colonies, however, Coke's doctrine was to be far more powerful. Coke's writings – both the *Reports* and the *Institutes* – had dominated colonial legal education,[205] and continued to have an influence after independence when the courts of the new republic in a famous series of judgements worked out the doctrine that they might declare a law unconstitutional.[206] This was more persuasive since American courts could by then appeal to a shared awareness of continental European natural law, acquired during the eighteenth century. It allegedly influenced the minds of patriots like James Otis, who, recorded Adams, was

> a great master of the laws of nature and nations. He had read Pufendorf, Grotius, Barbeyrac, Burlamaqui, Vattel, Heineccius; and, in the civil law, Domat, Justinian, and, upon occasions, consulted the Corpus Juris at large. It was a maxim which he inculcated on his pupils . . . *'that a lawyer ought never to be without a volume of natural or public law, or moral philosophy, on his table or in his pocket'.*[207]

This new element in colonial law was not in itself decisive. Natural law did not at once point to colonial independence, and it was with difficulty that colonial theorists framed the argument that they already inhabited a federal empire in which subordinate bodies possessed absolute and

---

[204] *The Eighth Part of the Report of Sir Edward Coke, Kt.* (In the Savoy, 1738), p. 118a. For this, see Theodore F. T. Plucknett, 'Bonham's Case and Judicial Review', *Harvard Law Review* 40 (1926–7), 30–70.

[205] Adams, *Political Ideas*, p. 41; Edward Dumbauld, *Thomas Jefferson and the Law* (Norman, Oklahoma, 1978), pp. 11–17.

[206] Adams, *Political Ideas*, pp. 142–3; Charles Grove Haines, *The American Doctrine of Judicial Supremacy* (New York, 1914), pp. 73–121 and passim.

[207] John Adams to Hezekiah Niles, 14 Jan. 1818: Adams, *Works*, vol. 10, p. 274.

devolved sovereign authority of their own in certain respects.[208] This option was first explored by reaction, when the British claim of a right to tax America was extrapolated in American imaginations into something much more extensive. John Dickinson seized on the consequential British Act suspending the legislation of New York after that colony had declined to comply fully with a requisition in aid of British troops: 'If the parliament may lawfully deprive *New-York* of any of *her* rights, it may deprive any, or all the other colonies of *their* rights';[209] Dickinson began to work out a conception of the parts of the empire each possessing separate rights, the central authority possessing a co-ordinating right only. This was difficult to make plausible if, as he admitted, Parliament 'unquestionably possesses a legal authority to *regulate* the *trade* of *Great-Britain*, and all her colonies . . . We are but parts of a *whole*; and therefore there must exist a power somewhere to preside, and preserve the connection in due order. This power is lodged in the parliament . . . ' Dickinson could at most draw an elaborate and unconvincing distinction between regulating trade by a duty and raising revenue by a tax.[210] He quoted a recent historian of New York: 'The state of our laws opens a door to much controversy . . . The common law of *England* is generally received . . . but our courts EXERCISE A SOVEREIGN AUTHORITY, in determining *what parts of the common and statute law* ought to be extended . . .'[211] It was an implausible boast, and despite this argument ready to hand, Dickinson only noticed it in passing: even for Americans, the idea of a federal empire embodying a divided sovereignty was not yet clearly

---

[208] E.g. [John Dickinson], *Letters from a Farmer in Pennsylvania* (Philadelphia, 1768); [John Joachim Zubly], *An Humble Enquiry* ([Charleston], 1769): cited Bailyn, *Ideological Origins*, pp. 215–17. For the origins of the theory that the colonies owed allegiance to the king and were not bound by acts of the Westminster Parliament, see Edmund S. Morgan, 'Colonial Ideas of Parliamentary Power, 1764–1766', reprinted in idem, *The Challenge of the American Revolution* (New York, 1976), pp. 3–42, and Greene, *Peripheries and Center*, pp. 79–104. Morgan emphasises the unimportance for practical men of the theoretical distinction between any British right to levy external as opposed to internal taxation. For colonial theorists its importance may however have been greater.

[209] [John Dickinson], *Letters from a Farmer in Pennsylvania, To the Inhabitants of the British Colonies* (Philadelphia, 1768), p. 5 (letter I).

[210] Ibid., p. 7 (letter II). He rejected (p. 18, letter IV) the distinction between internal and external *taxes* on the grounds, drawn from specific legal precedent rather than natural right, of 'a total denial of the power of parliament to lay upon these colonies any '*tax*' whatever'.

[211] Ibid., p. 46 (letter IX), quoting William Smith, Jr, *The History of the Province of New-York* (London, 1757), ed. Michael Kammen (2 vols., Cambridge, Mass., 1972), vol. 1, p. 259. Smith had however ascribed this situation to legal uncertainty rather than to a deliberate federalism. He was also obliged to argue (ibid., p. 238) that the English common law did not sanction the establishment of the Anglican Church, rather than claim that New York courts could upset such a provision, which the common law was ordinarily assumed to contain.

conceptualised as an alternative to an empire dominated formally (if not always in actuality) by the common-law sovereign.

A colonial critic of the *Farmer's Letters*, in moving further towards such a federal concept, first accepted Dickinson's premise that 'in every government, there must be a supreme absolute authority lodged somewhere', but denied that this conceded the British case: each part of the empire 'may enjoy a distinct complete legislature, and still good government may be preserved, everywhere'.

> It is in vain to assert, that two or more distinct legislatures cannot exist in the same state. If, by the same state, be meant the same individual community, it is true. Thus, for instance, there cannot be two supreme legislatures in Great-Britain, or two in New-York. But, if, by the same state, be understood a number of individual societies, or bodies politic, united under one common head, then, I maintain, that there may be one distinct compleat legislature in each: Thus there may be one in Great-Britain, another in Ireland, and another in New-York, and still these several parts may form but one state . . . there can never be said to be two sovereign powers, in the same state; while *one common king* is acknowledged, by every member of it.[212]

An empire centred on the monarch but with a variety of representative assemblies of equal status was as far as the argument developed: but from an English perspective, this already meant precisely that division of sovereignty which colonists shied away from naming. English commentators had at most framed projects for imperial union which would allow the colonies representation at Westminster within the still-undivided sovereignty which the common law made axiomatic. In 1768, Thomas Pownall's intelligent and well-informed scheme of imperial union envisaged granting the colonies 'a share in the legislature of Great-Britain, by having Knights and Burgesses of their own election, representing them in parliament'. Nevertheless, Pownall accepted as his major premise, citing Blackstone:

> There is no doubt, but that in the nature, reason, justice and necessity of the thing, there must be somewhere, within the body politic of every government, an absolute power. The political freedom of Great Britain, consists in this power's being lodged no where but in King, Lords and Commons in parliament assembled.

Pownall's object was to end the anomaly created by this supremacy by incorporating the colonies within the realm.[213]

---

[212] [Alexander Hamilton], *The Farmer Refuted: or, A more impartial and comprehensive View of the Dispute between Great-Britain and the Colonies* (New York, 1775), pp. 16–17.

[213] Thomas Pownall, *The Administration of the Colonies. Wherein their Rights and Constitution Are discussed and stated* (4th edn, London, 1768), pp. xv, 130, 133.

Before independence, colonists never appealed to the Holy Roman Empire as a model, as some were to do in the debates over the Articles of Confederation and, later, the Constitution of 1787. Anti-Catholicism was generally far more prevalent and more vivid in the colonies than in England, and prevented colonists from exploring the federal implications of Roman-law traditions: federalism was not a common topic of American speculation before 1776. The claim that the American colonies were not subject to the King-in-Parliament could not initially be framed as an argument that sovereignty was divisible, as in continental European juristic traditions; it had to be framed as a suspiciously anachronistic argument that the colonies were immediately dependent on the Crown, like the Channel Islands and the Isle of Man. This was a minority position in Britain, although Lord Camden made the point in the debate on the repeal of the Stamp Act.[214] Richard Bland made this claim for Virginia with sensationally greater force when he supported it by appeal to natural law: Englishmen excluded from direct representation by the introduction of the forty-shilling franchise in the reign of Henry VI retained a 'natural Right' to 'retire from the Society, and to settle in another Country'. Those who remained were bound by British laws not by being virtually represented in Parliament but because they had 'implicitly' consented to them; but by leaving the realm they 'recover their natural Freedom and Independence: The Jurisdiction and Sovereignty of the State they have quitted ceases'. This principle Bland established by ignoring the common-law doctrine that allegiance was indelible and arguing: 'As then we can receive no Light from the Laws of the Kingdom, or from ancient History, to direct us in our Inquiry, we must have Recourse to the Law of Nature, and those Rights of Mankind which flow from it.'[215]

Benjamin Franklin, then in England, began similarly to react against the Blackstonian doctrine. In manuscript annotations to his copy of the anonymous *An Inquiry into the Nature and Causes of the Disputes between the British Colonies in America and their Mother Country* (London, 1769) he challenged its doctrine that 'Supreme power and authority must not, cannot, reside equally everywhere throughout an empire': 'Writers on this subject often confuse themselves with the idea', maintained Franklin, 'that all the King's dominions make one state, which they do not, not ever did since the conquest. Our kings have ever had dominions not subject to the English Parliament', like Scotland before the Union or contemporary

---

[214] *Parl. Hist.*, vol. 16, col. 169.
[215] Richard Bland, *An Inquiry into the Rights of the British Colonies, Intended as an Answer to The Regulations lately made concerning the Colonies, and the Taxes imposed upon them considered* (Williamsburg, 1766), pp. 10, 12, 14, 27.

Hanover; 'Ireland the same in truth, though the British Parliament has *usurped* a dominion over it.' Among these dominions 'Their only bond of union is the King.' The author of *An Inquiry* had maintained that the first settlers in the colonies knew that 'they were to continue the subjects of the same government'. Franklin replied:

> They well knew the contrary. They would never have gone, if that had been the case. They fled from your government, which oppressed them. If they carried your government with them, and of course your laws, they had better have stayed and endured the oppression at home, and not have added to it all the hardships of making a new settlement. They carried not your laws; but, had they carried your government and laws, they would now have been subject to spiritual courts, tithes, church acts of Parliament, game acts, &c. &c., which they are not, and never were since their being *out of the realm.*[216]

It was a position far removed from colonists' former claims against metropolitan taxation on the grounds that they *had* carried with them the rights, and laws, of Englishmen.

One American actually accepted assimilation with the case of Ireland, relying on a natural-law argument for a defence. 'They were both conquered countries, peopled by English subjects' admitted Arthur Lee; but natural law, operating everywhere, made taxation without consent inexpedient because unjust.[217] This was unusual: conquest was normally denied by those American jurists who in the 1770s discovered the argument that the colonies were in the same position as the Channel Islands, the Isle of Man and Ireland: part of the king's dominions, owing allegiance to him as monarch, but not subject to the legislation of the Westminster Parliament. James Wilson pointed out that the colonies were in some ways *more* independent: appeals from the Court of King's Bench in Ireland were heard by the Court of King's Bench, and finally the House of Lords, in England, but colonial appeals lay with the King in Council. And if Ireland had been held to be not bound by the statutes of the Westminster Parliament because it had no representatives there, this was true of the American colonies also.[218] Wilson recognised that Sir Edward Coke had conceded the authority of Westminster over Ireland if

[216] Franklin's annotations, printed in Franklin, *Works*, vol. 4, pp. 281–2, 288–9.

[217] [Arthur Lee], *An Appeal to the Justice and Interests of the People of Great Britain, in the Present Disputes with America, by an Old Member of Parliament* (4th edn., London, 1776), p. 15.

[218] James Wilson, *Considerations on the Nature and Extent of the Legislative Authority of the British Parliament* (1774), in Robert Green McCloskey (ed.), *The Works of James Wilson* (2 vols., Cambridge, Mass., 1967), vol. 2, pp. 735, 737, citing *Calvin's Case* (1608), *The Seventh Part of the Reports of Sir Edward Coke Kt.* (In the Savoy, 1738), p. 22b; Sir Edward Coke, *The Fourth Part of the Institutes of the Laws of England* (London, 1669), p. 356; Danby Pickering (ed.), *Modern Reports* (7 vols., In the Savoy, 1757), vol. 4, p. 225.

the latter were specifically named in an Act, that this derived from the conquest of Ireland, and that Blackstone had repeated the same argument of conquest to explain British authority over America; but Wilson challenged the historical accuracy of the claim that the colonies or Ireland had been conquered.[219] Allegiance, he argued, was owed to the Crown, in return for protection; allegiance was not owed to the Parliament, for the colonies were unrepresented there.[220] So the American case had turned the natural, indefeasible allegiance of the common law into a tenuous, conditional relationship which the catalogue of George III's alleged misdeeds in the Declaration of Independence would make void.

It was late in the contest when the shared legal tradition was sharply polarised into an antithesis between a common law and a natural law understanding of sovereignty, but when this occurred the results were catastrophic. The immediate occasion was a move to shield judges in Massachusetts Bay from local pressures by granting them royal salaries. This stimulated a local petitioning movement, led by Samuel Adams, and a committee whose report embodied a declaration of principles, ratified by a Boston town meeting on 20 November 1772, explicitly founded on natural law:

> Among the natural Rights of the Colonists are these: First, a Right to Life; secondly, to Liberty; thirdly, to Property; together with the Right to support and defend them in the best Manner they can . . . All Men have a Right to remain in a State of Nature as long as they please: And in case of intolerable Oppression, civil or religious, to leave the Society they belong to, and enter into another. When Men enter into Society, it is by voluntary Consent; and they have a Right to demand and insist upon the Performance of such Conditions and previous Limitations as form an equitable original Compact.[221]

Lieutenant Governor Thomas Hutchinson, historian and lawyer, was appalled: the *Votes and Proceedings* clearly pointed to independence. It was essential, he thought, to bring the issues clearly and finally into focus in order to isolate the extremists and check the advance of a movement to endorse Boston's position. Calling a special meeting of both Houses of the Assembly, he delivered an address which, to the horror of the London authorities,[222] revealed how Anglo-American difficulties had become expressed as a stark antithesis in a way which effectively prevented future

---

[219] Wilson, *Considerations*, loc. cit., pp. 738–9, citing Blackstone, *Commentaries*, vol. 1, pp. 104–5.

[220] Wilson, *Considerations*, p. 743.

[221] *The Votes and Proceedings of the Freeholders and other Inhabitants of the Town of Boston, In Town Meeting assembled, According to Law* (Boston, 1772; Dublin, 1773), p. 2.

[222] Bailyn, *Ordeal of Thomas Hutchinson*, pp. 206–20.

compromise.[223] As a Whig on the principles of 1688, Hutchinson interpreted Massachusetts' 'Grant and Charter from the Crown of England' of 1691, when accepted by the colonists, as an acknowledgement of 'the supreme Authority of Parliament'. Colonists could not claim exemption from its authority 'as Part of their Rights by Nature', since all government involved the surrender of natural rights. Consequently,

> I know of no Line that can be drawn between the supreme Authority of Parliament and the total Independence of the Colonies. It is impossible there should be two independent Legislatures in one and the same State, for although there may be but one Head, the King, yet the two Legislative Bodies will make two Governments as distinct as the Kingdoms of England and Scotland before the Union.[224]

Hutchinson introduced this position without defence; it was his major premise, bluntly stated as a self-evident truth.

Within the mental world of the Assembly, no such answer was self-evident: to the Council, what Hutchinson termed Parliament's '*Supreme* Authority' meant '*unlimited* Authority'; and if Hutchinson were right that no line could be drawn, then 'a Denial of that Authority in any Instance whatever implies and amounts to a Declaration of total Independence'. This, they professed to deny. Hutchinson's position was not self-evident to the Council because it conflicted with their own broadest theological premise: 'Supreme or unlimited Authority can with Fitness belong only to the Sovereign of the Universe.' Only after establishing this premise did the Council explain the colonial sense of grievance at being taxed without direct representation in Parliament: the 'Right to Representation' was 'so essential and indispensable in Regard of all Laws for levying Taxes' that it could not be given up 'without making a Breach on the essential Rights of Nature'.[225]

The Massachusetts House of Representatives made a similar use of a point of substance. The 'great Design of our Ancestors, in leaving the Kingdom of England, was to be freed from a Subjection to its spiritual Laws and Courts, and to worship God according to the Dictates of their Consciences'. They would not have left, the House claimed, had the jurisdiction of Parliament extended to the colonies, so that Parliament 'might make what ecclesiastical Laws they pleased, expressly to refer to them, and place them in the same Circumstances with Respect to religious

---

[223] *The Speeches of His Excellency Governor Hutchinson, to the General Assembly Of the Massachusetts-Bay. At a Session begun and held on the Sixth of January, 1773. With the Answers of His Majesty's Council and the House of Representatives Respectively* (Boston, 1773), reprinted as John Phillip Reid (ed.), *The Briefs of the American Revolution* (New York, 1981).

[224] Reid (ed.), *Briefs*, pp. 15, 20.

[225] Ibid., pp. 34–6, 42.

Matters, to be relieved from which was the Design of their Removal'.[226]
Like the Council, the House of Representatives observed that Hutchinson's position entailed that either 'the Colonies are the Vassals of the Parliament, or, that they are totally Independent'; the House's position was to seize the option of Hutchinson's model of England and Scotland before the Union, 'united in one Head and common Sovereign', but, if that were impossible, independence was better than 'the Consequences of absolute uncontrouled Supreme Power, whether of a Nation or a Monarch'.[227]

The problem arose because, after the foundation of the American colonies, the dominant legal definition of sovereignty in England evolved under the impact of the civil war, the Restoration and the Glorious Revolution; colonists meanwhile sought to take their stand on an early-seventeenth-century understanding, that, as Thomas Pownall explained it, the colonies

> were dominions of the King of England; although, according to the language of those times, 'not yet annexed to the crown'. They were under the jurisdiction of the King, upon the principles of foedal sovereignty: although considered *'as out of the jurisdiction of the kingdom'*. The parliament itself doubting, at that time, whether it had jurisdiction to meddle with those matters, did not think proper to pass bills concerning America

until, at the Restoration, 'the constitution of the colonies, received their great alteration: the King participated the sovereignty of the colonies with the parliament'. As a Whig, Pownall condemned the doctrine that overseas territories were, in his own day, held directly of the Crown: to him, the tripartite nature of the sovereign (which he dated to 1660) was the basis of English liberties.[228]

In order to argue that the colonies' relationship with Britain was via the crown only, colonists inconveniently had to accept the validity of feudal tenures: as Arthur Lee put it, 'By the feudal law as it has been adopted into our constitution, all territory taken possession of in any manner whatsoever, by the king's subjects, rests absolutely in him . . . It is therefore that the king has ceded, given, or granted such territory to whom he pleased, and in what manner he pleased, without the intervention or consent of the state.'[229] To Thomas Hutchinson, this doctrine was unacceptable: it would turn the English constitution from a mixed into an absolute monarchy, for 'in absolute Monarchies the Legislative and

---

[226] Ibid., pp. 70–2.
[227] Ibid., pp. 70–2.
[228] Thomas Pownall, *The Adminstration of the Colonies*, pp. 48–9, 125, 138–9; cf. Reid (ed.), *Briefs*, pp. 80–1.
[229] Arthur Lee to Samuel Adams, 11 June 1773, quoted in Reid (ed.), *Briefs*, pp. 121–2.

executive Powers are united in the Prince or Monarch'. This, argued Hutchinson as a resolute Whig, had never been the medieval English constitution, despite the Conquest: the legislative and the executive were distinct powers.[230] But having accepted that this was indeed the law at the time the colonies were settled, so that the king's grant of them to the settlers conferred no rights over the colonies to Englishmen remaining in England, the Massachusetts House of Representatives could at once begin subtly to undermine the force of this monarchical tie by employing the arguments of John Adams's *Dissertation on the Canon and Feudal Law*: feudalism was not a system that successfully guarded liberty and property; as Rousseau said, it 'shamefully degraded' human nature; it had been 'aided by the Canon Law, calculated by the Roman Pontiff, to exalt himself above all that is called God'; it had been progressively dispelled since the Reformation as 'Knowledge' had 'darted its rays upon the benighted World'. How the feudal monarch acquired his 'absolute Right' to the lands in his dominions was still a 'Mystery', not justified by 'Nature and Reason'. However, claimed the Massachusetts House of Representatives, 'our Predecessors wisely took care to enter into Compact with the King' to limit his government of the colonies to the principles of the English constitution as outlined in Magna Carta and similar documents.[231]

So it was that Americans accepted the monarchical tie only in order to exploit its apparent weaknesses, and open the way for a natural-law rejection of the common-law sovereign. The process was powerfully advanced when Jefferson argued that since America had never been conquered by William I, colonists held their lands by the same absolute tenure as Saxons before 1066: the feudal principle that all lands were held mediately or immediately of the king would not apply in America and was, indeed, not the norm according to the common law in England.[232] Since the Saxon constitution was scarcely known, the way was clear to infer its provisions from the dictates, now self-evident truths, of natural law. By 1774, natural law arguments took precedence over all others.[233]

[230] Ibid., pp. 148–52.
[231] Ibid., pp. 126–9.
[232] [Thomas Jefferson], *A Summary View of the Rights of British America* (Williamsburg, [1774]), p. 20.
[233] [Alexander Hamilton], *A Full Vindication of the Measures of Congress from the Calumnies of their Enemies* (New York, 1774) in Henry Cabot Lodge (ed.), *The Works of Alexander Hamilton* (9 vols., New York, 1885), vol. 1, pp. 4, 6, 11; [idem.], *The Farmer Refuted; or, A more comprehensive and impartial View of the Disputes between Great Britain and the Colonies*: ibid., pp. 59–61, 65, 83, 97, 108; [Thomas Jefferson], *A Summary View of the Rights of British America* (Williamsburg, 1774), pp. 5–6, 22 ('a free people claiming their rights, as derived from the laws of nature, and not as the gift of their chief magistrate'); James Wilson, *Considerations on the Nature and Extent of the Legislative Authority of the British Parliament* (Philadelphia,

The natural law argument soon led to far more extensive conclusions than a distinction between internal and external taxation. The Scots lawyer and failed Presbyterian minister James Wilson[234] began a constitutional investigation, like his legal mentor John Dickinson, with

> a view and expectation of being able to trace some constitutional line between those cases in which we ought, and those in which we ought not, to acknowledge the power of parliament over us. In prosecution of his inquiries, he became fully convinced that such a line does not exist; and that there can be no medium between acknowledging and denying that power in *all* cases.[235]

Wilson established the option of total submission by quoting Blackstone's *Commentaries* and its famous definition of sovereignty; but he subordinated this sovereign to natural law and the foundation of government on consent, citing Burlamaqui and turning Blackstone's dictum against himself: 'The law of nature is superior in obligation to any other.'[236]

The first Continental Congress, meeting in Philadelphia on 5 September 1774, saw a conflict, as John Adams recorded, on 'Whether we should recur to the law of nature, as well as to the British constitution, and our American charters and grants. Mr. Galloway and Mr. Duane were for excluding the law of nature. I was very strenuous for retaining and insisting on it, as a resource to which we might be driven by Parliament much sooner than we were aware.' The law of nature was backed by Jay, Colonel Lee and William Livingston; Sherman similarly argued that 'The Colonies adopt the common law, not as the common law, but as the highest reason.'[237] The Continental Congress debated at length the problem of 'describing with Certainty

---

1774) in Wilson, *Works* (ed. McCloskey), vol. 2, pp. 723 (the law of nature 'must control every political maxim: it must regulate the legislature itself'), 735; John Adams, *Novanglus: or, a History of the Dispute with America, from its Origin, in 1754, to the Present Time* (letters printed in the *Boston Gazette*, 23 January – 17 April 1775; collected edn., London, 1783) in Adams, *Works*, vol. 4, pp. 15, 37, 79–84, 122.

[234] James Wilson (1742–98); born St Andrews; educated for the Presbyterian ministry at St Andrews, Glasgow and Edinburgh; emigrated to America 1763; teacher of law; member of the provincial convention at Philadelphia, 1775, and of the Continental Congress; helped frame constitution; a Justice of the Supreme Court. See Charles Page Smith, *James Wilson Founding Father (1742–1798)* (Chapel Hill, 1956); Geoffrey Seed, *James Wilson* (Millwood, N.Y., 1978).

[235] James Wilson, *Considerations on the Nature and Extent of the Legislative Authority of the British Parliament* (1774) in Wilson, *Works* (ed. McCloskey), vol. 2, pp. 721–46, at 721.

[236] Ibid., p. 723, citing Blackstone, *Commentaries*, vol. 1, p. 41: 'This law of nature, being co-eval with mankind and dictated by God himself, is of course superior in obligation to any other.'

[237] John Adams, *Diary*, 8 Sept. 1774, and Autobiography, in Adams, *Works*, vol. 2, pp. 370–4.

the Rights of *Americans*'; on 14 October they adopted their 'DECLARA-
TION and RESOLVES' which rested the colonists' claims on all
available grounds: 'the Inhabitants of the *English* Colonies in *North
America*, by the immutable Laws of Nature, the Principles of the *English*
Constitution, and the several Charters or Compacts, have the following
RIGHTS . . .'[238] But natural law, once admitted, soon swept all before
it.

The glories of the law of nature rapidly became a trope of colonial
discourse. They could be echoed even by the eighteen-year-old Alexander Hamilton, arguing against Samuel Seabury's *Farmer's Letters* in
The Farmer Refuted (1775). 'I would recommend to your perusal, Grotius,
Puffendorf, Locke, Montesquieu, and Burlamaqui', suggested the teen-
age patriot. Invoking this natural-law pantheon, Hamilton stressed that
all human rights were derived immediately from natural law, which
he identified with divine law, and that the duty of statute law was
merely to safeguard these rights.[239] The common tradition was shared
no longer: it had been polarised into two irreconcilable alternatives.
But this process of polarisation, though sudden, was late. It seems
that no inner logic drove the common law tradition to polarise in this
way, and no such development was observable in England in the
decade before 1776. In England, the common law was indeed developing in the opposite direction: even Anglicans like Sir Robert Chambers
were beginning to play down the natural law inheritance by associating
it with utilitarianism,[240] and even in the 1760s the tide had already
set strongly in the direction of Benthamite positivism.[241] The evolution
of legal thought is insufficient in itself to explain the outbreak of
revolution: grievances legally expressed demanded legal redress, but
did not entail independence.[242] Natural law and natural rights doctrines
proved explosive, but they did so when ignited by adjacent beliefs. To
explain both why the shared legal tradition was polarised in the
American colonies, and why a revolution was thereby precipitated, the
reaction against the common-law doctrine of sovereignty must be
replaced in its denominational setting.

[238] *Journals of Congress. Containing the Proceedings From Sept. 5. 1774. to Jan. 1. 1776*, vol. 1
(Philadelphia, 1777), pp. 12, 27–31.
[239] [Alexander Hamilton], *The Farmer Refuted* in Lodge (ed.), *Works of Alexander Hamilton*, vol.
1, pp. 59–60.
[240] Chambers, *A Course of Lectures on the English Law*, vol. 1, pp. 83–94.
[241] David Lieberman, *The Province of Legislation Determined: Legal Theory in Eighteenth Century
Britain* (Cambridge, 1989).
[242] As a legal historian has concluded, 'The case for independence could not be made in
legal terms': Thomas C. Grey, 'Origins of the Unwritten Constitution: Fundamental Law
in American Revolutionary Thought', *Stanford Law Review* 30 (1977–8), 843–93, at 890.

V. SOVEREIGNTY, DISSENT AND THE AMERICAN REJECTION OF THE BRITISH STATE

Law did not exist in an intellectual vacuum. Not only its structure but the pattern of its evolution was profoundly influenced by the currents of thought around it and, especially, by the religious context in which it was located. Especially was this true of the question of sovereignty explored in part IV, and especially relevant was the fact than the legal conflict possessed the same emotional charge for many colonists as it possessed for English Dissenters.

This state of mind, was, moreover, of long standing. The Blackstonian definition of sovereignty was more than an abstraction, recently devised for theoretical purposes in an Oxford college or an Inn of Court; it was the embodiment of attitudes to authority and state formation which were of ancient origin and which were widespread within England on the level of popular attitudes. In 1767 Benjamin Franklin, in London, predicted that Britain would refuse the colonies representation in the Westminster Parliament: 'the Pride of this People cannot bear the Thoughts of it. Every Man in England seems to consider himself as a Piece of a Sovereign over America; seems to jostle himself into the Throne with the King, and talks of OUR *Subjects in the Colonies.*'[243] To the Deist Franklin, such English attitudes seemed mere condescension. He failed to appreciate their extreme antiquity and permeation not only of English law but of public formulations of English identity. The common-law doctrine of sovereignty was not entertained as a legal doctrine alone: it penetrated popular discourse as an assumption, a necessary truth. Parliamentary supremacy arose, as a loyalist explained, 'from the nature and reason of civil society'; to divide this unitary authority, 'the most beautiful and regular political system in the world', was mere barbarism.[244]

Colonial empires, like composite states, were unified by doctrines of sovereignty; but these were seldom received without resistance by some of the minorities of which they consisted, however confident their articulation at the centre or within hegemonic discourse.[245] Colonial Americans

---

[243] 'The Sovereignty of the King is . . . easily understood. But nothing is more common here than to talk of the *Sovereignty of Parliament*, and the *Sovereignty of this Nation* over the Colonies; a kind of Sovereignty the Idea of which is not so clear, nor does it clearly appear on what Foundations it is established': Franklin to Lord Kames, 25 Feb. 1767: Franklin, *Papers*, vol. 14, p. 62.

[244] [Joseph Galloway], *A Reply to an Address To the Author of a Pamphlet, entitled, 'A Candid Examination of the Mutual Claims of Great Britain and her Colonies'*, &c. (New York, 1775), pp. 9, 20.

[245] These issues were classically explored in a debate between Charles Howard McIlwain, *The American Revolution: A Constitutional Interpretation* (New York, 1923) and Robert Livingston Schuyler, *Parliament and the British Empire: Some Constitutional Controversies Concerning*

found an even greater emotional resonance in these legal definitions, and from the 1760s were acutely aware of the implications of English doctrines of sovereignty for their practical positions. In America, resistance to the English formulation of sovereignty came first from those, especially Calvinist Dissenters, who came for new reasons to perceive in it an affront to God's sovereignty as expressed in fundamental law.

It was this predisposition which linked them to a much older context, for the idea of fundamental law long preceded the reception in the colonies of the natural law arguments of Barbeyrac and Pufendorf and, indeed, created the setting in which those natural law doctrines would be found congenial. Although the term 'fundamental law' was widespread and diffuse in its meaning by the late eighteenth century, its inception was more clearly defined. In France, the term *loix fondamentales* first occurred in the Calvinist and Huguenot supporter Theodore Beza's *Du droit des magistrats* (1572), a work written in the aftermath of the Massacre of St Bartholomew to justify resistance and limit the sovereignty of the ruler; only later did the term come to refer to the framework of government.[246] In England, the term was applied inconsistently as early as the seventeenth century: sometimes it meant the whole common law, sometimes specific provisions; sometimes it was synonymous with natural law, sometimes with the ancient constitution.[247] This diversity of usage deprived 'fundamental law' of much of its specific force for many Englishmen.

For Calvinists, however, the idea had a greater significance. The sovereignty of the people, under God, was an idea which led away from the ancient constitution or from English liberties as a set of positive privileges and immunities, and towards a unified society whose fundamental laws, of general applicability, mirrored and expressed the eternal principles of natural law. In 1688, the ancient constitution and the traditional rights of Englishmen proved sufficient grounds for a successful resistance to James II: fundamental law was therefore in decline in England throughout the succeeding century as an argumentative strategy. Among colonial Americans, however, it survived and was given a new lease of life when fundamental law allowed the

---

Imperial Legislative Jurisdiction (New York, 1929). See also Harvey Wheeler, 'Calvin's Case (1608) and the McIlwain-Schuyler Debate', *AHR* 61 (1956), 587–97. These works have less often been invoked in studies of political and religious discourse.

[246] Thompson, 'Fundamental law', 1105–6, 1109. Thompson identifies the context in which the concept of fundamental law emerged in terms of 'two basic metaphors' of political thought (p. 1111), and does not examine theological issues.

[247] J. W. Gough, *Fundamental Law in English Constitutional History* (Oxford, 1955); Pocock, *The Ancient Constitution and the Feudal Law*, pp. 48–50.

absorption of what seemed to be a congruent European school of natural-law theory from the pens of men like Pufendorf, Rutherforth, Burlamaqui and Vattel.[248]

The heightened rhetoric of the years of the revolution similarly echoed the idea of fundamental law, but combined it with new themes. George III 'having, contrary to his oath, his duty, and the fundamental laws of God and the realm, sent an army of mercenary soldiers to America', colonial resistance was argued to be no rebellion; such laws were synonymous with 'the laws of God, nature, reason, state and nations'.[249] The language of natural law, when it arrived, did not necessarily mean a new reliance on, or even much knowledge of, continental European natural-law theorists. It was already an old term in denominational discourse:

> Law was given to man. The original law our Maker gave us, commonly called *the law of nature*, was not a blind law of instinct, but *the eternal rule of righteousness*, the *moral law* ... The spirit of this law was written on the heart of innocent man ... Man is still bound by the same authority ...[250]

In this tradition the terms natural law, moral law, fundamental law and divine law were often virtually synonymous, and were invoked together for rhetorical force rather than for precision of argument. Colonial polemicists acquired the habit of parading strings of authorities, like Grotius, Pufendorf, Locke, Burlamaqui and Vattel; this compulsive name-dropping did not mean that those authors had been widely read or deeply understood.

What mattered was less the way in which political lessons could validly be derived from the metaphysical realm, rather the content of those lessons which a long-familiar Calvinism shaped. Puritan preachers had conventionally waxed lyrical on the omnipotence of God, which made him 'an *Eternal Sovereign*; and we at His absolute and uncontrolable dispose'.[251] God possessed 'supream, universal and absolute *Dominion* over all Worlds', so that the '*Potentates* of this World are *little* parcels of Dust, and Worms before HIM'. While God was self-sufficient, 'Earthly *Kings* are supported in their Magnificence by their Subjects'; '*Kings* are also *limited* by God both as to the Extent and

---

[248] Grey, 'Origins of the Unwritten Constitution' at 860–5, for the way in which such writers went far beyond the claims made for fundamental law within Anglo-American discourse.

[249] *The Crisis* no. 14 (New York, 1775), pp. 114–5.

[250] Peter Powers, *Jesus Christ the true King and Head of Government. A Sermon ... March 12, 1778* (Newbury Port, 1778), p. 9.

[251] Jonathan Dickinson, *The Reasonableness of Christianity, in Four Sermons* (Boston, 1732), pp. 23–4, 32.

Exercise of their Power' because 'God is the only *absolute* Lord and Sovereign.'[252] 'Methinks I see crowns and sceptres thrown away as vile refuse', announced one preacher. Christ himself was 'our king'; 'Surely there is no king like the king of America who lives and reigns for ever and ever.'[253] In due course, after the surrender of Cornwallis at Yorktown, Americans were assured that 'the glorious Sovereign of the earth and heavens ... hath saved you by his right hand'.[254] The idea of independence itself, going far beyond the redress of grievances, was attributed to divine inspiration: 'What but the mighty operations of providence inspired us with magnanimity and resolution to declare ourselves INDEPENDENT ...?'[255]

These ideas were revitalised for many colonists in a denominational setting long before the question of political independence arose. From the 1740s, and increasingly into the 1750s and 1760s, Calvinists in the American colonies, and especially in New England, saw themselves fighting a rearguard action against rising tides of Arminianism, associated with the threat of an Anglican establishment. It was even worse elsewhere, thought New Englanders. The Anglican clergy in Virginia, claimed a New Side Presbyterian minister, had 'universally, as far as my Intelligence extends, ... embraced the modish System of *Arminian Divinity*'.[256] The reaction of Calvinist predestinarians was initially theological, but had inescapable political implications. The doctrine that 'The Mercy of God to any of his sinful Creatures hath it's Foundation and takes it's Rise from his mere sovereign, arbitrary good Pleasure' was emphasised to be 'wholly subversive of all carnal Dependance'. Arminian (and Anglican) doctrines that all men might be saved were countered by reassertions of the sovereignty of the Deity,[257] and of the

---

[252] Benjamin Colman, *God is a Great King. A Sermon Preached (in part) at Boston May 13. 1733* (Boston, 1733), pp. 1–3, 9; cf. Peter Raynolds, *The Kingdom is the Lord's, or God the Supreme Ruler and Governor of the World. A Sermon ... May 12th, 1757* (New London, Conn., 1757).

[253] Powers, *Jesus Christ the true King*, pp. 12, 29–30.

[254] Robert Smith, *The Obligations of the Confederate States of North America to Praise God. Two Sermons ... December 13th, 1781* (Philadelphia, 1782), p. 4; 'The rankest deist can scarcely deny the hand of Providence in our successes', p. 28; Joseph Huntington, *God ruling the Nations for the most glorious end. A Sermon ... May 13th, 1784* (Hartford, 1784).

[255] Benjamin Trumbull, *God is to be praised for the Glory of his Majesty, and for his mighty Works. A Sermon ... December 11, 1783* (New Haven, 1784), p. 15.

[256] Samuel Davies, *The State of Religion among The Protestant Dissenters in Virginia* (Boston, 1751), p.4.

[257] Samuel Cooke, *Divine Sovereignty in the Salvation of Sinners, consider'd and improv'd. In a Sermon ... July 29th. 1741* (Boston, 1741), p. 8; Edward Wigglesworth, *The Sovereignty of God in the Exercises of his Mercy ... Two Publick Lectures at Harvard College in Cambridge* (Boston, 1741); Moses Dickinson, *A Discourse Shewing that the Consideration, of GOD's Sovereignty, in working Grace in the Souls of Men, is so far from being a Discouragement ...* (Boston, 1742); [Thomas Prince], *The Sovereign GOD Acknowledged and Blessed, both in Giving and Taking away. A Sermon ...* (Boston, 1744). Arminians were obliged to argue that their doctrines

ubiquity and power of divine Providence.[258] Theological and political struggles went hand in hand. This pattern of reaction was found more widely than the colonies. The English Baptist minister Caleb Evans advanced an identical doctrine:

> Perhaps you will say, The SUPREME POWER in every government, must be lodged somewhere, and this power must be OMNIPOTENT and UNCONTROLLABLE. I allow it. But the glory of the British constitution is, that the PEOPLE have never parted with this power, but have most religiously kept it in their own hands. You will tell me, probably, that they *do part with it*, when they elect representatives, and that the *supreme power* in Great Britain, most unquestionably resides in King, Lords, and Commons. I answer, such a portion of it only as is within the limits of the fundamental laws and constitution of the kingdom.[259]

Evans too was a Calvinist, and a lifelong assailant of the Arianism and Socinianism which he feared were subverting the cause of Dissent.

This desperate and losing rearguard action was not only theological and political; it was moral also, and the moral dimension was prominent in New England. To fight against this doctrine was held to be in itself proof of moral corruption: 'The reason why we dislike and disrelish this divine sovereignty, is because we have corrupted ourselves, and our hearts are disaffected to God: we don't like God should be all; and that his will should be an absolute rule to us.'[260] To overcome this, sinners – even if predestined – must strive all the harder towards salvation.[261]

Because of these ulterior objectives, colonial discourse conventionally conflated 'absolute' with 'arbitrary' in a way which Blackstonian analysis implicitly denied:

> If we consider absolute Sovereignty in the same View in which it is ascribed to Men; a Prerogative or Power to do whatever a Man will, controlled by

were indeed consistent with God's sovereignty, e.g. [Samuel Johnson], *A Letter from Aristocles to Authades Concerning the Sovereignty And the Promises of God* (Boston, 1745), replied to by Jonathan Dickinson, *A Vindication of GOD's sovereign free Grace* (Boston, 1746), and the subject of a pamphlet controversy. Other denominations witnessed the same Calvinist rearguard action against encroaching Arminianism, including the Baptists: e.g. Isaac Backus, *The Doctrine of Sovereign Grace Opened and Vindicated* (Providence, 1771).

[258] John Witherspoon, *The Dominion of Providence over the Passions of Men. A Sermon preached at Princeton, On the 17th of May, 1776* (Philadelphia, 1776), p. 26: 'there is often a discernible mixture of sovereignty and righteousness in providential dispensations'; cf. Abraham Keteltas, *God Arising and Pleading His People's Cause . . . A Sermon Preached October 5th, 1777* (Newbury Port, 1777).

[259] Caleb Evans, *A Reply to the Rev. Mr. Fletcher's Vindication of Mr. Wesley's Calm Address to Our American Colonies* (Bristol, [1776]), p. 71.

[260] Moses Mather, *Divine Sovereignty displayed by Predestination; Or, the Doctrine of the Decrees Considered in its Proper Light, and Real Tendency* (New Haven, 1763), pp. 18, 25.

[261] William Tennent, Jr, *God's Sovereignty, no Objection to the Sinner's Striving. A Sermon, preached at New-York, On the 20th of January, 1765* (New York, 1765).

no Reason, Law or Right, but his Will to do so, merely because he will: I
suppose it to be the worst Idea that can be formed of GOD, or of Government. But absolute Sovereignty consisting in a Power and Prerogative to
act in all Things, according to the immutable Rules of Justice, Truth,
Righteousness and Goodness; to be determined in all its Operations by
perfect Wisdom, I conceive to be the most glorious Character of GOD; and
the best Government that possibly can be in the World. Now such is the
divine Government: And in this View, GOD is the absolute and sovereign
Ruler of the World.[262]

The success of the Revolution seemed to confirm the triumph of natural-
law principles by emancipating Americans from past experience. 'When
this Revolution was yet incompleat', urged one analyst, 'it was a common
practice to revert to Grecian, Roman and British customs, for precedents
and models'; now, independence meant that it was 'our business, without
confining ourselves to imitate such wretched exemplars, to recur immediately' to the 'great Law of Nature'.[263] Yet if self-evident in retrospect,
Calvinism had co-existed with a Hanoverian monarchy for many decades
before its revolutionary potential was unlocked. From the mid-eighteenth
century, however, American colonial polemic increasingly began to depict
English rule as a claim of the divine right of kings and to reject it as
'blasphemy' on the grounds that it infringed the prior sovereignty of God,
'whose *Kingdom ruleth over all*'.[264] Jonathan Mayhew, the Arian author of
that remark, was, ironically, able to denounce Trinitarian Anglicans by
appeal to his Trinitarian Congregationalist colleagues' own ideals: an
Arian, by demoting the Son, was free to offer larger compliments to the
Father.

So both Arians and Trinitarians joined in the denunciations of Anglicans which Arians had often initiated. The Congregationalist James
Otis, famously denouncing British policy before the passage of the Stamp
Act, was giving a new expression to an old Dissenting tradition with his
dictum:

> To say the parliament is absolute and arbitrary, is a contradiction. The
> parliament cannot make 2 and 2, 5: Omnipotency cannot do it. The

---

[262] Solomon Williams, *The Greatness and Sovereignty of God, sufficient Reason to silence Man's
Complaints of his Providence . . . A Sermon . . . December 3, 1775* (Norwich, Conn., [1777]), p.
15.

[263] *Rudiments of Law and Government, deduced from The Law of Nature; Particularly addressed to the
People of South Carolina, But composed on Principles applicable to Mankind* (Charlestown, 1783),
pp. iii, xiii. The author supported his scheme by citations from Montesquieu, *Cato's
Letters*, Beccaria, Blackstone, Cicero, Sallust, Pufendorf, and Robertson's *History of Charles
V.*

[264] Jonathan Mayhew, *A Discourse concerning Unlimited Submission and Non-Resistance to the Higher
Powers* (Boston, 1750), pp. 26, 35–6.

supreme powers in a state, is *jus dicere* only: – *jus dare*, strictly speaking, belongs alone to GOD.[265]

The common law had had an immutable quality in the early seventeenth century, eloquently stressed by Coke; but by the age of Blackstone the supremacy of the King-in-Parliament and the parliamentary sovereign's busy programme of legislation led Englishmen rather to stress the law's moral content and equity between individuals as sources of its merit. To Blackstone, the law's morality and the natural-law restrictions on the sovereign were equally identified by the Anglican ascendancy, the union of Church and State. Colonists, especially Dissenters, had no such confidence.

Otis reviewed the four main theories of the origin of government – divine grace, conquest, compact or property – and showed how each was inadequate, despite his deference for Locke on contract and for 'the incomparable Harrington', who had demonstrated 'that Empire follows the balance of *property*'.[266] Otis emphasised that government had, rather, 'an everlasting foundation in the *unchangeable will of GOD*'. It was only because he emphasised God's superintenting Providence that Otis could concede 'that an original supreme Sovereign, absolute, and uncontroulable, *earthly* power *must* exist in and preside over every society; from whose final decisions there can be no appeal but directly to Heaven'. Given this concession, it was his denominational heritage, not secular political science, which made Otis deduce that sovereign power was '*originally* and *ultimately* in the people'. It was his qualification ('earthly power') which proved dispensable.

Critics of British policy had at the outset to be even louder in their professions of loyalty to the British state. Otis argued against the expedience, not the legality, of the Stamp Act:

> It is certain that the Parliament of Great-Britain hath a just, clear, equitable and constitutional right, power and authority, to bind the colonies, by all acts wherein they are named. Every lawyer, nay every Tyro knows this. No less certain is it that the Parliament of Great-Britain has a just and equitable right, power and authority, to *impose taxes on the colonies, internal and external, on lands, as well as on trade.* This is involved in the idea of a supreme legislative or sovereign power of a state. It will however by no means from thence follow, that 'tis always expedient, and in all circumstances equitable for the supreme and sovereign legislative to tax the colonies, much less that 'tis reasonable this right should be practised upon without allowing the colonies an actual representation.

[265] James Otis, *The Rights of the British Colonies Asserted and proved* (Boston, 1764), p. 47.
[266] Ibid., pp. 1, 5, 8–9.

The alternative was *'imperium in imperio*, the greatest of all political sol-
ecisms'.[267] Natural law, not colonial charters, checked the sovereign
power; to deny this was to run into 'absurd treasonable doctrines', namely
'all the vagaries of Filmer, Mannwaring and Sibthorp'. The heart of
Otis's critique was that this doctrine was not merely incorrect but a
'Horrid blasphemy' since 'The Lord omnipotent reigneth' and had not
deputed to any Filmerian sovereign a power which contradicted natural
law.[268] It was the ardently anti-Stuart, anti-Catholic orientation of colonists which initially bound them, like English Whigs, to the common-law
doctrine of sovereignty, for to accept the Revolution of 1688 was to accept
also 'the act of Queen Anne, which makes it high treason to deny 'that
the King with and by the authority of parliament, is able to make laws
and statutes of sufficient force and validity to *limit* and bind the crown,
and the descent, limitation, inheritance and *government* thereof'': the
Regency Act of 1707. To say otherwise was to 'serve the cause of the
Pretender'.[269] Otis trusted to the rights of Englishmen under a sovereign
limited by natural law. Just administration would confirm the colonies
in their loyalty.[270]

In the 1760s, after the common-law sovereign of King, Lords and Commons had become the target for this ancient but now reactivated and
redirected critique,[271] it was natural for Dissenters to rediscover an alternative *locus* of sovereignty in the people, under God:

> The power of GOD almighty is the only power that can properly and
> strictly be called supreme and absolute. In the order of nature immediately
> under him, comes the power of a simple *democracy*, or the power of the whole
> over the whole.[272]

When the solidly Congregationalist people of Boston were encouraged by
Samuel Adams to agree that

> The Legislative has no Right to absolute arbitrary Power over the Lives
> and Fortunes of the People; Nor can Mortals assume a Prerogative, not only
> too high for Man, but for Angels; and therefore reserved for the Exercise of
> the Deity alone[273]

---

[267] [James Otis], *A Vindication of the British Colonies, Against The Aspersions of the Halifax Gentleman, in His Letter to a Rhode-Island Friend* (Boston, 1765), pp. 4–5, 14. Otis was now able
to cite Blackstone's recently-published *Commentaries* in his support (p. 10).

[268] [Otis], *Vindication*, pp. 10–11.

[269] Otis, *Rights of the British Colonies*, pp. 32, 34–5; 6 Anne, c. 41.

[270] Ibid., p. 51.

[271] The ecclesiological and theological causes of this reactivation are discussed in chapters
3 and 4 below.

[272] Otis, *Rights of the British Colonies*, p. 9.

[273] *The Votes and Proceedings of the Freeholders and other Inhabitants of the Town of Boston, In Town
Meeting assembled, According to Law* (Boston, 1772; Dublin, 1773), p. 7.

armed rebellion was not far away. The Massachusetts General Court's proclamation of 19 January 1776, justifying resistance, similarly derived its doctrine of sovereignty explicitly from a theological premise:

> It is a maxim, that, in every Government there must exist, some where, a supreme, sovereign, absolute, and uncontrollable power; but this power resides, always, in the body of the people, and it never was, or can be delegated to one man or a few; the great Creator having never given to men a right to vest others with authority over them unlimited, either in duration or degree.[274]

Popular sovereignty was then confirmed when the realities of military conflict gave a focus to providentialist rhetoric, long implicit in several strands of colonial discourse, which nothing else had ever done. American newspapers consistently invoked Divine Providence to explain revolutionary victories; American soldiers on the eve of battle were spurred on by their preachers[275] in the belief that, as Joab Trout insisted before the battle of Brandywine, 'God is with you! The eternal God fights for you! He rides on the battle-cloud; he sweeps onward with the march, or the hurricane charge! God, the awful and the infinite, fights for you, and will triumph!'[276] If Americans regularly resorted to the grandiose imagery of the Book of Exodus to explain God's miraculous deliverance of the new Israel out of the hands of Egyptian slavery,[277] Blackstone's careful apologia could only seem at best parochial, at worst heretical.

This cosmic scenario naturally engaged with the critique of the Anglican version of sovereignty framed by Dissenters in England. The failed Presbyterian minister James Burgh directly challenged Blackstone: 'The truth is, therefore, that the learned judge has placed sovereignty wrong, viz., in the government; whereas it should have been placed in the people, next and immediately after God.'[278] A similar rhetoric could commend itself to Low Church Anglicans in the reforming camp: Granville Sharp repeatedly denounced Justinian's dictum, quod principi placuit legis habet vigorem, as 'IMPIOUS AND UNJUST', since

> even the ALMIGHTY SOVEREIGN OF THE UNIVERSE, to whose WILL alone such deference is justly due, hath not so dealt with his creature

---

[274] Peter Force (ed.), *American Archives*, 4th series (5 vols., Washington, 1837–44), vol. 4, col. 833.

[275] Catherine L. Albanese, *Sons of the Fathers: The Civil Religion of the American Revolution* (Philadelphia, 1976), pp. 81–111.

[276] Joab Trout, 'A Sermon Preached on the Eve of the Battle of Brandywine, September 10, 1777' in [Lydia Minturn Post], *Personal Recollections of the American Revolution*, ed. Sidney Barclay (New York, 1859), cited in Albanese, *Sons of the Fathers*, p. 86.

[277] Albanese, *Sons of the Fathers*, pp. 88–9.

[278] James Burgh, *Political Disquisitions, or an Enquiry into Public Errors, Defects and Abuses* (3 vols., London, 1774), vol. 3, p. 278.

Man, enforcing his Will for his Reason; but, on the contrary, hath mercifully
condescended to convince us (his frail mortal subjects) that REASON is
his WILL.

It followed that the doctrine of 'the omnipotence of Parliament' was 'A
kind of Popery in Politics'.[279] However limited in its effect in England,
this became a commonplace of colonial discourse, because it was able to
draw on far more powerful sectarian sources.

If denominational discourse explains the legal activation of the American patriot case, a second development had given to the first the support
of analogy. From the 1740s colonial religious revivalism and its challenge
to the regenerate to separate from 'slothful' and 'carnal' congregations
posed repeatedly, at grassroots level, the question: was *ecclesiastical* authority indivisible? This had not always been clearly decided. Protestant sects,
by separating from the Church of England, had not necessarily become
pluralist: on the contrary, they often sustained, in the American colonies,
their seventeenth-century English, Scots or Irish assumptions that their
own polities provided a model for their society at large. These monopol-
istic instincts were now challenged within Presbyterianism and Congregationalism by New Lights who put theology above ecclesiastical polity.
Revivalists in turn were denounced as promoting faction. Their reply was
necessarily systematic: 'beginning in the 1740s and continuing into the
next decade, Presbyterian and Congregational separatists constructed a
defense that stressed the rights of minorities against majorities, and of
individuals against the whole, in matters of conscience'.[280]

Colonial defences of a right of ecclesiastical separation initially
appealed to Anglican latitudinarians like William Chillingworth and John
Tillotson; but in the heat of debate, New Lights displayed a 'propensity
to cast their defense of religious rights in an increasingly political idiom'.[281]
The revivalist Samuel Blair, pastor of a largely Scots-Irish congregation
at New Londonderry, complained that he was wrongly charged 'that we
deny all Authority of Government to Church Judicatures', and claimed
that the New Lights only 'oppose the Exorbitancy of Church Power'.
The Old Light Synod of Philadelphia had proceeded upon 'the absurd
tyrannical Maxim of, *sic volo, sic jubeo, stet pro Ratione voluntas*'. Blair's
position was different: 'Is there no Authority besides absolute and unlimited?'[282] New Light sectaries did not yet extend the ecclesiastical right of

---

[279] Granville Sharp, *A Declaration of the People's Natural Right to a Share in the Legislature*
(London, 1774), pp. xxvi, xxix.
[280] Bonomi, *Cope of Heaven*, pp. 153–4.
[281] Ibid., p. 155.
[282] Samuel Blair, *A Vindication of The Brethren who were unjustly and illegally cast out of the Synod
of Philadelphia ... From maintaining Principles of Anarchy in the Church ...* (Philadelphia,
1744), pp. 11, 15, 21.

secession to the civil sphere, where, as the Congregationalist Elisha Williams admitted, 'the Right of each Individual is subjected to the Body, or so transferred to the Society, as that the Act of the Majority is legally to be considered as the Act of the whole, and binding to each Individual';[283] but the practical impact of religious revivalism clearly pointed in that direction.

The legal and religious ties between colonies and metropolis were powerfully grounded: it would take powerful forces within law and religion to break them. Outright independence was a goal formulated with reluctance or intellectual difficulty, and only late in the long saga of colonial grievances against British policy. In October 1774, Washington reassured a serving British officer about the intentions of Massachusetts: 'I think I can announce it as a fact, that it is not the wish or interest of that government, or any other upon this continent, separately or collectively, to set up for independency'; as late as April 1776, he acknowledged how 'My countrymen I know, from their form of government, and steady attachment heretofore to royalty, will come reluctantly into the idea of independence.'[284] Even Jefferson, in August 1775, noted that he 'would rather be in dependence on Great Britain, properly limited, than on any nation upon earth, or than on no nation'.[285] The Founding Fathers in general were slow to take that step: the natural law tradition suggested at most a federal relationship; independence implied that this was impossible and that the Blackstonian formula was inescapable except by a final separation.

Independence implied also a united polity; this did not yet exist. On 28 June, 1, 2 and 4 July 1776, Congress debated whether to issue the Declaration of Independence. John Dickinson of Pennsylvania opposed it as untimely:

> The formation of our government and an agreement upon the terms of our confederation ought to precede the assumption of our station among sovereigns. A sovereignty composed of several distinct bodies of men not subject to established constitutions, and not combined together by confirmed articles of union, is such a sovereignty as has never appeared.[286]

Without unity, independence seemed logically impossible; but without the legal framework of nationality provided by the doctrine of monarchical

---

[283] [Elisha Williams], *The essential Rights and Liberties of Protestants. A seasonable Plea for The Liberty of Conscience, and The Right of private Judgement, In Matters of Religion, Without any Controul from human authority* (Boston, 1744), pp. 48–9; Bonomi, *Cope of Heaven*, p. 156.

[284] Washington to Captain Robert Mackenzie, 9 Oct. 1774; Washington to Joseph Reed, 1 Apr. 1776; in John C. Fitzpatrick (ed.), *The Writings of George Washington* (39 vols., Washington, 1931–44), vol. 3, p. 244; vol. 4, p. 452.

[285] Jefferson to John Randolph, 25 Aug. 1775: Jefferson, *Papers*, vol. 1, p. 240.

[286] Quoted in W. P. Breed, *Presbyterians and the Revolution* (Philadelphia, 1876), pp. 159–60.

allegiance, no unity could emerge. Americans were moved to resistance when natural-law checks on the common-law sovereign were perceived to be insufficient; but it was the sectarian element, working on the natural law tradition, which created this perception. Before the Declaration of Independence, English sovereignty was therefore chiefly countered in the colonies by warnings against or denunciations of 'tyranny', the preoccupation of denominational discourse, rather than by the elaboration of federal schemes for imperial devolution. The full doctrine that each colony was an independent state, united to the empire only by allegiance to a common monarch, was not given clear expression until 1774.[287]

Contract theory was, meanwhile, widespread in transatlantic arguments. Yet this too derived its force from sectarian tradition, revitalised by successive waves of migrants, as in the teaching of John Witherspoon, a Presbyterian minister brought from Scotland in 1768 to head the College of New Jersey. To a succession of pupils who were to emerge as leaders of the revolution, Witherspoon taught that

> Though people have actually consented to any form of government, if they have been essentially deceived in the nature and operation of the laws, if they are found to be pernicious and destructive of the ends of the union, they may certainly break up the society, recall their obligation, and resettle the whole upon a better footing.

This doctrine, insisted Witherspoon, made Blackstone's conception of the sovereign not untrue, but ultimately inconclusive:

> It is frequently observed, that in every government there is a supreme irresistible power lodged some where, in king, senate, or people. To this power is the final appeal in all questions. Beyond this we cannot go. How far does this authority extend? We answer as far as authority in a social state can extend, it is not accountable to any other tribunal, and it is supposed in the social compact that we have agreed to submit to its decision. There is however an exception, if the supreme power wherever lodged, come to be exercised in a manifestly tyrannical manner, the subjects may certainly if in their power, resist and overthrow it. But this is only when it becomes manifestly more advantageous to unsettle the government altogether, than to submit to tyranny. This resistance to the supreme power however, is subverting the society altogether, and is not to be attempted till the government is so corrupt as that anarchy and the uncertainty of a new settlement is preferable to the continuance as it is.

The remoteness of this ultimate sanction was diminished by the historical concreteness given to the contract in the Presbyterian world view:

---

[287] In James Wilson, *Considerations on the Nature and Extent of the Legislative Authority of the British Parliament* (written in 1768), and, shortly afterwards, in John Adams's *Novanglus Letters*.

Dominion, it is plain from all that has been said, can be acquired justly only one way, viz. by consent. There are two other ways commonly mentioned, both of which are defective, inheritance and conquest. Hereditary power which originally rose from consent, and is supposed to be founded on the continuance of consent (as that of the hereditary power in a limited monarchy) is as lawful as any, but when they pretend such a right from nature, is independent of the people, it is absurd.

This doctrine of private judgement, Witherspoon admitted, would make the people 'both judge and party', but there was little danger in this: only the rebellion of a whole people, proving that 'they have received very great provocation', would be successful. 'There are occasional and partial insurrections in every government. These are easily raised by interested persons, but the great majority continues to support order.'[288] Four Presbyterian ministers in Philadelphia similarly addressed the Blackstonian model in writing to rally support from their co-religionists in North Carolina:

> it is said, that the Parliament of England has supreme power, and that no one ought to resist. This we allow, while they make Acts that are reasonable, and according to the British Constitution; but their power has bounds and limits, that they must not exceed: they are limited by the Laws of God and of reason; they are limited by the fundamental laws of the Constitution, and by the Great Charter of England.[289]

Both in England and the thirteen colonies, it was Dissenters and especially men of heterodox views in religion who were most articulate against the Blackstonian conception of sovereignty, since it was they who were most sensitive to its essentially Anglican nature. Sometimes they disclosed this by the images they chose to denounce it. The 1730s Deist William Pitt, now first Earl of Chatham, found an apt form of words to repudiate the Blackstonian theory: that he would 'as soon *subscribe to Transubstantiation as to Sovereignty (by right)*, in the Colonies'.[290] Where such theological proclivities were shared, the Dissenting critique of unitary sovereignty could commend itself to Low Church Anglicans also. David Griffith, an Anglican rector from Virginia, explicitly linked the American cause to the campaign at Westminster to relieve heterodox Anglican clergy from the need to subscribe the Thirty-Nine Articles:

[288] Lecture 'Of Civil Society' in *The Works of the Rev. John Witherspoon* (2nd edn., 4 vols., Philadelphia, 1802), vol. 3, pp. 432, 436–8.

[289] Francis Alison, James Sprout [Sproat], George Duffield, Robert Davidson, 'An Address to the Ministers and Presbyterian Congregations in North Carolina', 10 July 1775: in William L. Saunders (ed.), *The Colonial Records of North Carolina* (Raleigh, 1890), vol. 10, p. 222.

[290] Chatham to Shelburne, 18 Dec. 1777: Lord Fitzmaurice, *Life of William Earl of Shelburne* (2nd edn, 2 vols., London, 1912), vol. 2, p. 9. For the intellectual origins of Pitt's position see Clark, *English Society 1688–1832*, pp. 279–307.

> In my opinion, the doctrine of transubstantiation is not a greater absurdity
> than the notion of America's being represented in the British parliament
> ... Many members of the British senate have, of late, interested themselves
> greatly to procure relief from subscription to the articles of our church; and
> for this reason, principally, that the doctrines they contain are incompre-
> hensible and absurd: Yet those very members, who wish to be excused from
> acknowledging, publickly, truths which they cannot comprehend, would
> compel the colonists to subscribe doctrines, which they are convinced, are
> neither just nor true.[291]

Where English administrators thought the supremacy of Parliament
(King, Lords and Commons) a self-evidently necessary framework for
English liberties, colonists like the Massachusetts Congregationalist minister William Gordon increasingly perceived and denounced it as entailing
'the once exploded, but again courtly, doctrines of passive obedience and
non-resistance'.[292] The heterodox were especially prominent in their insistence that sovereignty lay with the people, an idea which went inseparably
with contract theory. For the Deist Major John Cartwright, much of the
constitutional argument about American grievances was irrelevant:

> a title to the liberty of mankind is not established on such rotten founda-
> tions: 'tis not among mouldy parchments, nor in the cobwebs of a casuist's
> brain we are to look for it; it is the immediate, the universal gift of God,
> and the seal of it is that free-will which he hath made the noblest constituent
> of man's nature.

From these premises, it followed without argument that since these rights
were 'not derived from any one, but original in every one', that therefore
'The answer is obvious and short. The rights of sovereignty reside in the
people themselves.'[293] For the Arian Richard Price, it was equally 'obvious, that all civil government, as far as it can be denominated *free*, is the
creature of the people . . . If omnipotence can, with any sense, be ascribed
to a legislature, it must be lodged where all legislative authority origin-
ates; that is, the PEOPLE.'[294] For English Dissenting ministers, the issue
of taxation without representation was 'pivotal'; they 'viewed Parliament's assertions of absolute sovereignty as both unconstitutional and
unjust'.[295] One such was James Murray, who argued in 1781 that the

---

[291] David Griffith, *Passive Obedience Considered: in a Sermon Preached at Williamsburg, December 31st, 1775* (Williamsburg, [1776]), pp. 22–3.

[292] William Gordon, *A Discourse Preached December 15th 1774* . . . (Boston, 1775), p. 11.

[293] [John Cartwright], *American Independence the Interest and Glory of Great-Britain* (London, 1775), pp. 7, 9. For Cartwright, God's sovereignty, as revealed by 'the nature of man at his creation', rendered Magna Carta and the ancient constitution merely superstructural: ibid., p. 39.

[294] Richard Price, *Observations on the Nature of Civil Liberty, the Principles of Government, and the Justice and Policy of the War with America* (2nd edn, London, 1776), p. 6.

[295] Bradley, *Religion*, p. 152.

Americans were the victims of British policy: 'It is well known that there were no laws in existence that could make them rebels a few years ago; they were only created such, by the modern omnipotence of parliament.'[296] The wide employment of this Dissenting idiom in the colonies is no longer problematic: it supplied a perfect reply to the ideology which justified British authority.

VI. SOVEREIGNTY AND THE NEW REPUBLIC: THE AMERICAN CONSTITUTION IN TRANSATLANTIC PERSPECTIVE

After the Revolution, the English Deist Major John Cartwright drew the obvious lesson: Blackstone had failed in the *Commentaries* to distinguish between ordinary and constitutional law because of his arbitrary definition of sovereignty, and because he did not have the American republican example before his eyes. The idea of a constitution as a structure of devolved fundamental rights which overrode the absolute, centralising authority of the Blackstonian sovereign had been given concrete expression in the new American republic, thought Cartwright.[297] Not all Americans, however, shared the euphoric confidence of their British and French admirers that independence had solved all these problems at a stroke. The experience of the early Republic revealed instead the persistence of exactly those agonizing problems on the uniquely British nature of which the Revolution had been justified. It will be argued here that the debates on the American Constitution can be understood, among their other meanings, as a replay of the major issue at stake in the Revolution, and that the outcome in 1787 in a fundamental sense reversed the verdict of 1776.

The issues raised in the framing and ratification of the Constitution may helpfully be analysed as old issues, inescapably structural in the relations between centre and peripheries in the British Empire over the previous century and a half.[298] Yet Americans after 1776 normally failed to place their debate in that context: for them, as for many Englishmen after 1688 and Frenchmen after 1789, the Revolution counted as Year One, emancipating its devotees (as they supposed) from their historical

---

[296] James Murray, *Sermons for the General Fast Day* (London, 1781), pp. 36–7; 'Those who obey the fundamental laws of government cannot be rebels, though it is manifest that legislators that make laws contrary to natural justice and the law of God may be guilty of rebellion', p. 22.

[297] John Cartwright, *An Appeal, on the Subject of the English Constitution* (London, [1797]), pp. 23–4, 29.

[298] Greene, *Peripheries and Center*, pp. 181–211, at 182, 198.

burdens.[299] By forgetting their history, and forgetting it so quickly, Americans were doomed to repeat it.

The constitutional arrangements which grew up informally between the thirteen colonies in and after 1774 to allow them to organise a war of resistance, and which were imperfectly codified in the Articles of Confederation, partly mirrored in the relation between each colony and the Continental Congress the colonies' case against British rule.[300] James Madison accurately recorded the perspective of colonial patriots: 'the fundamental principle of the Revolution was, that the Colonies were co-ordinate members with each other and with Great Britain, of an empire united by a common executive sovereign, but not united by any common legislative sovereign'.[301] The second of the Articles of Confederation seemed to go further in providing that 'Each State retains its sovereignty, freedom and independence'.[302] Yet despite this extreme statement of an ideal, the practical division of governmental functions between the States and Congress which the Articles envisaged meant that 'a division of sovereignty was implicit in the structure of American federalism from its very inception'.[303] The Continental Congress deliberately shied away from discussion of this potentially explosive theoretical question between its creation and the adoption of the Articles in June–July 1778: practical co-operation in the midst of the revolutionary war took priority over all else.[304] Yet this rejection of Blackstonian doctrine was the point centrally at issue.

English reformers seldom sought to divide their unified polity: Bentham in his critique of Blackstone sought only to score an intellectual point, not to create a federal Britain. The practical division of a unitary state was however precisely the objective of the Founding Fathers. The Scots-American James Wilson, immersed in the practical business of state building, offered in his lectures of 1790 a far more extended account than Bentham's of the history and theory of confederacies: 'In some respects, such confederacies are to be considered as forming only one nation: in other respects, they are to be considered as still retaining their separate

---

[299] There were exceptions, some discussed here; but more striking is the lack of explicit reference in the America of c. 1776–87 to the British and historical dimensions of the momentous structural problems they addressed in framing a new polity.

[300] Jack N. Rakove, *The Beginnings of National Politics: An Interpretive History of the Continental Congress* (New York, 1979); Peter S. Onuf, *The Origins of the Federal Republic: Jurisdictional Controversies in the United States, 1775–1787* (Philadelphia, 1983); Greene, *Peripheries and Center*, pp. 153–80.

[301] Madison, 'Notes on the Resolutions', 1799–1800, in Madison, *Writings*, vol. 6, p. 373, cited in Greene, *Peripheries and Center*, p. 153.

[302] Merrill Jensen, *The Articles of Confederation* (Madison, 1966), p. 263.

[303] Rakove, *Beginnings of National Politics*, p. 162.

[304] Greene, *Peripheries and Center*, pp. 175–6.

political characters, rights, and powers.' So it was that the United States had been 'formed into one confederate republick; first, under the articles of confederation; afterwards, under our present national government'. Loyally defending his great experiment, Wilson drew no distinction between the two, and passed over in silence the stresses to which composite states were subject.[305] Already, however, the confederal polity of 1776 had been fundamentally modified. The exploration of these issues by the Founding Fathers was profound but, as events were soon to show, not conclusive.

The American colonial sense that they were already living in a quasi-confederal polity derived partly from assumptions predating the English Civil War about the indefeasible rights of certain agencies of government, partly from the theory that the colonies were immediately subject to the Crown but beyond the realm of Great Britain in which the Westminster Parliament's writ ran. But once independence had been achieved, and achieved through an upheaval in society, how was Britain's boasted division of powers between King, Lords and Commons to be preserved now that monarchy had been reviled and the social elite of inherited wealth and hereditary status rejected by a *de facto* egalitarianism?[306] How was sovereignty, now solely entrusted to the people, to be guarded against?

Robert Treat Paine, in his eulogy on Washington, recognised 'How novel, how aspiring, was the hope of connecting, under one compact code of general jurisprudence, so many distinct sovereignties, each jealous of its independence, without impairing their respective authorities!'[307] But in its novelty lay its difficulty. Americans had not opted for a previously-existing federal model linking the colonies; federalism had to be invented. The political and legal challenge gave birth to an attempt at codifying and republicanising American law which can properly be compared to Blackstone's monument of royalist codification. Its author was James Wilson, and the occasion (like Blackstone's) was the series of lectures given by Wilson, a Justice of the Supreme Court, as newly-appointed Professor of Law at the College of Philadelphia.

So dangerously attractive did the doctrines of Blackstone seem that Wilson devoted a long section of his lectures to extirpating them from the minds of citizens of the new Republic. He reminded his hearers of a former case. That other celebrated champion of the common law, Lord Chief Justice Hale (1609–76), had written passages which seemed 'to

[305] Wilson, *Works* (ed. McCloskey), vol. 1, pp. 247–69, at 247, 262–3.

[306] Gordon Wood, *The Radicalism of the American Revolution* (New York, 1992), passim.

[307] Robert Treat Paine, 2 Jan. 1800, quoted in Frank I. Schechter, 'The Early History of the Tradition of the Constitution', *American Political Science Review* 9 (1915), 707–34, at 727.

militate against the principles' of the subsequent Glorious Revolution. Seventy years after that event, Mr Justice Foster thought it still important to refute those passages, offering as a justification:

> The Cause of the Pretender seems now to be absolutely given up. I hope in God it is so. But whether the Root of Bitterness, the Principles which gave Birth and Growth and Strength to it, and have been Twice within our Memory made a Pretence for Rebellion at Seasons very Critical, whether those Principles be totally eradicated I know not. These I encounter . . . by shewing that certain Historical Facts which the learned Judge hath appealed to in support of them, either have no Foundation in Truth; or were they true do not warrant the Conclusions drawn from them.[308]

Did Blackstone similarly influence the early American republic? Foster admitted that Hale's passages 'have been cited with an uncommon degree of triumph by those, who, to say no worse of them, from the dictates of a misguided conscience, have treated the revolution [of 1688] and present establishment as founded in usurpation and rebellion; and they are in every student's hand'.[309] The expulsion of some American loyalists and the intimidation and silencing of others removed from the public life of the early republic a body of men who would have offered a fundamental critique of the constitution; but the clash of Federalist and Antifederalist nevertheless had explored similar issues, if in less historical depth.

Wilson saw that Blackstone's definitions of law as the command of a superior, and of sovereignty as something other than an attribute of the whole people, were linked: 'this notion of superiority contains the germ of the divine right'. Further, Wilson traced Blackstone's doctrine back to Pufendorf, Barbeyrac, Heineccius and Domat:

> Domat, in his book on the civil law, derives the power of governours from *divine* authority. 'It is always he (God) who places them in the seat of authority: it is from him alone that they derive all the power and authority that they have; and it is the ministry of his justice that is committed to them. And seeing it is God himself whom they represent, in the rank which raises them above others; he will have them to be considered as holding his place in their functions. And it is for this reason, that he himself gives the name of gods to those, to whom he communicates the right of governing and judging men'.[310]

---

[308] Wilson, *Works* (ed. McCloskey), vol. 1, pp. 194–5, citing [Michael Foster], *A Report of Some Proceedings on the Commission of Oyer and Terminer and Gaol Delivery for the Trial of the Rebels in the Year 1746* . . . (Oxford, 1762), p. vi. Foster was a Dissenter: Robbins, *Commonwealthman*, p. 433 n. 32. For Foster's anonymous attack on Edmund Gibson's account of ecclesiastical authority, see p. 171 below.

[309] Wilson, *Works*, vol. 1, p. 195.

[310] Wilson, *Works*, vol. 1, pp. 103, 105, 109, 111, 170, 186–7, citing Jean Domat, *The Civil Law in its Natural Order: Together with the Publick Law* (2 vols., London, 1722), vol. 1, p. xxii.

By repudiating the European natural law tradition for its associations with Popery, the Scots Presbyterian Wilson, like many of his generation of Americans, neglected the best available route to a viable federalism.

'The position', concluded Wilson, 'that law is inseparably attached to superiour power, was the political weapon used, with the greatest force and the greatest skill, in favour of the despotick claims of Great Britain over the American colonies.'[311] Why, demanded Wilson, had that principle been introduced into English laws, where it lacked all precedent and authority? There was, of course, Coke's dictum, 'Of the power and jurisdiction of the Parliament, for making of laws in proceeding by Bill, it is so transcendent and absolute, as it cannot be confined either for causes or persons within any bounds';[312] but this, contended Wilson, only established Parliament as the 'legislative authority' of Britain, not of the colonies. Even within Britain, he continued in sectarian mode, history and law did not record any contract by which the people had invested Parliament with supreme authority.[313] Where Wilson in his *Considerations* of 1774 had been willing to appeal to natural law to limit the common-law sovereign, in his law lectures of 1790 he rejected much of the natural law tradition in the name of the new American conception of liberty, and of the immediate access of the virtuous American citizen to the true content of natural law as the will of God.[314]

James Wilson identified as 'the *vital* principle' of the American constitution the doctrine that 'the supreme or sovereign power of the society resides in the citizens at large'; a doctrine which Blackstone, denying Locke, 'treated as a political chimera, existing only in the minds of some theorists; but, in practice, inconsistent with the dispensation of any government upon earth'. Modern enquiry, insisted Wilson, had dispelled an ancient mystery: 'The dread and redoubtable sovereign, when traced to his ultimate and genuine source, has been found, as he ought to have been found, in the free and independent man.'[315] Blackstone's mistake, insisted Wilson, was to presume that sovereignty must reside in the legislature; with the supreme power entrusted to the sovereign people, Wilson was quite content.[316] This was to prove the undoing of his system, for the sovereignty of the people implied a supreme and unitary national government, drawing its authority from all the people equally, rather

---

[311] Wilson, *Works*, vol. 1, p. 112.
[312] Ibid., pp. 170–1, citing Coke, *Institutes*, vol. 4, p. 36; cf. Blackstone, *Commentaries*, vol. 1, p. 156.
[313] Wilson, *Works*, vol. 1, pp. 172–4.
[314] Ibid., vol. 1, pp. 126–47.
[315] Ibid., vol. 1, pp. 77, 81, citing Blackstone, *Commentaries*, vol. 1, p. 157.
[316] Wilson, *Works*, vol. 1, p. 169; cf. McCloskey, Introduction, p. 26.

than a confederate government, resting on the co-operation of independent States. Yet on this central issue the whole problem of framing the
polity of the new republic turned.

The debate on the framing and ratification of the Constitution has been
conventionally reconstructed as a unique and therefore largely self-
contained episode, American in its origins and reference, and explained
in largely functional terms.[317] The Antifederalists' profound aversion to a
national government has been referred to the material interests of democratic agrarians arrayed against Federalist commercial oligarchs, or to
Antifederalist doubts about the viability of republican government for a
large state,[318] or to their distrust of executive power;[319] in the absence of
a reconstruction of the pre-1776 debate over the Blackstonian conception
of sovereignty and its role in the Revolution, the coherence and context
of Antifederalist thought have been difficult to recover.[320]

Yet ideological conflicts over the Constitution proved with embarrassing clarity that the Revolution of 1776 had not emancipated Americans
from the old issues. The millenarian element in colonial discourse had
not of itself shaped a new polity; it had merely damaged the existing one.
The legal legacy of British rule could not easily be escaped. Consequently,
framing a new constitution proved to be a more difficult matter than
destroying the old. George Mason complained:

> The revolt from Great Britain and the formations of our new [state] govern-
> ments at that time, were nothing compared to the great business now before
> us; there was then a certain degree of enthusiasm, which inspired and
> supported the mind; but to view, through the calm, sedate medium of
> reason the influence which the establishment now proposed may have upon
> the happiness or misery of millions yet unborn, is an object of such magni-

---

[317] For a review of recent scholarship and an analysis of other influences on the Federalist
debate, see Daniel Walker Howe, 'Why the Scottish Enlightenment Was Useful to the
Framers of the American Constitution', *Comparative Studies in Society and History* 31 (1989),
572–87; idem, 'Anti-Federalist/Federalist Dialogue and its Implications for Constitutional
Understanding', *Northwestern Law Review* 84 (1989), 1–11; Morgan, *Inventing the People*, pp.
263–87.

[318] Cecilia Kenyon, 'Men of Little Faith: the Anti-Federalists on the Nature of Representative
Government', *WMQ* 12 (1955), 3–43.

[319] Jackson Turner Main, *The Antifederalists: Critics of the Constitution 1781–1788* (Chapel Hill,
1961), pp. 120–9 and passim.

[320] This theme is missing from even the most comprehensive modern account, Herbert
J. Storing (ed.), *The Complete Anti-Federalist* (7 vols., Chicago, 1981), vol. 1, *What The
Anti-Federalists were For*; Blackstone does not feature in such fine studies as Merrill Jensen,
The Articles of Confederation, Jackson Turner Main, *The Sovereign States, 1775–1783* (New
York, 1973) and Jack N. Rakove, *The Beginnings of National Politics*. For an important
exception, though organised around a different intellectual framework, see Greene, *Peri-
pheries and Center*.

tude, as absorbs, and in a manner suspends the operations of the human understanding.[321]

This awesome task was addressed at agonising length by the Convention which sat in Philadelphia from May to September 1787.

One of the key elements largely missing from the debate on the Constitution was an historical perspective which would have sufficiently clearly identified a centralised, unitary republic with the centralised, unitary monarchy it succeeded. The impact of war and revolution had, in some ways, made all things new: monarchy was now an irrelevance, and the Anglican model for America's future was smashed. In a secular republic a unitary, absolute sovereignty could no longer be denounced with the language of Popery and arbitrary power; and a purely functional critique of centralised government proved inconclusive. Without the denominational impetus to schism, the centralising imperative of the common law reasserted itself. The Articles of Confederation had been drawn up and ratified at the beginning of the revolution with very little discussion of the issue of sovereignty, since the Confederation was not intended (except by a few individuals) to be a single republic to which the States' sovereignty was transferred. It was a widespread argument that (following Montesquieu) liberty was to be preserved by a division of sovereignty into small republics, for only in small polities could republicanism be sustained. Thanks to the opposition of anti-Blackstonians like Jefferson (himself in France from 1785 to 1789), the power and governing role of Congress fell into decay after the end of the war; but this opened the States' assemblies to challenges from 'the people'[322] and these pressures finally allowed centralisers to contrive the summoning of the Philadelphia Convention.

'Federal' and 'confederal' were initially synonymous. Partly the problem in 1787 was the increasingly uncertain and diverging meaning of these terms, as Gouverneur Morris (Pennsylvania) pointed out on 30 May: 'foederal', he urged, ought to mean a national government with power to compel obedience.[323] Although 'federal' and 'confederal' were still often used as synonyms, some men now wished to draw a distinction between them. Alexander Hamilton (New York) defined his terms in this way:

> A *federal* Govt. he conceived to mean an association of independent Communities into one. Different Confederacies have different powers, and exercise

---

[321] George Mason to George Mason Jr, 1 June 1787: Max Farrand (ed.), *The Records of the Federal Convention of 1787* (4 vols., New Haven, 1966), vol. 3, p. 32.
[322] Gordon S. Wood, *The Creation of the American Republic 1776–1787* (Chapel Hill, 1969), pp. 354–63.
[323] Farrand (ed.), *Records*, vol. 1, p. 43.

them in different ways . . . Great latitude therefore must be given to the signification of the term.[324]

Rufus King (Massachusetts) 'conceived that the import of the terms 'States' 'Sovereignty' *'national'* 'federal', had been often used & applied in the discussion inaccurately & delusively': the states were, in important ways, already without sovereignty in the Confederation, he argued.[325]

Edmund Randolph (Virginia) listed for his fellow delegates the defects of the existing confederation. They stemmed from its weakness: 'No judge will say that the *confederation* is paramount to a State constitution'; though his desire for a mechanism to give more federal power to larger states than to smaller overrode the objection that 'Sovereignty is an integral Thing – We ought to be one Nation.'[326] This was, indeed, the crucial point. On 30 May Gouverneur Morris used 'federal' in the old sense; he

> explained the distinction between a *federal* and national, supreme, Govt.; the former being a mere compact resting on the good faith of the parties; the latter having a compleat and *compulsive* operation. He contended that in all communities there must be one supreme power, and one only

which, as James Madison (Virginia) pointed out, implied different numbers of representatives from each state, 'as from Counties of different extents within particular States'.[327]

The national legislature needed a power of veto over state legislation, urged Charles Pinckney (South Carolina) on 8 June; 'such a universality of the power was indispensably necessary to render it effectual; that the States must be kept in due subordination to the nation'. James Wilson (Pennsylvania) agreed: 'the surrender of the rights of a federal government' to the States he would regard as 'a surrender of sovereignty'. Federal (i.e. national) sovereignty must be safeguarded:

> In the Establishment of society every man yields his life, his liberty, property & Character to the society. There is no reservation of this sort, that the individual shall be subject to one and exempt from another Law – Indeed we have seen the Legislatures in our own Country deprive the citizen of Life, of Liberty, & property we have seen Attainders, Banishment, & Confiscations. If we mean to establish a national Govt. the States must submit themselves as individuals.

John Dickinson (Delaware) echoed the old debate about internal and external taxation: 'There can be no line of separation dividing the powers of legislation between the State & Genl. Govts. The consequence is inevit-

[324] Ibid., p. 283.
[325] Ibid., pp. 323–4.
[326] Ibid., pp. 26–7 (29 May).
[327] Ibid., pp. 34, 37.

able that there must be a supreme & august national Legislature.'[328]

For the Antifederalists William Paterson (New Jersey) argued against a representation of the States in proportion to their populations: the Federal Convention had authority only to amend the Confederation, not abolish it;

> We are met here as deputies of 13 independent, sovereign states, for federal purposes. Can we consolidate their sovereignty and form one nation, and annihilate the sovereignty of our states who have sent us here for other purposes?

Paterson denied it. He outlined the principle:

> A confederacy [i.e. federal union] supposes sovereignty in the members composing it & sovereignty supposes equality. If we are to be considered as a nation, all State distinctions must be abolished, the whole must be thrown into hotchpot . . . It was once proposed by Galloway & some others that America should be represented in the British Parlt. and then be bound by its laws. America could not have been entitled to more than 1/3 of the no. of Representatives which would fall to the share of G.B. Would American rights & interests have been safe under an authority thus constituted?[329]

The colonists' use of the natural law tradition against the common law formulation of sovereignty carried over to support an appeal against the creation of a sovereign national government. Luther Martin (Maryland) cited Locke, Vattel, Lord Somers and Priestley to prove 'that individuals in a State of nature are equally free & independent'. Then, 'To prove that the case is the same with States till they surrender their equal sovereignty, he read other passages in Locke & Vattel, and also Rutherford:[330] that the States being equal cannot treat or confederate so as to give up an equality of votes without giving up their liberty.'[331]

Alexander Hamilton threw his weight against William Paterson's plan for merely strengthening the Confederation on 18 June, 'being fully convinced, that no amendment of the confederation, leaving the States in possession of their sovereignty could possibly answer the purpose . . . Two Sovereignties cannot co-exist within the same limits.' Reviewing the arguments, he included the historical examples that had interested Bentham.

> The amphyctionic council of Greece had a right to require of its members troops, money and the force of the country. Were they obeyed in the exercise of those powers? Could they preserve the peace of the greater states and

[328] Ibid., pp. 164, 170, 172.
[329] Ibid., pp. 177–9, 182 (9 June).
[330] Thomas Rutherforth, *Institutes of Natural Law* (2 vols., Cambridge, 1754).
[331] Farrand (ed.), *Records*, vol. 1, pp. 437–8.

republics? or where were they obeyed? History shows that their decrees were disregarded, and that the stronger states, regardless of their power, gave law to the lesser.

The 'German Confederacy', united under Charlemagne, had then been impaired by the advance of 'feudal chiefs', which 'reduced the imperial authority to a nominal sovereignty', unable to prevent wars among the electors. Similarly, 'The Swiss cantons have scarce any Union at all, and have been more than once at war with one another – How then are all these evils to be avoided? only by such a compleat sovereignty in the general Govermt. as will turn all the strong principles & passions above mentioned on its side.'[332] So the Convention reported to Congress, enclosing its suggested draft of a constitution: 'It is obviously impracticable in the foederal government of these States, to secure all rights of independent sovereignty to each, and yet provide for the interest and safety of all.'[333]

There were strong grounds for arguing that this constituted an abandonment of the central principle on which the revolution had been fought. It generated a sense of indignation and betrayal which, in tension with the powerful idea of a unitary state, produced a moral dilemma unprecedented in the English-speaking world since 1688 and gave rise to America's one acknowledged classic of political theory. *The Federalist* essays, written by Alexander Hamilton, John Jay and James Madison, appeared in the New York press between 27 October 1787 and 2 April 1788 with the intention of countering a rising tide of anti-Federal writing and recommending to the people of New York the Constitution just submitted to Congress. In these essays the anonymous authors rehearsed for a wider public many of the arguments that had been urged in the Philadelphia Convention behind closed doors and under an order of secrecy.

They initially and too candidly framed the choice as a stark alternative between 'one foederal Government' and a division into 'distinct confederacies or sovereignties', each of which 'will be *distinct nations*'.[334] The idea of a confederacy as an equal association of States in which the central government dealt only with State governments, not with their inhabitants individually, was an 'arbitrary' scheme, insisted *The Federalist*: most such governments had indeed operated in that manner, but there had been 'extensive exceptions' which proved that there was 'no absolute rule on the subject'. The historic examples were again rehearsed (the Amphyctionic Council, the Achaean league, the German empire, Switzerland);

---

[332] Ibid., pp. 283–7, 296, 302–3, 319.
[333] Federal Convention to Congress, 17 Sept. 1787, in Farrand (ed.), *Records*, vol. 2, p. 666.
[334] *The Federalist*, ed. Jacob E. Cooke (Middletown, Conn., 1961), pp. 8 (no. 2), 26 (no. 5).

but where Bentham used them as evidence of the feasibility of divided sovereignty, *The Federalist* used them to prove its weakness:

> The history of Germany is a history of wars between the Emperor and the Princes and States; of wars among the Princes and States themselves; of the licentiousness of the strong, and the oppression of the weak; of foreign intrusions, and foreign intrigues; of requisitions of men and money, disregarded, or partially complied with; of attempts to enforce them, altogether abortive, or attended with slaughter and desolation, involving the innocent with the guilty; of general imbecility, confusion and misery.[335]

As the extremely sensitive nature of the issue became clear, successive issues of *The Federalist* began to evade or disguise the point by talk of mixed or shared sovereignty, a doctrine which Madison privately regarded as 'absurd and self-contradictory'.[336] Rather than admit his real intentions, the new Constitution had to be smuggled through as if it were essentially like the old:

> The proposed Constitution, so far from implying an abolition of the State Governments, makes them constituent parts of the national sovereignty by allowing them a direct representation in the Senate, and leaves in their possession certain exclusive and very important portions of sovereign power.[337]

Equal voting by States in the Senate would preserve States' rights; from this and other causes, the central government 'appears to be of a mixed character presenting at least as many *federal* as *national* features'.[338] But this was not what the authors really meant, and their real beliefs sometimes slipped out. They adhered to the idea of indivisible sovereignty, which entailed that Antifederalists 'cherish with blind devotion the political monster of an *imperium in imperio*'. The Constitution explicitly made itself and federal law 'the supreme law of the land', overriding State constitutions and legislation; otherwise, the new nation would have been 'a monster in which the head was under the direction of the members'. The President would necessarily be the commander in chief of the armed forces, just as Blackstone had recognised the same prerogative in the king.[339] *The Federalist* defined law in Blackstonian terms as command; 'Government implies the power of making laws'. Each nation must con-

---

[335] Ibid., pp. 110–23 (nos. 18, 19). For the misrepresentation of German history by the authors of *The Federalist*, see Helmut Neuhaus, 'The Federal Principle and the Holy Roman Empire', in Hermann Wellenreuther (ed.), *German and American Constitutional Thought: Contexts, Interaction, and Historical Realities* (New York, 1990), pp. 27–49.

[336] Pole, 'The Politics of the Word 'State' ', p. 9.

[337] *The Federalist*, p. 55 (no. 9).

[338] Ibid., p. 255 (no. 39).

[339] Ibid., p. 465 (no. 69).

tain one court with final jurisdiction.[340] The national government must
have the power to raise revenue: the Antifederalists' distinction between
internal and external taxation was invalid.[341] All these characteristics were
wholly Blackstonian. The Revolution was not what it claimed to be in
this key respect: Americans' use of natural law tropes as a critique of
the common-law sovereign had, after all, been only skin deep. American
revolutionaries' use of natural rights was indeed devastating in its results;
but it was temporary, for political argument in the new republic quickly
reverted to controversy over the specific meaning of a written constitution,
and it was to a large degree cosmetic, for it redescribed and derived its
force from the idea of fundamental law within colonial denominational
traditions.

Nor had natural-rights discourse entailed much real knowledge of how
continental European polities reflected their juristic traditions. Once the
Revolution had been won, Americans lapsed back into their familiar den-
igration of Roman law as akin to Popery. Americans' own use of the key
term therefore took on a new meaning. The term 'federal' was subject to
a 'deft and sudden abduction': during the years 1787–8, 'a word clearly
connoting decentralisation, state supremacy and particularism in current
politics mysteriously emerged from the Federal convention as the designation of a party devoted to the idea of consolidation and delocalisation'.[342]
At the time of the debates on the Union with Scotland, Englishmen could
still use the term 'federal' to mean a loose association of relatively independent parts. Now, contemplating the new republic, they increasingly
saw a federal union as one in which those parts were drawn inexorably
into a new unitary state. Only in continental Europe did the old usage
still dominate and 'federal' mean a division, not an amalgamation, of
authority.[343]

Federalists and Antifederalists, and their historical exponents, each
sought to ground their case in the prior existence of the agency of government, central or local, which they championed. Neither argument was a
wholly adequate description of the historical processes at work. As legal
authority broke down in the Revolution, the question of allegiance and
sovereignty was thrown into flux. National sovereignty in the name of
'the people', expressed in the Continental Congress, did not precede and
create State sovereignty; but neither did State sovereignty, the legacy of
the legislative separateness of each colony, precede and create national

---

[340] Ibid., pp. 93, 95, 143, 306, 542 (nos. 15, 22, 44, 81).
[341] Ibid., p. 190 (no. 30).
[342] Schechter, 'Early History of the Tradition of the Constitution', 714.
[343] It was later still that the pressures of bureaucratic centralisation overrode and reversed
this continental European usage.

sovereignty.[344] Rather, both came into existence together in the form of groups of men in different institutional settings laying claims to authority in the wake of the withdrawal of British rule. Although Federalists and Antifederalists sought to fill a gap so created, it was British rule that defined the shape of the problem.

Antifederalists reacted against the proposed Constitution with a rhetoric whose extremism matched that of 1776. Elbridge Gerry compared the issues of 1788 with those of 1776, and stigmatised the Constitution by raising fears of centralised power: the new federal government would be 'a consolidated fabrick of aristocratick tyranny'; its advocates 'tell us republicanism is dwindled into theory – that we are incapable of enjoying our liberties – and that we must have a master'. The proposed federal constitution would be only a 'Republican *form* of government, founded on the principles of monarchy'.[345] But this ancient rhetoric warning against absolute power in the hands of the executive was strangely ineffective in its new post-revolutionary context.

A more powerful defence was mounted by the individual States. Did the new Constitution destroy State sovereignty? Yet it was possible, by a play on definitions, to deny it. John Dickinson argued that there was no reason to expect that the Federal government would so destroy the States;

> it requires an extinction of *the principle of all society*: for, the subordinate sovereignties, or, in other words, the *undelegated rights* of the several *states*, in a *confederation*, stand upon the very same foundation with the *undelegated rights* of *individuals* in a *society*, the *federal sovereign will* being *composed* of the *subordinate sovereign wills* of the several confederated states.[346]

So natural rights doctrine, once held to be embodied in the new republic, could be used to justify any of the republic's actions. It was now even possible openly to appeal to the 'so much boasted British form of government' in recommending the newly-drafted Constitution, since it could be argued that 'we did not dissolve our connection with that country so much on account of its constitution, as the perversion and mal-administration of it'. Once reformed, especially by breaking the link of Church and State and eliminating the hereditary principle, America could enjoy all the other benefits of the British Constitution.[347]

Breaking the Anglican, monarchical nexus meant that the new Consti-

---

[344] Greene, *Peripheries and Center*, pp. 178–80.

[345] [Elbridge Gerry], *Observations On the new Constitution, and on the Federal and State Conventions. By a Columbian Patriot* [Boston, 1788], pp. 3, 5, 14.

[346] [John Dickinson], *The Letters of Fabius, in 1788, on the Federal Constitution* (Wilmington, 1797), p. 23 (originally newspaper articles of 1788).

[347] [Tench Coxe], *An Examination of the Constitution for the United States of America* (Philadelphia, 1788), pp. 5–6.

tution could be shielded from historical analysis by the doctrine of American exceptionalism. This represented no shallow propaganda trick; it accompanied a serious attempt to Americanise the law of the new nation, to reconstruct the common law legacy in accordance with the principles of the revolution.[348] It was a campaign destined to enjoy only partial success, as the record of a key state revealed. On 15 November 1776, the General Assembly of Virginia appointed a committee including Thomas Jefferson, charged with reforming state laws to bring them into line with republican principles and eliminate all traces of monarchy. They agreed quickly on those items closest to Jefferson's heart, the abolition of English land law, especially the principles of primogeniture and entail, and the Statute on Religious Freedom, which destroyed the established status of the Church of England. More difficult was whether, as Edmund Pendleton proposed, the committee should draw up a new compendium of Virginia law on the model of Justinian, Bracton and Blackstone; but the scale and difficulty of the task deterred the committee. Their recommendations were for piecemeal reforms, leaving the English common law as the basic source. Jefferson recorded that, in respect of a bill on punishments, 'it gave me great satisfaction to find that in general I had only to reduce the law to its ancient Saxon condition, stripping it of all the innovations and rigorisms of subsequent times, to make it what it should be'.[349] But this bill eventually failed when presented to the Assembly in 1786, so that, as Madison reported, 'Our old bloody code is by this event fully restored.'[350]

If the enlightened co-operation of the *bienpensants* of 1776 failed to transform the criminal law, public law too remained in thrall to English precedents.[351] Blackstone's *Commentaries* therefore enjoyed a huge vogue in the new nation, and eventually prompted the Deist St George Tucker to attempt to defuse them by publishing a revised version, stripped, as he thought, of its unacceptable implications.[352] It was too late. An observer

[348] See, in general, William E. Nelson, *Americanisation of the Common Law: The Impact of Legal Change on Massachusetts Society, 1760–1830* (Cambridge, Mass., 1975) and Morton J. Horwitz, *The Transformation of American Law 1780–1860* (Cambridge, Mass., 1977).

[349] Edward Dumbauld, *Thomas Jefferson and the Law* (Norman, Oklahoma, 1978), pp. 132–5. It seems that primogeniture and entail were exceptional and unimportant in Virginian society, and still less important in other colonies: ibid., pp. 152, 243 n. 99; C. Ray Keim, 'Primogeniture and Entail in Colonial Virginia', *WMQ* 25 (1968), 545–86. But they played a major part in Jefferson's heated imagination as constitutive elements of English tyranny.

[350] Dumbauld, *Jefferson*, p. 138.

[351] For the large currency of English law after independence, see Elizabeth Gaspar Brown, *British Statutes in American Law 1776–1836* (Ann Arbor, 1964).

[352] Craig Klafter, 'Reason over Precedents: The Origins of American Legal Thought' (Oxford D.Phil. thesis, 1990).

like Jefferson, sensitive to the issues involved, saw and (independently of the critiques of Blackstone offered by Bentham or Priestley) deplored the influence of the *Commentaries*. In 1826 he reminded Madison that the professor of law to be appointed at the University of Virginia had to be of politically correct views:

> You will recollect that before the revolution, Coke [upon] Littleton was the universal elementary book of law students, and a sounder whig never wrote, nor of profounder learning in the orthodox doctrines of the British constitution, or in what were called English liberties. You remember also that our lawyers were then all whigs. But when his black-letter text, and uncouth but cunning learning got out of fashion, and the honied Mansfieldism[353] of Blackstone became the student's hornbook, from that moment, that profession (the nursery of our Congress) began to slide into toryism, and nearly all the young brood of lawyers now are of that hue. They suppose themselves, indeed, to be whigs, because they no longer know what whigism or republicanism means.[354]

The outcome was not at once obvious. The new nation could indeed claim, echoing *The Federalist*, that it possessed (to use the new vocabulary) both federal and confederal elements; but the course of events, confirmed by a second civil war in the 1860s, was to prove that the confederal element was ultimately subordinate.[355] The division of powers between President, Congress, the Supreme Court and the States endowed the republic with a system of government which was merely cumbersome, not one in which sovereignty was effectively divided. The American Revolution had not been as carefully legalistic as its advocates had claimed. It had begun amid expressions of the most lofty ideals; but it was soon dragged back to the compromises, expediencies and necessities of daily politics (if indeed it had ever left them). It was because the Revolution was at its ideological heart a war of religion that the federal experiment failed: the theological setting of the argument over sovereignty prevented Americans from exploiting those rival traditions, tainted as they thought by Roman Catholicism, within which authority might have

---

[353] William Murray (1705–93), 1st Earl of Mansfield, of a Jacobite family and loyalty when young, Lord Chief Justice 1756–d., an opponent of the American Revolution.

[354] Jefferson to James Madison, 17 Feb. 1826, in Jefferson, *Writings* (Ford), vol. 10, p. 375; Julius S. Waterman, 'Thomas Jefferson and Blackstone's Commentaries' in David H. Flaherty (ed.), *Essays in the History of Early American Law* (Chapel Hill, 1969), pp. 451–88.

[355] The federal or confederal significance of the Constitution was an unresolved issue in the early decades of the nineteenth century, Jefferson's presidency seeing an important swing away from central power; this was definitively reversed in the 1860s. For an argument that the Antifederalist movement rested on the enormous growth in evangelical sects (Baptists, Methodists) from the 1780s, see Stephen A. Marini, 'Political Theologies of the American Revolution' (forthcoming).

been lastingly divided. The unitary republican state, too, could now be expressed in idealistic terms. The Federalists, to secure the adoption of the Constitution, had argued, and argued indelibly, that the power of the people was 'paramount to every constitution, inalienable in its nature, and indefinite in its extent'.[356] Sovereignty in the United States therefore proved to be as transcendent and absolute, as despotic and uncontrollable as in the United Kingdom; the final irony of the American Revolution was that Sir William Blackstone's analysis prevailed in the end.[357]

---

[356] Quoted in Morgan, *Inventing the People*, p. 281. It was similarly argued by Federalists that since the sovereign was the people collectively, a bill of rights would be a contradiction in terms, the whole Constitution taking its place (ibid., p. 283), the same argument which explained to Englishmen why a bill of rights was a solecism within the Blackstonian sovereign state.

[357] For a rare anticipation of this point, see H. J. Laski, *The Foundations of Sovereignty and Other Essays* (London, 1931), pp. 126–30. Laski did not appreciate that the American Revolution had been a protest against this legal formulation.

2

The conflict between denominations: the religious identity of early modern societies

If national identity in early-modern societies was determined by the modes of discourse hegemonic within them, eighteenth-century England had few powerful alternatives to its Anglican, monarchical self-image. It has rightly been observed that 'there existed from before 1662 until sometime after 1800 a coherent and widely accepted body of establishment social theory rooted in catholic ecclesiology, ultimately biblical in origin, transmitted unimpaired to the post-Reformation Church of England, and expressed most authoritatively in the *Book of Common Prayer*'.[1] The centrality of the hierarchical and hereditary ethos and of the Anglican clergy have led historians to characterise eighteenth-century England as an 'ancien régime' and 'a confessional state'.[2] It was a social formation which proved consistent with, indeed was reinforced by, growing agrarian and commercial prosperity, a proliferating print culture, the development of state bureaucracies and military power; but in respect of political languages, few inconsistent alternatives to this hegemonic discourse of the Anglican, monarchical, hereditary order were available.

The discourse of commercial prosperity did not originate or proliferate

[1] 'Hence there is a clear conceptual nexus running from the Trinity and orthodox christology through Pauline soteriology, catholic ecclesiology, post-Reformation ecclesiastical and civil polity, to the political doctrines arising from and conveniently labelled by the 'grand principle of subordination' ': A. M. C. Waterman, 'The Nexus between Theology and Political Doctrine in Church and Dissent', in Knud Haakonssen (ed.), *Enlightenment and Rational Dissent* (forthcoming). Waterman provides the clearest analysis available of this nexus, although I would add that eighteenth-century Anglicans did believe that they derived their ecclesiastical polity from their ecclesiology.

[2] For both terms, see Linda Colley, 'Whose Nation? Class and National Consciousness in Britain 1750–1830', *P&P* 113 (1986), 107. For an exploration of this characterisation of eighteenth-century Ireland, see C. D. A. Leighton, *Catholicism in a Protestant Kingdom: A Study of the Irish Ancien Regime* (London, 1993).

in the 1760s. It was already an old one, and had proved remarkably consistent with other discourses: the merchant community was royalist and republican, Christian and Jew, Anglican and Dissenter, English, Dutch and Huguenot.[3] The discourses of ancient constitutionalism and natural rights were similarly employed by every interest group, though used in different ways by each: all sides successfully sought to use the catch-words of the day. The discourses which proved most resistant to this appropriation by established authority were, of course, denominational; and in that respect colonial societies differed most profoundly both from each other and from their mother country. England since the Reformation had witnessed a variety of competing bids by men within its Church seeking to use the machinery of state to impose a uniform version of their vision of the truth: the Puritan enterprise of the late sixteenth century did not obviously come to an end with the Presbyterian regime of the 1650s. With the Restoration, it was not at once clear that the policy referred to as comprehension could not incorporate this strand of orderly if anti-prelatical discourse. Rigid Presbyterians were amazed as events in the early 1660s took a very different direction, and the Act of Uniformity of 1662 gave exclusive legal authority to the liturgy, theology, ecclesiastical polity, civil polity and social teaching summed up in the *Book of Common Prayer*. Religious conflict was henceforth set in denominational moulds, which failed attempts at comprehension and substantial but partial toleration after 1688 failed to break. Dissent now more widely assumed a sectarian character, definitively composed of gathered churches which accepted their status as separate sects rather than as pressure groups within, and seeking to reform, a universal Church.

This pattern of discourse, set in the 1660s, challenged but defended in the 1680s, remained substantially unrevised in England until the 1830s. The process of its revision in that decade was partly political.[4] Partly, too, it went with a momentous reconceptualisation of political and social life which divided Victorian England from what soon came to be seen, and via new categories to be condemned, as an old order.[5] The historical recovery of that old order requires the deletion from our vocabulary of a whole series of terms, invented or given new meanings in the early nine-

---

[3] Gary S. De Krey, *A Fractured Society: The Politics of London in the First Age of Party 1688–1715* (Oxford, 1985), pp. 74–120; Robert Brenner, 'The Civil War Politics of London's Merchant Community', *P&P* 58 (1973), 53–107.

[4] Clark, *English Society 1688–1832*, chapter 6.

[5] It has been rightly observed by J. G. A. Pocock that the term '*ancien*' in '*ancien régime*' means 'former', not 'old' as in, for example, the 'ancient constitution'. It is argued here that the world before 1832 (or 1776) was not distinguished by archaism or anachronism from that which came after. The reverse is closer to the truth.

teenth century, which, as now used, obscure much of what was fundamentally different about early-modern consciousness. Such a re-ordering is more than an exchange of synonyms: it reveals how idioms of political discourse worked differently within the 'old society' both in Britain and America, and how religion in the form of denominational discourse was able to play a much larger role than the thesis of natural and progressive secularisation predicts.

Most of the important innovations in political vocabulary emerged from within Britain and, specifically, from England. The American Revolution cannot be ascribed to some prior colonial invention of a modern and newly-powerful language of liberty: none such emerged.[6] The adjective 'radical' (meaning from the root, fundamental) was long familiar in English discourse, and did not become joined in the phrase 'radical reform' until the 1790s; 'radical reformer' had been shortened to the substantive, 'a radical', only by c. 1802. When these usages were adopted in the United States in the 1810s, they initially referred to English politics, not to a native American tradition. 'Radicalism' followed these earlier usages, in England in c. 1820, in the USA only in the 1830s.[7] 'Liberal' was, similarly, a familiar eighteenth-century adjective (meaning open, generous) which did not emerge in its substantive form, 'a liberal', until the rivalry of the Spanish political parties, *serviles* and *liberals*, was taken up first into French, then into English, with the Peninsular War; in the United States its earliest usage has been traced to 1839. 'Liberalism' has been identified in England from 1819; in early-nineteenth-century America it does not appear to have registered.[8]

Significant innovations in political vocabulary long continued to emanate from England; they enjoyed no easy or automatic currency in Amer-

---

[6] Noah Webster's *A Compendious Dictionary of the English Language* (Hartford, Conn., 1806) gives 'liberal' in the conventional eighteenth-century definition as an adjective, meaning 'generous, bountiful, free, genteel', but not as a noun; 'liberalism' too is absent. 'Radical' as an adjective is given as 'original, implanted by nature, inborn', and as a noun meaning 'a radical word, root, primary element', but similarly without political meaning. 'Radicalism' and 'individualism' are absent. No new political meanings are added to these terms even in Webster's much larger *A Dictionary of the English Language* (2 vols., New York, 1828; repr. 3 vols., London, 1832).

[7] The introduction of the anachronistic term 'radicalism' has its effect on the historiography (e.g. Bradley, *Religion*, p. 137) by implying the existence of a common denominator between orthodox and heterodox, Anglican and Dissenter, so that radicalism's theoretical roots must be in that shared and presumably secular feature. The deletion of such anachronistic terms reveals how heterodox Christology and ecclesiastical polity, both among Anglicans and Dissenters, could act to promote political mobilisation and define eighteenth-century ideologies.

[8] *Oxford English Dictionary*; Hans Sperber and Travis Trittschuh, *American Political Terms: An Historical Dictionary* (Detroit, 1962).

ica.[9] 'Socialist' as a noun has been traced in England only to 1827, and 'socialism' did not follow until 1837. 'Industry' before about the 1840s still meant the virtue of hard work rather than a particular form of manufacturing (the term 'capitalism' has similarly been dated only from 1854). 'Industrialism' (1831) was followed by the modern sense of 'exploitation' (1841), but 'industrial revolution' only arrived in the 1880s. 'Individualism' was imported into England by translation from the French in 1840 and taken up as an antithesis to 'socialism'; 'communist' and 'communism' equally date from 1840, but 'collectivism' waited until 1880 and 'egalitarian' until 1885.[10] A further characteristic distinguished the 'old society' from the new: the weakness of those institutions which, in a later age, were to be redefined as intermediate agencies. Here again, language provides a clue to a quite different understanding of the world. Readers of Alexander Cruden's definitive *Concordance* (1738, and many later editions) would find no Biblical anticipations of the twentieth-century usages of 'community', 'class' or 'society'. Instead of 'classes' or 'communities', the basic units of Anglican thought were families and denominations, pictured in a Providential hierarchy of ranks, orders and degrees: secular political ideologies had no place in this world.

Equally, the old order was not defended by 'conservatives'. 'Conservatism' was a response to English circumstance, those crucial party-political changes which came in 1828–32. The repeal of the Test and Corporation Acts in 1828, and Catholic Emancipation in 1829, shattered the coalition which had been in office for most of the previous half century. 'Tory', by the late 1820s, signified the old Anglican political theology, the exclusive link of Church and State, defended at Westminster by a loose and unstructured governing coalition assembled by the crown. Now the old ideology had been made irrelevant by the final, sweeping, victory of the Whigs; party discipline and an official party name suddenly became a necessity for a group newly out of office. A new, more neutral, more pragmatic title was felt by some to be appropriate for a new organisation. In 1830 an anonymous writer in the *Quarterly Review* (now identified as John Miller of Lincoln's Inn) famously sought to argue for continuity in declaring his loyalty to 'what is called the Tory, and which might with

[9] For a contrasting claim of the novelty of colonial political language see Bailyn, *Ideological Origins*, p. 161.

[10] Anna Bezanson, 'The Early Use of the Term Industrial Revolution', *Quarterly Journal of Economics* 36 (1922), 343–9; Arthur E. Bestor, 'The Evolution of the Socialist Vocabulary', *Journal of the History of Ideas* 9 (1948), 259–302. Bestor illustrates the brief lives of many other new terms, since deceased: guarantism, pantisocracy, serigermy, phalanstery. Equally with liberalism, radicalism and conservatism, these terms do not identify timeless dispositions.

more propriety be called the Conservative, party'. Others, like Robert Peel, instinctively hostile to the Ultras of 1832, intended a clearer break from old Anglican commitments; he sought to ground political action on secular expediency. 'Conservatism' was a deliberate invention in this new world, and can be traced only from its use by Thomas Arnold in 1835.[11]

It quickly gained currency as the name of the creed of the newly-organised Conservative party. By 1844, the Tory sympathiser Benjamin Disraeli could condemn the shortcomings of the new doctrine in *Coningsby*: Peel's Tamworth Manifesto of 1834 'was an attempt to construct a party without principles . . . Conservatism discards Prescription, shrinks from Principle, disavows Progress; having rejected all respect for Antiquity, it offers no redress for the Present, and makes no preparation for the Future.'[12] In his Preface to the fifth edition of 1849, Disraeli made his intention clear: 'in considering the Tory scheme, the author recognised in the CHURCH the most powerful agent in the previous development of England, and the most efficient means of that renovation of the national spirit at which he aimed'. It was too late: Anglican hegemony had been destroyed. Despite Disraeli's critique, the term 'conservatism' therefore took on the appearance of self-evidence, as if it were an unchanging attitude to politics. Yet it was as much a specific formation as any of the others, and in Peel's formulation it would have seemed unfamiliar and unappealing to the eighteenth-century ruling elite. Such men neither discarded prescription, nor shrank from principle, nor disavowed progress. Their problems were differently defined. The American Revolution, like other political confrontations in the English-speaking world, was not a conflict between 'conservatism' and 'radicalism'. 'Lockeian liberalism' and 'bourgeois radicalism' were terms devised in a later age: they were unknown to the transatlantic Englishmen of the seventeenth and eighteenth centuries, and played no part in the political conflicts discussed here. The intellectual origins of those conflicts must be sought elsewhere.

The analysis of discourse has revealed how such reifications as 'radicalism', 'liberalism' and 'conservatism' were coined in the 1810s, 20s or 30s to address specific tactical needs of political and social polemic in those decades. Those terms, like others, were specific in meaning and period, not eternal verities of timeless application. This insight simplifies the historical problem: no longer must a complex mix of economic and social

---

[11] *Oxford English Dictionary; Quarterly Review* (January 1830), 276; Robert Stewart, *The Foundation of the Conservative Party 1830–1867* (London, 1978), p. 69; Wilfred S. Dowden (ed.), *The Journal of Thomas Moore* (6 vols., Newark, 1983–91), vol. 3, p. 1287; James J. Sack, *From Jacobite to Conservative: Reaction and Orthodoxy in Britain, c. 1760–1832* (Cambridge, 1993), p. 5.

[12] Benjamin Disraeli, *Coningsby*, book 2, chapter 5.

causes be devised to account for the confused emergence of eighteenth-century 'radicalism'. The distinctive identity of groups and doctrines need no longer be submerged in order to give historiographical substance to this nebulous anticipation of a nineteenth-century category. Once the analysis of terms has established that radicals and radicalism did not yet exist, the way is clear to take seriously those groups and doctrines whose political languages are undoubted.[13] Chief among them were the legal codes, and the rival churches, of western Christianity.

If the classic terms of political analysis devised in the early nineteenth century are stripped away, the conflict of denominations assumes a new importance. From being merely the leading theme of denominational history (either an embarrassing obstacle to ecumenism or a defining myth of sectarian origins), the conflict among different persuasions of Christians is revealed as a chief determinant of the idioms of discourse within which all political conflicts were articulated.[14] These survivals had consequences for language which in turn had political implications. If millennial eschatology survived long into the eighteenth century for colonial Americans, so too did the ancient exegetical device of typology, employed, as in past centuries, to define that vision. Typology had, indeed, been transformed since the seventeenth century 'from a literal and historical exegesis of Scripture to an allegorical symbolism', but this evolution only restored to it 'the authority of prophecy'.[15] The rich symbolism of the era of the American Revolution did not emerge from nowhere; nor was it without its political effects.

Denominational conflict was, furthermore, a determinant which mobilised far larger numbers of men than any secular ideology was to do in later centuries. This mobilisation allowed churchmen to emphasise that the state was substantially, not merely nominally, Anglican. It was not, argued Bishop Horsley, the requirement to take the oaths of allegiance and supremacy, and subscribe the declaration against transubstantiation, that kept Roman Catholics out of the House of Commons.

---

[13] The thesis advanced here is not, therefore, that theological heterodoxy was the sole cause of 'political radicalism', but that political 'radicalism' had not yet been conceptualised as anything distinct from the intellectual structures of disaffection within the 'old society'. It was theological heterodoxy, therefore, which generated the categories which in England underpinned new understandings of democratic representation: Clark, *English Society 1688–1832*, chapter 5; cf. Waterman, 'The Nexus between Theology and Political Doctrine'.

[14] Sidney E. Mead, 'Denominationalism: The Shape of Protestantism in America', *Church History* 23 (1954), 291–320; Timothy L. Smith, 'Congregation, State, and Denomination: The Forming of the American Religious Structure', *WMQ* 25 (1968), 155–76.

[15] Mason I. Lowance, Jr, 'Typology and Millennial Eschatology in Early New England', in Earl Miner (ed.), *Literary Uses of Typology from the Late Middle Ages to the Present* (Princeton, 1977), pp. 228–73, at 228.

The notoriety of their Popery, and the dread and abhorrence of the principles of the church of Rome, which the people of this country in general
entertain, have been the real, oaths and declarations have been only the
apparent means of their exclusion from the House of Commons . . . so great,
even in these times of indifference, is the dread of Popery, that were a
reputed Papist to become a candidate to represent the most corrupt borough
in the kingdom, it would be impossible that he should carry his election.[16]

Anti-catholicism was sufficiently established for an English audience.
It could be tapped on the level of popular prejudice. It could also be
invoked in scholarly renditions. Bishop Stillingfleet

> hath clearly *prov'd*, and sufficiently *expos'd*, the *Fanaticism of the Romish
> Church*, in his *Incomparable Discourse concerning their Idolatry*; hath shewn to
> what *Extravagant heights* it has been carried, how peculiarly *encouraged by the
> Popes*; hath been the foundation of their several *Religious Orders, and Societies*;
> and the *engine* for introducing their *false, superstitious, and Idolatrous Doctrines,
> and Practises*.

Since 'the *spirit of Enthusiasm* is always the same', it could seem credible
to apply the same stigma to other sects also.[17]

Methodists likewise were credited with a defining style: 'affected
phrases, fantastical and unintelligible notions, whimsical strictnesses,
loud exclamations against some trifling and indifferent things', religious
melancholy, antipathy to fine clothes and bodily cleanliness, innocent
recreations and personal wealth; their restless urge to travel, desire to
suffer persecution and physical mortification; their stress on the need for
sudden conversion, claim of an assurance of salvation, and belief in the
immediate presence of Christ; their '*extraordinary Inspiration*' in preaching
and boasts of '*immediate Revelation*' – all these could be documented from
the recent writings of the Methodists, and matched, by Anglican scholarship, with strikingly similar passages from lives of the saints and martyrs
of the Roman Church.[18]

Bishop Lavington did not discuss the social impact of Methodism,
and ignored also the greatly enhanced role of religious revivalism in the
American colonies. He might, however, have found confirmation in a
recent tract by colonial America's greatest theologian. Jonathan Edwards,

---

[16] [Samuel Horsley], *A Review of the Case of the Protestant Dissenters; with reference to the Corporation
and Test Acts* (London, 1790), pp. 7–8.

[17] [George Lavington], *The Enthusiasm of Methodists and Papists, compar'd* (3 parts, London,
1749–51), Part I, Preface, sigs. A1v, A2r.

[18] [Lavington], *Enthusiasm of Methodists and Papists*, Part I, pp. 18, 20, 22, 24, 26–7, 40, 43,
50, 61, 67. Lavington's massive compendium was reprinted in Boston in 1750, shortly
following the 1749 Philadelphia reprint of George Whitefield's defence, *Some Remarks on a
Pamphlet, Entituled, The Enthusiasm of Methodists and Papists compar'd* (London, 1749). Lavington's identification of idioms of discourse was clearly relevant for colonists also.

commending the religious revivals in New England later known as the Great Awakening,[19] admitted that the Devil had formerly subverted such movements by a design 'to improve the indiscreet Zeal of Christians, to drive them into those three Extremes, of *Enthusiasm, Superstition,* and *Severity towards Opposers*', to such effect that 'Spiritual Pride disposes to speak of other Persons Sins, their Enmity against GOD and his People, the miserable Delusion of Hypocrites and their Enmity against vital Piety, and the Deadness of some Saints, with Bitterness, or with Laughter and Levity, and an Air of Contempt.' These attitudes had a profound impact on discourse: such zealots would

> speak of almost every Thing that they see amiss in others, in the most harsh, severe and terrible Language. 'Tis frequent with them to say of others Opinions or Conduct or Advice, or of their Coldness, their Silence, their Caution, their Moderation, and their Prudence, and many other Things that appear in them, that they are from the Devil, or from Hell; that such a Thing is devilish or hellish or cursed, and that such Persons are serving the Devil or the Devil is in them, that they are Soul-Murtherers and the like; so that the words *Devil* and *Hell* are almost continually in their Mouths. And such Kind of Language they will commonly use, not only towards wicked Men, but towards them that they themselves allow to be the true Children of GOD, and also towards Ministers of the Gospel and others that are very much their Superiours.[20]

It was the heightened language of 1776, already fully formed as a language of spiritual liberty.

With remarkable prescience, Edwards offered a taxonomy of the political dispositions of 1776 foreshadowed in the spirituality of 1742.

> Spiritual Pride is very apt to suspect others . . . Spiritual Pride commonly occasions a certain Stiffness and Inflexibility in Persons, in their own Judgement and their own Ways . . . Spiritual Pride disposes Persons to affect Separation . . . Spiritual Pride takes great Notice of Opposition and Injuries that are received, and is apt to be often speaking of them, and to be much in taking Notice of the Aggravations of 'em, either with an Air of Bitterness or Contempt . . . Another Effect of spiritual Pride is a certain unsuitable

---

[19] For an argument of the 'fundamental transformation of popular consciousness' as a result of the novel language and rhetoric of religious revivalism, 'an innovative style of communications that redefined the social context in which public address took place', see Harry S. Stout, 'Religion, Communications, and the Ideological Origins of the American Revolution', *WMQ* 34 (1977), 519–41. Although this point is to be accepted, the present work supplements it with the contention that attacks on 'traditional conceptions of order, hierarchy, and deference' did not depend on revivalism alone, but were implicit in many strands of denominational discourse and could, in circumstances explored here, be made explicit.

[20] Jonathan Edwards, *Some Thoughts Concerning the present Revival of Religion in New-England* (Boston, 1742), pp. 190–1, 202, 204.

and self-confident Boldness before GOD and Men . . . It oftentimes makes it natural to Persons so to act and speak, as tho' it in a special Manner belong'd to them to be taken Notice of and much regarded.[21]

These dispositions proved persistent in both Britain and America. So apt did Lavington's picture of the psychological roots of Dissenting and Papist enthusiasm seem to Anglicans that it was republished by a Cornish vicar, Richard Polwhele, in 1820, reinforced by a 312-page Introduction reviewing the phenomenon since Lavington's day and displaying much less discrimination about its theological distinctions.[22] Polwhele accepted the tripartite classification of the *Report from the Clergy of a District in the Diocese of Lincoln*, but, again, with less charity towards its first innocuous category of occasional conformists: they too, argued Polwhele, promoted schism in the Church.[23] Polwhele agreed with Bishop Randolph in his *Charge* of 1808: 'By their constant inculcation of faith, as something opposed to good works, these Enthusiasts remove the only sure ground of moral conduct.'[24] According to Randolph, the enthusiasts' invention of the need for an adult experience of Conversion was meant to diminish the significance both of regeneration through infant baptism and of repentance; enthusiasts' over-emphasis on the legitimate doctrine of justification by faith diminished the significance of daily practical morality.[25] Enthusiasts' talk was of 'the grace of God, and the mercies of his covenant; (for such is their language) a covenant, as they preposterously call it, without conditions; flattering language indeed for the profligate and corrupt . . .'[26]

Apart from the long list of objections to forms and ceremonies, Dissenters in turn were alienated by the tone of the Church of England. Even the resolutely orthodox historians of Nonconformity concluded their catalogue of the corruptions of Anglicanism: 'After the enumeration of so many subjects of complaint, I must add, that I strongly object to the harsh, rigid, severe, and utterly unaccommodating spirit of the church of England.' Its denunciations were personified:

> I am the church of England: and it is universally acknowledged, that a more venerable matron does not exist. My sons tell me that I derive my

---

[21] Edwards, *Revival of Religion*, pp. 202, 208–9, 212, 216, 218.

[22] Polwhele pointed out the difference between Calvinist and Arminian Methodists, but neglected it on the grounds that 'Men of sense may deem it ridiculous to define at all, the religion of enthusiasts and hypocrites': R. Polwhele (ed.), *The Enthusiasm of Methodists and Papists Compared* (2nd edn., London, 1833), p. xxvi.

[23] Ibid., pp. lxxxv–lxxxix; for the *Report*, see p. 182–3 below.

[24] Ibid., p. xcix; John Randolph, *A Charge Delivered to the Clergy of the Diocese of Bangor* (Bangor, 1808).

[25] Ibid., pp. 16–19.

[26] Ibid., pp. 21–2.

descent by a pure and uninterrupted succession from the apostles: and they well know what they say, for none are better qualified, by their talents and learning, to investigate the subject. Such language as yours shocks me, and makes me lose all patience. I daily hear it asserted, that I am the purest church in Christendom, and that everything appertaining to me is primitive and apostolical; in short, just as it should be. It is not only my younger children, the rectors, vicars, and curates who say, so, but my elder sons, archbishops, bishops, and deans. They are continually saying so; and I believe them, for it must be true. Pray, sir, who are you, who dare treat me in so rude a manner? I suppose you are one of those whom I hear so frequently called by the name of fanatics and enthusiasts, people dangerous to the church, and disaffected to the government.

'An unhappy peculiarity of spirit, which may be denominated, 'stern severity', runs through the whole constitution of the English church', inferred the Dissenter.[27]

If Anglican manners grated on the sensibilities of Dissenters, Nonconformist discourse was equally and instinctively alien to churchmen. One indignant Scots Episcopalian anthologised Scots Presbyterian sermons, tracts and prayers as evidence of their 'whining Tone', 'Hypocrisy', 'canting', false teaching or 'Extemporary Gibberish'. Their differences were not merely political, but moral: 'such a book as *the Whole Duty of Man* is look'd upon with wonderful Contempt by them'. This had, he claimed, a political application: 'who knows not that despising of Dominions, speaking evil of Dignities, and rising in Arms against the Lord's Anointed, is with them but fighting the Battles of the Lord'. The battle of Bothwell Brig in 1679 was cited as an example of thousands whipped into frenzied rebellion 'by Sermons assuring them, that the very Windle-straws, the Grass in the field, and Stars in Heaven would fight for them: And that after the Victory they should possess the Kingdom themselves'.[28]

Texts like these are evidence less for the exact character of denominational discourse than for the sharp distinctions which rival churches perceived as dividing them. Religious denominations, Anglican, Catholic and Protestant Dissenting, had each a particular tone or manner, immediately recognisable to ally and critic alike, which marked off these social groups from each other in the ordinary business of life. Anglican social practice mixed the sacred unashamedly with the secular in a deliberate expression of the role of the eternal in daily affairs. In the colonies as in England, divine service on Sundays produced a gathering of the community which,

---

[27] David Bogue and James Bennett, *History of Dissenters, from the Revolution in 1688, to the Year 1808* (4 vols., London, 1808–12), vol. i, pp. 356–7, 359.

[28] *Scotch Presbyterian Eloquence Display'd: or, the Folly of their Teaching Discover'd, from their Books, Sermons, and Prayers* (London, 1692; repr. 1738), pp. 2–3, 7, 9, 23.

before and after prayers, soon turned to other things: vestry meetings, commercial transactions, sports.[29] This robust attitude, underpinned by sophisticated theory about the compatibility of reason, science and attainable morality, clashed with Methodist or Dissenting attempts at otherworldliness, which Anglicans stigmatised as unchristian misery and gloom; Methodists and Dissenters responded with denunciations of Anglican impiety and profanation of the Sabbath.[30] The lukewarmness of established religion was as much a complaint of evangelical New Lights in New England as in Anglican Virginia by the 1770s. The Congregationalist minister William Gordon demanded rhetorically: 'What is religion with the generality, more than being baptised, attending public worship stately on the Lord's day, owning the covenant, coming to the Lord's table, and then being orderly in outward deportment!'[31] To many Anglicans, this level of formal observance would have seemed highly reassuring.

Advancing Anglicanism attracted satire as well as fearful apprehension. One wit addressed a fictional potential convert: 'You would sometimes spend a tedious hour by taking an innocent game at *cards*, and a *glass of wine*, or by waiting on the *ladies*, which afforded me some hopeful symptoms, that such a *polite* young gentleman could not be greatly pleased with that *puritanical preciseness* which generally prevails among the *presbyterians* and *congregationalists* in *New-England*.' It was a '*principal advantage* of the *church of England*', claimed the anonymous author, '*that the religion which is generally practised by her members is perfectly agreeable to polite gentlemen*', whereas the doctrines of Dissenters, taught to students, 'make them unsociable, and unfit them for *all genteel* company'.[32] Arminian Anglican priests increasingly stressed the merits of charity and moral living; they sought to co-operate with their parishioners' better instincts rather than expect or seek to produce a moral transformation. To Dissenters in England and America, this could too easily seem a laxity of life and doctrine: the personal unworthiness, worldliness or lack of spirituality of established clergy was a constant refrain of colonists too who separated from the

[29] Charles Sydnor, *Gentleman Freeholders: Political Practices in Washington's Virginia* (Chapel Hill, 1952), pp. 83–4; Rhys Isaac, *The Transformation of Virginia 1740–1790* (Chapel Hill, 1982), pp. 58–65.

[30] W. K. Lowther Clarke, *Eighteenth Century Piety* (London, 1944), pp. 1–29; Henry May, *The Enlightenment in America* (New York, 1976), pp. 66–87; Butler, *Awash in a Sea of Faith*, pp. 167–8.

[31] William Gordon, *A Discourse Preached December 15th 1774* . . . (Boston, 1775), p. 19.

[32] [Noah Welles], *The Real Advantages Which Ministers and People may enjoy especially in the Colonies, by Conforming to the Church of England; faithfully considered, and impartially represented, in a Letter to a Young Gentleman* ([New York], 1762), pp. 3, 6; answered by John Beach, *A Friendly Expostulation, With all Persons concern'd in publishing A late Pamphlet* . . . (New York, 1763).

Anglican church. It was a major tenet of the New Light Presbyterians, claimed an Anglican incumbent in Virginia,

> That a true Christian may know whether a Minister be converted or not by hearing him preach or pray ... And thus by their pretended Spirit of discerning they apply the sentence of Condemnation to all ministers who are not of their way, and persuade as many as they can, to forsake their own Pastors as carnal graceless wretches, tho men of good principles and blameless lives.[33]

The Dissenters' ideal distinguished itself from Anglican practice, however much the reality of Nonconformists' daily conduct fell short. Their most famous English historians looked back to the early eighteenth century as a golden age of Dissenting piety. Family worship, and a strict observance of the Sabbath, were the norm. Secret devotions were 'universally adopted' among them. Such practices admittedly generated 'some peculiarities of conduct in the ordinary routine of life'. This 'marked the character of the dissenters of those days; and the peculiarity of their conduct rendered them the sport of the ungodly, and the mark of ridicule to the careless and profane'. It produced the strict regulation of families; 'diligence in business'; and a particular attitude to recreations.

> The amusements of the world, to which both the busy and the idle have recourse for pleasure, the dissenters of this period in general looked upon with disapprobation; and all, who made any pretensions to religion, abstained entirely from them. At a card table, at an assembly, and at the theatre, a dissenter, professing to be a man of piety, could not be found. Among the more sober delights of domestic life, they sought their pleasure. This was a general rule and a distinguishing feature of the sect.[34]

The historians offered no empirical evidence; but they reported a powerful myth.

Yet far more than tone was at stake. Dissenters possessed a distinct understanding of the nature of the Church which alike rejected both Richard Hooker's account of the integral relation of Church and State and William Warburton's doctrine of their alliance:[35] as the Dissenter William Belsham claimed in 1791,

> The spirit of the Church [of England], in a political view, differs indeed most essentially from the spirit of the Constitution, or rather, it is diametric-

---

[33] Patrick Henry, Sr, to William Dawson, Commissary of the Bishop of London, 13 Feb. 1745: *WMQ* 1 (1921), 261–6, at 263.

[34] Bogue and Bennett, *History of Dissenters*, vol. 2, pp. 171–4.

[35] [William Warburton], *The Alliance between Church and State, or, the Necessity and Equity of an Established Religion and a Test-Law Demonstrated, From the Essence and End of Civil Society, upon the Fundamental Principles of the Law of Nature and Nations* (London, 1736); for which, see Clark, *English Society 1688–1832*, pp. 139–41, 250, 305.

ally opposite to it. For the existence of its legislative powers, it is dependent entirely upon the Crown, which, by virtue of its supremacy, has wisely suspended, or rather annihilated the exercise of them. Its executive powers are subject to no regular superintendancy or controul, and are liable therefore to the most flagrant negligence or abuse: and its judicial powers are universally execrated, as dark, oppressive and despotic. The Church presumptuously claims, indeed, to be *an Ally* of the State, as if it were a co-ordinate or independent power: and talks of the two-fold nature of the Constitution, as if the Act of Toleration was not as much a part of the Constitution as the Act of Uniformity. But the Church is, in a civil view, the mere creation of the State, which supports what it originally formed, not as an ally, which is only a softer term for a rival to itself, but as a mere human institution, established for the purpose of instructing the people in the principles of morality and religion.[36]

There could, at times, be much ecumenical co-operation between the denominations of Protestants in the English-speaking world.[37] At other times, when sensibilities were aroused by the right stimuli, conflict could recur. Dissenters might once more seek to assimilate the Church to the status of a sect; they might again be profoundly alarmed when, in the colonies as at home, the Church of England lastingly persisted in behaving as if it were a church.[38]

II. ANGLICANISM AS AN AGENCY OF STATE FORMATION: THE QUESTION OF ESTABLISHMENT

Law and religion intersected at a number of points. On the level of jurisprudence, the most politically sensitive was the Anglican doctrine of sovereignty. From the parochial point of view, the most weighty was the legal code which conferred established status on the Church of England. Numbers were important, but not decisive, for the hegemony of the Church was expressed and enforced by the laws which defended its established status. In the colonies, similarly, the numerical balance of denominations did not in itself decide the political outcome: the extreme numerical weakness of the Church of England in many colonies at the beginning

[36] [William Belsham], *Observations on the Test Laws, in reply to 'A Review of the Case of the Protestant Dissenters'* (London, 1791), p. 26.

[37] James E. Bradley, 'Toleration, Nonconformity, and the Unity of the Spirit: Popular Religion in Eighteenth-Century England', in James E. Bradley and Richard A. Muller, *Church, Word, and Spirit* (Grand Rapids, Michigan, 1987), pp. 183–99.

[38] For the lasting anxiety produced among colonial Dissenting ministers by militant Anglicanism's disbelief in the validity of their orders, see Charles Chauncy, *The Validity of Presbyterian Ordination Asserted and Maintained* (Boston, 1762); Ezra Stiles, *The United States Elevated to Glory and Honour. A Sermon . . . May 8th, MDCCLXXXIII* (2nd edn., Worcester, Mass., 1785), pp. 101–16.

of the eighteenth century[39] was not interpreted in London as a signal of an impending Dissenting takeover. Establishment could still secure hegemony. This was not, however, a parish matter alone: it was imposed from above, part of the process of state formation itself. The Anglican ascendancy offered, in Ireland as in America, the basis for a dynamic and successful society in which law and theology provided a theoretical underpinning for self-interest and altruism, privilege and opportunity, tradition and innovation.[40] England's American colonies equally had access to a doctrine of identity, origins, purpose and destiny as a new Israel, a chosen people defined by religious allegiance and practice.[41] It was a religious identity which, in 1642, 1688, 1715 and 1745, even overrode the claims of dynastic allegiance for many Englishmen; the American Revolution in turn directed such religious sensibilities against the mother country. These self-images were seldom pluralist: they were fragmented, each rival vision competing for monopoly.

Anglicanism provided an ideological imperative in the creation of the kingdom out of its component parts. Within the realm, the Church's teaching was uniquely monarchical. From Elizabeth's reign, many Anglican divines praised their Church as following a *via media* between the extremes of Rome and Geneva, each of which taught a right of rebellion against unjust princes. Civil war in the 1640s emphasised this denominational threat with brutal clarity. In response the Church of England, by taking as its earthly head the monarch, committed itself to an increasing endorsement of the institution of monarchy as such, a trend which naturally reached its apogee after the Restoration of 1660. Robert South[42] gave famous and succinct expression to the doctrine in a sermon:

> The church of *England* glories in nothing more than that she is the truest friend to kings, and to kingly government, of any other church in the world; that they were the same hands and principles that took the crown from the king's head, and the mitre from the bishops. It is indeed the happiness of some professions and callings, they can equally square themselves to and thrive under all revolutions of government: But the clergy of *England* neither

---

[39] For which, see 'An Account of the State of the Church in North America, by Mr. George Keith and Others' [1702] in *HMPEC* 20 (1951), 363–71.

[40] S. J. Connolly, *Religion, Law and Power: The Making of Protestant Ireland 1660–1760* (Oxford, 1992).

[41] E.g. Ernest Lee Tuveson, *Redeemer Nation: The Idea of America's Millennial Role* (Chicago, 1968); John F. Berens, *Providence & Patriotism in Early America 1640–1815* (Charlottesville, 1978); Ruth Bloch, *Visionary Republic: Millennial Themes in American Thought, 1756–1800* (Cambridge, 1985).

[42] For whom, see Gerard Reedy, SJ, *Robert South (1634–1716): An Introduction to His Life and Sermons* (Cambridge, 1992), pp. 53–87.

know nor affect that happiness, and are willing to be despised for not doing so.[43]

Like the great majority of his fellow clergy, he believed that 'monarchy, or kingly government is the most excellent, and best adapted to the ends of government, and the benefit of society'.[44] The Church of England was

> the only church in Christendom we read of, whose avowed principles and practices disown all resistance of the civil power; and which the saddest experience, and the truest policy and reason will evince to be the only one, that is durably consistent with the *English* monarchy. Let men look both into its doctrine, and into its history, and they will find neither the *Calvins*, the *Knoxes*, the *Junius Brutus's*, the *Synods*, nor the holy Commonwealths of one side, nor yet the *Bellarmines*, the *Escobars*, nor the *Mariana's* of the other.[45]

So the Laudians, restored in the 1660s, were able to answer for a church which was, in its composition, far more diverse.[46]

The dominant Anglican theory of kingship came in the Restoration to rest on interlinked components: divine, indefeasible, hereditary right.[47] If obedience to lawful commands was an aspect of Christian duty, resistance and rebellion were sinful as well as unlawful. What were the limits of obedience? The doctrine of passive obedience taught to disaffected religious minorities the lesson that unjust (even impious) commands were not to be obeyed, but that the subject should accept the penalties for non-compliance rather than rise in rebellion and involve the nation in the greater evils of civil war. What, then, were unjust commands? They proved, in the reign of James II, to be commands which conflicted with established Anglicanism. The Revolution of 1688 was nevertheless a step which involved damage to both Church and monarchy. The Church lost its power to compel regular mass attendance at its services; the monarchy

---

[43] Robert South, 'The Duties of the Episcopal Function: A Sermon Preach'd at Lambeth-Chapel, On the 25th of November, 1666. Upon the Consecration of the Right Revd Father in God John Dolben, Lord Bishop of Rochester' in South, *Sermons Preached Upon Several Occasions* (6 vols., London, 1737), vol. 1, p. 190.

[44] 'The Peculiar Care and Concern of Providence for the Protection and Defence of Kings. A Sermon Preached at Westminster-Abbey, Nov. 5, 1675', ibid., vol. 3, p. 476; 'Ecclesiastical Policy the best Policy: Or, Religion the best Reason of State: A Sermon Preach'd before the Honourable Society of Lincoln's-Inn', ibid., vol. 1, p. 117.

[45] 'Pretence of Conscience, no Excuse for Rebellion. A Sermon Preach'd before King Charles II. At his Chapel in Whitehall, on the Thirtieth Day of Jan. 1662/3', ibid., vol. 5, pp. 97–8.

[46] Robert S. Bosher, *The Making of the Restoration Settlement: The Influence of the Laudians 1649–1662* (London, 1951); John Spurr, *The Restoration Church of England, 1646–1689* (New Haven, 1991). For the lasting influence of Whig High Churchmen, even after 1714, see Clark, *English Society 1688–1832*.

[47] E.g. John Kettlewell, *The Measures of Christian Obedience* (London, 1681), continued in a Nonjuror application in idem., *The Duty of Allegiance Settled upon its True Grounds* (London, 1691).

was restricted by a new libertarian rhetoric, even though the ideas of an original contract and of natural rights were not entrenched in English law. If a minority of republicans and Jacobites believed that the changes had been fundamental,[48] however, the mainstream Anglican position denied this. Of the components of late-Stuart kingship – divine, hereditary, indefeasible right – most strands of political discourse sought to argue that 1688 had modified only 'indefeasible'.[49] Into the early nineteenth century, the Church of England therefore continued to insist that the state in general and sometimes that the existing form of government in particular had received divine sanction.[50]

It was this establishment which confronted, or could be argued was confronting, colonial Americans. A loyalist was incredulous that any colonial Anglicans could be found to side with the rebellion:

> The principles of submission and obedience to lawful authority, are as inseparable from *a sound, genuine member* of the Church of *England*, as any religious principles whatever. This Church has always been famed and respected for its *loyalty*, and its regard to order and government. Its annals have been never stained with the history of plots and conspiracies, treasons and rebellions. Its members are instructed in their duty to government, by Three *Homilies* on *Obedience*, and six against *Rebellion*, which are so many standing lessons to secure their fidelity. They are also taught to pray in the Litany, that the Almighty would preserve them, 'from all sedition, privy conspiracy and rebellion'. And more than one solemn office is provided, for the annual commemoration of former deliverances from the power of those, whether *Papists* or *Protestants*, 'who turn religion into rebellion, and faith into faction'.[51]

Before the nineteenth century, neither the kingdom of England nor its Church were, in their dominant self-images, pictured as voluntary societies. Men were, in law, born members of both. In the Middle Ages, this duality was not complicated by religious diversity. As Archbishop Garbett observed, 'There is no special moment in English history of which it can be said that the Church was established when previously it had no connection with the state. The [medieval] controversies between the Church and the State were between different sets of officials within the nation, representing respectively ecclesiastical and secular interests.'[52]

---

[48] The legitimist reading of Anglican political theology was summed up in Nonjuror works like Abednego Sellar's *The History of Passive Obedience Since the Reformation* (2 parts, Amsterdam, 1689–90).

[49] William Sherlock, *The Case of Allegiance due to Sovereign Powers* (London, 1691); Clark, *English Society 1688–1832*, pp. 119–98.

[50] Robert Hole, *Pulpits, Politics and Public Order in England 1760–1832* (Cambridge, 1989).

[51] [Myles Cooper], *A Friendly Address to All Reasonable Americans, On the Subject of our Political Confusions* (New York; repr. London, 1774), pp. 49–50.

[52] Cyril Garbett, *The Claims of the Church of England* (London, 1947), pp. 184–5.

After the Reformation, this ideal was re-expressed, not abandoned. The Statute of Appeals of 1533 outlined the Henrician doctrine of England as an independent 'body politick', 'an empire', governed in its spiritual aspect in the Church, in its secular aspect in the State, both under the monarch. This doctrine recognised the Church as what it had always been: it was never 'established', endowed or chosen for a special position from among competitors, by any Act of Parliament. The term first appeared in canon 3 of 1604: 'the Church of England by Law established under the King's Majesty'; but this recognised the situation as it already was.

A full account of the legal framework of the Establishment and of the apologias for its preservation turning on Anglican ecclesiology are beyond the scope of the present study.[53] Nevertheless, certain texts in both genres had, by the eighteenth century, achieved classic status and by their practical importance shaped the idioms of political discourse for far larger numbers of men than ever read them. The foundation document, in Anglican perception, had been provided by Richard Hooker (c. 1554–1600). *Of the Laws of Ecclesiastical Polity*, the first and greatest apologia for Anglicanism, was published in instalments (1594, 1597, 1648, 1662); the political Book VIII countered the hostile thesis that 'unto no civil prince or governor there may be given such power of ecclesiastical dominion as by the laws of the land belongeth unto the supreme regent thereof'. It proceeded from the assumption that 'there is not any man of the Church of England but the same man is also a member of the commonwealth; nor any man a member of the commonwealth, which is not also of the Church of England' (ch. 1.2). This, indeed, constituted the political aspect of the Anglican *via media*. Hooker argued (ch. 1.7) that

> within this realm of England . . . from the state of pagans we differ, in that with us one society is both Church and commonwealth, which with them it was not; as also from the state of those nations which subject themselves to the bishop of Rome, in that our Church hath dependency upon the chief in our commonwealth, which it hath not under him. In a word, our estate is according to the pattern of god's own ancient elect people, which people was not part of them the commonwealth, and part of them the Church of God, but the selfsame people whole and entire were both under one chief Governor, on whose supreme authority they did all depend.[54]

Political involvement in the life of the Church could not validly be described as Erastianism, it was argued. The monarch was anointed and

---

[53] For a fuller account of tensions within Anglican discourse on this subject see Spurr, *Restoration Church of England*, pp. 105–65 and passim.
[54] *The Works of . . . Mr. Richard Hooker* (2 vols., Oxford, 1865), vol. 2, pp. 485, 493.

clothed in priestly vestments at his coronation; Parliament was a lay synod. Both were part of the Church, not separate and secular agencies subordinating the Church to their control.[55] But Hooker's doctrine contained a fatal flaw: it was ambiguous about the title of the 'chief Governor' on whom the whole system depended, and even appeared to recognise conquest and *de facto* power.[56] Providence, though heavily emphasised, might point in more than one direction.

Such views were re-expressed in Bishop Overall's *Convocation Book*, the composition of the Convocation of 1606, published in 1690 and given the imprimatur on 24 June 1689 by William Sancroft, still Archbishop of Canterbury but now a Nonjuror under the new regime. Overall's text, though lacking Hooker's wide circulation, had a powerful influence on the terms of the ecclesiastical controversies of the reigns of William III and Anne, and helped to shape the political discourse of the succeeding century.[57] Emphatically patriarchal and providentialist, it nevertheless argued against the indefeasibility of kingly authority in a way which proved unacceptable in the reign of James I but essential in that of William III. It contained a long and careful deduction of political and ecclesiastical authority from Adam and Noah and of the divine sanction of forms of ministry; it argued against the authority of the Pope to depose princes. The Anglican Establishment was thereby set once again in the broadest theological and philosophical setting. Deduction proceeded from an anti-contractarian account of the origins of government which became Anglican as well as Nonjuror orthodoxy:

> If any Man shall therefore affirm, that Men at the first, without all good Education, or Civility, ran up and down in Woods, and Fields, as Wild Creatures, resting themselves in Caves, and Dens, and acknowledging no superiority one over another, until they were taught by Experience the necessity of Government; and that thereupon they chose some among themselves to order and rule the rest, giving them power and authority so to do; and that consequently all civil Power, Jurisdiction, and Authority was first derived from the people, and disorder'd multitude; or either is originally still in them, or else is deduced by their consents naturally from them; and

---

[55] G. W. O. Addleshaw, *The High Church Tradition* (London, 1941), chapter 6.

[56] Hooker (*Laws*, Book VIII, ch. 2.5) outlined the different origin of governments in consent, conquest, and 'divine right' through God's 'special appointment', but added: 'By which of these means soever it happen that kings or governors be advanced unto their states, we must acknowledge both their lawful choice to be approved of God, and themselves to be God's lieutenants, and confess their power his': *Works*, vol. 2, pp. 496–7.

[57] John Kenyon, *Revolution Principles: The Politics of Party 1689–1720* (Cambridge, 1977), pp. 26–7; J. H. Overton, *The Nonjurors* (London, 1902), pp. 36–7; L. M. Hawkins, *Allegiance in Church and State: The Problem of the Nonjurors in the English Revolution* (London, 1928), p. 64; Gordon J. Schochet, *Patriarchalism in Political Thought* (Oxford, 1975), pp. 92–5.

is not God's Ordinance originally descending from him, and depending upon him, he doth greatly Erre.[58]

This doctrine was difficult to reconcile with Locke's that 'in the beginning all the World was *America*':[59] as the 'state of nature' became less and less of an episode in divine history, more and more a sociological component of a stadial view of human progress,[60] the assumptions embodied in Overall's account increasingly conflicted with those which seemed to be echoed in Locke's.

The Convocation had developed a broad political and social theory on this initial insight. Men were born members of families, and familial authority was affirmed as the model for civil authority.[61] From there it proceeded to argue for the authority of the civil magistrate in ecclesiastical affairs:

> As it is apparent in the Scriptures, that the Israelites generally, as well the Priests as the People, were equally bound, as Subjects, personally to honour, reverence, and obey their Kings: So it is there also as manifest, that the Authority of their Soveraigns over them, did not only extend to civil Causes, but in like manner to Causes Ecclesiastical. For as it was then the duty of Parents, so by the Law of Nature, was it of good Kings and Civil Magistrates, to bring up their Children and subjects, in the true service and worship of God; as having a care committed unto them, not only of their Bodies but likewise of their Souls. In which respect the chief charge that all Subjects and inferior Persons, of what condition soever, should diligently observe the said Law of Nature (being the very same in substance that God, writing with his own Finger, gave unto *Moses*, and stiled by the name of his *Ten Commandments*) was principally imposed upon Kings and civil Rulers.

Thirdly, it insisted on the special appropriateness of monarchy. God had indeed instituted monarchy among the Israelites. Other nations had chosen differently;

> Whereupon divers other kinds of Governments, termed according to their Temper, *Aristocratical, Political, Tyrannical, Oligarchical or Democratical*, &c. were afterwards setled in many places. The Inconveniences of which Forms of Government being found (upon many occasions oftentimes) to be very

---

[58] [William Sancroft (ed.)], *Bishop Overall's Convocation-Book, MDCVI. Concerning the Government of God's Catholick Church, and the Kingdoms of the Whole World* (London, 1690), pp. 3–4.

[59] John Locke, *Two Treatises of Government* (1690), ed. Peter Laslett (2nd. edn, Cambridge, 1967), p. 319.

[60] H. V. S. Ogden, 'The State of Nature and the Decline of Lockian Political Theory in England, 1760–1800', *AHR* 46 (1940–1), 21–44.

[61] For the colonial reaction see Jay Fliegelman, *Prodigals and Pilgrims: The American Revolution Against Patriarchal Authority, 1750–1800* (Cambridge, 1982). The argument of this work may be weakened by positing as its starting point a predominant 'Lockean paradigm'.

great; the People have been driven, of necessity, in sundry Countries, to frame them again, as near as they could, to the *Monarchical* Government.

Even so, *de facto* power was acknowledged as divinely sanctioned: 'When any . . . new Forms of Government, begun by Rebellion, are after thoroughly settled, the Authority in them, is . . . of God.'[62]

Even in Hooker's day, this ideal was challenged by the separate existence of Roman Catholic recusants; increasingly through the seventeenth century, it was challenged by the proliferation of varieties of Protestant Dissent. James II's policies on toleration, and the outcome of the Glorious Revolution, placed permanently beyond reach the project of Archbishops Sheldon (1663–77) and Sancroft (1677–90) for the recreation of a practical identity between the Church of England and the nation. Yet, despite the *de facto* recognition of Nonconformity given by the 'Toleration' Act of 1689, the ideal of the Church as the highest and all-encompassing religious expression of the nation survived. That ideal was given most cogent expression in the defences mounted by Anglicans of the Test Act (1673) and Corporation Act (1661), those lasting monuments of Restoration exclusiveness, in which a militantly Anglican Parliament had sought to restrict office in central and local government to Churchmen.

The attempt of the early 1660s to reassert the Anglican identity of England was, in some ways, strikingly successful. Legal persecution combined with the exhaustion of the springs of action within the sects reduced Dissenters to about six per cent of the population of England, even on their own estimates, by the second decade of the eighteenth century. Decline continued despite the freedom of worship guaranteed by the Toleration Act.[63] For some denominations the decline was catastrophic. By 1690 the number of Baptist congregations was only a third of what it had been in 1660; almost all of these were smaller than they were, and the movement was damagingly split between Calvinists, Arminians and Sabbatarians.[64]

This sense of decline created the defensive note in repeated Dissenting justifications of the legitimacy of their separation. Edmund Calamy's account of the principles of the ejected ministers of 1662 called forth confident Anglican replies. The Rev. John Ollyffe's view was premised

---

[62] [Sancroft (ed.)], *Bishop Overall's Convocation-Book*, pp. 32–3, 56, 59.

[63] Michael Watts, *The Dissenters* (Oxford, 1978), p. 270; Roger Thomas, 'The Break-up of Nonconformity' in Geoffrey Nuttall et al. (eds.), *The Beginnings of Nonconformity* (London, 1964), pp. 33–60; R. Tudur Jones, *Congregationalism in England 1662–1962* (London, 1962), pp. 46–145; C. G. Bolam et al., *The English Presbyterians from Elizabethan Puritanism to Modern Unitarianism* (London, 1968), pp. 73–218.

[64] Alfred C. Underwood, *A History of the English Baptists* (London, 1947), pp. 130–2; W. T. Whitley, *The Baptists of London, 1612–1928* (London, [?1928]), pp. 47–8.

on the necessity of subscriptions as such, 'without which there could be no agreement nor owning any thing in common amongst Men'. Dissenters surely admitted this in subscribing thirty-six of the Thirty-Nine Articles, and to these, moderate conformists desired assent in 'the best and most candid construction . . . that the words will properly and fairly bear', not in a narrow literalism.[65] This was a telling answer since most of the Prayer Book's teachings on order and ceremony could be interpreted in a relaxed sense, and although Calamy had objected to the Athanasian Creed, it was its 'Damnatory Sentences' which he rejected as too 'harsh', not its Trinitarianism.[66]

Benjamin Hoadly was similarly moved to rebut Calamy, for even Low Churchmen might initially subscribe to Anglican views on establishment. Indeed Hoadly's attitude to Dissenters was as benign as to High Churchmen it was hostile. 'We cannot but heartily wish they would unite with us', he wrote of the former; 'and there is somewhat both in the principles and practice of these persons, which suffers me not to think it altogether an hopeless attempt.' Hoadly was a Low Churchman, often cited by sympathisers in the colonies, but on the question of establishment he echoed standard Anglican doctrine. In a two-part tract totalling 392 pages, Hoadly summarised the case for conformity framed by Anglican apologists from Hooker, through Bradshaw and others in the 1640s, to Stillingfleet and Sherlock in the 1690s.[67] Hoadly's case for the Church of England was substantive: setting aside Nonconformists' scruples, 'Are there any means necessary to the Peoples Salvation wanting in the *Church of England*? . . . Is there any thing in the administration of the Sacraments, contrary to the main design of the Gospel, or destructive of Salvation?'[68]

Dissenters nevertheless inevitably felt their position insecure if Anglican intellectuals continued, with immense erudition and polemical zeal, to deny the validity of Presbyterian ordination from the evidence of scripture, the early Church, and the Fathers.[69] The Dissenting interest was

---

[65] John Ollyffe, *A Defence of Ministerial Conformity to the Church of England: In Answer to the Misrepresentations Of the Terms thereof By Mr. Calamy In the tenth Chapter of his Abridgement of the History of Mr. Baxter's Life and Times* (London, 1702), pp. 14–15.

[66] Ibid., pp. 79–81; cf. Benjamin Hoadly, *A Defence of the Reasonableness of Conformity to the Church of England, &c. In Answer to the Objections of Mr. Calamy In his Defence of Moderate Non-Conformity* (London, 1705), pp. 102–3.

[67] Benjamin Hoadly, *The Reasonableness of Conformity to the Church of England, Represented to the Dissenting Ministers. In Answer to the Tenth Chapter of Mr. Calamy's Abridgement of Mr. Baxter's History of his Life and Times*, Part I (2nd edn; London, 1703), sig A4r.

[68] Ibid., p. 11.

[69] E.g. Zachary Grey, *The Ministry of the Dissenters Proved to be Null and Void, From Scripture and Antiquity. In Answer to Dr. Calamy's Sermon: Entitled, The Ministry of the Dissenters Vindicated, &c.* (2nd edn., London, 1725).

kept fully briefed about its history and its origins in Anglican persecution. These could be rehearsed both in lengthy works of scholarship like Daniel Neal's *The History of the Puritans or Protestant Non-Conformists, from the Reformation* (4 vols., London, 1732–8) and in pocket compendia like Samuel Palmer's *The Protestant-Dissenter's Catechism* (London, 1774). Such Nonconformist works themselves drew the sharpest distinction between the Church of England and Dissent. Congregationalists, Presbyterians and Baptists, insisted Samuel Palmer, agreed in the direct accountability of each congregation to Christ; but 'The church of England is not a voluntary society, the whole nation being considered as members of it, whether professedly so or not; and obliged by law (except those included in the toleration-act) at least thrice in the year, to communicate with it in the Lord's supper.' Moreover, the Anglican Church could not vote: 'the several congregations of which it consists, are equally destitute of this liberty, being all obliged to an absolute uniformity in faith, worship, and discipline'.[70]

The fears of colonial Dissenters that the Church of England sought to secure established status and practical dominance in America were not without foundation. Just such a campaign to replicate the Church's rights, privileges and assets was conducted in South Carolina as early as the years 1708–16 by the Bishop of London's Commissary, Gideon Johnston.[71] He candidly pursued 'such a Settlement of the Church, & Regulation of Ecclesiastical Discipline, as shou'd be Conformable to that great Pattern the Church of England at home',[72] and although colonial Anglicans achieved only limited success in implementing this extensive ambition, it remained the goal which generations of colonial Dissenters thought they saw behind Anglican requests for the ordination of a colonial bishop.[73]

Precisely who was included in the benefits of the Toleration Act was consequently a matter of lasting importance. In the American colonies the problem was far greater, made urgent and momentous by the upsurge in Dissenting revivalism and itinerancy from the 1740s onwards. The difficulty arose since, as one Anglican incumbent pointed out in complaining to the Bishop of London's Commissary about the 'Intrusions' of

---

[70] [Samuel Palmer], *The Protestant-Dissenter's Catechism. Containing, I. A Brief History of the Nonconformists: II. The Reasons of the Dissent from the National Church* (London, 1774; 2nd edn., 1774), pp. 28–9.

[71] Frank J. Klingberg (ed.), *Carolina Chronicle: The Papers of Commissary Gideon Johnston 1707–1716* (Berkeley, 1946).

[72] Gideon Johnston to SPG, 27 Jan. 1710/11, in Klingberg (ed.), *Johnston*, pp. 66–92, at 74.

[73] Carl Bridenbaugh, *Mitre and Sceptre: Transatlantic Faiths, Ideas, Personalities, and Politics 1689–1775* (New York, 1962).

unlicensed preachers into his parish, 'Tis a Doubt, I am told, with some worthy Members of your honorable Bench, whether the Act of Toleration extends to the Plantations.' He was, perhaps, too optimistic in expecting a clear ruling on this convenient ambiguity, even though he professed his personal goodwill: 'Not that I would be fond of seeing these or any other nonconforming Teachers molested purely for their religious tenets; but of seeing the Privileges of both Churchmen & Dissenters so precisely ascertained, as to leave no Room for Controversy in the Case.' The Anglican *via media* was, by the eighteenth century, a delicate and narrow line between persecution and the condoning of Dissent. As the Rev. James Maury (1718–69) expressed it in a remote corner of the Bishop of London's diocese,

> I trust I am far from the inhuman & uncharitable Spirit of Persecution. No Man either professes or thinks himself a warmer Advocate for Liberty of Conscience, that natural Right of Mankind. But when Men under Pretence of asserting & exercising this Right, sow the Seeds of Discord & Confusion: when they so industriously propagate heterodox opinions in a Manner, inconsistent with & repugnant to, the formal Sanctions of Government & Law; none, surely, not their most zealous adherents, nor even themselves, can justly complain, should they be laid under just & equitable Restraints. Such, as dissent from the established Church, & are indulged by the Government publicly to teach those of their own Communion under certain wise & moderate Restrictions, would, one would think, if influenced either by Modesty or Prudence be cautious of transgressing the Bounds, markt out to them by such wholsome & tolerating Laws; which, as they, on one Hand grant them all reasonable Indulgences, in Condescension to their scrupulous Consciences, so, on the other, must be thought just in wisely providing for the Peace, Unity & Order of the national Church, for the Security of which they have been chiefly calculated.[74]

The Church of England was a state church, not a 'gathered church', and was explicitly aware of what this entailed. The three premises of such a view were set out by Edmund Gibson:

> Religion, and the general Practice of it in a Nation, is the surest Establishment of States and Kingdoms. That therefore, in every Nation, it is the proper Business of the Civil Magistrate, as such, to vindicate and maintain the Honour of Religion. That without a serious Regard

---

[74] James Maury to [? William Dawson], Fredericsville, 6 Oct. 1755: *WMQ* 1 (1921), 277. After his father's death, Thomas Jefferson lived with Maury as his pupil for two years from the age of 14 (1757–9). This was the Anglican orthodoxy against which the Deist Jefferson rebelled. Maury was a prominent campaigner to advance the status and independence of the clergy, and in 1763 became a famous litigant in the disputes over clerical incomes known as the Parsons' Cause: John Frederick Woolverton, *Colonial Anglicanism in North America* (Detroit, 1984), pp. 204–6.

to the Moral and Spiritual Duties of Religion, the greatest Zeal in other Matters, even tho' it be for the establish'd Worship of God, will not secure the divine Favour and Protection, either to Persons or Nations.

It followed that

in a Christian Country, every *Civil* Magistrate is obliged to consider himself also as a *Christian* Magistrate; as one, who has not only received a Commission from the Prince, to maintain Peace and Order in the State; but who has also, thro' the hands of the Prince, received a Commission from God, to maintain the Honour of his Religion upon Earth.[75]

This being so, defence of the Anglican ascendancy could proceed from the Hookerian premise that 'We are obliged to receive the Sacrament in *the Church of Christ* in obedience to an institution of Christ; and consequently we are supposed to be in Communion with that visible part of the Church with which we receive the Sacrament.' As the Litany in the *Book of Common Prayer* made explicit, the Church and State were one not because of the Church's Erastian subordination to the State but because all the members of the State were deemed to be included in the Church as the body of Christ.[76] Schism and the threat of rebellion attendant on schism challenged this picture, however. The sacramental test was uniquely effective as a test of allegiance; and, consistently with this ecclesiology, it was a central tenet of Anglican apologists that this did not misuse a divine ordinance for profane ends:

That receiving the Sacrament, *according to the Usage of the Church of* England, is not the qualification for an Office, within the intent of the Act, but only the proof of such qualification: The qualification required is, That the Person be well affected to the Ecclesiastical State and Constitution of these Realms; and the receiving the Sacrament according to the Rites of the establish'd Church is, the proof or Test required that he is so.[77]

The Church's claims to Apostolic authority were bound up with this mode of defending its position:

What then shall exclude the Papists, if the Sacramental Test be abolished? Not Oaths, nor Declarations, which it is plain the Legislature at that Time looked upon as dispensable Matters, and such Securities as might be broke thro' for the Good of the Catholick Cause. But their joining with the Church of *England* in the most solemn Act of Christian Worship, is a Bar of the strongest kind; it is an open and publick Acknowledgement, that our

[75] Edmund Gibson, *Religion, the best Security to Church and State. A Sermon Preach'd at the Assizes Held at Kingston in Surrey, March the 10th 1714/15* (London, 1715), pp. 7, 13.
[76] Waterman, 'The Nexus between Theology and Political Doctrine'.
[77] Thomas Sherlock, *A Vindication of the Corporation and Test Acts. In Answer to the Bishop of Bangor's Reasons For the Repeal of Them* (London, 1718), pp. 9, 72.

Church is a true Church, and our Ministry a true Ministry, and We True
Members of the Catholick Church of Christ; notwithstanding our Separation from the Church of *Rome*.

Anglicans thereby derived, or thought they derived, their ecclesiastical
polity from their ecclesiology.[78] Where Dissenters subordinated divine
rights to natural rights, thought Anglicans, they themselves treated natural rights as a lesser expression and anticipation of divine rights. Such
was a premise of the establishment:

> In the Books which have been written upon this Subject, in Favour of the
> Dissenters, we have heard much of *Natural Rights*, and the unjust Invasion
> of those Rights by the Corporation and Test Acts. But is not Society and
> Government itself founded in an *Abridgement* of Natural Rights, in such
> Instances and such Degrees, as in the Judgement of the Legislature the
> Safety and Welfare of the *whole* requires?[79]

If such an abridgement of natural rights were legitimate, then a distinction could be sustained between toleration of Dissenters' private worship,
and their admission to political power:

> In framing the Test Act, both Houses of Parliament put a just Distinction
> between the relieving of *Conscience*, and the entitling to Power; the same
> Distinction that was afterwards made in framing the Act of Toleration,
> which gives Relief to Conscience, but expressly debars from Temporal
> Power.[80]

Thus expressed, the case for Anglican ascendancy became a well-
rehearsed orthodoxy, readily and ably expounded, often in the same
terms. Apologetics such as these were reprinted on the occasion of later
attempts to repeal the Acts: Sherlock's *Vindication* in 1787, 1790 and 1827,
his *History of the Test Act* in 1790, and Gibson's *Dispute Adjusted* in the same
year. Samuel Horsley, the ablest Anglican apologist of the latter part of
the century, endorsed and restated the same case in 1790, looking equally
to the efficacy of legislation. If repeal passed, he predicted, 'Government
will have thrown down the best barrier it had to oppose to innovation;
and the work of reformation will go on, without obstruction, till one
stone will not be left standing upon another of the admired fabrick of the
BRITISH CONSTITUTION.'[81]

[78] I differ here from the admirable analysis of Waterman, 'The Nexus between Theology
and Political Doctrine'.
[79] [Edmund Gibson], *The Dispute adjusted, about the Proper Time Of Applying for a Repeal of the
Corporation and Test Acts: By Shewing, That No Time is proper* (London, 1732), pp. 10–11.
[80] [Thomas Sherlock], *The History of the Test Act: In which the Mistakes in some late Writings
against it are rectified, and the Importance of it to the Church explain'd* (London, 1732), p. 9.
[81] [Samuel Horsley], *A Review of the Case of the Protestant Dissenters; with reference to the Corporation
and Test Acts* (London, 1790), p. 59.

Did the ambitions of Dissenters cease with toleration and an admission to civil offices? Churchmen doubted it.

> The public hath been told, that it would be but equitable, that one church, at least, in every considerable town should be set apart for the Dissenters; and that such a portion of the tithes, ET CAETERA, of that district should be alloted to the Minister, as should be proportioned to the numbers of his followers. It hath even been suggested, that a time may come, and may be at no great distance, when a *portion* of the Tithes and the ET CAETERA will not suffice: When under the authority of an Arian or Socinian Parliament (which nothing indeed might so soon produce as the repeal of the Corporation Act) the rash defenders of the present system, deposed from their dignities, and plundered of the emoluments, may be thankful if they escape the horrors of a jail.[82]

Dissenters consistently professed their loyalty to the House of Hanover, their adherence to Revolution principles, and their peaceful demeanour; the repeal of the Test and Corporation Acts could scarcely 'be imagined to introduce universal confusion into our civil constitution, and utterly dissolve the frame of our government'.[83] But this argument was only effective on the Dissenters' own premise of the proper separation of Church and State. To an Anglican, by contrast, 'The Church of England is part of the Constitution. Every Dissenter, if he be an honest and conscientious man, must be an enemy to it, as what he deems to be wrong; and will endeavour it's destruction, in order to introduce what he deems to be right.'[84]

Dissenters in particular stressed the language of liberty. Anglicans might reply that 'religious liberty can alone exist under an establishment of religion, as civil liberty most certainly can have no existence, unless under the protection of law and civil government'. The alternative was 'confusion and wild extravagance'. It could be taken as a starting point that

> religion has, more or less, entered into the constitution of every civil society, that has ever existed . . . Until therefore the experiment of a state subsisting without any establishment in matters of religion be tried, it is impossible to contravert the argument from general practice in their favor, or to say, that the great ends of civil society can be obtained without them.

---

[82] Ibid., p. 58, referring to Joseph Priestley, *The Importance and Extent of Free Inquiry in Matters of Religion: A Sermon . . . November 5, 1785* (Birmingham, 1785), pp. 44–6, and Priestley, *Letters to Dr. Horsley, Part II* (Birmingham, 1784), p. 88.

[83] Samuel Palmer, *A Vindication of the Modern Dissenters against the Aspersions of the Rev. William Hawkins MA* (London, 1790), p. 34.

[84] [George Horne], *Observations on the Case of the Protestant Dissenters with Reference to the Corporation and Test Acts* (Oxford, 1790), p. 7.

England's constitution was fully defensible: it combined the security of the establishment with the absence of persecution.[85] Anglicans continued, as a truism, to link two propositions: 'in no well-governed State has religious indulgence gone so far, as in our own', and 'Religion cannot subsist in the world without some public Rules, nor these again without public Authority.'[86]

Establishment still implied not only the practical advantages of official recognition – the privileges, immunities or material rewards. It meant also the claim that the Church represented the nation in its spiritual aspect, the two united in the person of an anointed king rather than by parliamentary statutes ensuring the payment of clergy. It was this second 'sense of the state as a single, corporate religious body' which was 'gradually, though unevenly, lost' in the colonies, leaving the first, the system of legal privileges, more clearly defined and more dangerously isolated.[87] Its destruction in the Revolution only reinforced the Anglican account of social order in the minds of its adherents. To the social theorists of the English establishment, one proposition could be taken as central:

> For a state to exist without a religion of some sort being united to it, is a solecism in the world; the new revolutionary democracy of America being the first that ever attempted it: so that the experience of four thousand years in every corner of the globe, might have taught some diffidence to those who fondly dream that the Christian religion would thrive equally well if the king were an atheist, and if it had no more protection or encouragement from him than Mahometanism, Judaism, or Deism. Woe be to that king and to that nation in which such maxims shall ever prevail.[88]

From the Anglican perspective, a secular republic could not, by definition, offer the prospect of a stable order.

III. CANON LAW, HETERODOXY AND THE AMERICAN PERCEPTION OF TYRANNY

Heterodoxy identified the Anglican enemy more vividly than any other development in denominational discourse and created a scenario of world history which, in the American colonies, steadily grew in its ability to persuade. The Arian John Adams, writing in the *Boston Gazette* of August

---

[85] Nathaniel Forster, *The Establishment of the Church of England defended upon the Principles of Religious Liberty. A Sermon Preached at the Triennial Visitation of the ... Bishop of London* (London, 1770), pp. 9–10, 13.

[86] Peter Williams, *A Short Vindication of the Established Church: in which the objections of Methodists, and Dissenters, are dispassionately considered* (Oxford, 1803), pp. 13, 29.

[87] Woolverton, *Colonial Anglicanism in North America*, p. 19 and passim.

[88] [Henry Drummond], *Social Duties on Christian Principles* (London, 1830), pp. 155–6.

1765, believed he derived his insight from an historical analysis: 'Since the promulgation of Christianity, the two greatest systems of tyranny that have sprung from this original, are the canon and the feudal law.'[89] Adams supplied no historical references, however. Evidence was replaced by anti-Catholic invective, which stigmatised the canon law, and by a claim that feudal law was a 'system' which was 'similar in many respects to the former' and served 'the same purposes of tyranny, cruelty and lust'. The 'two systems of tyranny' had historically formed 'a wicked confederacy', diminished in England by the Reformation but evidently not abolished, 'till at last, under the execrable race of the Stuarts, the struggle between the people and the confederacy aforesaid of temporal and spiritual tyranny, became formidable, violent, and bloody. It was this great struggle that peopled America',[90] and guaranteed that the successors of the early settlers were unambiguously identified with the cause of liberty.

Where most early-seventeenth-century Puritans had imagined themselves to remain within the Church of England, and to differ from it only on some reformable points of ecclesiastical polity, Adams's analysis presumed an unaltered canon law and allowed for no distinction between episcopalian Anglicanism and Popery.[91] With only a perfunctory allusion to the Revolution of 1688, Adams could therefore proceed from rhetorical assertion via an absence of evidence to a conclusion:

> There seems to be a direct and formal design on foot, to enslave all America. This, however, must be done by degrees. The first step that is intended, seems to be an entire subversion of the whole system of our fathers, by the introduction of the canon and feudal law into America. The canon and feudal systems, though greatly mutilated in England, are not yet destroyed. Like the temples and palaces in which the great contrivers of them once worshipped and inhabited, they exist in ruins; and much of the domineering spirit of them still remains. The designs and labours of a certain society, to introduce the former of them into America, have been well exposed to the public by a writer of great abilities; and the further attempts to the same purpose, that may be made by that society, or by the ministry or parliament, I leave to the conjectures of the thoughtful.

The Stamp Act had the same aim, he asserted, by restricting knowledge and introducing the 'inequalities and dependencies of the feudal system'. John Adams's authority and his target were made clear on his last page: the Arian Congregationalist minister Jonathan Mayhew, and his tirade

---

[89] John Adams, *A Dissertation on the Canon and Feudal Law* in *Works*, vol. 3, pp. 445–64, at 449. The title was supplied by Thomas Hollis, who arranged for the piece's republication in London.
[90] Ibid., pp. 450–1.
[91] Ibid., pp. 435, 453.

against the Society for the Propagation of the Gospel for its efforts to secure an Anglican bishop in New England.[92]

Nor was the Stamp Act the last legislation to engage with these denominational anxieties. Benjamin Franklin's 'Rules for Reducing a Great Empire to a Small One', written for the London *Public Advertiser* in October 1773, made plain how extensive was the threat posed by the 1766 Declaratory Act's claim

> 'that King, Lords, Commons had, have, and of right ought to have, full power and authority to make statutes of sufficient force and validity to bind the unrepresented provinces in *all cases whatsoever.*' This will include spiritual with temporal, and, taken together, must operate wonderfully to your purpose; by convincing them, that they are at present under a power something like that spoken of in the Scriptures, which can not only kill their bodies, but damn their souls to all eternity, by compelling them, if it pleases, to worship the Devil.[93]

In a functional perspective, this preoccupation with ecclesiastical power presents a paradox. In England, ecclesiastical courts were in marked decline from the 1680s in their function as allies of the parochial clergy in their pastoral duties. Part of the reason for the falling off of their case load was that Parliament in the 1690s provided a quick and cheap method for the recovery of tithes before two JPs. But there were profounder causes in the ecclesiastical policy of James II, the advantage widely taken of the Toleration Act not to attend church, and the increasing use of parliamentary statutes to reprove moral offences like sabbath-breaking and drunkenness. Nevertheless, the courts remained, exercising with devolved power what John Cosin identified as the right of a bishop 'to correct, deprive, suspend, excommunicate and stop the mouths of offenders'[94] – a discipline which almost all other denominations exercised over their members,[95] but which Dissenters, and especially heterodox Dissenters, were indignant should remain in the hands of the Church which they rejected.

The authority of the Church displayed the characteristics of the social order of which it was part.[96] On the level of high theory, it was upheld as hegemonic. The Toleration Act only provided that Dissenters who took the oaths which it contained 'shall not be prosecuted in any ecclesiastical court for or by reason of their non-conforming to the Church of England';

---

[92] Ibid., p. 464.
[93] Franklin, *Works*, vol. 4, p. 393.
[94] M. G. Smith, *Pastoral Discipline and the Church Courts: The Hexham Court 1680–1730*, Borthwick Papers no. 62 (York, 1982), pp. 2, 5.
[95] Watts, *The Dissenters*, pp. 319–36.
[96] Spurr, *Restoration Church of England*, pp. 209–19, shows how imperfectly the system had worked even before 1688.

but this still left them theoretically open to Church discipline on many other matters. At local level, that discipline was subject to all the vagaries of exception and evasion: 'to speak freely', announced a standard handbook, 'no wise Man has any reason to hope that Church-Discipline can be restored in such an Age as this'. Ecclesiastical laws were still current, but there was no '*spirit in the* English *People*' for the enforcement of laws against vice:

> One is too Rich to be prosecuted, and no Officer dare meddle with him; another is too Poor, and if he be prosecuted he will run away, and leave his Family to the Parish; and if a wealthy Man be presented, he gets the Information withdrawn by feeing some Officer: if a poor Man, then no Ecclesiastical Officer will prosecute him, because he can get nothing by it; and the Church-Wardens, or Parish will not be at twenty Shillings Charge to bring an Offender to Penance.[97]

Inefficiently, and with a bias to the poor, church courts continued to hear cases of moral transgressions and to punish them either with fines or the infliction of public penance, until the Act of 1787[98] which effectively ended their power to act in cases of defamation and fornication. To Anglicans it appeared an imperfect system which fell well short of its ideals; to the licentious and to the heterodox, it was a lasting threat.

Yet in the American colonies, none of this applied. No separate Anglican church courts had ever been established there. In their absence, their probate jurisdiction was vested by the crown in the royal governors; but in many colonies, especially in New England, probate questions were settled in local common law courts, and lawyers seldom needed to buy texts on ecclesiastical law: absent from colonial libraries were 'detailed treatises on the canon law, regulations concerning the clergy, treatises on church court punishments for defamation, blasphemy, and related offenses, and similar works prepared and published in great numbers by the learned members of the Doctors' Commons of England'.[99] Canon law texts seem to have been of interest chiefly to the intelligentsia rather than to the generality of practising attorneys: Richard Burn's *Ecclesiastical Law* (1st edn, 1763, 2nd edn, 1767) was owned by Thomas Jefferson and John Adams, Edmund Gibson's *Codex* (1st edn., 1713) by Jefferson.[100]

These were, however, important texts. At the zenith of the High Church

---

[97] [John Johnson], *The Clergyman's Vade-Mecum: Or, An Account of the Ancient and Present Church of England; The Duties and Rights of the Clergy; And of Their Privileges and Hardships* (1706; 6th edn., London, 1731), pp. 301–2.

[98] 27 Geo. III, c. 44.

[99] Herbert A. Johnson, *Imported Eighteenth-Century Law Treatises in American Libraries 1700–1799* (Knoxville, 1978), p. xx.

[100] Ibid., pp. 11, 24.

revival under Queen Anne, Edmund Gibson, chaplain to the Archbishop of Canterbury, produced in 1713 a massive compendium and systematisation of ecclesiastical law. Its object was candidly avowed: Gibson had undertaken it 'purely for the Service of the Clergy, and in Support of the Rights and Privileges of the Church'. It plainly asserted 'the Right which the Bishops of the Church of *England* have, to Exercise Discipline upon the foot of *Divine*, as well as Human, Authority', openly challenging the opponents of divine right and those who held that the Reformation had made 'the *Jurisdiction* of our Bishops *meerly human*'. Church courts were therefore defended by Gibson as being on a par with temporal courts, each with their proper jurisdictions.[101]

The implications of Gibson's position were extensive. Not only might foreign canon law have acquired currency in England as common law, by long acceptance and usage, but

> *England* is governed by two distinct Administrations: one *Spiritual*, for matters of a spiritual nature; and the other *Temporal*, for matters of a Temporal nature. And for the same ends, it hath two *Legislatures*, the one consisting of persons Spiritual, and the other of persons Temporal; whose business it is, to frame Laws for the Government of Church and State: and these Laws being Enacted and Confirmed by the Prince, as *Sovereign*, and *Supreme Head*, become obligatory to the People, and Rules for the Administration of Justice in Spiritual and Temporal Matters.

Legislation in the Convocations of Canterbury and York, in other words, was binding on the laity, whether Anglican, Dissenter or atheist, provided that that canon was 'not contrary to the Prerogative Royal, nor to the Statutes and Customs of the Realm'. Ecclesiastical law was a more complete and 'effectual' system than many supposed, concluded Gibson, were 'every Person to be constrained to a vigorous Execution of the part which belongs to him'.[102] Gibson's *Codex* could therefore come under attack from those, like the Dissenting lawyer Michael Foster, who subscribed to Hoadly's doctrine that Christ's kingdom was 'not a Kingdom *of this* World'. The opposite doctrine, with which Foster involved Gibson in guilt by association, was popery, the 'most impious and oppressive Tyranny that ever exercised the Patience of God or Man'. Gibson too was aiming at 'a sacerdotal Empire'.[103]

Gibson had been the target of sustained hostility in the 1730s, charged with an attempt to arrogate the nomination of bishops, reminded of the

---

[101] Edmund Gibson, *Codex Juris Ecclesiastici Anglicani: or, The Statutes, Constitutions, Canons, Rubricks and Articles, of the Church of England* (2 vols., London, 1713), pp. i, xvii, xx.

[102] Ibid., pp. xxviii–xxix, xxxi.

[103] [Michael Foster], *An Examination Of the Scheme of Church-Power, Laid down in the Codex Juris Ecclesiastici Anglicani, &c.* (London, 1735), pp. 1–3.

Commons' charge in the impeachment of Laud, a 'Usurpation of a *Papal and Tyrannical Power*', and accused of being, thirty years before, 'a most virulent *Jacobite*'.[104] Gibson was defended, together with the clergy: 'the Nation never had less reason to be Angry with that Body of Men than at present, I believe every cool, impartial, and temperate Man, is fully convinced that the Heat, and Pride, and Passion, and Intemperance, which might be the Sins of their Forefathers, are almost banished entirely from that Order of Men in this Age'.[105] But it was a defence unlikely to weigh with Dissenters.

Under the impact of a Whig regime lasting throughout the reigns of the first two Georges, ecclesiastical lawyers were obliged to adapt and restate Gibson's position. Richard Burn, vicar of Orton in Cumberland, the author of an enthusiastically royalist survey of ecclesiastical law which achieved a prominence little short of Blackstone's *Commentaries*, was equally clear about the diverse ancestry of his subject:

> The ecclesiastical law of England is compounded of these four main ingredients; the *Civil* law, the *Canon* law, the *Common* law, and the *Statute* law . . . By the CIVIL law is meant, the law of the ancient Romans . . . And generally, the whole civil law, in use at this day, is comprized in those four books of Justinian; the *Code*, the *Digest*, the *Institute*, and the *Novels* . . . the canon law being in great measure founded upon the civil law, and so interwoven with it in many branches thereof, that there is no understanding the canon law rightly without being very well versed in the civil law.[106]

Burn's *Ecclesiastical Law* reminded its owners of the Act of 25 Henry VIII, c. 19, which confirmed the validity of 'such canons, constitutions, ordinances, and synods provincial, being already made, which will not be contrariant or repugnant to the laws statutes and customs of this realm' until reviewed and revised by a royal commission (which had not assembled until the reign of Edward VI and whose report had never received royal confirmation). Canon law not repugnant to statute, common law or royal prerogative 'is recognised and enacted to be in force by authority of parliament', concluded Burn.[107] So that although he accepted and quoted Lord Hardwicke's judgement in Middleton v. Croft (1736) that canon law passed by Convocation alone did not bind the laity, he emphasised that this was not the case of 'the ancient canon law

---

[104] [William Arnall], *A Letter To the Reverend Dr. Codex* (London, 1734), pp. 15, 32; [idem], *A Short and Plain Answer to the Modest Reply of Dr. Codex* (London, 1734).

[105] *A Modest Reply, To the Author of the Letter to Dr. Codex* (London, [1734]), p. 10.

[106] Richard Burn, *Ecclesiastical Law* (2 vols., London, 1763), vol. 1, pp. i, iv–v. Burn's account continued to be accepted as standard on this point; cf. David Williams, *The Laws relating to the Clergy* (London, 1813), p. 1.

[107] Burn, *Ecclesiastical Law*, vol. 1, pp. ix, xi.

received here before the said statute of the 25 Hen. 8'. And there was an exception: in the case of laymen who were officers of ecclesiastical courts (registers, proctors, apparitors and also churchwardens), 'the temporal courts in the adjudications which have been made, do proceed upon a supposition that these canons are in force'.[108]

Burn's sympathies were evident. Although he accepted Hale's arguments about the ultimate supremacy of the common law and the derivation of the jurisdiction of ecclesiastical courts from the crown, Burn entered his protest against the 'prejudice' and 'byass' of lord chief justices Coke and Holt towards those courts. Now, however, the 'ferments' of those times had subsided, the conflict of civil and ecclesiastical jurisdictions had abated, 'and we shall naturally recur to the state wherein popery took us up, in which there was no thwarting between the two jurisdictions, but they were amicably conjoined, affording mutual help and ornament to each other'.[109]

The ownership of such texts by Jefferson and Adams had a practical purpose which the absence of a separate Anglican legal agency obscured. The issue of ecclesiastical authority was one which allowed the heterodox intelligentsia to play on the fears of the denominations. It was also an issue which Anglicans obligingly kept on the agenda. The missionary purpose of the Society for the Propagation of the Gospel embraced in a single imperial vision all the British colonies on the North American mainland and in the West Indies. It evoked a similar colonial response: Nicholas Trott, Chief Justice of South Carolina, provided a codified review of the laws on religious establishment and the regulation of public worship which made clear how much ground had been won, and what remained to be accomplished.[110]

Dissenters still perceived the Church as an agent of persecution and tyranny; or, at least, they could say that they so perceived it, for they could point to the fact that the Church still preserved, in England, much of its ancient structure of canon law and ecclesiastical courts. Moreover, non-Anglicans could argue that the Church's claim to spiritual authority for such institutions was compromised, and the link between ecclesiastical and civil tyranny established, by an Erastian subordination of the spiritual to the secular. Where did authority reside in the Church of England? Dissenters into the eighteenth century could still cite the Act of 26 Henry VIII, cap. 1: the king

---

[108] Ibid., vol. 1, pp. xiv–xv.
[109] Ibid., vol. 1, pp. 425–6.
[110] Nicholas Trott, *The Laws of the British Plantations in America, Relating to the Church and the Clergy, Religion and Learning* (London, 1721). The work was dedicated to the Archbishop of Canterbury, the Bishop of London and the SPG.

> is vested with all power to exercise all manner of ecclesiastical jurisdiction;
> and Archbishops, Bishops, Archdeacons, and other ecclesiastical persons,
> have no manner of jurisdiction ecclesiastical, but by and under the King's
> majesty, who hath full power and authority to hear and determine all
> manner of causes ecclesiastical, and to reform and correct all vice, sin,
> errors, heresies whatsoever.

But this left the bishops with extensive temporal powers:

> They have their respective courts of judicature held in their cathedrals, and
> issue out writs, not in the King's name, (as other courts do) but in their
> own. They depute Chancellors to act as Judges; whose jurisdiction extends
> to all causes concerning marriages, last wills, administrations, etc. as well as
> to persons accused of various crimes, on which they pass sentence without a
> jury, and for which they inflict very heavy secular punishments. The
> Bishops also are Lords of Parliament, and as such have a seat in the House
> of Lords.[111]

The Church of England was, from its outset, governed by its own
system of law. The medieval English church had accepted its canon law
on the authority of Rome.[112] With the Reformation, that body of canon law
remained in force, modified only by the new doctrine of royal supremacy.
Successive sixteenth-century attempts at a fundamental revision of canon
law failed. What changed was the source of this authority: retrospectively,
it was claimed that canon law had, and had always had, validity in
England on the authority of English provincial synods. This remained
the official Anglican version throughout the eighteenth century. Its effect
was to assimilate canon law to the common law: both derived their
authority and their merits from custom and ancient usage.

From 1534 to 1833 the supreme ecclesiastical court of appeal, replacing
appeals to Rome, was the High Court of Delegates; it was served by
ecclesiastical lawyers gathered in Doctors Commons, their equivalent of
an Inn of Court.

> Professional honour made them preserve the ecclesiastical law as a separate,
> and independent system . . . They naturally tended to interpret the ecclesi-
> astical law in agreement with the *jus commune* of the western Church and to
> treat it as a part of western canonical jurisprudence . . . an independent
> ecclesiastical judicature and a body of professional ecclesiastical lawyers,
> like Doctors Commons, were the corner stones in the High Church concep-
> tion of the oneness of Church and State; they ensured that the community
> had a legal system suited to its nature as a Church. The substitution of the

---

[111] [Samuel Palmer], *The Protestant-Dissenter's Catechism* (2nd edn., London, 1774), pp. 30–1,
38.
[112] Frederic William Maitland, *Roman Canon Law in the Church of England* (London, 1898),
pp. 1–99.

Privy Council in 1833 for the High Court of Delegates, as the supreme ecclesiastical court of appeal, meant that a temporal court with temporal judges tried ecclesiastical cases and interpreted the ecclesiastical law according to rules and maxims alien to its ethos. The doctrine of binding precedents, a doctrine alien to the ecclesiastical law, compelled the diocesan and provincial courts to follow the opinions of the Privy Council, and administer a law, which was nothing but a secular law attempting to deal with spiritual things.[113]

English ecclesiastical courts shared the fate of the social order of which they were part: long defended in terms of their ancient texts, long the target of reformers, they were the subject of a Royal Commission appointed in 1830 and reporting in 1832[114] which abolished the jurisdiction of the Court of Delegates. It led in due course to further reconstruction with the Ecclesiastical Courts Bill of 1843, and to a classic example of the Victorian high-minded belief that what was in fact being abolished was really being revitalised.[115]

Until the reforms of the 1830s, ecclesiastical law was one area in which a hegemonic order found expression. The rejection both of absolutely binding precedent and of unconstrained reason had been given classic expression by bishop Robert Sanderson (1587–1663) in his Preface to the 1662 *Book of Common Prayer*:

> It hath been the wisdom of the Church of *England*, ever since the first compiling of her Public Liturgy, to keep the mean between the two extremes, of too much stiffness in refusing, and of too much easiness in admitting any variation from it ... Yet so, as that the main Body and Essentials of it (as well in the chiefest materials, as in the frame and order thereof) have still continued the same unto this day, and do yet stand firm and unshaken, notwithstanding all the vain attempts and impetuous assaults made against it, by such men as are given to change, and have always discovered a greater regard to their own private fancies and interests, than to that duty they owe to the publick.

Sound doctrine as identified by living tradition, rather than formal precedent or ahistorical reason, identified the Anglican *via media*; its existence encouraged the development of the law of equity to soften the formal rigours of the common law.

Richard Hooker had similarly avoided the Scriptural literalism of the Puritans by positing in its place an overarching natural law, conceived as the expression of God's reason: Scripture was to be interpreted, and

---

[113] Addleshaw, *High Church Tradition*, pp. 172–5.
[114] *The Special and General Reports made to His Majesty by the Commissioners appointed to enquire into the Practice and Jurisdiction of the Ecclesiastical Courts* (London, 1832).
[115] Robert Isaac Wilberforce, *Church Courts and Church Discipline* (London, 1843).

civil laws framed, in the light of this natural law. In place of a rigid and mechanical adherence to the text of Scripture, Hooker posited the Church of England as an organic and developing institution, possessing an essential continuity with the medieval church. Scriptural literalism and abstract natural rights were both replaced by Anglican tradition as the yardstick to which the content of legislation was referred. The state therefore embodied and enacted specific and positive views on what counted as acceptable religious doctrine. The Act of 1 W & M, c. 18 was inappropriately nicknamed the 'Toleration Act': toleration was not mentioned either in its title or its text, which consisted of a mere suspension of penalties incurred under still-unrepealed legislation.[116] Moreover, its benefits were confined to Trinitarian Protestant Dissenters: Roman Catholics and anti-Trinitarians were still held to be beyond the pale, and continued to enjoy only *de facto* sufferance, not legal protection. This interpretation of the 'Toleration Act' makes intelligible the Blasphemy Act of 1698, which provided penalties for those who 'deny any one of the persons in the Holy Trinity to be God, or shall assert or maintain there are more gods than one, or shall deny the Christian religion to be true, or the holy scriptures of the old and new testament to be of divine authority'.[117] Socinians, Deists and their publishers might sometimes find themselves the subject of legal proceedings into the early nineteenth century.

Anglicans regarded their exclusiveness as fully consistent with their praise of the libertarian nature of the constitution. William Blackstone merely reflected widespread opinion in announcing that 'the idea and practice of this political or civil liberty flourish in their highest vigour in these kingdoms, where it falls little short of perfection'.[118] He modified the common law doctrine of binding precedent by Hooker's doctrine of law as a reflection of natural law, and natural law as (in Blackstone's words) 'dictated by God himself'. Man 'must necessarily be subject to the laws of his creator, for he is entirely a dependent being'.[119] Revelation, revealed law, was a reiteration of natural law. 'Upon these two foundations, the law of nature and the law of revelation, depend all human laws; that is to say, no human laws should be suffered to contradict these.' Divine law ultimately overrode even precedent itself.[120]

This was the theological context for Blackstone's account of the criminal law relating to religion. 'Of Offences against God and Religion',

---

[116] Especially the Acts of 5 Eliz. I, c. 1 and 13 Car II. st. II, c. 1.
[117] 9 & 10 Will. III, c. 32, in Danby Pickering (ed.), *The Statutes at Large*, vol. 10 (Cambridge, 1764), p. 177.
[118] Blackstone, *Commentaries*, vol. 1, pp. 122–3.
[119] Ibid., vol. 1, pp. 38–41, 69–70.
[120] Ibid., vol. 1, pp. 42, 70.

chapter 4 of the fourth volume of the *Commentaries*, was the first of his categories of specific crimes, even taking precedence over High Treason. Blackstone professed that 'the preservation of Christianity, as a national religion, is, abstracted from its own intrinsic truth, of the utmost consequence to the civil state': the law protected religion because of its social utility. Nevertheless, the forms which that protection took were hardly distinguishable from a defence of Anglican Christianity as a body of dogmatic truth. First of the offences against religion was, therefore, apostasy, an offence once cognisable in the ecclesiastical courts, which had grown 'obsolete' there, but which had been (argued Blackstone) implicitly re-enacted as a criminal offence in the Blasphemy Act of 1698. Apostasy was a total rejection of Christianity ('if any person educated in, or having made profession of, the Christian religion, shall by writing, printing, teaching, or advised speaking, deny the Christian religion to be true, or the holy scriptures to be of divine authority . . .'); a partial denial constituted heresy, left as an offence at common law alone by the Act of Supremacy of 1559, which repealed all former statutes, and subjected to lesser penalties by the Heresy Act of 1678, which abolished the ancient writ *de haeretico comburendo*.[121] With these limitations, believed Blackstone, 'it seems necessary for the support of the national religion, that the officers of the church should have the power to censure heretics, but not to exterminate or destroy them'. Hence, he claimed, the propagation of anti-Trinitarian doctrines were made subject to the same offences as apostasy by the Blasphemy Act.

Offences against the established church took two forms. Reviling its ordinances was the first:[122] such laws had been necessary, suggested Blackstone, to defend the English liturgy against the 'utmost bitterness' of Rome and Geneva. They

> proved a principal means, under providence, of preserving the purity as well as the decency of our national worship. Nor can their continuance to this time be thought too severe and intolerant; when we consider, that they are levelled at an offence, to which men cannot now be prompted by any laudable motive; not even by a mistaken zeal for reformation: since from political reasons . . . it would now be extremely unadvisable to make any alterations in the service of the church; unless it could be shewn that some manifest impiety or shocking absurdity would follow from continuing it in its present form. And therefore the virulent declamations of peevish or opinionated men on topics so often refuted, and of which the preface to the

[121] 1 Eliz. I, c. 1; 29 Car. II, c. 9.
[122] Reviling Holy Communion was punishable by fine and imprisonment under 1 Edw. VI, c. 1 and 1 Eliz. I, c. 1; 1 Eliz. I, c. 2 defended the Prayer Book from criticism by the penalties, in the last resort, of forfeiture of goods and life imprisonment.

liturgy is itself a perpetual refutation, can be calculated for no other purpose, than merely to disturb the consciences, and poison the minds of the
people.

The second type of offence against the established church was nonconformity. Those who 'absent themselves from the divine worship in the
established church, through total irreligion, and attend the service of no
other persuasion' were liable to heavy fines.[123]

> The second species of non-conformists are those who offend through a
> mistaken or perverse zeal. Such were esteemed by our laws, enacted since
> the time of the reformation, to be papists and protestant dissenters: both
> of which were supposed to be equally schismatics in departing from the
> national church; with this difference, that the papists divide from us upon
> material, though erroneous, reasons; but many of the dissenters upon mat-
> ters of indifference, or, in other words, upon no reason at all. However the
> laws against the former are much more severe than against the latter; the
> principles of the papists being deservedly looked upon to be subversive of
> the civil government, but not those of the protestant dissenters. As to the
> papists, their tenets are undoubtedly calculated for the introduction of all
> slavery, both civil and religious: but it may with justice be questioned,
> whether the spirit, the doctrines, and the practice of the sectaries are better
> calculated to make men good subjects. One thing is obvious to observe,
> that these have once within the compass of the last century, effected the
> ruin of our church and monarchy; which the papists have attempted indeed,
> but have not yet been able to execute.

The sin of schism, in itself, was beyond the scope of the civil magistrate:

> If through weakness of intellect, through misdirected piety, through per-
> verseness and acerbity of temper, or (which is often the case) through a
> prospect of secular advantage in herding with a party, men quarrel with
> the ecclesiastical establishment, the civil magistrate has nothing to do with
> it; unless their tenets and practice are such as threaten ruin or disturbance
> to the state. He is bound indeed to protect the established church, by
> admitting none but its genuine members to offices of trust and emolument:
> for, if every sect was to be indulged in a free communion of civil employ-
> ments, the idea of a national establishment would at once be destroyed,
> and the episcopal church would no longer be the church of England.

Hence the penalties imposed on Protestant Dissenters by sixteenth- and
seventeenth-century Acts;[124] hence, too, the mere suspension of these statutes by the Toleration Act. Meanwhile, the Test and Corporation Acts
were fully justified. Given the interdependence of civil and spiritual jurisdiction which they underpinned, both the civil and ecclesiastical courts

[123] By the Acts of 1 Eliz. I, c. 2, 23 Eliz. I, c. 1 and 3 Jac. I, c. 4.
[124] 31 Eliz. I, c. 1; 17 Car. II, c. 2 and 22 Car. II, c. 1.

in England were able to punish a range of 'general immoralities' including swearing, cursing, witchcraft, simony, sabbath-breaking, drunkenness, lewdness and, most notably,

> *blasphemy* against the Almighty, by denying his being or providence; or by contumelious reproaches of our Saviour Christ. Whither also may be referred all profane scoffing at the holy scripture, or exposing it to contempt and ridicule. These are offences punishable at common law by fine and imprisonment, or other infamous corporal punishment: for Christianity is part of the laws of England.[125]

Blackstone echoed a maxim of Lord Chief Justice Coke (1552–1634), which Coke intended to reinforce natural-law limitations on the sovereign but which common-law judges during the Restoration converted into a practical weapon against blasphemy.[126] In a case of 1676 in the Court of King's Bench, Chief Justice Sir Matthew Hale ruled that

> such Kind of wicked blasphemous words were not only an Offence to God and Religion, but a Crime against the Laws, State and Government, and therefore punishable in this Court. For to say, Religion is a Cheat, is to dissolve all those Obligations whereby the Civil Societies are preserved, and that Christianity is Parcel of the Laws of England; and therefore to reproach the Christian Religion is to speak in Subversion of the Law.[127]

In the trial of the Deist Thomas Woolston in 1729, Lord Chief Justice Robert Raymond relied on the same doctrine:

> Christianity in general is Parcel of the Common Law of England, and therefore to be protected by it; now whatever strikes at the very Root of Christianity, tends manifestly to a Dissolution of the Civil Government . . . so that to say, an Attempt to subvert the establish'd Religion is not punishable by those Laws upon which it is establish'd, is an Absurdity.

Blasphemy remained an offence at common law, Raymond insisted, despite the more specific additional provisions of the 1698 Blasphemy Act.[128] Even the repeal in 1813 of its clause punishing anti-Trinitarianism,[129] at the instigation of Dissenters, left in place not only the rest of the Act,

---

[125] Blackstone, *Commentaries*, vol. 4, chapter 4.

[126] Courtney Kenny, 'The Evolution of the Law of Blasphemy', *Cambridge Law Journal* 1 (1922), 127–42, argued that this rested on a mistranslation or misquotation of a ruling of Judge Prisot in 1458, rightly construed as the doctrine that canon law formed part of the common law only if it had been customarily received, not that the common law punished offences against Christianity.

[127] *The Reports of Sir Peyton Ventris Kt.* (2 vols., London, 1726), vol. 1, p. 293.

[128] John Fitz-Gibbons, *The Reports Of Several Cases Argued and Adjudged in the Court of King's Bench* (London, 1732), pp. 65–61.

[129] By the Act of 53 Geo. III, c. 160.

penalising even inoffensive denials of Christianity, but also the common-law offence of blasphemous libel, and prosecutions of unbelievers under this heading, citing Woolston's case, reached a peak during the tenure of Lord Eldon as Lord Chancellor. Only from the 1830s in England did the Church progressively lose this power to enforce its doctrine, not because of a repeal of the rest of the Blasphemy Act but because of the political impossibility of prosecutions under it.[130] In England, the pattern was one of tactical retreat. In America, the threat posed by the Nonconformist and heterodox challenge to collective Anglican religiosity was vivid and immediate; far from fading away, the hegemony of the Anglican order was violently broken in 1776.

The common-law doctrine that Christianity was part of the law of England was anathema to the Deist lawyer Thomas Jefferson. His volume of Virginia law reports, posthumously published,[131] included a tract by the author himself on 'Whether Christianity is a part of the Common Law'.[132] Jefferson indignantly denied this: the judges had no authority for this 'adoption in mass of the whole code of another nation', the Jews. Old Testament laws were made 'for the Jews alone'; New Testament laws were 'intended by their benevolent author as obligatory only *in foro conscientiae*'. The alliance between Church and State in England made the judges accessories in the frauds of the clergy.[133] But although Jefferson broke the link between Church and State in America, the great majority of his countrymen did not share his Deistic views, and moved further from them in the half-century after independence. Consequently, and with unconscious irony, the courts of the early Republic continued to repeat the doctrine that Christianity was part of the common law, even though professing the Anglican defence that the law punished sin only because of its civil consequences.[134]

IV. THE ANGLICAN ASCENDANCY AS THE HEGEMONY OF DISCOURSE

Successive waves of migrants to the American colonies carried with them

[130] William H. Wickwar, *The Struggle for the Freedom of the Press 1819–1832* (London, 1928); Kenny, 'Law of Blasphemy', 132–3.

[131] Thomas Jefferson, *Reports of Cases Determined in the General Court of Virginia* (Charlottesville, 1829). For Jefferson's historical argument on the misquotation of Prisot (echoed by Kenny, 'Law of Blasphemy'), see Gilbert Chinard (ed.), *The Commonplace Book of Thomas Jefferson* (Baltimore, 1926), pp. 351–6.

[132] In Jefferson, *Writings* (Ford), vol. 1, pp. 453–70; Edward Dumbauld, *Thomas Jefferson and the Law* (Norman, Oklahoma, 1978), pp. 76–83.

[133] Jefferson, *Writings* (Ford), vol. 1, pp. vi, 142.

[134] Cases cited in Dumbauld, *Jefferson*, pp. 77–8.

the image of a militant Anglicanism.[135] Yet their image of Anglicanism as akin to Popery needs to be interpreted in the light of the theology of the Dissenters themselves, and their linked image of Anglicanism as a persecutory creed equally needs to be modified: the Anglican ascendancy is to be understood as securing its position by the techniques of hegemony rather than by those of Counter-Reformation Roman Catholicism.

The most obvious aspect of the question was quantifiable: the immense numerical preponderance of the Church of England in its ancient heartlands. Aside from its own political and doctrinal divisions, the parochial position of the Church in many areas of early-eighteenth-century England was still one of immense strength, and the confidence expressed by prelates in the lowland shires, remarkably similar to that of the Virginian clergy, reflected the numerical as well as theoretical weakness of Dissent.[136] Thomas Secker, Bishop of Oxford, discovered this in his new diocese in 1738. In the questionnaire his clergy received, one section read:

> Are there any Persons in your Parish who profess to disregard Religion, or who commonly absent themselves from all publick Worship of God on the Lord's Day? And from what Motives and Principles are they understood to do so? And what is the Number of such Persons, and is it increased of late? And of what Rank are they?

Their replies revealed not only the massive numerical prevalence of Anglican allegiance but, more significantly, the considerable uniformity in Anglican perception of the nature of the problems they still confronted. Atheism was not among them. John Edwardes, Rector of Brightwell, replied: 'There is no professd Atheist in the Parish that I know of; There are indeed too many here as in all other places, who thro' inconsideration as I suppose rather than any fixd hatred of religion commonly absent themselves from the worship of God on the Lords day.' Robert Pargeter, Vicar of Bloxham, echoed him: 'I know of None but what go to Some publick Worship of God on the Lords Day. I know of none that profess

---

[135] For the intelligentsia, see Arthur Sheps, 'Ideological Immigrants in Revolutionary America' in P. Fritz and D. Williams (eds.), *City and Society in the Eighteenth Century* (Toronto, 1973), pp. 231–46; for a later period, Michael Durey, 'Thomas Paine's Apostles: Radical Emigrés and the Triumph of Jeffersonian Republicanism', *WMQ* 44 (1987), 661–88. A study is needed of the commitments and beliefs that formed the ideological baggage of rank-and-file migrants.

[136] It was, of course, a church in which laymen, especially owners of advowsons and tithes, exercised considerable power against local incumbents: G. F. A. Best, *Temporal Pillars* (Cambridge, 1964), pp. 35–77. Best argues (p. 70) that 'Church and state, which had nearly split apart in the revolutions of the seventeenth century, were brought back into close connexion with each other [from the reign of George II]; clergy and laity adopted the same ideals and almost the same conduct; the spiritual and temporal estates became again what they had always been in medieval theory, twin dimensions of an indivisible unity.'

to disregard Religion from any other motive than laziness.'

Haviland Hiley, Vicar of Goring, underlined the lack of principled protest: 'There are none who profess a Disregard for Religion, tho' there are some who often absent themselves from the Publick Worship of God on the Lord's Day. I can't understand that they do this on any Principles; but only from the Motives of Negligence and Want of due Regard and lively Sense of their Duty.' The absentees were always described as 'of the lowest rank' (John Edmonds, Vicar of Bampton); 'of the meaner sort' (Thomas Hunt, Vicar of Bix).[137] A movement founded in apathy and without structured leadership seemed to pose little danger. Nor was such a picture confined to the south. At York in 1743, Archbishop Herring's enquiries revealed a similar pattern. Parish after parish recorded few or no Dissenters.[138] By the early nineteenth century, this picture had indeed changed: but what emerged from visitation returns of that age was neither a growth of atheism, nor of undeferential friction between proletarians and Anglican clergy as such, but the proliferation and growth of a variety of Dissenting sects.[139]

In numerical terms, the steep rise in English Dissent (as opposed to Methodism nominally within the Church of England) came in the opening decades of the nineteenth century. Even in 1800, the classic report of the clergy of Lincoln into the decline of Anglican attendance in their diocese analysed the problem in terms largely drawn from the world inhabited by respondents to the visitation returns of Bishop Secker six decades earlier. In their list of causes, the new element in the scene came first:

> The circulation of profane, obscene, and seditious writings, tending to impair the religious sentiments, morals, and loyalty of the people, and to prejudice them against the present establishment both civil and ecclesiastical: but we are happy to add, that it also appears that the circulation of these pernicious productions hath of late been much discountenanced, and diminished.

The 1790s counter-offensive against Jacobinism had, thought many Anglicans, been widely successful. That threat disposed of, the other causes cited by the clergy of Lincoln had a timeless air about them: the 'irregular

---

[137] *Articles of Enquiry Addressed to the Clergy of the Diocese of Oxford at the Primary Visitation of Dr. Thomas Secker, 1738*, ed. H. A. Lloyd-Jukes (Oxford, 1957), pp. 4–6, 13, 17, 22, 24, 69. For the successfully inclusive Anglicanism of Brightwell in the Restoration, and the viability of the unitary ideal, see Spurr, *Restoration Church of England*, pp. 166 ff, 232.

[138] *Archbishop Herring's Visitation Returns 1743*, ed. S. L. Ollard and P. C. Walker (5 vols., Wakefield, 1928–31).

[139] *The Diocese of Exeter in 1821: Bishop Carey's Replies to Queries before Visitation*, ed. Michael Cook (2 vols., Torquay, 1958–60).

management of ale-houses'; farm labour on Sundays; wakes, feasts, danc-
ing, fairs, markets, cock-fights; 'the slackness of churchwardens'. By contrast, the threat posed by old Dissent was played down: 'the number of
real Dissenters is small, and by no means increasing. They are chiefly
Baptists or Independents, and a few Quakers. These behave in general
with great decency, and manifest no asperity towards the Clergy or other
members of the establishment.'

The major threat was perceived to be the enemy within: revivalist
Methodism. Its adherents ranged from friends through misguided separatists to open enemies. They were ranked in three groups:

1   Persons who profess to be members of the Church of England, and
    regularly attend divine service at Church, and partake of the Holy
    Sacrament; but have places set apart for additional exercises of
    devotion, at such hours as do not interfere with the Church service.

2   Such as rarely, if ever, attend the Church service, and are regardless
    of the hour at which it is celebrated in the appointment of their
    separate time of meeting, and have also of late taken upon
    themselves to administer and receive the Holy Sacrament at such
    meetings.

3   Those who attend and encourage a wandering tribe of fanatical
    teachers, mostly taken from the lowest and most illiterate classes of
    society; among whom are to be found raving enthusiasts, pretending
    to divine impulses of various and extraordinary kinds, practising
    exorcisms, and many other sorts of impostures and delusions, and
    obtaining thereby an unlimited sway over the minds of the ignorant
    multitude.

These itinerant preachers might 'sometimes' be aided in subverting a
parish 'by the remembrance of some former dispute on matters of property'; but with that perfunctory exception, the clergy's analysis was wholly
ecclesiastical. It owed nothing to any perception of economic change,
urbanisation or class formation. Despite the shock waves created by the
French Revolution, the report displayed no assumption that any watershed divided its authors from a world before 1789.[140]

Trade and commerce multiplied; the ideals of material acquisition and
improvement were increasingly dwelt on by observers. It is difficult, how-

[140] *Report from the Clergy of a District in the Diocese of Lincoln, Convened for the Purpose of Considering
the State of Religion In the Several Parishes in the Said District, as well as the best Mode of promoting
the Belief and Practice of it; and Of guarding, as much as possible, against the Dangers arising to
the Church and Government of this Kingdom, from the alarming Increase of Profaneness and Irreligion
on the one Hand, and from the false Doctrines and evil Designs of Fanatic and Seditious Teachers on
the Other* (London, 1800), pp. 7–9, 15.

ever, to see these developments as in any necessary sense hostile to Anglican hegemony; property (or luxury), consumption (or profligacy) were
most clearly associated with the middle ground of the established order,
and the social commentators who deplored them, like Richard Price and
James Burgh, were generally Dissenters or High Churchmen.[141] Individuals caught up in business expansion were not prominent in revising
the intellectual framework of their world. The specific case is, as always,
a revelation of what was possible in the old order. Thomas Turner (1729–
93), shopkeeper of East Hoathly in Sussex, traded in a wide range of mer-
chandise.[142] His financial dealings ran throughout his locality, but induced
in him no sense of regional distinctiveness or cohesion. His religiosity,
too, must be balanced against the familiar equation of shopkeeper with
Dissenter, for he was both an Anglican and a regular attender at church
(absence without cause on a Sunday gave him attacks of conscience).[143]
Spirituality bulked large in his private life. Large parts of the diary consist
of Turner's 'moralizing reflections after having heard a striking sermon,
read a stirring passage from some improving work, or suffered pangs of
conscience after either a quarrel with his wife or a heavy evening's
drinking'.[144] With such views, Turner did not try to manipulate his relationship with his rector, the Rev. Thomas Porter, and even found him at
times too worldly for Turner's tastes rather than too pious. Despite his
unwearied economic endeavour, Turner accepted Anglican social teaching in one crucial respect: 'I will make it my greatest endeavour to be
content with that station which it shall please God to appoint for me, and
if it be my fortune to be poor and low in the world (as I can have no
other hopes), I will endeavour to meet my fortune with pleasure. For thou,
O Lord, knowest what is best for me.'[145]

Piety did not confine itself to submission. It produced in addition both
a moral critique of society, and patriotism. Turner was a strict attender

---

[141] John Sekora, *Luxury: The Concept in Western Thought, Eden to Smollett* (Baltimore, 1977) and
Albert O. Hirschmann, *The Passions and the Interests: Political Arguments for Capitalism before
its Triumph* (Princeton, 1977) fail to record the origins of the 'luxury' debate in conflicts
of Anglican and Dissenting social teaching. For the High Church critique see James E.
Bradley, 'The Anglican Pulpit, the Social Order, and the Resurgence of Toryism during
the American Revolution', *Albion* 21 (1989), 361–88, and for the wider setting James
Raven, *Judging New Wealth: Popular Publishing and Responses to Commerce in England, 1750–
1800* (Oxford, 1992). For the religious context of this debate in the colonies, Edmund S.
Morgan, 'The Puritan Ethic and the American Revolution' in idem, *The Challenge of the
American Revolution* (New York, 1976), pp. 88–138.
[142] *The Diary of Thomas Turner 1754–1765*, ed. David Vaisey (Oxford, 1984).
[143] Turner, *Diary*, p. 36, 21 March 1756.
[144] Vaisey, Introduction, ibid., p. iv. For such reflections, pp. 65, 113, 127, 162, 184, 228,
319.
[145] Turner, *Diary*, p. 82, 28 Jan. 1757.

at services on days of 'public fast and humiliation' to implore military victory, like that on 6 February 1756 or 16 February 1759. On 17 February 1758

> The fast-day to all outward appearance has (in this parish) been observed with a great deal of decorum and, I hope, true piety, the church in the morning being more thronged than I have seen it lately. Oh, may religion once more rear up her head in this wicked and impious nation and triumph over vice and immorality! Then may we once more hope for success from our fleets and armies when our commanders shall be inspired with the love of God and his most holy religion. Then (and not till then) will all private interest and connection of friends give way and become subordinate to the love of king and country.[146]

Not were such attitudes unreflective. On the contrary, Turner's reading is an eclectic catalogue of the major works of Anglican theology in his age. To *The Whole Duty of Man* (1658) and *The New Whole Duty of Man* (1744) he added William Beveridge, *Private Thoughts upon Religion* (1709) and *Works* (1720); Gilbert Burnet, *The History of the Reformation of the Church of England* (1679); William Derham, *Physico-Theology* (1713); Daniel Dobel, *Primitive Christianity Propounded* (1755); Charles Drelincourt, *The Christian's Defence against the Fears of Death* (translated from the French, 1675); Edmund Gibson, *The Evil and Danger of Lukewarmness in Religion* (1748) and *Trust in God the best Remedy against Fears of All Kinds* (4th edn, 1749); James Hervey, *Meditations Among the Tombs* (1746); Anthony Horneck, *The Great Law of Consideration* (1677); Robert Nelson, *A Companion for the Festivals and Fasts of the Church of England* (1704); John Sharp, *Works* (1749); Thomas Sherlock, *Sermons on Various Subjects* (1747) and *A Letter . . . to the Clergy and People of London and Westminster; on Occasion of the late Earthquakes* (1750); William Sherlock, *A Practical Discourse Concerning Death* (1689) and *A Practical Discourse Concerning a Future Judgement* (1692); John Tillotson, *Sermons* (various collections from 1671); William Wake, *The Principles of the Christian Religion Explained* (1699); James Walder, *The Ax Laid to the Root; or, a Preservative against the Erroneous Doctrines of the Methodists* (1763); and Robert Warren, *The Devout Christian's Companion* (2nd. ed., 1733).[147] It need not be suggested that Thomas Turner was representative in the range and depth of his reading;[148] but the specific case is good evidence for the poten-

---

[146] Turner, *Diary*, pp. 36, 137, 175.

[147] Turner, *Diary*, pp. 347–53. The dates of first publication are given where known; many of these titles were frequently reprinted.

[148] Comparisons are difficult: surviving accounts seldom bear on the points at issue, e.g. *An Eighteenth-Century Shopkeeper: Abraham Dent of Kirkby Stephen*, ed. T. S. Willan (Manchester, 1970). Against this must be set evidence for provincial literacy in theological and Latin classics: for Manchester, in *The Private Journals and Literary Remains of John Byrom*, ed. Richard Parkinson (2 vols., Chetham Society, Manchester, 1854–7); for Lichfield, in

tial extent of the reading of a member of the provincial middle orders, and good evidence against Anglican ascendancy necessarily resting on unthinking acceptance or deference.

Such a nexus of ideas was not confined to the south of England, as Archbishop Herring's visitation returns also attest. It could be entertained by a Yorkshire hardware manufacturer like Thomas Butler (b. 1773), son of a Methodist trustee and himself an assiduous hearer of Methodist sermons.[149] His diary records no conflict with orthodox Anglican clergy, no systemic class friction, and no perceptions of secularisation. Butler indeed looked with some scepticism on the effects of secular ideologies.[150] He preferred to celebrate George III's birthday;[151] but a focus of his public morality, like Thomas Turner's, was evidently provided by public fasts. On 9 March 1796 he recorded:

> This is a day appointed by proclamation for a General Fast, & Humiliation before Almighty God, and to send up our Prayers & Supplications before the Divine Majesty, for obtaining pardon of our Sins & for averting those heavy Judgements, which hang at present over our heads, & which we have most righteously deserved, and imploring Blessings and Assistance on the Arms and Fleets of our Sovereign both by Sea & Land and for restoring, and perpetuating, Peace, Safety & prosperity to Himself, and His Kingdoms.
>
> I do not doubt but many a sincere and Ardent prayer, has ascended to the Arches of Heaven, from the Hearts of Thousands & Tens of Thousands of Loyal Subjects on behalf of our King ...

Butler was evidently untroubled by fears that this Providential perspective was not shared by his countrymen; and in due course he and others could believe that their prayers had been answered. On 18 December 1797 he wrote:

> Today is appointed by Royal Proclamation to be a day set apart to return thanks to Almighty God for his Wonderful deliverances wrought for us in Giving us three Such Signal Victories over our Enemies at Sea – viz: Over the French on the 1 June 1795 – by the Fleet commanded by Lord Howe – Over the Spaniards on the 17 Feb. 1797 – by Sir J. Jarvis – and over the Dutch on the 11 Octo. 1797 – by Admiral Duncan.
>
> The King in all his Royal Attire: With all the Peers in their Robes &c.

James L. Clifford, *Young Samuel Johnson* (London, 1955). See also C. J. Hunt, *The Book Trade in Northumberland and Durham to 1860* (Newcastle, 1975) and John Feather, *The Provincial Book Trade in Eighteenth-Century England* (Cambridge, 1985).

[149] *Diary of Thomas Butler of Kirkstall Forge, near Leeds, Yorkshire. From March 8, 1796, to December 31, 1799* (privately printed [London, 1906]).

[150] On 5 February 1798 he dined with a Mr Ingham, 'very arbitrary in his Family: will bear no Contradiction – NB – he is a Democrat. – All violent Democrats are Tyrants over their Inferiors. Tis almost an invariable Rule': Butler, *Diary*, p. 196.

[151] Ibid., p. 39.

&c. &c. are to March in procession to St Pauls – and there to dedicate to
the Lord the Colours taken in the forementioned Engagements: at the same
time to render thanks to the Almighty for such remarkable Instances of his
favor: and humbly to Implore Divine assistance in future: so that our Enemies may never have power over us.

Mr. Miles gave us an excellent Sermon this morning on the Occasion.

Almighty God – vouchsafe to Accept the praises that will be uttered with
unfeigned Lips by thousands and tens of thousands this day and Graciously
attend to the supplications of thy people – and Grant that in future We
may All trust in thee; And then we shall never be confounded.

Amen & Amen

Anglicanism itself could be the matrix for a fervent patriotism, chastened
by defeat in the American War, heightened again in the wars against
revolutionary France. On 31 December 1801, William Holland, an Anglican incumbent in Somerset, penned an eulogy of his country's heroic
success in checking revolutionary frenzy.

> After this the preliminaries to Peace were soon signed Glory be to God.
> Long live great George our King. May French principles, Atheism and Irre-
> ligion vanish from the face of the Earth, Amen . . . I had a nice woodcock
> this day for dinner which I am very fond of.[152]

English discourse could be nearly as Providentialist as colonial American
discourse; but England's Providence was an Anglican one, established by
the Church's claim to be the Church of all Englishmen.

During the American war, public opinion in the north of England
moved as decisively against the colonists as it did in the south.
Birmingham, Bradford, Halifax, Huddersfield, Leeds, Manchester, Nottingham and Wakefield were all successfully encouraged to petition in
favour of the enforcement of coercive legislation, though counter-petitions
from such towns often warned of economic dislocation.[153] In the latter part
of 1775 the loyal petitions became a flood, and in the early years of the war
proministerial support was strong in the provinces, despite the alternative
structure given to opinion by Dissent.[154] Expanding English manufacturing towns, if they lacked their own MPs, were not markedly polarised by
political conflicts echoing parliamentary alignments until the 1820s or
after: without such a matrix, English provincial consciousness could not

[152] Holland, *Diary*, p. 62 (see p. 191, n. 165 below).

[153] Lawrence Henry Gipson, *The British Empire Before the American Revolution* (15 vols., New York, 1958–70), vol. 12, pp. 288–93; Colin Bonwick, *English Radicals and the American Revolution* (Chapel Hill, N.C., 1977), pp. 84–6.

[154] John Money, *Experience and Identity: Birmingham and the West Midlands, 1760–1800* (Manchester, 1977); Dora Mae Clark, *British Opinion and the American Revolution* (New Haven, 1930); and, especially, James E. Bradley, *Popular Politics and the American Revolution in England: Petitions, the Crown, and Public Opinion* (Macon, Georgia, 1986).

develop in ways which its nineteenth-century flowering implies. One student has concluded that 'a majority' of Leeds merchants were Church and King loyalists, in power until they met 'crushing defeat' in 1832, and thereafter replaced by 'a profusion of Whig Dissenting merchant-manufacturers, engineers and retailers – a class largely created after the 1780s'.

> Until its dissolution the old corporation continued to be dominated by a caucus of Tory, Anglican merchants, who only admitted new common-councilmen of their own breed and on their own terms . . . The Tory merchants opposed every petition for peace before 1815, and every motion for reform after the war. Their great dinners on the Prince Regent's birthday, and the meetings of the Pitt and True Blue clubs, were concluded with vast speeches and innumerable toasts that called for support of the Constitution, the Established Church and the preservation of social order. Dissent they regarded as a peculiar form of Anglicised Jacobinism.[155]

This social formation, alternatively pictured as 'Church and King' or 'Old Corruption', was intelligible in all parts of England (in Scotland, Ireland and Wales it took different forms); it was this which reformers agreed in taking as their target.[156]

The parochial manners on which this public order was premised were not ones of servility. This question was indeed addressed within Anglican theory under another heading which illuminates the modern concept of hegemony. Seventeenth-century Anglicans faced with a monarch unacceptable on religious grounds had worked out a theory of the limits of disobedience (confusingly redescribed by its enemies as 'passive obedience'); Anglicans under George III, including George Horne, William Smith and William Stevens, merely dwelt on the related positive duty of obedience to acceptable monarchs. In 1776, the heterodox Richard Watson interpreted this emphasis to mean that the state was being defended with a claim of unlimited obedience. The doctrinally orthodox William Stevens protested: 'I never heard of any who maintained it. If by *unlimited*, he means *passive obedience*, which I suspect he does from his using the term as synonymous to *non-resistance*, I am sorry, that a master in Israel should not know these things better. There is surely an essential

[155] R. G. Wilson, *Gentlemen Merchants: The Merchant Community in Leeds 1700–1830* (Manchester, 1971), pp. 172–3, 181–2.

[156] Classically in [John Wade], *The Extraordinary Black Book: An Exposition of the United Church of England and Ireland; Civil Lists and Crown Revenues; Incomes, Privileges, and Power, of the Aristocracy . . . Presenting a Complete View of the Expenditure, Patronage, Influence, and Abuses of the Government, in Church, State, Law and Representation* (London, 1831); cf. W. D. Rubinstein, 'The End of 'Old Corruption' in Britain 1780–1860', *P&P* 101 (1983), 55–86, and the extended context given to this point in Clark, *English Society 1688–1832* and *Revolution and Rebellion* (Cambridge, 1986).

difference between obeying unlawful commands, implied by unlimited obedience, and patient suffering for not obeying them, which is, properly speaking, *passive obedience*.'[157] The expression of such doctrines during the American war was merely a deployment of a long-established rationale for the state, preached repeatedly by orthodox Whigs under George I and George II. If the experience of the reigns of the first two Hanoverians is omitted, then Anglican preaching of the 1770s appears to be new in converting monarchical divine right into the divine right of lawful government;[158] but this was already an ancient strategy in the Anglican repertoire, not confined to any group anachronistically labelled 'Tory'.

In traditional early-Hanoverian Whig fashion, Anglican clergy during the American war identified monarchical protection with the rule of law and the liberties of the constitution and valued the dynasty as the deliverer and guarantor of England's Protestant freedoms. Such a self-image, entrenched by the legal facts of Anglican privilege, enjoyed a position which can usefully be analysed as hegemonic:[159] it was one of several alternatives; it was dominant; it owed its dominance to cultural and intellectual victory rather than to naked power (matched by coerced submission) alone. For the same reason, to describe Anglicanism as hegemonic within England is to record that it faced continued challenges. No assumption of stasis in social forms need be integral to the concept of hegemony, though the continuance of such a situation is likely to require that change proceed by evolution rather than transformation. Transformation was not the experience of Anglicans in England during the American Revolution: the diaries, discussed below, of James Woodforde (1740–1803) and William Jones (1755–1821) display no sense of a watershed in popular sentiment or allegiance during the 1770s, although those of William Holland (1746–1819), Benjamin Newton (1761–1830) and John Skinner (1772–1839) record just such pessimistic judgements on local phenomena during and after the Napoleonic War.

During the American conflict, Anglican clergy continued to deplore (what with reference to their precommitments they perceived as) licentiousness and insubordination; but it would be difficult to read off from their rhetoric any simple increase in the incidence of either.[160] A more

---

[157] [William Stevens], *The Revolution Vindicated, and Constitutional Liberty Asserted* (Cambridge, 1777), pp. 13–14.

[158] Paul Langford, 'Old Whigs, Old Tories and the American Revolution', *Journal of Imperial and Commonwealth History* 8 (1980), 106–30, at 124.

[159] For an exploration of the concept of hegemony, see Joseph V. Femia, *Gramsci's Political Thought* (Oxford, 1981), pp. 23–60; J. C. D. Clark, 'Reconceptualising Eighteenth-Century England', *British Journal for Eighteenth Century Studies* 15 (1992), 135–9.

[160] If it were possible to do so, it would have to be conceded also that the rapid advance of Anglican evangelicalism from the 1790s, and the associated changes in public morals,

valid exercise is to ask how these threats were pictured.[161] Political disaffection was conventionally traced to a right of private judgement rather
than to proletarian self-consciousness. The secular ideas which accompanied it were seen as ones of natural rights, defined in opposition to
duties. Rank and property were depicted as antithetical to licentious egalitarianism and levelling rebelliousness. Stock phrases characterising a
'mutinous licentious spirit' or a 'restless and factious spirit' disclosed an
understanding of the problem as intellectual or moral, and as a frenzy
rather than the cool effects of popular political organisation or a rational
reaction to violated constitutional liberties. The persistence of denunciation in such similar terms is evidence for Anglican hegemony rather than
monopoly, but an hegemony challenged by religious heterodoxy or disengagement, and confronted by what Anglicans pictured as their political
consequences, 'faction' and 'disaffection'. These two things were defined
and denounced in ways which clearly disclosed the continued supremacy
in England of the ideal of a unitary state. The hegemony of Anglican
discourse is clearly reflected in the defence of a vision of social organisation, whatever the number of Dissenters outside it. Zealous Anglicans
could continue to present an inclusive vision of their church's role: regular
attendance at her services was a 'duty'; churchwardens had a 'duty' to
see that none absented themselves 'without sufficient reason', and present
any who did; the parochial system constituted a 'beautiful and rational
system of dependence', which was 'essential to the convenience and per-
manence of society'.[162]

V. THE ANGLICAN DREAM: HARMONY AND CONFLICT IN THE
ENGLISH PARISH

It is suggested above that religious discourse was not an anachronism in
the 'old society'; that Anglicanism had been a powerful agency of state
formation; that the law relating to establishment profoundly expressed
the Church's conception of itself; that canon law still provided a target
for the disaffected; and that, on the level of abstract political theory,
Anglican discourse may rightly be analysed as hegemonic. It remains to
be traced how these forms received their concrete expression in the daily
life of English and American parishes. In both, of course, the situation

actually strengthened the hegemony of the Church as the catastrophe of 1828–32
approached.
[161] For a different interpretation, to which the present is indebted, see James E. Bradley, 'The
Anglican Pulpit, the Social Order and the Resurgence of Toryism during the American
Revolution', *Albion* 21 (1989), 361–88.
[162] John Moir, *The Parish Church. A Discourse* ... (London, 1802), pp. 3, 11, 64.

on the ground presents a picture of fragmentation and diversity which challenges any easy classification. The English and American experiences demand a comparison of these local features if any argument for the overarching validity of legal or religious discourse is to be sustained.

In the aftermath of the Restoration and Glorious Revolution the Church of England was profoundly weakened by two schisms: the exclusion of some 1,700 clergy who refused to comply with the Act of Uniformity of 1662, and the haemorrhage of a body of Nonjurors, who refused the new oath of allegiance to William and Mary in 1689, or the Abjuration Oath of 1701, or the oath of allegiance to George I in 1714.[163] If a precondition of political upheaval in the early-modern world was ordinarily a divided elite, English parishes also were no strangers to the local manifestations of religious schism. Nonjurors had their impact mostly via institutions (especially the universities) and the written word, but the denominations of 'Old Dissent' – Presbyterians, Congregationalists, Baptists, Quakers – could be found at work in many parishes. A divided Church of England, weakened by an outflow of supporters if strengthened by greater consistency, faced lasting denominational conflict as well as the less newsworthy effects of English popular anticlericalism.

Short of schism, factional disunity at the end of the eighteenth century once more weakened the parochial position of the Anglican clergy. As a High Churchman complained, 'The Clergy, instead of uniting in a cause dear to all who have any regard for an establishment which they have sworn to defend, and by which they live, are divided into two parties – the one *canonical* – the other self-named *Evangelical*.'[164] From the 1770s, the rise of an Evangelical party within the Church of England again led Anglicans to think of themselves as divided into parties, and arguably to expend more emotional energy on the 'enemy within' than on the general position of religion in their society.

Does the extent of these problems invalidate the thesis of Anglican hegemony? The search for a yardstick by which to assess its validity has led to the diaries[165] of Anglican clergymen. They are a unique source, but

---

[163] The number of Nonjurors is far harder to estimate than that of incumbents ejected from their livings during the Commonwealth or under Charles II. J. H. Overton, *The Nonjurors* (London, 1902), pp. 467–96, lists 584 English clerical and lay Nonjurors. John Findon, 'The Nonjurors and the Church of England 1689–1716' (Oxford D.Phil. thesis, 1978), pp. 193–243, identifies 530 clergy, schoolmasters and dons. Many more evaded rather than refused the oaths; others took them with mental reservations. Scotland contributed another unknown number.

[164] R. Polwhele (ed.), *The Enthusiasm of Methodists and Papists Compared: by Bishop Lavington* (London, 1833), p. ccxv.

[165] *The Bletchley Diary of the Rev. William Cole MA FSA, 1765–67*, ed. Francis Griffin Stokes (London, 1931); *The Diary of a Country Parson: The Reverend James Woodforde*, ed. John Beresford (5 vols., Oxford, 1924); *The Diary of the Revd. William Jones 1771–1821*, ed. O. F.

one which poses problems of interpretation. If they contain evidence of parochial disharmony and conflict, is this strong evidence against the local dominance of ideals of hierarchy, deference, patriarchalism or Anglican hegemony? Were these diaries biassed against the inclusion of such evidence of conflict, so that its presence is even more telling against a model of local piety and tranquillity? Yet an opposite hypothesis seems as plausible: diarists often confided their sufferings to their journals, and in the case of the clergy these sufferings might often have arisen from affronts to the ideals to which they considered respect was due. Their journals might be biassed in favour of the inclusion of exceptions to the norm. Their sense of what the norm was, however, did not evidently change in this period: what is known of diaries from the seventeenth and nineteenth centuries does not support a thesis of the collapse of Anglican dominance in the eighteenth.[166] Similarly, if the parochial position of the state church is held to have been profoundly different in continental Europe then such an argument could not be sustained without a comparison of the diaries of English and continental clergy.[167] Moreover, society's public affirmations about its structure and ruling values embodied in law, theology and political ideology will not easily be tested by the level of parochial conflict alone. The thesis that a law was in force is not immediately refuted by the observation that that law was sometimes broken, and, similarly, the hegemonic position of Anglican, aristocratic values was not in any immediate or obvious sense refuted by the existence of insubordination and disrespect. The questions to be asked about that process which finally undermined it are of two sorts. When and through what events did this loss of hegemony occur? Second, within what categories did dissidence fall?

It is conventional, especially in the age of the American Revolution, to

---

Christie (London, 1929); *Paupers and Pig Killers: The Diary of William Holland a Somerset Parson 1799–1818*, ed. Jack Ayres (Gloucester, 1984); John Skinner, *Journal of a Somerset Rector 1803–1834*, ed. Howard and Peter Coombs (Bath, 1971); cited and discussed by John Phillips, 'The Social Calculus: Deference and Defiance in Later Georgian England', *Albion* 21, 3 (1989), 426–49.

[166] The very different literary conventions which governed earlier diaries would make such a thesis of decline difficult to frame: see, for example, Alan Macfarlane (ed.), *The Diary of Ralph Josselin 1616–1683* (London, 1976). Josselin, vicar of Earl's Colne, Essex, from 1641 to 1683, scarcely conceived of his relations with his parishioners in terms other than those of providence, sin, grace and redemption, all within a strong millenarian framework. This unthreatened nexus was evidently not eroded by the 'revolution' of the 1640s; the change came through the forms of mass religious disengagement from formal observance witnessed in the eighteenth century.

[167] The subject still awaits its historian, though Françoise Deconinck–Brossard, *Vie Politique, Sociale et Religieuse en Grande Bretagne d'après les Sermons prêchés ou publiés dans le Nord de l'Angleterre 1738–1760* (2 vols., Paris, 1984), depicts a church deeply involved in all aspects of social life in a way reminiscent of the Catholic Church in France before 1789.

relate much to the rise of 'individualism', set over against 'deference'. Deference is depicted as a veneer; the reality beneath was individualistic in the sense of morally autonomous, egalitarian, secular, resistant to leadership, unconstrained by inherited identities or allegiances. Nonconformity is held to have mattered not as religion but as a way of achieving personal advancement and social levelling.[168] This allegedly new pattern of social relations, summed up in the modern meanings of 'individualism', may indeed have a revolutionary origin. From his observations on a visit to the United States from May 1831 to February 1832, Tocqueville reflected that

> 'Individualism' is a word recently coined to express a new idea. Our fathers only knew about egoism . . . Individualism is a calm and considered feeling which disposes each citizen to isolate himself from the mass of his fellows and withdraw into the circle of his family and friends . . . Individualism is of democratic origin and threatens to grow as conditions get more equal . . . aristocratic institutions have the effect of linking each man closely with several of his fellows . . . Aristocracy links everybody, from peasant to king, in one long chain. Democracy breaks the chain and frees each link.[169]

This was not the case in England, he discovered in 1833: 'The English aristocracy in feelings and prejudices resembles all the aristocracies of the world'; it has 'even in our time a power and a force of resistance which it is very difficult for a Frenchman to understand'. Only in recent years was its position challenged by 'that democratic spirit which in Europe one calls the French spirit'.

Despite being based on 'the riches and the *instincts* of the nation', the English aristocracy, insisted Tocqueville, was threatened by a wave of reform: 'all the secondary abuses upon which the aristocracy leans, are falling'. 'For three years now the House of Lords has seemed isolated in the country.'

> If any fundamental change in the law, or any social transformation, or any substitution of one regulating principle for another is called a revolution, then England assuredly is in a state of revolution. For the aristocratic principle which was the vital one of the English constitution, is losing strength every day, and it is probable that in due time the democratic one

[168] Phillips, 'Deference and Defiance'; Roy Porter, *English Society in the Eighteenth Century* (Harmondsworth, 1982).

[169] Alexis de Tocqueville, *Democracy in America*, ed. J.P. Mayer and Max Lerner (2 vols., London, 1968), vol. 2, part 2, chapter 2 (first published 1835). For an argument that 'individualism' in this sense has been an historical episode in American history rather than an eternal verity see Stephanie Coontz, *The Social Origins of Private Life* (London, 1988); cf. Y. Arieli, *Individualism and Nationalism in American Ideology* (Cambridge, Mass., 1964). For the European concept see Colin Morris, *The Discovery of the Individual 1050–1200* (London, 1972).

will have taken its place ... In past times what most distinguished the
English people from any other was its satisfaction with itself ... Today
everything has changed. In the England of our times a spirit of discontent
with the present and hatred of the past shows itself everywhere.

The revolution had not yet been completed: 'I was singularly struck
during my stay in this country by the extent to which the aristocratic
principle affected manners.' But 'the revolution is on the move'. With the
aristocracy might fall the church, for in its wealth, its abuses and its
political power, the Church of England 'finds itself much in the position
of the Catholic Church in France before the revolution of 1789'. The
division between Church and Dissent was politicised: 'Thus you not only
have a political aristocracy and democracy, but also an aristocratic religion and a democratic one. Religious tensions are going in the same
direction as political ones; a grim symptom for the future.'[170]

'Individualism', as a secular term, did not arrive in English discourse
until the 1840s. In the old world its closest equivalent was the Protestant
right of private judgement. This, however, could be far more subversive
of established forms than the merely negative model of human relations
encapsulated in 'individualism' was to be. The heterodox Dissenting minister Samuel Palmer explained in 1774 why the 'right of private judgement
and liberty of conscience', central to the Dissenting position, entailed that
'all human laws, which are inconsistent with the divine, ought to be
disobeyed':

> Q.3. *But is every private man to judge for himself, whether the laws of his country
> are agreeable to the laws of God?*
> A. Certainly in the affairs of religion, every man ought to judge for himself,
> since every man must give an account of himself to God, who has given us
> an infallible rule in his word to guide us, and reasonable faculties to under-
> stand it; which private persons are as capable of using, to discover the way
> of truth and duty, as magistrates and large bodies of men.[171]

Secular individualism was politically quietist, never elevated into a creed;
Dissent was a clearly-formulated doctrine, containing a right of resistance.
Adjustment is necessary before we apply nineteenth-century American
conceptions of individualism to England before the 1830s; it is not a
concept which obtrudes itself from the record of Anglicanism's parochial
role. Its records disclose that Anglican vicars sometimes met with disrespect from some of their parishioners. We might infer that the vicars

---

[170] Alexis de Tocqueville, *Journeys to England and Ireland*, ed. J. P. Mayer (London, 1958), pp.
50, 59–61, 64, 66–72, 79. These perceptions support my conclusions in *English Society
1688–1832*, chapter 6.
[171] [Samuel Palmer], *The Protestant-Dissenter's Catechism* (2nd edn., London, 1774), p. 24.

expected to be treated with more respect; that disrespect violated a social code; that they could only respond with indignation; that they lacked effective powers of coercion. Their position, in other words, was hegemonic.

The extent of conflict should not be overstated.[172] William Cole was on familiar terms with his neighbours and servants, and recorded many instances of the local poor dining in his kitchen. James Woodforde's tithe audits were generally agreeable (perhaps because he only collected half the sums which Mr Dell, his successor, was to demand), but he congratulated himself on the harmony of his tithe dinners nevertheless. William Holland, like William Cole, found his difficulties arose largely from one obstreperous tenant farmer in his parish;[173] most of Holland's tithe days recorded in his diary were peaceful. Social conflict in Benjamin Newton's diary was not prominent. Only the profoundly unhappy John Skinner pictured himself as surrounded by daily antagonism, and this might be accounted for not least by his troubled personality. Even so, Skinner's knowledge of his parishioners of all social classes was encyclopaedic: he was continually among the poor. At its best, parochial life could be far more agreeable, as John Trusler found when he arrived in the living of Ockley, Surrey, in 1759:

> In this parish, where I continued more than a year, I received great civilities

[172] Social conflict is a theme markedly absent in many other clerical diaries. See the diary of John Thomlinson (1692–1761), a curate in Co. Durham 1717–20, rector of Glenfield, Leicestershire 1720–61, printed for 1717–22 in J. C. Hodgson (ed.), *Six North Country Diaries* (Surtees Society, vol. 118, London, 1910), pp. 64–167; *The Diary of Benjamin Rogers Rector of Carlton, 1720–71*, ed. C. D. Linnell (Bedfordshire Historical Record Society, vol. 30, Streatly, Beds., 1950), printed for 1727–40; *Recreations and Studies of a Country Gentleman of the Eighteenth Century. Being Selections from the Correspondence of the Rev. Thomas Twining, M.A.* (London, 1882), the record of a Rector of St Mary's, Colchester (b. 1735, d. 1804); *Diaries of William Johnston Temple 1780–1796*, ed. Lewis Bettany (Oxford, 1929): Temple (1739–96) was incumbent of parishes first in Devonshire, then Cornwall; *Memoirs of the Life and Writings of the late Rev. Henry Tanner, of Exeter*, ed. Robert Hawker (London, 1811): Tanner (1718–1805) here writes a journal of spiritual introspection prompted by George Whitefield; John Freeman, *Life of the Rev. William Kirby, MA* (London, 1852), Rector of Barham, Norfolk; *The Journal of the Rev. William Bagshaw Stevens*, ed. Georgina Galbraith (Oxford, 1965), which covers the years 1792–1800; *The Diary of a Cotswold Parson: Reverend F. E. Witts, 1783–1854*, ed. David Verey (Gloucester, 1980), printed for the years 1820–52; *Reminiscences Personal and Bibliographical of Thomas Hartwell Horne, BD, FSA*, ed. Sarah Anne Cheyne (London, 1862). David Davies, Rector of Barkham, Berkshire 1782–1819 and author of the classic *The Case of Labourers in Husbandry Stated and Considered* (London, 1795) seems to have enjoyed equally good relations both with his poor parishioners and with the tenant farmers from whom he derived his tithe: Pamela Horn, *A Georgian Parson and His Village: The Story of David Davies (1742–1819)* (Abingdon, 1981).

[173] Cf. Richard Gough, *The History of Myddle*, ed. David Hey (Harmondsworth, 1981). Gough (1635–1723), of Myddle in Shropshire, 'was writing from the point of view of the small freeholder and orthodox Anglican, who upheld the moral code of the church and preached the virtues of hard work and obedience ... his scathing denunciations were aimed at relatively few individuals' (p. 10).

from the people in general, and many acts of friendship from individuals, so as to enable me, on a curacy of £40 a year, to live comfortably and keep two saddle-horses. One lent me a house, another furnished it, a third supplied me with coals, a fourth with wine, a fifth with poultry; one with vegetables, another with fruit, and two days in the week we had the use of a gentleman's carriage, to go wherever we pleased: my wife was as much beloved as myself, and these friends studied to bestow what they meant to give, in a delicate way, so as neither to hurt my pride nor my feelings: so much is the curate of a country parish befriended, where he is liked.[174]

Did this situation systematically change after some mid-century idyll? The nature of the frictions recorded by Cole, Woodforde, Jones, Holland and Skinner do not, in general, suggest this. Many of the incidents of petty conflict they lamented had to do with over-zealous choirs or too-enthusiastic bellringers, the sort of conflicts which occur when popular participation is at a high, not a low, level. Other problems arose from intoxicated congregations: but it was remarkable that men should be so determined to attend their parish church, even though drunk, or even if sufficiently rough in their manners to fight each other. This suggests a popular church, deeply rooted in society, not the preserve of an elite alone. We discover that popular religion had a streak of anticlericalism; but this, of course, had even preceded the Reformation.[175]

If parochial life witnessed conflict between the Church and the Nonconformists, the latter were just as prone to conflict within their own congregations. Benjamin Hoadly warned that the same spirit of faction could be observed even in those few Anglican parishes where the incumbent was elected:

> in *Parishes*, and places where the *People* chuse their own *Ministers*, there are the greatest divisions, and quarrels, the greatest feuds, and passions remarkable; as *Unqualified Ministers*, as in other places; and, perhaps it may be said also, the greatest number of *Dissenters* from the *Established Church*. Nothing hath been the *Cause* of greater variance and strife, and illwill amongst neighbours, than this Choice, and the time of *Election* is commonly the time of heat, and anger; and it ends often in a *bad Choice*, and in the

---

[174] *Memoirs of the Life of the Rev. Dr. Trusler . . . Written by Himself* (Bath, 1806), p. 146.

[175] Tithe conflicts, too, were as old as the parochial system: see the difficulties and legal arguments recorded in *Extracts from the Diary of the Rev. Robert Meeke, Minister of the Ancient Chapelry of Slaithwaite, near Huddersfield*, ed. Henry James Morehouse (London, 1874), p. 33 and passim, and the journal of the Rev. William Sampson 1672–1701, printed as *The Rectors Book Clayworth Notts*, ed. Harry Gill and Everard Guilford (Nottingham, 1910), pp. 23, 30, 44–5, 57, 78–80, 94, 135, 146–53. Tithe disputes did not prevent Sampson from knowing his parishioners closely and recording their churchgoing in detail. The same minute knowledge of a congregation, and exact records of charity distributed to the poor, can be found in the notebook of the Rectors of Lower Heyford, Oxfordshire 1730–80, begun by the Rev. Thomas Leigh: Bodleian MS Top. Oxon. f. 50.

alienation of the minds of many Men from their *Brethren*, and from their *Minister*, worthy, or not worthy.[176]

The right of election could not have been central to Dissenters' separation from the Church, Hoadly inferred: democracy as such was not their goal.

'Subordination is lost': phrases like this echoed through clerical diaries. This was the most common theme of complaint in a society whose hegemonic self-image was that of a hierarchy. Order was threatened by disrespect; examples of disrespect were to be recorded and deplored. Such evidence is evidence on both sides: insolence, rough manners and obscenity clearly existed; but the mode in which they were complained of is evidence for the supremacy of the values of hierarchy. Within this social order these texts are all, in their different ways, spiritual autobiographies. Not secular diaries like those of Pepys or Evelyn, nor abstract works of spiritual introspection, they (like their American counterparts) belong to a genre of their own: specific, practical records of attempts to live a Christian life, and to minister to a congregation, amid the mundane difficulties of the real world.[177] In that context, three points emerge about the world view which these diaries disclose.

First, the social purposes of parishioners. It has been suggested that the conflicts visible in their pages are not essentially about theology, but concern 'the use of existing religious diversity by elements of the population to achieve something closer to social parity'.[178] Nevertheless, it seems that these clergymen perceived threats to their social standing in terms of rival sectarian allegiance,[179] not just in terms of proletarian rebellion against 'deference'. Theology, too, was visible at parochial as well as at metropolitan level: the reception of itinerants could be traced to the doctrinal alignment of the local residents. At Nottingham, where Charles Wesley was stoned in 1744, he had no expectation of legal redress: 'What justice could be expected from the chief men of this place, if, as I am

---

[176] Benjamin Hoadly, *The Reasonableness of Conformity to the Church of England*, Part II (2nd edn., London, 1703), pp. 151–2.

[177] A. Tindal Hart, in *The Country Priest in English History* (London, 1959), wrote (p. 18) of the 'continuity' of pastoral care 'persisting substantially unaltered for nearly a thousand years from the Norman Conquest to the Great War of 1914–18'. The genre includes works of the obscurity of the Rev. William Boys Ellman's *Recollections of a Sussex Parson* (London, 1912) and minor classics like *Kilvert's Diary: Selections from the Diary of the Rev. Francis Kilvert 1 January 1870–13 March 1879*, ed. William Plomer (3 vols., London, 1938–40), an innocent and idyllic vision without any perception of systemic, structural social conflict. The last clerical diary in this idiom is probably *Echoes of the Great War: The Diary of the Reverend Andrew Clark 1914–1919*, ed. James Munson (Oxford, 1985).

[178] Phillips, 'Deference and Defiance', 434.

[179] For a major aspect of this, the Anglican campaign against Methodism, see Arthur Warne, *Church and Society in Eighteenth-century Devon* (Newton Abbot, 1969), pp. 106–28.

informed, they are mostly Arian Presbyterians?'[180] William Cole (1714–82), from his new parish of Waterbeach, lamented the sectarian basis of its tensions:

> But the Greif of Greif is yet behind: the Parish swarms with Methodists: my 2 neighbours on each side of me are such, & opposite to me the same: & indeed, look which way I will, the same Heresy stares me in the Face. Yet such is my wretched Situation, that I am obliged to be more than ordinary Civil to these Enemies of the Church and Clergy. Only think how this must mortify my High Church Spirit? For having no Place to lay my Dunghill in, on one Side, I am obliged to pay Court, & hire a Bit of a Yard of a methodistical or presbyterian Baker, who gives leave to clear my Stable by a Back Door into it: on the other side, divided from him by a slight Paling, I am forced to go Cap in Hand to a little Pert Teacher among them, by Profession a Collar Maker: this Brother Preacher accommodates me with his Barn for my Chaise to stand in, for the Lodge or Hovel built for it by my Landlord, happens to be neither lofty nor deep enough to receive it. I leave you to guess how agreeable these things must be to my orthodox Stomach! especially when I can't cross the Yard to go into my poor Business of a Garden, but this mechanical Teacher, with the usual puritanical Assurance and Forwardness, must needs greet me every Time he sees me with Good Morrow! or How d'ye, Neighbour?[181]

William Holland was more concerned about the sectarian implications of Methodism than about its potential as a source of disrespect to himself: Methodists

> do a great deal of harm, they pretend to great sanctity, but it is ostentation, not reality. They draw people from the Established Church, infuse prejudices in them against their legal Pastors and of late they are all Democratic and favourers of French Principles and I suspect that some of the Philosophers get among them under the character of Celebrated Preachers and so poison their minds against the Established Church.[182]

This role could be traced to their theology: 'These Methodists preach Salvation through Faith in Christ without Repentance from Sin and I Preach Repentance from Sin and then Salvation through Christ.'[183]

'New Light' Presbyterian preaching in Virginia had had a similar effect, according to an Anglican clergyman:

> Both Preachers and people are great boasters of their assurance of salvation. They are so full of it here that the greatest number of those who have lately left the Church, and followed those Enthusiastick Preachers, last, as if they

---

[180] Thomas Jackson, *The Life of the Rev. Charles Wesley, MA* (2 vols., London, 1841), vol. 1, p. 367.
[181] Cole, *Diary*, p. 307, Cole to Mrs Barton, 25 Dec. 1767.
[182] Holland, *Diary*, p. 33, 11 May 1800.
[183] Holland, *Diary*, p. 270, 3 March 1816; cf. p. 292.

were there already; nay some people here who have always been justly reputed guilty of several immoralities such as do confidently assert that they are as sure of going to Heaven at cheating, lying, and even theft, and whose practices (I well know) are the same now as before, these very men do boast as much of their assurances, as others who are reckond blameless in their conversation: where such as these are so confident or rather impudent, you'l be less surpriz'd at what follows, viz, That their Preachers publickly tell their hearers, that they shall stand at the right hand of Christ in the day of Judgement, and condemn all of them who do not come to him at their call.[184]

The Rev. John Skinner reacted similarly after the death of a collier named Lockyear in 1809: 'I find that William Hill, a Methodist collier, had been with him in his last moments and extorted from him a declaration that he had faith in Christ, which is considered as a sufficient satisfaction for an ill-spent life and as a sure passport to Heaven. What delusive, what diabolical doctrines both for those who die and those who live!'[185] A collier named Cottle, who converted from the Church of England to the Methodists and finally to the Baptists in pursuit of worldly advantage, ended by drowning himself; his children too came to bad ends. Skinner drew the moral: 'Such are the consequences of instability, in religion it cuts at the root of all order and morality among the people.'[186] At the other end of the spectrum of respectability, popular knowledge of theological questions could easily reach a level at which bitter personal and familial conflict at the end of the century could be expressed by the participants as a clash between Calvinists and Arminians, each regarding the other as heretical.[187]

Secondly, with notable uniformity, these Anglican clergy subscribed to orthodox doctrine on the integral constitutional union of Church and State. William Cole, whose early-Hanoverian Tory background encouraged him to point out 'the Fallacy of vaunting ourselves of the Blessedness of our English Constitution' when it came to the actual working of jury trials and parliamentary elections,[188] nevertheless idealised the Anglican constitutional monopoly, assailed by the

> restless & indefatigable Rage & Disposition of the Fanatics of all sorts, united with their good Friends & allies the Deists and Atheists of the Age, who are out of measure uneasy at the undisturbed Quiet which they them-

---

[184] Patrick Henry, Sr, to William Dawson, Commissary of the Bishop of London, St Pauls parish, Hanover County, 13 Feb. 1745: *WMQ* I (1921), 261–6, at 264.

[185] Skinner, *Journal*, p. 26.

[186] Ibid., p. 27.

[187] E.g. in *Autobiography of Thomas Wright, of Birkenshaw, in the County of York. 1736–1797*, ed. Thomas Wright (London, 1864).

[188] Cole, *Diary*, p. 88, 11 Aug. 1766.

selves & the Catholics enjoy under a mild & moderate Administration . . . The great Enquiry, which is never thought of,[189] should be after the Enemies of the Established Church, under every Denomination of Presbyterian, Independent, Quaker, Deist, Atheist, &c., &c., &c., all in league to over-turn the Establishment, & rather than that [attempt] should fail, Christian-ity itself.[190]

A Yorkshire rector, Benjamin Newton, described the social structure which, he considered, lent solidity to Anglican ascendancy:

> It has occurred to me that one of the strongest parts of our Constitution, at least one which is the greatest security against revolutions, is that which merges all the younger sons of Nobles into the mass of the people, by which the Nobles and Commoners are linked in the strongest possible manner together, and the marriage of the clergy not allowed in Catholic countries cements that body to the laity and in the present times to the most powerful and respectable part of the laity, the great merchants or the country gentle-men from whose families the clergy and their wives (with very few exceptions) are now almost universally taken.[191]

This was the image of the social order, at once mobile and hierarchical, most often advanced by Anglican apologists. Highly unequal rewards within the Church allowed a liaison between the higher clergy and the elite: if those rewards were levelled,

> All those gentlemanly, honourable feelings, which, under the guidance of the Christian religion, now produce such happy effects upon society, must entirely disappear. The profession must be wholly degraded, must fall a prey to the frantic enthusiasm of some, the low and sordid interests of others, and to the ignorance of all. Its influence upon the higher, and middling classes would altogether vanish; and gradually, as it became filled with half-educated coarse-bred men, would cease to command the respect of the people.[192]

The tripartite, interlocking system which Newton pictured was one of great strength; but, should any of its components be impaired, the whole might suddenly shatter. So it seemed to Newton in 1817, when his eye was caught by the analysis of Edward Gibbon in a letter to Lord Sheffield

---

[189] This 1760s unpreparedness was soon modified by the Subscription Controversy of the early 1770s.

[190] Cole, *Diary*, p. 178, 24 Jan. 1767; cf. p. 253, 21 Aug. 1767.

[191] *The Diary of Benjamin Newton Rector of Wath 1816–1818*, ed. C. P. Fendall and E. A. Crutchley (Cambridge, 1933), p. 61, 5 March 1817. The Archdeacon of Merioneth similarly argued that civil and ecclesiastical government could not have 'too many degrees of subordinate ranks in its members. The more numerous the degrees of ranks, provided they be respect-able, and filled by men of sense and character, the more fences do they furnish against the abuses of the individual': Peter Williams, *A Short Vindication of the Established Church*, p. 26.

[192] Francis Thackeray, *A Defence of the Clergy of the Church of England* (London, 1822), p. 145.

of 30 May 1792: 'if you admit the smallest and most specious change in our parliamentary system', Gibbon had written, 'you are lost. You will be driven from one step to another, from principles just in theory to consequences most pernicious in practice.' England's tripartite social order would then collapse, as France's had just done. Gibbon had continued: 'Remember the proud fabric of the French Monarchy. Not four years ago it stood founded as it might seem on the rock of time force and opinion, supported by the triple Aristocracy of the Church, the Nobility and the Parliaments. They are crumbled into dust, they are vanished from the earth.'[193]

The Church clearly had its problems at local level, but into the 1820s these could seem to Anglicans to have more to do with the Church's incomplete coverage of new concentrations of population than with its failure in old strongholds. In 1822, the Rev. Francis Thackeray wrote of the Church's undermining at parochial level as a danger still some way off:

> There are prejudices at this time existing as to the duties and rights of the Clergy of the Church of England. They may not, at present, affect the pecuniary interests of that body, they may not apparently injure the stability of that Church; but, if uncorrected, they may gradually undermine, and ultimately destroy both. At all events, they are productive of many inconveniences, and much unpleasant feeling.[194]

The attention of Anglicans was focused on systemic breakdown above all by the repeal of the Test and Corporation Acts in 1828 and Catholic Emancipation in 1829. As the destruction of the Anglican ascendancy unfolded, Skinner privately lamented the partial burning of York Minster as 'a token and omen of the destruction of a great part of the Protestant Church – the purest and most enlightened, and I may add too the most adorned establishment of any in Christendom'.[195]

Thirdly, although these country clergy were fully aware of the conflicts and frustrations at parish level which their diaries record, none of these difficulties prevented them from subscribing to an ideal of social order which might, in its broadest political sense, be described as patriarchal. In 1797 the Rev. Legh Richmond became curate of Brading and Yaver-

---

[193] Newton, *Diary*, p. 61, 6 March 1817. Gibbon to Lord Sheffield, 30 May 1792, in *The Letters of Edward Gibbon*, ed. J. E. Norton (3 vols., London, 1956), vol. 3, p. 257.

[194] Thackeray, *Defence of the Clergy*, p. iii. For an argument that the 'decisive period' in the decline of clerical power and status came between 1828 and 1840, see Peter Virgin, *The Church in an Age of Negligence: Ecclesiastical Structure and the Problems of Church Reform 1700–1840* (Cambridge, 1989).

[195] Skinner, *Journal*, p. 379, 8 Feb. 1829; cf. 12 May 1825, p. 284.

land on the Isle of Wight; his church stood on high ground, overlooking the surrounding roads.

> From a point of land which commanded a view of all these several avenues, I used sometimes for a while to watch my congregation gradually assembling together at the hour of Sabbath worship . . . Gratifying associations of thought would form in my mind, as I contemplated their approach and successive arrival within the precincts of the house of prayer . . . How beautifully does this represent the effect produced by the voice of 'the good Shepherd', calling his sheep from every part of the wilderness into his fold![196]

This ideal could even extend to, and be illustrated from, the natural world. The image provided the troubled John Skinner with moments of mental peace:

> After dinner this evening there were lying on the rug before the fire my three dogs and a pet lamb of my daughter's, also a large tom cat, and at the window presented itself a tame jackdaw; all these different creatures were perfectly quiet, and to all appearances good friends. If my son and daughter and myself, perhaps, had left the room for any time the discordant dispositions of these inmates would have produced mischief, since all these creatures are as happy as creatures can be under our protection, and I may ask, were not my fellow creatures far more happy under the protection of their more powerful superiors years ago when the laws were duly executed than they are now amidst that great diversity of parties in religion and politics?[197]

Contentment, social order and spiritual consolation were the goals of these men; occasionally we have a glimpse of their attainment. William Jones could write: 'I know not what envy means. I know not the human being with whom I would exchange situation. I *have* everything which I can wish for, or at least which I *ought* to wish for.'[198] In 1800 William Holland paid a visit to his other living at Monkton Farley. Pluralism, he found, had not led to disaffection. 'Every one grinned and seemed pleased to see us and the poor seemed very respectful and did not make such dismal complaints of the times as I had expected. We returned to Bath in good time through a land of curtesies and bows and greetings.'[199]

[196] T. S. Grimshawe, *A Memoir of the Rev. Legh Richmond, AM* (3rd edn., London, 1828), pp. 40–1.

[197] Skinner, *Journal*, p. 429, 30 April 1831; cf. Keith Thomas, *Man and the Natural World: Changing Attitudes in England 1500–1800* (London, 1983), pp. 41–50. 'In early modern England human rule over the lower creatures provided the mental analogue on which many political and social arrangements were based . . . Domestication thus became the archetypal pattern for other kinds of social subordination. The model was a paternal one, with the ruler a good shepherd, like the bishop with his pastoral staff' (p. 46).

[198] Jones, *Diary*, p. 127, 7 Sept. 1801.

[199] Holland, *Diary*, p. 31, 27 April 1800; cf. W. R. W. Stephens (ed.), *The Life and Letters of Walter Farquhar Hook* (2 vols., London, 1878), vol. 1, p. 251.

Such passages are subjective testimony to the persistent power of an ideal, a personal vocation, a private vision of social order; but they are less subjective as evidence of the currency and power of idioms of political discourse. The persistence of such idioms was for a time consistent with ugly material realities, especially in the aftermath of the Napoleonic War, like the East Anglian 'bread or blood' riots of 1816 or the more widespread 'Captain Swing' riots of 1830–1. But it seems clear that the targets of such rural violence were landowners as such, and rarely clergy as such. In Anglican England, even under the grinding restraints of war, unemployment and hunger, rural violence was not easy to translate into political rebellion. To produce the events of 1776 in America and 1798 in Ireland, more was necessary than material grievance alone.[200] To undo the Anglican hegemony in England, more would be necessary than parochial friction. Even the profoundly unhappy John Skinner, writing his will two months before his suicide in 1839, recognised the power of this vision:

> I bequeath all the books [his journals] to the British Museum for my countrymen's benefit. May they know how to value such a territory as this as it ought to be valued, and unite in maintaining its ancient institutions inviolate to the last. England, I love thee still![201]

VI. THE ANGLICAN NIGHTMARE: SECTARIAN DIVERSITY IN COLONIAL AMERICA

No Anglican consensus ever embraced the whole of the diverse populations of the British Isles. Even within England, the position of the Church was hegemonic, not consensual: a part stood proxy for the whole, using its established status, legal entrenchment, material resources and intellectual dominance to persuade or to overawe. In England especially, that hegemony was successfully maintained into the early nineteenth century; but in the American colonies the picture was very different. In England, the Church long retained its numerical preponderance; in the thirteen colonies it was steadily overtaken and reduced to a minority position by 1776. Parochial conflict in England did not overset hegemony; in colonial America, hegemony was insecure even in those colonies where the Church was nominally established. Parochial conflict therefore had a far greater significance.

Ambrose Serle, observing the Revolutionary war in New York in 1776, drew attention to a cause of the rebellion 'now overlooked . . . This is

---

[200] For the clergy's role in countering rural disorder see Virgin, *Age of Negligence*, pp. 7–11; for the Church's more general problems, Best, *Temporal Pillars*, pp. 137–84.
[201] Skinner, *Journal*, p. vi.

the Circumstance of Religion, added to the very active and unbecoming
Part, the Preachers here of all Denominations have taken in these
Controversies.'

> The great Source of this religious Contention and Disorder lies in the defect-
> ive Constitution of our colonial Policy. Every Church has its pretensions
> to take the Lead; because nothing truly decisive has been done to give any
> one a real Superiority. The Church of England is by Law the established
> Church, and, as far as merely declarative Law can hold where no Law of
> Britain has been rigidly observed, asserts her Pre-eminence. The Congrega-
> tionalists, on the other hand, plead Numbers, and look with a kind of
> envious Disdain upon the Episcopalians in all their Pretensions of Preced-
> ency. These latter [Congregationalists] are, as Your Lordship knows, for
> the most part Calvinists with respect to *Discipline*, and of course have a
> pretty strong Inclination to every sort of Democracy . . . The War is . . .
> at the Bottom very much a religious War; and every one looks to the
> Establishment of his own Party upon the Issue of it. And indeed, upon the
> Issue, some one Party ought to predominate, were it only for the Conserva-
> tion of Peace. It is perhaps impossible to keep the ecclesiastical Polity out
> of the Settlement, without endangering the permanency of the civil.

Serle expected an early victory and an opportunity 'to fix the Constitution
of America in all respects agreeable to the Interests and Constitution of
Great Britain'.[202]

It was too late, not least because denominational differences had
become in many ways more marked in the American colonies. Where
commentators on English parliamentary elections would identify a bloc
of votes simply as 'Dissenters', the sects presented themselves separately
in the colonies. Ezra Stiles numbered the non-Congregationalist freemen
of Newport, Rhode Island, in 1758 clearly under the headings of Baptists,
Quakers, Episcopalians and Presbyterians: the normal size of each congregation, and the names of their adherents, were well known in settled
communities.[203] Social development did not produce harmony, but
increasing opportunities for sectarian antagonism. The conflict of denominations meant competition between ministers for congregations and
resources; both could ebb or flow with the calibre of individuals, the
acceptability of their theology, or the advent of rivals. Most denominations tended to be drawn into this pattern. The power of Anglican vestries
to elect their clergy, and so increasingly to keep them on uncertain tenure
pending confirmation, assimilated the Church to the sects in this key

---

[202] Ambrose Serle to Earl of Dartmouth, 8 Nov. 1776, in Stevens (ed.), *Facsimiles*, vol. 24,
no. 2045.
[203] Franklin Bowditch Dexter (ed.), *Extracts from the Itineraries and other Miscellanies of Ezra
Stiles, D.D., LL.D. 1755–1794* (New Haven, Conn., 1916), p. 103 and passim.

respect.[204] Jonathan Parsons, a Presbyterian minister in New England, complained of the 'spiritual tyranny' of Congregationalists and argued that it was his own denomination's polity which conformed to Calvin's design. But this claim was ineffective in America, he lamented, where all men could appeal to scripture and avoid tests and creeds.

> We are fully persuaded that it is owing to the random way of settling ministers and churches, together with a vile contempt of creeds and confessions, that has been the guilty cause of the many confusions and distresses in the land. No sort of church government fixed, but all is managed to suit the taste of the party concerned; and all confessions of faith, by which the sense and meaning of scripture may be known, are set aside. – Hence, all seem to jumble together, and make meer *hodge podge*.[205]

The pattern of settlement in the colonies was always marked by religious diversity, but in the first half of the eighteenth century sectarian pluralism 'exploded', especially in the middle colonies.[206] For this challenge the decentralised, parish-based colonial Church of England was largely unprepared, and in most colonies its success in dealing with proliferating diversity, increasing with each new wave of immigration, was limited. Just as the Board of Trade consistently sought to redefine all colonies as royal colonies, so the Church sought, wherever possible, to reproduce the English pattern of endowment and establishment. As a state church, this pressure was evident first at the level of colonial government; parochial provision lagged behind. A British undersecretary of state, William Knox, described during the Revolution how colonial self-government had been promoted by the absence of religious prescription in colonial charters: 'Every Man being thus allowed to be his own Pope, he becomes disposed to wish to be his own King, and so great a latitude in the choice of a religious system naturally begets republican and independent ideas in politics.' Even where Anglicanism gained a foothold, 'the Church itself was still kept out of sight, and its alliance with Monarchy totally dissolved. There was no Hierarchy or degrees of Eminence among the Clergy, no distinction of Bishops, Priests and Deacons, no Rule or Order, no Deans Chapters or Archdeacons.' Even the practice of Bishops of London appointing commissaries had been discontinued.[207]

---

[204] S. Charles Bolton, *Southern Anglicanism: The Church of England in Colonial South Carolina* (Westport, Conn., 1982), pp. 62–85.

[205] Jonathan Parsons, *Freedom from Civil and Ecclesiastical Slavery, the purchase of Christ. A Discourse . . . On March the Fifth, 1774, At the Presbyterian Meeting-House, in Newbury-Port* (Newbury-Port, [1774]), pp. 7–9.

[206] Jon Butler, *Awash in a Sea of Faith: Christianizing the American People* (Cambridge, Mass., 1990), p. 175.

[207] William Knox, 'Considerations on the great Question, what is to be done with America' [c.1779], ed. Jack P. Greene, *WMQ* 30 (1973), 293–306, at 303–4.

This organisational failure was more evident in retrospect, however. Earlier observers could often be optimistic about the long-term fortunes of the Church of England in the colonies, despite the proliferation of other sects.

Although the sects sought to strengthen their organisation, their potential members often displayed, before their recruitment, a weak sense of denominational identity. Some spiritually restive members of the Church of England in Hanover County, Virginia, were turned into seceders in 1743 by reading a volume of George Whitefield's sermons, printed at Glasgow and brought to the colony by a recent Scots emigrant. Challenged by the local court to declare their reasons for their absence from church, they were uncertain until, 'recollecting that *Luther* was a noted Reformer, and that his Doctrines were agreeable to our Sentiments, and had been of special Service to us, we declared our selves *Lutherans* and thus we continued 'till Providence afforded us an unexpected Opportunity of hearing the Rev. Mr. *William Robinson*', whereupon they became Presbyterians.[208]

In rural Virginia, the nominal Anglican Devereux Jarratt (1733–1801) experienced a religious rebirth: his

> first awakening to any sense of religion, was by means of a *Presbyterian*, and all the years, I had lived, since I made a profession, were among the people of that *denomination* – till I went to learning. Indeed, I knew of no other *people*, that had any real appearance of religion; and my sentiments, for want of a more liberal education, were exceedingly contracted. I scarcely thought there was any religion but among the *Presbyterians* – I imbibed all their tenets – and became such a rigid *Calvinist*, that I condemned all men and books, which said any thing against *Election* and *Predestination*. I had contracted a prejudice against the *Church of England*, not only on account of the loose lives of the Clergy, and their cold and unedifying manner of preaching, but also by reading some books, and especially a book,[209] called *the dissenting gentleman's answer to Mr. White's three Letters*.

From this position he was only recalled by further study of Anglican authors like Hervey, Wesley and Whitefield, until he decided that the Church 'contained an excellent system of doctrine and public worship – equal to any other in the world'.

So believing, 'the general prejudice of the people, at that time, against dissenters, and in favour of the church, gave me a full persuasion, that I could do more good in the church than any where else'. He made the voyage to England, was ordained an Anglican priest, and spent the rest

---

[208] Samuel Davies, *The State of Religion among The Protestant Dissenters in Virginia* (Boston, 1751), pp. 10–11.
[209] For Micaiah Towgood's tract, see pp. 28n, 211, 322–3.

of his life as rector of Bath parish, Dinwiddie County, Virginia, where he preached human depravity, conversion and the new birth, encouraged Methodists, and was increasingly drawn to act as an itinerant in the surrounding counties of North Carolina and Virginia. Despite his ecumenical New Light sympathies, Jarratt shared the attitudes imposed by competition between sects, deploring the growth of the Baptists. When they secured a foothold in one corner of his parish it 'proved detrimental to the interests of *religion* . . . from that time it began to decline in that place. So fatal are the effects of church divisions.' He lived to see the devastation of the Anglican order in Virginia after the Revolution, the proliferation of Dissent, and the decimation of his once-overflowing congregations.[210]

Large numbers of the unchurched who were open to this sort of conversion might be won back, and others confirmed in an Anglican identity, given proper organisation: so, at least, it might appear to hopeful churchmen. Governor Tryon reported from North Carolina in 1765 that Anglicans were already a majority, and that 'when a sufficient number of clergy as exemplary in their lives, as orthodox in their doctrine; can persuade themselves to come into this Country, I doubt not but the larger number of every sect would come over to the established religion'. But of 32 parishes in the colony, only 5 had resident clergy.[211] Anglicans in the colonies contrasted their own proliferating numbers with their lack of organisation and structure. The SPG missionary Henry Caner warned of a Dissenting bid for control of the vast new territories conquered in the Seven Years' War and complained in 1763: 'we are a Rope of Sand; there is no union, no authority among us; we cannot even summon a Convention for united Counsell and advice, while the Dissenting Ministers have their Monthly, Quarterly, and Annual Associations, Conventions, &c., to advise, assist, and support each other in any Measures which they shall think proper to enter into'.[212]

To some degree, the conversion of colonists to Anglicanism represented the strengthening of the transatlantic tie. Elsewhere, however, it could have an opposite effect. The conversion of aspiring and prospering Bostonians was part of a process of geographical relocation and social with-

---

[210] *The Life of the Reverend Devereux Jarratt . . . written by himself* (Baltimore, 1806), pp. 40, 46, 52, 56–9, 97, 106. Jarratt was initially convinced that 'the Methodists were really sincere in their professions of attachment to the church', p. 110.

[211] Governor Tryon to SPG, 31 July 1765, in W.L. Saunders (ed.), *The Colonial Records of North Carolina*, vol. 7 (Raleigh, N.C., 1890), p. 102.

[212] Caner to Archbishop of Canterbury, 7 Jan. 1763: W. S. Perry (ed.), *Historical Collections Relating to the American Colonial Church*, 4 vols. in 5, (Hartford, Conn., 1870–8), vol. 3, p. 489.

drawal from the populist politics of town life. If the Anglican church, in such societies, was building up a powerful interest, increasingly self-referential, endogamous and identified with royal office-holding, this only strengthened its sense of distance from other elements in the colonial population.[213] Meanwhile, colonial Dissent proliferated.

In the first half of the eighteenth century, Presbyterianism and Baptism in the colonies took on a vitality almost wholly absent in England. The ethnic as well as the politico-theological mix of the colonies was progressively diversified by the arrival of Scots and Scots Irish (Quakers, Episcopalians, but especially Presbyterians), Huguenots, Germans ('Dunkers', Moravians, Reformed and Lutherans) and Swiss, and given scope for expression by a surge of migration into the backcountry of the middle and southern colonies in particular. Increasing geographical mobility provided ever more frequent occasions for sectarian friction. This had been anticipated, but on a far smaller scale, within the British Isles. English Dissenters gave a cool reception to 'stroling *Scotch*-Ministers', Presbyterians seeking congregations south of the border. 'The power of their Kirk-Sessions, Presbyteries, &c. runs too much in their Heads; and the general Fire of their Tempers is too great, to fit them to deal with *English* Constitutions, and to act upon Dissenting Principles.'[214] English Presbyterianism was conducted on rather different principles. English Dissenters were generally alienated by the much tighter ideas of church discipline and polity entertained by Scots Presbyterians. In the colonies these contrasts, and antagonisms, were even more marked.[215]

Not only settled Presbyterian ministers, but itinerants also, continued to be drawn from the old world. One such was John Cuthbertson, born in Ayr in 1719, a theology student at Glasgow, ordained at Braehead in 1747, who spent a year's ministry among the Irish Reformed Presbyterians, descendants of the Covenanters, before emigrating to America in 1751 at the behest of the Reformed Presbyterian synod.[216] There, from 1751 to 1773, he lived the arduous life of an itinerant minister in the backcountry from Pennsylvania to New England, travelling more than 69,000 miles before settling down in the latter year in charge of a congregation at Middle Octorara, Lancaster County. He continued to minister until his death in 1791, retailing a mixture of Covenanting predestin-

---

[213] William Pencak, *America's Burke: the Mind of Thomas Hutchinson* (Washington, 1982), pp. 5–6.
[214] *Some Observations upon the Present State of the Dissenting Interest, And the Case of those Who have lately deserted it* (London, 1731), p. 32.
[215] G. S. Klett, *Presbyterians in Colonial Pennsylvania* (Philadelphia, 1937), pp. 224–41 and passim.
[216] W. M. Glasgow, *History of the Reformed Presbyterian Church in America* (Baltimore, 1888).

arian doctrine and primitive medicine which bordered on the occult. Throwing his weight behind the Revolution, in 1777 he enlisted in a militia company and 'Beswore fidelity to the state' despite the Reformed Presbyterian opposition to oaths.[217]

Religious revivalism was a deliberate step back, a rejection of modernising Anglican ideas like 'politeness' and 'civility', which found similar expression in the campaigns of the 1760s to boycott imported English luxuries. When the Anglican clergyman Charles Woodmason met a 'large Body of Baptists and New Lights', he 'found them exceeding Vain and Ignorant . . . I found their Reading to be of no greater Extent than the Pilgrims Progress and Works of John Bunyan'.[218] By contrast – so he believed – the impact of Anglicanism in promoting civic virtue was profound: 'These Congregations being settled – their Children Baptiz'd, and the people rouz'd from their Insensibility – A New System of Things, and an entire Alteration in the Minds of Individuals, seem'd to take place from this Period.'[219] The main problem, he thought, was the itinerant preachers of the sects: 'I find them a Sett of Rhapsodists – Enthusiasts – Bigots – Pedantic, illiterate, impudent Hypocrites – Straining at Gnats, and swallowing Camels, and making Religion a Cloak for Covetousness Detraction, Guile, Impostures and their particular Fabric of Things.'[220] Itinerancy in time posed a similar threat in England too; but in England it arrived later, was regionally concentrated, and limited in its impact.[221] In colonial America it was present from an early date and became a defining characteristic of social consciousness. 'The spread of the gospel is somewhat like the spread of fire', observed an early historian of itinerancy and revivalism in the southern backcountry; 'It does not in all cases advance regularly; but a spark being struck out, flies off and begins a new flame at a distance.'[222] Such a phenomenon could not be contained either by persecution or toleration.

In England, religious conflict was mainly between High and Low Churchmen; in colonial America all sects were in conflict with each other, and often experienced schism under the impact of revivalism and itinerant

---

[217] William L. Fisk, Jr. (ed.), 'The Diary of John Cuthbertson, Missionary to the Covenanters of Colonial Pennsylvania', *Pennsylvania Magazine of History and Biography* 73 (1949), 441–58.

[218] Richard J. Hooker (ed.), *The Carolina Backcountry on the Eve of the Revolution: The Journal and Other Writings of Charles Woodmason, Anglican Itinerant* (Chapel Hill, 1953), 3 May 1767, p. 22.

[219] Ibid., p. 27.

[220] Ibid., p. 42.

[221] Deryck W. Lovegrove, *Established Church, Sectarian People: Itinerancy and the Transformation of English Dissent, 1780–1830* (Cambridge, 1988).

[222] Robert B. Semple, *A History of the Rise and Progress of the Baptists in Virginia* (Richmond, 1810), p. 13.

preaching. These threats, catalysed by the visits of George Whitefield, tore apart colonial Presbyterianism in 1741. The same process was repeated within New England Congregationalism following Whitefield's visit to Boston in 1740, with open division between Old and New Lights in 1742.[223] Inter-denominational conflict occurred between Quakers and Presbyterians in Pennsylvania in the 1760s,[224] between Presbyterians or Baptists and Anglicans in Virginia from the 1740s,[225] between Congregationalists and Separates, Baptists and Anglicans in New England. Against this background, future patriots combined a sense of the growing moral depravity of society with a perception of mounting persecution. The Virginian Anglican James Madison, aged 22, complained in 1774 how 'Poverty and luxury prevail among all sorts; pride, ignorance and knavery among the priesthood, and vice and wickedness among the laity.' Worse still, a 'diabolical, hell-conceived principle of persecution rages among some', as a result of which 'There are at this time in the adjacent country not less than five or six well-meaning men in close jail for publishing their religious sentiments, which in the main are very orthodox.'[226] The Anglican establishment in Virginia reacted against itinerant Baptist preachers in ways very similar to their English brethren's resistance to Methodists, or to other denominations' itinerants from the 1790s.

The geographical pattern of establishment, dissent and rival ethnic groups was far more complex in the colonies than in England. Denominationalism was most marked in that free market of competing sects, the middle colonies and southern backcountry; but it spread to the tidewater south also with the rise of denominations which fought against Anglican ascendancy in a way reminiscent of English Dissent, and it eventually transformed even the tight Congregational monopolies of New England, shattered by schism and revivalism and challenged by imported episcopalianism.[227] Not all New England Congregationalists were initially hostile to Anglicanism. 'Where there was Honey to be extracted I have not refused to Suck even the Common Prayer Book of the Church of England', confided to his diary Ebenezer Parkman (minister of Westborough, Mas-

---

[223] Bonomi, *Cope of Heaven*, pp. 139–52.

[224] Ibid., pp. 171–6.

[225] Rhys Isaac, 'Religion and Authority: Problems of the Anglican Establishment in Virginia in the Era of the Great Awakening and the Parsons' Cause', *WMQ* 30 (1973), 3–36; George William Pilcher, *Samuel Davies, Apostle of Dissent in Colonial Virginia* (Knoxville, 1971).

[226] James Madison to William Bradford, 24 Jan. 1774: Madison, *Writings*, vol. 1, p. 18.

[227] Clarence C. Goen, *Revivalism and Separatism in New England, 1740–1800* (New Haven, Conn., 1962); William G. McLoughlin, *New England Dissent, 1630–1833* (2 vols., Cambridge, Mass., 1971); James West Davidson, *The Logic of Millennial Thought: Eighteenth-Century New England* (New Haven, 1977); Stephen A. Marini, *Radical Sects of Revolutionary New England* (Cambridge, Mass., 1982).

sachusetts, 1724–82) in 1726.[228] In 1759 Jacob Bailey, a Congregational schoolmaster and minister of Gloucester, Massachusetts, had his objections against episcopal ordination and conformity to the Church of England fully answered when Henry Caner lent him Archbishop Potter's *Church Government*;[229] Bailey then took Anglican orders and became himself an SPG missionary in Maine, only to find his congregation undermined by the harassment of a wealthy local Dissenter circulating Towgood's *The Dissenting Gentleman's Answer, to The Rev. Mr. White's Three Letters and other tracts*.[230] After Ebenezer Parkman's ecumenical confession, the progress of theological heterodoxy among Congregationalists after the Seven Years' War[231] reacted with the missionary activity of the SPG to inflame sensibilities. Other denominations proliferated too in what had been a virtual Congregationalist monopoly. By 1776, New Hampshire supported one hundred and eighteen churches: eighty-four Congregational, fifteen Presbyterian, eleven Baptist, four Quaker, three Episcopal. From the religious revivals of 1780–1, the number of sects burgeoned; nevertheless, not until the Toleration Act of 1819 did the dominant Congregationalists surrender their attempts to extract tithes from the reluctant members of other sects.[232]

In the middle colonies, diversity was even greater by an earlier date. Michael Schlatter, minister of the German Reformed Church, arrived at Philadelphia as an itinerant missionary in 1746. He found a city of some 10,000 inhabitants served by a spectrum of churches: Anglican, Swedish, German Evangelical (Lutheran), Presbyterian, German Reformed, Roman Catholic, Anabaptist and Moravian, plus two Quaker meetings. Schlatter, commissioned by the Synods of South and North Holland, duly reported back on the 'destitute congregations' of German and Dutch Reformed in the colonies, 'exposed to all kinds of sects and errorists' who led them astray with 'sugared poison'.[233] This rivalry of denominations had its usual effects. Dissenters, complained an Anglican clergyman, were 'taught to keep at a Distance from me, and beware of my Conversation'. 'Some of the wicked Books scattered about among you, would perswade you, *That our Church is little better than* Popery, *and symbolises with the Church*

---

[228] Francis G. Walett (ed.), 'The Diary of Ebenezer Parkman', *Proceedings of the American Antiquarian Society* 71 (1961), 93–227, at 140.

[229] Jacob Bailey to Henry Caner, 24 Sept. 1759, in William Bartlett, *The Frontier Missionary: A Memoir of the Life of the Rev. Jacob Bailey, A.M.* (Boston, 1853), p. 43.

[230] Ibid., p. 94.

[231] See chapter 4, part V (C) below.

[232] Richard Francis Upton, *Revolutionary New Hampshire* (Port Washington, N.Y., 1970), pp. 208–9.

[233] Henry Harbaugh, *The Life of Rev. Michael Schlatter* (Philadelphia, 1857), pp. 49, 118–20, 144, 202.

of Rome.' The political analogue of this was equally wounding: 'it is insupportably abusive in any of you, as some do, to charge us with being *High-flyers* and *Jacobites*, when you know in your Consciences, that we constantly pray for our most Gracious Sovereign King GEORGE'.[234]

In the tidewater of the southern colonies, the migration of English and Scots-Irish Presbyterians, Huguenots and Germans had similarly created acute religious diversity from an early date. The Anglican priest Francis Le Jau, an SPG missionary, complained from South Carolina how 'there is a mixture of Dissenters and among them hardly two of the same Opinion'; their quest for public maintenance moved him to add: 'wee see what they love best I fear it is Profit more than truth . . . You can't imagine how they are Cheated here by false Prophets.'[235] The inhabitants were

> miserably divided among themselves, I thought at first those who call themselves the Dissenting Party were of sober meek Charitable Principles as some which I have none [known] in Europe, but it is not so here . . . it vexes me to the heart to see some Clergymen here openly to disobey the Superior Authority in things very good of themselves & revile them with Gross Language to their faces, and declare in writing that obedience or disobedience to them are things indifferent & arbitrary.[236]

Le Jau acknowledged that

> there has been a mixture of good & Evil in all Partys, but those who call themselves the dissenting party here are a Strange sort of People. I have known some Dissenters in Europe & have had a great respect for their interior Disposition of Soul which I found to be really Sober, humble, patient, poor in Spirit, & of great Charity but it is quite another thing here among the Leaders of the Party: for some of their meanest sort of people seem to be better disposed. I pretend to no Skill in those Political Affairs & converse with few persons without necessity but the Effects of those men's designs are so violent and Scandalous that one must take notice of it whether he will or no.[237]

In the same colony, Commissary Johnston complained of what was already, in 1708, the plural nature of the colonial population,

> being a perfect Medley or Hotch potch made up of Bank[r]upts, pirates, decayed Libertines, Sectaries and Enthusiasts of all sorts who have transported themselves hither from Bermudas, Jamaica, Barbadoes, Montserat, Antego, Nevio, New England, Pensylvania &c; and are the most factious

---

[234] [Samuel Johnson], *A Letter from a Minister of the Church of England to his Dissenting Parishoners* (New York, 1733), pp. 3–5, 8.

[235] Le Jau to Philip Stubs, 15 April 1707: Frank J. Klingberg (ed.), *The Carolina Chronicle of Dr. Francis Le Jau 1706–1717* (Berkeley, 1956), p. 23.

[236] Le Jau to SPG, 30 June 1707: ibid., p. 25.

[237] Le Jau to Philip Stubs, 3 July 1707: ibid., p. 28.

and Seditious people in the whole World. Many of those that pretend to be Churchmen are strangely cripled in their goings between the Church and Presbytery, and as they are of large and loose principles so they live and Act accordingly . . .

It was a rivalry importantly different from that which prevailed in England: 'the debates and Contests, that are on foot here, are not between High and Low Churchmen; but between the dissenters and the Church . . .'[238]

In tidewater Virginia, the Baptist and Presbyterian critique of Anglicanism had extended by mid-century to 'alienation from opulent gentry culture, from private as well as public gentry behaviour, and from gentry attitudes about the social order' expressed in the common law and enforced by Justices of the Peace.[239] But by far the most acute problem of sectarian pluralism was developing in what was to be a distinct and decisive theatre of the Revolutionary war, the newly-settled backcountry of the middle and southern colonies.[240] Charles Woodmason, Anglican priest and rare Anglican itinerant of that area, recorded his profound concern for its inhabitants, 'without Law, Gospel, Trade or Money'. He was himself

> Insulted by a Pack of vile, levelling common wealth Presbyterians In whom the Republican Spirit of [16]41 yet dwells, and who would very willingly put the Solemn League and Covenant now in force – Nay, their Teachers press it on them, and say that [it] is as binding on the Consciences of all the Kirk, as the Gospel it Self, for it is a Covenant enter'd into with God, from which they cannot recede.[241]

Despite the ignorance of the backcountry, antipopery sentiments were strong. Woodmason recorded the reaction of one congregation to his ministry: 'the Presbyterians disliked the Service and Sermon of the Day [All Saints] saying it was Popish &c'. On another occasion, he had 'but a small Congregation and 5 Communicants – The Name of the Holy Sacrament frightened them all away.' On Good Friday 1768, 'Had but very few

---

[238] Gideon Johnston to Gilbert Burnet, Bp of Salisbury, 20 Sept. 1708, in Klingberg (ed.), *Johnston*, p. 19.

[239] A. G. Roeber, *Faithful Magistrates and Republican Lawyers: Creators of Virginia Legal Culture, 1680–1810* (Chapel Hill, 1981), pp. 137, 169. Local courts had been prominent in prosecuting moral offences: the most common Grand Jury presentments in the period 1720–50 were for missing church, swearing, and having a bastard child. In 1750–70 these continued, with the notable (Dissenting) addition of 'not listing tithables': ibid., pp. 141–2. Cf. James P. Walsh, "Black Cotted Raskolls': Anti-Anglican Criticism in Colonial Virginia', *Virginia Magazine of History and Biography* 88 (1980), 21–36.

[240] Ronald Hoffman, Thad W. Tate and Peter J. Albert (eds.), *An Uncivil War: The Southern Backcountry during the American Revolution* (Charlottesville, 1985).

[241] Woodmason, *Journal*, August 1768, p. 55.

at Service – The Sectaries deeming it savour'd of Popery.'[242] Commissary Johnston similarly complained of the 'Strange Notions & Whims' of South Carolina's mixed population about the Sacraments: they 'have fallen into such a Comprehensive and Latitudinarian way, that it is the hardest thing in the World to perswade 'em out of it'. Most Dissenters 'are a sort of people not to be reason'd with, and are generally uncapable of Argument'. His preferred strategy accepted this fact: 'the shortest way with the Dissenters wou'd be to strike at the very root of the Schism, by directly attacking their Ministers in the first place; and once these are gained, many of the rest will in all humane probability follow'.[243]

In this anticlerical environment, the attachment of Dissenting congregations to their ministers could be oddly tenacious. Woodmason found that Presbyterians would pay for a Presbyterian schoolmaster and refuse Woodmason's offer of his services free: 'Such is their attachment to their Kirk: – Some call me a Jesuit – and the Liturgy the Mass.'[244]

> Another Time (in order to disappoint me of a Congregation, and to laugh at the People) they posted a Paper, signifying, That the King having discovered the Popish Designs of Mr Woodmason and other Romish Priests in disguise, to bring in Popery and Slavery, had sent over Orders to suspend them all, and to order them to be sent over to England, so that there would be no more preaching for the future. This was believed by some of the Poor Ignorants, and kept them at home.[245]

Behind the formal professions of Presbyterian officialdom lay the daily conflicts of the denominations, particularly evident in areas of recent settlement. Far from becoming swiftly secularised, or experiencing a metamorphosis into a newly American religious mode, the sects exploited their relative license in the colonies in order to exaggerate their existing characters: 'the perverse persecuting Spirit of the Presbyterians, displays it Self much more here than in Scotland', wrote Woodmason.

> It is dangerous to live among, or near any of them – for if they cannot cheat, rob, defraud or injure You in Your Goods – they will belye, defame, lessen, blacken, disparage the most valuable Person breathing, not of their Communion in his Character, Good Name, or Reputation and Credit . . .
> These Sects are eternally jarring among themselves – The Presbyterians

---

[242] Ibid., 1 Nov. 1767, 27 Dec. 1767, 1 April 1768. For a demonstration that 'Catholic ecclesiology, soteriology and orthodox christology are interdependent. All three were handed down from patristic and medieval times to the post-Reformation Church of England and its 'popish liturgy'', see Waterman, 'The Nexus between Theology and Political Doctrine'.

[243] Gideon Johnston to SPG, 5 July 1710, in Klingberg (ed.), *Johnston*, pp. 34–62, at 39, 53–4.

[244] Woodmason, *Journal*, p. 45 (n.d.).

[245] Ibid., p. 45 (n.d.).

hate the Baptists far more than they do the Episcopalians, and so of the Rest – But (as in England) they will unite altogether – in a Body to distress or injure the Church establish'd.[246]

From a close acquaintance he thought 'these Northern Scotch Irish . . . certainly the worst Vermin on Earth', 'a Sett of the most lowest vilest Crew Breathing'.[247]

When Woodmason drafted for his aggrieved parishioners the Regulator 'Remonstrance', read in the Lower House of the Carolina Assembly on 7 November 1767, he added a note to the copy he forwarded to the SPG to amplify the remonstrance's complaint against the proselytising activities of the sectaries:

> Great, and Successful have their Endeavours on this Head been – Not less than 20 Itinerant Presbyterian, Baptist and Independent Preachers are maintain'd by the Synods of Pensylvania and New England to traverse this Country Poisoni[n]g the Minds of the People – Instilling Democratical and Common Wealth Principles into their Minds – Embittering them against the very Name of Bishops, and all Episcopal Government and laying deep their fatal Republican Notions and Principles – Especially – That they are a free People – That they are to pay allegiance to King George as their Sovereign – but as to Great Britain or the Parliament, or any there, that they have no more to think off or about them than the Turk or Pope – Thus do these Itinerant Preachers sent from the Northern Colonies pervert the Minds of the Vulgar.[248]

The establishment of an Anglican parochial structure was essential for the pacification of the backcountry, he urged. It was a plea which went unheeded: Woodmason's itinerancy was rare among non-Methodist Anglicans, and his departure from South Carolina in 1772 left a void still unfilled at the Revolution. It was a void, however, assiduously filled by others. In July 1775 the Presbyterian minister William Tennent, together with William Drayton, was entrusted with a mission by the South Carolina Committee of Safety to the backcountry of the colony to convert the inhabitants to the cause of independence. Tennent undertook the task like a revivalist itinerant, recording how he repeatedly 'harangued' groups of doubters, especially congregations of worshippers, until he awakened their zeal.[249]

For Anglican commentators like Ambrose Serle, this denominational

[246] Ibid., p. 43 (n.d.).
[247] Ibid., 17 July 1768, p. 50; 25 Jan. 1767, p. 14.
[248] Ibid., p. 240–1; Richard Maxwell Brown, *The South Carolina Regulators* (Cambridge, Mass., 1963), pp. 41–3. For the Regulator movement see below, pp. 266–9.
[249] 'A Fragment of a Journal kept by Rev. William Tennent' in R. W. Gibbes (ed.), *Documentary History of the American Revolution* (New York, 1855), pp. 225–39.

structure came as an unpleasant surprise. To what extent the sectarian situation in the colonies was appreciated by different groups in England at different times is a complex question. From the early eighteenth century, Church authorities in England had been warned of the problem of Dissent in America: in Pennsylvania, not only threats from Quakers but 'great opposition also from all other Dissenters, as Presbyterians, Independents and Anabaptists, who daily increase in other Provinces, as well as Pensilvania, for want of an established Ministry of the Church in those Parts'; persecution from Dutch and Quakers in New York; 'but slender hopes' in New England thanks to the legal entrenchment of Dissent. This was offset, however, by a perception of the widespread welcome given to Anglican worship and doctrine where sectarian commitments did not intervene.[250]

If the Society for the Propagation of the Gospel was systematically briefed, and sympathetic bishops, especially Bishops of London, took care to inform themselves, it is likely that knowledge was diluted with increasing distance from these sources. The wider English public was far less aware of the dynamics of sectarian conflict in the American colonies, and the sources to which laymen had access increasingly played these down. Even itinerant missionaries, like the Presbyterian Charles Beatty, chose to emphasise the peaceful reception of their message by the well-meaning and neglected communities of the backcountry, and gave priority to the Christian evangelical mission to the Indians which denominational divisions only hindered.[251] Even an SPG missionary adopted this convention in arguing for bishops to be sent to America not to quell inter-sectarian strife but because colonial Dissenters were already tranquil and therefore well-disposed to their episcopalian neighbours.[252] If this literature was representative of the published information, it is less surprising that so

---

[250] 'An Account of the State of the Church in North America, by Mr. George Keith and Others' [1702], in *HMPEC* 20 (1951), 363–71, at 368. George Keith, *A Journal of Travels from New-Hampshire to Caratuck, On the Continent of North-America* (London, 1706), reprinted ibid., 372–487, at 430. Keith recorded the preoccupation of an SPG missionary with the Quaker threat but disclosed his conviction that Quakers could be converted to the Church by theological argument.

[251] Charles Beatty, *The Journal of a Two Months Tour; with a view of Promoting Religion among the Frontier Inhabitants of Pennsylvania, and of Introducing Christianity among the Indians to the Westward of the Alegh-geny Mountains* (London, 1768). The publication of this work was in reality part of a fund-raising campaign undertaken to enlist practical support from Presbyterian coreligionists in England: Guy Souliard Klett (ed.), *Journals of Charles Beatty 1762–1769* (University Park, Pennsylvania, 1962). For Beatty's awareness of the SPG's hostility in England to colonial Presbyterianism, ibid., p. 82.

[252] Thomas Bradbury Chandler, *An Appeal to the Public, in Behalf of the Church of England in America* (New York, 1767), p. 115: 'It is . . . rash and injurious to charge any with Disaffection to the Government, at this Day, because they dissent from the national Religion.'

many Englishmen imagined that the greatest disaster to Church and State since the 1640s came out of a clear blue sky.

3

Predispositions: rebellion and its social constituencies in the English Atlantic Empire, 1660–1832

If law and religion followed the patterns already outlined, it remains to trace their impact in the daily political events of the English-speaking world and, especially, in those crises on both sides of the Atlantic which saw the established order repeatedly, and sometimes successfully, challenged. Yet acts of resistance to constituted authority within the hegemonic political and ecclesiastical order described in this book pose a special problem for historical analysis, since modern historiography has until recently marginalised those very features of the social order which were the targets of resistance and defined its nature. Moreover, the main category of explanation has itself been reified: 'revolution' has been turned from an explanation into a thing to be explained, and 'rebellion' reduced to a pejorative and diminutive term. Consequently, revolutions are conventionally explained by reference to a timeless model of what revolutions are or should be; rebellions are dismissed as minor challenges to governments, unsuccessful because not equipped with the appropriate ideological charge. It is assumed here, by contrast, that a series of contingent features, especially political and military contingencies, ensured that episodes like 1660, 1688 and 1776 should succeed while those of 1685, 1715, 1744 and 1798 did not: a revolution is not essentially different from a successful rebellion, and no explanation is or can be offered of the nature of revolutions 'as such'.

The nature of those contingencies is at the centre of this study; yet the histories of western societies after the French Revolution have masked some of the early-modern characteristics of political mobilisation. Once 'revolution' was reified, as it was after 1776,[1] and more widely after 1789, it was transformed from a catastrophe into a rite of passage: societies were held to undergo fundamental reconstruction through experience of these watershed events. In the period addressed here, by contrast, no such assumption informed a differently-structured debate on the meaning and interrelation of rebellions. That debate turned on ideological and ecclesiastical rather than social-structural features. All parties to many different disputes claimed the 'rights of Englishmen' or appealed to the libertarian inheritance of the Reformation; but they interpreted these things in different ways. Within the English-speaking world, debate was for decades preoccupied by the meaning and implications of the shatteringly divisive events of 1688–9. In those years the American colonies seemed to triumph in the success of the Glorious Revolution;[2] in 1776, from the British perspective, they seemed to rebel against the polity which the Glorious Revolution had established. From the American perspective, by contrast, 1776 might be claimed as the fulfilment of the promise of 1688, the vindication of its principles (even if the Constitution of 1787 then went on to embody quite different, republican, principles).[3] Such a connection between the events of 1688 and 1776 was asserted by Americans. Arthur Lee, rehearsing a natural-law account of 'the American claim' against taxation without representation, extrapolated these principles backwards not only to 1688 but to the Civil War: if those principles were

> fallacious, then were our own claims usurpations upon the crown, and the glorious revolution itself was nothing more than a successful rebellion; Hampden, Pym, Sidney and Russel, than whom Greece with all her patriots, and Rome with all her heroes, produced no men who trod this mortal stage with more dignity, or quitted it with greater lustre, were sturdy traitors.[4]

Within the idiom of secularised constitutional history, it has been shown how patriots and loyalists in 1776 derived different answers from

---

[1] For the new meanings attached to the term, part of 'the semantic transformation to the modern world', see Horst Dippel, 'The American Revolution and the Modern Concept of 'Revolution'' in Erich Angermann (ed.), *New Wine in Old Skins* (Stuttgart, 1976), pp. 115–34.

[2] David S. Lovejoy, *The Glorious Revolution in America* (1972; 2nd edn., Middletown, Conn., 1987). For a study linking interpretations of the Civil War, 1688 and 1776 in an ecclesiastical setting, see Richard L. Greaves, 'Radicals, Rights and Revolution: British Nonconformity and Roots of the American Experience', *Church History* 61 (1992), 151–68.

[3] Greene, *Peripheries and Center*, p. 133; 'For the colonists, resolution of their dispute with the metropolis had never seemed to require much more than the rationalisation of existing political arrangements within the empire', p. 137.

[4] [Arthur Lee], *An Appeal to the Justice and Interests of the People of Great Britain, in the Present Disputes with America, by an Old Member of Parliament* (4th edn., London, 1776), p. 21.

a common inheritance; but why the two parties to the conflict should diverge has not been elucidated except in terms of the correctness or otherwise of the argument from that inheritance. A wider frame of reference, however, sets the secular constitutional arguments about taxation and representation in the context of the sectarian explanations for those many episodes of insurrection which threatened, which erupted, which succeeded or were suppressed in the English-speaking world over two centuries. Analysts of 'revolution' have debated whether a particular episode was a restoration of the *status quo ante*, especially as a Machiavellian *ridurre ai principii*, or whether they were watershed events which made all things new; and they have sought to date (often in 1776 or 1789) a moment when the first sort of episode gave way to the second. This study suggests that the religious dimension, and especially apocalyptic or millenarian elements within it, shows how early-modern rebellions might be both.

The myth of the uniqueness of the American Revolution indeed took its rise from the colonists' claims never to have been taxed by Britain. John Dickinson claimed that history proved that Britain's supremacy was fully consistent with not levying taxes; it showed the colonies' 'filial submission' to British rule 'without a single rebellion, or even the thought of one, from the first emigration to this moment'.[5] This image of a peaceful, settled, libertarian polity, finally driven in 1776 to vindicate its customary liberties by resistance to a novel tyranny, is at odds with the evidence, rehearsed here, of intermittent social conflict and insurrection over many decades. Only by an historiographical tradition have the events of 1688 and 1776 been isolated from this turbulent story and redefined as two validating examples in a tradition of secular constitutional evolution, indeed two unrevolutionary efforts to defend that tradition against counter-revolution. This isolation itself establishes a major premise of British and American history: the belief that both societies have pursued the uninterrupted evolution of a secular, libertarian, constitutional ideal, and that its progressive implementation has progressively freed them from internal revolutionary threat.

In the shadow of that premise, Monmouth's rebellion in 1685 has been claimed as the last popular rebellion in England: the Glorious Revolution was interpreted as glorious partly because popular insurrection was not unleashed. Civil war in Ireland and Scotland is generally omitted from the histories of that episode. Political stability, in this account, then blanketed the country with a benign somnolence. English democracy found

[5] [John Dickinson], *Letters from a Farmer in Pennsylvania, To the Inhabitants of the British Colonies* Boston, 1768), p. 52.

its early promise blighted during 'pudding time'; colonial administration similarly luxuriated, or languished, beneath a policy of 'salutary neglect'. Eighteenth-century riots never graduated beyond local disturbances in Britain or America. English insurrectionaries were only 'primitive rebels', clumsily anticipating glories to come in a later era. Intimations of rebellion in the Captain Swing riots of 1830–2 and the Chartist disturbances never came to fruition. By such arguments the threat of massive disruption inherent in the English Atlantic empire from the outset has been made marginal to what are conventionally presented as its central developmental themes. All the many instances of rebellion throughout the late seventeenth and eighteenth centuries are explained away as exceptions to the rule. Insurrections which failed to anticipate twentieth-century norms are marginalised as anachronistic. English sectional or local disorders, the result of economic stress, allegedly had 'no national character' until 'a working-class consciousness was created in the early nineteenth century'. Equally, if 1685 is defined as 'the last occasion when a cause which was basically religious created a popular movement',[6] then we know in advance that the 'long' eighteenth century will contain little of relevance.

For 1776 as for 1688, the causes of resistance have conventionally been located in innovations of British policy, both within the framework of older constitutional history and within the paradigm of 'Commonwealth' ideology; yet this self-evidence itself needs to be explained. In the early-modern period the most effective rhetorical strategy was generally an appeal to ancient custom, law and convention in which one's opponents were depicted as the innovators.[7] At its most inflamed, this rhetoric has seemed from a modern perspective to end in a paranoid fear that cherished values were threatened by an international conspiracy and undermined by domestic traitors.[8] It is argued here that the thesis of the psychological disturbance of many of the figures who acted as catalysts of rebellion needs to be reformulated: what were most at issue on both sides of the Atlantic were not the ailments conceptualised by twentieth-century psychoanalysis, but the categories, commitments and stresses of early-modern religion. These stresses were fully sufficient to generate the most lurid theories of conspiracy, betrayal and persecution. So it was in 1641,

---

[6] Robin Clifton, *The Last Popular Rebellion: The Western Rising of 1685* (London, 1984), pp. 282–3.
[7] Robert Ashton, 'Tradition and Innovation and the Great Rebellion', in J. G. A. Pocock (ed.), *Three British Revolutions: 1641, 1688, 1776* (Princeton, 1980), pp. 208–23.
[8] Gordon Wood, 'Conspiracy and the Paranoid Style: Causality and Deceit in the Eighteenth Century', *WMQ* 39 (1982), 401–41; Richard Hofstadter, *The Paranoid Style in American Politics* (New York, 1965).

1688 and 1776; and the continuity of rhetoric ensured that in the later crises men appealed to earlier ones as instances of resistance to the same peril. Such rhetoric is apt to be misleading: it is likely, taken in isolation, to identify royal or metropolitan initiatives as the only new elements in the scene. The inclusion of the realms of law and religion now allows us to decode that rhetoric by answering a further question: what was it that, at various periods, made its exponents so frenzied in their perception of such threats? Why did an ostensibly conservative, defensive disposition turn at times into paranoia, mass hysteria, virulent hostility to certain ancient institutions?

To explain these periodic transformations, the appropriate frame of reference must be expanded geographically and thematically as well as chronologically to allow the removal of early modern risings from an explanatory scheme perhaps instituted in 1789, certainly codified in modern political science. The contrast between the nature of insurrections in the old world and the new was captured by Edmund Burke. Writing in 1790, Burke already sensed that the French Revolution was essentially different from previous revolutions:

> All other nations have begun the fabric of a new government, or the reformation of an old, by establishing originally, or by enforcing with greater exactness some rites or other of religion. All other people have laid the foundations of civil freedom in severer manners, and a system of a more austere and masculine morality. France, when she let loose the reins of regal authority, doubled the licence, of a ferocious dissoluteness in manners, and of an insolent irreligion in opinions and practices.[9]

Burke inevitably intended 'all other nations' to include the United States. Yet, in postponing this dethroning of religion until the years after 1789, Burke's analysis has now an air of paradox. It comes at the end of a century conventionally depicted as the era of secular Enlightenment, in which political upheaval has been explained in terms of rising gentry, declining gentry, Court v. Country, bourgeois revolution, the triumph of secular contractarianism, urban radicalism, industrial stress, incipient nationalism. None of these things were central to Burke's account of what had happened in France in 1789–90; and despite his fascination with the events of 1688–9, and his personal involvement with the American Revolution, Burke insisted that the novelty of the French Revolution lay,

---

[9] Edmund Burke, *Reflections on the Revolution in France, and on the Proceedings in Certain Societies in London relative to that Event* (London, 1790), p. 54. For the uniquely anti-Christian element in the French Revolution, see Michel Vovelle, *The Revolution against the Church: From Reason to the Supreme Being* (Cambridge, 1991); for the millenarian element see Clarke Garrett, *Respectable Folly: Millenarians and the French Revolution in France and England* (Baltimore, 1975).

by contrast, in the priority of irreligion over religious and legal reformation.

Despite this insight, the assumption prevailed within nineteenth- and twentieth-century social science that religion as such was irrelevant to definitions of revolution, except in the tenuous sense in which Jacobinism and Marxism themselves were reminiscent of religions.[10] In an extreme form, this emerged as the claim that, because of the assumed secularisation of politics after the Reformation, even revivalist religion had been 'politically without consequences and historically futile' in its contribution to modern revolutions:

> Secularisation, the separation of religion from politics and the rise of a secular realm with a dignity of its own, is certainly a crucial factor in the phenomenon of revolution. Indeed, it may ultimately turn out that what we call revolution is precisely that transitory phase which brings about the birth of a new, secular realm. But if this is true, then it is secularisation itself, and not the contents of Christian teachings, which constitutes the origin of revolution.[11]

In this form the analysis of social science endorsed a growing historiographical consensus.[12]

The analysis offered here instead begins with a functional approach: it seeks to review, in order to compare, all the major instances of violent resistance to political and ecclesiastical authority on both sides of the Atlantic from the Restoration to the end of the eighteenth century. By including episodes hitherto isolated through being assigned to categories which are by definition incommensurable, it is possible to elucidate some of the common features of resistance in the early-modern Atlantic world. This comparative perspective reveals something of the preconditions of rebellion; it suggests that rebellions launched with a measure of success generally drew on a relatively clearly-defined social constituency which was often denominational in nature, and that acts of resistance which failed in this way to appeal to a group and to a tradition had different and markedly less successful track records. A simplistic dualism of 'pre-

---

[10] Crane Brinton, *The Anatomy of Revolution* (revised edn, New York, 1965), pp. 182–7, 196. Brinton's stress on an *analogy* between religion and revolution implied a denial of any direct relationship. For a critique of social scientists' analyses of revolution, see Ian R. Christie, *Stress and Stability in Late Eighteenth-Century Britain: Reflections on the British Avoidance of Revolution* (Oxford, 1984), pp. 3–14.

[11] Hannah Arendt, *On Revolution* (New York, 1963), pp. 18–19. For the survival of the historiographical setting of this thesis, see C. John Sommerville, *The Secularisation of Early Modern England: From Religious Culture To Religious Faith* (New York, 1992).

[12] It did not, of course, remain a consensus within sociology. For the development of theory on this question, see Bruce Lincoln (ed.), *Religion, Rebellion, Revolution* (London, 1985), pp. 3–11, 219–92.

conditions' and 'triggers' is to be avoided; rather, the analysis of the political discourses of law and religion suggests a hierarchy of causation in which denominational polities often established the boundaries of and potential for political mobilisation; theological developments, acting on those polities, acted as accelerators; practical grievances over land and defence, justice and taxation, religious discrimination and the perceived threat of 'Popery and arbitrary power' acted as catalysts; but a long chronological perspective suggests too that practical grievances were seldom sufficient to activate those preconditions without specific triggers of the right of resistance. Even anti-Catholicism was not an autonomous variable. Briefly reviewed here and examined in greater depth for the American Revolution in chapter 4, those triggers are found to be integrally related to the theological inheritance and internal development of those denominations which carried a right of resistance as part of their definitions of their ecclesiastical polities.

The political implications of those ecclesiastical polities were by no means simple, however, and few sects or theological schools were ever easily mobilised into rebellion. Even Calvinism, the most often cited candidate for that role, was not necessarily republican. In response to Henri IV's granting of religious toleration by the Edict of Nantes in 1598, Huguenot theorists like many English Protestants were encouraged in a direction of extreme royalism, expressed as a rebuttal of the claims for papal authority expressed by Cardinal Bellarmine and Franciscus Suarez. In order to distance themselves from English republicanism and regicide of the 1640s, Huguenot royalism briefly exceeded even that of Catholic lawyers like Cardin Le Bret's *Traité de la souveraineté du roy* (1632).[13] But Louis XIV's Catholicism, like the Arminianism or the Catholicism of some of the Stuarts, increasingly polarised Calvinists on both sides of the English Channel into a stance of presumptive alienation from a monarchical regime. In England and America, that pressure steadily forged an alliance between opposition and Calvinist Dissent which some more active catalyst might tip over into armed resistance.[14] Preconditions and catalysts

---

[13] Guy Howard Dodge, *The Political Theory of the Huguenots of the Dispersion With Special Reference to the Thought and Influence of Pierre Jurieu* (New York, 1947), pp. 4–6.

[14] Some historians of the sixteenth century have argued for a specifically Calvinist origin of the early-modern doctrine of a right of rebellion, e.g. Michael Walzer, *The Revolution of the Saints* (Cambridge, Mass., 1965). This has been powerfully denied for a later period by an argument which locates as its end point the 'classic formulation' of John Locke's *Two Treatises*, 'a fully secularised and populist theory of revolution', and then discovers the origins of both the secular and populist elements in the previous century: Quentin Skinner, 'The Origins of the Calvinist Theory of Revolution' in Barbara C. Malament (ed.), *After the Reformation* (Manchester, 1980), pp. 309–30; idem, *The Foundations of Modern Political Thought* (2 vols., Cambridge, 1978), vol. 2, pp. 239–41, 338–9. It is suggested that our new understanding of the religious dimension of Locke's thought has reopened this question.

can both be identified within the realms of law and religion; and these realms were inseparably joined.

II. COVENANTERS, PRESBYTERIANS AND WHIGS: RESISTANCE TO THE STUARTS IN ENGLAND AND SCOTLAND, 1660–1689

The thesis of the secularisation of politics was not devised by contemporary observers of the period examined here. The preoccupation of each denomination with its history, its ecclesiastical polity and its theology ensured that the transatlantic arena was one in which the sacred was challenged, disputed and defended, not ignored. Even the minority theme of millenarian expectations initially proved a very visible transatlantic link. The interdependence of religion and revolution in seventeenth-century Britain and America was evident in the first insurrection to follow the Restoration, an abortive rising of Fifth Monarchists in London. Its leader, Thomas Venner, was a New Englander by birth, a Puritan by background; after his migration to London in the late 1640s, he became a Fifth Monarchist by religious inspiration, and one of the minority of that sect committed to instituting the thousand-year reign of Christ on earth by a rebellion of His saints. The early decades of the seventeenth century witnessed not just emigration from England to New England, but an important interchange of religious zealots and activists between the two societies. Like Hugh Peter, an English Puritan who had avoided the personal rule of Charles I by spending the years 1629–41 in more congenial surroundings in Massachusetts,[15] the Civil War in the British Isles gave Venner the required scope to develop the implications of his theology. By 1657, he was impatient with Cromwell's rule also, and his planned *coup* was only frustrated by the government's intelligence service. After a year spent in the Tower, Venner tried again in 1661. Using his position as a preacher to incite his followers to 'fight for King Jesus', he led forty or fifty of his fellow fanatics in a rising which lasted for three days of street fighting in the City of London. The executions of Hugh Peter, Thomas Venner and Sir Henry Vane marked the government's continued awareness of the insurrectionary potential of sectarian fanaticism; but, for the moment, repression was effective.[16]

The issue of ecclesiastical polity was still momentous. It was the occa-

---

[15] William L. Sachse, 'The Migration of New Englanders to England, 1640–1660', *AHR* 53 (1948), 251–78; Philip F. Gura, *A Glimpse of Sion's Glory: Puritan Radicalism in New England 1620–1660* (Middletown, Conn., 1984), pp. 142–4.

[16] David S. Lovejoy, *Religious Enthusiasm in the New World: Heresy to Revolution* (Cambridge, Mass., 1985), pp. 103, 107–10; C. Burrage, 'The Fifth Monarchy Insurrections', *EHR* 25 (1910), 722–47; P. G. Rogers, *The Fifth Monarchy Men* (London, 1966), pp. 110–22.

sion of the principled secession of some 1,700 Presbyterians and Independents who had obtained Anglican livings under the Commonwealth when the Act of Uniformity of 1662 demanded their assent to the episcopalian structures embodied in the *Book of Common Prayer*. Yet these men, in many other respects orthodox in their belief, did not go on to foment rebellion against the state, however much they constituted a disaffected community whose resentments could potentially be tapped. Like the English Nonjurors of 1688, the ejected ministers of 1662, mostly Presbyterians, found their practical grievances largely overridden by the otherworldly imperatives of theological orthodoxy. Disaffection carried to the length of armed resistance was associated with more extreme minorities defined now as small sects and generally failing to mobilise larger and more moderate denominations.[17] Even the Quakers, who officially adopted a stance of political pacifism in the wake of Venner's rebellion, contained within their ranks minorities still involved in armed conspiracy: such men can be traced in their contacts with John Locke and Algernon Sidney, the Rye House Plot and Monmouth's rising.[18]

The survival of these minorities meant that the sectarian sources of insurrection did not disappear. A conspiracy intended to unite Presbyterians and Anabaptists in Co. Durham and Yorkshire was planned for 1663; its alleged objects, if the evidence of an informer is reliable, highlighted the necessary relation of the sacred and the secular. The godly were

> to rise in rebellion against the government, and to destroy Parliament, and murder all Bishops, Deans, and Chapters, and all other ministers of the Church; to break all organs, and further to kill all the gentry that should either oppose them, or not join with them, and to destroy the Common Prayer Book, and to pull down all Churches.

The rising was ultimately intended to be simultaneous in every county and in London; when the relation between the northern conspirators and other parts of the plan became known, John Cosin, Bishop of Durham, declared the northern rising to be only 'the first discovery of this late intended plot in other places',[19] and the authorities continued to believe in the possibility of a nationwide conspiracy on the part of surviving

---

[17] Richard L. Greaves, *Deliver Us From Evil: The Radical Underground in Britain, 1660–1663* (New York, 1986); idem, *Enemies Under His Feet: Radicals and Nonconformists in Britain, 1664–1677* (Stanford, 1990); idem, *Secrets of the Kingdom: British Radicals from the Popish Plot to the Revolution of 1688–89* (Stanford, 1992).

[18] Richard L. Greaves, 'Shattered Expectations? George Fox, the Quakers, and the Restoration State, 1660–1685', *Albion* 24, 2 (1992), 237–59.

[19] Henry Gee, 'The Derwentdale Plot, 1663', *TRHS*, 3rd Ser., 11 (1917), 125–42, at 125.

republicans and sectaries.[20] Schemes to assassinate the king and restore a godly commonwealth continued: the plots of 1662 led by Thomas Tong involving Congregationalists and Baptists, and 1665 led by the Baptist Henry Danvers, ended in the capture and execution of many of the ringleaders.[21] The elite had massively abandoned such movements during the 1650s. With the Popish Plot and Exclusion Crisis, however, plebeian millenarianism once more acquired aristocratic patrons. It was to the survivors and heirs of the Fifth Monarchists and Levellers that the Earl of Shaftesbury turned in seeking a social base for his opposition to Charles II,[22] and the threat of an attempt by surviving regicides to overthrow the monarchy was a source of constant anxiety to both Charles and James II.

In Scotland, similar problems were repeated but in a more acute form: just as rebellion had been possible to organise amidst the religious tensions of the 1630s, so rebellion was a major threat after the Restoration.[23] In England the sectarian legacy of the 1640s was largely driven from the public arena after 1660; in Scotland, by contrast, a more militant mainstream Protestantism was potentially available for exploitation by sectaries. That mainstream had been given special force by Scots history since the 1630s. The National Covenant of 1580, re-subscribed in 1638, had been designed as a unifying document and was in intention neither anti-monarchical nor anti-episcopal; but the religious issue led to war with England nevertheless, and the Solemn League and Covenant of 1643 went far further, entailing a commitment to a crusade for the imposition of Presbyterian church government, doctrine and liturgy in all three kingdoms. It was this document and these aims that Charles II was obliged to subscribe as the price of Scots support in 1650, and which he later abandoned as the price of restoration to the English throne. When episcopacy returned to Scotland with a Stuart monarch, a Scottish Act of 1662 duly condemned as 'rebellious and treasonable' the doctrine 'That it is lawfull to subjects upon pretence of reformation, or other pretence whatsoever, to enter into leagues & covenants, or to tak[e] up armes against the King', and condemned as unlawful oaths both the National

---

[20] B. S. Capp, *The Fifth Monarchy Men: A Study in Seventeenth-Century English Millenarianism* (London, 1972), pp. 195–227; W. C. Abbott, 'English Conspiracy and Dissent, 1660–1674', *AHR* 14 (1908–9), 503–28, 696–722; Rogers, *Fifth Monarchy Men*, pp. 123–33.

[21] For a range of other conspiracies, see especially Greaves, *Deliver Us from Evil*, *Enemies Under His Feet*, and *Secrets of the Kingdom*, passim.

[22] Richard Ashcraft, *Revolutionary Politics & Locke's 'Two Treatises of Government'* (Princeton, 1986), pp. 30, 54, 149–80, 247–50 and passim.

[23] See, in general, Ian B. Cowan, *The Scottish Covenanters 1660–1688* (London, 1976); Julia Buckroyd, *Church and State in Scotland 1660–1681* (Edinburgh, 1980).

Covenant as sworn in 1638 and the Solemn League and Covenant itself.[24] The settlement was widely accepted; by contrast, the minorities of extremists, who maintained their protest against prelacy and Erastianism, remained committed to contract theories of government for overtly theological reasons.

Ecclesiastical polity was still an area of bitter conflict: when an Act of 1662 sought to regularise the position of incumbents who had acquired their livings since the last episcopal regime, some 270 ministers in Scotland declined to seek episcopal collation and were deprived. Equipped with a very different theology, their catalytic effect was vastly greater than that of their 1,700 deprived English colleagues. Informal gatherings for worship known as conventicles became common in the areas in which the ejected ministers were concentrated, especially the south-west, and from this movement sprang the minor Pentland Rising of 1666.[25] It was followed by a policy of conciliation inspired by Lauderdale and pursued in London by the Cabal; but the growth of conventicles and unauthorised preaching put this policy into reverse by 1674. Under official discouragement, conventicles in the south-west increasingly took on a military character: steps to repress them came too late to prevent the murder of Archbishop Sharp in May 1679 and an armed rebellion at Rutherglen. A 'standing army', that bogey of denominational discourse, again showed its power: after one pitched battle won by the rebels at Drumclog, they were defeated and dispersed by the Duke of Monmouth's regular troops at the battle of Bothwell Brig on 22 June 1679. Like the Battle of the Boyne in Ireland, this obscure skirmish passed into the folk memories of the Scottish sects.

Scots Whig historians therefore sought to minimise the significance of these risings. Robert Wodrow, the historian of Scots Presbyterianism, denied the claims of English pamphleteers that there was 'a close Correspondence 'twixt *Shaftsbury* and the *Scots* Rebels': there was no evidence of such a link, Wodrow bravely urged, and 'to me it appears almost incredible, that a Handful of poor insignificant Country People, hearing and following some Field-Preachers, with no other View, than to have the Benefit of the Gospel, and preserve it in the Land, should enter into a

---

[24] 'ACT for preservation of his Majesties Person, Authoritie and Government', in *The Acts of the Parliaments of Scotland* (11 vols, Edinburgh, 1844–75), vol. 7, pp. 377–9 (hereafter *APS*).

[25] The rebels protested against the abandonment by Charles II of the National Covenant and the Solemn League and Covenant. They acknowledged the King's authority, but asserted 'the Lawfulness of sinless Self-Defence': Robert Wodrow, *The History of the Sufferings of the Church of Scotland, from the Restauration to the Revolution* (2 vols., Edinburgh, 1721–2), vol. 1, pp. 245–6.

Concert with the *English Peers*'.[26] This argument is open to doubt. *The Declaration and Testimony of Some of the True Presbyterian Party in Scotland, published at Rutherglen, May 29. 1679*[27] protested only against legislation bearing on religion in Scotland since 1660, without reference to English affairs, but *The Declaration of the oppressed Protestants now in Arms in Scotland*[28] announced that it was 'now more than ever apparent to us, that there is a formed and universal Plot carried on, for Subversion of the Protestant Religion, and for subjecting these Lands under the antichristian Bondage of Popery, as by secret undermining and murderous Practices in *England*, so by the open Introduction of Slavery and tyrannical Government in *Scotland*' and affirmed as one of their goals 'The diverting of the Succession from falling in the Person of a notorious Popish Plotter': James, Duke of York, now completed the equation of Popery with arbitrary power for Scots Presbyterians as well as English Dissenters.

Only a small minority known as Cameronians after Richard Cameron, one of their leading preachers, remained in active disaffection after the defeat at Bothwell Brig. Under persecution, they maintained a sharply-defined political theory which, appealing to the covenants, rejected the authority of the civil power over church government and threatened 'the Overthrow of the Kingdom of Darkness', including its symptoms – 'Popery', 'Prelacy' and 'Hierarchy', imposed via an Erastian settlement by 'a lustful and arbitrary Tyranny'. It was explicitly anti-democratic. Church government 'ought distinctly to be exercised, not after a carnal Manner by the Plurality of Votes, or authority of a single Person, but according to the Word of God; so that the Word makes and carries the Sentence, and not Plurality of Votes'.[29] After Charles II's renunciation of the Covenants, the Cameronians held themselves 'made free by God and their [the King and allied authorities'] Doings . . . loosed from all Obligations both Divine and Civil to them', and accordingly vowed to

> set up over our selves, and over what God shall give us Power of, Government and Governors according to the Word of God . . . we shall no more commit the Government of our selves, and the making of Laws for us, to any one single Person or lineal Successor . . . this Kind of Government by a single Person being most liable to Inconveniencies, and aptest to degenerate into Tyranny, as sad and long Experience hath taught us.[30]

These positions were repeated in the 'Sanquhar Declaration', a declaration of war dated 22 June 1680, announcing Charles II's title 'forfeited

[26] Wodrow, *Church of Scotland*, vol. 2, p. 42.
[27] Printed ibid., vol. 2, p. 44.
[28] Ibid., vol. 2, pp. 59–61.
[29] 'Queensferry *Paper*' (1680) in ibid., vol. 2, Appendix xlvi, pp. 43–7.
[30] 'Queensferry *Paper*', loc. cit.

several Years since, by his Perjury and Breach of Covenant both to God and his Kirk, and Usurpation of his Crown and Royal Prerogatives therein, and many other Breaches in Matters Ecclesiastick, and by his Tyranny and Breach of the very leges regnandi in Matters Civil'.[31] This rebellion too was suppressed by force: Richard Cameron was killed at the battle of Aird's Moss (21 July 1680); Donald Cargill, the other leading preacher, was executed in July 1681. Their martyrdom did not extinguish the Cameronians. Persecution was met with threats of armed resistance, and a renunciation of James II on his accession as a 'murderer', 'idolater' and 'a subject of Antichrist'.[32]

The Scots nation in general was enthusiastically loyal to James, despite this minority of extreme Presbyterians: Argyll's rebellion in May 1685 quickly collapsed for lack of support.[33] It was this loyalty which James II forfeited by measures favouring Roman Catholicism: toleration was initially extended to that church and to Quakers, but not to frequenters of conventicles. This distinction was then dropped by a sweeping royal Indulgence of June 1687 which extended toleration to Presbyterians also, so undoing long attempts at comprehension: from this point the Presbyterians gathered strength. Following the Glorious Revolution, the Scottish Convention, which met on 14 March 1689, was soon left in the hands of a Whig rump when the Jacobite minority seceded. In Scotland as elsewhere, the Glorious Revolution owed its success to militant armed minorities. In the northern kingdom one minority in particular played a decisive part: the Scottish Convention carried on its deliberations defended by the Cameronians in arms, and it was they who checked Viscount Dundee's counter-revolution in favour of James, after Dundee's victory at Killiecrankie, by their crucial defence of the town of Dunkeld on 21 August.

Under the aegis of resurgent Presbyterianism, the Scots went further than the Westminster Parliament in their constitutional claims of 1689. The Scottish Claim of Right adopted the general form of the English Declaration of Rights, but differed importantly from it.[34] The English document dropped all mention of the king having broken an original

---

[31] 'Sanquhar *Declaration*, 1680': Wodrow, *Church of Scotland*, vol. 2, Appendix xlvii, pp. 47–8.

[32] 'The Sanquhar Protestation', 28 May 1685, in W. C. Dickinson and G. Donaldson (eds.), *A Source Book of Scottish History*, vol. 3 (2nd edn, London, 1961), pp. 182–4.

[33] Wodrow (*Church of Scotland*, vol. 2, p. 530) excused the Presbyterians for not more effectively backing Argyll: they were 'sorely broken . . . perfectly dispirited under Twenty four Years sore Sufferings'. It has been suggested that Argyll's 'ambitions for a quasi-independent fiefdom in the Highlands were too transparent for him to be trusted by the Lowlanders, who aimed principally at restoring Presbyterianism': Clifton, *Western Rising*, p. 150.

[34] For the Claim of Right, see *APS*, vol. 9, pp. 37–40.

contract and took refuge behind the idea that James had abdicated, an abdication which (by a syntactical ambiguity) might be ascribed to his flight rather than to his misrule. The Scots Claim of Right, by contrast, ignored James's flight and fictional abdication; listed his offences against Protestantism; and concluded:

> THERFOR the Estates of the kingdom of Scotland Find and Declaire That King James the Seventh being a profest papist, Did assume the Regall power and acted as king, without ever takeing the oath required by law, and hath by the advyce of Evill and wicked Counsellors, Invaded the funda-mentall Constitution of the Kingdome, and altered it from a legall limited monarchy to ane arbitrary despotick power, and hath Exercised the same, to the subversione of the protestant religion, and the violation of the lawes and liberties of the Kingdome, inverting all the Ends of Government, wherby he hath forfaulted the right to the Croune, and the throne is become vacant.

The 'fundamentall Constitution', identified with denominational commit-ments and echoing English Calvinists' use of 'fundamental law', was a formula which owed more to the Covenanters' Sanquhar Declaration than to the English Declaration of Rights. The Claim of Right went much further, again, in condemning an institution whose legality was still unquestioned by the Anglican majority in England:

> THAT Prelacy and the superiority of any office in the Church, above pres-byters is, and hath been a great and insupportable greivance and trouble to this Nation, and contrary to the Inclinationes of the generality of the people ever since the reformatione (they haveing reformed from popery by presbyters) and therfor ought to be abolished.

It may have been an attempt to commit William to a Presbyterian settle-ment by implicitly linking it with the offer of the Crown. Thirdly, the Claim of Right demanded that 'Parliaments ought to be frequently called, and allowed to sit', i.e. to run out their term; by contrast the English House of Lords had deleted the final phrase from the draft of the Declara-tion of Rights, leaving discretion over dissolution in the hands of the monarch. Whatever their importance and *de facto* indispensability, English (and after 1707 British) parliaments at Westminster continued to be called and dissolved by royal command: in England and beyond into English spheres of influence, the definition of sovereignty remained mon-archical, and representative assemblies tried with difficulty to find space for an overriding conception of natural or fundamental law.

In passing the Declaration of Rights, the Westminster Parliament had deliberately omitted from the longer draft list known as the 'Heads of Grievances' those complaints which would require new law; but two days after passing the Claim of Right, the Scots Convention voted its own Articles of Grievances, including, principally, a condemnation of the Act of Supremacy of 1669 as 'Inconsistent with the Establishment of the Church Government now desyred and ought to be abrogated'.[35] The Act of Supremacy (1669) had firmly recorded 'that his Maiestie hath the Supream Authority and Supremacie over all persons & in all causes ecclesiasticall within this Kingdom; And that be vertew therof the ordering and disposall of the Externall Government and policie of the Church Doth propperlie belong to his Maiestie and his Successours As ane inherent right to the Croun'.[36] Scots Presbyterians now bid for a reversal of this principle in the context of a successful rebellion against monarchy.

William was initially favourably disposed, owing to the influence of exiled Presbyterians in Holland before the invasion; but the drive of the Presbyterians in Scotland for revenge, and the need not unnecessarily to alienate the large body of Scots Episcopalians, meant that William was reluctant to establish Presbyterianism until the Episcopalians' Jacobitism became inescapable. Alexander Rose, Bishop of Edinburgh, sent south to negotiate for the Scottish Church, later recorded that William had commanded Compton, the Bishop of London, to tell Rose

> that he now knows the state of Scotland much better than he did when he was in Holland; for, while there, he was made believe that Scotland generally all over was Presbyterian, but now he sees that the great body of the nobility and gentry are for Episcopacy, and 'tis the trading and inferior sort that are for Presbytery: wherefore he bids me tell you, that if you will undertake to serve him to the purpose that he is served here in England, he will take you by the hand, support the Church and Order, and throw off the Presbyterians.

Rose offered his opinion that his fellow Scots bishops 'will not serve the prince so as he is served in England, that is (as I take it), to make him their king, or give their suffrage for his being king'. His loyalties were clear. The next day Rose saw William; but to the *de facto* king's direct question about Rose's conduct, the bishop could only answer 'Sir, I will serve you so far as law, reason, or conscience shall allow me.'[37]

William realistically interpreted these three massive reservations as plain symptoms of Jacobitism. An Act abolishing prelacy, as foreshadowed in the Articles of Grievances, followed in 1689;[38] in 1690, by the threat of withholding supply, the Edinburgh Parliament forced

---

[35] The Articles of Grievances, *APS*, vol. 9, p. 45.

[36] *APS*, vol. 7, p. 554.

[37] Alexander Rose to Bishop Archibald Campbell, 22 Oct. 1713: Robert Keith, *An Historical Catalogue of the Scottish Bishops* (Edinburgh, 1824), pp. 65–72.

[38] *APS*, vol. 9, p. 104.

through an Act establishing Presbyterianism.[39] It was a compromise settlement; still Erastian, it left unrepealed the Act condemning the Covenants; founded Presbyterianism on general consent rather than divine ordination; and fell short of the popular election of ministers. Such a settlement the Cameronians refused to accept. On the other hand, the Presbyterians, including prominently the survivors of the ministers ejected in 1662, set about using a settlement moderate in principle to purge large numbers of Episcopalians. In England, by evasion and equivocation, many men unhappy with the outcome of 1688 avoided being forced into the open as Nonjurors; but in Scotland a large disaffected intelligentsia was swiftly created by ruthless persecution. Armed with its traditional legitimist ideology, it provided both a social constituency and the major rationale for repeated Scots rebellions[40] over the next half century; but in that role it suffered from a major disadvantage. Scots Nonjurors, like their English brethren, possessed a keen sense of the sacred nature of certain interlocking forms in ecclesiastical and civil polity, especially that of sacred monarchy; but their theology was in other respects scarcely distinguishable from orthodox positions. Without the crucial catalyst of heterodoxy the millennial note undoubtedly present in Jacobitism never became prominent, and the movement's large social constituency was never effectively mobilised. Minorities of religious extremists continued to pose the greater threat. Meanwhile, Covenanter theology had created a libertarian interpretation of the settlement of 1689 which differed sharply from the English interpretation, which proved intolerable to Westminster (leading to union in 1707), and which was to find powerful re-expression in those American colonies to which successive waves of emigrants carried it.

In England, the sectarian impetus to rebellion and social upheaval of the 1640s and 50s was reformulated in the 1670s in the course of a dynastic crisis.[41] During the Exclusion Controversy, that quasi-revolutionary attempt by English Whigs to bar James, Duke of York, from the succession as an agent of 'popery and arbitrary power', open attacks on monarchy as such were necessarily limited. Whig praise of the ancient constitution implied a balance between its elements, one of them monarchical,

---

[39] *APS*, vol. 9, pp. 133–4.

[40] Bruce Lenman, *The Jacobite Risings in Britain, 1689–1746* (London, 1980).

[41] The characteristic dynastic and anti-Catholic political vocabulary, which extends for more than a century from this crisis, was classically expressed in such texts as [Earl of Shaftesbury], *A Letter From a Person of Quality, To His Friend in the Country* (n.p., 1675) and [Andrew Marvell], *An Account of the Growth of Popery, and Arbitrary Government in England* ('Amsterdam', 1677).

and a right of redressing an imbalance: exclusion could only profess to be restorative. Could it be

> the duty of either *English* men or Christians, to have that zeal for a corrupted leprous Branch of Royalty, that we must ruine both Religion, Government, and Majesty it self, to support him? How much more consistent would it be with the honest, prudent, and lawful means of a Nations preservation, to take out one link out of the whole Chain of Succession, than, by preserving that, to break the whole to pieces?[42]

If monarchy as such could almost never be denounced, the religious dimension was openly rehearsed. Vitriolic assaults on the character of the Duke of York and on Catholicism were combined with professions of respect for the monarchy, and even for its basis in religious obligation: 'Religion, consider'd only in a Politick Sense, is one of the chief Supports of Civil Government', maintained one Exclusion tract with a mixture of platitude and qualification. More specifically, of course, Protestantism was professed as the touchstone of Whig integrity. Even in Catholic France, religion overrode the hereditary principle: 'Let these Assertors of Divine Right tell me, if in *France*, at this day the most Absolute Monarchy in *Europe*, and where the Succession is held most Sacred, a *Protestant* Prince would be admitted to the Crown.'[43]

Royalists by contrast dwelt on the implausibility of the Whig claim that their objection was limited to the person of the heir, and did not extend to the institution of monarchy. Contract theory in an extreme form was indeed prevalent among Whig exclusionist polemics: it potentially undermined the title of any heir, not just a Popish one. Tories also saw the hand of the men of 1648 in the support given to Monmouth: legitimacy so defended might be a screen for republicanism. In fact, few parliamentary Whigs ever backed Monmouth.[44] The proposed Association to defend the succession after the failure of parliamentary attempts at exclusion was condemned as the work of '*Associators,* or *Covenanters,* call them what you will',[45] 'only a Prologue to a Rebellion'.[46] The Association document indeed took the form of an oath to defend 'the True Protestant religion against Popery . . . the power and priviledge of Parliaments, the lawfull Rights and Liberties of the Subject, against all Incroachments and

---

[42] [Elkanah Settle], *The Character of a Popish Successor, and What England May Expect From Such a One* (London, 1681), pp. 22–3.

[43] *Reasons for his Majesties Passing the Bill of Exclusion* (London, 1681), pp. 3–4.

[44] O. W. Furley, 'The Whig Exclusionists: Pamphlet Literature in the Exclusion Campaign, 1679–81', *Cambridge Historical Journal* 13 (1957), 31; J. R. Jones, *The First Whigs: The Politics of the Exclusion Crisis 1678–1683* (London, 1961), pp. 14, 69, 179.

[45] *A Plea for Succession, In Opposition to Popular Exclusion* (London, 1682), p. 4.

[46] [Roger L'Estrange], *A Brief History of the Times, &* (London, 1687), p. 6.

Usurpation of Arbitrary power whatsoever', and to resist the accession of James, Duke of York, or any other Papist 'by force of Arms, if need so require'.[47] It was indeed a threat of rebellion.

From 1679 to 1681 the Whigs in Parliament concentrated on Exclusion: they thereby made all other issues in their ideology depend on the religious issue. A dynastic rearrangement was affirmed to be the only effective means by which other Whig goals could be secured.[48] In the debate on the Exclusion Bill of 2 November 1680, several speakers preferred the prospect of civil war to a popish monarch. One such was Sir Thomas Player: 'As for that one argument, of a Civil War that may come upon this Exclusion, I would let the World know, that we are not afraid of War upon that occasion.' John Trenchard added: 'when a Popish King comes to the Crown, either we must submit, and change our Religion, or resist'.[49] Rebellion was thus implicit in the Whig position from the outset, and their stance inevitably provoked analogies with the Covenanters' rebellion of June 1679. The centrality of religion in the Covenanters' case, and the swift suppression of their rebellion by Charles's efficient standing army at the battle of Bothwell Brig, strengthened the analogy. Scots, including the fugitive Earl of Argyll, naturally joined the Earl of Shaftesbury's conspiracy for an insurrection in 1682–3.[50]

Like the Covenanters, the Whig Exclusionists were anti-Catholic rather than pro-democratic. The popular appeal of both groups had little initially to do with the extent of the franchise or the wide representational function of parliaments. Indeed, Shaftesbury's proposals for parliamentary reform (prudently left unpublished in his lifetime) were aimed at bolstering the independence of the MP against the monarch by eliminating dependent voters: a revaluation of the ancient forty-shilling freehold franchise to adjust for inflation would have reduced the electorate, predicted Shaftesbury, by about three quarters.[51] Appropriately, his closest collaborator and paid retainer, John Locke, did not construct his political theory around a democratic objection to monarchy. The guiding themes in Locke's intellectual development were theological. Shaftesbury con-

---

[47] Printed ibid., pp. 100–6.
[48] Jones, *The First Whigs*, p. 67; Ashcraft, *Revolutionary Politics*, p. 393, for the absence of franchise reform as an Exclusionist principle.
[49] Anchitell Grey (ed.), *Debates of the House of Commons, From the Year 1667 to the Year 1694* (10 vols., London, 1749), vol. 7, pp. 406, 410, 413.
[50] Ashcraft, *Revolutionary Politics*, p. 354. The Scots initially asked the English conspirators for £30,000 to finance the rising north of the border: ibid., pp. 361 ff. For Scots involvement in the Rye House Plot and for Argyll's intended rebellion see A. Ian Dunlop, *William Carstares and The Kirk by Law Established* (Edinburgh, 1967), pp. 40–2.
[51] Lord Shaftesbury, *Some Observations Concerning the Regulating of Elections for Parliament* (London, 1689), pp. 11–12.

fessed to a fellow conspirator, while in exile, that he owed his Socinian opinions in religion to Locke's influence:[52] it was such views which identified even an Anglican episcopal, not merely a papist, regime as tyrannical. Anglicans sought not merely to impose a theology, but a theology which Socinianism identified as anathema. Furthermore, it was in the context of the Exclusion Crisis that John Locke, in the circle of extremists associated with Shaftesbury, evolved political views which were 'vehemently supportive of armed resistance'. Shaftesbury's essential principle was that the imposition of arbitrary government and popery under Charles II meant that the government was dissolved, and the people free to settle another government.[53] This was precisely the central point of Locke's *Two Treatises*, and the most extreme position conceivable in the context of Restoration England.

Out of the Exclusion Crisis arose a heightened awareness not only of the institution of monarchy, but specifically of the succession issue, both in Scripture and in English history. John Somers's *Brief History of the Succession* established the case for the Crown descending to illegitimate sons, and so provided a legitimist rationale for Monmouth's rebellion. Monmouth's pretended title to the crown was by inheritance: if he were Charles II's legitimate son, he would take precedence over Charles's brother James. The future Whig Lord Chancellor was (perhaps in consequence) unable to break from the common law's traditional definition of sovereignty. Somers argued that anarchy could only be avoided by 'a supreme uncontroulable power lodged somewhere'; that in England it was lodged 'in the King, Lords and Commons in Parliament'; that, therefore, '*the Succession was wholly under the Controul of Parliament*'.[54] The Glorious Revolution, similarly, was dominated by legitimist rather than contractarian interpretations of the significance of what had occurred. Claims that the crown was or had been made elective were generally resisted in England; the implications of rebellion were sometimes avoided, not by a confusion of mind but by an English adherence to Anglican doctrine which kept at bay the republican implications of a break in the succession.

Monmouth may have been a Protestant symbol, but he fell also into the category of opportunist adventurer, whose elite supporters too were 'young hotheads, extravagant and in some cases desperate for want of money . . . essentially of the fashionable class of courtiers, whose opposi-

---

[52] Ashcraft, *Revolutionary Politics*, pp. 327, 375.
[53] Ibid., p. 392.
[54] [John, Lord Somers], *A Brief History of the Succession, Collected out of the Records, and the most Authentick Historians*, n.p., n.d. [London, 1681], pp. 12, 15.

tion was that of opportunists or frondeurs'. Had the king died during his acute illness of August 1679, a military coup by Shaftesbury and Monmouth would have been a possibility.[55] Similarly, Monmouth's progress through the northern counties in September 1682 'may have been a feeler; at times it had the appearance of an abortive rebellion'.[56] Schemes of insurrection were now under discussion in Monmouth's entourage, involving (among others) Argyll and Scots who had fled after the battle of Bothwell Brig.[57] From this notion of the right of resistance emerged the Rye House Plot, a plan for a general insurrection after the murder of Charles II, timed for October or November 1682, postponed to April 1683, and, when that plan proved abortive, for a rising by Monmouth timed to coincide with that of Argyll in 1685.

If Monmouth's elite backers were often rakes, cynics and opportunists, his rank and file were exceptionally thoughtful and pious.[58] From their perspective, the rebellion took the form of a crusade against popery. Yet this was more than the common coin of English Protestantism, for the itinerary of Monmouth's rising was deliberately chosen to pass through strongholds of Dissent; and three quarters of Somerset Dissenters after 1660 were Presbyterians. Dissent correlated in that county with the sharpest form of political alienation. Somerset Quarter Sessions informations after the Restoration record a

> flow of disgruntled, quasi-seditious, talk . . . Never sufficiently organised or serious to merit the term conspiracy, sometimes vengeful and sometimes boastful, now expressing a startling contempt for the King's government, now simply hoping for stirring times once more, these depositions suggest how attitudes formed during the Civil War and Interregnum lived on after 1660.[59]

Such attitudes in the West had been inflamed by the Popish Plot and encouraged by such local Whig magnates as Shaftesbury, whose seat was at nearby Wimborne St Giles, and John Trenchard, earlier implicated in the Rye House plot.[60] The rising duly combined legitimist and republican strands: Monmouth did not claim the throne on his landing but only during the course of the rebellion, when the republicans among his supporters had no option but to agree; his commanders included the Fifth Monarchist Colonel Venner, kinsman of the rebel of 1661; the disposition

[55] Jones, *The First Whigs*, pp. 82, 87–8.
[56] David Ogg, *England in the Reign of Charles II* (2nd edn, Oxford, 1956), p. 646.
[57] Ibid., p. 647; Ashcraft, *Revolutionary Politics*, pp. 354–405.
[58] The element both of Anglican and Dissenter anti-popery among the rank and file is emphasised by Peter Earle, *Monmouth's Rebels* (London, 1977).
[59] Clifton, *Western Rising*, pp. 46, 52.
[60] Ibid., pp. 58, 60; Earle, *Monmouth's Rebels*, pp. 29–30.

of the rank and file is suggested by the party of rebels who, passing through Wells, paused to smash the monuments in the Cathedral.[61]

This last did not represent an echo of a world which had been lost: through all the vicissitudes of English politics from the 1530s to the 1830s and beyond, the most consistent theme both of popular sentiment and of ideological exegesis was anti-Catholicism.[62] It was not always the most prominent theme; but its periodic prominence was associated with political crises and episodes of paranoia, from the Marian executions of 1555–8 through the Gunpowder Plot of 1605 to the Popish Plot of 1678, which demonstrated its ability to reassert itself. From the sixteenth century, Englishmen pictured the Roman Church not merely as a system of cruelty and intolerance, but as an international conspiracy operating through secret agents and with the covert sympathy of fellow travellers. Events as far removed as Spanish invasion attempts on England and Ireland, and the Massacre of St Bartholomew, were depicted as the personal schemes of the Pope. Deliverances were attributed to equally direct divine intervention in favour of Protestant England.[63] An apocalyptic or even millenarian perspective on England's history was generated principally in the context of Protestantism's conflict with Rome. The seventeenth century fuelled this with repeated panics of Catholic plots, insurrections and massacres. Groundless reports of Catholic massacres far outnumbered actual rebellions by Protestants, and their strange currency has prompted the suggestion that popular political vocabulary was largely expressed in a dichotomy of papist and anti-papist.[64] The apotheosis of this tradition in England was the Glorious Revolution; in the new world, the American Revolution.

This resilient tradition resolves a paradox of late-seventeenth-century

---

[61] Clifton, *Western Rising*, pp. 168, 192. Clifton argues against economic recession or class antagonism as sources of the rebellion, notes that the evidence does not establish that Dissenters formed a majority of the rebel army, and emphasises a shared anti-Catholicism (pp. 270, 275).

[62] For the survival of this nexus into the eighteenth century, see Colin Haydon, *Anti-Catholicism in Eighteenth-Century England, c. 1714–1780: A Political and Social Study* (Manchester, 1993) and M. Dorothy George, *English Political Caricature* (2 vols., Oxford, 1959); for its subsequent expression, E. R. Norman, *Anti-Catholicism in Victorian England* (London, 1968); J. Wolffe, *The Protestant Crusade in Great Britain, 1829–1860* (Oxford, 1991), and work cited.

[63] Carol Wiener, 'The Beleaguered Isle. A Study of Elizabethan and Early Jacobean Anti-Catholicism', *P&P* 51 (1971), 27–62. The author drew a parallel with Richard Hofstadter's analysis of modern American anti-communism in *The Paranoid Style in American Politics*. For a corrective on the theme of millenarianism, see Richard Bauckham, *Tudor Apocalypse* (Abingdon, 1978), pp. 208, 227–8.

[64] Robin Clifton, 'The Popular Fear of Catholics During the English Revolution', *P&P* 52 (1971), 23–55; J. P. Kenyon, *The Popish Plot* (London, 1972); Jonathan Scott, 'England's Troubles: Exhuming the Popish Plot', in Tim Harris, Paul Seaward and Mark Goldie (eds.), *The Politics of Religion in Restoration England* (Oxford, 1990), pp. 107–31.

political discourse. The late Stuart monarchy had been steadily strengthened. Bureaucratic, financial and military reforms, continued from the 1650s, gave greater solidity to the institutions of government; the royal prerogative was put to more vigorous use, and its legality clarified; Parliament's institutional role was not allowed to develop. Yet little opposition was aroused to the prospect of a stronger, better organised state until 'popery' identified a reformed monarchy as an agency of 'arbitrary power'. The prospect of a Catholic successor in James, Duke of York, generated a nexus of ideas to check the Crown and regulate its succession even before his specific policies could be known: the mass hysteria of the Exclusion Crisis and the Popish Plot, and the fully developed Whig doctrine of a right of rebellion, preceded James's accession. The religious policies of his reign, whether or not they aimed beyond pluralism and toleration to the establishment of Catholic hegemony, could hardly fail to threaten a similar crisis by activating these more extreme responses; and policies which failed to endorse the position of the established Church forfeited the support of Tories and Anglicans. This combination of an alienated though passive majority with violently disaffected minorities created a situation in which foreign military intervention might succeed.[65]

The unfolding events of the Glorious Revolution showed how Englishmen's hostility to Popery was both spontaneous and manipulable. Its manipulation for tactical advantage was evident after the landing of William of Orange: in York, on 22 November 1688, a meeting of a hundred of the country gentry threatened to get out of hand and pass a loyal address to King James, when on a pre-arranged signal a Whig rushed into the room, shouting that 'the papists were risen and had fired at the militia troops'. Untrue as the report was, it was sufficient to break up the meeting and allow the Williamites to seize the city.[66] In the North West, Protestant opinion was polarised behind William by the 'Irish Fright', an equally groundless rumour that an army of 10,000 Irish Catholics was on the loose, burning Birmingham, Wolverhampton or other towns and concerting a massacre of Protestants.[67] On 13 December 1688 the City of London was convulsed by reports of an Irish massacre actually in progress, led by James's Catholic troops at Uxbridge; from London the rumour spread widely over the southern counties, with similar wild alarms that whole towns had been burned. Indeed, there is evidence that the reports were regarded by some as deliberately spread by supporters

[65] John Miller, *Popery and Politics in England 1660–1688* (Cambridge, 1973).
[66] Andrew Browning (ed.), *Memoirs of Sir John Reresby* (Glasgow, 1936), p. 528.
[67] Eveline Cruickshanks, 'The Revolution and the Localities: Examples of Loyalty to James II', in Cruickshanks (ed.), *By Force Or By Default? The Revolution of 1688–1689* (Edinburgh, 1989), pp. 28–43, at 37.

of William of Orange.[68] Such heightened emotions meant that the invasion of 1688 was a desperate gamble carried through at a time of widespread panic – fear of a Catholic monarch's subversion of the constitution, fear of a military coup by a Catholic standing army, fear of a massacre by Irish Catholics. In such a frenzied setting, a moderate outcome proved impossible to achieve. The attempt to undo James's religious reforms ended in something that few men foresaw or advocated before William's landing: his succession to the throne.

III. COLONIAL AMERICAN REBELLIONS 1660–1689 AND TRANSATLANTIC DISCOURSE

Seventeenth- and early-eighteenth-century America displayed the problems of England, Scotland and Ireland in a more acute form. The practical weakness of central government was matched by the survival of substantial power in the hands of local magnates. The theoretical authority of the centre was similarly contradicted and sometimes challenged by powerfully-rooted doctrines of a right of resistance. In this setting the relatively undeveloped state of the institutions of government gave scope for opportunist coups: this was the age of the adventurer, the unquiet spirit. Colonial Americans preserved with even greater clarity than the English the sanguinary expectations of the seventeenth century. Thomas Smith, Congregational minister of Portland, Maine, lamented news of the Jacobite rising of 1745, believing that 'the rebels, having taken Edinburg ... made a bloody sacrifice of all the people within thirty miles',[69] a belief which at least harmonised with the regular minor massacres of New England's Indian wars for more than a century past.

Even after the reassertion of royal authority in 1660, the American colonies were torn by a succession of violent, personalised but ideologically charged disturbances which surpassed in sectarian and anti-Catholic zeal those seen in the British Isles. On behalf of the Puritan interest, Josias Fendall was briefly successful in attempting to overthrow the Catholic proprietary government of Maryland in 1660,[70] and success attended the anti-quitrent rebellion in New Jersey in 1672 until Dutch reconquest in 1673 and the restoration of an English governor in 1674

---

[68] George Hilton Jones, 'The Irish Fright of 1688: Real Violence and Imagined Massacre', *Bulletin of the Institute of Historical Research* 55 (1982), 148–53.

[69] William Willis (ed.), *Journals of the Rev. Thomas Smith, and the Rev. Samuel Deane* (Portland, Maine, 1849), p. 122.

[70] Wesley Frank Craven, *The Southern Colonies in the Seventeenth Century 1607–1689* (Baton Rouge, 1949), pp. 297–9. Fendall escaped punishment and later associated with the followers of Nathaniel Bacon and with John Coode: *DAB*.

swamped these issues.[71] The Protestant rebellion led by William Davyes and John Pate in Maryland in 1676 against the ideas of absolute rule which lay behind the proprietorship of Charles Calvert, third Lord Baltimore, was a failure, ending in the execution of its two instigators,[72] but Nathaniel Bacon's rebellion in Virginia the same year temporarily captured power and was terminated only by Bacon's illness and death. A rebellion in North Carolina in 1677–8 now associated with the name of John Culpeper was briefly successful, though Culpeper was acquitted at his eventual trial in England at the instigation of the Carolina proprietors themselves.[73] A second rising led by Fendall against the authorities of Maryland in 1680–1 was a failure, however, as was Edward Gove's rebellion in New Hampshire in 1683 (a rebellion against Edward Cranfield, Governor of New Hampshire, on the grounds that his commission as vice-admiral of the colony was illegal, being signed by a papist, James Duke of York).[74] Equally unsuccessful was the Essex County rebellion in Massachusetts in 1687 (a tax strike, partly led by the Puritan minister John Wise).[75]

The events of 1688–9 in England then provided the inspiration and the inducement for a series of rebellions appealing for their justification to the English model: Jacob Leisler was temporarily successful in New York; in Boston, Massachusetts, the Governor of the new Dominion of New England was overthrown; in Maryland, John Coode seized power, continuing an anti-Catholic struggle which had already produced coups in 1660, 1676 and 1680–1; in North Carolina Governor Seth Sothel was ousted, as was Governor John Colleton in South Carolina.[76] After the Glorious Revolution, however, colonial governors steadily strengthened their positions: the opportunist coup became slowly but steadily more unlikely. The rebellion against Governor Andrew Hamilton in New Jersey in 1699 failed, and Thomas Cary's rebellion of 1709–11 in North Carolina,

[71] Richard P. McCormick, *New Jersey from Colony to State 1609–1789* (Princeton, 1964), pp. 24–7.

[72] Craven, *Southern Colonies*, p. 411; Charles M. Andrews, *The Colonial Period of American History* (4 vols., New Haven, Conn., 1934–8), vol. 2, pp. 325–79.

[73] Wesley Frank Craven, *The Colonies in Transition 1660–1713* (New York, 1968), pp. 156–60; Hugh F. Rankin, *Upheaval in Albemarle: The Story of Culpeper's Rebellion, 1675–1689* (Raleigh, 1962).

[74] J. M. Sosin, *English America and the Restoration Monarchy of Charles II* (Lincoln, Nebraska, 1980), pp. 268–71.

[75] George Allan Cook, *John Wise: Early American Democrat* (New York, 1952), pp. 43–58. Wise's writings were on questions of church government rather than democracy in civil society.

[76] Political conflict in South Carolina from c. 1670 into the early eighteenth century was essentially between the Anglican ('Goose Creek') and Dissenter parties: M. Eugene Sirmans, *Colonial South Carolina: A Political History 1663–1763* (Chapel Hill, 1966), pp. 17, 40, 48–9, 75–6 and passim.

which arose from a conflict between Quaker and Anglican parties,[77] highlighted the growing infrequency of such risings. The overthrow of the
proprietary government in South Carolina in 1719 was the last of its
type.[78] Thereafter the arena of action until the 1760s steadily moved from
east coast capitals to the backcountry. How do we explain these cases?
Do they have common features?

For as long as the familiar teleological account of the Anglo-American
past appeared self-evident, it seemed natural to explain 'early' (and therefore generally unsuccessful) rebellions as anticipations of a late (and naturally successful) revolution. If their causes were assumed to be similar,
the rising led by Nathaniel Bacon in Virginia in 1676 could be made to
act out the libertarian, patriotic scenario of 1776;[79] clearly, that scenario
itself is in question if Bacon's like other rebellions could be explained as
a conflict between rival elements within the elite.[80] Yet local lawlessness
involving both religious and economic grievances, culminating in coups
rather than democratic or libertarian endeavour, was the normal mode
of political trauma in colonial society. The emphasis by figures of authority in the old world on the urgent need for subordination and obedience
was given point by the record of old world rebellion, but even more point
by the remarkable record in this respect of new world settlers. Social
conditions in Virginia and Carolina predisposed them to stability from
the 1680s;[81] other colonies were not so fortunate. In a society which saw
widespread grievances over labour conditions, land tenure and local
administration, religion might provide an intellectual framework, identifying the tyrannical nature of a ruling elite or providing a stimulus to
collective action. It duly did so, the catalyst being the person of the émigré
dissident Nathaniel Bacon.

Anticipations of the constitutional demands of 1776 could indeed be

---

[77] Hugh T. Lefler and William S. Powell, *Colonial North Carolina: A History* (New York,
1973), pp. 195–7.
[78] Sirmans, *Colonial South Carolina*, pp. 125–8, argues that the catalyst for this rebellion was
a rumour of an impending Spanish (and Catholic) invasion of the colony; it was 'not a
revolt against tyranny'.
[79] The recent invention of an historiography explaining 1676 as a proto-democratic movement is documented and corrected by Wilcomb E. Washburn, *The Governor and the Rebel:
A History of Bacon's Rebellion in Virginia* (Chapel Hill, 1957).
[80] Bernard Bailyn, 'Politics and Social Structure in Colonial Virginia' in James Morton
Smith (ed.), *Seventeenth Century America* (Chapel Hill, 1959), pp. 90–115. Warren M. Bill-
ings, in 'The Causes of Bacon's Rebellion: Some Suggestions', *Virginia Magazine of History
and Biography* 78 (1970), 409–35, emphasises and elaborates a similar interpretation,
adding that the Assembly held under Bacon's aegis in June 1676 'was not a force for
radical change' and pointing to local complaints against 'too frequent Assembly sessions
. . . a curious objection for people supposedly concerned with their liberties' (pp. 432–3).
[81] T. H. Breen, 'A Changing Labor Force and Race Relations in Virginia, 1660–1710',
reprinted in idem, *Puritans and Adventurers* (New York, 1980), pp. 127–47.

found in the Virginia of 1676, but they were voiced by the colonial authorities against which Bacon rebelled. His actions made still more difficult
the attempt of Virginian agents in London in 1674–6 to obtain a royal
charter confirming what they took to be their liberties, including security
of landownership against royal grants to proprietors, the legislative
authority of the Virginia Assembly, and taxation only with the colonists'
agreement via their Assembly. It was a demand to possess 'the same
liberties and privileges as Englishmen in England'. Direct dependence on
the crown rather than on proprietors would guarantee the colonists, they
claimed,

> those just rights and privileges as were their due whilst they lived in Eng-
> land, and which they humbly hope that they have not lost by removing
> themselves into a country where they hazarded their lives and fortunes, so
> much more to the advantage of the crown and kingdom, than to their own.

These rhetorical demands defended also the perquisites and profits of
office, licit and illicit, built up by the colonial elite and now threatened
by a reassertion of royal power. It was this elite against which Bacon's
rebellion was directed, and it was the Privy Council's belief 'that the
Rebellion of Virginia was occasioned by the Excessive power of the
Assembly' which explained the much more limited nature of the charter
granted to that colony in 1676. If land tenures were confirmed, the claim
of sovereign authority in the Assembly was ignored, and a right of no
taxation without consent was not established. The constitutional position
of a colony was to be a subordinate one.[82] This pattern of dual rebellion –
the efforts of the backcountry settlers against the coastal elites, and of the
latter against the transatlantic authorities – was therefore to persist long
after 1676 and even after 1783.

The rhetoric employed by the backcountry rebels against the tidewater
elite echoed that used by that elite against the British authorities. Nathaniel Bacon would readily 'harangue' his hearers 'on the Preserving our
Lives from the Indians, Inspecting the Publick Revenues, th' exorbitant
Taxes and redressing the Grievances and Calamities of that Deplorable
Country', while Richard Lawrence, who may have masterminded the
rebellion, sought 'to See those abuses rectified that the Countrey was
oppress'd with through (as he said) the frowardness avarice and french

---

[82] David S. Lovejoy, 'Virginia's Charter and Bacon's Rebellion', in Alison Gilbert Olson
and Richard Maxwell Brown (eds), *Anglo-American Political Relations, 1675–1775* (New Brunswick, 1970), pp. 31–51; Stephen Saunders Webb, *The Governors-General: The English Army
and the Definition of the Empire, 1569–1681* (Chapel Hill, N.C., 1979); idem, *1676: The End of
American Independence* (New York, 1984). On the last two titles, see Richard R. Johnson,
'The Imperial Webb: The Thesis of Garrison Government in Early America Considered',
WMQ 43 (1986), 408–30.

Despotick Methods of the Governour'. The elite's use of executive authority, and the elite's international affiliations, were already linked in backcountry rhetoric: 'Popery and arbitrary power' was an identity easily imported from England.[83] Bacon himself was a recent emigrant to the colonies after being withdrawn from Cambridge University by his father for having 'broken into some extravagancies'; once in Virginia he was reported to be 'of a pestilent and prevalent logical discourse tending to atheisme in most companyes'.[84] Not all politically engaged men were distinguished by theological heterodoxy; the vast majority were not. But smaller minorities acted as catalysts, and the role of religion in their activation establishes a lasting character type. This pattern of religious dissident turned rebel leader was to persist from Thomas Venner and Nathaniel Bacon through John Coode and Jacob Leisler to Tom Paine, Samuel Ely and Ethan Allen.

These insurrections were challenges initially and principally to the authority of a newly-emergent east-coast oligarchy of gentry landowners. Sometimes, as with the rebellions of 1676 or 1719, the occasion was an Indian war: the need to defend the backcountry settlers from attack, or the demands of new settlers for liberty to make incursions into Indian settlements.[85] Yet if the practical circumstances of life in mainland America differed so much from those at home, the differences of politics and religion were less marked. News of Monmouth's rebellion triggered similar reactions in many American colonies – colonies whose local problems were unrelated to those of Somerset except by issues of the dynasty and religion. Legitimism and militant Protestantism led men to toast Monmouth and acknowledge him as rightful king in colonies as far apart as Massachusetts, New Hampshire and New York; Maryland and Virginia; and even the West Indies. As the Governor of Bermuda reported, 'It was whispered about the country that now or never was the time, that the Duke [of Monmouth] was rightful king and no papist, and that the Pope

---

[83] [Thomas Mathew], 'The Beginning, Progress, and Conclusion of Bacon's Rebellion, 1675–1676', in Charles M. Andrews (ed.), *Narratives of the Insurrections, 1675–1690* (New York, 1915), pp. 30, 40.

[84] Washburn, *Bacon's Rebellion*, p. 18; 'A True Narrative of the Rise, Progresse, and Cessation of the Late Rebellion in Virginia . . . by his Majestyes Commissioners', in Andrews (ed.), *Narratives*, p. 110.

[85] Later historians idealised the frontiersman and depicted him as a champion of freedom and democracy; the violent and aggressive reality was very different. In Virginia, for example, 'it was the tyranny of the temporarily enraged frontiersman against which [Governor] Berkeley was struggling in 1676 . . . The record of the June assembly proves that the real grievance against Governor Berkeley was not that he refused to defend the country against the Indians – a ridiculous charge . . . but that he refused to authorise the slaughter and dispossession of the innocent as well as the 'guilty'': Washburn, *Bacon's Rebellion*, p. 163.

was the whore of Babylon and drunk with the blood of the saints, and much more such stuff.'[86]

Thanks to the religious conformity successfully imposed by a confessional polity, the New England colonies enjoyed relative internal stability from the 1630s to the 1680s, challenged principally by the catastrophic irruption of periodic wars with the Indians:[87] this was now to be disrupted by the similarly-perceived intrusion of English issues. By the late seventeenth century, anti-Catholic paranoia was even stronger in America than in England, despite the presence in the colonies of an even smaller Catholic minority. This heightened sensibility reacted strongly against the innovative exercise of executive power by James II and produced a situation of extreme tension: in 1689 news of events in England was followed by violent rebellions in three colonies – Massachusetts, New York and Maryland – and peaceful changes of government where the authorities did not resist the proclamation of William and Mary.[88] The Massachusetts rebellion was aimed at restoring Puritan hegemony and local autonomy, enjoyed from Charles I's charter of 1629 until its cancellation when the colony was unwillingly incorporated in the Dominion of New England in 1684. Its Governor, Sir Edmund Andros, was imprisoned on news of William of Orange's landing, and the colonists ostentatiously resumed their former constitution. This swift and violent reaction was in part a response[89] to a theory of popish conspiracy, manifest in recent English history:

> We have seen more than a decad of Years rolled away since the English World had the Discovery of an horrid Popish Plot; wherein the bloody Devotees of Rome had in their Design and Prospect no less than the Extinction of the Protestant Religion . . . And we were of all Men the most insensible, if we should apprehend a Countrey so remarkable for the true Profession and pure Exercise of the Protestant Religion as New-England is, wholly unconcerned in the Infamous Plot.

The cancellation of Charles I's charter was merely one stage in the con-

---

[86] J. W. Fortescue (ed.), *Calendar of State Papers, Colonial Series, America and West Indies, 1685–1688* (London, 1899), pp. 41–2, 95, 97, 136, 151, 158, 243, 606.

[87] T. H. Breen and Stephen Foster, 'The Puritans' Greatest Achievement: A Study of Social Cohesion in Seventeenth-Century Massachusetts', *Journal of American History* 60 (1973), 5–22.

[88] See, in general, Lovejoy, *The Glorious Revolution in America*; Michael G. Hall, Lawrence H. Leder and Michael G. Kammen (eds.), *The Glorious Revolution in America: Documents on the Colonial Crisis of 1689* (New York, 1964).

[89] For the colonists' practical grievances, especially against Andros's land policy, see T. H. Breen, *The Character of the Good Ruler: A Study of Puritan Political Ideas in New England, 1630–1730* (New Haven, Conn., 1970), pp. 134–79.

spiracy; it identified Andros' government as 'absolute and arbitrary'.[90] Here, as elsewhere, it was their religious implications which raised practical grievances to a higher plane of collective action.

The revolution was marked, according to the loyalists, by particular hostility to Anglicans: on 18 April 1689, the mob allegedly 'secured most [men] of the Church of England (who were the only persons sought for) . . . one of the Preachers was for cutting the throats of all the Established Church and then (said he very religiously), wee shall never be troubled with them again'.[91] Another observer identified a Puritan propaganda campaign: just before the rising

> a most scandalous Pamphlet was . . . Printed and Published by Cotton [sc. Increase] Mather . . . intituled the unlawfulness of the Common-prayer Worship, wherein he affirms, and labours to prove the same to be both Popery and Idolatry, and several scandalous Libels both against the Church and Government were spread and scattered up and down the Country, insinuating into the Common People, that the Governor and all of the Church of England were Papists and Idolaters, and to stir them up to Faction and Rebellion, for which the said Cotton Mather, and others, were bound over to answer according to Law; but was suspended by their Insurrection.[92]

In New York, tensions had built up between factions of local magnates: the abolition of the Assembly when the colony was incorporated in the Dominion of New England blocked the advance of the group still excluded. The rebellion, headed by Jacob Leisler, was in part an ethnic Dutch backlash against English encroachment since the conquest of the colony in 1664,[93] in part an attempt by one set of magnates to dispossess another set of the spoils of office. Nevertheless, the popish phobia created a political idiom in New York and could be exploited.[94] Trouble began

---

[90] 'The Declaration of the Gentlemen, Merchants and Inhabitants of Boston, and the Country adjacent, April 18, 1689' in Andrews (ed.), *Narratives*, pp. 175–7.

[91] 'A Particular Account of the Late Revolution, 1689', in Andrews (ed.), *Narratives*, pp. 196, 207. A Puritan colonist confessed that 'the Worship of the Church of *England* had the disadvantage with us, that most of our Late Oppressors were the great and sole Pillars of it there': 'An Account of the Late Revolutions in New-England by A. B.' (Boston, 1689) in W. H. Whitmore (ed.), *The Andros Tracts* (3 vols., Boston, 1868–74), vol. 2, pp. 191–201, at 199.

[92] 'New England's Faction Discovered . . . in a Letter from a Gentleman of that Country, to a Person of Quality' in Andrews (ed.), *Narratives*, pp. 258–9.

[93] The Dutch dimension is emphasised in Thomas J. Archdeacon, *New York City, 1664–1710: Conquest and Change* (Ithaca, NY, 1976). David Voorhees, 'In Behalf of the True Protestants Religion: The Glorious Revolution in New York' (Ph.D. thesis, New York University, 1988), analyses the contending groups as Anglicans and Anglicising (Arminian) Dutch versus Calvinist Dutch Reformed.

[94] Jerome R. Reich, *Leisler's Rebellion: A Study of Democracy in New York 1664–1720* (Chicago, 1953), pp. 52, 73 and passim; Robert C. Ritchie, *The Duke's Province: A Study of New York Politics and Society, 1664–1691* (Chapel Hill, 1977), p. 219: 'Rumours and plots to scize New

when Leisler, a merchant and a deacon of the Dutch church, refused to pay a customs bill of £100, 'alledging, The Collector, being a Papist, was not qualified to receive it, denying the then power to be legal; but whether for that or his own private interest let the impartial judge'. After the proclamation of William and Mary, Leisler 'endeavours afresh to inflame the common people, by branding those who were in commission of the Peace with being Popishly affected, for no other reason than that they would not join with him in violating all our Laws and Liberties'.[95]

Sceptics claimed that Leisler and his deputy Jacob Milborne 'did not from pure zeal for their Majesties Interest, and the Protestant Religion, but being of desperate Fortune, thrust themselves into Power, of purpose to make up their wants by the Ruin and Plunder of his Majesties Loyal Subjects'.[96] The rebels commanded a powerful political rhetoric, however. Jacob Milborne harangued 'the Common People' with the claim that

> now it was in there powr to free themselfs from tht Yoke of arbitrary Power and Government under which they had Lyen so long in the Reign of tht Illegall king James, who was a Papist, Declareing all Illegall whatever was done & past in his time, yea the Charter of this Citty was null & void Since it was graunted by a Popish kings governour & that now the Power was in the People to choose both new Civill and Military officers as they Pleased, challenging all them that had bore office in king James Time to be Illegall, and therefore they must have a free Election, and much Such like Discourse.[97]

Leisler and Milborne were executed as rebels when a London-authorised government was restored, instantly creating the image that Leisler was a 'Martyr to Jacobite Revenge'. James II's Governor Thomas Dongan (1682–8), claimed the Leislerians, had ruled under the terms of a commission whereby 'the will of the Prince became the Law'.[98] Leislerians attempted to prove the identity of their cause with that of the English Whigs, 'We having also long groaned under the same oppression, having been governed of late, most part, by papists who had in a most arbitrary

York blossomed constantly in the hot summer weather of 1689 . . . They lived in a world filled with catastrophe, evil, and, in the end, hatred.'
[95] 'A Modest and Impartial Narrative Of Several Grievances and Great Oppressions . . . By the Extravagant and Arbitrary Proceedings of Jacob Leysler and his Accomplices' in Andrews (ed.), *Narratives*, pp. 322, 331.
[96] 'A Letter from a Gentleman of the City of New-York to Another, Concerning the Troubles which happen'd in that Province in the Time of the late Happy Rebellion', in Andrews (ed.), *Narratives*, p. 370.
[97] E. B. O'Callaghan (ed.), *The Documentary History of the State of New York* (4 vols., Albany, 1850–1), vol. 2, p. 64.
[98] 'Loyalty Vindicated from the Reflections of a Virulent Pamphlet . . .' in Andrews (ed.), *Narratives*, pp. 376, 393.

way subverted our ancient priviledges, making us in effect slaves to their will contrary to the laws of England.'[99]

All shortcomings in the administration of proprietary Maryland could be similarly attributed to the religion of its administrators, and political parties were already polarised on sectarian lines. By 1689, this division had generated rhetorical complaints of 'Not only private but publick outrages, & murthers committed and done by papists upon Protestants without redress, but rather connived at and tolerated by the chief in authority'.[100] In March 1689 the colony was gripped by a rumour that the Catholic ruling group was conspiring with the Indians to massacre the Protestants.[101] According to the Council's report to London, people had 'gathered themselves together in great parties to defend themselves, as they were persuaded, against a groundless and imaginary plott and designe contrived against them as was rumoured and suspected by the Roman Catholicks inviting the Indians to joyne with them in that detestable and wicked Conspiracy'. This groundless rumour was 'fomented by the Artifice of some ill minded persons who are studious and ready to take all occasions of raising a disturbance for their own private and malitious interest'.[102]

John Coode, leader of the Maryland rebellion, has been claimed to fit into a category: 'certain types of popular movements of dissent . . . offer special opportunities to agitators with paranoid tendencies, who are able to make a vocational asset out of their psychic disturbances'.[103] The religious dimension offers a more authentic insight, however: Coode was a rogue Anglican priest who migrated to Maryland after being 'turned out' of his living in Cornwall, and was later accused of open atheism and blasphemy.[104] His anti-Catholicism, whatever its personal origins in Coode's irreligion, was an effective catalyst. The failure of the governor

---

[99] Address of the New York militia to William III, June 1689, in Hall, Leder and Kammen (eds.), *Glorious Revolution*, p. 109.

[100] W. H. Browne (ed.), *Archives of Maryland: Proceedings of the Council of Maryland 1687/8–1693*, vol. 8 (Baltimore, 1890), p. 104.

[101] Michael G. Kammen, 'The Causes of the Maryland Revolution of 1689', *Maryland Historical Magazine* 55 (1960), 293–333.

[102] Browne (ed.), *Archives of Maryland*, vol. 8, pp. 86–7, 91. When John Coode seized power, he attempted to justify the scare, 'well remembering the incursion and invade of the said Northern Indians in the year 1681, who were conducted into the heart of this Province by French Jesuits': 'The Declaration Of the reason and motive for the prest. appearing in arms of His Majtys Protestant Subjects in the Province of Maryland', ibid., pp. 101–7, at 106.

[103] Kammen, 'Maryland Revolution', 317, 322–4, quoting Richard Hofstadter, *The Age of Reform* (New York, 1956), p. 71.

[104] David W. Jordan, 'John Coode, Perennial Rebel', *Maryland Historical Magazine* 70 (1975), 1–28; W. H. Browne (ed.), *Archives of Maryland: Proceedings and Acts of the General Assembly of Maryland September 1693–June 1697*, vol. 19 (Baltimore, 1899), pp. 436–40, 478–82.

to proclaim William and Mary (Lord Baltimore's messenger with instructions on this point had died en route) was at once interpreted by Protestants as overt loyalty to James II; John Coode successfully whipped up anti-Catholic feelings to the point of a rebellion against the proprietor in July 1689.

IV. THE RIGHTS OF ENGLISHMEN, THE RHETORIC OF SLAVERY, AND REBELLIONS IN BRITAIN AND AMERICA, 1689–1760

These three groups of rebels, in Massachusetts, New York and Maryland, appealed to William III to endorse their causes: they claimed merely to have re-enacted the principles of the Glorious Revolution in a transatlantic setting. The risings in the colonies came after a series of constitutional claims formulated in c. 1675–85 and at that time rejected in London: the American risings of 1689 could therefore be made to seem practical vindications of these claims. Yet if colonists saw themselves asserting the rights of Englishmen against tyrannical attempts to deprive them of those rights, William III did not formally endorse this picture. In Massachusetts, the Congregational confessional state implied by the 1629 charter was not fully restored when a new charter was granted, and imperial authority was again asserted via a crown-appointed Governor. In New York, the element of popular violence and vengeance in 1689 was disavowed by the execution of the two leading rebels: the old ruling group returned to power, but with animosities heightened by the executions an opposition had been created which was soon to bring them down and inflict vengeance in its turn. In Maryland, the destruction of the Proprietor's political power was endorsed in London, and the rebels gained an opportunity to revise the colony's statutes; but a working definition of autonomy did not emerge.

So the imperial government saw itself as asserting control and imposing standard institutions on previous diversity: a royal governor, an appointed council, and an elected assembly.[105] The prevalent English assumption was that a rational, reformed administration confirmed the colonies in their subordination. The prevalent colonial assumption, on the contrary, was that by their independent initiatives in 1689, the English, and perhaps the Scots, principles of the Glorious Revolution had been upheld in the colonies also. The structural occasions for conflict nevertheless remained. In England, the later-Stuart strengthening and reorganisation of the machinery of state carried over to the Williamite

[105] Lawrence H. Leder, 'The Glorious Revolution and the Pattern of Imperial Relationships', *New York History* 46 (1965), 203–11.

regime and even accelerated in the 1690s. Its effects extended to America via a new Navigation Act (1696), the Board of Trade (1696), and a system of vice-admiralty courts. In some ways the royal prerogative in the colonies even strengthened after 1689: Americans had rehearsed certain libertarian issues in 1689, but they had not obtained all or even most of what they had sought.

The seventeenth-century idioms of political discourse therefore persisted into the eighteenth; but their significance was reversed by the change of dynasty. No longer could antipopery sentiments transform practical objections to English rule into rebellion: William III's Calvinism aligned him squarely with New England Puritanism, and the Lutheranism of George I and George II was similarly sufficient to establish their credentials. The enemy was henceforth defined as an external one.[106] If the practical threat of popery receded, it did not disappear: in Europe the Protestant interest often seemed on the defensive until the Seven Years' War; French Canada and Spanish Florida similarly served as reminders to Americans. These denominational orientations were heightened but not realigned by the experience of religious revivalism. American revivals, like those in England, were episodic and scattered both geographically and between sects; not until 1842 were they reified into a single movement,[107] the Great Awakening, which (if so conceived in the 1740s) could have provided a unifying identity for some nascent inter-colonial American consciousness. No such sense bound together the revivalists of the last half-century of the American colonial experience.[108] Until the early 1760s, even those New England clergy most touched by millennial expectations framed their historical and theological scenario as a titanic struggle between Protestantism and the Antichrist of Rome.[109] In that uncertain struggle, Canterbury was too powerful an ally to dispense with or to disparage. It was an ideological polarity which affected all issues of power which came within its field of force. One in particular was strangely caught up with this frenzied anti-Catholicism and now began to prey on the psyche of the southern colonist:[110] the fear that he

[106] For an alternative reading of the Glorious Revolution in America, emphasising the crucial role of 1689 as a transition away from theological imperatives to godly rule towards a secular defence of colonial liberty and property, see Breen, *The Character of the Good Ruler*.

[107] Joseph Tracy, *The Great Awakening: A History of the Revival of Religion in the Time of Edwards and Whitefield* (Boston, 1842).

[108] For a different interpretation, see especially Alan Heimert, *Religion and the American Mind from the Great Awakening to the Revolution* (Cambridge, Mass., 1966) and Bonomi, *Cope of Heaven*.

[109] Nathan Hatch, 'The Origins of Civil Millennialism in America: New England Clergymen, the War with France, and the Revolution', *WMQ* 31 (1974), 407–30.

[110] Herbert Aptheker, *American Negro Slave Revolts* (New York, 1943), emphasises 'the widespread fear of servile rebellion ... There is also evidence that this fear existed quite independent of any connection with an actual outbreak' (pp. 18–19).

would be murdered by the negro slave population, either in an isolated incident or as part of a mass insurrection which would necessarily result (as anti-Catholic phobias recorded or predicted) in a general massacre of white Protestants. Isolated incidents certainly occurred.[111] Would they run together to constitute a slave revolution?

The early Hanoverian era saw a series of plots or uprisings by black slaves in America, brutal alike in what provoked them, in their impact and in the punishments with which they were repressed. Conspiracies were discovered and rebellion prevented in Virginia in 1687 and 1709, South Carolina in 1720, New Jersey in 1734, Maryland in the late 1730s, South Carolina in 1740 and elsewhere. Violent rebellions occurred or were allegedly thwarted in New York City in 1712 and 1741, in South Carolina (the Stono Rebellion) in 1739 and on other occasions.[112] South Carolina society had been destabilised by the King of Spain's edict, published in Spanish Florida, offering freedom to all slaves who deserted from the English colonies; in September 1739 a Catholic priest was arrested in Georgia, allegedly 'employed by the Spaniards to procure a general Insurrection of the Negroes'; the Stono Rebellion occurred when news arrived in South Carolina of the outbreak of war between England and Spain, and involved an attempt by a party of slaves to march to St Augustine, Florida. English colonists perceived in the rebellion an ancient Catholic threat; the negroes were more likely to have been inspired by tribal cults among recent arrivals from Africa.[113] Even a Marxist analysis acknowledges that 'until the nineteenth century, and even then albeit with altered content, religion provided the ideological rallying point for revolt'.[114] The situation was similar in Jamaica, where obeah (witchcraft) 'functioned largely in the numerous rebellions of the slaves ... in the plotting of these rebellions the obeah-man was essential in administering oaths of secrecy, and, in cases, distributing fetishes which were supposed to immunize the insurgents from the arms of the whites'.[115] On the colonial

---

[111] Edmund S. Morgan, *American Slavery American Freedom: The Ordeal of Colonial Virginia* (New York, 1975), pp. 308–9, argues for the weakness of the threat; 'No white person was killed in a slave rebellion in colonial Virginia.' It follows that the phenomenon is significant chiefly as a trigger to a much older body of ideas, initially formed, it may be suggested, around Roman Catholics.

[112] Aptheker, *Slave Revolts*, pp. 162–208; Richard Maxwell Brown, 'Violence and the American Revolution' in Stephen G. Kurtz and James H. Hutson (eds.), *Essays on the American Revolution* (Chapel Hill, N.C., 1973), p. 87.

[113] Peter H. Wood, *Black Majority: Negroes in Colonial South Carolina From 1670 through the Stono Rebellion* (New York, 1975), pp. 308–26; William C. Suttles, Jr, 'African Religious Survivals as Factors in American Slave Revolts', *Journal of Negro History* 56 (1971), 97–104; Gayraud S. Wilmore, *Black Religion and Black Radicalism* (2nd edn., New York, 1983).

[114] Eugene D. Genovese, *From Rebellion to Revolution: Afro-American Slave Revolts in the Making of the Modern World* (Baton Rouge, 1979), p. 28 and passim.

[115] Orlando Patterson, *The Sociology of Slavery* (London, 1967), pp. 182–215 at 192, 260–83.

mainland, in the 1730s and 40s slave disorder has been linked to the evangelical movement now known as the Great Awakening:[116] the first movement to sweep large numbers of negroes into sectarian participation, it acted to challenge hierarchical distinctions of white and black even more forcibly than those of white and white.

Despite the special circumstances of individual slave revolts, religion could be decisive both in their motivation and in the white response. In 1730 conspiracies were triggered in Virginia by a rumour that the newly-arrived Governor Spotswood came with the king's command to emancipate all slaves who had been baptised as Christians.[117] Revivalism and anti-Catholicism were more familiar catalysts, however. In 1741 New York was convulsed by fears of a negro insurrection: outbreaks of arson and robbery seemed to be its preliminaries; informers fuelled the panic, and trials rehearsed the issues in the public eye. Paranoia now inflated public disorder into a full-scale conspiracy. Much of the blame was attributed to revivalist religion, ignited by the recent visit of the Calvinist George Whitefield, and directed to the subversive end of the conversion of blacks as well as whites. Wartime conflict between Spanish Florida and the colony of Georgia soon introduced another ancient preoccupation into the mounting New York frenzy: the Catholic plot. Suspicion of the enthusiasm or superstition which was seen as common to both Methodism and Catholicism now joined with the ancient horror of a Catholic massacre: 1641, the Popish Plot, the Massacre of St Bartholomew. These events were seen as part of the divine scenario: 'so bloody and Destructive a Conspiracy was this, that had not the mercifull hand of providence interposed and Confounded their [the negroes'] Divices, in one and the Same night the Inhabitants would have been butcher'd in their houses, by their own Slaves, and the City laid in ashes'.[118] Within such a context, New York's response to this fictional conspiracy is revealing of motive rather than of mere rhetoric: 4 whites were hanged as conspirators; so were 18 blacks; and 13 more negroes were burnt at the stake.[119]

---

[116] The punishments inflicted on convicted rebel slaves, including burning at the stake, burning over a slow fire, and breaking on the wheel, echoed the practices which were held to characterise Roman Catholic persecution of Protestants: Winthrop D. Jordan, *White over Black: American Attitudes Toward the Negro, 1550–1812* (Chapel Hill, N.C., 1968), pp. 116, 120, 212–15.

[117] Aptheker, *Slave Revolts*, p. 179.

[118] Daniel Horsmanden to Cadwallader Colden, 7 Aug. 1741, quoted in Jordan, *White over Black*, p. 117.

[119] Lovejoy, *Religious Enthusiasm*, pp. 201–6; J. T. Headley, *The Great Riots of New York 1712 to 1873* (New York, 1873, 1971), pp. 24–45; Daniel Horsmanden, *The New York Conspiracy* (1810), ed. Thomas J. Davis (Boston, 1971); Edgar J. McManus, *Black Bondage in the North* (Syracuse, NY, 1973), pp. 133–9; idem, *A History of Negro Slavery in New York* (Syracuse, 1966), pp. 126–38; Ferenc M. Szaz, 'The New York Slave Revolt of 1741: A

Similar conspiracies continued to be uncovered up to and long after the Revolution. Practical grievances were little changed, but a catalyst remained necessary; as with the insurrections of white colonists, a denominational constituency and charismatic religious leaders provided a common formula. Gabriel's rebellion (Virginia, 1800), 'lacking a sacred dimension, was without a Moses, and therefore without a following': it was unsuccessful because it failed to exploit the potential for collective action opened up by religious revivalist movements. Nevertheless, 'religious and eschatological elements often generate the large-scale rebellions of pre-industrial folk'; these were successfully exploited in the Methodist Denmark Vesey's rebellion (South Carolina, 1822), and, still more spectacularly, in the Baptist Nat Turner's rebellion (Virginia, 1831): 'Religion and magic sustained Nat Turner's rebellion.'[120] The principles of 1776 were as lofty and idealistic as Protestantism's case against the Church of Rome; they were given emotional force and a social constituency by emotions more powerful but less rational. The Declaration of Independence hinted at these ancient phobias, but uncandidly shied away from naming the threat: its final charge against George III, that he 'has excited domestic insurrections amongst us', referred to the attempts of Lord Dunmore, Governor of Virginia, to free and arm the slaves.[121]

In England, millennial expectations receded after the disillusion of the revolutionary sects in the 1650s; in the colonies, even the socially stable Puritan New England,[122] they evolved into the eighteenth century as a still-relevant part of political discourse. New England society had earlier come close to being a theocracy; the sense of America as a religious experiment, as the new Israel, still gave practical content to millenarian hopes in a society whose domestic stabilities were often overset by war with the Indians.[123] In the southern colonies, these traditions may have been refreshed by the Presbyterianism of successive waves of Scots and Scots-Irish immigrants.[124] The same was true of the massive migration of Huguenot and German refugees from French or Imperial persecution who carried to both England and the American colonies detailed and

Re-Examination', *New York History* 48 (1967), 215–30; Thomas J. Davis, *A Rumor of Revolt: The 'Great Negro Plot' in Colonial New York* (New York, 1985).

[120] Gerald W. Mullin, *Flight and Rebellion: Slave Resistance in Eighteenth-Century Virginia* (New York, 1972), pp. 140–63; Wilmore, *Black Religion*, pp. 53–73.

[121] Sidney Kaplan, 'The 'Domestic Insurrections' of the Declaration of Independence', *Journal of Negro History* 61 (1976), 243–55.

[122] Michael Zuckerman, *Peaceable Kingdoms: New England Towns in the Eighteenth Century* (New York, 1970).

[123] Michael J. Crawford, *Seasons of Grace: Colonial New England's Revival Tradition in its British Context* (New York, 1991), pp. 28–36, 42–51, 65–80.

[124] Ruth M. Bloch, *Visionary Republic: Millennial Themes in American Thought, 1756–1800* (Cambridge, 1985), pp. 10–14.

recent reports of what appeared to be the undiminished rigour of Roman Catholic cruelty. English readers had access to accounts of Catholic atrocities against French and German Protestants which resembled Foxe's *Book of Martyrs*, presented as a campaign of persecution which intensified rather than began with the revocation of the Edict of Nantes.[125] This consciousness helped sustain on both sides of the Atlantic a sense of Protestantism as a minority movement in urgent danger but with a world-wide mission.[126]

English identifications of the main threats to Church and State were evidently divided and conflicting in 1715, but partly thanks to a sustained propaganda campaign by the Hanoverian regime over the next three decades, the '45 witnessed a '*grande peur*': 'the full horror of Popery seems to have reasserted itself in most sections of the popular mind, ensuring that 1745 witnessed the peak of eighteenth-century anti-Catholic feeling'. As in the New World, these phenomena in the English shires were mostly triggered by the threat of the intrusion of sinister outsiders into the local community rather than any activity by the well-known local Catholic individuals – the threat, in other words, of a reified international Popery with all its historical and apocalyptic overtones.[127]

Religious revival in the 1740s engaged with these anxieties; when it lost its first impetus, England's wars of the 1740s and 1750s against France and Spain renewed the identification of Antichrist with Catholicism[128] and revitalised the old images of Catholic persecution. At issue was not military conflict alone, momentous though this could be for local communities, but its religious and dynastic consequences. As a New England preacher warned, reviewing English history since the accession of Charles I and repeated Jacobite conspiracies since the Glorious Revolution, 'our inveterate and *popish* Enemies both without and within the Kingdom, are restless to enslave and ruin us'. The enemy within was made up of 'many wretchedly deluded *half-way nominal Protestants* in divers Parts of Britain'. A Jacobite victory would allow the Highlanders 'and

[125] E.g. *The History of the Persecutions of the Reformed Churches in France, Orange and Piedmont From the year 1655. to this time* (London, 1699); Elias Neau, *An Account of the sufferings of the French Protestants, Slaves on Board the French Kings Galleys* (London, 1699), continued by works like Charles Owen, *An Alarm to Protestant Princes and People, who are all struck at in the Popish cruelties at Thorn* (London, 1725).

[126] W. R. Ward, *The Protestant Evangelical Awakening* (Cambridge, 1992), pp. 15–31.

[127] Haydon, *Anti-Catholicism in Eighteenth-Century England*, chapter 4.

[128] Bloch, *Visionary Republic*, pp. 15–20, 42–50; Heimert, *Religion and the American Mind*, pp. 324–50; Nathan O. Hatch, *The Sacred Cause of Liberty: Republican Thought and the Millennium in Revolutionary New England* (New Haven, 1977), pp. 36–41; Melvin B. Endy, Jr, 'Just War, Holy War, and Millennialism in Revolutionary America', *WMQ* 42 (1985), 3–25; Harry S. Stout, *The New England Soul: Preaching and Religious Culture in Colonial New England* (New York, 1986), pp. 233–55.

other numerous Papists thro' the Nation, at once to *massacre* all the chief Friends of the *Hanover Succession*'; London would 'run down with *Blood*'; its Protestant families would be 'beggared and ruined'. A Stuart monarchy would have to repay its debt to its chief ally, so that 'even all the *British America*, would either by Gift, Sale, or Conquest, be soon subjected to the Power of *France*'; 'Cruel *Papists* would quickly fill the *British Colonies*, seize our Estates, abuse our Wives and Daughters, and barbarously murder us; as they have done the like in *France* and *Ireland*'.[129]

The menace of a Jacobite restoration sustained a rhetorical hysteria which was merely re-directed after 1760. With the advance of Anglicanism, ancient fears of a general massacre began to be projected on to the Church. At the outbreak of the Seven Years' War, complained an Anglican clergyman, 'while we were all under a deep concern, all that was precious to us in the world being at stake, to increase our trouble, some of the dissenters said, that as soon as the *French* army should come into the country, all the churchmen would join with them, & cut all the *Presbyterian's* throats'.[130] So the fortunes of Dissenting denominations in America were locked in a dramatised long-term scenario; and their idioms of political discourse displayed a striking continuity from the early seventeenth century into the eighteenth.

The Protestant interest in Europe, as on the North American continent, was seen to be on the defensive if not in imminent danger of extinction from at least the 1720s to the 1750s. Even during the Seven Years' War, an English clergyman hailed Frederick the Great not just as an ordinary ally; 'The protestant reformed cause is nearly interested in his affairs; because, at present, he is its champion and defender; and if he should, at last be overpowered, popery, it is much to be feared, will once more, overwhelm the empire.'[131] The survival of a sense of the Jacobite menace in colonial America was similarly determined by European diplomacy and by events in England and Scotland. To record the survival of Jacobitism is to record that there was no single English or Scots interpretation of 1688: Jacobites denounced it as a clear rejection of the divine basis of

[129] Thomas Prince, *A Sermon Delivered at the South Church in Boston, N.E. August 14. 1746. Being the Day of General Thanksgiving for The great Deliverance of the British Nations by The glorious and happy Victory near Culloden* (Boston, 1746), pp. 12–14, 18. For the survival of the anti-Catholic phobia in England, see Jeremy Black, 'The Catholic Threat and the British Press in the 1720s and 1730s', *Journal of Religious History* 12 (1983), 364–81; idem, 'The Challenge of Autocracy: The British Press in the 1730s', *Studi Settecenteschi* 3–4 (1982–3), 107–18; and idem, *Natural and Necessary Enemies: Anglo-French Relations in the Eighteenth Century* (London, 1986), pp. 160–71.

[130] John Beach, *A Friendly Expostulation, With all Persons concern'd in publishing A late Pamphlet . . .* (New York, 1763), p. 21.

[131] J. Williams, *The Favours of Providence to Britain in 1759. A Sermon . . . On the 29th Day of November 1759, Being the Day of General Thanksgiving* (London, 1759), p. 21.

monarchical legitimacy; extreme Whigs hailed it as the final embodiment
of contract theory in the constitution. Neither group upset the ambiguous
compromise of 1689, for England (though not Scotland) was distinguished
by the existence of a large middle ground, open to influence by both
extremes, which nevertheless attempted to stress the continuities between
their world before and after 1688: England was still monarchical; the
monarchy was hereditary; it was Anglican; it claimed a divine sanction,
and thereby validated social hierarchy.[132] Jacobites and republicans had,
in the abstract, powerful cases against this centrist argument, but cases
which most Englishmen sought to deny. Jacobite conspiracies and rebellions thus received considerable but finally inadequate support in England; it was to the unforgiving and embittered culture of Scotland that
both sides looked for fulfilment.[133] The Stuarts' social constituencies in
England were wide but, thanks to the weakness and further decline of
Nonjurors and Roman Catholics, finally inadequate.

Meanwhile, the dynastic issue, with its explicitly religious overtones,
was the precondition for a series of unsuccessful conspiracies, invasion
attempts and rebellions in 1689 (Viscount Dundee), 1708 (an invasion
force of 6,000 French infantry, led by James III in person), 1715 (a
domestic Scots rising), 1717 (a plot for a rising with Swedish aid), 1719
(a Spanish invasion attempt, carrying 5,000 troops, of whom only 307
reached Scotland to trigger an abortive rebellion), 1720–2 (the Atterbury
plot), 1731–5 (Lord Cornbury's plot), 1744 (a massive French invasion
attempt) and 1745 (Charles Edward's unsupported rebellion).[134] The
record of Jacobitism as a source of armed rebellion was considerably more
successful than that of British Jacobinism in the 1790s: where Jacobinism
appealed to men as men, citizens of the world undifferentiated by social
rank, geography or religion, Jacobitism addressed social constituencies
clearly defined by observable criteria of which religion was the most
salient.

Only in the last domestic English conspiracy was a different Stuart
perception of the potential constituency observable; and this attempt to
exploit a different basis of support was markedly less successful than
previous attempts. The 'Elibank Plot', or rather series of conspiracies in

---

[132] For the importance of moderate opinion, see Clark, *English Society 1688–1832*, pp. 119–98.
[133] For the reappearance of Jacobitism within an historiographical frame of reference which
now attends to religion, see J. C. D. Clark, 'On Moving the Middle Ground: The Significance of Jacobitism in Historical Studies', in Eveline Cruickshanks and Jeremy Black
(eds.), *The Jacobite Challenge* (Edinburgh, 1988), pp. 177–88.
[134] George Hilton Jones, *The Main Stream of Jacobitism* (Cambridge, Mass., 1954); Lenman,
The Jacobite Risings in Britain, 1689–1746; Eveline Cruickshanks, 'Lord Cornbury, Bolingbroke and a Plan to Restore the Stuarts 1731–1735', *Royal Stuart Papers* 27 (1986).

1749–53, was premised on an appeal by Prince Charles Edward not to the geographically or socially marginal groups – Scots or Catholics – but to the disaffected of the metropolis, disillusioned with Hanoverian rule and uncommitted either to Prince Frederick and his son Prince George or (in the sometimes-discussed event of a coup) to the Duke of Cumberland as possible successors to the ageing George II. The Elibank plot was a carefully prepared revolution that never happened: it nevertheless revealed Charles Edward's appreciation of the religious key to his potential social constituency. At a church in the Strand, he was received into the Church of England in September 1750; but so *politique* a conversion was counter-productive, and organised backing was not forthcoming in sufficient quantity from London.[135] When an invasion was next seriously planned by France, the earlier assumptions of substantial domestic Jacobite support were revised downwards. In the 1720s and 1730s, Jacobites appealed for in the order of only 6–10,000 foreign troops,[136] and in 1744 the French force indeed numbered some 10,000 men;[137] in 1758–9 the total land forces, French, Swedish and Russian, were to number 90,000.[138] England would now need to be conquered: it was not enough to hope to topple a weakly-supported government, as in the 1690s. With the fading of domestic religious schism, the potential for revolution within England herself (as opposed to Ireland and Scotland) diminished markedly; not until the rise in the 1790s of a Jacobin movement did this situation change, and in England Jacobinism was fatally compromised by the contradiction (disguised in America in the 1770s) between the heterodox religious commitments of many of its potential leaders and the open atheism of its French exemplar. It was not to be England which experienced the full consequences of shared transatlantic stresses.

V. THE RIGHT OF RESISTANCE AND ITS SECTARIAN PRECONDITIONS IN NORTH AMERICA, 1760–1799

In the 1740s and 50s, Britain overcame the major threat to her internal stability – a threat to the religious and dynastic order. Fewer groups became willing to invoke a right of resistance. In Ireland, these ancient conflicts of political discourse were muted after the 1690s but unresolved.

---

[135] Frank McLynn, *Charles Edward Stuart* (London, 1988), pp. 395–414.

[136] Jeremy Black, 'Jacobitism and British Foreign Policy Under the First Two Georges 1714–1760', *Royal Stuart Papers* 32 (1988); idem, 'Jacobitism and British Foreign Policy, 1731–5' in Cruickshanks and Black (eds.), *The Jacobite Challenge*, pp. 142–60.

[137] Eveline Cruickshanks, *Political Untouchables: The Tories and the '45* (London, 1979), p. 54.

[138] Claude Nordmann, 'Choiseul and the Last Jacobite Attempt of 1759' in Eveline Cruickshanks (ed.), *Ideology and Conspiracy: Aspects of Jacobitism, 1689–1759* (Edinburgh, 1982), pp. 201–17.

In the American colonies they survived; indeed they were exacerbated. Apart from the conflict of loyalist and republican, in the four decades following the Peace of Paris in 1763 a common thread ran through the conflicts which saw colonial Americans in armed conflict with each other: the clash of material interests and political commitments between the pioneers, the new arrivals in the western backcountry, and the long-established settlers of the eastern seaboard with their control first of colonial, then of republican State government. This applied to the march of the Paxton Boys against Philadelphia (1764); the Regulator movement in North and South Carolina (1768–71); the clashes in the Wyoming Valley of Pennsylvania between Pennamite and Yankee (1770–1);[139] and the disorders of the Green Mountain Boys[140] in Vermont (early 1770s). In 1784, four western counties of North Carolina sought to secede and establish a separate state, which they wished to call Franklin; the rebellion collapsed in 1787. In the same year the settlers of the Wyoming valley attempted to secede from Pennsylvania, an attempt frustrated only by armed force. These backcountry tensions, common to several states, were expressed also by Shays' Rebellion in Massachusetts (1786–7); the Whiskey Rebellion in Pennsylvania (1794); and Fries' Rebellion (1799). Such conflicts were once held to owe everything to the material grievances of the backcountry and equally little either to the pursuit of secular constitutional ideals or to formal sectarian allegiance. These instances of civil disobedience can now be seen also to share important features with other colonial insurrections since 1676, especially their religious constituencies; their social composition brings their sectarian element into sharp relief, and establishes a clearer relation between rhetoric and motive.[141]

These rebellions took place against the background of a development which had no parallel in early-eighteenth-century England. Where English Dissent was progressively eroded numerically and largely failed to devise structures to give better expression to its principles of ecclesiastical polity, the opposite in both respects was true in the American colonies. There, denominational boundaries generally clarified over time as colonial society became more settled and formalised. It has been argued that the years between 1680 and 1760 witnessed not only a vigorous revival

---

[139] Discussed in James Kirby Martin, 'The Return of the Paxton Boys and the Historical State of the Pennsylvania Frontier, 1764–1775', *Pennsylvania History* 38 (1971), 117–33.

[140] For their charismatic leader, author of an aggressively Deist tract entitled *Reason, the Only Oracle of Man*, see Charles A. Jellison, *Ethan Allen: Frontier Rebel* (Syracuse, New York, 1969); cf. Irving Mark, *Agrarian Conflicts in Colonial New York 1711–1775* (New York, 1940), and David M. Ludlum, *Social Ferment in Vermont, 1791–1850* (New York, 1939).

[141] For the backcountry of the middle and southern colonies, see David Hackett Fischer, *Albion's Seed: Four British Folkways in America* (New York, 1989), pp. 765–82.

of the state church tradition in Virginia and New England, but an adoption of 'authority and coercion' by colonial Dissenters as they built up institutional frameworks for their denominations. Although not normally Anglican, American religious life therefore 'emerged as establishmentarian rather than Dissenting, coercive rather than voluntary, and institutional rather than individualistic'. Only the Church of England was prevented from matching its programme of church building with the creation of a colonial framework of authority and discipline. Ironically, the Church of England failed in England's transatlantic colonies, 'a failure caused not by its inability to adjust to American individualism but by its inability to transplant its institutional authority in the ways the Dissenters did so successfully'.[142]

Even areas of recent settlement witnessed the effects of coherent sectarian identity at grassroots level, despite the efforts of a denomination's nominal leaders normally to put a brake on the process of political mobilisation and rebellion. Pennsylvania from the 1750s witnessed a succession of savage clashes between frontiersmen and Indians which in turn induced powerful tensions within the colony's politics. The grievances of the increasingly populous backcountry regions against east coast dominance reached a head after the Assembly's failure to defend the frontier settlers against Indian attack during Pontiac's War of 1763. Early in 1764 the inhabitants of Donegal, Paxton and other western townships were organised to march on Philadelphia with the immediate aim of completing the massacre of a group of Indians whom the government had taken into its protection, the more general aim of breaking the grip on government of the Quakers, a minority of the colony's population but a majority in the unicameral Assembly.

The composition of the insurgents was largely Scots-Irish, and they engaged the sympathy of the New Light faction among their fellow Presbyterians of the east coast.[143] Thanks to a mission from the Governor and Council led by Benjamin Franklin, the column of Paxton Boys was persuaded to turn back before reaching a Philadelphia now armed to resist them; but the movement nevertheless produced its statement of principles and complaints.[144] These echoed a constitutionalist tradition,

---

[142] Jon Butler, *Awash in a Sea of Faith: Christianizing the American People* (Cambridge, Mass., 1990), pp. 98–128; for England, Michael Watts, *The Dissenters*, vol. 1 (Oxford, 1978), pp. 382–93.

[143] Peter A. Butzin, 'Politics, Presbyterians and the Paxton Riots, 1763–64', *Journal of Presbyterian History* 51 (1973), 70–84, for the priority of religion in alignments and arguments, despite the complexity of factions.

[144] In *Minutes of the Provincial Council of Pennsylvania*, vol. 9 (Harrisburg, Pa., 1852), pp. 138–45; printed as *A Declaration and Remonstrance of the distressed and bleeding Frontier Inhabitants of the Province of Pennsylvania* (1764), reprinted in John R. Dunbar (ed.), *The Paxton Papers*

but it was their ethnic and religious context which mobilised the settlers for action. With fulsome professions of loyalty to George III, they expressed the frontiersmen's sense of a deprivation of their rights 'as Free-Men and *English* Subjects' by the coastal government and condemned the numerically inequitable distribution of seats in the assembly as 'oppressive, unequal and unjust, the Cause of many of our Grievances, and an infringement of our natural Privileges of Freedom and Equality'. These demands were nevertheless received with horror: such reforms, it was objected, would 'enable them to return a majority of their Presbyterian friends for Representatives'. Quakers therefore resisted any change in the structure of representation: they responded instead by committing themselves more strongly to royal authority, bidding for a royal government to replace the existing proprietary government.[145] Backcountry Presbyterian rebellion would henceforth increasingly be focused on the imperial link itself. One of Franklin's associates foresaw this:

> The legislature here in England may do well to think of some Checks to the Torrent of Presbyterian Power which prevails in the Governments to the Eastward of Pennsylvania – they still have Oliverian spirit in them, and if ever a Revolution is attempted to sett up themselves independent of their Mother Country, it will arise from this prevailing Presbyterian Faction.[146]

Presbyterians differed. In 1710 the Anglican Commissary in South Carolina reported that Ebenezer Taylor, the Presbyterian minister of Charlestown, was 'of a very peaceable temper, and greatly abhors and disapproves of that restless and ffactious Spirit those of his Party are possessed with'; he later conformed to the Church. Two of his fellow ministers, however, were 'fierce men'; 'Mr Taylour says that place can never be easy or quiet, where there is a Scotch Presbyterian Minister.' He urged that only English Presbyterian ministers be sent to the colony, 'it being unreasonable to subject the Presbyterians Interest and Cause in this Province to the Presbyterian Government in Scotland, which is the thing the Scotch Dissenting Ministers here are driving at, with all their might and main . . .'[147] Already, saw Commissary Johnston, Scots Presby-

---

(The Hague, 1957), pp. 99–110. For an argument that democratic representation was not the issue directly contended for, see James E. Crowley, 'The Paxton Disturbance and Ideas of Order in Pennsylvania Politics', *Pennsylvania History* 37 (1970), 317–39.

[145] Brooke Hindle, 'The March of the Paxton Boys', *WMQ* 3 (1946), 461–86; Esmond Wright, *Franklin of Philadelphia* (Cambridge, Mass., 1986), pp. 133–8; Charles H. Lincoln, *The Revolutionary Movement in Pennsylvania, 1760–1776* (Philadelphia, 1901), pp. 97–113.

[146] P. Collinson to E. Hyde, 11 Oct. 1764, quoted in William S. Hanna, *Benjamin Franklin and Pennsylvania Politics* (Stanford, 1964), p. 157.

[147] Gideon Johnston to SPG, 5 July 1710, in Frank J. Klingberg (ed.), *Carolina Chronicle: The Papers of Commissary Gideon Johnston 1707–1716* (Berkeley, 1946), pp. 34–62, at 58.

terian ministers were 'Pouring in' to the colony, the beginning of a tide of migration from Ulster which was to transform the middle and southern colonies, and especially their backcountry, by 1776.[148]

Faced by this rising tide of immigration, Pennsylvania Quakers remained keenly aware of the political proclivities of Presbyterians. Daniel Morris emigrated from Scotland in 1770 aged 14, and, 'my father not being able to pay for my passage', he recorded, 'I was sold' as an indentured servant to John Garrett. After the British evacuated Philadelphia, and Washington's army was approaching, wrote Morris

> I told my Master, who was a Quaker, of it. He said, 'Does thee not wish that they would come and press my horse and wagon and press thee to drive it?' I told him I did. I had a whip in my hand which he took from me and gave me several lashes with it and said, 'Thee Scotch rebel, thou was a rebel in thine own country, and now thou has come here to rebel.' So I was determined to leave him, which I did

– and enlisted in the revolutionary army.[149]

The emotional temperature even of east coast political discourse had steadily risen as issues of imperial taxation engaged with much older traditions of ideas. A Philadelphia Stamp Commissioner complained to London in 1766 that the Presbyterians had become 'as averse to Kings, as they were in the Days of Cromwell, and some begin to cry out, *No King but King Jesus*'.[150] Such manifestations were uncommon before the 1770s, but showed the persistence both of the expectations aroused by the religious revivals of the 1740s and, residually, of a much older inheritance. The wide availability of sectarian idioms meant that British legislation on the American colonies in the 1760s could at once be seen in an 'apocalyptical perspective'. The Stamp Act revealed the sudden and astonishing reversal of a whole nexus of ideas which had grown up in a fervent identification of civil and religious liberty with British rule, and had been so expressed during the Seven Years' War.[151] George Grenville's stamps were described in the language of the Book of Revelation as 'the mark of the beast'; in cartoons, British policy was often personified as the devil. This paranoia had been expressed again in the New England controversy of 1763–5 over the threatened appointment of an Anglican bishop. In 1774 it received an immense boost: the Quebec Act, granting toleration to Canadian Catholics, was taken as proof of an imperial plot

[148] Gideon Johnston to SPG, 20 April 1711: ibid., pp. 93–8, at 97.
[149] John C. Dann (ed.), *The Revolution Remembered: Eyewitness Accounts of the War for Independence* (Chicago, 1980), p. 162.
[150] Quoted in Edmund S. and Helen M. Morgan, *The Stamp Act Crisis: Prologue to Revolution* (New York, 1963), p. 321.
[151] Bloch, *Visionary Republic*, p. 54; Hatch, *Sacred Cause*, pp. 51–4.

to promote popery. From the 1740s, American imagery had steadily strengthened the identity between tyranny and sin, civil liberty and grace.[152] This profound shift in colonial discourse was partly a consequence of a religious revivalist movement affecting several denominations in the 1740s and sufficiently dramatic to acquire a capitalised name in nineteenth-century historiography: the Great Awakening.[153]

Several decades before British political authority was systematically challenged in the colonies, a similar challenge was launched against conventional ecclesiastical authorities of several denominations, especially Presbyterians and Congregationalists, by the 'New Light' preachers of religious rebirth. The significance of their appeal to personal revelation, a right of private judgement and a duty of secession from sinful congregations was interpreted by existing Dissenting denominational authorities in the same terms as was the critique of the rebels of 1776 by civil authorities. The New Light clergy were denounced as 'Innovators, disturbers of the peace, of the church, sowers of heresies and seditions'; they were 'foremost in propagating the Principles of Sedition, and Disobedience to Authority'.[154] George Whitefield recorded in 1739 the unpopularity of the New Light ministers who graduated from William Tennent's famous Log College: 'Carnal ministers oppose them strongly; and, because people, when awakened by Mr. Tennent or his brethren, see through them, and therefore leave their ministry, the poor gentlemen are loaded with contempt, and looked upon as persons who turn the world upside-down.'[155] Despite their anti-establishment orientation, sectarian authoritarianism was generally promoted rather than undermined by the sporadic but persistent religious revivals of the early and middle eighteenth century.[156] Especially was this true of the Presbyterian schism of 1741, provoked by the intolerance of the 'New Lights' towards what they perceived as the unacceptable moral laxity of the 'Old Light' Synod of Philadelphia, given organisational expression by the creation of the more rigorous Synod of New York, and finally settled on New Light terms by the reunion of 1758. For the Presbyterians especially, revivalist frenzy and a disciplined ecclesiastical polity increasingly worked together.

Revivalist religion on both sides of the Atlantic had much in common in its manifestations: the mass hysteria, the individual experience of new

---

[152] Bloch, *Visionary Republic*, pp. 61–2.
[153] See, most recently, Bonomi, *Cope of Heaven*, pp. 131–60.
[154] Quoted in Alice M. Baldwin, 'Sowers of Sedition: The Political Theories of Some of the New Light Presbyterian Clergy of Virginia and North Carolina', *WMQ* 5 (1948), 52–76, at 52.
[155] L. Tyerman, *The Life of the Rev. George Whitefield* (2 vols., London, 1876–7), vol. 1, p. 332.
[156] Butler, *Awash in a Sea of Faith*, pp. 180–93.

birth. Its nature and impact were, however, far more diverse than the strange uniformity of these symptoms suggests. In some contexts revivalism acted as a social solvent, with political implications; elsewhere it was politically neutral, or failed to establish an organisational base. New England's first wave of revivalism in c. 1736–45, associated with George Whitefield and Jonathan Edwards, brought into being nearly one hundred new churches of Separate Congregationalists; but it was a movement which faded, its followers often returning to the Congregational fold or joining the Baptists. The Separates' case was an ecclesiological one: they 'did not take issue with the basic theological tenets of Calvinism', and without this theological imperative the ecclesiological reasons for division proved difficult to sustain. New England's first massive experience of anti-Calvinist sectarian proliferation – the Shakers, Universalists and Freewill Baptists – came in the 'paroxysm' of c. 1778–82, and coincided, in a complex relation, with war and revolution.[157] The 'Great Awakening' is not an immediate or sufficient explanation of the Revolution. Joseph Pilmore, an English Methodist itinerant sent to the colonies in 1769, remained firmly within the Anglican Church but found that his revivalism transcended denominational boundaries: 'The love of God shed abrode in the heart makes all needless distinctions void.'[158] Pilmore however was politically quietist, and his diary ignored public affairs: revivalism unified colonial denominations only as long as politics did not intrude. Devereux Jarratt, the revivalist Virginian Anglican rector, complained in 1776 how 'the late work' had reached only seven or eight of the colony's fifty-two counties, and even then only via itinerant preachers, leaving the rest 'still in a very dark and deplorable condition'. Revivalists, too, neglected politics: 'The unhappy disputes between *England* and her Colonies, which just before had ingrossed all our conversation, seemed now in most companies to be forgot, while things of far greater importance lay so near the heart.'[159]

Revivalism in colonial America, like other religious and political phenomena, was swept along in denominational channels: direct connections

---

[157] Stephen A. Marini, *Radical Sects of Revolutionary New England* (Cambridge, Mass., 1982), pp. 4, 6, 19, 136–55 and passim; for the fading of the Separatist churches, Edwin Scott Gaustad, *The Great Awakening in New England* (New York, 1957), p. 115.

[158] Frederick E. Maser and Howard T. Maag (eds.), *The Journal of Joseph Pilmore Methodist Itinerant For The Years August 1, 1769 to January 2, 1774* (Philadelphia, 1969), pp. 51, 75–6, 135–6. Pilmore however recorded doctrinal challenges from Old Lights in a variety of denominations (pp. 48, 58, 61, 85–6, 120), and shared in the prevalent anti-Catholicism (pp. 81, 101).

[159] [Devereux Jarratt], *A Brief Narrative of the Revival of Religion in Virginia* (London, 1778), pp. 11, 26. For other instances of political engagement by New Light clergy see Donald Weber, *Rhetoric and History in Revolutionary New England* (New York, 1988).

can for example be established between the recrudescence of enthusiasm in early-eighteenth-century Scotland, especially the events known as the 'Cambuslang revivals',[160] the revivals in New England,[161] and events in those areas of the middle and southern colonies that received successive waves of Scots Presbyterian emigrants. Evangelicalism then came to eclipse ethnicity as the basis for denominational identity: 'What had begun as a Scottish evangelical movement became a Presbyterian movement, dominated by Scotsmen, attracting members of several ethnic groups. The acceptance of Scottish revivalist religion, rather than actual Scottish descent, became the principal criterion for inclusion in the religious community.'[162] To observers from other denominations, colonial Presbyterianism increasingly meant militant, Scots Presbyterianism.

Few of the implications of New Light theology were brought to bear against British rule before the early 1760s: until the conclusion of the Seven Years' War, the threat to liberty, property and Protestantism clearly emanated from French Canada. In New England especially, Britain was depicted as the main bulwark of freedom against the antichrist of Rome. British victory in the Seven Years' War, militarily resplendent, territorially extensive and seemingly irreversible, transformed the outlook of colonials and metropolitans alike. British administrators were confronted by new challenges, and approached them with a new spirit of confident interventionism. Colonists meanwhile were liberated from the imperatives which had kept them tied to the House of Hanover: from the mid-1760s, they were free to redirect what has been termed their new rhetoric, the product of religious revivalism,[163] as well as their old rhetoric of Protestant virtue. In this they were encouraged both by theological innovation, explored in chapter 4 below, and by the perspective of still more recent waves of immigrants from Scotland and Ireland, including the clergymen John Witherspoon and Alexander Craighead, who re-emphasised the Covenanter roots of political contractarianism. Witherspoon exercised his influence as President of Princeton from 1768 to 1794, Craighead in more humble surroundings as a minister in Meckl-

---

[160] For which, see [James Robe], *A Short Narrative of the Extraordinary Work at Cambuslang in Scotland* (Philadelphia and Boston, 1742); Edward Fisher, *The Marrow of Modern Divinity* (London, 1646; Edinburgh, 1718; Boston, 1743); *A Letter from a Gentleman in Scotland, to his friend in New-England. Containing an Account of Mr. Whitefield's Reception and Conduct in Scotland . . . and also of the work at Cambuslang* (Boston, 1743); Alexander Webster, *Divine Influence the True Spring of the Extraordinary Work at Cambuslang* (Edinburgh, 1742; Boston, 1743).

[161] Ward, *Protestant Evangelical Awakening*, pp. 335–9.

[162] Ned C. Landsman, *Scotland and Its First American Colony, 1683–1765* (Princeton, 1985), pp. 227–55.

[163] Bonomi, *Cope of Heaven*, p. 158.

enburg County, North Carolina, from 1755 to his death in 1766. Craighead had already been expelled from ministering in two presbyteries for preaching without licence and other irregularities: his affinities with the Cameronians made him a difficult neighbour. Among the Scots-Irish of the backcountry, however, he found a receptive audience. To them he appealed both by his preaching and his published works. Craighead carefully prepared his flock in their knowledge of the history and meaning of covenantal theology. If he explicitly renounced the commonly-held idea that Covenanters 'are obliged to rise in Rebellion against his present Majesty King *George*',[164] this was not true of the anonymous pamphlet *Renewal of the Covenants* (Philadelphia, 1743, 1748).[165]

The pamphlet records the renewal of the Covenant by a congregation at Middle Octorara, Lancaster County, Pennsylvania, on 11 November 1743. That Covenant reiterated the Cameronians' violent rejection of and persecution by Charles I, Cromwell and Charles II, and extended this saga as a reason for denying allegiance to George I and George II, they

> being sworn Prelaticks, the Head of Malignants, and Protectors of Sectarian Hereticks, and Electory Princes of *Brunswick*, in chusing of new Emperors, which is their giving their Power to the Beast; and for their Confederacy with Popish Princes, directly contrary to the second Commandment; and for want of their Scriptural and national Qualifications . . . and for their being established Head of the Church by the Laws of *England*.

Its signatories rejected also the Revolution settlement of 1689,

> which established an Erastian power in the Kings Hands (as they term him) to appoint Time and Place, when and where General Assemblies should be holden, and obliged Presbyteries to settle such qualified Preachers (as they call them) to vacant Congregations, as should be presented by the pretended King or Laick Patrons.[166]

It was a vivid anticipation of that more famous renewal of a covenant which was the American Revolution.

In 1764 Governor Dobbs of North Carolina asked the SPG in London for an Anglican missionary to be sent to Mecklenburg county, whose

---

[164] Alexander Creaghead [sic], *A Discourse Concerning the Covenants: containing The Substance of Two Sermons, preached at Middle-Octarara, January 10 and 17. 1741, 2* (Philadelphia, 1742), p. 32.

[165] Baldwin, 'Sowers of Sedition', 64–71.

[166] *Renewal of the Covenants, National and Solemn League; A Confession of Sins; An Engagement to Duties; and a Testimony; as they were carried on at Middle Octorara in Pennsylvania, November 11, 1743* (n.p., 1748), printed in part in Maurice W. Armstrong et al., (eds), *The Presbyterian Enterprise* (Philadelphia, [1956]), pp. 57–60 and Gaius Jackson Slosser (ed.), *They Seek a Country. The American Presbyterians: Some Aspects* (New York, 1955), p. 108; it is not listed in Evans, *American Bibliography*.

inhabitants 'are mostly now Presbyterians'. When the Rev. Andrew Morton arrived, he learned that

> the Inhabitants of Mecklenburg are entire dissenters of the most rigid kind – That they had a solemn leag[u]e and covenant teacher settled among them. That they were in general greatly averse to the Church of England – and that they looked upon a law lately enacted in this province for the better establishment of the Church as oppressive as the Stamp Act and were determined to prevent its taking place there, by opposing the settlement of any Minister of the Church of England that might be sent amongst them – In short it was very evident that in Mecklenburg County I could be of little use to the honorable Society and I thought it but prudent to decline embroiling myself with an infatuated people to no purpose . . .

He settled in Northampton county instead, 'vastly well received by the people'.[167]

Like the Covenanters, Craighead preached to his congregation in Mecklenburg county the necessity to 'declare a defensive War against all Usurpers of the Royal Prerogative of the glorious Lamb of God'.[168] After his death, this message was sustained by other New Light clergy in the neighbourhood, like the influential David Caldwell: their teaching flowed directly into the Regulator movement. Although other denominations including New England Congregationalism shared this religious impetus to political engagement, the popular movement known as the Regulation had a special place in the tradition of disorder. The history of colonial British America was punctuated with a series of backcountry rebellions against east coast authorities. The last and greatest of these occurred only shortly before the larger Revolution of 1776, for from 1768 until their military destruction at the battle of Alamance in May 1771 the piedmont of North and South Carolina was increasingly under the control of the self-styled Regulators, local activists usurping by force the authority of colonial magistrates and tax officials. The nature of this disorder, so closely anticipating the events of 1776, has long been debated. Statistical analysis has now shown that the Regulators drew their active supporters from all social strata: a class explanation no longer does justice to the evidence.[169] Demographic and social explanations are clearly important in explaining the turmoil of a backcountry region which was inundated

---

[167] Andrew Morton to SPG, 25 Aug. 1766, in W.L. Saunders (ed.), *The Colonial Records of North Carolina*, vol. 7 (Raleigh, N.C., 1890), p. 252.

[168] 'This our active Testimony commences from the Year 1680', noted Craighead – the year of the Queensferry Paper and the Sanquhar Declaration. *Renewal of the Covenants*, in Armstrong, *Presbyterian Enterprise*, pp. 58–9.

[169] James P. Whittenburg, 'Planters, Merchants and Lawyers: Social Change and the Origins of the North Carolina Regulation', *WMQ* 34 (1977), 215–38.

by waves of migrants after c. 1740,[170] but these new masses had one other important characteristic: their ethnic and religious composition marked them off sharply from the older settlers of the east.

The Regulators are fitted, but too easily, into that system of beliefs and attitudes now conventionally termed 'Commonwealth' ideology. The petty corruption of executive officials, in this perspective, was a threat both to their property and their liberty: 'slavery' would be their fate if they submitted to 'tyranny'.[171] Arriving as migrants, above all from Scots-Irish Pennsylvania, the new settlers in North Carolina demanded of the eastern authorities a range of political practices already common in other colonies.[172] On one level, the disputes arose from backcountry complaints about 'the Malpractices of the Officers of our County Court, and the Abuses that we suffer by those that are impowered to manage our publick Affairs', as a petition from Granville county complained.[173]

Yet the Regulation went much further, and was given millennial expression by the interaction of the settlers' background with the issue of the demand of tithes for the Church of England. Hermon Husband, the movement's only contemporary defender in print, echoed the Scots Dissenter James Murray: 'In Britain, the clergy endeavor to make us believe that tithes and church rates are of divine institution. This pretended right of demanding church dues, more than the secular power gives, is treating men like asses.' It was a charge valid against all ecclesiastical authority: 'The Jure Divino of episcopacy and presbytery are pieces of furniture that prophets prepare for their asses.'[174] So extensive an assertion of a right of private judgement led Husband to add a millennial expectation as the outcome of the redress of specific grievances: 'Methinks when a Reformation can be brought about in our Constitution by a legal and constitutional Manner, then will commence that Thousand Years Reign with Christ, and utter downfall of Mystery *Babylon*, who has truly made

[170] H. R. Merrens, *Colonial North Carolina in the Eighteenth Century: A Study in Historical Geography* (Chapel Hill, 1964), pp. 53–81.

[171] Many Regulator complaints against the dishonesty or incompetence of government officers in the backcountry were clearly well founded; but it has been suggested that one cause of the rebellion was the settlers' 'general reluctance to accept any bridling of their hitherto unrestricted freedom in the interest of what seems reasonable to any proponent of a well-ordered society', including the payment of colony taxes: Carl Bridenbaugh, *Myths and Realities: Societies of the Colonial South* (Baton Rouge, 1952), p. 161.

[172] A. Roger Ekirch, 'The North Carolina Regulators on Liberty and Corruption, 1766–1771', *Perspectives in American History* 11 (1977–8), 199–256; idem, *'Poor Carolina': Politics and Society in Colonial North Carolina, 1729–1776* (Chapel Hill, N.C., 1981), pp. 161–211.

[173] [Hermon Husband], *An Impartial Relation of the First Rise and Cause of the Recent Differences, in Publick Affairs, in the Province of North-Carolina* (n.p., 1770), reprinted in William K. Boyd (ed.), *Some Eighteenth Century Tracts Concerning North Carolina* (Raleigh, 1927), pp. 247–333, at 254–5.

[174] Ibid., pp. 320, 328.

the Nations of the Earth drunk, poysoned their Understandings, and bereaved them of Sense as much as strong Drink will do.'[175] Husband was an ex-Anglican, a convert to New Light Presbyterianism, inspired by Gilbert Tennent and George Whitefield to reject his first church as corrupt and unspiritual;[176] he ended his career as a participant in the Whiskey Rebellion of 1794.[177] If the Regulator case was given its most principled expression in the idiom of religious dissent, the Governor's case was similarly articulated by a missionary Anglican cleric from the Society for the Propagation of the Gospel, preaching a sermon on the classic text of Romans XIII, 1–2.[178]

Rebellion was not necessarily intended to be destructive of all authority; rather it might imply the claim of a right to transfer or appropriate authority. The right of resistance envisaged by a variety of sectarian traditions was invoked with a view to better order, not less order: it envisaged a godly reformation, not John Locke's extreme scenario in which a monarch's breach of the original contract released his subjects back into a state of nature, free to make all things new. The Regulator movement of 1768–71 in South and North Carolina claimed to be the response of the 'respectable' to a breakdown of law in the aftermath of an Indian war: an association of property owners responded with force against known criminals in an effective vigilante campaign. Despite this professed reverence for the rule of law, most of the Regulators sided with the Revolution.[179] The notion of popular sovereignty which their culture sustained meant, at local level, informal collective retributive violence ranging from tarring and feathering to that peculiar American institution, lynching.[180] (Its only parallel in the English Atlantic empire was the

---

[175] [Hermon Husband], *Continuation of the Impartial Relation of the First Rise and Cause of the Recent Differences, in Publick Affairs, In the Province of North-Carolina, &c.* ([New Bern, N.C.], 1770), p. 15.

[176] For his spiritual autobiography, see [Hermon Husband], *Some Remarks on Religion, With the Author's Experience in Pursuit thereof* (Philadelphia, 1761), reprinted in Boyd (ed.), *Tracts Concerning North Carolina*, pp. 193–246.

[177] Thomas P. Slaughter, *The Whiskey Rebellion: Frontier Epilogue to the American Revolution* (New York, 1986), pp. 216, 276. For Hermon Husband's involvement in the Whiskey Rebellion, William Findley, *History of the Insurrection in the Four Western Counties of Pennsylvania: in the Year M.DCC.XCIV* (Philadelphia, 1796), p. 212.

[178] George Micklejohn, *On the important Duty of Subjection to the Civil Powers. A Sermon Preached before his Excellency William Tryon, Esquire, Governor, and Commander in Chief of the Province of North-Carolina, and the Troops raised to quell the late Insurrection* (New Bern, 1768), reprinted in Boyd (ed.), *Tracts Concerning North Carolina*, pp. 393–412.

[179] Richard Maxwell Brown, *The South Carolina Regulators* (Cambridge, Mass., 1963), pp. 123–6 and passim. Brown observes (p. 139) that the South Carolina Regulators 'never once complained against this stiff requirement [the high qualification for a seat in the Assembly: 500 acres of land and 10 slaves]; theirs was a not a democratic movement'.

[180] James E. Cutler, *Lynch-Law: An Investigation into the History of Lynching in the United States* (New York, 1905); Fischer, *Albion's Seed*, pp. 765–71.

system of private violence that prevailed time out of mind in Ireland.)

The North Carolina Regulators were defeated and scattered by troops under the command of Governor William Tryon at the battle of Alamance on 16 May 1771. In 1776 the old Regulators were divided: some responded with loyalty to the new Governor, Josiah Martin, who had attempted to redress their grievances, but there are grounds for thinking that most fought for independence.[181] Some of the Mecklenburg county resolutions of 31 May 1775 echoed Regulator grievances, and a link is undeniable.[182] In reaction to the news of the Boston Port Bill, a general convention of representatives from North Carolina met in August 1774 and provided, *inter alia*, for the continuing existence of county committees. On 31 May 1775 the committee for Mecklenburg county passed its famous Resolves. They responded to the Address to the King of both Houses of Parliament on 10 February 1775, declaring the New England colonies to be in a state of rebellion, and deduced: 'we conceive that all Laws and commissions confirmed by, or derived from the Authority of the King or Parliament, are annulled and vacated, and the former civil Constitution of these Colonies for the present wholly suspended'. They then went on to make provision for the administration of justice within the county and the collection of arms and ammunition, the Resolves to apply 'until Instructions from the General Congress of this Province, regulating the Jurisprudence of this Province, shall provide otherwise, or the legislative Body of *Great-Britain* resign its unjust and arbitrary Pretentions with Respect to *America*'.

The Governor of the colony at once denounced it as a 'most treasonable publication ... explicitly renouncing obedience to His Majesty's Government and all lawfull authority whatsoever'.[183] In this he went beyond the text of the Resolves, but contributed to a later tradition which saw them as a full and final declaration of independence. The Resolves themselves were subtly different in their argument: they claimed that British actions had 'annulled and vacated' British authority. The terms of the complaint are more reminiscent of the Scots Convention's charge in 1689 that James II had 'forfaulted' the Crown than of the language of Jefferson's Declaration of Independence. Soon

---

[181] A heavy predominance of Regulators in support of the Revolution is argued by Elmer D. Johnson, 'The War of the Regulation' (MA Thesis, Univ. of N. Carolina, 1942); these figures are challenged by Marvin L. Michael Kay, 'The North Carolina Regulation, 1766–1776: A Class Conflict' in Alfred F. Young (ed.), *The American Revolution: Explorations in the History of American Radicalism* (De Kalb, Illinois, 1976), pp. 71–123, at 105.

[182] Kay, ibid., pp. 105, 107.

[183] A.S. Salley, jr., 'The Mecklenburg Declaration: The Present Status of the Question', *AHR* 13 (1907), 16–43, shows how a spurious text of the Resolves was later invented and propagated.

a draft of instructions to the County's delegates in framing the State's constitution, in September 1775, proposed:

> 1. You are instructed to vote that the late Province of North Carolina is and of right ought to be a free and independent state invested with all the powers of Legislation capable of making laws to regulate all its internal policy subject only in its external connections and foreign commerce to a negative of a continental Senate. 2. You are instructed to vote for the Execution of a civil Government under the authority of the People for the future security of all the Rights Privileges and Prerogatives of the State and the private natural and unalienable Rights of the constituting members thereof either as Men or Christians.[184]

The draft instructions in fact said little about the secular rights of man; 'unalienable right' chiefly concerned religion. Protestantism might be established, in so far as the Thirty-Nine Articles were compatible with that Presbyterian yardstick the Westminster Confession of Faith (1646), itself a response to the Scottish Solemn League and Covenant (1643). A 'confession and profession of the Religion so established shall be necessary in qualifying any person for public trust in the State', the instructions continued;

> You are to oppose to the utmost any particular church or set of Clergymen being invested with power to decree rites and ceremonies and to decide in controversies of faith to be submitted to under the influence of penal laws ... You are moreover to oppose the establishing an ecclesiastic supremacy in the sovereign authority of the State. You are to oppose the toleration of the popish idolatrous worship.[185]

Mecklenburg county's instructions to its delegates to the Continental Congress in November 1776 were a list of technical constitutional provisions, including the aim 'that the Government be a simple Democracy or as near it as possible'; but they prominently reiterated the injunction that

> any person who shall hereafter profess himself to be an Atheist or deny the Being of God or shall deny or blaspheme any of the persons of the Holy Trinity or shall deny the divine authority of the Old and New Testament or shall be of the Roman Catholic Religion shall not sustain hold or enjoy any office of trust or profit in the State of North Carolina.[186]

---

[184] 'Instructions for the Delegates of Mecklenburg County proposed to the Consideration of the County', [n.d.] in William L. Saunders (ed.), *Colonial Records of North Carolina* (Raleigh, 1886–90), vol. 10, p. 239.

[185] Ibid.

[186] Ibid., pp. 870a, 870d. By contrast, although the North Carolina State constitution somewhat widened the franchise, it did not eliminate the disproportionate representation of the tidewater counties. 'Representation in proportion to population was not even recognised in principle ... Apparently it was the indifference of the piedmont to the issue rather than any opposition from tidewater conservatives which was responsible for the

It was as well that the authors of the document were unaware of the heterodox private beliefs of most of the Founding Fathers.

What prompted certain Americans to rebel? The old constitutional scenario of a sinister and concerted attempt by George III to resurrect monarchical absolutism is now untenable; so is the related notion that the ministry of Lord North rested on a revived Tory party.[187] Nevertheless, the historiographical tradition which made a Commonwealth libertarianism into the almost universal American idiom even before 1776 required that the precipitant of revolution should be external to the colonies. It was still, therefore, located (though now rather on the level of ideology) as a 'mid-eighteenth-century English reactionary shift in both the theory and the practice of government'.[188] A fuller picture of the monarchical, Anglican nature of the early-Hanoverian regime[189] removes the significant structural elements in this contrast between the years before and after 1760, and reopens the question of internal colonial precipitants to the rebellion of 1776. Those precipitants, like innovations in British policy in the 1760s, can now be seen to have engaged with certain distinctive predispositions.

Before the 1760s, the main idioms of political discourse in most mainland colonies had echoed English norms: they were determined by the dynastic and religious questions fought over by Englishmen since 1679.[190] The first two Georges undoubtedly enjoyed widespread public acclaim in America. Yet fears of royal tyranny were as vivid in the colonies as in England: indeed, the colonies had been subject to the more creative and unrestrained exercise of Stuart executive privilege. The level of those fears

failure to reform the existing system': Elisha P. Douglass, *Rebels and Democrats: The Struggle for Equal Political Rights and Majority Rule During the American Revolution* (Chapel Hill, 1955), pp. 131–2.

[187] For the creation of the myth of a new absolutism, see J. C. D. Clark (ed.), *The Memoirs and Speeches of James, 2nd Earl Waldegrave, 1742–1763* (Cambridge, 1988) and Ian R. Christie, 'George III and the Historians – Thirty Years On', *History* 71 (1986), 205–21; for the non-party basis of North's ministry, see Ian R. Christie, 'Was There a 'New Toryism' in the Earlier Part of George III's Reign?', *Journal of British Studies* 5 (1965–6), 60–76, and idem, 'Party in Politics in the Age of Lord North's Administration', *Parliamentary History* 6 (1987), 47–68.

[188] Lawrence Stone, 'The Results of the English Revolutions of the Seventeenth Century' in Pocock (ed.), *Three British Revolutions*, p. 99. For a full discussion of the 'neo-Whig' historiography of the colonies, see Gordon S. Wood, 'Rhetoric and Reality in the American Revolution', *WMQ* 23 (1966), 3–32.

[189] Advanced in, for example, Clark, *English Society 1688–1832*.

[190] Neo-Harringtonian emphases (the corruption of the legislature by the executive, the superiority of militias to standing armies, the threat to agrarian virtue posed by finance, commerce and luxury) were congruent with this basic polarity and derived force from it. Cf. Jack P. Greene, 'Political Mimesis: A Consideration of the Historical and Cultural Roots of Legislative Behaviour in the British Colonies in the Eighteenth Century', *AHR* 75 (1969–70), 359.

therefore followed for a time a similar path on both sides of the Atlantic: rising in the 1670s and 1680s, subsiding after 1688, but never wholly absent in the first half of the eighteenth century.[191] The charge of arbitrary power, an allegation with immediately recognisable dynastic implications, remained available for use against the executive in the colonies also. But why was it thought appropriate by some people after c.1760 to use Whig rhetoric against a Whig regime? It is now apparent how, after the end of the Seven Years' War, the pattern in the New World again corresponded closely to that in the Old. The old external threats disappeared, together with the internal polarity they had induced. The confluence of former Whigs and Tories in support of George III simultaneously reawakened old fears and provided new targets for existing opposition rhetoric.

From the Exclusion Crisis, that idiom[192] had pictured one group of men as patriotic upholders of an ancient constitution, endeavouring to defend it against or to retrieve it from its secret enemies, themselves engaged in a conspiracy for the introduction of Popery and arbitrary power. Whatever the possibilities of a forcible reconversion of the nation to Roman Catholicism, the daily experience of the 1660s and 1670s was an Anglican campaign for religious uniformity associated with Archbishops Sheldon and Sancroft. In the colonies the same idiom survived, confirmed by the revolution of 1688, war and religious revival in the 1740s, to form a staple of revolutionary rhetoric in 1776. Within the sectarian vision, one component in particular still acted as a powerful emotional predisposition: the fear of Popery. Its role was already an ancient one. The New England colonies were founded at a time of frenzied anti-Catholicism in England, and carried this inheritance as a lasting and vivid theme in their moral and political discourse. Laudian persecution of Puritans added to their extreme sensitivity to anything which could be defined as religious persecution. Consequently, the imperial challenges of the 1670s and 80s produced an even more rhetorically heightened reaction in the colonies than in England, but with one characteristic especially accentuated: in the absence of significant numbers of colonial Catholics, the popish threat had even more to be depicted as covert, hidden, disguised. Such fears and accusations found prominent expressions in the risings of 1689. By the mid-eighteenth century, the vocabulary of tyranny, slavery and arbitrary power was still grounded on the meanings of the key term 'popery';

---

[191] For an exploration of 'monarchical culture', and the options which it provided for politicians, see Richard L. Bushman, *King and People in Provincial Massachusetts* (Chapel Hill, N.C., 1985).

[192] Classically explored by J. G. A. Pocock, 'Machiavelli, Harrington and English Political Ideologies in the Eighteenth Century' (1965), reprinted in idem, *Politics, Language and Time* (London, 1972), pp. 104–47.

but, under the impact of such early-eighteenth-century English texts as *The Independent Whig*, these meanings could be stretched to cover the exercise of power by any established, episcopal church.[193] The remarkable and novel depiction of British policy of the 1760s and 1770s in terms of 'popery and arbitrary power' justified, and was reinforced, by New Englanders insisting on a parallel with the events of the 1680s.[194]

Yet here the English and American experiences profoundly diverged. In the three decades following the '45, the strident and widespread English denunciation of Catholicism was fragmented and considerably muted: pragmatic co-existence, the disappearance of the strategic threat of a Stuart restoration and the advance of ideals of politeness and civility predisposed many men, at least many Anglicans, to reconsider England's penal code and explore ways of relaxing it.[195] This reorientation found its expression in colonial policy too with the Quebec Act of 1774, belatedly giving effect to the requirements of the Treaty of Paris in 1763 regarding the free exercise of their religion by the newly-conquered French Canadians. In colonial America, by contrast, no such relaxation of these ancient animosities occurred: on the contrary, the issues of the 1760s gave them new if implausible targets, and the Quebec Act of 1774 unleashed furious denunciation.[196]

Religious predispositions among anti-Catholic colonists acted to translate practical problems into triggers of armed resistance. In both 1688 and 1776, the constitutional issues raised by questions of taxation, executive prerogative and parliamentary jurisdiction were turned from negotiable ones into non-negotiable grievances which evoked the passionate, uncalculating commitment of great numbers of ordinary men by their engagement with a much wider nexus of ideas and feelings. Contemporaries, both loyalists and rebels, recognised the part played by religious enthusiasm in the American cause: the sectarian contribution was clear. For a minority, 'enthusiasm' now came to take on a wider secular meaning: John Adams echoed Shaftesbury's eulogy of 'noble enthusiasm' as a qual-

---

[193] T. M. Brown, 'The Image of the Beast: Anti-Papal Rhetoric in Colonial America' in Richard O. Curry (ed.), *Conspiracy: The Fear of Subversion in American History* (New York, 1972), pp. 1–20.

[194] E.g. Increase Mather, *A Narrative of the Miseries of New-England, by reason of an Arbitrary Government erected there under Sir Edmund Andros* (London and Boston, 1688; reprinted Boston, 1775); *The Revolution in New-England Justified, and the People there Vindicated* (Boston, 1691; reprinted Boston, 1773).

[195] Haydon, *Anti-Catholicism in Eighteenth-Century England*, chapter 5.

[196] The virulence and power of popular American anti-Catholicism is the suppressed theme of colonial history, and the studies which seriously address it are forgotten books: Sister Mary Augustina Ray, *American Opinion of Roman Catholicism in the Eighteenth Century* (New York, 1936); Charles H. Metzger, *The Quebec Act* (New York, 1936); idem, *Catholics and the American Revolution* (Chicago, 1962).

ity which 'raised the imagination to an opinion or conceit of something
majestic and divine'.[197] But its secular sense had most importance only
to the small circle of men who formed part of the Jeffersonian Enlightenment. The political commitments of most men were still an aspect of
their religion; this was already taking forms which were in some ways
distinctively American and which powerfully aided the political mobilisation of the sects.

Sectarian discipline and inter-denominational competition meant that
rates of church attendance were strikingly higher in the American
colonies than in England.[198] More was involved, however, when in
1776 Richard Price sensed that the American colonies were 'animated
by piety'.[199] By 1776, religious revivalism had inspired in a minority
of the most frenzied colonists a vision of an imminent millennium, in
the majority a heightened sense of the colonies' place in an international
moral drama. The expectation of a future moral transformation was
matched by a condemnation of the sinfulness, luxury and corruption
of past life, and, especially, of English and Anglican modes. It was this
revivalistic, evangelical and sectarian impulse which gave immediacy to
the critique of 'corruption', and the denominational social constituency
of the evangelical movement which gave these religious insights their
populist focus as an attack on privilege and hierarchy, an assertion of
divinely-sanctioned popular sovereignty against the divine right of the
English monarchy.[200] Millennial themes, where available, were quickly
transposed to the civil realm, but theological arguments for the immin-
ence of the Second Coming were not the dominant idiom of 'patriot'
preachers during the revolutionary war: it has been suggested that only
a sixth of such writings employed these motifs.[201] Most denominational
invective stressed the corruption that Dissenters perceived in Anglicanism; the right of resistance with which the sects distinguished them-

---

[197] Lovejoy, *Religious Enthusiasm in the New World*, p. 228.
[198] Patricia U. Bonomi and Peter R. Eisenstadt, 'Church Adherence in the Eighteenth-
    Century British American Colonies', *WMQ* 39 (1982), 245–86.
[199] Richard Price, *Observations on the Nature of Civil Liberty, the Principles of Government, and the
    Justice and Policy of the War with America* (2nd edn., London, 1776), p. 98: 'From one end
    of North-America to the other, they are FASTING and PRAYING. But what are we
    doing? – Shocking thought! we are ridiculing them as *Fanatics*, and scoffing at religion.'
[200] Rhys Isaac, 'Preachers and Patriots: Popular Culture and the Revolution in Virginia' in
    Young (ed.), *The American Revolution*, pp. 124–56, at 128; idem, 'Evangelical Revolt: The
    Nature of the Baptists' Challenge to the Traditional Order in Virginia, 1765–1775', *WMQ*
    31 (1974), 345–68; idem, *The Transformation of Virginia, 1740–1790* (Chapel Hill, N.C.,
    1982); Alan Heimert, *Religion and the American Mind From the Great Awakening to the Enlighten-
    ment* (Cambridge, Mass., 1966), pp. 12–14, 21, 59–60, 354, 453, 460–3 and passim.
[201] Melvin B. Endy, Jr, 'Just War, Holy War, and Millennialism in Revolutionary America',
    WMQ 42 (1985), 3–25.

selves from Anglican ecclesiastical polity; the tyranny which those sects had embodied in the myths of their flight to the promised land to escape episcopal persecution; the association of 'popery and arbitrary power' which the sectarian perspective led them to perceive in Britain's balanced constitution and its Warburtonian Church establishment; and the Dissenting use of contract and voluntary association as a critique of the Anglican, common-law conception of sovereignty.[202] Denominational doctrine could have major consequences even in the absence of millenarianism and revivalism.

In the decade before 1776, one aspect of this denominational rhetoric of the American clerical intelligentsia subtly changed. The familiar jeremiad about the sins of God's chosen people and the need for a collective act of repentance and atonement was increasingly combined with an implication that that repentance had already been demonstrated by a defiance of tyranny, so that Providence was now enlisted in the cause of resistance. The doctrine that God stood in a contractual relation with His chosen people – a doctrine found in most denominations, but especially emphasised in New England Congregationalism and in Presbyterianism – became more generally available to all Americans, and the burden of guilt for the breach of this eternal contract was by implication transferred to the mother country: 'this coalescence of abnegation and assertion, this identification of Protestant self-distrust with confidence in divine aid, erected a frame for the natural rights philosophy wherein it could work with infinitely more power than if it had been propounded exclusively in the language of political rationalism'.[203]

Indeed, argued Perry Miller, it was not the 'genial Anglicanism' of the established clergy nor the 'urbane rationalism' of the Washingtons, Jeffersons and Franklins that

> brought the rank and file of American Protestants into the war. What aroused a Christian patriotism that needed staying power was a realisation of the vengeance God denounced against the wicked; what fed their hopes was not what God promised as a recompense to virtue, but what dreary fortunes would overwhelm those who persisted in sloth; what kept them going was an assurance that by exerting themselves they were fighting for a victory thus providentially predestined.[204]

It has been suggested that colonial Americans were able to mobilise so quickly between 1773 and 1776 because a millennial tradition of thought

---

[202] See chapter 1 above.
[203] Perry Miller, 'From the Covenant to the Revival' in idem, *Nature's Nation* (Cambridge, Mass., 1967), pp. 90–120, at 101.
[204] Ibid., p. 102.

was available for instant activation, overriding the tradition of a remedy for present corruption in the return to former virtue;[205] but the unanimity and speed of this mobilisation is called in question by the military history of a fragmented and ambiguously-motivated civil war[206] and by the evidence, presented in chapter 4 below, of the self-doubt and internal conflicts within several denominations about joining in armed resistance. Yet these doubts were finally swept aside, and for far more colonists than subscribed to millenarian ideas. However seldom expressed in a strict sense or widely influential in a general sense millenarianism was, colonial denominations sustained many other traditions of thought about their histories and ecclesiastical polities which, although at times ambiguous, were activated with ultimately decisive effect. Mobilisation on the scale of 1776 is evidence against religious imagery being mere rhetoric. A break in the tie with Britain, a renunciation of existing rationales for American society, demanded and was given an alternative rationale, a Biblically-supported vision of a new future. Euphoria therefore began with rebellion: it did not have to wait for military victory.

In America, the combined effects of long-standing denominational discourse, religious revivalism and theological heterodoxy gave a particular structure to the most extreme frequencies of political debate. This heightened emotional temperature acted to sweep up and distort patterns of argument which might otherwise have provided grounds for caution rather than insurrection. American rhetoric in the 1760s and 1770s combined the same potentially inconsistent elements as did that of England: beside contract theory and natural rights theory went the doctrine of the ancient constitution, all covered by the ambiguous idea of 'fundamental law'. This last necessarily referred to 1688 as one of the episodes by which that constitution had been defended or repaired. As important as the specific form of the ancient constitution was the long record of sacrifice in its defence: colonists revered the 'ancestors [who] have liberally shed their blood to secure to us the rights we now contend for'; but such a rhetoric carried the implication that the constitution could only be maintained 'at the hazard of our lives and fortunes'.[207] A theory of past achievement became itself an incitement to present excess: in the heat of an evangelical religious movement, the theory of the ancient constitution was made to demand sacrifice and atonement rather than negotiation, compromise or humility. Millennial religion and civil liberty had been linked in such a way that, 'With remarkable consistency, those clergymen

---

[205] Bloch, *Visionary Republic*, pp. 75–7.
[206] See chapter 4, part I.
[207] Quoted Rhys Isaac, 'Preachers and Patriots', p. 149.

most prone to apocalyptic interpretations expressed the most fear that grandiose plots were afoot against the ancient constitution. Those who most vigorously recounted their forefathers' errand into the wilderness argued most emphatically for the civic virtues of republicanism.'[208]

From soon after the accession of George III, English Dissenters co-operated with their colonial co-religionists to confirm and strengthen the Americans in their belief that a transatlantic conspiracy was being hatched against both civil and religious liberty.[209] These issues were revitalised, for English Dissenters also, by the Anglican church's intermittent moves to appoint a bishop for the colonies. Such plans existed, but only when viewed against the background of the history of English, Irish and Scots sectarian emigration to the colonies did this modest proposal assume the sinister shape of a bid to reimpose those claims which the Americans had fled their homelands to escape.[210] For those sharing this mind-set the Wilkes affair and Anglican resistance to the Feathers Tavern petition against subscription to the Thirty-Nine Articles fell into place as episodes in the royal conspiracy.

It required the Dissenting perspective to arrange these unconnected incidents into a scenario of impending tyranny. Anglicans explained the innocence of a scheme for a bishop in America: 'it could make no Alteration with respect to the Civil Governm[en]t, or to the People', as Bishop Secker petitioned in 1759; as a memorandum of Shelburne re-emphasised in 1764, it was proposed to 'model every thing upon the most extensive Principles of the *Toleration* . . . No Coersive Powers are desired over the Laity.' But the ancient intolerance of New England Congregationalism was given a new object by the loyal behaviour of Anglican clergy during the Stamp Act crisis; by 1771 the clergy of New York and New Jersey, petitioning once more for a bishop, could warn that 'Independency in Religion will naturally produce Republicanism in the State.'[211] Although still expanding in numbers and cultural influence, Anglicanism had progressively softened the appearance of being a persecutory creed which it had given as recently as Anne's reign; yet colonial Dissenters still largely

---

[208] Hatch, *Sacred Cause*, p. 69.
[209] E.g. [Joseph Priestley], *The Present State of Liberty in Great Britain and Her Colonies. By an Englishman* (London, 1769), in J. T. Rutt (ed.), *The Theological and Miscellaneous Works of Joseph Priestley* (n.p., n.d.), vol. 22, pp. 380–98.
[210] Andrew Kippis, *A Vindication of the Protestant Dissenting Ministers With Regard to their late Application to Parliament* (2nd edn, London, 1773), pp. 101–2. Kippis was in the difficult position of demanding an extension of toleration to Dissenters in England while denying a similar freedom of religious practice to Episcopalians in America. He reconciled the two by raising fears of an extension of Anglican 'ascendancy and dominion'.
[211] Quoted in Jack M. Sosin, 'The Proposal in the Pre-Revolutionary Decade for Establishing Anglican Bishops in the Colonies', *Journal of Ecclesiastical History* 13 (1962), 76–84.

lived with their ancient shibboleths, nursing long-standing hatreds which any stimulus might reactivate – especially the appearance of Anglican intolerance created by the magnifying lens of Dissenting theological heterodoxy.

The main occasions on which these hatreds were expressed were, of course, provided by the issues of executive accountability, land grants, customs and taxation. From the Stamp Act crisis onwards, Edmund Burke's main engagement with the American question was on those issues. This remained true in 1775: recognising American indebtedness to English precedents, Burke believed that 'the great contests for freedom in this country were from the earliest times chiefly upon the question of Taxing'. Nevertheless, he acknowledged the close relation of the colonists' conception of liberty to their religion. As yet, Burke only half understood the reasons for this: 'I do not think, Sir, that the reason of this averseness in the dissenting churches from all that looks like absolute Government is so much to be sought in their religious tenets, as in their history.' The results, however, were clearer to him:

> the dissenting interests have sprung up in direct opposition to all the ordinary powers of the world; and could justify that opposition only on a strong claim to natural liberty. Their very existence depended on the powerful and unremitted assertion of that claim. All protestantism, even the most cold and passive, is a sort of dissent. But the religion most prevalent in our Northern Colonies is a refinement on the principle of resistance; it is the dissidence of dissent; and the protestantism of the protestant religion. This religion, under a variety of denominations, agreeing in nothing but in the communion of the spirit of liberty, is predominant in most of the Northern provinces; where the Church of England, notwithstanding its legal rights, is in reality no more than a sort of private sect, not composing most probably the tenth of the people. The Colonists left England when this spirit was high; and in the emigrants was the highest of all: and even that stream of foreigners, which has been constantly flowing into those Colonies, has, for the greatest part, been composed of dissenters from the establishments of their several countries, and have brought with them a temper and character far from alien to that of the people with whom they mixed.[212]

Burke's appreciation of theology was more limited than it was to become by 1790; so was his understanding of the colonists' ethnic diversity.[213] But his appreciation of the sectarian predispositions which elevated taxation into so momentous an issue was sound. So was his appreciation of the

---

[212] *The Speech of Edmund Burke, Esq.; on Moving his Resolutions for Conciliation with the Colonies, March 22, 1775* (London, 1775), pp. 16–18.
[213] He had begun: 'First, the people of the Colonies are descendants of Englishmen': ibid., p. 16. Burke used 'Englishman' as a portmanteau term: 'Are not the people of America as much Englishmen as the Welsh?': ibid., p. 40.

role of the English Dissenting clerical intelligentsia: they swiftly drew the appropriate conclusions from American independence,[214] though Dissenting laymen seem to have been less eager to follow them.

Within the culture of the international Enlightenment, the right of rebellion became an article of the new faith, self-justifying and immune to historical review. The Deist Thomas Jefferson, among congenial company in Paris in 1787, commended Shays' rebellion and looked forward to another clearing of the air:

> The spirit of resistance to government is so valuable on certain occasions, that I wish it to be always kept alive. It will often be exercised when wrong, but better so than not to be exercised at all. I like a little rebellion now and then. It is like a storm in the Atmosphere.[215]

The 'interpositions of the people' in America were sometimes 'irregular', but always had the good effect of checking their rulers; in European states, whose basis was not 'the opinion of the people', the governors had degenerated into 'wolves', but the 'errors' of the people could always be corrected by the diffusion of information on affairs of state: 'experience declares that man is the only animal which devours his own kind, for I can apply no milder term to the governments of Europe, and to the general prey of the rich on the poor'.[216] Rebellions were minor events, even natural responses to and proofs of the existence of tyranny.

In this way the Jeffersonian perspective blocked any deeper understanding of the causes of rebellion even for Americans themselves. At the same time, a right of rebellion, asserted so successfully, had been reaffirmed as part of American culture: it could not be removed by Britain's recognition of the independence of thirteen of her colonies in 1783. Rebellions therefore continued, adding to fears that the new republic would break into its component parts, either between northern and southern or between eastern and western states. In Shays' Rebellion (1786), the Whiskey Rebellion (1794),[217] and Fries' Rebellion (1799), Americans fought Americans in a continuing conflict over the issues that had been at stake in 1776;[218] but now it was a US Federal government which

---

[214] E.g. Richard Price, *Observations on the Importance of the American Revolution, and The Means of Making it a Benefit to the World* (London, 1785), pp. 34–49.

[215] Thomas Jefferson to Abigail Adams, 22 Feb. 1787, in Jefferson, *Papers*, vol. 11, p. 174.

[216] Jefferson to Edward Carrington, 16 Jan. 1787, ibid., p. 48.

[217] For these two episodes, see Barbara Karsky, 'Agrarian Radicalism in the Late Revolutionary Period (1780–1795)' in Angermann (ed.), *New Wine in Old Skins*, pp. 87–114.

[218] Almost twenty years after the Declaration of Independence, 'they were still fighting about taxes, still burning politicians in effigy, still tarring and feathering tax collectors, planting liberty poles, circulating petitions of protest, and again forming political action societies to defend the cause of liberty against its enemies in government. Something had clearly gone wrong, or so at least some Americans believed': Thomas P. Slaughter, *The Whiskey Rebellion: Frontier Epilogue to the American Revolution* (New York, 1986), p. 227.

asserted its authority with the whisky excise of 1791, and the stamp and land taxes of 1798. This continuing conflict sets 1776 once again in the perspective of a civil war rather than a war of national liberation, a war to emancipate a pre-existing nation.[219] Moreover, if the analysis presented above[220] is correct, the conflicts of 1861–5 are more intelligible as the second American civil war; the attempted secession of the South begins to seem more like a delayed stage of the conflict between Federalist and Antifederalist over the inevitability of the Blackstonian sovereign state.

Shays' rebellion[221] began in western Massachusetts but was part of a widespread phenomenon that swept the backcountry not only of that state but of Maine, Vermont and New Hampshire; only a failure of leadership stood in the way of a more effective movement.[222] Its wide potential was created partly by disillusion at the unfulfilled millennial promises of the Revolution, partly by a similar social constituency. Shays' rebellion, like those fomented by Coode, Leisler or Ethan Allen, came after the material grievances of the New England backcountry had been inflamed by a failed clergyman. Samuel Ely (1740– post 1797), a Yale graduate, was minister of Somers, Connecticut for six months in 1765 until discharged for his vices. Timothy Dwight credited him with 'the arts, of a demagogue, in an unusual degree. He was voluble, vehement in address, bold, persevering, active, brazen-faced in wickedness ... At the same time he declared himself, everywhere, the friend of the suffering and oppressed, and the champion of violated rights.'[223] Obliged to seek his fortune, Ely embarked on a career of armed rebellion and pillage which ended finally in politics.

Joseph Hawley, the Massachusetts patriot, warned the Boston authorities in June 1782 of the extent of backcountry dissatisfaction: people were 'perpetually taught that they were horribly deceived and deluded by those who first contended with Bernard and Hutchinson'. They were, moreover, inadequate patriots: 'They have no Sense or value for liberty – They are principally affected with present immediate feelings.'[224] In October 1786, 'a Regulator' wrote in the *Hampshire Gazette*: 'how did we know in the year 1774 it would be best to revolt

---

[219] See chapter 1, part I.
[220] See chapter 1, parts IV–VI.
[221] Robert J. Taylor, *Western Massachusetts in the Revolution* (Providence, R.I., 1954), pp. 128–67. David P. Szatmary, *Shays' Rebellion: The Making of an Agrarian Insurrection* (Amherst, Mass., 1980), p. xiv, locates 'the roots of the insurrection in a clash between a traditional, agrarian way of life and an ever-encroaching commercial society'.
[222] Slaughter, *Whiskey Rebellion*, pp. 48–9.
[223] Timothy Dwight, *Travels in New England and New York* (2 vols., London, 1823), vol. 2, pp. 275–6, quoted in Robert E. Moody, 'Samuel Ely: Forerunner of Shays', *New England Quarterly* 5 (1932), 105–34, at 106.
[224] Quoted in Moody, 'Ely', p. 113.

from Great Britain? We did not; but there was many clever things said of our future glory and we were induced to put to sea without a compass.' The problems had not been solved; another revolution might solve them.[225] However urgent the material needs of a poor backcountry region under the pressure of wartime taxation and inflation, a specific social constituency more clearly identified the incidence of political mobilisation: 'underlying the rebellion was the cardinal backcountry assumption that citizens should resist or separate from governments that did not serve local interests', and this assumption was held with particular vividness by those new sects, like Shakers, Universalists and Freewill Baptists, whose proliferation and migration had transformed the social structure of that region since the late 1770s.[226]

A lack of denominational evidence obscures the Whiskey Rebellion in the Pennsylvania backcountry in 1794; but despite the familiar pattern of material grievance, evidence does survive of the rebels identifying the cause of their east coast opponents with Antichrist.[227] Many rebels were active Presbyterians, and although their church officially disavowed rebellion, the religious element continued to do more than strengthen their group identity.[228] Even Fries' Rebellion contained an echo of dynastic, anti-Anglican fears. It arose among the Pennsylvania Germans of the backcountry as an anti-tax protest, and culminated in 1798–9 when John Fries led a party of armed men to release from prison two tax evaders, lodged there by a US marshal. The protest took place against a background of fears of monarchical tendencies in the Federal government, including a wild rumour that President Adams was conspiring to found an American royal dynasty by marrying his daughter to a son of George III.[229] Just as the separation of Church and State did not release American politics from religious pressures, so neither did the creation of a republic

[225] Quoted in Bloch, *Visionary Republic*, p. 110.

[226] Stephen A. Marini, *Radical Sects of Revolutionary New England* (Cambridge, Mass., 1982), pp. 25–39; George Richards Minot, *The History of the Insurrections, in Massachusetts In the Year MDCCLXXXVI, and the Rebellion Consequent Thereon* (Worcester, Mass., 1788), p. 17: 'With such high wrought notions of freedom in the people, it was difficult for the legislature either to govern without appearing to tyrannise, or to relieve without appearing to be overcome.'

[227] Bloch, *Visionary Republic*, p. 181.

[228] Leland D. Baldwin, *Whiskey Rebels: the Story of a Frontier Uprising* (Pittsburgh, 1939), pp. 81–2, 205; Ronald W. Long, 'The Presbyterians and the Whiskey Rebellion', *Journal of Presbyterian History* 43 (1965), 28–36.

[229] Adams, *Works*, vol. 8, p. 644; Bernard C. Steiner, *The Life and Correspondence of James McHenry* (Cleveland, 1907), pp. 432–5; John R. Howe, Jr, *The Changing Political Thought of John Adams* (Princeton, 1966), pp. 178–86; Louise Burnham Dunbar, *A Study of 'Monarchical' Tendencies in the United States from 1776 to 1801* (Urbana, Illinois, 1922), pp. 119–26; Alexander Graydon, *Memoirs of His Own Time. With Reminiscences of the Men and Events of the Revolution*, ed. J. S. Littell (Philadelphia, 1846), pp. 392–3.

sanitise American politics from those familial and charismatic features that European states continued to find focused in their dynasties.

VI. THE RHETORIC OF RESISTANCE AND ITS SOCIAL
CONSTITUENCIES IN ENGLAND AND IRELAND, 1733–1832:
SOME TRANSATLANTIC ANALOGIES

The Presbyterian political idiom of the Whiskey rebels bound them closely into a transatlantic tradition. Opposition to internal taxes in England in the 1730s, as in the colonies in the 1760s and 1790s, was articulated by the elite in the familiar terms of arbitrary power. A high incidence of taxation was seldom analysed in relation to the government's share of the national product, but was inextricably linked with Roman Catholicism and was symbolised by the poverty ('wooden shoes') it was held to entail for its subject populations. Popular perceptions showed why such language was activated: according to Lord Hervey, during the Excise Crisis of 1733 'the universal cry of the kingdom was 'No slavery, no excise, no wooden shoes".[230] The *London Journal* claimed that the opposition had spread the effective rumour 'that a great many Pair of *Wooden Shoes* were lately *imported*, on purpose to be carried about the City on Poles or Sticks, as *Emblems* or *Signs* to the People, of what a dismal State they are coming to'.[231]

Given that popular discourse remained within this framework, it becomes more evident why Real Whig ideology was not a far more powerful weapon against the Walpolian regime than it proved to be. Whigs in opposition after the Glorious Revolution sought with very limited success to use this idiom against successive Whig ministries: the threat of a restored Stuart dynasty and of all that it might entail was too real until the 1750s for a mode of political dissatisfaction ever to turn into a rhetoric of rebellion. Opposition Whigs, and even the most extreme 'Real Whigs', never envisaged armed resistance from the accession of William III to the death of George II. From the early 1760s, however, English Dissenters (independently of developments in America) began a great political reorientation: their early-Hanoverian commitment to the king's Whig ministers was, within a decade, transformed into an equally marked commitment to the opposition. This transformation has been quantified,[232] but not yet fully explained. Nevertheless, there is strong evidence to link it

[230] John, Lord Hervey, *Some Materials Towards Memoirs of the Reign of King George II*, ed. Romney Sedgwick (3 vols., London, 1931), vol. 1, p. 147.
[231] Herbert M. Atherton, *Political Prints in the Age of Hogarth* (Oxford, 1974), pp. 156, 172. For a full study see Haydon, *Anti-Catholicism in Eighteenth-Century England*.
[232] John A. Phillips, *Electoral Behavior in Unreformed England* (Princeton, 1982).

chiefly to the evolution of Dissenters' ideas rather than to their passive response to external events. First, the transformation can be observed initially among English Dissenters marked by theological heterodoxy, men like James Murray, Joseph Priestley, Joseph Towers.[233] Second, the rank and file of Dissenters were relatively little involved with the conflicts triggered in the 1760s by the career of John Wilkes; their real entry into public debate came with the subscription controversy of the early 1770s, and with the willingness of some of them to forge an alliance with their fellow Dissenters in the American colonies against an imagined recrudescence of 'popery and arbitrary power' in the person of George III.[234]

In the 1770s, the intelligentsia among the opposition in England and the supporters of independence in the American colonies imagined themselves to be engaged in a common cause.[235] This profound congruence of outlook, extending even to shared imaginings of persecution and to conspiracy theory, is the more remarkable since overt acts of public policy on either side of the Atlantic had had few points of similarity in the previous decade, despite assiduous attempts by some contemporaries to emphasise those analogies which could be found. The cry of 'no taxation without representation' had produced a strictly muted reaction when imported into English politics in the 1760s,[236] and the general election of 1774 revealed the failure of this issue to generate a nationwide response on the scale of the Sacheverell disturbances of 1710, the Excise crisis of 1733, or the Jew Bill agitation of 1753.[237] There was no debate in England about the role of subordinate legislatures, and no significant alarm about the undermining of judicial independence by the Crown. Borough charters were not being suspended; royal assent was not refused to parliamentary legislation. Despite conflicts over the general warrants, a minor affray labelled the St George's Fields 'massacre' or the Middlesex election, the Declaration of Independence, with its brief, generalised introduction and

[233] This thesis is more fully outlined in chapter 4, part IV below.
[234] For a different interpretation see Bradley, *Religion*, pp. 58–60.
[235] See especially Robbins, *Commonwealthman*; Bailyn, *Ideological Origins*; Colin Bonwick, *English Radicals and the American Revolution* (Chapel Hill, N.C., 1977); John Sainsbury, *Disaffected Patriots: London Supporters of Revolutionary America 1769–1782* (Kingston and Montreal, 1987); Bradley, *Religion*.
[236] For a different interpretation, John Brewer, *Party Ideology and Popular Politics at the Accession of George III* (Cambridge, 1976), pp. 201–16; cf. Clark, *English Society 1688–1832*, pp. 321–4 and Bradley, *Religion*, pp. 147–58.
[237] Geoffrey Holmes, 'The Sacheverell Riots: The Church and the Crowd in Early-Eighteenth-Century London' in Holmes, *Politics, Religion and Society in England 1679–1742* (London, 1986), pp. 217–47; George Rudé, "Mother Gin' and the London Riots of 1736' and 'Wilkes and Liberty, 1768–9' in *Paris and London in the Eighteenth Century: Studies in Popular Protest* (London, 1971), pp. 201–67; Paul Langford, *The Excise Crisis* (Oxford, 1975); T. W. Perry, *Public Opinion, Propaganda and Politics in Eighteenth Century England: A Study of the Jew Bill of 1753* (Cambridge, Mass., 1962).

its long, implausible catalogue of grievances, created few echoes within English political discourse, and was not taken up as a cult document either by the elite or the populace.[238] The sense of common cause felt by some Englishmen and Americans in the 1770s had its origins elsewhere, in a shared history, shared political discourse and, fundamentally, in shared positions in theology and ecclesiastical polity.[239]

By contrast, even the most 'advanced' figures in English politics, if they were not within this denominational nexus, tended not to feel any unusual affinity with Americans. The Deist John Wilkes, taking refuge from the law in Paris, wrote in November 1765: 'If I am to be an exile from my native London, it shall not be in the new world: so far I can command'; when back in the King's Bench Prison, he disappointed an eager Bostonian admirer in April 1769, who reported that Wilkes 'often with a Sneer enquires after his Friends in the Howling Wilderness as he terms us'.[240] Wilkes's later support for the American cause related to tactical expediency, not prior commitment. Nor was Dissent alone sufficient to produce alignment among Englishmen with the American cause: the Protestant Dissenting Deputies, the London-based committee organised in 1732 to represent the interests of Presbyterians, Congregationalists and Baptists, failed to address the American issue during the revolution.[241] More was needed: and the new feature was what marked out heterodox from orthodox. Even this was insufficient to sustain insurrection without the sort of social constituency that denominational identity most commonly supplied. A minority tradition within English Dissent sustained a reactivated millenarian tradition from the 1760s; but this was countered by the forces of order in public debate in ways which limited the expression of that tradition to individual eccentricities.[242] Dissent had its main impact via its weight in parliamentary elections, and here it was

---

[238] Remarkably, America scarcely features in the voluminous evidence presented by E. P. Thompson, *The Making of the English Working Class* (London, 1963). The American rebellion or its heroes similarly did not feature as images in the threatening letters sent by English plebeians to their masters, although the Jacobite menace had been so used, and the Jacobin threat shortly would be: E. P. Thompson, 'The Crime of Anonymity' in Douglas Hay (et al., eds), *Albion's Fatal Tree: Crime and Society in Eighteenth-Century England* (London, 1975), pp. 255–344.

[239] For the traditional explanation, which sees major similarities between the opposition grievances of the 1760s in England and the conventionally-rehearsed secular causes of the American Revolution, see Sainsbury, *Disaffected Patriots*, pp. 13–21; Pauline Maier, *From Resistance to Revolution: Colonial Radicals and the Development of American Opposition to Britain, 1765–1776* (London, 1973).

[240] Quoted in Sainsbury, *Disaffected Patriots*, pp. 33, 244.

[241] Ibid., p. 81.

[242] Clark, *English Society 1688–1832*, pp. 276–348; Garrett, *Respectable Folly*, pp. 121–230; E. P. Thompson, *The Making of the English Working Class*.

the alignment of whole denominations, not minorities of extremists, which mattered.

Popery and poverty meanwhile remained as much a popular identity as a literary trope, as the Gordon Riots of 1780 once more emphasised.[243] These riots, massive in their scope and potentially destabilising of the government, were a reaction to the Catholic Relief Act of 1778, inopportunely passed when the entry into the war of France and Spain allowed the old anti-Catholic phobias to be expressed once more in the guise of conspiracy theory. Although the riots occurred in London, however, the message was far more effective in Scotland than in the English regions, and the propaganda work of its pressure group, the Friends to the Protestant Interest in Scotland, far more effective than that of the Protestant Association south of the border. In England, the petitions of 1779 for repeal of the Relief Act often correlated with centres of Dissent, and this social constituency was insufficient to achieve its ends or to fuel significant disorder in the provinces. The great scale of violence in the London disturbances of June 1780, which left 285 dead and much property destroyed, went far beyond these denominational sources: it revealed instead, in the metropolis as simultaneously in America, the way in which predispositions to resist authority with force, once activated by minorities, could swiftly escalate into a catastrophe which swept along large numbers of bystanders, driven by emotions only tenuously connected with the constitutional point at issue.[244]

If this discourse was more effective in Scotland than in England, it was more momentous again in Ireland. There, Presbyterians had compensated for their exclusion from political participation under the Anglican ascendancy by sustaining an ecclesiastical polity in internal exile, the Synod of Ulster, preoccupied, on a theoretical level, by the issues of church-state relations. During the exceptional stresses produced by the American war, the differences of view which that denomination contained were resolved into a militant hostility to British rule, and the Presbyterian population was 'transformed . . . into a citizen army', the Volunteer movement,[245] which threatened to prise Ireland free from English control at the same time as it defended Protestantism from the surrounding Cath-

[243] J.P. de Castro, *The Gordon Riots* (Oxford, 1926); John Stevenson, *Popular Disturbances in England, 1700–1870* (London, 1979), pp. 76–90.

[244] This paragraph draws on the results of Colin Haydon, *Anti-Catholicism in Eighteenth-Century England*, chapter 5. Haydon emphasises the mob's desire to legitimate their actions, to echo the due processes of law, to be selective in its targets and to be unwilling to take life: all features, it may be suggested, which characterised the mass action of the early stages of the revolution in America.

[245] Peter Brooke, *Ulster Presbyterianism: The Historical Perspective 1610–1970* (Dublin, 1987), p. 113.

olic majority. This same sense of a denominationally-defined society in arms was carried to America in the massive wave of emigration from Ulster which reached its height in the early 1770s and broke in 1776.

By the 1790s, the nature of the revolutionary stresses in England is more clearly evident in those instances where a threat became a reality. The naval mutinies[246] at Spithead and the Nore in 1797 encapsulated in enclosed communities the patterns more diffusely evident in the nation at large: material suffering, the combination of men in situations which facilitated both organisation and mass emotion, the catalysing role of leaders with particular identities. But the Spithead mutiny was quelled by swift practical concessions, and even the Nore mutineers were eventually persuaded to return to duty and to carry out the executions of the ring-leaders on board their own ships. Such a pattern does not suggest the prior existence of widespread Jacobin organisation or principled commitment among the seamen, however explosive their practical grievances might become if a catalyst were present.[247]

The most likely problem was again within a denominational social constituency, the substantial Irish Catholic contingent on board the fleet, and the catalyst was provided by the presence among them of committed United Irishmen. These activists injected a distinctively sectarian element into the violent and unstable world of the lower decks: it proved decisive. Evidence for 1797 is inconclusive, but clearer for incidents in 1798.[248] On board HMS Cambridge, leading mutineers administered an oath to the crew 'to be United Irishmen, equal to their brethren in Ireland, and to have nothing to do with the King, or His Government'. Despite the interdenominational basis of the United Irish movement at its inception,[249] one of the ringleaders, Michael Butler, was testified to have declared

> that there ought to be a Catholic Government in Ireland; that the Protestants should be expelled; and that the English had no right to be there: he also wished to be in Ireland to assist in the rebellion, and to recover the title and estate of Ormond, of which, he said, his family had been unjustly

[246] B. Dobrée and G. Mainwaring, *The Floating Republic* (3rd edn., London, 1937); J. Dugan, *The Great Mutiny* (London, 1966).

[247] The applicability of this pattern to the rest of English society is suggested by the evidence deployed in Christie, *Stress and Stability*, and John Bohstedt, *Riots and Community Politics in England and Wales, 1790–1810* (Cambridge, Mass., 1983).

[248] Marianne Elliott, *Partners in Revolution: the United Irishmen and France* (New Haven, Conn., 1982), pp. 134–44; Roger Wells, *Insurrection: The British Experience 1795–1803* (Gloucester, 1983), pp. 79–109, 145–51.

[249] W. D. Killen, in J. S. Reid and W. D. Killen, *History of the Presbyterian Church in Ireland* (3 vols., Belfast, 1867), argued that Presbyterian involvement in the United Irish movement was largely confined to the anti-Trinitarian New Light wing of Presbyterianism. For a different interpretation see Brooke, *Ulster Presbyterianism*, pp. 129–30.

deprived by the English ... that he should never die easy till he swam in English blood.

Similarly, mutineers on board HMS Defiance had allegedly taken an oath

> to be true to the Free and United Irishmen, who are now fighting our cause against tyrants and oppressors; and to defend their rights to the last drop of my blood, and to keep all secret; and I do agree to carry the ship into Brest the next time the ship looks out a-head at sea, and to kill every officer and man that shall hinder us, except the master; and to hoist a green ensign with a harp on it; and afterwards to kill and destroy all the Protestants.[250]

The naval mutinies acted out, in miniature, the most likely scenario of revolution in 1790s England. For the chief threat to English domestic stability was that variant of Jacobinism which might be imported from Ireland; and that variant (unlike the French original) was given its distinctiveness in a sectarian context.

Protestant ascendancy in eighteenth-century Ireland was defended by the evocation of horrific memories of Catholic self-assertion, from the massacre of Protestants in 1641 to the civil war of 1689–91. Popular stories of murder and outrage, still widely in circulation, were complemented by a literature which kept the events of 1641 at the centre of debate.[251] Sir John Temple's history of that episode, a 'large collection of lurid and harrowing stories of boiling, stoning, stripping, disembowelling, mutilating, hanging, whipping and drowning', performed for Irish Protestants what Foxe's *Book of Martyrs* performed for English Protestants: it provided at once an heroic self-image and a warning of the unchanging nature of an ancient enemy. Fear of a Catholic massacre of the Protestants survived and could be reactivated by every instance of an armed disturbance.[252] Like the stresses induced in the American colonies by negro slavery, unreconciled denominational divisions in Ireland drew on ancient discourse and revitalised ancient images.

From the Gordon riots and their revelation of the lasting force of English plebeian anti-Catholicism it was a short step to the most sanguinary example of insurrection in the British Isles since the war of 1689–91 and the one which came closest to overthrowing the English, Anglican hegemony. In the Irish rebellion of 1798 many thousands of men, women and children lost their lives in circumstances of the most extreme sectarian

---

[250] *Report of the Committee of Secrecy of the House of Commons. Ordered to be Printed 15th March, 1799* (London, 1799), pp. 72–3.

[251] Sir John Temple's *The Irish Rebellion* (London, 1646) was repeatedly reprinted through the eighteenth century and countered by a succession of authors arguing the Catholic case. Cf. David Berman, 'David Hume on the 1641 Rebellion in Ireland', *Studies* 65 (1976), 101–12.

[252] Thomas Bartlett, 'A New History of Ireland', *P&P* 116 (1987), 213–16.

savagery.[253] Nevertheless, the increasingly sectarian nature of the rebellion came as an unwelcome surprise to many. Even in the mid-1790s, it was claimed in Ireland that relations between Catholic and Protestant were good; that Irish aspirations had been caught up in a non-denominational Jacobinism as the natural culmination of modern libertarian or heterodox ideals. Yet beneath the euphemisms of *bienpensant* opinion, peasant violence, including sectarian conflict, had been growing since the 1760s;[254] the slight predominance of Catholics in the leadership of the Dublin United Irishmen gave scope for a sectarian motivation from the outset,[255] even before 1798 reasserted the polarities of 1641. Ulster 'New Light' Presbyterians had grown increasingly restive at the survival of the Anglican ascendancy;[256] the early union of Catholic and Presbyterian in the United Irish movement was impelled more by sectarian motives of a combination against the Church of Ireland than the rhetoric of the movement implied.

The outbreak of fighting in May 1798 quickly exposed the apocalyptic fury which drove the rank and file on each side. Catholic peasant insurrections singled out local Protestant targets for sudden massacre. The Catholic bishop of Wexford, Dr Caulfield, was aghast at the nature of the popular passions now unleashed: 'The People could not be described . . . in reality the Devil was roaring among them . . . they would make it a religious War which would ruin them.'[257] In turn, the Protestant forces reacted to the threat and the reality of massacre with similar acts of sectarian violence. Thanks to this traumatic episode, nineteenth century Irish self-images were to take shape within a matrix of Catholic sectarian allegiance rather than Enlightenment secularism; and it was a Catholicism activated by a powerful millenarian dynamic. Into the 1840s, apocalyptic overtones of holy war against Protestants were recurring themes in

---

[253] Thomas Pakenham, *The Year of Liberty: The Story of the Great Irish Rebellion of 1798* (London, 1969); Elliott, *Partners in Revolution*, pp. 165–240; Wells, *Insurrection*, pp. 131–61. Casualties are often put in the region of 20–30,000, but accurate records are not available.

[254] Maureen Wall, 'The Whiteboys' in T. D. Williams (ed.), *Secret Societies in Ireland* (Dublin, 1973), pp. 13–25; J. S. Donnelly, 'The Whiteboy Movement, 1761–5', *Irish Historical Studies* 21 (1978), 20–54; Michael Beames, *Peasants and Power: The Whiteboy Movements and their Control in Pre-Famine Ireland* (Brighton, 1983), pp. 21–41; Jim Smyth, *The Men of No Property: Irish Radicals and Popular Politics in the Late Eighteenth Century* (London, 1992), pp. 33–51.

[255] R. B. McDowell, 'The Personnel of the Dublin Society of United Irishmen, 1791–4', *Irish Historical Studies* 2 (1940–1), 12–53; A. T. Q. Stewart, "A Stable and Unseen Power': Dr. William Drennan and the Origins of the United Irishmen' in J. Bossy, (et al., eds), *Essays Presented to Michael Roberts* (Belfast, 1976), pp. 80–92; M. Wall, 'The United Irish Movement', *Historical Studies* 5 (London, 1965), 122–40.

[256] H. Senior, *Orangeism in Ireland and Britain, 1795–1836* (London, 1966); Elliott, *Partners in Revolution*, pp. 20–1.

[257] Quoted in Pakenham, *Year of Liberty*, p. 190. For the recent debate on the extent of sectarian motivation in the rebellion see Smyth, *The Men of No Property*, pp. 178–81.

proletarian Irish Catholic culture.[258] This seventeenth-century commitment found its modern expression in Daniel O'Connell's movement for Catholic 'Emancipation': O'Connell appealed to the electors of County Clare in 1828 not on the basis of democratic theory but in order to sweep away the oath required of Westminster MPs, including the proposition, to Roman Catholics blasphemous, 'That the sacrifice of the Mass and the invocation of the blessed Virgin Mary and other saints as now practiced in the Church of Rome are impious and idolatrous.'

The poll was attended by 'processions of freeholders, with their parish priests at their heads ... marching like troops to different quarters' beneath banners with such messages as 'Vote for Your Religion'. Appropriately, O'Connell called the County Clare election 'in reality, a religious ceremony, where honest men met to support upon the altar of their country, the religion in which they believed'. Such threats were effective political levers because they drew on memories of agrarian insurrection since 1798: Wellington at once saw that 'We have a rebellion impending over us in Ireland.'[259] Emancipation failed to assuage these ancient hatreds, which passed at once into the land war. A threatening handbill from Cashel, Co. Tipperary, in 1836 spoke of something more momentous than the tithes dispute which was its formal occasion: 'Heretics prepare for death ... The day is approaching when we will root the bloody heretics out of the world ... Let them prepare to meet the flaming devils.'[260] The nineteenth century had opened amid much rhetoric about improvement and the march of mind; but the elemental forces which now threatened to destroy modern achievements indicated a pattern of idioms of discourse not as different from those which disturbed the Restoration period as the rhetoric of polite and commercial sociability would suggest.

Scotland meanwhile remained undisturbed by rebellion during the reign of George III, its dynastic framework for resistance dismantled by the dispersal of the Jacobite challenge. Yet the theological preconditions for a remarkable Scots counter-offensive against Anglican England in the 1820s and 30s were already present. Anti-Trinitarianism had initially been a capital offence in Scotland, as the execution of the student Thomas Aikenhead in 1697 demonstrated; but thereafter Arianism made steady headway among the definers of 'politeness'. The trial for heresy of John Simson, professor of theology at Edinburgh, revealed the influence of the writings of the English Arian Dr Samuel Clarke. Simson taught Francis

[258] S. J. Connolly, *Priests and People in Pre-Famine Ireland 1780–1845* (Dublin, 1982), pp. 12–13, 110.
[259] Quoted in Fergus O'Ferrall, *Catholic Emancipation: Daniel O'Connell and the Birth of Irish Democracy 1820–30* (Dublin, 1985), pp. 193, 197, 200, 203.
[260] Quoted in Connolly, *Priests and People*, p. 13.

Hutcheson (1694–1746); when the chair of theology at Glasgow fell vacant in 1743, Hutcheson in turn secured the appointment of his pupil William Leechman; it was through Leechman that 'the opinions of the English Arians came to be popular in Scotland, and he may be regarded as one of the founders of the school of Moderatism'. As Leechman's protégé William MacGill's *A Practical Essay on the Death of Jesus Christ* (Edinburgh, 1786) demonstrates, 'the Arian Movement in England and Moderatism in Scotland were identical'.[261] The devastatingly effective military conquest of Scotland in 1745–6, and that country's re-education in Whig principles thereafter, were lessons to colonial Americans of what they could expect if armed resistance in 1776 failed. Military repression postponed the impact of the Scottish 'Enlightenment' on England for a generation; but the effects of the extreme views of the 'Moderate' party were at length registered in the pages of the *Edinburgh Review* and given their impact at Westminster through the role at Holland House, the London salon of the Whig opposition, of angry Scots zealots like Sir James Macintosh, Henry Brougham, Robert Allen and James Mill.[262]

VII. DENOMINATIONS, SOCIAL CONSTITUENCIES AND THEIR ACTIVATION

Many denominational groups had been led to emigrate to America by their religious perceptions of mission or of persecution; but the experience of geographical mobility, upheaval, loss and uncertainty gave an immense impetus to ethnoreligious commitment. Within the British Isles only the geographically mobile and denominationally articulate Scots Irish displayed these characteristics to a marked degree, but through the experience of migration many other denominations came to share them. This created a new society which exaggerated rather than escaped certain characteristics of the old society; a new society whose denominational components were more, not less, open to political mobilisation. It was this potential for mobilisation which was challenged by its negation in Anglican political theology, and this ethnoreligious pluralism which was threatened by those great homogenising systems, the Church of England and the common law.

Increasing waves of immigration swamped many of the English colonies of seventeenth-century settlement and turned their populations, by

---

[261] J. Hay Colligan, *The Arian Movement in England* (Manchester, 1913), pp. 130–1.
[262] See Clark, *English Society 1688–1832*, pp. 349–420; idem (ed.), *Waldegrave Memoirs*, pp. 112–34; William Thomas, *The Philosophic Radicals: Nine Studies in Theory and Practice 1817–1841* (Oxford, 1979); Biancamaria Fontana, *Rethinking the Politics of Commercial Society: The Edinburgh Review 1802–1832* (Cambridge, 1985).

the 1770s, into societies more ethnically diverse than any other of the English-speaking world. It was in this setting of bewildering and increasing ethnic diversity that denominational affiliation took on an increasing role in defining ethnoreligious boundaries. The principles of voluntary association and providentially-reinforced collective authority were thereby reconciled, at the same time as the experience of uprooting and the attendant motivations to cling to familiar religious certainties led to a heightened stress in each denomination on correct behaviour.[263] America's denominational culture was even more ethical than those of its parent societies; for that reason also it was more open to political mobilisation.

None of these developments were contradicted by transatlantic trends in war, trade or administration. England's Atlantic empire during the seventeenth and eighteenth centuries presents a picture of dynamic social development offset by long continuities in political discourse, carefully nurtured and deliberately preserved. Conflict, massacre, schism and sometimes successful rebellion were set against structural change and commercial development, substantial though irregular and always threatened by the stresses and outcomes of war or insurrection.[264] Rebellions and the threat of rebellion were not daily occurrences; but they were frequent enough that they cannot be dismissed as exceptions to a norm in which the right of resistance was either absent from the dominant traditions of political discourse, or (as in ministerial English Whig discourse) had been reduced to a remote and theoretical abstraction. The boundaries within which those rights of resistance were defined, and the means by which social groups thus demarcated were mobilised, are central questions for the history of the Atlantic world.

The persistent advocacy of such a right of resistance had wide implications for the social dynamics of early-modern societies, and justifies the characterisation of those dynamics as essentially denominational. Where rebellion was avoided, it has never been demonstrated that its absence is chiefly to be explained in terms of the inner workings of parliamentary institutions: these failed to provide a remedy for the ills which assailed England's territories. 'Political stability' is a term appropriate, if at all, only for a period of single-party domination of English ministries between the 1720s and 1750s; but it was an ascendancy so widely challenged from without and so often contested from within that this period displays no

---

[263] Timothy L. Smith, 'Religion and Ethnicity in America', *AHR* 83 (1978), 1155–85, at 1168, 1175.

[264] Peter Laslett, *The World We Have Lost Further Explored* (London, 1983), pp. 182–209; N. F. R. Crafts, *British Economic Growth During the Industrial Revolution* (Oxford, 1985); E. A. Wrigley, *Continuity, Chance and Change: The Character of the Industrial Revolution in England* (Cambridge, 1988).

fundamental contrast with the period before 1714 or after 1760. Political parties were no magic inventions to still this maelstrom, but vehicles for ideological and denominational antagonism.[265] Far from an Anglophone constitutional tradition having eliminated revolutionary challenges after 1688, continuities of ideology and religious discourse show how rebellions were linked by common features of denominational identity in the communities on which those rebellions drew for their support. As long as this sectarian pattern persisted, the secular, constitutional structures of political authority remained at risk because they acted as channels or agents for these mass passions; representative assemblies and courts of law, though they drew on an ancient mythology which in the nineteenth century was to endow them with secular authority, did not yet operate in a world in which religious ideology had come to an end.

Rebellions, then, although not a single sequence, were related to each other by their social constituencies; 1688 and 1776 were not the only two instances of rebellion to be so related, and the inclusion of the many other instances of insurrection in the English-speaking North Atlantic world reveals some unfamiliar patterns of causation. The familiar legal and constitutional tradition, dating back to early Stuart conflicts, was clearly still current;[266] but evidence for the social constituencies of rebellions sheds light on when and why that tradition was activated or turned from a defensive to an offensive creed, and why, at some times but not at others, numbers of men, and sometimes great numbers, were gripped by revolutionary frenzy. From the tiny Venner's rising of 1661 to the catastrophic Irish rebellion of 1798 and beyond, denominational discourse and its activation offers a common thread.[267] Moreover, however important were denominational differences within England, they were far more vivid in Scotland and Northern Ireland, from which a heavy preponderance of emigrants originated after c. 1680, and more pronounced again in the American colonies. If the impetus to the organisation and strengthening of the components of Anglo-Irish Protestant Dissent came from within the colonies rather than from parent bodies in the old world, the capacity of those denominations to act as political agents is less remarkable.[268]

[265] Eveline Cruickshanks, 'Religion and Royal Succession – The Rage of Party' in Clyve Jones (ed.), *Britain in the First Age of Party 1680–1750* (London, 1987), pp. 19–43.

[266] Margaret Atwood Judson, *The Crisis of the Constitution: An Essay in Constitutional and Political Thought in England 1603–1645* (New Brunswick, 1949); most recently emphasised by John Philip Reid, *Constitutional History of the American Revolution*, vol. 1, *The Authority of Rights*, vol. 2, *The Authority to Tax*, vol. 3, *The Authority to Legislate* (Madison, Wisconsin, 1986, 1987, 1991).

[267] Hannah Arendt, *On Revolution*, p. 19: 'no revolution was ever made in the name of Christianity prior to the modern age'.

[268] Timothy L. Smith, 'Congregation, State, and Denomination: The Forming of the American Religious Structure', *WMQ* 25 (1968), 155–76, at 169.

Denominational dynamics have been explained in these pages chiefly on the level of high theory, by drawing legal and theological disputes into the arena of the history of political thought. The same insight, however, could also be expressed in local studies of alignments and conflicts, drawn from evidence of settlement patterns and voting records. For Pennsylvania, whose extreme demographic diversities had not been homogenised in the 'melting pot' of later republican myth, the ethnic-religious lines of division are demonstrable.[269] Theological commitments, especially to or against Calvinism, acted to encourage alliances between denominations where major issues presented men with a clear binary choice.

In local colonial electoral districts, the propensity of each sect to vote as a unit was pronounced, overriding economic, occupational, geographic or class considerations. The fluctuations in the fortunes of these groupings were as marked as their clarity of definition: the years after the Tea Party crisis of 1773–4 saw the steep decline of the Quaker-Anglican alliance in the face of the astonishing rise of the Presbyterians and, within that denomination, of the hitherto politically-reticent Scots-Irish component.[270] Not least of the effects of the American Revolution within America was an irreversible transfer of power from the denominations implicated in the old order to expanding or newly-political denominations which defined themselves in antithesis to a government which was ultimately identified with an Anglican establishment. This transfer of power occurred in local patterns of great complexity which varied from colony to colony; but the common features of the process are established by the denominations' consistency across the colonies, and indeed across the Atlantic, in their attachment to certain characteristic assumptions and traditions concerning power, authority and liberty.[271] Even where specifically ecclesiastical issues like toleration or establishment were not the subject of action by the States, the denominations displayed an awareness of their collective identity which derived from the major premises with which their religious traditions provided them.

To successive threats framed in these sectarian terms, English (and Anglican) hegemony was forewarned but vulnerable. To a marked degree, England's hold over her dependencies rested on recognised authority

---

[269] Owen S. Ireland, 'The Ethnic-Religious Dimension of Pennsylvania Politics, 1778–1779', *WMQ* 30 (1973), 423–48; Wayne L. Bockelman and Owen S. Ireland, 'The Internal Revolution in Pennsylvania: An Ethnic-Religious Interpretation', *Pennsylvania History* 41 (1974), 125–59; O. S. Ireland, 'The Crux of Politics: Religion and Party in Pennsylvania, 1778–1789', *WMQ* 42 (1985), 453–75.

[270] Bockelman and Ireland, 'Internal Revolution', pp. 133, 141, 149.

[271] From a different perspective, see David Hackett Fischer, *Albion's Seed: Four British Folkways in America* (New York, 1989), which traces these distinctions primarily to regionally-demarcated and materially-defined cultures within the British Isles but acknowledges the power of the religious determinants of those cultures (p. 795).

rather than on military power, and civil authority was closely bound up with the authority of its legitimating Church of England. (Scotland, where episcopalianism took a Jacobite direction, was an exception.) The government of England's Atlantic empire rested chiefly on the acceptance of the legitimacy first of the Restoration of 1660, then of the Revolution settlement of 1689. Acceptance of both civil and religious settlements was extensive; but rejection too was extensive, and took various forms. The parochial realities of Anglican hegemony and inter-denominational conflict in England and the thirteen colonies have already been outlined.[272] This diverse denominational pattern emphasises that Anglicanism was never a monopoly except in particular localities and cannot be described as a consensus; denominational diversity produced a conflicting range of political discourses in which those of the Church of England and the common law exercised an uneasy hegemony. As in other post-revolutionary regimes, open criticism of the state from fundamentally different premises was suppressed. But this merely diverted criticism into a second channel: the Glorious Revolution was accepted, but successive governments condemned for falling short of its ideals.

This rhetoric is not, however, evidence for the intrinsically libertarian nature of the constitutional rearrangements of 1689: no shared, constitutional libertarianism abolished the significance of denominational divisions. Indeed, in America more even than in England, 1689 deserved the label 'revolution' in its traditional meaning in that it substantially restored the *status quo ante* James II. This did not prevent the continued evolution of the functional realities of royal administration. In America, a tightening of English administration and a reassertion of English sovereignty equally followed the conflicts of 1641–60 and 1756–63. Colonial resistance equally followed in 1689 and 1776. But from the English perspective, nothing that happened in the colonies in 1689 had been allowed to overturn the late-Stuart claim of England's absolute sovereignty.[273] Thus in 1776 Englishmen could believe they were maintaining the settlement of 1689; colonists might think they were asserting the principles of 1689 against a resurgent absolutism. It is those perceptions which require explanation. Perceptions of tyranny, and the social constituencies around which resistance to tyranny might be organised, were both, it has been argued, often explicable in terms of denominational distinctions: practical cohesion, and political discourse, often followed the boundaries of churches or sects. This is, however, to frame the question as much as to answer it. For if, by implication, the familiar material grievances of Amer-

---

[272] See above, chapter 2, parts IV–VI.
[273] See above, chapter 1, parts II–III.

ican settlers or of English, Scots or Irish proletarians are held to have been insufficient in themselves to mobilise insurrection, the problem is transposed rather than resolved: how was denominational discourse activated?[274]

This is the question next to be addressed. Yet not every revolution is a civil war: the term 'revolution' is often reserved for episodes of national emancipation from foreign oppression or from an outdated and fragile social structure. Neither of these characterisations is particularly helpful in explaining the conflicts addressed in this book, and to appreciate the profound social divisions which made the events of 1776–83 a civil war but not a revolution, the interplay of denominational discourse must now occupy a central place.

---

[274] It has rightly been observed that study of the relationship between religion and ethnicity has shown the inadequacy of the metaphors of 'melting pot' and 'mosaic', and led towards a picture of 'kaleidoscopic change', not reducible to any 'set of fixed primordial realities [which] lies behind . . . changing ethnoreligious relationships': Smith, 'Religion and Ethnicity in America', 1185. Political mobilisation now emerges as one aspect of that kaleidoscopic change.

4

Political mobilisation: the American Revolution as a war of religion

I. THE AMERICAN REVOLUTION AS A CIVIL WAR

The passionate commitments on both sides of the Atlantic which made armed conflict unavoidable, and the loyalties in America and Britain which the conflict promoted, obscured in retrospect an important truth: in functional terms, the American Revolution shared most of the characteristics of a civil war.[1] One such characteristic was the way in which both sides seemed to appeal to a common tradition. In 1774 a loyalist addressed the Congress: 'You may still profess yourselves to be his *Majesty's most dutiful and loyal subjects*, as you did in your late RESOLVES, and as the leaders in the grand rebellion of 1641 did, in their messages to the King immediately after the battle of *Edge Hill*, where they had fought against him in person'; but this would not save America from the 'desolation and slaughter' of a civil war.[2] Between Washington's assuming command of the Continental Army in July 1775 and the Declaration of Independence on 4 July 1776, he and his officers professed their continuing allegiance to George III in a way which indeed recalled the rhetoric of Parliamentary forces in the 1640s.

For similar reasons many English officers refused to accept a command in America, like General Lord Frederick Cavendish and Admiral Keppel, or spoke against the war in Parliament, like General Henry Seymour Conway; few of those in the field had much stomach for the conflict.[3]

---

[1] The profound divisions in English opinion have attracted few historians. For the best study, though focused on 1775 alone, see James E. Bradley, *Popular Politics and the American Revolution in England: Petitions, the Crown, and Public Opinion* (Macon, Georgia, 1986); cf. Dora Mae Clark, *British Opinion and the American Revolution* (New Haven, 1930).

[2] *A Friendly Address to All Reasonable Americans, On the Subject of our Political Confusions* (New York; repr. London, 1774), p. 32.

[3] Don Higginbotham, *The War of American Independence: Military Attitudes, Policies, and Practice, 1763–1789* (New York, 1971), pp. 124–6, 129; Jeremy Black, *War for America: The Fight for Independence 1775–1783* (Stroud, 1991).

Some resigned their commissions, like Lord Effingham,[4] who protested to the Secretary at War: 'the very same principles which have inspired me with these unalterable sentiments of duty and affection to his Majesty, will not suffer me to be instrumental in depriving any part of his people of those liberties which form the best security for their fidelity and obedience to his government'.[5] Elite opinion fractured: the reviled Earl of Bute's fourth son served honourably in North America;[6] the patriot Earl of Chatham's eldest son,[7] hiding behind his father's fame and exploiting his mother's influence, abandoned his duties under General Guy Carleton in Canada, returned to England with despatches, and withdrew from active service.[8]

Popular opinion in England was divided also, and part of it, especially among Dissenters, was nearly as virulently disaffected as that in America. John Wesley, who had evidently moved in Dissenting circles, warned the ministry (though with evident agitated overstatement) of his impressions of the country during the previous two years: the widespread decay of trade; popular disaffection focused on the person of the king:

> the people in general all over the nation, are so far from being well satisfied that they are far more deeply dissatisfied than they appear to have been even a year or two before the Great Rebellion, and far more dangerously dissatisfied. The bulk of the people in every city, town, and village where I have been, do not so much aim at the ministry, as they usually did in the last century, but at the king himself. He is the object of their anger, contempt and malice. They heartily despise his majesty; and hate him with a perfect hatred. They wish to imbrue their hands in his blood; they are full of the spirit of murder and rebellion, and I am persuaded, should any occasion offer, thousands would be ready to act what they now speak.[9]

On both sides of the Atlantic, a Dissenting idiom of political discourse had been given focus, as in Tom Paine's *Common Sense*, in a bitter anti-monarchical diatribe. Within the British Isles beyond England, the divisions were more serious still. Scotland, conquered in 1745 and re-educated

---

[4] Thomas Howard (1747–91), 3rd Earl of Effingham. Old Etonian, Freemason and sloven, he was later rumoured to have taken part in fomenting the Gordon Riots.

[5] Lord Effingham to Lord Barrington, 12 April 1775, in [John Almon], *The Remembrancer, or Impartial Repository of Public Events*, vol. 1 (London, 1775), pp. 165–6.

[6] See the letters of Col. Charles Stuart to Bute in Mrs E. Stuart-Wortley (ed.), *A Prime Minister and His Son* (London, 1925), pp. 66–176.

[7] John Pitt (1756–1835), 2nd Earl of Chatham; he re-entered the army in 1778 and thereafter, until 1812, enjoyed a spectacularly undistinguished military career.

[8] Countess of Chatham to General Carleton, 14 Feb. 1776, in W. S. Taylor and J. H. Pringle (eds.), *Correspondence of William Pitt, Earl of Chatham* (4 vols., London, 1838–40), vol. 4, p. 420.

[9] John Wesley to Earl of Dartmouth, 23 Aug. 1775: Historical Manuscripts Commission. Fifteenth Report, Appendix, Part I. *The Manuscripts of the Earl of Dartmouth*, vol. 3 (London, 1896), p. 220.

in English Whig values thereafter, began to stir. Ireland, similarly conquered in 1689–93, partly betrayed by the biassed interpretation of the Treaty of Limerick and heavily garrisoned into quiescence in the following decades, seized its opportunity and almost broke free from the control of Westminster.[10] It was only when Britain's major military antagonists became, once again, the Catholic powers of France and Spain that the division of opinion within the British Isles over the wisdom and justice of reconquering America was smothered.

Within the colonies, the degree of support for the war varied greatly from region to region: as in the English Civil War, substantial numbers of Americans were neutral, lukewarm, or compelled to side with the victors in their localities.[11] From the Stamp Act in 1765 to the outbreak of fighting in 1775, loyalists had been menaced, victimised and intimidated at local level, in a pattern of collective patriotic action (or mob violence) which must have both provided a framework for popular sentiments of independence, and offered long and lurid warnings not to oppose future such expressions of the popular will. Given the early success of the patriot cause in mobilising the colonial militia in 1775, it is remarkable how large a section of the colonial population openly declared themselves principled loyalists[12] against their own interests: it is estimated that some 19,000 colonists enlisted in the Provincial Service in corps like Benedict Arnold's 'American Legion', Benjamin Thompson's 'King's American Dragoons' and Sir John Johnson's 'Royal Regiment of New York', together with at least thirty nine other smaller units, a figure which has been extrapolated to yield an estimate of about 500,000 loyalists in a population of the thirteen colonies of some 2,500,000 in 1775.[13] Of these it has been estimated that at least 60,000 (perhaps as many as 100,000) were forced into exile, losing their property; a figure, in relation to the American population, five times higher than that of the émigrés after the French Revolu-

---

[10] For the Scots and Irish dimension see John Cannon, *Parliamentary Reform 1640–1832* (Cambridge, 1973), pp. 98–115; Owen Dudley Edwards and George Shepperson (eds.), *Scotland, Europe and the American Revolution* (Edinburgh, 1976); David Noel Doyle, *Ireland, Irishmen and Revolutionary America, 1760–1820* (Dublin, 1981).

[11] John Shy, *A People Numerous and Armed: Reflections on the Military Struggle for American Independence* (revised edn., Ann Arbor, 1990), pp. 235–6.

[12] William H. Nelson, *The American Tory* (New York, 1961), p. 92, estimates loyalist support as half the population in New York, a quarter to a third in the South, a tenth in New England.

[13] Paul H. Smith, 'The American Loyalists: Notes on their Organisation and Numerical Strength', *WMQ* 25 (1968), 259–77. Support on this scale casts doubt on an alternative characterisation of the Revolution: Thomas C. Barrow, 'The American Revolution as a Colonial War for Independence', *WMQ* 25 (1968), 452–64.

tion. The financial losses of loyalists in both cases, judged by later compensation, were comparable.[14]

British officers serving in America, royal governors and colonial loyalist spokesmen consistently and disastrously overestimated potential loyalist military support;[15] but they had good reason for thinking that substantial loyalist sympathy could be evoked, however difficult it was to quantify.[16] Only a ruthless campaign of proscription succeeded in containing the loyalist threat: in each new state, the 'Revolutionary regimes stifled free expression, ordered arrests, impressed goods, confiscated land, and exiled their opponents'. Oaths of loyalty were drafted by state authorities and imposed on free male inhabitants on pain of disenfranchisement, prosecution, legal disability, penal taxation, confiscation of property, and finally exile. In New York, New Jersey and Pennsylvania committees of public safety sustained an inquisition into suspected loyalism, often themselves assuming judicial powers. In providing armed backing for these kangaroo courts the local militias found their most effective role[17] as 'a police force and an instrument of political surveillance'. Elsewhere,

> Wherever the British and their allies were strong enough to penetrate in force – along the seacoast, in the Hudson, Mohawk, and lower Delaware valleys, in Georgia, the Carolinas, and the transappalachian West – there Toryism flourished. But geographically less exposed areas, if population density made self-defence feasible – most of New England, the Pennsylvania hinterland, and piedmont Virginia – where the [British] enemy hardly appeared or not all, there Tories rather ran away, kept quiet, even serving in the rebel armies, or occasionally took a brave but hopeless stand against Revolutionary committees and their gunmen.[18]

Beside the official conflict between Washington's Continental army and his French allies, and British regular troops and their German allies, ran a desperate and more vicious guerilla war between loyalist and revolution-

[14] R.R. Palmer, *The Age of the Democratic Revolution* (2 vols., Princeton, 1959–64), vol. 1, pp. 188–90. The relative ease of emigration to Canada is a caution against treating these figures as directly comparable.

[15] Higginbotham, *War of American Independence*, pp. 134–7, 181, 241; for the adverse impact of this overestimate on British military strategy, Paul H. Smith, *Loyalists and Redcoats: A Study in British Revolutionary Policy* (Chapel Hill, 1964); Shy, *A People Numerous and Armed*, pp. 182–212.

[16] British officers consistently reported that loyalist support could be mobilised only by the presence of regular troops in sufficient numbers to protect the loyalists against local retribution; but such numbers were seldom available. Smith, *Loyalists and Redcoats*, pp. 12, 14–15, 62–3.

[17] Higginbotham, *War of American Independence*, pp. 257–87; Charles Royster, *A Revolutionary People at War: The Continental Army and American Character, 1775–1783* (Chapel Hill, N.C., 1979), pp. 105–7.

[18] Shy, *A People Numerous and Armed*, pp. 175–9; Nelson, *The American Tory*, pp. 85–115.

ary; as a South Carolina loyalist officer described it, 'the whole province resembled a piece of patch work, the inhabitants of every settlement, when united in sentiment being in arms for the side they liked best & making continual inroads into one anothers settlements'; both parties were 'equally afraid of the other', alternately terrorised and terrorising, in 'every other part of the province wherever it was checquered by this intersection of Whig & Tory settlements'.

> The cruelties the Whigs exercised upon the Tories, which seemed to be carried to their utmost excess under the auspices of Genl Green when he invaded the province, were now returned upon them with interest, and both parties in this petty, but sanguinary war displayed prodigies of military skill & address & seemed to breathe the extirpation of their enemies.[19]

Reports of the 'savage fury' of these parochial conflicts are linked with the understanding that principle, not just private vendetta, was at issue in the 'murderous suppression of loyalism'.[20]

Loyalists themselves, often victims of violence or the destruction of property, responded in kind and their counter-terrorism was often beyond the control of the British authorities. As Sir Henry Clinton explained in reticent language, the Loyalist refugees of South Carolina were

> a class of . . . men of a more ardent and enterprizing disposition, whose zeal and courage I have not yet been able to bend to the useful purposes they are by many thought equal to. Their former stations in life were above the level of the private soldier, and their spirits are not such as will permit them to submit totally to military control. Stung with resentment at the ignominious treatment they have received, and urged by indigence to venture their lives for the supply of their wants, their wish was to gratify their double impulse, and to ravish from their oppressors the property which had often in fact been their own. Such dispositions, as far as they induced the capture of obnoxious persons, of militia, and other soldiers, of forage wood, cattle and property of persons in rebellion, I was willing to encourage . . . But fearing indiscriminate depredations, and having some cause to suspect that a spirit of licentiousness was the chief motive with many adventurers of this class, I endeavoured to restrain their irregularities . . . These efforts have not as yet had the wished for effect.[21]

Lord Howe's secretary reported from New York how the revolutionaries'

---

[19] 'Colonel Robert Gray's Observations on the War in Carolina', *South Carolina Historical and Genealogical Magazine* 11 (1910), 139–59, at 153–4.

[20] Royster, *Revolutionary People*, pp. 278–82. Part of the later myth of the American Revolution was that popular political action was marked by a low level of personal violence. However true of the 1760s, this picture of events after 1776 is difficult to reconcile with military historians' accounts of the atrocities perpetrated by regular and irregular forces on both sides.

[21] Clinton to Lord George Germaine, 15 Dec. 1779, quoted in Shy, *A People Numerous and Armed*, pp. 208–9.

guerilla warfare tactics had provoked even regular troops to give no quarter: 'Tis truly shocking to hear what often passes on both Sides; and the Notion of Humanity and Kindred Blood begins to wear away.' He blamed the rebels: 'They rob, they imprison, and they murder, like Madmen: And the Ardor of our Troops begins to rise in Proportion.'[22]

Yet this savagery was not mere random violence. The antagonism and drive for vengeance of local communities had its inner logic, and one which contributed to British defeat: as a distinguished military historian has noted, 'close study of the areas committed to one side or the other supports the view that ethnic and religious differences were important determinants of Revolutionary behaviour'.[23] For the common soldier on the republican side, the call to war, the sense of personal obligation to fight, the nature of that American virtue which was to be vindicated and the happy future which victory would guarantee, were often expressed in religious terms.[24] This was the result not least of preaching which differed widely from the caution of denominational leaders. Lord Dartmouth was informed that one patriot minister

> told his Congregation, that 'the Man, who was able in this Country to wield a Sword and did not endeavor to stain it with the Blood of the King's Soldiers and their Abettors, would be renounced by the Lord Jesus Xt at the Day of Judgement'. Your Lordship can scarcely conceive, what Fury the Discourses of some mad Preachers have created in this Country . . . Low as my Opinion is of Man's fallen Nature in general, I never expected to find such uncommon Instances of Duplicity, Villainy, and Malice, as I have heard of and seen, in America, which has been so much talked of for Religion.[25]

The physical facts of suffering and death in battle were swamped by religious euphemism: 'Liberty or death was not a rhetorical exaggeration when the choice referred to the revolutionaries' minds . . . Slavery meant an infinite, hereditary misery, while death in resistance meant bliss.'[26]

Such men were fighting a holy war, either in the literal sense that their religion identified their enemy, predisposed them to resistance and vastly heightened the emotional temperature, or in the more general sense that patriotic zeal derived its force by analogy with religious enthusiasm. Emotional excess, a stress on moral absolutes of black or white, moral ardour,

[22] Ambrose Serle to Earl of Dartmouth, 20 March 1777, in Stevens (ed.), *Facsimiles*, vol. 24 (London, 1895), no. 2052.
[23] Shy, *A People Numerous and Armed*, p. 317.
[24] Royster, *Revolutionary People*, pp. 13–23, 152–89.
[25] Ambrose Serle to Earl of Dartmouth, 20 March 1777, in Stevens (ed.), *Facsimiles*, vol. 24 (London, 1895), no. 2052.
[26] Royster, *Revolutionary People*, pp. 32, 145–6.

uplifting goals and a reckless sacrifice of means to ends transported large numbers of men out of the cautious world of discourse populated by such idioms as the ancient constitution, chartered rights and common-law freedoms into an extravagant mind set within which killing was no murder. The *New Jersey Journal* of 4 May 1779 encapsulated this attitude in quoting 'A Jersey Soldier' on the reasons for the endurance of American troops in the previous two years: 'nothing but a kind of enthusiasm, in the sacred cause of freedom, could have secured their continuance in the army until this time'; they were engaged in effecting a 'glorious revolution'.[27] From the Coercive Acts to the end of the war, colonial loyalists too, though less often and with less fervour, drew on a providential interpretation of the British empire and God's purposes for it:[28] here too, a division within a shared body of ideas gives the Revolution the character of a civil war. For loyalists, however, it was the sin of rebellion which called down a Providential judgement on an erring people. It was Dissenting accounts of the active role of Providence which had been mobilised; Anglican accounts were on the intellectual defensive.

This influenced the shape of the new society as well as the inception of the rebellion. One characteristic of a civil war, fought on principles more than on material self-interest, is a capacity to divide communities. Exactly this was sensed by Crèvecoeur after the Revolution: 'The rage of civil discord hath advanced among us with an astonishing rapidity. Every opinion is changed; every prejudice is subverted; every ancient principle is annihilated . . . the son is armed against the father, the brother against the brother, family against family; the nearer the connexion, the more bitter the resentment, the more violent the rage of opposition.'[29] The Hessian Lieutenant Colonel von Dincklage observed the same thing during the course of the war. Whatever the outcome, he predicted, the Americans

> may have peace but not happiness when the war is over. It matters little whether the Americans win or lose. Presently this country is the scene of the most cruel events. Neighbours are on opposite sides, children are against their fathers. Anyone who differs with the opinions of Congress in thought or in speech is regarded as an enemy and turned over to the hangman, or else he must flee . . . If peace comes after an English victory, discord between the two parties will flare up underneath the ashes and nobody will

[27] William Nelson (ed.), *Documents Relating to the Revolutionary History of the State of New Jersey*, vol. 3 (Trenton, N.J., 1906), p. 307.

[28] John F. Berens, "A God of Order and Not of Confusion': The American Loyalists and Divine Providence, 1774–1783', *HMPEC* 47 (1978), 211–19.

[29] J. Hector St John de Crèvecoeur, *Sketches of Eighteenth-Century America*, ed. Albert E. Stone (Harmondsworth, 1981), pp. 342–3.

be able to resolve it. If the rebels should win, they will break their necks, one by one. What misery the people have plunged themselves into![30]

If a civil war was the shape of conflict within societies on both sides of the Atlantic which were mobilised as and by denominations, how was that result achieved?

II. PREDISPOSITIONS, ACCELERATORS AND CATALYSTS: THE ROLE OF THEOLOGY

Law and religion, in uniting the New World with the Old, both show how the theses of British and American exceptionalism could only begin to seem plausible after 1783. Colonial America indeed had its differences from its parent societies, just as the British kingdom had from the monarchies of France and Spain; but these differences did not make Britain essentially and fundamentally different from its continental European neighbours, and the image of America as a wholly new, unindebted and morally free-standing culture from the outset of colonisation is similarly untenable. Far from being unique, and therefore self-sufficient, even social and political innovations in the American colonies can only be explained within a transatlantic dimension. The American Revolution was no exception to this rule: like the other insurrections discussed in this book, it drew on the transatlantic social constituencies which the denominations identified. Yet 1776 was by far the largest of these episodes, not just in its consequences but in the way in which so many social groups and traditions of political discourse were activated and directed to a common end. 1776 therefore performs for both British and American historiography the same role which 1789 performs for their French counterpart: the most momentous problems of causation are brought to a single focus.

How were great masses of men mobilised in the early-modern transatlantic world? How were the political predispositions set by and within denominations activated, accelerated, and finally precipitated into the cataclysm of civil war? These vast processes have many aspects, political, military, and logistic prominent among them; but the present study is concerned to elucidate the intellectual pathways along which this process of mobilisation developed. The transatlantic setting is once more relevant. It has been argued, for late-eighteenth-century England, that there is a strong correlation – both a conceptual link and an identity of personnel – between heterodoxy in theology (but especially in Christology) and those new notions of individual political status which produced new doctrines

[30] New York Public Library, Hessian mss. no. 26, printed in Ernst Kipping, *The Hessian View of America 1776–1783* (Monmouth Beach, N.J., 1971), pp. 34–5.

of parliamentary representation; that these led to a profound religious critique of the 'Protestant Constitution' in Church and State and, eventually, to a movement for parliamentary reform. This model entails that, since 'radicalism' had not been conceptualised by 1800, it was heterodoxy which played a central role in activating principled opposition to the established order; by implication, that disaffection was not the simple reflex of material deprivation or disadvantage per se; similarly, that it was not the status of Dissenters as *the excluded* alone that *drove* them into disaffection. It was not that they were denied civil liberties, but, rather, that they came to define those liberties in new ways that produced a surge of political activism in England from the 1760s onwards.[31] Against this thesis, it has been argued that it was indeed the Dissenters' marginal location which drove them to such vocal political action, and that it was therefore their ecclesiastical polity and ecclesiology rather than their Christology[32] which was centrally at issue. Deprivation and exclusion have been reintroduced by another route, and the colonial identification of British rule with 'arbitrary power' has been significantly reinforced.[33]

In whichever way these explanations are to be balanced for late-eighteenth-century England, one consequence of their investigation is now apparent. In the context of this recovery of neglected idioms of political discourse, the events of the 1770s and 80s in America become once more intelligible in ways later obscured beneath layers of interpretation. This was sensed by John Adams in his advice to the historian Hezekiah Niles in 1818, a passage which recalls Burke's insight[34] into the French Revolution:

> But what do we mean by the American Revolution? Do we mean the American war? The Revolution was effected before the war commenced. The Revolution was in the minds and hearts of the people; a change in their religious sentiments of their duties and obligations.[35]

Adams's remark has indeed been quoted or partly quoted by later scholars, but with reference to 'hearts and minds', not 'religious senti-

---

[31] Clark, *English Society 1688–1832*.

[32] Christology has been defined as 'The study of the Person of Christ, and in particular the union in Him of the Divine and human natures': F. L. Cross and E. A. Livingstone, *The Oxford Dictionary of the Christian Church* (2nd edn, Oxford, 1974), p. 281. Ecclesiology is here taken to be the study of the ontological nature of the Church. Ecclesiastical polity, by contrast, is the structure and government of the Church on earth, in human history.

[33] This argument has been pioneered by James E. Bradley, most notably in *Religion, Revolution and English Radicalism: Nonconformity in Eighteenth-Century Politics and Society* (Cambridge, 1990). The debate has been importantly focused by A. M. C. Waterman, 'The Nexus between Theology and Political Doctrine in Church and Dissent' in Knud Haakonssen (ed.), *Enlightenment and Rational Dissent* (forthcoming). The present study addresses this debate in a transatlantic setting.

[34] See p. 222 above.

[35] John Adams to Hezekiah Niles, 13 Feb. 1818: Adams, *Works*, p. 282.

ments'. Yet because of the truth of his insight, the American Revolution displays, on a vast canvas, all these ancient British and ecclesiastical conflicts played out to a conclusion: militant imperial Anglicanism versus sectarianism and ethnic diversity; heterodoxy and what we know as the international Enlightenment versus dour, tradition-conscious orthodoxy, both Anglican and Calvinist; religious exclusiveness versus demands for toleration and the separation of Church and State; the right of rebellion versus the duty of allegiance: all these momentous issues made the American Revolution (among its other aspects) the last great war of religion in the western world, and potentially offer a more accessible set of indices to the roles of religious ideologies than the reform movements of late-eighteenth-century England, belated and poorly supported as, in comparison, they were.

Other developments in the historiography of early-modern England have also placed the American Revolution in a different setting. The political thought of the Revolution of 1688 and of the reigns of William and Anne has been profoundly reassessed.[36] An historical Locke has been recovered, not the successful framer of a new consensus but the frustrated planner of an older form of insurrection.[37] The early-Hanoverian Tory party has been rehabilitated, and its revolutionary potential explored.[38] The early-Hanoverian establishment is now visibly much more indebted to Whig High Churchmen than once it appeared;[39] the monarchy is now at the centre of our picture, and it is a resolutely traditionalist monarchy and its attendant court society which has been depicted.[40] From the standpoint of parliamentary political history, the large degree of continuity between the Pelhamite Whigs of George II's reign and the ministry of Lord North has been revealed.[41] For all these mutually-supporting reasons, it is much harder to sustain an argument for the 'resurgence of Toryism' in the reign of George III.[42] The result for the historiography

---

[36] J. P. Kenyon, *Revolution Principles: The Politics of Party 1689–1720* (Cambridge, 1977).

[37] Richard Ashcraft, *Revolutionary Politics and Locke's 'Two Treatises of Government'* (Princeton, 1986).

[38] Eveline Cruickshanks, *Political Untouchables: The Tories and the '45* (London, 1979); Linda Colley, *In Defiance of Oligarchy: The Tory Party 1714–60* (Cambridge, 1982); Paul Monod, *Jacobitism and the English People, 1688–1788* (Cambridge, 1989); Ian R. Christie, 'The Tory party, Jacobitism and the 'Forty-five: A Note', *HJ* 30 (1987), 921–31.

[39] S. J. C. Taylor, 'Church and State in England in the Mid Eighteenth Century: the Newcastle Years 1742–1762' (Cambridge Ph.D. thesis, 1987).

[40] Edward Gregg, *Queen Anne* (London, 1980); Ragnhild Hatton, *George I, Elector and King* (London, 1978); J. C. D. Clark (ed.), *The Memoirs and Speeches of James, 2nd Earl Waldegrave, 1742–1763* (Cambridge, 1988), Introduction.

[41] Ian R. Christie, 'Party Politics in the Age of Lord North's Administration', *Parliamentary History* 6 (1987), 47–68.

[42] James E. Bradley, 'The Anglican Pulpit, the Social Order and the Resurgence of Toryism during the American Revolution', *Albion* 21 (1989), 361–88 argues that contemporaries

of colonial America is to make the Revolution correspondingly harder to explain as a response to major innovations from Britain: British civil policy now seems more convincingly explicable in functional terms as a series of pragmatic responses to administrative problems.[43]

The thesis of discontinuity and British innovation has therefore been transferred to the sphere of political discourse. Yet religious affairs, similarly, do not easily illustrate a new authoritarianism. Many of the strongest expressions of Anglican resentment against rebel colonists were made by clergy who themselves had had experience as missionaries in America and were now either émigrés or had in other ways been targets of violence or abuse: Myles Cooper, East Apthorpe, Andrew Burnaby. Others, like those of Archbishop Markham and Bishop Thomas, dwelt on the sufferings of their fellow clergy in the colonies in ways which reflected reawakened memories of the 1640s. Writing like theirs is evidence for the widespread and violent targeting of loyalist episcopalians in the colonies rather than for a rise of ecclesiastical authoritarianism at home to which rebellion was a reaction.[44] Expressions of monarchical allegiance by English clergymen like John Coleridge, John Fletcher, George Horne and Richard Hurd have been advanced as evidence of 'an impressive resurgence of Tory ideas in the Anglican pulpit';[45] yet the novelty of their views has been greatly weakened by recent emphasis on the monarchical politics of Whig High Churchmen during the reigns of George I and George II. Prelates like Edmund Gibson (1669–1748), John Potter (?1674–1747) and Thomas Sherlock (1678–1761) supported a Whig regime with arguments drawn from a stock common to Whigs and Tories, but from which Whigs drew a conclusion which favoured the Hanoverian rather than the Stuart dynasty.[46] The novel elements in the scene, the innovations which transformed transatlantic relationships in the 1770s, are principally evident in

perceived a 'resurgence of authoritarianism', not without reason, since the preaching of such men as Thomas Nowell, Myles Cooper, John Fletcher, George Horne and others meant that 'during the American crisis Tory ideology was current once again', a 'political persuasion that in structure, content and tone was genuinely menacing to Dissenters and Commonwealthmen'. G. M. Ditchfield, 'Ecclesiastical Policy under Lord North', in John Walsh, Stephen Taylor and Colin Haydon (eds.), *The Church of England c. 1689 – c. 1833. From Toleration to Tractarianism* (Cambridge, 1993), argues for the lack of a persecutory spirit in the church, and in North's ecclesiastical policy, especially by comparison with the earlier part of the century. If so, we must trace the growing perception of authoritarianism to changes in the viewpoint of the political and religious opposition rather than to new initiatives by the establishment.

[43] Robert W. Tucker and David C. Hendrickson, *The Fall of the First British Empire: Origins of the War of American Independence* (Baltimore, 1982).

[44] Ditchfield, 'Ecclesiastical Policy under Lord North', passim.

[45] Bradley, *Religion*, p. 162.

[46] Clark, *English Society 1688–1832*, pp. 136–41; for an earlier period see George Every, *The High Church Party 1688–1718* (London, 1956).

the inner dynamics of life in the American colonies. Yet those dynamics were not self-sufficiently American, insulated from developments on the eastern side of the Atlantic. American and English innovations were, on the contrary, profoundly analogous. They differed in their scale and in their combinations rather than in their essence.

The pattern of political evolution of the American colonies demands also an explanation of their ethnic and, therefore, their sectarian dynamics: 1776 must be located within the long-term patterns of evolution of the North American settlements as well as within the short-term patterns of the evolution of colonial attitudes. New England and Virginia, beginning in the early seventeenth century as colonies of the English, united in many respects though divided in religion, were increasingly supplemented by waves of settlers who not only were not Anglican, but were not even English: lowland Scotland, and in even larger numbers Ulster, provided successive waves of migrants in the eighteenth century which profoundly modified not only the ethnic nature of the American population, but, more potently, its sectarian composition. By 1776 the colonies displayed neither that uniform, homogeneous society of Anglican High Churchmen's dreams, nor the homogeneous melting pot of later American legend, but a kaleidoscope of conflicting denominations – Anglicans, Congregationalists, Presbyterians, Baptists, Quakers, with a few Catholics, Huguenots and German Protestants, all subject to theological influences mostly emanating from Europe and all challenged by the Deism and scepticism of the international *bienpensants*. The American Revolution was doubly a civil war in that it tended to divide social groups in Britain as well as America: few ranks, professions or denominations even approached unanimity. Nevertheless, intellectual and practical leadership were not equally distributed. In England, 'the majority of English pro-Americans were Anglicans, and yet the Dissenters provided both the dominant ideology of opposition and the bulk of charismatic leadership for the pro-American agitation'.[47] Small groups of men precipitated the American rebellion and organised support for it, though they did so by playing successfully on the dispositions of the masses.

These popular dispositions generally had a large religious underpinning. Church polity was only the most visible outward sign of religious belief: each Dissenting sect necessarily defended its integrity first and foremost by defending its principle of church order. In any collision between denominations, it would be this around which controversy first turned: ecclesiastical polity, and perhaps ecclesiology, formed the outer

[47] Bradley, *Religion*, p. 158.

defences of Dissent. It did not follow that these were the first or original things at issue. For Protestant Dissenters, some doctrinal difference from Anglicanism was generally at the root of their wish to separate; a theory of church polity which permitted that separation was a means to an end, however much the course of controversy later made it appear an end in itself. And to the apparent priority of ecclesiastical polity there was one immense exception. The Church of England, after the Reformation, insisted for centuries, and with striking unanimity among its Trinitarian members, that it had no special doctrine of the nature of the Church to mark it out from Rome; that it was merely the local branch of that one holy, Catholic and Apostolic Church which it daily affirmed itself to be in its liturgy. The relations of Protestant Dissenters with the Church of England were essentially unlike the relations of the Church of England with the Roman Catholic Church. Anglicans were amazed and incomprehending when anti-papist hysteria was turned against them; but Protestant Dissenters perceived an essential truth when they saw that Anglican attachment to an episcopalian, hierarchical church order (and social order) was more than a contingent fact.

If ecclesiastical polity was the outward sign of the integrity of a denomination, Christology was its inner core. On this question, largely evaded during the English Reformation, raised in the 1640s in the work of men like John Biddle (1615–62) and John Fry (1609–57), suppressed by the Act of Uniformity of 1662 but explosively recurring after the Glorious Revolution,[48] everything else depended. To this degree, the doctrinal controversies begun in England in the 1690s were at least as momentous as those of the 1530s, and their practical consequences were far greater. They had practical consequences because they explored facets of what was still a single entity, the Anglican association of Church and State. Orthodox Christian theology too formed an interlocking system: the doctrine of predestination was bound up with those of the Incarnation and the Atonement; these in turn related to the doctrine of the Trinity. Calvinists suspected Arminians of holding a position which led swiftly to irreligion by denying the doctrine that salvation was offered only to the elect. From Bethesda, Georgia, the Calvinist George Whitefield made exactly this charge against the Arminian John Wesley in 1741: 'Infidels of all Kinds are on your Side of the Question. Deists, *Arians, Socinians*, arraign

---

[48] Robert Wallace, *Antitrinitarian Biography* (3 vols., London, 1850), vol. 1, pp. 138–392; Herbert John McLachlan, *Socinianism in Seventeenth-Century England* (Oxford, 1951); Gerard Reedy, S.J., *The Bible and Reason: Anglicans and Scripture in Late Seventeenth-Century England* (Philadelphia, 1985), pp. 119–41.

God's Sovereignty, and stand up for *Universal Redemption*.'[49] Arminians resisted this conflation; Wesley replied:

> you rank all the maintainers of *universal redemption* with Socinians themselves. Alas, my brother, do you not know even this, that the Socinians allow *no redemption* at all? That Socinus himself speaks thus: '*Tota redemptionis nostra per Christum metaphora*'? And says expressly, Christ did not die as a ransom for any, but only as an *example* for all mankind?[50]

On points of doctrine other than ecclesiastical polity and the Trinity,[51] the degree of common ground between the Church and the orthodox, Trinitarian sects was considerable: even the Westminster Assembly's *Confession of Faith* of 1647 taught a doctrine of the Eucharist indistinguishable from that of moderate Anglicanism.[52] Yet other differences between Nonconformists and Anglicans were often perceived to be large, and were keenly debated. In particular, this study focuses on two areas of difference: how far was it heterodoxy in Christology and how far long-standing Dissenting views on ecclesiology which provided the common factor among both colonists joining the revolution and English Anglican and Dissenting sympathisers with America, especially that smaller group in England which continued to support the Americans when an argument which began over civil liberties within the empire ended in armed conflict aimed at destroying it? In America similarly, Anglicans and Dissenters were divided: although a majority of loyalists were Anglicans, many Dissenters also joined them, and a similar balancing of explanations has to be made. Along what lines did the populations of England and America fracture? What similarities and what contrasts can be observed in the two examples? How can the political conduct be explained of those colonists who, although apparently orthodox in their religious belief, nevertheless fought for independence?

---

[49] George Whitefield, *A Letter to the Reverend Mr John Wesley: In Answer to his Sermon, entituled, Free-Grace* (London, 1741), p. 22.

[50] John Wesley to George Whitefield, 27 [sc. 28] April 1741, in Frank N. Baker (ed.), *The Works of John Wesley*, vol. 26, *Letters II 1740–1755* (Oxford, 1982), pp. 58–61.

[51] Epistemological debates over revelation between Deists, orthodox and evangelicals did not generally follow denominational boundaries: H. D. McDonald, *Ideas of Revelation: An Historical Study A.D. 1700 to A.D. 1860* (London, 1959).

[52] C. W. Dugmore, *Eucharistic Doctrine in England from Hooker to Waterland* (London, 1942), pp. 64–5; F. C. Mather, *High Church Prophet: Bishop Samuel Horsley (1733–1806) and the Caroline Tradition in the Later Georgian Church* (Oxford, 1992), pp. 5–6, 17–20. Caroline High Churchmen had a philosophical problem in expressing an understanding of the real presence which only began to be resolved by the early-Hanoverian Nonjurors (Dugmore, *Eucharistic Doctrine*, p. 153); until then, the degree of agreement within the Church of England was considerable. A new synthesis which lasted into the nineteenth century was attained, though with controversy, in the doctrine of Daniel Waterland (1683–1740), (ibid., pp. 167–83).

Schism, or the rise of new sects, could seem to owe everything to ecclesiology and might, in the short run, leave theology untouched. Political mobilisation, however, was a further step and was not obviously the result of innovations in ecclesiology alone: it will be argued below that in the 1760s and 1770s heterodoxy often acted as an accelerator of grievances long latent in denominations' inherited ideas on polity. For these reasons it seems an overstatement rather than a misapprehension to treat the 'Great Awakening' as 'in a vital respect an American declaration of independence from Europe', an agency for the Americanisation of the colonies.[53] The effects of revivalism were indirect, acting within and among denominations to erode arguments for sacred authority and only by implication for civil authority also. If revivalist fervour was not directed against British rule before 1763, some controlling reason must account for its redirection thereafter. On both sides of the Atlantic, religious revivalism was sometimes enlisted in support of governments, at other times pitted against them; the similarities of its symptoms fail to explain the diversities of its political results.[54] To explain these diversities, a more complex picture is needed of the evolution of those doctrinal questions which stood at the centre of denominational attention.

Nevertheless, it is undoubtedly true that far more men were mobilised in support of the revolutionary war after 1776 than subscribed to the latest fashionable heterodoxies, and some denominations in which those new movements of ideas are hard to trace were enlisted also in the cause of independence. Why was it that the activation of doctrines of ecclesiastical polity within particular denominations acted to mobilise both the orthodox within those denominations and also other, adjacent denominations preoccupied with other issues? One argument, identifying common features in Dissenters' economic situation or social marginalisation, fails to date the outbreak of insurrections or to explain the large degree of surviving Christological conflict between Dissenting denominations, both in Britain and America, whose objective social circumstances were similar. A fuller answer would stress the ecclesiological common ground between the sects, common ground which strengthened in the colonies under the stimulus of events but which in Britain developed along different paths, sometimes supportive of rather than undermining the regime.

---

[53] Alan Heimert, *Religion and the American Mind: From The Great Awakening to the Revolution* (Cambridge, Mass., 1966), p. 14.
[54] For England, from an extensive literature, see Eric Hobsbawm, 'Methodism and the Threat of Revolution in England' (1957), reprinted in idem, *Labouring Men* (London, 1964), pp. 23–33; E. P. Thompson, *The Making of the English Working Class* (London, 1963); Alan D. Gilbert, 'Methodism, Dissent and Political Stability in Early Industrial England', *Journal of Religious History* 10 (1978–9), 381–99.

One aspect of that common ground has been identified with the inclusive term 'providential thought'.[55] Revivalism and millennialism joined in the more general perception of Providence dealing with nations as well as with individuals, and when theological developments prompted a more strident colonial rejection of Anglican hegemony, the sense could be fostered that America itself might be a nation; that individual denominations' sense of being a people, a New Israel, might be projected on to the colonies as a whole in the dramatic scenario of international politics. Just such a scenario was provided by Britain's wars against France of 1739–48 and 1756–63, which (unlike earlier wars with American Indians) promoted the sense of an intercolonial common interest against the French and Spanish military threats at the same time as they identified the colonies as essentially libertarian and Protestant against a threat from without that was the opposite of these things.[56] It was above all denominational discourse, however, which increasingly placed Britain in France's role after 1763, for Providential libertarianism during the Seven Years' War had been as enthusiastically pro-British as it was later to be hostile to British rule. Although denominations shared much in their ecclesiastical polities and other doctrines, the issues which divided them, though fewer in number, were decisive in preserving their divisions and demanding that, if their very different track records are to be understood, they be analysed separately.

III. HETERODOX AND ORTHODOX IN THE CHURCH OF ENGLAND

In many sections of English society, opinion from 1776 was heavily against the independence of the colonies. It is true that American grievances in the 1760s, phrased as appeals to the rights of Englishmen and to the ancient constitution, had elicited substantial sympathy for the colonists. A body of moderate opinion had sought a negotiated settlement which would preserve Parliament's authority,[57] but once fighting began

---

[55] John F. Berens, *Providence & Patriotism in Early America 1640–1815* (Charlottesville, 1978). Berens writes of undifferentiated 'Americans' and does not examine the denominational divisions stressed in the present work.

[56] Ibid., pp. 32–50. Nathan O. Hatch, *The Sacred Cause of Liberty: Republican Thought and the Millennium in Revolutionary New England* (New Haven, Conn., 1977), p. 53 and passim, attributes political mobilisation in this period to a 'civil millennialism' rather than to the 'Great Awakening'. The nature of 'civil millennialism' might be further clarified if it is resolved into its denominational components. For a critique of the 'civil religion' thesis, see Harry S. Stout, *The New England Soul: Preaching and Religious Culture in Colonial New England* (New York, 1986), pp. 7, 271.

[57] It has been established that the Dissenting ministers subscribing pro-American petitions to the Crown in the 1770s included large numbers of the doctrinally orthodox: James E. Bradley, *Popular Politics and the American Revolution* (Macon, Georgia, 1986). But only a

support for the American cause fell away. This lent sharp definition to the remaining minorities whose former identification with American constitutional grievances now extended far further, to condoning armed rebellion itself.

Those minorities, whether Anglican or Dissenter, were not defined in England in ecclesiological terms. Men from all denominations, including the established Church, sided with the colonists. Late-eighteenth-century Anglicans did not often give priority to a doctrine of ecclesiastical polity, nor did they tend to offer a rigid interpretation of such a doctrine. Much of the alleged latitudinarianism of that Church derived from its relaxed stance on this matter of church order rather than from its more frequently cited source, heterodoxy on central doctrinal and Christological issues. Attention to questions of ecclesiastical polity usually related to only one facet of that question, the Church in its relations with the State; and here the tactical compromise of William Warburton deliberately steered discussion away from the nature of the Church as such. Although a High Churchman by background, even John Wesley's attitude to church polity was remarkably pragmatic. In January 1746 he recorded reading Lord King's tract on the primitive church,[58] published in 1691, and being persuaded by it that 'bishops and presbyters are (essentially) of one order, and that originally every Christian congregation was a church independent on all others!'[59] It authorised Methodist congregations to worship separately and use lay preachers, Wesley thought; but although he accepted the Presbyterian theory of ordination, he did not act on it in England until 1788–9.[60] Henceforth, his position was: 'Whether it be *lawful* or no (which itself may be disputed, being not so clear a Point as some may imagine) it is by no Means *expedient* for us to separate from the Establish'd Church.'[61] John Wesley's resolute opposition to the American rebellion strongly suggests that his flexible approach to church polity was not a contributory cause of pro-Americanism in the Anglican communion at large.

What part, then, did doctrinal heterodoxy play in shaping the political

---

smaller group supported armed rebellion, and they had a much clearer association with minority heterodox positions.

[58] [Peter, Lord King], *An Enquiry into the Constitution, Discipline, Unity & Worship of the Primitive Church, That Flourish'd within the First Three Hundred Years after Christ* (2 parts, London, 1691); esp. part 1, pp. sig. A2, 20, 32, 35, 49, 73–4, 83–4, 101, 106, 187, 191, 193.

[59] Quoted in Henry D. Rack, *Reasonable Enthusiast: John Wesley and the Rise of Methodism* (London, 1989), p. 292. Wesley had earlier read Bishop Stillingfleet's *Irenicum*, which he interpreted as proving that no form of church government was divinely ordained.

[60] Rack, *Reasonable Enthusiast*, p. 520.

[61] John Wesley, *Reasons Against a Separation from the Church of England* (London, 1758; 2nd edn., 1760), p. 3.

alignment of Churchmen? By the 1770s, the Dissenting minister Micaiah Towgood could attribute the generally-admitted decline in religion to the hypocrisy of Anglican clergy, forced to subscribe Articles 'which they do not *really believe*'. The Thirty-Nine Articles were 'strongly, what is called, *Trinitarian* and *Calvinistic*. Little less notorious is it, that the *Clergy* are, generally, gone far from the *religious sentiments* which the Articles express, and are many, or even most of them either *Unitarian* or *Arminian*.'[62] But there is evidence that he vastly exaggerated. Only some two hundred out of ten thousand Anglican clergy supported the Feathers' Tavern Petition for relief from subscription,[63] and fewer still left the Church after the petition's rejection: the doctrinal orthodoxy of mainstream Anglicanism distinguished it from its colonial counterpart.[64]

A large majority of laymen were Anglicans; Anglican clergy greatly outnumbered Dissenters. Yet only a small minority of Anglican clergy in England identified themselves as 'friends of America': 'The fact that some of them were tainted with the anti-Trinitarianism fashionable in the 1770s confirmed the impression that sound churchmanship and political orthodoxy went hand in hand.'[65] Since English sympathisers with the American cause included both Anglicans and Protestant Dissenters, ecclesiastical polity does not offer a very close correlation with political stance. Orthodox Anglicans were, however, sensitive to the issue of Christology within Anglican ranks as well as among Dissenters; perhaps alarms over the 'enemy within' were more urgent. Joseph Price observed in 1770 of his colleague Thomas Thompson, now Vicar of Elham after returning from six years with the Society for the Propagation of the Gospel as a missionary in New Jersey: 'Half a dissenter owing to having been in America.' And soon he discerned the nature of Thompson's dissent: 'Favourable to Arians. Talks of the liberty of private opinion ... '[66]

[62] [Micaiah Towgood], *Serious and Free Thoughts on the Present State of the Church, and of Religion* (4th edn., London, 1774), pp. 7, 9.

[63] R. B. Barlow, *Citizenship and Conscience: A Study in the Theory and Practice of Religious Toleration in England during the Eighteenth Century* (Philadelphia, 1962), pp. 150–1.

[64] F. C. Mather, 'Georgian Churchmanship Reconsidered: Some Variations in Anglican Public Worship 1714–1830', *Journal of Ecclesiastical History* 36 (1985), 255–83; idem, *High Church Prophet: Bishop Samuel Horsley (1733–1806) and the Caroline Tradition in the Later Georgian Church* (Oxford, 1992); E. A. Varley, *The Last of the Prince Bishops: William Van Mildert and the High Church Movement of the Early Nineteenth Century* (Cambridge, 1992); Peter Nockles, *The Oxford Movement in Context: the Transformation of Anglican High Churchmanship, 1760–1857* (Cambridge, forthcoming).

[65] Paul Langford, 'The English Clergy and the American Revolution', in Eckhart Hellmuth (ed.), *The Transformation of Political Culture: England and Germany in the Late Eighteenth Century* (Oxford, 1990), p. 277.

[66] G. M. Ditchfield and Bryan Keith-Lucas (eds.), *A Kentish Parson. Selections from the Private Papers of the Revd Joseph Price Vicar of Brabourne, 1767–1786* (Stroud, 1991), p. 40.

If the country clergy were vigilant on these issues, the university intelligentsia was even more aware. At Cambridge, added Joseph Price, John
Jebb's lectures 'had made so much noise' because he 'had been charged
with propagating Socinianism and Fatalism ([to] which Mr. Locke's
chapter on power is thought to look)'.[67] This was the Jebb whom John
Nichols called both 'a professed Arian' and 'a warm friend to the cause
of America against England, an incessant advocate for annual parliaments and universal suffrage'.[68] Richard Watson, later Bishop of Llandaff,
a reputed Socinian at Cambridge, backed the American cause in his
Cambridge sermon of 1776, *The Principles of the Revolution vindicated*, which
called on 1688 implicitly to validate resistance in 1776.[69] Watson later
denied that he was 'an Unitarian', but his tract *An Apology for Christianity*
of 1776 was welcomed on its publication by the Socinian John Jebb since,
as Jebb wrote, 'it will I trust remove the prejudices of many well disposed
Deists, and be the happy mean of converting them to the truth'.[70] Watson
largely avoided committing himself on his theological opinions while writing his *Memoirs*, or omitted the subject in revising them. Some evidence
remains: his *A Collection of Theological Tracts* (6 vols., Cambridge, 1785)
drew the thanks of the Dissenting minister Dr Edward Harwood for
recommending '*my five dissertations*, which completed my downfal among
the bigots at Bristol', chiefly on the strength, it seems, of the 'second
dissertation . . . of the *Socinian scheme*'. In 1790, Watson and the Socinian
Duke of Grafton had decided on 'the introduction of a Bill into the House
of Lords, for expunging the Athanasian Creed from our Liturgy'; only
the progress of the French Revolution led them to drop the idea. Watson
stressed the points of doctrine on which the churches agreed, and declared
their differences to be 'of less importance'.[71]

This eirenic exterior concealed positive views. As an absentee, mostly
resident in the Lake District, he had among his neighbours Thomas de
Quincey, who recorded that the bishop 'talked openly, at his own table,
as a Socinian; ridiculed the miracles of the New Testament, which he
professed to explain as so many chemical tricks, or cases of legerdemain;
and certainly had as little of devotional feeling as any man that ever

[67] Ibid. p. 71.
[68] John Nichols, *Literary Anecdotes of the Eighteenth Century* (7 vols., London, 1812–13), vol. 1,
p. 571.
[69] Richard Watson, *The Principles of the Revolution vindicated* (Cambridge, 1776); [W. Stevens],
Strictures on a Sermon, entitled, The Principles of the Revolution vindicated . . . (Cambridge,
1777), p. 37, stigmatised Watson's arguments as 'heretical doctrines', the result of his
relative ignorance of Scripture.
[70] *Anecdotes of the Life of Richard Watson, Bishop of Landaff: written by himself at different intervals
and revised in 1814* (London, 1817), pp. 47, 63.
[71] Watson, *Anecdotes*, pp. 138, 241–2, 413.

lived'.[72] When the Socinian and vegetarian Gilbert Wakefield dedicated his *An Enquiry into the Opinions of the Christian Writers of the First Three Centuries concerning the Person of Jesus Christ* (London, 1784) to Watson, the Bishop replied praising its 'erudition' and offering only a mild protest in favour of the Arian position on 'the pre-existence of Jesus'. In 1791 Watson joined with the openly Socinian Duke of Grafton in subscribing to Wakefield's translation of the New Testament.[73]

William Paley, later accused of anti-trinitarian heterodoxy,[74] supported American resistance, although often expressed in terms of contract theory, despite his scepticism of the social contract in general.[75] Heterodoxy led others, like the American colonists themselves, to target the Blackstonian conception of sovereignty, formulated as it was in essentially Anglican terms.[76] The heterodox Bishop Shipley[77] contended that the argument from the inviolability of sovereignty 'has something in it that sounds pleasant to the ears of Englishmen, but is otherwise of little weight'. Unlimited sovereignty was a 'vain phantom'. America was 'the only great nursery of freemen now left upon the face of the earth': England's state could only be darkly hinted at. Shipley hoped that 'heaven will take part' against 'a plan' for 'enslaving' the colonies.[78]

English lay supporters of American independence invoked a much older Whig clerical canon which had been similarly marked by its Trinitarian heterodoxy. When on 30 May 1777 the House of Lords debated Chatham's motion to address the king to end the war in America, the Socinian Duke of Grafton reproached Archbishop Markham's strongly anti-American sermon to the SPG of 21 February for betraying Revolution principles and advised him to read Hoadly (1676–1761) and Burnet (1643–1715).[79] Dissenters could do the same. Micaiah Towgood made 'a Country Gentleman' complain: 'I own I have lately read with Attention and Pleasure the *Bangorian Controversy*, and am thence fully convinc'd, that no Powers upon Earth, neither Ecclesiastical nor Civil, nor king nor Parliament, nor Councils nor Synods have any the least Authority in

---

[72] Thomas de Quincey, *Recollections of the Lakes and the Lake Poets* (Edinburgh, 1862), p. 111.
[73] John T. Rutt and Arnold Wainewright, (eds)., *Memoirs of the Life of Gilbert Wakefield, BA* (2 vols., London, 1804), vol. 1, pp. 249, 355–6, 509–10; vol. 2, p. 312.
[74] G. A. Cole, 'Doctrine, Dissent and the Decline of Paley's Reputation, 1805–1825', *Enlightenment and Dissent* 6 (1987), 19–30.
[75] William Paley, *The Principles of Moral and Political Philosophy* (London, 1785), pp. 416–17, 429–30.
[76] See chapter 1, parts III and V above.
[77] For whom see Peter Brown, *The Chathamites* (London, 1967), pp. 325–38.
[78] [Jonathan Shipley, Bishop of St Asaph], *A Speech Intended to have been spoken on the Bill for Altering the Charters of the Colony of Massachusetts Bay* (2nd edn., London, 1774), pp. 19, 24, 31–2, 34.
[79] *Parl. Hist.*, vol. 19, cols. 323–30.

Matters of Religion.'[80] For laymen as for clerics, the issues of 1688 and 1714 were still the common currency of debate.

Anglicans who sympathised with the American cause were, in general, Low Churchmen and had Low Church views about ecclesiastical polity; but these views were a symptom rather than a cause of contention. The Church of England was not rocked by debates over its internal organisation – by calls for the abolition of bishops, the establishment of presbyterian ordination, or the introduction of synodical government.[81] The major source of contention in the Church during the 1770s was, rather, an attack on doctrinal uniformity: the attempt to modify or abolish clerical subscription to the Thirty-Nine Articles, culminating in the Feathers Tavern petition of 1772. This was not a move by Anglicans or Dissenters to reform Church polity. The impetus behind it came from Arians and Socinians among Anglican clergy, and it was Socinian clergy like Theophilus Lindsey, John Jebb and John Disney who left the Church after the rejection of the petition placed their consciences under strain.[82]

The chronology of individuals' experiences provides an important clue to causation. Gilbert Wakefield, while still an Anglican curate in Liverpool, found his sympathies inclining towards the colonists in the American war. Some time before giving up his curacy in June 1779,

> the thunder of the church was launched in a sanguinary prayer against the *Americans*. I read this prayer in its order, but with the omission of all those unchristian words and damnatory clauses which constituted the very life and soul of the composition, and the essence of edification, to the generality of my hearers.

The episode is undated in his *Memoirs*, but seems to have accompanied a shift in his theological opinions which he did date: 'December, 1778. Began to conclude from Scripture that Christ had no existence prior to his conception; and that the *spirit of God*, according to the *Hebrew idiom*, means only *God*.'[83] Until then Wakefield, though increasingly troubled by doubts over subscription while at that future centre of Unitarianism, Jesus College, Cambridge, had recorded no evidence of commitment to opposition causes; henceforth he became a reformer. By comparison, his interest in ecclesiological questions was small. In 1786 he confessed:

---

[80] [Micaiah Towgood], *High-Flown Episcopal and Priestly Claims Freely Examin'd: In a Dialogue betwixt a Country Gentleman and a Country Vicar* (London, 1737), p. 10.

[81] Convocation had been suspended in 1717 by the Hanoverian Whig regime. The only pressure for its restoration came from High Churchmen, whose Trinitarian orthodoxy was seldom at issue.

[82] Clark, *English Society 1688–1832*, pp. 212–13, 250–2, 314–15.

[83] Rutt and Wainewright (eds.), *Memoirs of the Life of Gilbert Wakefield*, vol. 1, pp. 184, 198, 276; elsewhere (ibid., p. 467) Wakefield dated the beginning of his doubts on the Holy Spirit to 1775 or 1776.

I never did read *ecclesiastical* history in my life, except ten years ago at college, when I read Mosheim[84] and Jortin;[85] and was so thoroughly disgusted with the former, as to resolve never to look at him again. Such minute details of the frivolous reveries of ideots and knaves – such accounts of sects, which ought to have no existence but in a name – made me set down this branch of study (except as far as it was respectably treated by Eusebius, Sozomen, and Socrates, for the three first centuries, and by others for the three last,) as unworthy the attention of every man, who made pleasure or profit the object of his enquiries.[86]

Wakefield's new theological views then led him to join a sect and take his place in the story recorded, or lamented, by Mosheim and Jortin.

IV. THE DIVISIONS AND DISRUPTIONS OF ENGLISH DISSENT

If Christology predominated over ecclesiology in explaining alignments within the mainstream Anglican tradition, the picture is far more complicated within the minority that was English Dissent. Issues of ecclesiastical polity had had a far greater salience in the seventeenth century. Even by the late eighteenth, it has been well argued, it was their egalitarian and congregational ecclesiastical polity and ecclesiology that were central to the Dissenters' separation from the Church, and provided them with a permanent and ineradicable inclination not just to political opposition but to disaffection from the whole hierarchical social structure.[87] Certainly, Dissenters entertained clear ideas on questions of polity; yet some themes were nevertheless absent from the copious literature on the subscription question in the 1760s and 70s. It was not argued that material disadvantage, or a location within certain trades or professions, or place of residence, predisposed men to membership of any denomination of Protestant Dissent. Nor was it argued that exclusion from office under the Test and Corporation Acts, or the seldom-invoked penalties against Dissent, were significant material burdens that pushed Dissenters into poverty. Even tithes were resented as a religious affront: it was not a contribution to religion which gave offence, but a *compulsory* contribution to the *wrong* religion. These arguments, however much they were later integrated into a saga of marginalisation and deprivation, were, in themselves, insufficient to lead eighteenth-century Englishmen into political opposition, still less armed rebellion. The concentration of certain denominations in the

---

[84] Johann Lorenz von Mosheim, *An Ecclesiastical History, ancient and modern, from the birth of Christ to the beginning of the present century*, trans. A. Maclaine (2 vols., London, 1765).

[85] John Jortin, *Remarks on Ecclesiastical History* (5 vols., London, 1751–73).

[86] Wakefield to Rev. Mr Gregory, 25 March 1786: Rutt and Wainewright (eds.), *Life of Wakefield*, vol. 1, pp. 545–6.

[87] Bradley, *Religion*, p. 4.

middle and lower ranks of society, and even the marked inconveniences which arose from a refusal to swear oaths or pay tithes, did not consistently dispose even Quakers to hostility to the regime. Under the later Stuarts they had indeed conducted a campaign of civil disobedience and were persecuted as a subversive force;[88] during the American Revolution, English Quakers maintained a quietist pacifism despite their early efforts to promote a negotiated settlement.[89]

It may seem that Dissenters' doctrines of ecclesiastical polity ought to have committed them to a lasting militancy against a hierarchical society and its political rulers. Yet the hostility of some Dissenters to Lord North's ministry (or even George III's monarchy) during the American war is the more remarkable because of its contrast with the support, even fervent loyalty, which almost all Dissenters had offered to George II.[90] Dr John Taylor, tutor of the Dissenting Warrington Academy, reminded his hearers in 1756 that

> Under the just, mild and auspicious Government of his present Majesty, and that of his illustrious Father . . . Clear of all unnatural Restraints or Discouragements, from public Authority, Understanding and Conscience have been in full Liberty; and every Person hath been perfectly free to be wise, pious, good and virtuous, under the Direction of the best Light he could discover . . . *George* the First, and *George* the Second . . . have not given the least Countenance to any species of spiritual Tyranny . . . religious Liberty was never in any Period before, allowed to our Nation so fully and extensively.[91]

Taylor's ecumenical optimism was possible because of his downplaying of the sources of division: 'Episcopalians, Presbyterians, Independents, Baptists, Calvinists, Arminians, Arians, Trinitarians, and others, are Names of religious Distinctions. But, however we may commonly be ranked under any of these Divisions, we reject them all . . . We are *Christians*, and only *Christians*.'[92] Taylor was a model of kindness and moderation, except in one respect. 'If ever he expressed an uncommon warmth and honest indignation against anything, it was against *Athanasianism*, which he thought one of the greatest corruptions of pure and genuine Christian-

---

[88] Richard Clark, "The Gangreen of Quakerism': An Anti-Quaker Anglican Offensive in England after the Glorious Revolution', *Journal of Religious History* 11 (1980–1), 404–29.

[89] Arthur J. Mekeel, *The Relation of the Quakers to the American Revolution* (Washington, 1979), pp. 113–28.

[90] Barlow, *Citizenship and Conscience*, pp. 98–131.

[91] John Taylor, *The Glory of any House erected for Public Worship, and the True Principles, religious, civil, and social of Protestant Dissenters. Represented in a Sermon . . . May the 12th, 1756.* (London, 1756), p. 18; cf. the pro-Hanoverian views of John Toland in 1717, Richard Price in 1759 and Thomas Hollis in 1760, quoted in Clark, *English Society 1688–1832*, pp. 315–16.

[92] Taylor, *Glory*, p. 13.

ity, as this doctrine entirely subverts the unity of God . . .'[93] The potential for the bitter late-eighteenth-century rejection of the establishment was already present in the work of such men, but suppressed by the political imperatives which bound them so desperately to the House of Hanover.

Dissenters who sought relief from subscription to the Thirty-Nine Articles could draw on powerful Anglican scholarly support for the claim that Anglicans themselves had agreed on their original meaning, which had been determined by the prevalent Calvinism of the Reformation Church.[94] But this support was available only on the premise, which was John Angell's conclusion, that

> the principal Differences amongst the several Denominations of Protestant Churches, consists not in any essential and fundamental Points, but in one or other of these particulars, *viz.* different Apprehensions, with respect to the original Constitution and Government of the Christian Church; different sentiments with respect to some abstruse Points of Doctrine, in which the Essence of Religion does not, cannot consist; or else their Difference respects the positive Institutions, as to their Form and Manner, Importance or Insignificance, or of certain Rites and Ceremonies of less Importance; and that notwithstanding their separation in Communion, and very often reproaching each other, they agree in the main essential points of Religion, in 'all such Points as are abundantly sufficient to preserve the Knowledge and Practice of Religion in the World'.[95]

Early-Hanoverian Dissenters normally claimed that they withdrew from the Church on grounds of ritual, liturgy or ecclesiastical polity, not Christology. Orthodox Dissenters had traditionally turned the XIXth Article of the Church of England against its parent to argue for the autonomy of each congregation and the inability of any human organisation to require 'unnecessary Things' of men; the laity, it was argued, were at liberty to choose good ministers as they chose good doctors.[96] Points of difference on Christological questions were avoided; on the contrary, Edmund Calamy praised the Toleration Act as giving Dissenters liberty

[93] Edward Harwood, *A Sermon Occasioned by the Death of the Rev. John Taylor, D.D.* (London, 1761), p. 40; John Taylor, *The Scripture-Doctrine of Original Sin Proposed To Free and Candid Examination* (London, 1740; 3rd edn., 1750); idem, *The Scripture-Doctrine of Atonement Examined* (London, 1751).

[94] [John Angell], *The History of Religion: Particularly of the Principal Denominations of Christians* (4 vols., London, 1764), vol. 1, p. vi and passim. Angell's conclusion was that '*Antiquity is a wretched Guide to a Searcher after Truth; and that human Formularies of Faith are a chief Obstacle to real knowledge*' (ibid., vol. 1, p. x).

[95] Ibid., vol. 1, p. xviii, quoting Edmund Gibson, *The Bishop of London's Second Pastoral Letter to the People of his Diocese* . . . (London, 1730).

[96] [Charles Owen], *Plain Reasons I. For Dissenting from the Communion of the Church of England. II. Why DISSENTERS are not, nor can be guilty of SCHISM, in peaceably Separating from the Places of Publick Worship in the Church of England. And III. Several Common OBJECTIONS, brought by Churchmen against Dissenters, Answer'd* (23rd edn. (sic), London, 1736), pp. 5–7.

of conscience in matters of religion, 'provided they own'd the Doctrine of the Trinity, as they of whom I am giving here an Account did, and do universally'.[97] Despite some differences, Dissenters 'generally agree in the Doctrinal Articles of the *Church of England*, (which they subscribe) the Confession of Faith, and larger and smaller Catechisms compil'd by the Assembly of Divines at *Westminster*, and the Judgement of the *British* Divines at the Synod of *Dort*, about the *Quinquarticular Controversies*'.[98] An orthodox Dissenter like Edmund Calamy could argue against conformity by stressing that the call to ordination among the modern Nonconformists as in the Primitive Church came directly from the Holy Ghost, a position not easily compatible with unitarianism[99] and vulnerable once unitarianism began to advance within the ranks of Dissent.

Such views were the staple of Dissenting apologetic into the 1740s. Samuel Chandler was expressing familiar sentiments when in 1748 he wrote:

> I think myself obliged, as a Christian and Protestant, *peaceably to withdraw* from an Establishment, which . . . alters the Nature of indifferent Things, and makes new Rites and Postures in Religion, which are allowed to be indifferent, necessary Terms of receiving her Sacraments, and joining in the Privileges of her Worship; and which thus subjects herself to the Magistrate, as to make his Law, in the Appointment of Rites and Ceremonies in the Worship of God, obligatory upon the Consciences of all her Members.[100]

Reliance on the words of Scripture gave eirenically-inclined Dissenters the means of evading the problem of heterodoxy. As Chandler explained,

> whether there be few Heresies or many Heresies, *Socinian*, or *Arian*, or *Athanasian*, or *Sabellian*, or *Tritheistick*, or *Arminian*, or *Lutheran*, or *Cavinistick*, or *Popish* Heresies, this single Rule is universally applicable to them: *Hold fast the Apostle's Form of sound Words*. Judge all these Heresies by them . . . And if this Model be inviolably preserved, 'tis as impossible the Purity of the Christian Doctrine should be lost, as that the Light should perish while the Sun shines, or a Man should be blind whilst he hath the full Use of his Eyes.[101]

---

[97] Edmund Calamy, *A Letter to a Divine in Germany, giving a brief but true Account of the Protestant Dissenters in England*, reprinted as an appendix to *Plain Reasons*, p. 5.

[98] Ibid., p. 8.

[99] Edmund Calamy, *The Principles and Practice of the Moderate Nonconformists with respect to Ordination, Exemplify'd: In a Sermon Preach'd at the Ordination of Mr. John Munckley* . . . (London, 1717), passim; for his rejection of the doctrines of 'Deists, *Socinians*, *Arrians*, or *Papists*', p. 30.

[100] Samuel Chandler, *The Case of Subscription to Explanatory Articles of Faith, as a Qualification for Admission into the Christian Ministry, Calmly and Impartially Review'd* (London, 1748), p. 10.

[101] Samuel Chandler, *The Case of Subscription*, pp. 70–1.

This facile optimism about the ease of securing agreement nevertheless already disclosed a certain indifference about the nature of the outcome. But such views did not necessarily entail disaffection from or hostility to the Church of England. Chandler wrote to this effect at the end of friendly discussions with Anglican bishops Gooch and Sherlock, and Archbishop Herring,[102] in which they had embraced his hopes of comprehension and had been checked in that design only by political problems.[103] Chandler was not alienated: he still looked forward to comprehension through the action of 'Moderation, Benevolence, Charity, Tenderness to the Consciences of Men, Desire of Peace and Love of Liberty' on the minds of Anglicans.[104]

Yet the doctrinal position of Dissent was rapidly evolving. By the end of the eighteenth century, churchmen insisted on the changes which had transformed English Nonconformity since the days of Charles II:

> The Dissenters from the Church of England, in the times of the Stuarts, were Calvinists in doctrine, in discipline Presbyterians. What are our modern Non-conformists? In doctrine, Arians, Socinians, Pelagians, Necessarians, Materialists, Antinomians; any thing but Calvinists. What are they in discipline? Anything but Churchmen, or Presbyterians; no less enemies to Presbytery than to the established Church.

The author of this passage pointed as evidence to the virulent denunciation of Presbyterian polity in the Baptist minister Robert Robinson's *A Plan of Lectures on the Principles of Nonconformity* (Cambridge, 1778), a popular, frequently published tract, endorsed by a self-styled synod of Nonconformists meeting at Harlow in Essex.[105] It was undeniable that

---

[102] Chandler had presumably commended himself to the orthodox for his tract *Reflections on the Conduct of the Modern Deists, In their late Writings against Christianity* (London, 1727), but for Samuel Chandler's indebtedness to the Arian Dr Samuel Clarke, see J. Hay Colligan, *Eighteenth Century Nonconformity* (London, 1915), p. 41.

[103] Barlow, *Citizenship and Conscience*, pp. 113–16. For those negotiations, see J. Barker to Philip Doddridge, 2 Feb. 1748, in Thomas Stedman (ed.), *Letters to and from the Rev. Philip Doddridge, D.D.* (Shrewsbury, 1790), p. 112. Not all Dissenters were as pleased with the prospect of comprehension as Archbishop Herring, recorded their minister Barker: 'I have smiled at some who seem mightily frighted at it; and who are very angry with Mr. Chandler, and cry out, 'We wo'n't be comprehended, we wo'n't be comprehended.' One would think they imagined, it was like being electrified, or inoculated for the small-pox' (p. 116).

[104] Chandler, *Case of Subscription*, p. 147. For similar justifications of separation largely on grounds of ecclesiastical polity, see John Gill, *The Dissenters Reasons For Separating from the Church of England* (4th edn., London, 1760); for Gill's orthodoxy, see Colligan, *Eighteenth Century Nonconformity*, p. 40. The chief theological point which intrudes into such texts is a complaint against the lapse of the Church of England into Arminianism, a Calvinist code-word for Arianism.

[105] [Samuel Horsley], *A Review of the Case of the Protestant Dissenters; with reference to the Corporation and Test Acts* (London, 1790), pp. 22–3.

Dissent had undergone changes even more extensive than those experienced by the Church of England.

The case for a link between the growing heterodoxy of English Dissenters and their growing commitment to the opposition at home and the American cause abroad is greatly strengthened by the close chronological parallel of the two processes. By contrast, ecclesiological issues alone did not produce disaffection, still less rebellion. This was as true of lay Dissenters as of their ministers: at the outset of George III's reign, English Dissenters voted much like a cross section of the electorate as a whole, but between the general elections of 1774 and 1780 they moved strongly to align themselves with opposition as against ministerial candidates, and strengthened this adherence in subsequent polls.[106] Clearly the American Revolution had a profoundly important parallel in England. English Dissenters' political alignment cannot have been 'grounded primarily in polity, only secondarily in theology'[107] if almost all Dissenters were pro-government before 1760 and some remained so after 1770, and if many Anglicans backed the American cause while nevertheless remaining within the Church of England. Anglicans' and Dissenters' ideas on church polity were relatively stable throughout the reigns of George II and George III; it was their theology which changed.

Orthodox and heterodox Dissenters alike could nevertheless continue to offer the same account of their reasons for not conforming to the Church of England: as the Arian Micaiah Towgood[108] listed them, the civil magistrate had no 'right, authority, or power over the consciences and religion of men'; the Church had not, as its Article XX claimed, 'power to decree rites and ceremonies, and authority in controversies of faith'; its clergy had not, as the offices of Ordination and the Visitation of the Sick claimed, power to forgive or retain sins; salvation did not depend on belief in the doctrines contained in the Athanasian Creed, as the *Book of Common Prayer* maintained. Such Popish doctrines cut away the foundation of the Church in the Reformation. But here the new Dissenter stuck on a difficulty which did not confront most of his early-Hanoverian predecessors:

---

[106] John A. Phillips, *Electoral Behavior in Unreformed England* (Princeton, 1982), pp. 286–305. Dissenters, Philips found, continued meanwhile to mirror the occupational distribution of their localities.

[107] Bradley, *Religion*, p. 138.

[108] For Towgood's Arianism, see David Bogue and James Bennett, *History of Dissenters, from the Revolution in 1688, to the Year 1808* (4 vols., London, 1808–12), vol. 3, pp. 379–80; J. Hay Colligan, *The Arian Movement in England* (Manchester, 1913), pp. 127–8; James Manning, *A Sketch of the Life and Writings of the Rev. Micaiah Towgood* (Exeter, 1792), pp. 9, 128, 132–44; for his millennialism, p. 154. On Towgood's theology in general, see Alan P. F. Sell, 'A Little Friendly Light: the Candour of Bourn, Taylor and Towgood', *Journal of the United Reformed Church History Society* 4 (1991–2), 517–40, 580–613.

it was the 'inexplicable mystery' of the doctrine of the Trinity, contained in the Athanasian creed, which Micaiah Towgood singled out as its chief stumbling block.[109]

This was not, indeed, a point which Towgood could insist on; indeed he attempted to disguise it. 'You will be pleased, Sir, to observe that the objections of the Dissenters as such, to this part of the Church's doctrine, did not arise from their disbelief of the doctrine of Trinity: but to make the belief of any human explications of it, especially those of that proud and ignorant man (whoever he was) who fabricated this [Athanasian] Creed, absolutely and indispensably necessary to salvation, and to pronounce *all* who do not receive it, most certainly and eternally damned, this to us appears an act of such profane rashness and presumption as every good Christian should from his soul abhor.'[110] To benefit from the Toleration Act, Dissenters still had to subscribe thirty-five of the Thirty-Nine Articles, including an Article affirming the doctrine of the Trinity. It was this insistence on enforcing creeds and ceremonies of no divine authority, reinforced by the Act of Uniformity, that had deprived the Church of England of so many Dissenters, he claimed: Towgood listed Mathew Henry, Isaac Watts, Philip Doddridge, Henry Grove, Samuel Chandler, James Foster, John Leland, John Abernethy, Thomas Pierce, Joseph Hallet, James Duchal, Moses Lowman, Nathaniel Lardner and John Taylor.[111] Towgood did not point out how many of this list had entertained heterodox understandings of the Trinity.

Would not the abolition of subscription open the pulpit to scoffers at religion? A lay Dissenter, Israel Mauduit, was explicit: the doctrine of

[109] [Micaiah Towgood], *A Calm and Plain Answer to the Enquiry, Why are you a Dissenter from the Church of England? . . . By the Author of the Dissenting Gentleman's Letters to White* (London, 1772), pp. 3, 6, 7. Towgood's picture of an intolerant and tyrannical Church of England was implausible: as John Crosse, in *A Reply to the Objections brought against the Church of England* (Bradford, 1798) emphasised, Towgood's interpretation of Article XX rested on selective quotation. Cf. John Landon, *An Answer to the Dissenting Gentleman's Third Letter to the Reverend Mr. White* (London, 1758), pp. 1 ff; John White, *A Defence of the Three Letters to a Gentleman Dissenting from the Church of England* (London, 1746), p. 8.

[110] [Towgood], *Calm and Plain Answer*, p. 8. Towgood had pursued this argument against Church power since the 1740s: [Micaiah Towgood], *The Dissenting Gentleman's Answer to the Reverend Mr. White's Three Letters; in which A Separation from the Establishment is fully justified* (London, 1746); [idem], *The Dissenting Gentleman's Second Letter to the Reverend Mr. White* (London, 1747); [idem], *The Dissenting Gentleman's Third and Last Letter to the Reverend Mr. White* (London, 1738 [sc. 1748]). In the *Third Letter* (pp. 77–8), Towgood insisted on the contradiction between the Athanasian Creed, assuring 'ALL *Arians* and *Socinians* that they CANNOT be saved', and the Burial Office, expressing a hope that they had been.

[111] Ibid., pp. 18, 63. Towgood's *The Dissenting Gentleman's Answer* became a classic, running through six editions; reprinted as *A Dissent from the Church of England, fully justified* this title reached a 12th edition by 1811. Its republication in Boston (where it reached a third edition) was due to the heavily-politicised Congregationalist minister Charles Chauncy, 'who became his frequent correspondent': Manning, *Towgood*, p. 32.

the Trinity was 'sufficiently guarded' by the Blasphemy Act of 1698 – 'a Doctrine, concerning which good Men in all Ages have been of different Opinions, and which many great Divines of the Church of *England* have not thought to be of so much Importance'.[112] The present application for relief from subscription arose from the fact that, since the passage of the Toleration Act, many clergy both Dissenting and Anglican, 'by studying the Scriptures more carefully, have found Reason to alter their Opinions as to many doctrinal Articles'.[113] It was in the interest of Dissenters to keep the argument on the grounds of church polity and away from heterodoxy. Robert Robinson, Baptist minster at Cambridge, claimed that polity explained the dispute:

> By a strange oversight in readers the real principles of this controversy are mistaken. A statesman suspects civil faction; a trinitarian complains of arianism; a calvinist urges the looseness of arminianism; an arminian the intolerance of calvinism. Surprizing! Was the dispute about a DOCTRIN, the divinity of Christ, and predestination might be canvassed, but the dispute is about church-DISCIPLIN. For shame gentlemen, don't mistake the question; the question is not WHAT, but WHY the church believes; whether by compulsion or choice.[114]

But Robinson had his own heterodoxy to conceal,[115] and such a position was only tenable if doctrinal points were, to his contemporaries, either unimportant or undecidable: orthodoxy was 'a very vague, equivocal word . . . In one latitude it means a belief of one thing, in another the belief of another thing, quite contrary.'[116]

Thanks partly to evasions like this, the Trinitarian orthodoxy of English Dissenters sympathetic to the American rebellion is still often overstated. It is true that, at the beginning of the century, Dissenting Arians like George Benson,[117] Samuel Chandler and Nathaniel Lardner, among other Presbyterian ministers, joined in the critique of the Deists.[118] Yet this tactical alliance did not reconcile Arians with orthodox; and the introduc-

---

[112] Israel Mauduit, *The Case of the Dissenting Ministers. Addressed to the Lords Spiritual and Temporal* (3rd edn., London, 1772), p. 9.

[113] Ibid., p. 16. Mauduit, to prove the services of Dissenters in the defence of Christianity, cited those of their number who had written against the Deists, including Chandler, Simon Brown, Dr Foster, Benson, Duchal and Abernethy. Among them he listed, without comment, the names of Arians like Lowman and Lardner: ibid., pp. 46–50.

[114] [Robert Robinson], *Arcana: or the Principles of the late Petitioners to Parliament for Relief in the Matter of Subscription* (Cambridge, 1774), p. v.

[115] See below, pp. 332–3.

[116] Robinson, *Arcana*, p. 72.

[117] Bogue and Bennett, *History of Dissenters*, vol. 3, pp. 379–80, claimed Benson as a Socinian.

[118] Olive M. Griffiths, *Religion and Learning: A Study in English Presbyterian Thought from the Bartholomew Ejections (1662) to the Foundation of the Unitarian Movement* (Cambridge, 1935), pp. 110, 130.

tion into the ranks of Dissenters of the Arian views of the Cambridge Anglican theologians William Whiston and Samuel Clarke began a process of conversion and controversy, marked by such internal Presbyterian crises as the Exeter subscription controversy of 1717 and the Salters' Hall Conference of 1719 which, in essence, failed to give Presbyterians the means of resisting the advance of Arianism within their denomination as a whole.[119]

After the Salters' Hall controversy, English Dissenters tended to realign themselves on doctrinal grounds rather than in respect of ecclesiastical polity: Presbyterians tended to be non-subscribers, Arian or Trinitarian (but increasingly Arian); Congregationalists were subscribers, of whom few were not Trinitarian. According to Joshua Toulmin, the 'two denominations of presbyterians and independents became distinct communities, and acted separately with respect to their own denominations. And the ground of this separation being in doctrinal sentiments, the terms came afterwards to signify not a difference in Church Government, according to their original meaning, but in doctrinal opinions.'[120] 'The question of polity among the Nonconformists would never have been raised after the Act of Uniformity had not theological differences appeared among them', suggested a recent historian: it was these theological differences which broke up the 1691 Agreement between Presbyterians and Congregationalists, and led to the reappearance of the competing labels by c. 1695. From the middle of the century, the term 'Presbyterian' had 'not a denominational but a doctrinal significance in England, and was generally connected with a theology implying something between Arianism and Unitarianism, including both these views'.[121] In the ordination of ministers, the practice of English Congregationalists drew closer to that of the Presbyterians; under the terms of the 1691 alliance of the two sects, neighbouring ministers were called in to 'consult and advise' on that ceremony. The distinction was less and less one of polity, more and more one of doctrine, as the advance of Arianism among Presbyterians led many of

---

[119] Ibid., pp. 111–18; Colligan, *Eighteenth-Century Nonconformity*, pp. 23–33.

[120] Joshua Toulmin, *An Historical View of the State of the Protestant Dissenters in England, And of the Progress of Free Enquiry and Religious Liberty, From the Revolution to the Accession of Queen Anne* (Bath and London, 1814), pp. 213–14.

[121] Colligan, *Eighteenth Century Nonconformity*, pp. 34, 37, 103–5, 108; idem, *The Arian Movement in England*, pp. 44–59. The 1691 Agreement is printed in Alexander Gordon (ed.), *Cheshire Classis Minutes 1691–1745* (London, 1919), pp. 110–17. Apart from the question of the ordination of ministers, this document hardly addressed, and therefore failed to resolve, the questions of ecclesiastical polity which divided Presbyterians and Congregationalists. See Roger Thomas, 'The Break–up of Nonconformity' in Geoffrey F. Nuttall et al. (eds.), *The Beginnings of Nonconformity* (London, 1964), pp. 33–60.

its ministers to conform to the Church of England, others to join the Congregationalists.[122]

These doctrinal conflicts broke the morale of English Nonconformists and blighted their hopes, in the wake of the Glorious Revolution, that a plan of comprehension might reconcile them to the Church of England, or that their own security under the Toleration Act would lead to a steady expansion in their numbers. On the contrary, the position of orthodox Dissent under the early Hanoverians was a weak one: Anglican tolerance, and the advance of heterodoxy within Nonconformist ranks, prompted many (especially Presbyterians) to conform to the Church of England.[123] One anonymous Dissenter admitted to fifty Dissenting ministers having done so in the years 1714–31 alone;[124] nor was it a matter of numbers only, for the converts included men of the calibre of Joseph Butler (later a bishop) and Thomas Secker (later an archbishop). The Dissenter Edmund Calamy conceded that the converts 'were, generally, persons of sobriety and unblemished character';

> it was easy to be observed, and much taken notice of, that most that con-
> formed about this time, complained much of a spirit of imposition working
> among the Dissenters, which discovered itself in the proceedings at Salters'
> Hall, and on other occasions, after the debates about the Trinity grew
> warm.[125]

Anti-Arian pressures within each congregation alone inhibited the advance of this school, and these safeguards often failed. In the south-west of England its advance was rapid in the years following the Salters' Hall controversy; elsewhere its spread was slower, but preceded by an increasing belief in a right of private judgement and a rejection of tests of orthodoxy as a solution to the doctrinal controversies which Arianism provoked.[126] By the mid eighteenth century, it has been suggested that Arianism was still the creed of only 'a small nucleus' of Presbyterians, though more were sympathetic; the swift conversion of large numbers to Socinianism was the work of the last half of the century.[127] Beginning with

---

[122] Bogue and Bennett, *History of Dissenters*, vol. 2, pp. 130–8; vol. 3, pp. 331–2; Duncan Coomer, *English Dissent under the Early Hanoverians* (London, 1946), p. 51.

[123] For an argument that the position of Christologically orthodox Dissenters was inconsistent, and that rationality would have led them either to the Church or to heterodox Dissent, see Waterman, 'The Nexus between Theology and Political Doctrine'.

[124] *Some Observations upon the Present State of the Dissenting Interest, And the Case of those Who have lately deserted it* (London, 1731), p. 10.

[125] Edmund Calamy, *An Historical Account of My Own Life . . . (1671–1731)*, ed. John Towill Rutt (2 vols., London, 1829), vol. 2, pp. 503–6.

[126] Griffiths, *Religion and Learning*, pp. 119–33.

[127] Ibid., pp. 134–50. Heterodoxy was influential beyond its numbers because it influenced especially the Dissenting intelligentsia. For the Sabellian beliefs of Philip Doddridge

Nathaniel Lardner's *Letter on the Logos*, published in 1759, and Moses Lowman's *Three Tracts* of 1756 (of which Samuel Chandler was a sympathetic editor), Presbyterians developed a 'large body of men whose Christology resembled closely that Socinianism which their fathers had considered heretical to the degree of blasphemy'.[128]

Such views were not the property of all Dissenters. The majority were still evidently orthodox. Involvement with American issues, too, was initially minimal. Of those conventionally identified as the English 'Commonwealthmen' and their circle, it has been suggested that only Thomas Hollis, John Almon and John Fothergill were active in the American cause in the early 1760s. The Dissenting intelligentsia still largely ignored the Stamp Act and its implications, for it did not engage with the major elements in their ideology. Of the three listed only Fothergill wrote a tract during the Stamp Act crisis, appearing anonymously as *Considerations Relative to the North American Colonies* (London, 1765).[129] For such men, involvement in American affairs was produced by an issue which did so engage, for in England it was above all the 'Commonwealthmen', more accurately identified as militant anticlericals, who engineered an outcry against the attempts of the 1760s to secure a bishop for the colonies.[130] Thomas Hollis used his contacts with Jonathan Mayhew to republish the American's tracts in London, and Hollis encouraged English friends to denounce the church once more in the new context of its American ambitions.[131] This press campaign was eventually collected and published in book form by the fundamentally alienated and presumably Arian Anglican clergyman Francis Blackburne.[132]

(1702–51), the most widely-read publicist of early-Hanoverian dissent, see Alexander Gordon, *Philip Doddridge and the Catholicity of the Old Dissent* (London, [1951]), pp. 13–14.

[128] Griffiths, *Religion and Learning*, p. 139.

[129] Colin Bonwick, *English Radicals and the American Revolution* (Chapel Hill, 1977), pp. 58–9 and bibliography.

[130] For which, see Arthur Lyon Cross, *The Anglican Episcopate and the American Colonies* (New York, 1902); Carl Bridenbaugh, *Mitre and Sceptre: Transatlantic Faiths, Ideas, Personalities, and Politics 1689–1775* (New York, 1962).

[131] John Sainsbury, *Disaffected Patriots: London Supporters of Revolutionary America 1769–1782* (Kingston, Ontario, 1987), p. 10 argues for the important role of the small group of propagandists who identified themselves as 'Real Whigs', but does not discern the significance of their theological commitments or explore the denominational dynamics which, it is suggested here, explain much of the alignment for and against the American cause in England. Sainsbury instead contends that Real Whig ideology was a successful mobiliser because it 'provided a world view which was thoroughly rational and persuasive to many of London's tradesmen in the light of their perceived economic and political victimisation by successive administrations' (pp. 18–19).

[132] [Francis Blackburne, ed.], *A Collection of Letters and Essays in Favour of Public Liberty, first published in the News-papers in the Years 1764, 65, 66, 67, 68, 69, and 1770. By an Amicable Band of Wellwishers to the Religious and Civil Rights of Mankind* (3 vols., London, 1774); Clark, *English Society*, p. 314. Blackburne stopped short of Socinianism, however; see his unpub-

If opposition opinion in general was hostile to Bute, it was this circle in particular in which anti-Stuart, anti-Jacobite, anti-popish hysteria reached its highest and most inventive pitch: in 1767 Sylas Neville noted Thomas Hollis's opinion that 'Bute intends making himself King, pretending to be descended from an elder branch than the banished [Stuart] family'. Appropriately, the Mr Fleming who told Neville in April 1768 that 'Bute and George Grenville are hatching a plan . . . to send Bishops to America and absolutely enslave that country' was the same Dissenting minister Caleb Fleming who, that February, 'declares himself a Unitarian before God and the world and indeed the Trinity has no other foundation but the Athanasian heresy'. Hollis, by contrast, was 'disgusted' at Fleming's preaching: 'I have always suspected Mr. Hollis of Deism', explained Neville.[133] Deists on the one extreme, and Arians or Socinians on the other, still had difficulty in making common cause except where their perceptions of episcopalian, orthodox tyranny coincided.

If ancient denominational kinship predisposed English Dissenters to sympathise with their American coreligionists, something more was needed in England as well as America to create the perception that the daily frictions of everyday politics on both sides of the Atlantic were really all products of a single cause; that there was one crisis, not many, produced by a single conspiracy against liberty throughout the empire. That additional element was initially provided by a clearly defined school of thought, whose alarm had been aroused by the bishopric issue of the early 1770s;[134] and it correlated with the rapid spread of theological heterodoxy among the Dissenters, especially Dissenting ministers, who formed the real social constituency which the term 'Commonwealthmen' less precisely describes.

It was this small group of zealots, many of them concentrated in London, who fashioned a pro-American policy which only subsequently influenced the rank and file of Dissenting laymen, a minority whose ideology or paranoia precommitted them to the blindly held belief that the *sole* cause of the conflict was the tyrannical policy of the British government, and that, as Thomas Hollis confided to his diary on 25 August

lished memo, 'Answer to the Question, Why Are You Not a Socinian?' in *The Works . . . of Francis Blackburne* (7 vols., Cambridge, 1805), vol. 1, pp. cxx–cxxvi.

[133] Basil Cozens-Hardy (ed.), *The Diary of Sylas Neville 1767–1788* (London, 1950), pp. 14, 30–1, 58.

[134] By contrast, they had largely ignored the Stamp Act and had 'responded somewhat mildly to the Wilkite affair': Bonwick, *English Radicals*, p. 117. For the belated but growing perception among English Dissenters of a link between the English and American cases, ibid., pp. 118–22.

1768, 'the whole Equity lies on the side of the North Americans'.[135] Yet the wider community of London Nonconformists did not necessarily share the instant and unnuanced hostility to the government of this small cadre. The pro-Americanism of famous figures like Burgh, Hollis, Price and Priestley has, suggested one historian, distracted attention from 'a significant trend. Less famous but equally important Dissenters steadily turned their backs on America during the later 1760s and 1770s.'[136] At Franklin's instigation, Priestley attempted to incite his co-religionists in *An Address to Protestant Dissenters of All Denominations* (London, 1774), reminding them of the 'strenuous exertions' of 'the old *Puritans* and *Nonconformists*', but, in general, English Dissenters were not enthusiasts for an independent America. Paine's obviously Deistic *Common Sense* was not well received by most of them.[137] John Adams later listed his acquaintance during his years as Minister in England from 1785 to 1788 – Theophilus Lindsey, John Disney, Hugh Farmer, Richard Price, Joseph Priestley, Andrew Kippis, John Jebb, Benjamin and William Vaughan, Edward Bridgen, Thomas Brand Hollis, Joseph Towers, Thomas Belsham: 'Unitarianism and Biblical Criticism were the great Characteristicks of them all . . . All professed Friendship for America, and these were almost all, who pretended to any such Thing.'[138] Socinians were never more than a minority among Dissenters, often reviled by their Trinitarian brethren, and destined to experience steep decline in the 1790s.[139] But in the 1770s, they were a vital catalyst.

A number of Calvinists have been cited as examples of English Trinitarian Dissenters who were pro-American, including Rees David, Caleb Evans, James Murray, Samuel Palmer, Robert Robinson, Benjamin Wallin and Samuel Wilton.[140] More work remains to be done on their

---

[135] Sainsbury, *Disaffected Patriots*, pp. 11–12, 38, 41, 69. Sainsbury's evidence confirms that, even by the general election of 1774, 'organised support for the colonists was largely confined to London'. See also Ian R. Christie, 'The Wilkites and the General Election of 1774' in *Myth and Reality in Late-Eighteenth-Century British Politics and Other Papers* (London, 1970), pp. 244–60.

[136] Michael G. Kammen, *A Rope of Sand: The Colonial Agents, British Politics, and the American Revolution* (Ithaca, NY, 1968), pp. 201–4 at 204: 'nonconformists in the colonies were in the vanguard of the revolutionary movement. Their willingness to sever ties with Britain, however, was strengthened by the cool treatment they received from dissenting organisations in London, most of which seemed conservative to their American brethren.'

[137] Sainsbury, *Disaffected Patriots*, pp. 81, 127–8.

[138] Adams to Jefferson, 25 June 1813: Lester J. Cappon (ed.), *The Adams-Jefferson Letters* (2 vols., Chapel Hill, 1959), vol. 2, p. 334.

[139] Anthony Lincoln, *Some Political & Social Ideas of English Dissent 1763–1790* (Cambridge, 1938), pp. 60–2.

[140] Bradley, *Religion*, pp. 127–31; idem, 'Heresy, Orthodoxy and Polity: The Ideological Origins of English Radicalism' (unpublished paper to the American Society of Eighteenth-Century Studies, March 1988).

theology; it seems possible that more evidence of heterodoxy will be uncovered for these often-obscure men, for evidence to the contrary already exists for at least three of them. If 'advanced' views in theology tended to go with a reforming stance in political or social matters, this link can be observed in the provinces also: it was not the prerogative of a metropolitan elite alone, however much Dissenting talent was concentrated in London. Newcastle, a centre of Wilkesite agitation in the 1760s, provides an accessible example. The Scot James Murray (1732–82), descended from an old Covenanter family, graduate of Edinburgh, dismissed after some unexplained doctrinal differences from his post as assistant minister at a meeting house at Alnwick in the early 1760s, collected his own congregation in that place, built a chapel, and, not being ordained by any presbytery, went into print to argue for the freedom of all congregations (except Roman Catholics) in matters of ecclesiastical polity. That teaching was so successful that in 1764 he gathered a larger and richer congregation who built for him the High Bridge Chapel in thriving Newcastle and maintained him as their minister until his death.[141]

As a Dissenting entrepreneur, with a strong financial inducement to comprehension, he emphasised 'the love and fellowship of all good men' above doctrinal distinctions which, he acknowledged, were still widely understood: 'The reproachful names of Arian, Socinian, Arminian, are, in his opinion, rather words of course, than any words of signification. Every malicious man gives them to those they do not love, because they know the common people hate the very sound of them.'[142] With heterodoxy thus excused, Murray could proceed to his central insight that 'All Europe, – yea the greatest part of the world have couched down between these two burdens of civil and religious oppression', and continue with denunciation of tests, subscription, creeds, establishment, tithes, electoral bribery, high taxation. In general, it was the alliance of church and state that he singled out as the '*principal cause of civil* and *religious oppression* wherever it takes place'.[143]

To what extent was Murray committed to opposition? His profession was that 'the people are as *wise, religious,* and *loyal* to the *government,* who

---

[141] Biographical details are drawn from the *Memoirs* prefixed to the edition of James Murray, *The Travels of the Imagination* (Newcastle, 1828).

[142] James Murray, *Select Discourses upon Several Important Subjects* (Newcastle, 1765), p. ii. Murray's doctrine of the Atonement appears to treat Christ in Arian fashion as a created (though divine) being, and to omit the third Person of the Trinity: James Murray, *An Essay on Redemption by Jesus Christ* (Newcastle, 1768), pp. 12–13, 15, 31–2.

[143] [James Murray], *Sermons to Asses* (London and Newcastle, 1768) pp. 5, 193; for his explicit attack on Bishop Warburton, [Murray], *Sermons to Doctors in Divinity* (London, 1771); on the Thirty-Nine Articles, Liturgy and Athanasian Creed, James Murray, *Lectures to Lords Spiritual* (London, 1774).

bear the *expense* of *their own religion,* and *pay their own teachers,* as *any* that are under the *nose* of *any bishop* in *England*'.[144] But Murray simultaneously extended these principles to a savage attack on George III and his minister the Duke of Grafton, both represented by the type of Eglon king of Moab (Judges III. 22).[145] Already, this issued in a veiled threat: a corrupt king's unsupervised ministers 'often raise such discontent in a nation, as nearly threatens a revolution in government. Under such an administration, every connection with such a kingdom is dangerous; for neither colonies nor allies can put confidence in a corrupt, selfish administration.'[146]

Even in 1768, the seeds of Murray's later pro-American stance had been sown; and with thinly-disguised political preferences went openly-acknowledged theological ones. Murray commended Thomas Chubb, Samuel Clarke and Lord Shaftesbury.[147] The Trinitarian controversy of the 1690s, and the attempts by Sherlock and South to defend the orthodox account of the Trinity, he dismissed: 'Whatever may be in those things, it is certain nobody ever understood them; and at best the whole controversy was a dispute about human inventions.'[148] William Whiston's revival of 'some of the doctrines of the arians' was sympathetically treated: his 'vindication of himself has been frequently caviled at, but has never been formally confuted'. John Simson, Professor of Divinity at Glasgow and the centre of a controversy in 1714–16 when 'called to account for reviving some of the arian doctrines', was similarly excused.[149] When Murray came to write on the American war, his position was hardly in doubt. Carefully avoiding treasonable expressions, he nevertheless depicted an alignment of forces in which coercion was supported in England by 'Jacobites', 'Tories' and 'Papists', ministerial policy was sacrificed 'at the shrine of dominion and despotism', and the 'American war, if continued, will either be the aera of liberty to them, or the aera of slavery to both them and us'.[150]

Samuel Palmer has similarly been claimed as simultaneously pro-American and an orthodox Calvinist Dissenter, expressing in his best-

---

[144] *Sermons to Asses,* pp. 197–8.
[145] [James Murray], *Sermons to Men, Women and Children* (Newcastle, 1768); republished as *ΕΙΚΩΝ ΒΑΣΙΛΙΚΗ* (Durham, 1773). Murray was presumably unaware of Grafton's Unitarian sympathies.
[146] [Murray], *Sermons to Men, Women and Children,* p. 9.
[147] *Sermons to Doctors in Divinity,* pp. 162, 174.
[148] [James Murray], *A History of the Churches in England and Scotland, From the Reformation to this present Time* (3 vols., Newcastle, 1771–2), vol. 3, p. 508.
[149] Ibid., vol. 3, pp. 511, 517.
[150] James Murray, *An Impartial History of the Present War in America* (2 vols., Newcastle upon Tyne, [1780]), vol. 2, pp. 572–6.

selling *Protestant Dissenter's Catechism* a claim that Dissenting principles resided only in such matters as 'the right of private judgement, and liberty of conscience, the acknowledgement of Christ alone as head of his church, and the sufficiency of the holy Scriptures as the rule of faith and practice'. Certainly, prudent Dissenters sought to found their case on arguments which would attract the widest sympathy, especially among Anglicans. Yet elsewhere he made his theological premises clear: 'I am indeed a *Unitarian*, as really as he [Priestley] is, since I believe *God is* ONE: i.e. one infinite being; but this I do not conceive to be inconsistent with the notion of a *Trinity.*' Rather than openly reject it, Palmer preferred to reinterpret the doctrine of the Trinity in the light of his Christology.[151]

A third Calvinist Dissenting minister can be shown to have developed anti-Trinitarian beliefs. Although the Baptist Robert Robinson formally defended the Trinity,[152] he was thought by the orthodox to hold 'this weighty doctrine with too loose a hand'. They had reason for their suspicion: George Dyer, Robinson's first biographer, discovered his subject's marginal annotations in a pamphlet on the subject 'which afford ample testimony that his idea of the nature of Jesus Christ was unsettled'. Robinson indeed, noted Dyer, always claimed his tract *A Plea for the Divinity* 'to be rather a Sabellian, than a Trinitarian book, that its object was not to defend the strictly orthodox side of the question'. Appropriately, Bishop Hinchliffe was among its admirers. Robinson began his career as a Baptist minister in Cambridge in 1761 with a strictly orthodox Confession of Faith;[153] but by the 1780s at the latest, 'he used to speak concerning the Trinity, not only with a degree of sceptical embarassment, but with a levity, inconsistent with the character of a sound believer . . . The cloven foot of heresy then began to make its appearance.'[154] In 1765, he qualified under the Toleration Act before the Cambridge JPs;[155] by

---

[151] Samuel Palmer, *A Vindication of the Modern Dissenters against the Aspersions of the Rev. William Hawkins, M.A.* (London, 1790), pp. 2–3.

[152] Robert Robinson, *A Plea for the Divinity of our Lord Jesus Christ, in a Pastoral Letter addressed to a Congregation of Protestant Dissenters at Cambridge* (Cambridge, 1776).

[153] George Dyer, *Memoirs of the Life and Writings of Robert Robinson* (London, 1796), pp. 45, 105–23, 365, 429–32.

[154] Ibid., p. 247. A leading Socinian, unaware of Robinson's manuscript doubts, nevertheless maintained that he 'changed his sentiments concerning the person of Christ' after publishing his *Plea for the Divinity* . . .: Joshua Toulmin, *Christian Vigilance. Considered in a Sermon, preached at the Baptist Chapel, in Taunton, on the Lord's Day, after the sudden Removal of the Learned and Reverend Robert Robinson* (London, 1790), p. 29.

[155] This involved taking the oath of allegiance, the oath renouncing the spiritual authority of all foreign powers (i.e. the Pope), subscribing the declaration against transubstantiation and the Thirty-Nine Articles (omitting numbers 34, 35, 36 and part of 20). The Toleration Act (clause XIV) explicitly denied 'any ease benefitt or advantage' to 'any person that shall deny in his Preaching or Writing the Doctrine of the Blessed Trinity' as contained in the rest of the Articles.

1774, he recorded in his church book, he would have '*run all hazards rather than have qualified thus*'.[156] Sabellianism, though a doctrine more uncommon at this time than Socinianism, could have similar effects in predisposing men violently to reject a Trinitarian established Church.

A number of orthodox Dissenters were nevertheless in some degree pro-American. The Calvinist Baptist Caleb Evans (1737–91) campaigned against Arians and Socinians,[157] including Priestley; but at the outset of the war he was drawn into controversy with John Wesley, John Fletcher and Josiah Tucker in which Evans came down clearly for the Americans on issues of taxation and virtual representation.[158] It seems likely that this was a libertarian affirmation provoked by the immediate controversy: Evans firmly repudiated the charge of republicanism and affirmed his support for the constitution. He professed that the only religious liberty Dissenters desired was 'the liberty we are this moment enjoying'; a Whig's 'utmost wishes with respect to *civil liberty*, are, that the *present constitution* may continue and flourish in its native original vigor to the remotest posterity'.[159] Evans professed to wish 'That a permanent peace and reconciliation may speedily take place betwixt us and our American Colonies, upon an honourable constitutional basis; and that our beloved Sovereign GEORGE the Third, may long live to sway the sceptre over an *united, harmonious, free* people.'[160] Orthodox Dissenters' sympathy for American grievances in the 1760s (a sympathy which they shared with orthodox Anglicans) did not normally carry over to support for American rebellion in the 1770s. In that decade, some English Dissenters supported the British case, like the layman Israel Mauduit[161] or ministers L.L. Peters, John Martin, Henry Hunter and others.[162] Caleb Evans maintained against

---

[156] Quoted in Toulmin, *Christian Vigilance*, pp. 44–5. Robinson's change of opinion on the Trinity evidently preceded 1774, but is difficult to date.

[157] E.g. Caleb Evans, *The Scripture Doctrine of the Deity of the Son and Holy Spirit, represented in two Sermons* . . . (Bristol, 1766). Evans did subscribe for a copy of Joshua Toulmin's *Memoirs of the Life, Character, Sentiments and Writings of Faustus Socinus* (London, 1777), but continued to write against Arianism and Socinianism, e.g. in Evans, *Christ Crucified; or the Scripture Doctrine of the Atonement briefly Illustrated and Defended* (Bristol, 1789), pp. 14–15, 39.

[158] For a different interpretation see Bradley, *Religion*, pp. 127–8, 136.

[159] Caleb Evans, *British Constitutional Liberty. A Sermon* . . . *November 5, 1775* (Bristol, [1775]), pp. 14–15.

[160] Caleb Evans, *A Letter to the Rev. Mr. John Wesley, Occasioned by his Calm Address to the American Colonies* (London, 1775), p. 24.

[161] Colin Bonwick, 'English Dissenters and the American Revolution' in H. C. Allen and Roger Thompson (eds.), *Contrast and Connection* (Athens, Ohio, 1976), pp. 88–112.

[162] Bradley, *Religion*, pp. 123–4. Lincoln, *Some Political & Social Ideas of English Dissent*, p. 22, listed as loyalists the Dissenting ministers Edward Pickard, John Martin, John Clayton and David Rivers.

Wesley's ally John Fletcher that Evans's Calvinism and Baptist polity were irrelevant:

> what relation my being a Calvinist, or a Baptist, has to the subject of my dispute with you, I am yet to learn. There are too many Calvinists and Baptists, some in the very society I serve, and several Baptist ministers with whom I am personally acquainted, who, through a mistaken view, as it appears to me, of our happy constitution and of the true meaning of the scriptures, contend earnestly for those very sentiments which you so strenuously defend. And with respect to the *Americans*, if you apply to the late Governor *Bernard* or Governor *Hutchinson*, they can inform you, from the best authority, that no one sect, in the *Massachusetts* colony particularly, have discovered so great a disposition to acquiesce in the measures of the ministry, as the Baptists.[163]

Observers in the 1770s already sensed a distinction between the political stance of orthodox and heterodox Dissenters, though some were as yet imprecise in analysing it. William Stevens observed in 1777 that

> The dissenters, who believe the Christian verities, are content with the toleration they now enjoy, and maintain their allegiance to their sovereign; but the Protestant succession in the house of Hanover would soon come to a fearful end, if it had no better support than the loyalty and zeal of the deistical tribe of separatists, a faction ever insatiable in their demands, implacable under disappointment, always tyrants when in power, and rebels when out of power.[164]

His language was rhetorically exaggerated, but the distinction which he sensed had some foundation. Jonathan Boucher, in a sermon of 1774 revised for publication in 1797, complained that 'Presbyterians are every where ignorantly and unjustly confounded with sectaries of a different description under the general name of Dissenters': on the issue of comprehension, a reunion of churches, 'there certainly is a much greater difference between the old, regular, Presbyterians and Modern Dissenters, than there is between Presbyterians and Churchmen'.[165] This distinction was refined in the *Anti-Jacobin* of December 1798. Writing of the attempted repeal of the Test and Corporation Acts in 1787, it analysed Protestant Dissenters into 'two general classes . . . the Socinians and Calvinists'. Had the latter

---

[163] Caleb Evans, *A Reply to the Rev. Mr. Fletcher's Vindication of Mr. Wesley's Calm Address to Our American Colonies* (Bristol, [1776]), p. 85. For the reluctance of colonial Baptists, who were firmly Trinitarian, to join the Revolution see part V (D) below.

[164] [William Stevens], *The Revolution Vindicated, and Constitutional Liberty Asserted. In answer to the Reverend Dr. Watson's Accession Sermon, Preached before the University of Cambridge, on October 25th, 1776* (Cambridge, 1777), pp. 64–5.

[165] Jonathan Boucher, *A View of the Causes and Consequences of the American Revolution; in Thirteen Discourses, Preached in North America between the Years 1763 and 1775* (London, 1797), p. 288.

disavowed all connection or concurrence of sentiment with republicans and degraders of the Saviour of the world, it is possible they might have been indulged; but as they took no such step to mark their disapprobation of Priestleian and Pricean doctrines, and Socinians and Democrats, it was impossible for the legislature to know that they were not of that description.[166]

The political consequences of 'rational' Dissent became fully apparent to contemporaries by the 1790s. Nevertheless, although tendencies to theological heterodoxy can be discerned among many more activists than first appears, very many orthodox Dissenters were also involved. This was inevitable, since it was the common inheritance of ecclesiastical polity which provided both orthodox and heterodox Dissenters with their public doctrine, their formal engagement with the political structure of established Anglicanism. Yet this inheritance was not in itself enough to commit Dissenters to opposition, still less to rebellion; it never had been. It required activation, acceleration, and, finally, a catalyst. In other centuries other issues had mobilised English Nonconformity; but in the 1760s and 70s a vital stimulus to political mobilisation appears to have been the evolving theological stance of the heterodox, which activated and mobilised the political engagement first of themselves and then, quickly spreading, a large part of orthodox Dissent as well. The ideological origins of what was in the 1820s to be termed 'radicalism' are not to be sought in some lowest common denominators uniting heterodox and orthodox Dissenters' views of ecclesiastical polity, especially if these denominators are found to reside in an almost secular insistence on equal opportunities and a protest that religious belief was an irrelevant ground for social exclusion; rather they are to be found in those new and sensational doctrines, in the writings and preaching of the heterodox, which were able to engage with and transform the body of inherited ideas of initially larger bodies of men who did not subscribe to the most extreme doctrines of the most extreme of their brethren. A reified ideological position was eventually created; but it was not inevitable that it should be, and not inevitable that those who were eventually persuaded that they shared a common cause should have been so persuaded.

V. HETERODOXY AND REBELLION IN COLONIAL AMERICA, 1760–1776

England displayed with remarkable conceptual and chronological clarity the role of theological issues as activators, mobilising among some Ang-

---

[166] *The Anti-Jacobin Review and Magazine*, I (London, 1799), 716.

licans and Dissenters, but never all of them, dispositions which had long
remained dormant in their inherited positions on church polity. Was the
pattern similar in America? Here the role of religion assumed a
heightened importance because of its involvement in the unexpected but
widespread phenomena of military conflict. It is easy to discern that the
rebellion of certain groups of colonists in the New World was *like* a war
of religion – alike in imagery, purpose and motivation. By 1776, the
American cause was an evangelical one, revivalistic with elements of millennialism, voluntarist in its bearing on social institutions, making explicit
play with the role of divine Providence and the predestined glory of a
liberated America. Colonists' zeal for liberty has most aptly been
described with a term drawn from religious revivalism, 'enthusiasm'.
Americans saw themselves fighting in a battle between the forces of light
and the forces of darkness, but it was churches or sects which drew the
distinction and vouched for the justice of the cause of God-fearing Americans. This revivalistic idiom is most often traced, not without cause, to
the positive affirmations of the religious revivals assembled by modern
convention under a single term, the Great Awakening.[167]

It had other sources too in the ancient negations sustained by the
denominations of Protestant Dissent which had flourished, and nurtured
their resentments, in a new soil. For these reasons, the American Revolution was more than analogous to a war of religion: it was to an important
degree such a war. Sectarian identity gave enthusiasm or millenarianism
a political application from the 1760s, where the activists of religious
revivals from the 1730s had refrained from any critique of the monarchy
or of the tie with Britain. The explicit attack on allegiance to a British
monarch, defined as that allegiance was in politico-theological terms,
came when the revivalist idiom, and anti-Anglican sectarian traditions of
ecclesiastical polity, were mobilised by men with profoundly different
theological positions, like the Arians Jonathan Mayhew and John Adams
or the Deist Tom Paine. Mobilisation meant the conversion of practical
but negotiable grievances into triggers of that right of resistance which

---

[167] See especially C. H. Maxson, *The Great Awakening in the Middle Colonies* (Chicago, 1920);
Wesley M. Gewehr, *The Great Awakening in Virginia, 1740–1790* (Durham, N.C., 1930);
Edwin Scott Gaustad, *The Great Awakening in New England* (New York, 1957); C. C. Goen,
*Revivalism and Separatism in New England, 1740–1800: Strict Congregationalists and Separate
Baptists in the Great Awakening* (New Haven, 1962); Alan Heimert, *Religion and the American
Mind from the Great Awakening to the Revolution* (Cambridge, Mass., 1966); William G.
McLoughlin, "Enthusiasm for Liberty': The Great Awakening as the Key to the Revolu-
tion', *Proceedings of the American Antiquarian Society* 87 (1977), 69–95; idem, *Revivals,
Awakenings, and Reform: An Essay on Religion and Social Change in America, 1607–1977* (Chicago,
1978); Bonomi, *Cope of Heaven*.

the sects had long preserved as a central definition of their independence from the Church of England.

Of the signers of the Declaration of Independence, covert or explicit theological heterodoxy has been alleged for John Adams, Josiah Bartlett, Benjamin Franklin, Stephen Hopkins, Thomas Jefferson, Robert Treat Paine, Benjamin Rush, Matthew Thornton and George Wythe. The orthodoxy or sincerity of James Madison, George Mason and George Washington has been questioned. Few of the Founding Fathers have been labelled 'conservatives in religion'.[168] Yet if the Founding Fathers were frequently heterodox, they prudently did not publicise their inclinations. In a world which valued their formal (if token) religious observance, they communicated their real feelings only to a small circle of like-minded men. Even after independence, Americans shied away from public discussion of an issue which was at the centre of open debate in England. George Washington continued, though unostentatiously, to avoid taking communion in the episcopalian church of which he was nominally a member.[169] Richard Price replied to the sympathetic American Benjamin Rush: 'You observe that in writing to the citizens of America it would be necessary that I should be silent about the disputed doctrines of Christianity, and particularly the Trinity. I am afraid that were I to write again, I should find this a hard restraint.'[170] The great mass of their American contemporaries was unaware of the contribution of religious doubt to the politics of the Founding Fathers: the public saw and responded to only the positive denunciations of prelacy, hierarchy and establishment which heterodoxy inspired. The mass of colonists was moved not by doubt but by belief, and their beliefs were relatively constant. It was their application which changed. Those beliefs were mobilised, turned from defensive to offensive creeds, by the private and generally unacknowledged dogmas of clerical and lay elites.

Richard Price was an Arian, stopping short of full Socinianism. Yet in December 1798, the *Anti-Jacobin* observed that it was his pro-American tract of 1776, *Observations on the Nature of Civil Liberty*, which in England 'contributed very much to the spreading among the dissenters (the Socinians at least,) those democratical principles to which Socinians are so prone'; the doctrines of the rights of man were 'heresiarchical chimeras ... the American contest added very much to the frequency and effect of such discussions, especially among the Socinian dissenters'.[171] But here

---

[168] Herbert M. Morais, *Deism in Eighteenth Century America* (New York, 1934), p. 17.

[169] Paul F. Boller, *George Washington & Religion* (Dallas, 1963), p. 15.

[170] Price to Rush, 30 July 1786, in Bernard Peach (ed.), *Richard Price and the Ethical Foundations of the American Revolution* (Durham, N.C., 1979), p. 336.

[171] *The Anti-Jacobin Review and Magazine* 1 (London, 1799), 714–15.

the differences in England between the English case and the American become crucial. The American Revolution was not inspired in the minds of colonists by a new doctrine of universal suffrage, the right of the individual to vote as an individual; nor was it a bid for colonial MPs at Westminster. The franchise in North American colonies was already wide, qualifications were seldom enforced, and the Revolution was not preceded by any significant drive to widen it further: not until the advent of Jacksonian democracy in the 1820s did the franchise become a matter of widespread contention in American politics.[172]

Late-eighteenth-century England began a new debate with Richard Price's assertion that a state is free 'in proportion as it is more or less fairly and adequately represented'. But late-eighteenth-century America was still conducting an old quarrel, strongly repetitive of the terms of debate in England between c. 1670 and 1730, in its critique of what were identified as absolute monarchy and arbitrary rule. In that critique, a number of streams converged. The best-known was, of course, the fashionable Deism personified in Jefferson and Franklin and popularised by Tom Paine's *Common Sense*. But by far the larger of the sources of this critique was its ancient derivation from the sects which had flourished on American soil, tending and ripening their seventeenth-century traditions, ideals and resentments. These were not immediately decisive: Dissent was not synonymous with republicanism or rebellion. Yet loyalists and patriots both obscured in retrospect the complexities of late-colonial alignments. By the late nineteenth century, most of the denominations in America had capitulated to the dominant myth of the Republic's origins. Each sought to reinterpret their own history, to represent colonial Episcopalians, Presbyterians, Congregationalists or Baptists as unanimous or nearly-unanimous in support of the Revolution, and to argue that the new polity was essentially indebted to the endeavours and the ideals of the one denomination whose achievements were being trumpeted.[173] The position in the 1770s was far more complex, however: the challenges of war induced in many men ambiguity and equivocation; many denomina-

---

[172] Chilton Williamson, *American Suffrage from Property to Democracy* (Princeton, 1960), pp. 43, 45–6, 77, 91–2, 117, 207; J. R. Pole, *Political Representation in England and the Origins of the American Republic* (London, 1966), pp. 543–64; R. J. Dinkin, *Voting in Provincial America: A Study of Elections in the Thirteen Colonies, 1689–1776* (Westport, 1977), pp. 28–49; idem, *Voting in Revolutionary America: A Study of Elections in the Original Thirteen States, 1776–1789* (Westport, 1982), pp. 27–43.

[173] E.g. W. S. Perry, 'The Faith of the Signers of the Declaration of Independence', *The Magazine of History* (Tarrytown, New York, 1926), 215–37 for the Episcopalians; W. P. Breed, *Presbyterians and the Revolution* (Philadelphia, 1876); William Cathcart, *The Baptists and the American Revolution* (Philadelphia, 1876): 'They were the seed-bearers of the Revolution', p. 114.

tions either divided or joined the fighting only after an agony of doubt, an agony which related to an internal debate about the lesson to be drawn from that sect's intellectual inheritance. To understand these processes, each denomination demands separate attention.

(a) THE AMERICAN ANGLICANS

A substantial proportion of American colonists was still Anglican; so was a majority of signers of the Declaration of Independence.[174] As in England, the alignment of and divisions within American Episcopalianism provides the larger part of the answer to the question of the relative priority of different religious motivations. These theological conflicts in themselves subverted an attempted Anglican hegemony in America, for the ecclesiastical dynamics of colonial society embraced some contradictory developments. Parallel to the growing sectarian diversity of the colonial population under the impact of successive waves of non-English immigration went a confident expansionary drive on the part of the Church of England. Anglicanism grew steadily in the American colonies during the eighteenth century, but from 1760 to the Revolution that growth powerfully accelerated. Whether in church building, in the number of clergy, or in higher education, the Church consolidated and strongly advanced its position. Outside New England, colonial taxes to finance the construction and endowment of new churches became the norm.[175] Despite the lack of resident bishops, the London-based Society for the Propagation of the Gospel played a dynamic role in sending and maintaining missionary clergy, mostly themselves High Churchmen. Yet this drive was to be resisted even within colonial Anglicanism.

The effect of religious establishments had become a cliché of colonial discourse, and a theme of college education even for Anglicans. James Madison, a graduate of Princeton in 1771, wrote from his native Virginia to a college friend in 1774: 'If the Church of England had been the established and general religion in all the northern colonies as it has been among us here, and uninterrupted tranquillity had prevailed throughout the continent, it is clear to me that slavery and subjection might and

---

[174] W. S. Perry, 'The Faith of the Signers of the Declaration of Independence', assigns the 56 signers: Episcopalians 34, Congregationalists 13, Presbyterians 6, Baptist 1, Quaker 1, Catholic 1. Of the 68 members of Congress on 4 July 1776, the imbalance was greater: Episcopalians 45, Congregationalists 14, Presbyterians 5, Quakers 2, Baptist 1, Dutch Reformed 1. The balance of the groups actually involved in fighting was to be quite different, however, with a heavy preponderance of non-Anglicans.

[175] Frederick V. Mills, 'Anglican Expansion in Colonial America 1761–1775', *HMPEC* 39 (1970), 315–24; Peter Doll, 'Imperial Anglicanism in North America, 1745–95' (Oxford D.Phil. thesis, 1989), pp. 157–275.

would have been gradually insinuated among us. Union of religious sentiments begets a surprising confidence, and ecclesiastical establishments
tend to great ignorance and corruption; all of which facilitate the execution of mischievous projects.'[176]

Yet despite these ecclesiological reasons for transatlantic solidarity,
Anglicanism was the most divided of all denominations in the Revolution,
a majority of the laity backing independence and only a narrow majority
of clergy being loyalists. Loyalism correlated with a number of factors.
The weaker the position of the Church in a colony, the more its members
had earlier supported an American episcopate, the more their churchmanship was 'high' rather than low or latitudinarian, the greater the
presence of the SPG, and the greater the number of recent converts, the
more Anglican laymen and, still more, clergy tended to be loyalists; the
opposite of these features produced a commitment in the other direction.[177] So the position varied from colony to colony: all of Connecticut's
20 Anglican clergy were loyalists, and New York and New Jersey each
produced only one republican priest; but of some 100 Virginia clergy, 74
have been identified as backing the rebellion against 20 loyalists.[178] The
division was a familiar one: 'although some High Church clergy supported the American side, the majority of the patriotic clergy seem to
have belonged either to the Latitudinarian or to the Low Church schools
of churchmanship'.[179] In Virginia especially, the absence of episcopal
authority and the dominance of a Latitudinarian laity produced a parochial pattern that was already quasi-Presbyterian in practice if not in
name.[180]

Episcopalians in the colonies spanned the same spectrum of churchmanship as churchmen in England, but with a greater Low Church (even
quasi-Dissenting) emphasis. Yet where in England the rivalry of Low and
High Church produced only minor gains and losses, in America a successful revolution altered the whole landscape and changed men's perspectives on what had gone before. Episcopalians in America were compelled

---

[176] James Madison to William Bradford, 24 Jan. 1774: Madison, *Writings*, vol. 1, p. 18.
[177] David L. Holmes, 'The Episcopal Church and the American Revolution', *HMPEC* 47
(1978), 261–91, at 265.
[178] Ibid., pp. 266–7.
[179] Ibid., p. 278. Holmes estimates (p. 283) that, overall, Anglican clergy in the 13 colonies
supported the loyalist cause by 150 to 123; Anglican laity supported the revolution by a
larger proportion.
[180] As the Bishop of London's Commissary in Virginia complained, 'the Vestries in general
do not care to appoint a person to a vacant living before they try him, that is, have heard
him preach, and according to his Voice and delivery he is received or rejected': William
Robinson to the Bishop of London, 23 May 1765: W. S. Perry (ed.), *Historical Collections
Relating to the American Colonial Church* (5 vols. in 4, Hartford, Conn., 1870–7), vol. 1, p.
503.

after 1783 to represent their denomination as overwhelmingly patriots; émigrés equally depicted colonial Anglicans as frustrated loyalists. Both views contained only part of the truth. There were certainly colonial clergy like Jonathan Boucher who attracted the revival of the old label 'Tory' by the propagation of such doctrine as 'A levelling republican spirit in the Church naturally leads to republicanism in the State.'[181] Yet even in New York, the loyalism of clergy like Charles Inglis and Samuel Seabury was countered by Dr Samuel Provoost, later bishop, or layman Alexander Hamilton, graduate of Anglican King's College, who wrote replies to Seabury's *Letters of a Westchester Farmer*. In Philadelphia, Anglican clergy took the side of Congress more often than in New York: ministers like William Smith, Thomas Coombe and Jacob Duché were vocal propagandists. But although Smith championed colonial grievances, he wrote against independence in a series of replies to Paine's *Common Sense*; Duché too deserted the rebel for the loyalist cause. Clerical alignments were not simple, and the churchmanship of individual clergy is often hard to establish; what is clear is their division.

Other clergy, especially in the south, were more clearly identified as Low Churchmen. The missionary Charles Inglis, of Trinity church in New York, reported pessimistically to the SPG in October 1776 of Virginia: 'For my part, I never expected much good of those clergy among them who opposed an American episcopate. If such should now renounce their allegiance, and abandon their duty, it is no more than what might naturally be looked for.'[182] The wide extent of Deist or similar sentiments among the Anglican gentry of Virginia[183] may have owed something to the penetration of fashionable ideas into seats of learning. It was at the College of William and Mary, alma mater of Thomas Jefferson from March 1760 to April 1762, that Edmund Randolph (a student from June 1770 to October 1771), as he later wrote, became 'a deist' under the influence of two of his 'preceptors, who, though of the ministry, poisoned me with books of infidelity'; Randolph was only converted to Christianity by his wife's orthodoxy.[184] The impact on Virginia society of two such men, perhaps the two who taught Randolph, is considered below.

Anglican Virginia had been no more tranquil in the parochial relations

---

[181] Boucher, *A View of the Causes and Consequences of the American Revolution*, p. 104.
[182] Ernest Hawkins, *Historical Notices of the Missions of the Church of England in the North American Colonies, Previous to the Independence of the United States: Chiefly from the Ms. Documents of the Society for the Propagation of the Gospel in Foreign Parts* (London, 1845), p. 332.
[183] Morais, *Deism*, pp. 113–19.
[184] William Meade, *Old Churches Ministers and Families of Virginia* (2 vols., Philadelphia, 1857; repr. Baltimore, 1966), vol. 1, p. 182; vol. 2, pp. 292–4; M. D. Conway, *Omitted Chapters of History Disclosed in the Life and Papers of Edmund Randolph* (New York, 1888), pp. 12, 156–66, 389.

of squires and parsons than the English countryside.[185] Conflicts over lay
control versus ministers' security of tenure soured the 1740s and 50s
with a series of legal suits collectively known as the Parsons' Cause.
Anticlericalism on the one side and a degree of militancy among the
clergy were the divisive results.[186] Anglican clergy sought to escape from
the depressed status which the undeveloped nature of the colony had
initially entailed, and aspired to enjoy the same rights to their incomes
as, under the tithe system, the clergy did in England. Lay vestrymen on
their side sought to defend traditional religion from the forces of itinerancy
and enthusiasm unleashed in religious revivals, especially those of the
Baptists. The result was lasting friction which divided the colony along
the familiar lines of churchmanship. Into this unstable situation a theological catalyst now intruded.

In 1771, the attempt of James Horrocks, the Bishop of London's commissary in Virginia, to organise a clerical petition for an Anglican bishop
to be sent to the colony was subverted by the opposition of a minority of
ministers. These clergy included two prominent new arrivals from England to chairs at the College of William and Mary, and their antecedents
reveal with unique clarity but with an unusual conclusion the impact of
heterodoxy within transatlantic Anglican debates on ecclesiastical polity.
Samuel Henley (b. 1744) had been educated as a Dissenter at Caleb
Ashworth's famous dissenting academy at Daventry, was ordained a Dissenting minister in 1768, and while exercising his ministry at St Neots
and living in Cambridge in 1768–9 cultivated Edmund Law and John
Jebb: they supported his application for Anglican ordination in 1769.[187]
Thomas Gwatkin (b. 1741) matriculated at Jesus College, Oxford in 1763
but never took a degree. He was ordained in 1767 by Robert Terrick
who, as Bishop of London, was chancellor of the College of William and
Mary, to professorships at which he nominated Gwatkin and Henley in
1769.[188]

Thomas Gwatkin had already employed the familiar rhetoric to argue
that 'many species of tyranny . . . prevail in the world', and that 'Among
a great variety of schemes employed for this purpose, none have been

---

[185] Eric J. Evans, 'Some Reasons for the Growth of English Rural Anticlericalism, c. 1750–
1830', *P&P* 66 (1975), 84–109; idem, *The Contentious Tithe* (London, 1976); John A.
Phillips, 'The Social Calculus: Deference and Defiance in Later Georgian England', *Albion*
21, 3 (1989), 426–49.

[186] Rhys Isaac, 'Religion and Authority: Problems of the Anglican Establishment in Virginia
in the Era of the Great Awakening and the Parsons' Cause', *WMQ* 30 (1973), 3–36.

[187] For biographical details, Fraser Neiman, 'Letters of William Gilpin to Samuel Henley',
Huntington Library Quarterly 35 (1971–2), 159–69.

[188] Rhys Isaac, *The Transformation of Virginia, 1740–1790* (Chapel Hill, 1982), pp. 181–6, 202–
3; Ray Hiner, Jr, 'Samuel Henley and Thomas Gwatkin: Partners in Protest', *HMPEC*
37 (1968), 39–50.

more successful in rivetting the chains of oppression, than the union of religion and civil policy.' A pagan invention, this device 'corrupted' Christianity where it became 'interwoven' with it.[189] Rather, Gwatkin aligned himself behind Francis Blackburne's *Confessional* and his bid to reform the English Church by the abolition of creeds and subscription to articles of faith.[190] Gwatkin believed that the 'much disputed doctrine of the Trinity owes its settlement to the manly reasoning of a *Dawson*'.[191] Dr Benjamin Dawson, who had published his work on the Trinity together with another dedicated to the heterodox Dr. Edmund Law,[192] Master of Peterhouse, had argued against the Arian doctrine of the pre-existence of Christ, preferred the Socinian position as 'more consistent than the *Arians*', and, while finding a formula to include Christ's exalted role, heavily stressed the unitary nature of God. Even the Athanasian creed, insisted Dawson with some verbal dexterity, announced the doctrine of '*One* God'. It was evidently an attempt to smuggle in a Socinian emphasis under cover of an eirenic defence of traditional formulae.[193] To these he was not strongly attached: born into a Presbyterian family in Halifax in 1729, Dawson had been educated at Caleb Rotheram's dissenting academy at Kendal and at Glasgow University before holding appointments as a Presbyterian minister; only in 1758 did he conform to the Church and in 1760 receive that Suffolk rectory where, secure from challenge, he wrote (though still anonymously) in support of Francis Blackburne's *Confessional*[194] and the Feathers' Tavern petition.[195]

It was appropriate that Dawson's unease over the central doctrines of Christianity should go together with unease over its established status. Even if, as a fellow cleric had argued, 'every state has a right to prevent the *ill consequences* of free opinion in matters of religion',[196] Dawson maintained that it was 'unproved' that 'any ill consequences can flow from

---

[189] [Thomas Gwatkin], *Remarks upon the Second and Third of Three Letters against the Confessional* (London, 1768), pp. 5–9.

[190] [Thomas Gwatkin], *Remarks upon the First of Three Letters against the Confessional* (London, 1768).

[191] [Thomas Gwatkin], *Remarks upon the Second and Third . . .* , pp. 17, 41.

[192] Benjamin Dawson, *Two Tracts Relating to the Doctrine of an Intermediate State*; for Law see Clark, *English Society 1688–1832*, pp. 311–13.

[193] Benjamin Dawson, *An Illustration of Several Texts of Scripture, Particularly Those in which the Logos occurs* (London, 1765), pp. 4–9, 94, 131, 233, index. The doctrine of the Church of England, insisted Dawson (p. 18) was 'that *God*, and no other Being, is our Saviour, and has been manifested to the World in the Flesh, by the *Man* Jesus Christ'.

[194] [Benjamin Dawson], *An Examination of Dr. Rutherforth's Argument Respecting the Right of Protestant Churches To require the Clergy to Subscribe to an Established Confession of Faith and Doctrines* (London, 1765).

[195] *DNB*.

[196] Dawson paraphrased Nathaniel Forster, *The Establishment of the Church of England defended upon the Principles of Religious Liberty. A Sermon Preached at the Triennial Visitation of the . . . Bishop of London* (London, 1770), p. 8.

free opinion'. Civil disorder arose from '*fanaticism*', not from '*freedom of opinion* in Religion'; these, Dawson maintained, were not the same.[197] The establishment of the Church of England could only be defended on 'a first principle of Protestantism ... *viz.* that, in the matter of Religion, and where Conscience is concerned, we are not accountable to any power upon earth'.[198] Dawson's principle of religious resistance thus introduced the trope which was to dominate colonial American reactions to Anglican and English authority: 'I am of opinion, that the Church of *England* is too firmly rooted in Protestant ground to be *essentially* endangered by any other principles whatever, than those of POPERY.'[199] Such was Thomas Gwatkin's guiding spirit.

Once in their new posts Henley and Gwatkin played on the latent anticlericalism of the Virginia gentry, and persuaded the House of Burgesses in July 1771 to condemn the proposed petition for a bishop as 'a Measure by which much Disturbance, great Anxiety, and Apprehension, would certainly take Place among his Majesty's faithful *American* Subjects'.[200] It was the threat of bishops *per se*, as agents of ecclesiastical authority, that dominated the hostile propaganda rather than the possible role of a bishop as the agent of a conspiracy by the king's ministers against American liberties: bishops as part of a 'mighty Torrent of spiritual Tyranny',[201] as the early-eighteenth-century Deists had depicted them. Anglicans could stigmatise the proposal for an American episcopate shorn of its temporal powers as smacking of the '*Jacobite* Church which flourished under the Hickses and the Leslies, and which you are labouring to set up in America'. Gwatkin cited Archbishop Secker's observation that '*a great Part of the Clergy who go to America are Scotch*', inferring that 'This is indeed a probable Account of the great Attachment that has lately been discovered in this Country to a NONJURING *Kind of Episcopate*, independent of, and unconnected with, the State.'[202] With such arguments, Gwatkin could play on the fears of Virginia Anglicans like Colonel Richard Bland, who announced: 'I profess myself a sincere son of the established church, but I can embrace her Doctrines without approving of her Hierarchy, which I know to be a Relick of the Papal Incroachments upon the Common Law.' Bland feared that the appointment in America

---

[197] [Benjamin Dawson], *A Free and Candid Disquisition on Religious Establishments in General, and the Church of England in Particular. Occasioned by a Visitation Sermon preached at Chelmsford, May 22, 1770* (London, 1771), pp. 10, 12.

[198] Ibid., p. 25.

[199] Ibid., p. 66.

[200] Isaac, *Transformation of Virginia*, p. 186.

[201] Ibid., pp. 187–9.

[202] Thomas Gwatkin, *A Letter to the Clergy of New York and New Jersey, occasioned by An Address to the Episcopalians in Virginia* (Williamsburg, 1772), pp. 19, 23.

of a bishop with 'any Jurisdiction at all' would produce 'greater convulsions than any thing that has ever as yet happened in this part of the Globe'. He generalised his point: 'a Religious Dispute is the most Fierce and Destructive of all others to the Peace & Happiness of Government'.[203]

So far, the conflict had seemed to turn on issues of ecclesiastical polity; yet this was soon to change. Heterodoxy had acted as a catalyst of wider assumptions, but now came under scrutiny itself. Although Henley was successful in raising a political obstacle to the consecration of an American bishop, the spotlight now turned on him. It began to be objected that he disbelieved in the Trinity. On 1 March 1772 he preached before the House of Burgesses a sermon soon published in Cambridge, England, and dedicated to 'a Friend', John Jebb, who was similarly labouring to 'strike off the shackles from the human mind . . . in the study of Revelation'. Henley argued for a complete separation of the sacred and the secular and for the purely secular ends of government; he condemned the state's practice of 'forcing a belief', so implicitly condemning everything being done in Virginia to check the wildfire growth of the Separate Baptists.[204] He or Gwatkin followed this with a letter to the press signed 'Hoadleianus' recommending the abolition of a 'Subscription to any of the Articles of the Church of England' as a condition for tolerating other denominations in Virginia.[205]

When the rectory of Bruton Church, Williamsburg, fell vacant, Henley's theological opinions were enquired into by the vestry in June 1773, it being recalled that Colonel Bland had complained to Henley that 'he explained the Scriptures as a Socinian' – that he was a 'Perverter of the sacred Text, in one of the most important Doctrines of the established Church, which it was his Duty to defend', i.e. that Henley had expounded the first chapter of Hebrews 'so as to deprive our Saviour of his Divinity'. John Page of Rosewell claimed he had heard Henley 'argue against the *Doctrine* of the ADORABLE TRINITY, and assert that by the *three Persons* was only meant the three *Characters* under which God had made himself known to Men, viz. as their *Creator, as the Means of their Redemption,* and *as inspiring them with good Thoughts*'; for that the Word *Person* was borrowed from *Persona,* which signified an *Actor's Mask*'.[206] The vestry chose another candidate. But the damage to the Church was done, one correspondent com-

[203] Bland to Adams, 1 Aug 1771: *WMQ* 1st ser., 5 (1896–7), 154.

[204] S. Henley, *The Distinct Claims of Government and Religion, Considered in a Sermon Preached before the Honourable House of Burgesses, at Williamsburg, in Virginia, March 1, 1772* (Cambridge, 1772), Dedication, pp. 6–8, 14.

[205] Isaac, *Transformation of Virginia*, pp. 218–40.

[206] Quoted ibid., p. 234.

plaining to the press that 'a general corruption of manners had diffused through . . . the lower parts of the country, whilst little else prevails in the upper counties . . . than an indissoluble aversion to, and an enthusiastic dissention from, the principles of our ecclesiastic establishment'.[207]

Open heterodoxy could still destroy clerical careers and define the heterodox against their persecutors. Henley raised the stakes yet further in a pamphlet designed to defend himself from these imputations; but its legalistic evasions and condescending tone towards his gentry critics did not promote reconciliation. Henley did not argue to establish his own orthodoxy, but to prove that the Church of England had always been in disagreement: Sherlock, South, Wallis, Bennet and Waterland had each maintained different positions on the Trinity without being branded as heretics.[208] Like Benjamin Dawson, Henley maintained that his own position was in fact that of the Thirty-Nine Articles, and demanded that his critics prove his teaching heretical from Scripture. Against the 'bigotry, ignorance and dulness' of the colonists, Henley boasted his metropolitan patriotism: he had written in the reign of a monarch 'of that ILLUSTRIOUS HOUSE which infused fresh vigour into every advocate for genuine Protestantism by the glorious protection of a CLARKE and a HOADLY'.[209] So embittered did relations with orthodox Anglican local gentry become that in 1775 Henley and Gwatkin took the British side and, with superb irony, had to be evacuated with the Governor, Lord Dunmore, on a British warship. In Virginia as elsewhere, a heterodox clerical minority played an important role in mobilising Low Church opinion against an Anglican polity; but the case of Henley and Gwatkin shows that the role of this minority was possible only as long as its critique was not focused on the colonial elite, and as long as its heterodox underpinning remained unknown to a wider audience.

The unmasking of Henley and Gwatkin was the reverse of typical, and the role of 'Enlightened' religion in the politics of Virginia Anglicans was better expressed in the career of Thomas Jefferson. Jefferson's formal Episcopalian attendance concealed distinct theological opinions, not secular unbelief; his views were heavily indebted to the English Deists like Lord Bolingbroke, Charles Blount, Conyers Middleton, Matthew Tindal and John Toland.[210] A close friend and admirer of Joseph Priestley and

[207] Quoted ibid.
[208] Samuel Henley, *A Candid Refutation of the Heresy Imputed by Ro. C. Nicholas Esquire to The Reverend S. Henley* (Williamsburg, 1774), pp. 24–5.
[209] Ibid., pp. 31, 67, 69, 72.
[210] Charles B. Sandford, *The Religious Life of Thomas Jefferson* (Charlottesville, 1984), pp. 13–14, 83–101.

later a member of his congregation in Philadelphia, Jefferson declined to act as a godfather in services of baptism because 'from a very early part of my life' he could not subscribe to the doctrine of the Trinity contained in the Apostles' Creed.[211] His great grandson claimed that the Virginian Robespierre was a

> conservative Unitarian ... He did not believe in the miracles, nor the divinity of Christ,[212] nor the doctrine of the atonement, but he was a firm believer in Divine Providence, in the efficacy of prayer, in a future state of rewards and punishments, and in the meeting of friends in another world.[213]

Unitarianism, Jefferson hoped, 'would become the general religion of the United States'.[214]

His religious views were largely unknown to his contemporaries. John Trumbull recorded his surprise to find himself at a 'freethinking dinner party' given by Jefferson at his house in 1793, where Senator William Giles of Virginia 'proceeded so far at last, as to ridicule the character, conduct, and doctrines of the divine founder of our religion – Jefferson in the mean time, smiling and nodding approbation on Mr. Giles', who finally blurted out:

> It is all a miserable delusion and priestcraft; I do not believe one word of all they say about a future state of existence, and retribution for actions done here. I do not believe one word of a Supreme Being who takes cogniz-ance of the paltry affairs of this world, and to whom we are responsible for what we do.

'I had never before heard, or seen in writing, such a broad and unqualified avowal of atheism', recorded Trumbull.[215] Appropriately, it was Jefferson who in 1801 invited Tom Paine to return to America, with his 'assurances of my high esteem and affectionate attachment'.[216]

Jefferson deliberately restricted knowledge of his religious opinions. These were only accidentally disclosed as asides in his *Notes on the State of Virginia*, written in 1781, printed in a limited edition of 200 copies after

---

[211] Jefferson to J.P.P. Derieux, 25 July 1788: Jefferson, *Papers*, vol. 13, p. 418.

[212] For which, Sandford, *Religious Life*, pp. 102–40, 174: 'It is probable that it was Jefferson's Christology which earned him his reputation as a religious radical more than his ideas about God ... ' Jefferson set out his position systematically in 'Syllabus of an Estimate of the Merit of the Doctrines of Jesus, compared with those of others', in Henry Stephens Randall, *The Life of Thomas Jefferson* (3 vols., Philadelphia, 1865), vol. 3, pp. 556–8. He praised the Socinian Joseph Priestley's *History of the Corruptions of Christianity* (London, 1782), which 'establishes the ground-work of my view of this subject'.

[213] Sandford, *Religious Life*, pp. 4–5.

[214] Jefferson to James Smith, 8 Dec. 1822: Jefferson, *Writings*, vol. 15, p. 409.

[215] Theodore Sizer (ed.), *The Autobiography of Colonel John Trumbull Patriot-Artist, 1756–1843* (New Haven, 1953), pp. 174–5.

[216] Jefferson to Paine, 18 March 1801: Jefferson, *Writings*, vol. 10, p. 223.

he replaced Benjamin Franklin in Paris in 1784, and published widely by the author only after a Paris printer brought out a pirated edition. Scattered through a work on Virginia's geography and natural history were doubts about such doctrinal tenets as the Flood and the origin of all mankind from a single couple, Adam and Eve. These doubts culminated in a round assertion of religious liberty:

> our rulers can have authority over such natural rights only as we have submitted to them. The rights of conscience we never submitted, we could not submit. We are answerable for them to our God. The legitimate powers of government extend to such acts only as are injurious to others. But it does me no injury for my neighbour to say there are twenty gods, or no god. It neither picks my pocket nor breaks my leg . . . Let us reflect that it [the earth] is inhabited by a thousand millions of people. That these profess probably a thousand different systems of religion. That ours is but one of that thousand.

Only free enquiry would purge the 'present corruptions' of Christianity.[217] Not until the 1800 presidential campaign, however, was Jefferson's irreligion drawn into political debate and used against him.[218] It then proved a major handicap. 'I dread the election of Mr. Jefferson', wrote the Rev. John Mason, 'because I believe him to be a confirmed infidel.' This had long been 'denied by his friends'; now his *Notes on Virginia* supplied proof. If the Federal Constitution made no acknowledgement of God, this 'reproach' of irreligion must be wiped off.[219]

Independence compelled Anglicans in the new states to redraft their polity,[220] but subjected them during that process once more to the forces which had divided them during the Revolution. Influential in the process of redrafting was the pro-revolutionary Samuel Provoost, who secured from these manoeuvres his consecration as Bishop of New York on 4 February 1787 but was meanwhile rector of Trinity Church in his native city. Provoost had been educated from 1761 to 1766 at Peterhouse, Cam-

[217] Thomas Jefferson, *Notes on the State of Virginia* (London, 1787), pp. 27, 46–8, 69, 165, 265–7.

[218] G. A. Koch, *Republican Religion: The American Revolution and the Cult of Reason* (New York, 1933), pp. 266–74.

[219] [John M. Mason], *The Voice of Warning, to Christians, on the Ensuing Election of a President of the United States* (New York, 1800), pp. 8, 33–4; [Clement Clarke Moore], *Observations upon certain passages in Mr. Jefferson's Notes on Virginia, which appear to have a tendency to Subvert Religion, and establish a False Philosophy* (New York, 1804), identified Jefferson's views as 'French Philosophy' (p. 6).

[220] William Stevens Perry, *The History of the American Episcopal Church 1587–1883* (2 vols., Boston, 1885), vol. 2, pp. 1–131. Clara O. Loveland, *The Critical Years. The Reconstitution of the Anglican Church in the United States of America: 1780–1789* (Greenwich, Conn., 1956) narrates this process but explains it as the transposition to the Church of 'John Locke's theory of government, on which the political framework of the United States was being formed' (p. 34).

bridge, during the disastrous mastership of the heterodox Edmund Law; there he had imbibed the fashionable doctrines as a contemporary of John Disney (a student 1764–8), who later forsook the Church for the newly-public Unitarian movement.[221] Equally influential was the pro-revolutionary William White, rector of Christ Church, Philadelphia, who later secured for himself the newly-created bishopric of Pennsylvania. In 1782 he published a tract which became a blueprint for the organisation of the new church: it envisaged all denominations being 'on a level' as voluntary associations, lay control over clergy and bishops, the equality of parishes, and 'a considerable latitude of sentiment' on the meaning of the Thirty-Nine Articles. Citing Hoadly and Tillotson, White argued for the authority of American clergy to consecrate their own bishops at once, without English involvement, and repudiated the idea that either bishops or monarchs exercised authority by divine right.[222] With members of this complexion, the first General Convention of the Protestant Episcopal Church of the United States of America met in Philadelphia from 27 September to 7 October 1785. The New England states, led by the loyalist High Churchman Samuel Seabury, newly consecrated bishop in the apostolic succession by the bishops of the Nonjuring Church of Scotland, did not attend. In the absence of this orthodox bloc the General Conference not only set up an almost Presbyterian system of church polity, giving substantial power to the laity; it also authorised a revised *Book of Common Prayer*,[223] altered 'in order to render the same conformable to the American Revolution and the Constitutions of the respective States'.

It went further still: since 'it is represented to this Convention to be the desire of the Protestant Episcopal Church in these States, that there may be further alterations of the Liturgy than such as are made necessary by the American Revolution', it proposed a whole series of doctrinal changes, to take effect when ratified by the constituent Conventions which had sent delegates to the General Convention.[224] These proposed changes give a unique insight into the mentality of the Anglican Low Churchmen in the central and southern colonies on whose support the Revolution had depended. They entailed, among an extensive list of amendments,

---

[221] *DAB, DNB.*

[222] [William White], *The Case of the Episcopal Churches in the United States Considered* (Philadelphia, 1782), pp. 8, 10, 13, 17, 19–20, 24.

[223] For this aspect of the Episcopalian church's redefinition, see Marion J. Hatchett, *The Making of the First American Book of Common Prayer* (New York, 1982), which examines the episode in a liturgical rather than a political or theological context.

[224] W. S. Perry, (ed.), *Journals of General Conventions of the Protestant Episcopal Church, in the United States, 1785–1835* (2 vols., Claremont, New Hampshire, 1874), vol. 1, pp. 21–3; *Fac-similies of Church Documents: Papers Issued by the Historical Club of the American Church. 1874–79* (Privately printed, [?1879]), nos. 10–47.

the reduction of the Thirty-Nine Articles to twenty (later to seventeen);[225] the replacement of the term 'priest' by 'minister'; the omission of 'He descended into Hell' from the Apostles' Creed; and the complete omission of the Nicene and Athanasian Creeds, the latter chiefly marked, according to the President of the Convention, by 'its protest against Arianism and Socinianism'.[226] John Page, graduate of the College of William and Mary in 1763 (and fellow-student with Jefferson), later Governor of Virginia, had even proposed (though unsuccessfully) 'to leave out the first four petitions of the Litany' and substitute another 'more agreeable to his ideas of the Divine Persons': the fourth petition was to be dropped as using the unscriptural term 'Trinity', the other three because, without that term, they implied the existence of three Gods.[227] Such fundamental changes produced a protest from the Archbishops of Canterbury and York, apprehensive of the ascendancy of clergy and laity over the bishops, specifically mentioning the deletion of an article from the Apostles' Creed 'which was thought necessary to be inserted, with a View to a particular Heresy,[228] in a very early Age of the Church', and calling for the restoration of that and the two deleted creeds.[229]

Under this pressure, the Convention reassembled in October 1786 and restored the 'Descent into Hell' to the Apostles' Creed; re-inserted the Nicene Creed; but again rejected the Athanasian Creed, New York, Pennsylvania and South Carolina voting against, New Jersey and Delaware being divided.[230] Some States had adopted the new prayer book, others not. Only after reunion with the Church in the New England States did the General Convention of 1789 agree on a revised Liturgy embodied in a *Book of Common Prayer* in a form which then became general throughout America.[231] In its liturgical omissions, especially the Athanasian

---

[225] Whatever was novel in the debates on the Articles, noted William White, President of the Convention, 'was taken from a book in the possession of the Rev. Dr. Smith. The book was anonymous, and was one of the publications which have abounded in England, projecting changes in the established articles': White, *Memoirs*, p. 120.

[226] E. F. Humphrey, *Nationalism and Religion in America 1774–1789* (Boston, 1924), pp. 218–19. For the text of the proposed changes see William White, *Memoirs of the Protestant Episcopal Church in the United States of America*, ed. B. F. De Costa (Philadelphia, 1820; New York, 1880), pp. 435–48; *Fac-similies of Church Documents*, nos. 32, 33.

[227] White, *Memoirs*, pp. 116, 135.

[228] 'The heresy of Apollinaris (Bishop of Laodicea, 362–382) who maintained that the Logos held in Christ the place of a rational soul, and that God was united in Him with the human body and the sensitive soul': B. F. De Costa, in White, *Memoirs*, p. 126.

[229] Perry, *Journals*, vol. 1, pp. 51–4; White, *Memoirs*, pp. 360–5; *Fac-similies of Church Documents*, no. 38.

[230] Humphrey, *Nationalism and Religion*, p. 225; White, *Memoirs*, p. 25.

[231] Philip Schaff, *A History of The Creeds of Christendom* (3 vols., London, 1877), vol. 3, *The Creeds of the Evangelical Protestant Churches*, pp. 487–516, prints the Anglican Thirty-Nine Articles and the American revision of 1801, retaining the Trinitarian Article but deleting the Athanasian Creed and suspending the application of the Book of Homilies, containing as it inconveniently did no. 21, 'Against Rebellion'.

Creed, it still fell far short of what the orthodox like Bishop Seabury desired.[232] This was not surprising. Three days before Provoost's consecration as bishop, his Unitarian student contemporary John Disney presented him with a transcription of Dr Samuel Clarke's manuscript alterations in the *Book of Common Prayer*, 'in the earnest hope that it might be useful, on a further revisal of the present Liturgy of the Protestant Church in America, so that they might in their public devotions acknowledge none other than the One only living and true God'.[233]

One scholar attributed the outcome of the 1789 Convention to this cause: such evidence establishes that 'the English Arians permanently influenced the Episcopal Church of the United States'.[234] It may not be unrelated that the form of church polity which it adopted has been described as 'in no proper sense of the word an episcopal government, but rather a classical and synodical government, according to the common type of the American church constitutions of the period';[235] by the election at various levels of the vestry, the clergy, the diocesan convention, the bishops and the General Convention, 'the principles of representative government controlled the Church as they controlled the State'.[236] The American bishop, elected by and ultimately answerable to his flock, acknowledged the division of ecclesiastical sovereignty among all the orders of the church: bishops, clergy and laity. The 'most monarchical and magisterial Protestant church in Europe' adapted itself to the west's first secular republic with a remarkable degree of willingness.[237]

(B) THE AMERICAN PRESBYTERIANS

Other denominations had been less hampered in their organisation than the Anglicans and, when the revolution came, were less divided in their attitude towards it. This was the case of the denomination of Dissenters most widely found throughout the colonies, the Presbyterians.[238] Their political weight was far greater than that of their English brethren; and this was a result of organisation as well as numbers. English Presby-

---

[232] Perry, *History of the American Episcopal Church*, vol. 2, pp. 119–24.
[233] Quoted in Colligan, *The Arian Movement in England*, pp. 132–3.
[234] Ibid., p. 133.
[235] L. W. Bacon, *A History of American Christianity* (New York, 1897), pp. 210–11.
[236] George Hodges, *Three Hundred Years of the Episcopal Church in America* (Philadelphia, 1906), pp. 95–7. 'In one respect, the Church was more democratic than the State; it gave no man executive authority.'
[237] John Frederick Woolverton, *Colonial Anglicanism in North America* (Detroit, 1984), pp. 234–8.
[238] Surveyed in Leonard J. Trinterud, *The Forming of an American Tradition: A Re-Examination of Colonial Presbyterianism* (Philadelphia, 1949).

terians, following the Toleration Act of 1689, had abandoned their plans to establish a national synod and remained content with an ecclesiastical polity similar to that of the Congregationalists except in respect of the ordination of ministers. In the American colonies, however, it was the Anglicans who were prevented from developing the appropriate infrastructure of their church. Presbyterians by contrast were unfettered, and developed a fully Presbyterian system of church polity matching that of their parent churches elsewhere in the British Isles. The first Presbytery was founded in 1706; after an influx of settlers from Scotland and Ireland, the first Synod was organised in 1717, and in 1729 it accepted the Westminster Confession of Faith of 1646 and the Larger and Shorter Catechisms as the yardstick of membership. When the schism of 1741 had been healed, symbolically by the formation of the Synod of New York and Philadelphia in 1758, Presbyterians had a united organisation and (at least outwardly) a common doctrine.

Their attention to their traditions of ecclesiastical polity was unusually coherent, enlivened rather than obscured by schism, and lay ready for activation by developments in the surrounding culture. Presbyterianism shows, in particular, how Dissenting potentialities could be aroused by sharing in the political mobilisation of denominations whose theological dynamics not all Presbyterians shared. Yet it also shows how difficult and belated such a mobilisation could be without the prominence of the crucial trigger of theological heterodoxy. Presbyterians eventually supported the cause of independence with substantial unanimity; but they were for long held back from commitment by the way in which their traditions of ecclesiastical polity pointed to an historic association with the House of Hanover. They were, nevertheless, drawn in another direction. Presbyterianism, as a system of ecclesiastical polity, had no obviously distinct theology; but American Presbyterians saw strong affinities between their polity and their Calvinism, the latter being an assertion of God's sovereignty and an understanding that He governed through fixed and eternal law, in accordance with a plan providentially foreordained. The connection between Calvinism and republicanism was not direct; but it was a shorter step to recognising that Presbyterianism implied republicanism, an identity easily adopted from the unfriendly pronouncements of the Calvinist James I and the Arminian Charles I,[239] or from the latter's chaplain, Peter Heylyn.[240]

[239] W. P. Breed, *Presbyterians and the Revolution* (Philadelphia, 1876), pp. 23–40.
[240] Peter Heylyn, *Aerius Redivivus; or, the History of the Presbyterians. Containing the Beginnings, Progress and Successes of that active Sect. Their Oppositions to Monarchical and Episcopal Government. Their Innovations in the Church: and, Their Imbroylments of the Kingdoms and Estates of Christendom in the pursuit of their Designes. From the Year 1536, to the Year 1647* (Oxford, 1670). In the

The alignment of Presbyterianism was particularly important since, by 1776, it was the most broadly diffused of the sects among the American colonies. Its adherents included English, Scots and Irish; they spanned the social range from indigent to prosperous. They had, moreover, arrived in five successive waves of migration since c. 1680: their life-experiences were therefore hardly uniform, but their denominational loyalties overrode this diversity. Presbyterians were the fastest-growing denomination in North America; they possessed a dynamism which had ebbed from Quakers and from New England Congregationalists. Presbyterianism also gave a single religious identity to two related ethnic groups, the Scots and Scots-Irish, who had flooded into the colonies after 1714. They not only brought with them a political theory with the strongest religious premises; in four colonies they amounted to large, distinctive political groupings. Pennsylvania, Virginia, North and South Carolina were to be a clearly-defined theatre of war after 1776, and the outcome hinged as much on American success there as in New England; of these colonies only Virginia (after Bacon's rebellion of 1676) had escaped a record of conflict between eastern elite and backcountry in which latter areas the Scots-Irish had already rehearsed their political mobilisation.

Denominations could be described by contemporaries in terms of their geographical origin as accurately as by their principles of polity. When in 1738 the Synod of Philadelphia approached Governor William Gooch of Virginia to petition for protection under the Toleration Act for Presbyterians newly migrating to that colony from Pennsylvania and Maryland, the Synod identified the settlers as those who 'are of the same persuasion as the Church of Scotland'. Their claim to favour was political: 'Your honour is sensible that those of our profession in Europe have been remarkable for their inviolable attachment to the house of Hanover, and have upon all occasions manifested an unspotted fidelity to our gracious sovereign, King George, and we doubt not but that these, our brethren, will carry the same loyal principles to the most distant settlements . . .'[241]

How far this ancestral identification of civil and religious liberties with William III or the Hanoverians was contradicted by theological innovation is a problem that has yet received little attention. The degree of Christological heterodoxy among colonial Presbyterians is still to be

Preface, Heylyn drew an analogy between the English Presbyterians and four groups of the theologically heterodox, 'that is to say, the practices of the *Novatians* in the North; the *Arrians* in the East; the *Donatists* in *Affrick*, or the Southern parts; and the *Priscillianists* in the Western'. Heylyn began his history with the Genevan Reformation and, especially, with Calvin.

[241] Charles F. James, *Documentary History of the Struggle for Religious Liberty in Virginia* (Lynchburg, Va., 1900), pp. 22–3.

established, but it seems unlikely that successive waves of emigrants did not carry with them the divisions over Arianism and subscription that divided early-eighteenth-century Scotland and Ulster.[242] The probability was greater since most colonial Presbyterian ministers were drawn from Northern Ireland until a late date. The Scottish Presbyterian church, too, re-echoed during the reigns of the first two Georges to charges and counter-charges of doctrinal error,[243] often initiated by the importation of Arian doctrine from south of the border.[244] It is probable, however, that more Scots emigrants came from the orthodox Evangelical wing of Scots Presbyterianism than from its heterodox Moderate wing, and for both groups theological disputes took their place within Dissenters' traditional litany of complaints against the overt structure of the Church of England. The Presbyterian minister William Tennent (1673–1746), arriving from Ireland in 1718, presented the Synod of Philadelphia with his credentials and his reasons for dissenting from the episcopal Church at home, in which he had formerly been ordained:

> *Imprimis.* Their government by Bishops, Arch-Bishops, Deacons, Arch-Deacons, Canons, Chapters, Chancellors, Vicars, wholly anti-scriptural.
>
> 2 Their discipline by Surrogates, and Chancellors in their Courts Ecclesiastical, without a foundation in the word of God.
>
> 3 Their abuse of that supposed discipline by commutation.
>
> 4 A Diocesan Bishop cannot be founded *jure divino* upon those Epistles to Timothy or Titus, nor anywhere else in the word of God, and so is a mere human invention.
>
> 5 The usurped power of the Bishops at their yearly visitations, acting all of themselves, without consent of the brethren.
>
> 6 Plurality of benefices.
>
> Lastly. The Churches conniving at the practice of Arminian doctrines

---

[242] E. H. Gillett, *History of the Presbyterian Church in the United States of America* (2 vols., Philadelphia, 1864), vol. 1, pp. 55–6, 67, 101–4; Robbins, *Commonwealthman*, pp. 167–76; A. W. Godfrey Brown, 'A Theological Interpretation of the First Subscription Controversy (1719–1728)' in J. L. M. Haire (et al.), *Challenge and Conflict: Essays in Irish Presbyterian History and Doctrine* (Antrim, 1981), pp. 28–43; Richard B. Barlow, 'The Career of John Abernethy (1680–1740) Father of Nonsubscription in Ireland and Defender of Religious Liberty', *Harvard Theological Review* 78 (1985), 399–419; Peter Brooke, *Ulster Presbyterianism: The Historical Perspective 1610–1970* (Dublin, 1987), pp. 79–92; Marilyn J. Westerkamp, *The Triumph of the Laity: Scots-Irish Piety and the Great Awakening, 1625–1760* (New York, 1988), p. 150; Richard B. Barlow, 'The Career of James Duchal (1697–1761)', *The Non-Subscribing Presbyterian* nos. 978, 979 (Newry, 1988), 26–9, 38–41.

[243] [John Angell], *The History of Religion: Particularly of the Principal Denominations of Christians* (4 vols., London, 1764), vol. 4, pp. 70–94. Intellectual influences are explored by Daniel Walker Howe, 'Why the Scottish Enlightenment was Useful to the Framers of the American Constitution', *Comparative Studies in Society and History* 31 (1989), 572–87.

[244] Colligan, *The Arian Movement in England*, pp. 129–31. For the presence in Pennsylvania in 1723 of one Presbyterian minister, a loyal former pupil of the heterodox John Simson, Professor of Theology at Glasgow, see Maurice W. Armstrong (et al., eds.), *The Presbyterian Enterprise: Sources of American Presbyterian History* (Philadelphia, 1956), p. 21.

inconsistent with the eternal purpose of God, and an encouragement of vice. Besides I could not be satisfied with their ceremonial way of worship. These, &c. have so affected my conscience, that I could no longer abide in a church where the same are practised.[245]

'Arminianism' was a term already used by Calvinists as synonymous with anti-Trinitarianism.[246] If the transfer of Irish controversies over ecclesiastical polity was immediate, so too was the transfer of other theological positions, orthodox as well as heterodox.

This transatlantic migration of dangerous innovations was initially resisted in the conservative colonies. The Presbyterian Synod in America early objected to the dilution of the Calvinist Trinitarianism of their forefathers: in 1735 Samuel Hemphill, recently arrived in the colonies with credentials from the Presbytery of Strabane, was convicted of preaching against the imposition of confessions of faith, and despite the support of the Deist Benjamin Franklin was suspended from preaching.[247] How typical this was is still unclear. Presbyterians' doctrine was kept in repair in its ancient formularies; but although these commanded obedience to the civil magistrate in terms quite sufficient to cover enthusiastic loyalty to George II, they contained the denunciations of 'an implicite Faith, and an absolute and blind Obedience' which were to have an opposite effect in the reign of George III.[248] The key to the Presbyterians' conduct was the way in which their ancient doctrines of ecclesiastical polity were activated, turned from reasons for loyalty into reasons for resistance.

Under George II, Presbyterians like other colonial Dissenters were as fervently loyal to the Crown as their English brethren. Samuel Davies (1723–61), evangelical Presbyterian, had been promoted from his ministry in Virginia to be President of the College of New Jersey in 1759. It was there that, in 1761, he preached a funeral sermon for his late sovereign:

[245] *Records of the Presbyterian Church in the United States of America* (Philadelphia, 1904), pp. 51–2.

[246] Conrad Wright, *The Beginnings of Unitarianism in America* (Boston, 1955), pp. 3–8, 200 ff. and passim.

[247] Richard Webster, *A History of the Presbyterian Church in America, from its Origin until the Year 1760* (Philadelphia, 1858), pp. 110–13. Jedediah Andrews, the Presbyterian minister at Philadelphia, claimed that Hemphill attracted a congregation of 'freethinkers, deists and nothings': for Andrews's articles on which Hemphill was tried, ibid., pp. 417–18. In the pamphlet debate which followed, it emerged that some of the sermons to which objection was made had been lifted from the published works of the English Arians Samuel Clarke and James Foster: ibid., p. 420.

[248] *The Confession of Faith, Agreed upon by the Assembly of Divines at Westminster,* in [William Dunlop], (ed.), *A Collection of Confessions of Faith, Catechisms, Directories, Books of Discipline, &c. Of Publick Authority in the Church of Scotland* (2 vols., Edinburgh, 1719), vol. I, pp. 102–4 (ch. 20), 123–8 (ch. 23).

His public and regal Virtues diffused their Beams to every Territory of His vast Dominions; and shone with efficacious, tho' gentle Force, even upon us, in these remote Ends of the Earth ... Can the *British* Annals, in the Compass of seventeen Hundred Years, produce a Period more favourable to Liberty, Peace, Prosperity, Commerce, and Religion?

It was as if Gibbon spoke of the age of the Antonines. Davies's analysis described the state by analogy with a gathered church, a voluntary association:

In this happy Reign, the *Prerogative* meditated no Invasions upon the Rights of the People; nor attempted to exalt itself above the Law. GEORGE the Great but Un-ambitious, consulted THE RIGHTS OF THE PEOPLE, as well as of the Crown; and claimed no Powers but such as were granted to Him by the *Constitution*: And what is the *Constitution*, but the voluntary Compact of Sovereign and Subject? And is not this the Foundation of their mutual Obligations?

Davies was open about the alternative: 'How different would have been our Situation under the baleful Influence of the ill boding Name of STUART!'[249]

In the early 1760s, the force of this early-Hanoverian loyalism was still sufficient to induce four Presbyterian ministers in North Carolina to censure the Regulator disturbances, especially since they could not deny that other Presbyterian ministers were implicated in them. They published a circular letter, nevertheless, as a recall to 'the peaceable Deportment and Loyalty of their Profession & Ancestors'. Citing the classic injunction to obedience in Romans 13, and the Westminster Confession of Faith and Catechism, they insisted that 'the remedy for Oppression is within the Compass of the Laws of your Country'. It was only the lack of churches and ministers in the areas of new settlement which obscured these truths: 'it must be confessed there are sundry, especially of the younger sort who have been bred up in this Wilderness, ignorant of the Principles and Practices of their Ancestors'; yet even these had been lured into the Regulator movement by 'the movers of the present Insurrection' who have 'put the cry of King, Loyalty, Allegiance, into the mouths of their unwary Adherents'.[250]

The official Presbyterian stance was still loyalist. The repeal of the Stamp Act, despite its accompanying Declaratory Act, was greeted by the Synod of New York and Philadelphia in effusive terms. Its pastoral

---

[249] Samuel Davies, *A Sermon delivered at Nassau-Hall, January 14, 1761. On the Death of His Late Majesty King George II* (New York, 1761), pp. 9–10.
[250] W. L. Saunders (ed.), *The Colonial Records of North Carolina*, vol. 7 (Raleigh, 1890), pp. 814–16.

letter dated 30 May 1766 invited Presbyterians to thank God for 'the paternal tenderness of the best of kings, and the moderation of the British Parliament'. They were called on to show 'a cheerful and ready obedience to civil authority'. They were reminded that 'A spirit of liberty is highly laudable when under proper regulations, but we hope you will carefully distinguish between liberty and licentiousness.'[251]

This official stance evaporated first amongst the intelligentsia, and with a speed which hints at the quite different dispositions which formal loyalty restrained. By 1769 the Philadelphian Presbyterian Francis Alison reported of Princeton: 'Our Jersey College is now talking as if she was soon to be the bulwark against Episcopacy: I should rejoice to see her Pistols, like honest Teagues, grown up into great Guns.'[252] Nor did he exaggerate: by the Commencement celebrations of September 1770, Principal Witherspoon was organising his students into publicly debating a series of patriotic theses, including 'The non-importation Agreement reflects a Glory on the American Merchants, and was a noble Exertion of Self-Denial and Public Spirit.'[253]

Such evidence, especially of Scots and Scots-Irish Presbyterian involvement, meant that from an English perspective, and to High Churchmen in particular, the American Revolution could easily seem a replay of the Civil War. Charles Inglis, incumbent of Trinity Church, New York drew the moral immediately after Washington's occupation of the city in his report to the SPG of 31 October 1776. The clergy had been

> everywhere threatened, often reviled with the most opprobious language, sometimes treated with brutal violence . . . Were every instance of this kind faithfully collected, it is probable that the sufferings of the American clergy would appear, in many respects, not inferior to those of the English clergy in the great rebellion of last century; and such a work would be no bad supplement to 'Walker's Sufferings of the Clergy'.[254]

'This has been a Presbyterian war from the beginning as certainly as that in 1641', declared William Jones of Nayland. Such reactions, by their vehemence, tended to neglect more complex questions of causation; they

---

[251] *Records of the Presbyterian Church in the United States of America*, pp. 362–3.
[252] Francis Alison to Ezra Stiles, 1 Aug. 1769: Franklin Bowditch Dexter (ed.), *Extracts from the Itineraries and Other Miscellanies of Ezra Stiles, D.D., LL.D. 1755-1794* (New Haven, Conn., 1916), p. 434.
[253] *Pennsylvania Chronicle*, 8–15 Oct. 1770, reprinted in *Journal of Presbyterian History* 52 (1974), 357.
[254] Hawkins, *Historical Notices*, pp. 329–30. John Walker's *An Attempt towards Recovering an Account of the numbers and sufferings of the clergy of the Church of England . . . in the . . . times of the grand rebellion* (London, 1714) was an Anglican classic. For similar evidence of the persecution of Anglican clergy, Hawkins, loc. cit., pp. 89, 139–40, 160–3, 244–58, 302–14, 317–22.

drew rather on an historical scenario, an undifferentiated account of the political consequences of the ecclesiastical polities of Dissenters as such. 'Presbyterian' had largely replaced 'Puritan', and was a term used with considerable imprecision. Hypocrisy, in this analysis, took the place of any more insightful account of the triggers of the right of rebellion: 'When it serves their turn', the Presbyterians 'will affect to be in the interest of the government, and yet never fail to oppose it, if its establishment is of service to any party but themselves.'[255] Anglican clergy in the colonies tended to advance a more differentiated analysis, or stress theological catalysts. Myles Cooper, formerly President of King's College, New York, though recognising that 'Many of the Colonists were of Republican Principles, and had an hereditary disaffection to the English constitution', used a sermon in Oxford to draw attention to Bishop Sherlock's warning in 1750 that 'the Press for many years past had swarmed with books, some to dispute, some to ridicule, the great truths of Religion . . . the Industry, used to disperse these books, both at home and abroad, and especially in our Plantations in America, were proofs of such Malice against the Gospel, and the holy Author of it, as would not have been borne even in a Mahometan Country'.[256]

The anguish of such men is readily explicable. During the Revolution Anglican clergy were singled out for harassment, and so given a particular insight into the motives of the rebels. Charles Inglis reported that the clergy were

> viewed with peculiar envy and malignity by the disaffected; for, although civil liberty was the ostensible object, the bait that was flung out to catch the populace at large and engage them in the rebellion, yet it is now past all doubt that an abolition of the Church of England was one of the principal springs of the dissenting leaders' conduct; and hence the unanimity of dissenters in this business. Their universal defection from government, emancipating themselves from the jurisdiction of Great Britain, and becoming independent, was a necessary step towards this grand object.

The decision of a Presbyterian synod to support the Continental Congress accounted for the complete uniformity of Presbyterian clergy on that side, Inglis reported. During Washington's occupation of New York from April to September 1776, 'members of the Church of England were the only

[255] 'An Address to the British Government on a Subject of Present Concern. 1776', in *The Theological, Philosophical and Miscellaneous Works of the Rev. William Jones* (12 vols., London, 1801), vol. 12, pp. 354–63, at 356.

[256] Thomas Sherlock, *A Letter from the Bishop of London, to the Clergy and People of London and Westminister; on occasion of the late earthquakes* (London, 1750), cited in Myles Cooper, *National Humiliation and Repentance recommended, and the Causes of the present Rebellion in America assigned, in a Sermon preached before the University of Oxford, on Friday, December 13, 1776* (Oxford, 1777), pp. 9, 13.

sufferers . . . The members of the Dutch church are very numerous there, and many of them joined in opposing the rebellion; yet no notice was taken of them, nor the least injury done to them.'[257]

The perceptions of émigrés and of churchmen in England were over-simplified, but contained an important element of truth. Local resolutions in the colonies in 1774–5, especially in communities with a strong Presby-terian presence, expressed a common dilemma: Presbyterians were torn between allegiance to the House of Hanover, the historic guarantor of their liberties, and the new implications of a rival historical scenario. The inhabitants of Fincastle County, Virginia, resolved on 20 January 1775:

> Many of us and our forefathers left our native land, considering it as a Kingdom subjected to inordinate power, and greatly abridged of its liber-ties; we crossed the Atlantic and explored this then uncultivated wilderness, bordering on many nations of Savages . . . but even to these remote regions the hand of unlimited and unconstitutional power hath pursued us to strip us of that liberty and property, with which God, nature and the rights of humanity have vested us.[258]

The closer approach of 'all the horrors of a civil war' appalled the Presbyterian synod, sitting at New York in May 1775. Their first instinct, in a pastoral letter, was to deny responsibility:

> we have not been instrumental in inflaming the minds of the people, or urging them to acts of violence and disorder. Perhaps no instance can be given on so interesting a subject, in which political sentiments have been so long and so fully kept from the pulpit, and even malice itself has not charged us with labouring from the press . . .

In a crisis, official Presbyterianism could exploit its traditional loyalties:

> In carrying on this important struggle, let every opportunity be taken to express your attachment and respect to our sovereign King George, and to the revolution principles by which his august family was seated on the British throne.

He, and even his ministers, had 'probably been misled'; 'the present opposition to the measures of administration does not in the least arise from disaffection to the king, or a desire of separation from the parent state'. Nevertheless, Presbyterians were charged to 'maintain the union which at present subsists through all the colonies', and to reverence the Continental Congress, whose delegates had been 'chosen in the most free and unbiassed manner, by the body of the people'. Their loyalty to the Crown was, necessarily, subservient to their religion. Implicitly, the

---

[257] Charles Inglis to SPG, 31 Oct. 1776: Hawkins, *Historical Notices*, pp. 328–9, 333.
[258] *Journal of Presbyterian History* 52 (1974), 373.

Synod sanctioned armed resistance provided it was accompanied by piety: 'there is no soldier so undaunted as the pious man, no army so formidable as those who are superior to the fear of death'.[259]

Presbyterians were divided; those in the south were particularly difficult to mobilise in 1775. From Philadelphia, four Presbyterian ministers wrote to rally their co-religionists in North Carolina. They began by stressing that the nature of their ambitions had been misrepresented:

> We are neither disloyal to our King, nor attempting, nor desiring to set up Governments independent of Britain, as they assert; we only desire to maintain the rights and privileges of Englishmen, but not to be their slaves, nor obliged to give them our money as oft as, and in what quantity, they please to demand it.

Their aim, as the Continental Congress had affirmed, was to vindicate their privileges as they stood before the Stamp Act. But they proceeded with a Scripturally-based account of political obligation which undermined the Blackstonian understanding of the rights of Englishmen and the claim of British parliamentary supremacy:

> To take any man's money, without his consent, is unjust and contrary to reason and the law of God, and the Gospel of Christ; it is contrary to Magna Charta, or the Great Charter and Constitution of England; and to complain, and even to resist such a lawless power, is just, and reasonable, and no rebellion.

A deep religious sense informed their perception of the corruption of Lord North and the House of Commons. This was confirmed by the similar reactions of their co-religionists: 'that we are wronged and injured, is believed and insisted on by the greatest and best men of all religious denominations on the Continent of America, who are firmly united in this glorious struggle for liberty'. It was a struggle which now came to be identified by those denominations in terms of their history:

> If we are now wrong in our conduct, our forefathers that fought for liberty at Londonderry and Enniskillen in King James' time, were wrong; nay, they were rebels, when they opposed, and set aside that bigotted Prince, and the Stewart family, and set the Brunswick family on the throne of England.

The ministry had 'established Popery in Quebec and the arbitary Laws of France; and why may they not do the same in Pennsylvania or North Carolina?' Although the authors spoke indiscriminately of 'British privil-

[259] 'A Pastoral Letter', 22 May 1775, *Records of the Presbyterian Church in the United States of America*, pp. 466–9.

eges and English liberty', they clearly understood these in the light of their sectarian inheritance. To those who refused to draw the same conclusion from these premises came a threat that sounded like excommunication: 'we can have no fellowship with you'.[260] The outbreak of fighting then polarised the options. The Synod of New York and Philadelphia abandoned its former scruples and by May 1778 was calling on fellow Presbyterians to pray for the success not only of rebel arms but of the armed forces of papist France.[261]

It was soon apparent that the early professions of official moderation were not representative of the actions of the rank and file. After Washington's occupation of New York in 1776 was over, the Anglican loyalist priest Charles Inglis reported to the SPG of Presbyterian ministers: 'I do not know one of them, nor have I been able, after strict inquiry, to hear of any, who did not, by preaching and every effort in their power, promote all the measures of the congress, however extravagant.'[262] In 1783 the 'Pastoral Letter' of the Presbyterian Synod agreed: 'We cannot help congratulating you on the general and almost universal attachment of the Presbyterian body to the cause of liberty and the rights of mankind. This has been visible in their conduct, and has been confessed by the complaints and resentment of the common enemy.'[263]

Despite the diversity of ethnic and religious groups on the side of independence, a recurring theme runs through British and loyalist accounts of the causes of the war: it was not the unanimous work of all Americans. Loyalists were candid in explaining how a large body of moderate opinion in the colonies, cautiously urging their grievances against Britain, had been silenced, tricked or rushed into much more extreme measures by small groups of extremists.[264] Some commentators like Joseph Galloway emphasised the manipulative role of small groups in repressing loyalists and seizing the means of communication. Loyalists observed that the practical points at issue were limited and should be negotiable: 'A small degree of reflection would convince us, that the grievances in question, supposing them to be real, are, at most, no more than a just ground for

---

[260] Francis Alison, James Sprout [Sproat], George Duffield, Robert Davidson, 'An Address to the Ministers and Presbyterian congregations in North Carolina', 10 July 1775, in William L. Saunders (ed.), *Colonial Records of North Carolina*, vol. 10 (Raleigh, 1890), pp. 222–8.

[261] *Records of the Presbyterian Church in the United States of America*, p. 481.

[262] Charles Inglis to SPG, 31 Oct. 1776: Hawkins, *Historical Notices*, pp. 329.

[263] *Records of the Presbyterian Church in the United States of America*, pp. 499–500.

[264] Delegates to the Congress in 1775 had been given strictly limited instructions by their colonies, but Congress greatly exceeded these instructions: [Thomas Bradbury Chandler], *What think ye of the Congress Now? Or, an Enquiry, how far the Americans Are Bound to Abide by, and Execute, the Decisions of the late Continental Congress* (New York, repr. London, 1775).

decent remonstrance, but not a sufficient reason for forcible resistance.'[265]
But these grievances had already engaged with much older bodies of ideas
which gave them momentous, even cosmic significance. Other observers
therefore stressed the minority religious alignment of the insurgents. As
a Hessian officer who had seen service in Pennsylvania wrote home: 'Call
this war, dearest friend, by whatsoever name you may, only call it not
an American Rebellion, it is nothing more nor less than an Irish-Scotch
Presbyterian Rebellion.'[266] To Professor August Ludwig Schlözer of Göt-
tingen he added: 'You know about the Huguenot wars in France. What
they called 'religion', is here 'liberty', the same fanaticism, the same furious events.'[267]

The American Presbyterian historian David Ramsay was clear about
the ethnic divisions of the colonial population.

> The [Scotch] Irish in America, with a few exceptions were attached to
> independence. They had fled from oppression in their native country, and
> could not brook the idea that it should follow them. Their national prepos-
> sessions in favour of liberty, were strengthened by their religious opinions.
> They were Presbyterians, and people of that denomination . . . were mostly
> whigs.[268]

Religion produced explicit apprehensions: 'religious bigotry had broken
in upon the peace of various sects, before the American war. This was
kept up by partial establishments, and by a dread that the Church of
England through the power of the mother country, would be made to
triumph over all other denominations.'[269] War then greatly heightened
those fears:

> The presbyterians and independents, were almost universally attached to
> the measures of Congress. Their religious societies are governed on the
> republican plan. From independence they had much to hope, but from
> Great Britain if finally successful, they had reason to fear the establishment
> of a church hierarchy.[270]

The Scotch-Irish duly played a hugely disproportionate role in manning
the Continental army and militia, and in driving armed conflict towards

---

[265] *A Friendly Address to All Reasonable Americans, On the Subject of our Political Confusions* (New
York; repr. London, 1774), p. 46.
[266] Heinrichs to Herr H, 18 Jan. 1778: 'Extracts from the Letter-Book of Captain Johann
Heinrichs of the Hessian Jäger Corps, 1778–1780', *Pennsylvania Magazine of History and
Biography* 22 (1898), 137–70, at 137.
[267] Heinrichs [or Hinrichs] to Schlözer, n.d., in Ernst Kipping, *The Hessian View of America
1775–1783* (Monmouth Beach, N.J., 1971), p. 34.
[268] David Ramsay, *The History of the American Revolution* (1789), ed. Lester H. Cohen (2 vols.,
Indianapolis, 1990), vol. 2, p. 626.
[269] Ibid., p. 631.
[270] Ibid., pp. 627–8.

a conclusion.[271] If east-coast, long-settled Presbyterians eventually though after misgivings sided with their traditions of ecclesiastical polity against their traditions of support for the House of Hanover, the choice was quick and emphatic for newly-arrived Presbyterians of the backcountry, especially those of other than English origin, and, above all, the Scots Irish. In New England, the disaffection of Presbyterians was attributed to their religion; in Pennsylvania and colonies to the south, Scots-Irish ancestry was the general designation.[272] But despite the diversity of the origins and life-experiences of colonial Presbyterians, they finally drew on a shared inheritance to make a nearly-unanimous commitment to the revolution.

(c) THE AMERICAN CONGREGATIONALISTS

Congregationalists, like Presbyterians, aroused ancient echoes and similar suspicions that those real purposes were being disguised in current controversies. As a Hessian officer serving in the Revolutionary war wrote,

> The resistance against illegal taxes was nothing more than a masquerade at the beginning. The plan of the rebellion is older and more deeply rooted. It was born primarily in the provinces of New England. Since these people are mostly Presbyterians and Puritans, every government on earth, especially that of a king, was a thorn in their sides because of their religious principles.[273]

Of all American denominations, this charge was least simplified as an account of the Congregationalists, the most homogeneous of the sects in sharing a similar stance on the issue of resistance to British rule. Like Presbyterians in all colonies, the Congregationalists of New England preserved through the seventeenth and eighteenth centuries the doctrine that their communities were settled as religious experiments;[274] some new development might always trigger a transition from recording that the early settlers had fled to escape religious persecution to asserting the renewal of that threat. Even in the years 1770–6, New England ministers

---

[271] E.g. Charles A. Hanna, *The Scotch-Irish* (2 vols., New York, 1902); Henry Jones Ford, *The Scotch-Irish in America* (Princeton, 1915); Wayland F. Dunaway, *The Scotch-Irish of Colonial Pennsylvania* (Chapel Hill, 1944); James G. Leyburn, *The Scotch-Irish: A Social History* (Chapel Hill, 1962); Maldwyn Jones, 'The Scotch-Irish in British America' in Bernard Bailyn and Philip D. Morgan (eds.), *Strangers within the Realm: Cultural Margins of the First British Empire* (Chapel Hill, 1991), pp. 284–313.

[272] James G. Leyburn, 'Presbyterian Immigrants and the American Revolution', *Journal of Presbyterian History* 54 (1976), 9–32, at 25.

[273] Undated, in Kipping, *Hessian View of America*, p. 34.

[274] J. W. Thornton (ed.), *The Pulpit of the American Revolution* (Boston, 1860), pp. xviii–xix.

did not celebrate civil liberties as such, in a secular context; 'Rather, they were presented as necessary instruments for the preservation of the gospel and New England's ongoing covenant with God.'[275]

This tradition was echoed even by the orthodox Trinitarian and Harringtonian Ezra Stiles, President of Yale, in his election sermon of 1783. The Congregational church had 'never been vested with any civil or secular power in New-England', he implausibly maintained;

> it is certain, that civil dominion was but the second motive, religion the primary one, with our ancestors, in coming hither and settling this land. It was not so much their design to establish religion for the benefit of the state, as civil government for the benefit of religion, and as subservient, and even necessary towards the peaceable enjoyment and unmolested exercise of religion – of that religion, for which they fled to these ends of the earth.[276]

Again, the problem is how these ancient principles of ecclesiastical polity were activated; and more clearly than in the case of Presbyterians, Christological heterodoxy contributed.

New England Congregationalists began to express their alarm at the growth of Arminian doctrines in their ranks in the 1730s, even before the Church of England began to make alarming inroads and give that doctrine a denominational vehicle.[277] By the 1740s this developed into suppressed unease at the possible spread of anti-Trinitarian ideas. By 1755, Jonathan Mayhew brought the issue into the open;[278] but Calvinists had been aware of the spread of heterodox theology at Harvard and Yale at least from the previous decade. In 1748 the Governor of New Jersey, Jonathan Belcher, a patron of the newly founded New Light college (later Princeton) complained to Jonathan Edwards: 'The accounts I receive from time to time give me too much reason to fear that Arminianism, Arianism, and even Socinianism, in destruction to the doctrine of the free

---

[275] Stout, *The New England Soul*, p. 271.

[276] Ezra Stiles, *The United States Elevated to Glory and Honour. A sermon ... May 8th, MDCCLXXXIII* (2nd edn., Worcester, Mass., 1785), pp. 125–6. For the claim that in New England, 'we have realised the capital ideas of *Harrington's* Oceana' in respect of the libertarian implications of freehold tenure, ibid., pp. 10–11. Harringtonian discourse in no way contradicted denominational discourse.

[277] E.g. John White, *New England's Lamentations* (Boston, 1734), pp. 16–17, 26; [Samuel Moody], *A Faithful Narrative of God's Gracious Dealings* (Boston, 1737), pp. 1, 7; cf. Wright, *Beginnings of Unitarianism in America*, pp. 21–2.

[278] Ibid., pp. 203–4. For the colonial (i.e. Puritan) assumption that Arminianism and anti-Trinitarianism were 'temperamentally and historically linked', ibid., pp. 200–1.

grace, are daily propagated in the New England colleges.'[279] In 1745 George Whitefield complained of Harvard: 'Tutors neglect to pray with and examine the Hearts of the Pupils. – Discipline is at too low an Ebb: Bad Books are become fashionable among them: *Tillotson* and *Clark* are read, instead of *Shepard*, *Stoddard*, and such like evangelical Writers.'[280] One practical result was the proliferation of other sects[281] which increasingly challenged the local hegemony of Congregationalists in New England and largely created their sense that they were threatened by rising tides of unspeakable evil even before the constitutional issues of the 1760s arose. A second result was theoretical. The impact of such doctrines can be traced in the life and work of three prominent Congregationalists: the ministers Andrew Eliot and Jonathan Mayhew, and the revolutionary leader John Adams.

Congregationalists influenced by these heterodox currents of ideas were not necessarily extremists by temperament. One such moderate was Andrew Eliot (1718–78), minister of the New North Church at Boston from 1742, friend and correspondent of Thomas Hollis, Thomas Brand Hollis and Francis Blackburne, eager student (and silent plagiarist) of the English Arian Samuel Clarke, and a propagandist (though an irresolute one) against plans for an Anglican episcopate in the colonies. Despite his benign character Eliot was led, as early as his election sermon of 1765, to invoke the most extreme rhetoric against the Stamp Act as, by implication, 'an offense against mankind' and 'an offense against God' which threatened to trigger the right of resistance. In correspondence with the two Hollises and with Francis Blackburne which followed the publication of the sermon, Eliot was persuaded that a dark conspiracy threatened transatlantic liberties; that, as Blackburne informed him in January 1767, the archdeacon was 'one among many others who think they have discovered the dregs of the Stuartine and Laudean ecclesiastical politics fermenting afresh in this country'; that a conspiracy was in train to promote Roman Catholicism; and that rebellion was indeed the appropriate response. Caught between the imperatives of this world view and

---

[279] Jonathan Edwards, *Works*, ed. E. Hickman (10th edn., 2 vols., London, 1865); vol. 1, p. cxliv, cited in Heimert, *Religion and the American Mind*, pp. 189–90. For the rise of anti-Trinitarian theology, and the influence of the 1756 Boston edition of Thomas Emlyn's *An Humble Inquiry into the Scripture-Account of Jesus Christ*, see Frank Hugh Foster, *A Genetic History of the New England Theology* (New York, 1963), pp. 273–7.

[280] George Whitefield, *A Letter To the Rev. the President, And Professors, Tutors, and Hebrew Instructor, of Harvard-College in Cambridge* (Boston, 1745), p. 12. For an attempted defence of orthodoxy by the President of Yale, see Thomas Clap, *A Brief History and Vindication of the Doctrines Received and Established in the Churches of New-England; with a Specimen of the New Scheme of Religion beginning to prevail* (New Haven, 1755).

[281] William G. McLoughlin, *New England Dissent 1630–1833: The Baptists and the Separation of Church and State* (2 vols., Cambridge, Mass., 1971), esp. pp. 421–587.

the fear of 'blood and slaughter' of civil war, still attached to Britain as 'my country' (as he described it in 1775), Eliot paid a high price in personal anguish during the British occupation of Boston. He has rightly been termed a 'reluctant revolutionary'.[282]

Jonathan Mayhew (1720–66) was long revered in one historian's telling image for having fired in 1750 'the morning gun of the Revolution, the *punctum temporis* when that period of history began'.[283] John Wingate Thornton wrote of Mayhew's Thirtieth of January sermon of 1749/50,[284] which broke with conventional Congregational performances in that idiom by its virulence, by the present rather than the hypothetical relevance of its message, and by redefining the right of resistance from a final resort into an immediate duty against evil rulers.[285] Mayhew had early acquired a reputation for heterodoxy. His ordination in 1747 as pastor of the West Church in Boston was delayed because his notoriety deterred other Congregational clergy from taking part. His *Seven Sermons* (Boston, 1749) was quickly praised by Bishop Hoadly, and was to be reprinted by American Unitarians in the 1830s.[286] Mayhew's next volume of *Sermons* (Boston, 1755) cast doubt on the doctrines of original sin and the atonement, and, in a passage which he later regretted publishing, rejected the doctrine of the Trinity as on a par with the Popish idolatry of the Virgin Mary. Neither Catholics nor Protestants should ever think 'that nonsense and contradictions can ever be too *sacred* to be *ridiculous*', he announced.[287]

Jonathan Mayhew was, by temperament, an extremist, an instinctive controversialist, an indignant and militant Arian. When his sermon of 25 August 1765 in the middle of the Stamp Act agitation on the text (Galatians 5. 12, 13) 'I would they were even cut off which trouble you

[282] Bernard Bailyn, 'Religion and Revolution: Three Biographical Studies', *Perspectives in American History* 4 (1970), 83–169, at 87–110. The evidence marshalled by Bailyn tells against his unsupported claims (pp. 88, 95, 97) that Eliot's political ideas and revolutionary sympathies were *not* a result of his religious beliefs.

[283] Thornton, *Pulpit*, p. 43. For his intellectual milieu, see Bernhard Knollenberg (ed.), 'Thomas Hollis and Jonathan Mayhew: Their Correspondence, 1759–1766', *Proceedings of the Massachusetts Historical Society* 69 (1956), 102–93.

[284] Jonathan Mayhew, *A Discourse Concerning Unlimited Submission and Non-Resistance to the Higher Powers* (Boston, 1750), reprinted in Thornton, *Pulpit*, and Bailyn (ed.), *Pamphlets*, 203–47. Bailyn (p. 205) wrote of Unitarianism as a 'gentle, creedless faith' and did not consider the question of theological triggers of the right of rebellion.

[285] Mayhew's text was substantially plagiarised from Hoadly's *The Measures of Submission to the Civil Magistrate Considered* and Trenchard and Gordon's *The Independent Whig*: Bailyn (ed.), *Pamphlets*, pp. 697–8.

[286] Alden Bradford, *Memoir of the Life and Writings of Rev. Jonathan Mayhew, D.D.* (Boston, 1838), pp. 87 ff; Charles W. Akers, *Called unto Liberty: A Life of Jonathan Mayhew 1720–1766* (Cambridge, Mass., 1964), pp. 47–52, 68–78.

[287] Jonathan Mayhew, *Sermons* (Boston, 1755), pp. 418, 433–4; Akers, *Called unto Liberty*, pp. 115–22.

for, brethren, ye have been called unto liberty' was followed the next day
by a renewed wave of mob violence, the most serious in the town's history,
which destroyed the house of Lieutenant Governor Thomas Hutchinson,
Mayhew attempted to justify himself to one of the congregation in ways
which implicitly acknowledged the impact his sermon had had on the
inflamed and already violent populace of Boston. Although the sermon[288]
warned against insurrections or rebellions, it hedged these warnings with
qualifications, condemning resistance only to '*lawful* rulers in the *due* dis-
charge of their offices'.[289] For the distinction between civil liberty and
'slavery' consisted, argued Mayhew, not in whether

> the laws by which they are governed, are made by a considerable number
> of persons instead of one, if they are thus governed, contrary to, or inde-
> pendently of, their own will & consent. The essence of civil liberty does not
> consist in, or depend upon, the number of persons, by whom a nation is
> governed; but in their being governed by such persons & laws, as they
> approve of.

Despite his cautions, Mayhew concluded his sermon in a way which
pointed clearly to resistance:

> some people might perhaps say, as they truly might, that a nation is some-
> times actually abused by their rulers to a great degree; and treated as if
> the people were made only to be subservient to their pride, pleasure and
> profit. And supposing this to be actually the case of any nation, the question
> was then proposed, Whether passive obedience and non-resistance were
> the duty of such a people; or Whether opposing such rulers, and the execu-
> tion of unrighteous & oppressive laws, could properly be accounted using
> liberty for an occasion to the flesh? This was answered in the negative
> . . . [290]

Mayhew effectively sanctioned resistance while washing his hands of
responsibility for the violence which accompanied it. In *The Snare Broken*,
a sermon on the same text preached on 23 May 1766 in celebration of
the repeal of the Stamp Act, Mayhew attempted to backtrack from the
dangerously exposed position in which he had found himself: social
stability was now presented as a precondition of political reform. Mayhew
himself, and the cause of resistance in general, had to bid for social
respectability if that cause were to retain its momentum.[291] After repeal,
he exhorted his countrymen to peace, industry, and to perform 'the duties
of our respective stations'. Nevertheless, he had recorded that he

---

[288] For Mayhew's memorandum of its text, see *Studies in American History* 4 (1970), 140–3.
[289] Ibid.; italics added.
[290] Ibid.
[291] Bernard Bailyn, 'Jonathan Mayhew' in 'Religion and Revolution: Three Biographical
Studies', *Perspectives in American History* 4 (1970), 83–169, at 111–24.

learnt from the holy scriptures, that wise, brave and vertuous men were always friends to liberty; that God gave the Israelites a King [or absolute Monarch] in his anger, because they had not sense and virtue enough to like a free common-wealth, and to have himself for their King; that the Son of God came down from heaven, to make us 'free indeed'; and that 'where the Spirit of the Lord is, there is liberty'.[292]

Appropriately, it was Mayhew who proposed to James Otis the idea of Committees of Correspondence to preserve the unity of the colonies following the repeal of the Stamp Act. He did so on an analogy drawn from ecclesiastical polity: 'You have heard of the *communion of churches* . . . the great use and importance of a *communion of colonies* appeared to me in strong light';[293] but he had chosen to activate these issues of ecclesiastical polity a decade before the beginning of the reign of George III and the issues of the 1760s which gave other men, orthodox in their Christology, grounds for thinking Mayhew's alarm plausible. 'Socinianism, Deism, and other bad principles find too much countenance among us', complained SPG missionary Henry Caner of the inhabitants of Boston in 1759.[294]

In New England, missionaries from the SPG reported in the 1740s on the growing goodwill of Dissenters to the Church of England, and their attendance at Anglican services;[295] by the early 1760s, even before the Stamp Act controversy, this had changed fundamentally. In New York, the Anglican clergyman John Beach was similarly concerned that a satirical attack on the Church of England should have been launched in 1763 'after so long a space, wherein nothing controversial had been written, and no provocation had been given, and a charitable temper between the different denominations hopefully began to prevail'.[296] Henry Caner complained from Boston of the Dissenters:

their Zeal is chiefly pointed at suppressing the Church of England . . . they are now reprinting here De Laune's Plea for the Non-conformists,[297] in

---

[292] Jonathan Mayhew, *The Snare broken. A Thanksgiving-Discourse, preached At the Desire of the West Church in Boston, N.E. Friday May 23, 1766. Occasioned by the Repeal of the Stamp-Act* (Boston, 1766), pp. 35, 41–2. The Stamp Act, Mayhew maintained, had been the invention of 'some evil-minded individuals in Britain . . . not improbably, in the interests of the Houses of Bourbon and the Pretender, whose cause they meant to serve, by bringing about an open rupture between Great Britain and her colonies' (p. 9).

[293] Mayhew to James Otis, 8 June 1766: Thornton, *Pulpit*, p. 44.

[294] Caner to the Archbishop of Canterbury, 7 April 1759: Perry (ed.), *Historical Collections*, vol. 3, p. 452. Caner requested the establishment of an Anglican Mission at Cambridge, Massachusetts, as an antidote.

[295] E.g. Timothy Cutler to SPG, 26 Dec. 1747; William McGilchrist to SPG, 21 June 1760: Perry (ed.), *Historical Collections*, vol. 3, pp. 417, 456.

[296] John Beach, *A Friendly Expostulation, With all Persons concern'd in publishing A late Pamphlet . . .* (New York, 1763), Advertisement.

[297] Thomas De Laune, *A Plea for the Non-Conformists, shewing The true State of their Case: And how far the Conformist's Seperation from the Church of Rome, for their Popish Superstitions, &c.*

order to give people the worst impressions of our Church; they have also lately printed a sermon[298] by Dr. Chauncy of this Town, in support of the validity of Presbyterian ordination, not without hard and ungenerous reflections upon Episcopal Government ... the principal attempt of this sermon is to Invalidate the Evidence of Ignatius's Epistles in favour of Episcopacy, by Renewing the charge of Spuriousness and Forgery, from which they have been so well vindicated by the learned Bishop Pearson. Another sermon was published the last year by one Styles, which was Entitled 'the Union', the author's intention being to invite all parties and sects in the Country to unite against the Church of England.[299]

Clearly, the Dissenters' target was the old one of ecclesiastical polity; but when Jonathan Mayhew launched an attack on the Cambridge Mission, the source of his disaffection was perceived to be Christological. Caner complained that Mayhew had

insulted the Missions in General, the Society [SPG], the Church of England, in short, the whole national establishment, in so dirty a manner, that it seems to be below the Character of a gentleman to enter into controversy with him. In most of his sermons, of which he published a great number, he introduces some malicious invectives against the Society or the Church of England, and if at any time the most candid and gentle remarks are made upon such abuse, he breaks forth into such bitter and scurrilous personal reflections, that in truth no one cares to have any thing to do with him. His Doctrinal Principles, which seem chiefly copied from Ld Shaftsbury, Bolingbroke, &c., are so offensive to the generality of the Dissenting Ministers, that they refuse to admit him a member of their association, yet they appear to be pleased with his abusing the Church of England.[300]

New England was distinctive within the British Empire for the high degree of its popular literacy on ecclesiastical questions. John Adams was as well-informed theologically as his fellow Congregationalists. In July 1813 he compared notes with Jefferson, boasting: 'For more than sixty Years I have been attentive to this great Subject. Controversies, between Calvinists and Arminians, Trinitarians and Unitarians, Deists and Christians, Atheists and both, have attracted my Attention, whenever the sin-

---

introduced into the Service of God, justifies the Non-Conformist's seperation from them (London, 1684; Boston, 1763).

[298] Charles Chauncy, *The Validity of Presbyterian Ordination Asserted and Maintained. A Discourse Delivered at the Anniversary Dudleian-Lecture, at Harvard-College in Cambridge New-England, May 12. 1762. With an Appendix, Giving a brief historical account of the epistles ascribed to Ignatius; and exhibiting some of the many reasons, why they ought not to be depended on as his uncorrupted works* (Boston, 1762).

[299] Caner to Archbishop of Canterbury, 7 Jan. 1763: Perry (ed.), *Historical Collections*, vol. 3, p. 489.

[300] Caner to Archbishop of Canterbury, 8 June 1763: ibid., vol. 3, p. 497.

gular Life I have led would admit, to all these questions.'[301] Adams was originally intended for the Congregationalist ministry but gave up that intention: 'the reason of my quitting divinity', he wrote, 'was my opinion concerning some disputed points', opinions which led him to admire Jonathan Mayhew and be accused of Arminianism.[302] Such opinions made Adams perceive an unacceptable 'spirit of dogmatism and bigotry in clergy and laity'. Those early tendencies were reinforced when he was articled to study law in Worcester, Massachusetts, where 'I found Morgan's 'Moral Philosopher',[303] which I was informed had circulated with some freedom in that town, and that the principles of deism had made a considerable progress among several persons, in that and other towns in the country.'[304] Under the influence of such doctrines, Adams rejected Calvinist tenets like election, predestination, man's total depravity, and the Trinity.[305] He believed that 'Human government is more or less perfect, as it approaches nearer or diverges further from an imitation of this perfect plan of divine and moral government';[306] but his conception of divine government was not Trinitarian or hierarchical. Rather, he believed, man must live 'under the monarchy of reason and conscience, within, as well as . . . a balance of power without'.[307]

John Adams read with approval the English Unitarian, ex-Anglican, minister John Disney, sided with that author's reproof of Arthur Ashley Sykes for stopping short at Arianism,[308] and went far beyond Disney in anticlericalism and antisacerdotalism.[309] The Church of England both at home and in the colonies provided him with ecclesiological targets; but these proved to be temporary ones. Adams lived to see his youthful heterodoxy rendered irrelevant by its very success. In 1815 he wrote:

> Where is the man to be found at this day, when we see Methodistical
> bishops, bishops of the church of England, and bishops, archbishops, and

[301] Adams to Jefferson, 18 July 1813: Cappon (ed.), *Adams-Jefferson Letters*, vol. 2, p. 361. Adams, like Jefferson, rejected the divinity of Christ: ibid., p. 359.
[302] Adams, *Works*, vol. 1, p. 41; vol. 2, pp. 10, 31. 'Arminianism' was a term used in Congregational circles by this period to include the school later termed Unitarian.
[303] Thomas Morgan, *The Moral Philosopher, in a dialogue between Philalethes a Christian deist, and Theophanes a Christian Jew* (3 vols., London, 1737).
[304] Adams, *Works*, vol. 1, p. 43.
[305] Howard Ioan Fielding, 'John Adams: Puritan, Deist, Humanist', *Journal of Religion* 20 (1940), 33–46, at 40. Fielding (p. 45) argues that Adams held consistently to 'a central body of principles, of which his political theory and his religious system are but different manifestations'.
[306] Adams, *Works*, vol. 2, p. 250.
[307] Ibid., vol. 4, p. 407.
[308] Zoltan Haraszti, 'John Adams on Religion', *More Books: Bulletin of the Boston Public Library* 9 (1934), 373–98, at 376, 394–5; idem, *John Adams & The Prophets of Progress* (Cambridge, Mass., 1952), pp. 49–79, 280–99.
[309] Ibid., pp. 384–6.

Jesuits of the church of Rome, with indifference, who will believe that the apprehension of Episcopacy contributed fifty years ago, as much as any other cause, to arouse the attention, not only of the inquiring mind, but of the common people, and urge them to close thinking on the constitutional authority of parliament over the colonies? This, nevertheless, was a fact as certain as any in the history of North America. The objection was not merely to the office of a bishop, though even that was dreaded, but to the authority of parliament, on which it must be founded. The reasoning was this:– . . . There is no power or pretended power, less than parliament, that can create bishops in America. But if parliament can erect dioceses and appoint bishops, they may introduce the whole hierarchy, establish tithes, forbid marriages and funerals, establish religions, forbid dissenters, make schism heresy, impose penalties extending to life and limb as well as to liberty and property.[310]

In other words, Parliament might define Adams's views as heterodox and impose civil penalties for their profession. Like others of the elite, Adams's perceptions had a heterodox basis.

The rank and file more often showed the potential of ideas of sectarian polity. Sermons of New England Congregationalists before and during the Revolution are remarkably consistent in their political teaching: that the people have the right to set up any form of government over themselves, change it or dissolve it at will.[311] Their consistency is explained by the fact that these were ancient tenets of Congregational ecclesiastical polity. Like their English brethren, the problem is how those relatively stable dispositions were activated, turned from a defensive to an offensive creed; but of the long survival of those dispositions there can be little doubt. In 1770, the Boston massacre, an accidental and unpremeditated clash between a mob and a party of regular soldiers, called forth from Congregationalist ministers 'a torrent of sermons and outcries which, for their sheer fury and blood revenge, exceeded anything in the annals of New England oratory'.[312] When the Boston Port Act forbade trade with that town until the East India Company had been compensated for its lost tea, Samuel Adams and his fellow activists on the Boston Committee of Correspondence responded with an agreement not to consume British products, or import them, after 31 August 1774: it was termed the Solemn League and Covenant.[313] The town of Concord, Massachusetts, drafted its own

[310] John Adams to Jedediah Morse, 2 Dec. 1815: Adams, *Works*, vol. 10, p. 185; Jedediah Morse, *Annals of the American Revolution* (Hartford, 1824), pp. 197–203.
[311] Humphrey, *Nationalism and Religion in America 1774–1789*, pp. 52–65.
[312] Stout, *New England Soul*, p. 272. For preachers' eager advocacy of war in their artillery election and militia muster sermons of 1774–5, ibid., pp. 287–9.
[313] Richard D. Brown, *Revolutionary Politics in Massachusetts: The Boston Committee of Correspondence and the Towns, 1772–1774* (Cambridge, Mass., 1970), pp. 178–200.

version, which attracted the signatures of eight out of ten adult males; of the nonsubscribers some held county appointments from the Crown, others were survivors of the 'Old Light' Congregationalists who had separated from their brethren when the 'New Lights', inspired by a visit from George Whitefield, had introduced turmoil and threatened social control in the 1740s.[314] Many towns thought the Covenant premature, and looked for an inter-colonial nonimportation agreement; a few were fervently enthusiastic, endorsing the Boston text and invoking ancestral opposition to 'the unlimited Prerogative, contended for by those arbitrary & misguided Princes, *Charles* the First & *James* the Second, for which the One lost his Life, & the Other his Kingdom'.[315]

Concord had been incited to armed resistance by its Congregational minister, William Emerson. On 13 March 1775 he had preached from 2 Chronicles 13.12 ('Behold, God himself is with us for our Captain and his Priests with sounding Trumpets to cry Alarm against you') a sermon which reminded his flock how an army so supported had defeated the forces, twice as numerous, of an 'idolatrous King'. As 'a Priest of the Lord who is under the Gospel Dispensation, I must say 'The Priests blow the Trumpets in Zion, stand fast, take the Helmet, Shield and Buckler and put on the Brigadine.'[316] On 19 April, he took part in the battle at Concord which began the Revolutionary conflict. By its anniversary, George III had joined James II in Emerson's demonology, and the facts of military conflict had taken their place as props and scenery in Emerson's imagined holy war against British blasphemy and sacrilege.[317]

(D) THE AMERICAN BAPTISTS

The Baptist catechism was firmly Trinitarian,[318] with all that that entailed for formal political orientation. Separate Baptists, most eloquently in the

---

[314] Robert A. Gross, *The Minutemen and Their World* (New York, 1976), pp. 20–3.

[315] Quoted Brown, *Revolutionary Politics*, p. 202.

[316] For the text of the sermon see Amelia Forbes Emerson (ed.), *Diaries and Letters of William Emerson 1743–1776* (privately printed, Boston, 1972), pp. 61–70. This clashed with Emerson's profession of loyalty to George III and resistance only to his 'most abandoned Ministry'.

[317] 'An Oration for the 19th of April 1776', ibid., pp. 89–97.

[318] *A Brief Instruction in the Principles of the Christian Religion, Agreeable to the Confession of Faith, put forth by the Elders and Brethren of many Congregations of Christians (Baptised upon Profession of their Faith) in London, and in the Country* (7th edn., Wilmington, 1763), p. 8 (citing the spurious text in I John 5.7); *The Baptist confession of faith: First put forth in 1643; afterwards enlarged, corrected and published by an assembly of delegates (from the churches in Great Britain) met in London July 3, 1689; adopted by the association at Philadelphia September 22, 1742; and now received by churches of the same denomination as most of the american colonies* (Philadelphia, 1765), p. 10.

works of Isaac Backus, were slow to argue for religious liberty in terms of the rights of man; they claimed religious liberty as a divine right, in obedience to God's command of a correct form of ecclesiastical polity.[319] This was not a powerful catalyst of revolution. Baptists did not explicitly champion democratic doctrine, but their ecclesiastical practice was immediately recognised as a challenge to the patterns of hierarchy and authority where Anglicanism or Congregationalism were established.[320] At first sight, Baptists ostensibly differed from other denominations on one point of church order alone, but their practice provoked the familiar charges of 'enthusiasm'.[321] In Virginia, the Baptist minister David Thomas, despite his overt Trinitarianism, had to defend his denomination from widespread charges of schism, heresy and apostasy; or, in non-technical language, that they were 'continual fomenters of discord and variance' whose 'noisy Religion' had 'broken the bonds of natural affection and bursted the strongest cords of relation asunder'. Thomas's answer to the charge pointed to a political future: critics enjoyed only a 'false peace' coming from 'ignorance and unbelief, and self love and carnal security' which 'must be broken in time, or it will most certainly terminate in an eternal war'.[322] But this implicit threat was translated into reality only late, and with reluctance.

Pennsylvania was unusual even by the 1770s in its tolerant stance on religion; elsewhere, intolerance often focused on this growing group. In 1774 James Madison warned a friend in Philadelphia that the Baptists' petition for religious liberty in Virginia was unlikely to succeed. It had failed the previous session: 'such incredible and extravagant stories were told in the House of the monstrous effects of the enthusiasm prevalent among the sectaries'; Baptists still had a 'bad name' with 'those who pretend too much contempt to examine into their principles and conduct'.

> The sentiments of our people of fortune and fashion on this subject are vastly different from what you have been used to. That liberal, catholic, and equitable way of thinking, as to the rights of conscience, which is one of the characteristics of a free people, and so strongly marks the people of

[319] William G. McLoughlin (ed.), *Isaac Backus on Church, State, and Calvinism: Pamphlets, 1754–1789* (Cambridge, Mass., 1968), p. 33.

[320] Isaac, *The Transformation of Virginia 1740–1790*, pp. 161–77.

[321] For the standard spiritual progression from Arminian confidence in the effect of good works, through doubt, guilt and despair to the new birth, membership of a Separatist congregation and finally of the Baptists, see the account of Connecticut farmer and carpenter Nathan Cole (1711–83): Michael J. Crawford (ed.), 'The Spiritual Travels of Nathan Cole', *WMQ* 33 (1976), 89–126.

[322] David Thomas, *The Virginian Baptist: or A View and Defence of the Christian Religion as it is Professed by the Baptists of Virginia* (Baltimore, 1774), pp. 39–42, 57.

your province, is but little known among the zealous adherents to our hierarchy.[323]

In the face of local persecution, the carefully orthodox David Thomas defended his sect as late as 1771 with the claim: 'We concern not ourselves with the government of the colony . . . We form no intrigues. We lay no schemes to advance ourselves, nor make any attempts to alter the constitution of the kingdom to which as men we belong. We profess a loyal subjection to his majesty; and are well satisfied with him as our earthly sovereign.'[324] In August 1775 the efforts of the Presbyterian minister William Tennent to stir up the South Carolina backcountry to rebellion were almost undone in one region by 'two gainsaying Baptist preachers'.[325]

In the southern colonies, Baptists quickly sided with the Revolution in reaction to Anglican persecution[326] and to the promises of Anglican Deists like Jefferson, proclaiming the natural rights of mankind. In the middle colonies the Baptists showed a 'strong tendency toward neutrality',[327] possibly in response to the encouragement from the Secretary for the Colonies, Lord Hillsborough, when the Baptist minister and loyalist Morgan Edwards was in London in 1769. Hillsborough, thought Ezra Stiles, had

> encouraged & promoted the complaints of the persecution of the Baptists by the Presbyterians in N. Engld, & directed him to collect & procure all Baptists Complaints, & send them home to Engd & they should be favourably heard, with Assurance of Redress. And this was a Scheme of the Ministry to set the Baptists against the Congregationists, & prevent the former from joyning the Latter in opposing an American Episcopate, under the notion that they should meet with more Liberty & less oppression under episcopal than presb. Government.[328]

Influenced by Edwards, the Philadelphia Baptist Association tried to apply a brake to the juggernaut of revolution.[329]

---

[323] James Madison to William Bradford, 1 April 1774: Madison, *Writings*, vol. 1, p. 22.

[324] David Thomas, *The Virginian Baptist* (Baltimore, 1774), p. 33.

[325] 'A Fragment of a Journal kept by Rev. William Tennent' in R. W. Gibbes (ed.), *Documentary History of the American Revolution* (New York, 1855), pp. 225–39, at 229.

[326] Robert B. Semple, *A History of the Rise and Progress of the Baptists in Virginia* (Richmond, 1810), pp. 14–35.

[327] McLoughlin, *New England Dissent 1630–1833*, vol. 1, p. 576.

[328] Franklin Bowditch Dexter (ed.), *The Literary Diary of Ezra Stiles, D.D., LL.D.* (3 vols., New York, 1901), vol. 1, p. 78: 26 Nov. 1770.

[329] McLoughlin, *New England Dissent*, vol. 1, p. 577.

This body had had very different concerns. In 1743 the ministers of the Philadelphia Baptist Association lamented that some of their flock had become 'so entangled and confused' in their inquiries 'as to question the Sonship of the second Person'; the ministers were 'fully united to repel, and put a stop to, as far as we may, unto the Arian, Socinian, and Antitrinitarian systems'.[330] In 1774 the same body was equally resolved to combat 'innovation in doctrine and practice'.[331] Accordingly, the Association's circular letter, drawn up on 12–14 October 1774, was an exposition and defence of the doctrine of the Trinity as 'a foundation, a corner stone in the Christian faith'.[332] So believing, the reaction of the Association meeting on 15–16 October 1776 to 'the awful impending calamities of these times' was to order four days of 'humiliation, fasting, and prayer'.[333]

New England Congregationalism had been able to contain many New Lights within it: the Baptist challenge, phrased as dissent from certain points of ecclesiastical polity, was initially weak.[334] Separate Baptists in New England may have drawn strength from their substantial similarity to their Calvinist Congregationalist neighbours. In so far as they drew on the theology of English co-religionists, American Baptists found strictly Calvinist reinforcement.[335] For that reason, the Baptists had no obvious and immediate anti-British orientation in the pre-Revolutionary decade: they still suffered considerable disabilities under the Congregational establishment and might realistically look to the Crown as a more likely guarantor of toleration; in some Baptist consciences, revivalist religion promoted pacifism rather than political engagement.[336] Isaac Backus (1724–1806), the most famous figure among New England Baptist ministers, was almost wholly preoccupied with the intricate issues dividing Arminian Old Baptists from Calvinist Separate Baptists, both sects from the pedobaptist Separates, and all three from the 'standing church' of the Congregationalists. Until 1774, politics seldom intruded into his con-

---

[330] A. D. Gillette (ed.), *Minutes of the Philadelphia Baptist Association, from A.D. 1707, to A.D. 1807* (Philadelphia, 1851), p. 48.

[331] Ibid., p. 136.

[332] Ibid., pp. 143–6. No political advice was offered to constituent Baptist congregations.

[333] Ibid., pp. 155–6. Not until Yorktown did the Association give thanks to God for a military victory (ibid., p. 174).

[334] Baptists endorsed the Savoy Confession of 1688, almost identical to the Congregationalists' Westminster Confession except on baptism and church structure. See Schaff, *Creeds of Christendom*, vol. 3, p. 741.

[335] John Gill, *A Body of Doctrinal Divinity* (London, 1769); Stephen A. Marini, *Radical Sects of Revolutionary New England* (Cambridge, Mass., 1982), p. 22.

[336] Marini, *Radical Sects*, p. 23.

cerns.[337] He was not moved to partisanship by news of the Boston riot against the Stamp Act, but rather to reflection that the crisis was a divine punishment for Americans having grown 'wanton' in the enjoyment of material affluence.[338]

The financial harassment of Separate Baptists by Congregationalists continued unabated. By 1770, Backus and his coreligionists were so offended that 'while our countery are pleading So high for liberty, yet that they are denying of it to their neighbours' that the Baptists were on the verge of appealing to England against Congregational persecution.[339] In 1773 the Warren Baptist Association, representing New England Baptists, decided to cease to seek tax exemption through local legal channels, abandon the goal of toleration in favour of that of religious freedom, and appeal to the crown for aid. It was this policy which the outbreak of the Revolution overtook. In 1774 Backus and the Warren Association appealed to Congress rather than to the crown against their persecution; but they were met by a New England delegation including John and Samuel Adams and Robert Treat Paine which argued that the Congregational establishment was only 'a very slender one', that it was not persecutory, and 'Mr. S. Adams tried to represent that regular baptists were easy among us, and more than once insinuated that these complaints came from enthuseasts who made a merit of suffering persecution, and also that enemies to these colonies had a hand therein.'[340]

News of the fighting at Lexington and Concord drew Backus reluctantly to side with the Revolution. On Sunday 23 April he preached from I Chronicles 12. 32,

> and after opening the words and the occasion of them, I endeavoured to apply them as a light to help us to answer these two questions, 1. Whether our present opposition to the power that is assusemed [? assumed] over us

---

[337] William G. McLoughlin (ed.), *The Diary of Isaac Backus* (3 vols., Providence, 1977), passim; idem (ed.), *Isaac Backus on Church, State, and Calvinism*. The evolution of Backus's position on Church-State relations in his writings between 1754 and 1768 entailed no commitment to or anticipation of colonial independence. Backus did, however, elaborate his interpretation of the erroneous nature of infant baptism into a critique of the whole Congregational establishment based on it (ibid., p. 33).

[338] Backus, *Diary*, 18 Aug. 1765, 31 Dec. 1765–2 Jan. 1766.

[339] Ibid., 11 Sept. 1770.

[340] Ibid., 14 Oct. 1774. It was a clash of conceptions of positive liberty. Robert Treat Paine had argued: 'they [the Baptists] plead for liberty of conscience and yet deny it; for we believe in our consciences that we ought to support ministers in that way [by compulsory taxes], and they will not allow us to do it': ibid., 19 Nov. 1774. The Congregational minister Ezra Stiles, briefed by Robert Treat Paine, thought that the Baptists still intended 'to complain to England of Persecution – because they hate Congregationalists': Dexter (ed.), *Literary Diary of Ezra Stiles*, vol. 1, p. 475.

be just or not? 2. How we ought to behave in the management thereof? As to the first I observed that the doctrine of passive obedience and non-resistance to kings, was, from bishop Bevereidge, published last Monday, i.e. in the Evening Post of that day,[341] which doctrine had been much preached up in James 2ds day, till the nation was brought so upon the brink of popery and slavery that the very biships who preached that doctrine up were forced to act against it; and I observed that if that doctrine were true, George the third and his grandfather and great grandfather and the glorious king William were all usurpers, and the pretender was the rightful heir of the crown. I noted that in Rom[ans] 13 the powers that we were required to submit to were ministers of God to the people *for good*, but that it was a foundation point in the constitution of the English government, that the peoples property shall not be taken from them without their consent, either by themselves or their representatives; but that the principle that all these proceedings are founded upon, which we oppose, is, 'That the British parliament have a right to bind America in all cases whatsoever'; which is an open violation of the essential rules of the English government. And I further said that George the third violated his coronation-oath which he had solemnly taken before God and his people in establishing popery in Canada.

Had Backus gone too far? 'On a review I have seriously thought that some of these expressions had better been omitted', he confessed; but the die was cast.[342] The spectre of Anglican hegemony was more terrifying than the present reality of Congregationalist persecution.

Writing the history of his denomination in 1784, Backus made this explicit, though more decisive in retrospect than it had been at the time. He listed his reasons for opposing British rule:

1. Where Episcopalians have had all the power of government, they have never allowed others so much liberty as we here enjoyed. In England all are taxed to their worship, while none are admitted into civil offices but communicants in their church. In Virginia they cruelly imprisoned Baptist ministers, only for preaching the gospel to perishing souls without license from their courts, until this war compelled them to desist therefrom. Of this we had incontestable evidence. Therefore we could have no rational hopes of any real advantage in joining with them. 2. The worst treatment we here met with came from the same principles, and much of it from the same persons, as the American war did . . . 3. The first Baptist minister in

---

[341] The *Boston Evening Post* of 17 April 1775 carried a quotation from Bishop William Beveridge (1637–1708).

[342] Backus, *Diary*, 17 Apr. 1775. The depth of the Calvinist Backus's doctrinal antipathy to Anglicanism was revealed when John Murray, an itinerant 'who preaches up universal salvation', visited Norwich and attracted the sympathy of the local episcopalian clergyman John Tyler, himself a convert from Congregationalism, although, as Backus put it, Murray's 'doctrine is really the same with that of the devil, *Ye shall not surely die*': *Diary*, 10 Oct. 1779.

America [Roger Williams] publicly held forth, that all righteous government is founded in compact, expressed or implied ... When therefore our countrymen adopted these principles, and founded their opposition to arbitrary claims wholly thereon, how could we avoid joining with them? For, 4. those claims appeared to us absolutely unjust, and a direct violation of the immutable rules of truth and equity ... 5. ... a strong hope was begotten of final deliverance to this land ...

It is all the more remarkable that so strong a case should have been ignored even by Backus before 1774. Ten years later he admitted: 'It is not pretended that our denomination were all agreed, or had equal clearness in these points; but a majority of them were, more or less, influenced thereby.'[343]

Other Baptists in New England were hesitant. Ezra Stiles collected evidence to prove that James Manning, president of the Baptist College (later Brown University) was 'a Tory, affecting Neutrality'. He had only prayed for Congress when Washington personally attended his meeting;

> But he & most of the Heads of the Baptists especially Ministers thro' the Continent are cool in this Cause, if not rather wishing the Kings side Victory ... Lately he was at Gov. Cooke's at Providence and making some sneering Reflexions on the public affairs – he suggested that this was a Presbyterian War – that the Congregationalists at the northward had prevailed upon the Ch[urc]hmen to the Southward to joyn them – & that it was worth considering who (viz Baptists) would be crushed between them both, if they overcome. This is the heart of the bigotted Baptist Politicians.[344]

Manning indeed lamented the outbreak of fighting as destructive of religious evangelism: 'the fatal 19th of April, the day of the Lexington battle, like an electric stroke put a stop to the progress of the work, in other places as here. Oh horrid war! How contrary to the spirit of Jesus!'[345] 'When one would have thought this would have promoted seriousness amongst us, it, strange to tell, operated the very reverse; for since the fatal day languor and abatement of zeal for God seem greatly to have obtained, and instances of conversion to Christ are rare.'[346]

[343] Isaac Backus, *A History of New England. With Particular Reference to the Denomination of Christians called Baptists*, ed. David Weston (2 vols., Newton, Mass., 1871), vol. 2, pp. 197–8.

[344] Dexter (ed.), *Literary Diary of Ezra Stiles*, vol. 2, p. 23: 16 July 1776; McLoughlin, *New England Dissent*, vol. 1, p. 579. Manning, like others, used 'Presbyterian' and 'Congregational' as synonyms.

[345] James Manning to John Ryland, 13 Nov. 1776, in Reuben Aldridge Guild, *Life, Times, and Correspondence of James Manning, and the Early History of Brown University* (Boston, 1864), p. 243.

[346] Manning to Benjamin Wallin, 12 Nov. 1776: ibid., p. 245.

Despite the sectarian intolerance they faced, Baptists aligned themselves with some uniformity on the side of the Revolution. On 16 August 1775 the Virginia Convention was addressed by the Baptists of the state, declaring themselves 'embarked in the same common Cause' and reporting that they 'had determined that in some Cases it was lawful to go to War, and also for us to make a Military resistance against Great Britain, in regard of their unjust Invasion, and tyrannical Oppression of, and repeated Hostilities against America'.[347] Doctrinal orthodoxy could not prevent this final step. The Baptist congregation founded at Haverhill, Massachusetts in May 1765 was explicitly Trinitarian in its creed.[348] Its organiser, Hezekiah Smith, nevertheless joined the Revolution, became a friend of Washington, and fought at Bunker Hill.

Only in 1775 did the New England Baptists swing clearly behind the cause of independence when their Association, based at Warren, Rhode Island, decided that liberty of conscience was more likely under a different regime. It was a gamble which failed. In Virginia, the leadership of Deists like Jefferson secured for the Baptists the religious liberty they sought; in New England the dominance of fervent (if sometimes heterodox) Congregationalists preserved a system of compulsory taxation for the support of the established church in the Massachusetts constitution of 1780. In Connecticut the establishment was dismantled in 1818; in Massachusetts in 1833. Nor did all Baptists follow this lead: although few became active loyalists, many more sought to preserve neutrality.[349] Of the five Baptist ministers in New Hampshire in 1776, three signed the 'Association Test' (the pro-revolutionary declaration drawn up by the Committee of Safety in April 1776); two refused, including the Baptists' leader in the colony, Samuel Shepard. The concentration of laymen refusing the oath was high in towns in which Baptists predominated.[350]

The frequent reticence or neutrality and occasional loyalism of American Baptists is more remarkable by comparison with the English Baptists' enthusiasm for the cause of American independence. Among English Baptist ministers, Robert Hall and John Ryland were open in siding with the Revolution. English Baptists shared in the general theological developments of their more sophisticated society: as one Baptist minister complained from London, 'Two things are threatening with us, – the

---

[347] Charles F. James, *Documentary History of the Struggle for Religious Liberty in Virginia* (Lynchburg, 1900), pp. 51–3, 218–19.

[348] Reuben Aldridge Guild, *Chaplain Smith and the Baptists: or, Life, Journals, Letters and Addresses of the Rev. Hezekiah Smith, D.D.* (Philadelphia, 1885), p. 80.

[349] Marini, *Radical Sects*, p. 24.

[350] Richard F. Upton, *Revolutionary New Hampshire* (Port Washington, N.Y., 1970), pp. 50, 61.

growth of Anti-Trinitarians, in a variety of forms, for they cannot agree
. . . The other is a popular ignorance of the authority of Christ . . .'[351] In
1784, the English Baptist minister John Rippon wrote from London to
James Manning:

> I believe all our Baptist ministers in town, except two, and most of our
> brethren in the country, were on the side of the Americans in the late
> dispute . . . We wept when the thirsty plains drank the blood of your depar-
> ted heroes, and the shout of a king was amongst us when your well-fought
> battles were crowned with victory. And to this hour we believe that the
> independence of America will for a while secure the liberty of this country;
> but that if the continent had been reduced, Britain would not long have
> been free.[352]

Baptist laymen in England, sharing less in the advanced views of their
ministers, were less committed.[353]

Once embarked, American Baptist laymen joined enthusiastically in
the war for the usual reasons. They even found a Baptist minister[354]
willing to suspend the pietism of his sect in favour of fierce exhortations
to join in the cause of liberty.[355] John Allen was unusual in his political
commitments, however. Indeed he had arrived in America only in
1771, having failed in business in London, spent time in the King's
Bench prison, published a Wilkesite pamphlet, been acquitted of forgery, and dismissed as minister of Baptist congregations in London
and Newcastle on grounds of doctrinal heterodoxy.[356] Despite his political activism, in 1773 the Second Baptist Church of Boston again
refused to accept him as its minister.[357] It was the onset of revolution
which gave Allen and others like him their chance, but it was revolution
also which wiped the slate clean and erased in retrospect the very
conflicts and equivocations which had brought it about. So Washington
addressed the Baptists in 1789 as having been 'throughout America,
uniformly and almost unanimously the firm friends to civil liberty, and

---

[351] Benjamin Wallin to James Manning, 30 July 1773, in Guild, *Manning*, p. 211. For the
advance of Arianism and Socinianism among the General Baptists, and even a few Particular Baptists, see A. C. Underwood, *A History of the English Baptists* (London, 1947),
pp. 127–8, 138–40, 156; W. T. Whitley, *A History of British Baptists* (2nd edn, London,
1932), pp. 200–3, 214, 228–9.

[352] Rippon to Manning, 1 May 1784, in Guild, *Manning*, p. 323.

[353] McLoughlin, *New England Dissent*, vol. 1, p. 583.

[354] John M. Bumsted and Charles E. Clark, 'New England's Tom Paine: John Allen and
the Spirit of Liberty', *WMQ* 21 (1964), 561–70.

[355] John Allen, *The American Alarm, Or The Bostonian Plea, For the Rights, and Liberties, of the
People* (Boston, 1773); idem, *An Oration, Upon the Beauties of Liberty, Or the Essential Rights
of the Americans* (Boston, 1773); idem, *The Watchman's Alarm to Lord N[ORT]H* (Salem,
1774). The *Oration* saw seven editions between 1773 and 1775.

[356] *DNB*; Bumsted and Clark, 'John Allen'.

[357] McLoughlin, *New England Dissent*, vol. 1, p. 584.

the persevering promoters of our glorious revolution'.[358] For the Baptists as for all other sects, the mutual self-congratulation which formed part of the early process of state formation had begun to obscure the mixed motives which had driven or hindered the rank and file. Symbolically, the secular halo was fastened on the Baptist brow by the nominal Episcopalian, George Washington.

---

[358] 'To the General Committee, Representing the United Baptist Churches in Virginia. May, 1789', in Washington, *Writings*, vol. 12, pp. 154–5.

CONCLUSION

'Desolating devastation': the origins of Anglo-American divergence

British and American society retained much in common in the centuries after 1783: more, indeed, than they were now concerned to assert or willing to admit. Both explored models of democratic politics, were swept by evangelicalism and unbelief, were dominated by the urban-industrial experience. Yet, inexorably, the two societies' self-images and interpretations of their histories drew apart in fundamental ways, so that the demonstration of a 'special relationship' required a reinterpretation of the perceived past as much as an evocation of it. Law and religion continued to shape this process by which both America and Britain devised partly-incompatible theories of their own exceptionalism. American understandings of the purpose of the Revolution quickly came after 1776 to turn on religious liberty as the antithesis of tyranny, and on law as the guarantor and definition of liberty; yet, paradoxically, the conflict of denominations steadily increased the authority of the group over the conscience of the individual, and the reconstruction of American law led the courts of the new Republic to develop a far more interventionist and innovatory attitude to their role.[1] Common lawyers in England, in the same half-century after American independence, were increasingly bound by the doctrine of strict construction: Benthamite utilitarianism, not Jeffersonian natural rights, came to describe the truths the English saw as self-evident.

The military outcome of the American Revolution had a profound impact on its interpretation. Its character as a civil war on both sides of the Atlantic was obscured and replaced by an image of a war of national or colonial liberation in which a morally united America fought a morally united Britain: American loyalists and British republicans were systemat-

[1] William E. Nelson, *Americanisation of the Common Law: The Impact of Legal Change on Massachusetts Society, 1760–1830* (Cambridge, Mass., 1975), pp. 89–116; Morton J. Horwitz, *The Transformation of American Law, 1780–1860* (Cambridge, Mass., 1977), p. 1 and passim.

ically excluded from their own society's vision. Within America, the course of the war meant that a national mythology was built around the ideology of triumphant New England, not devastated Virginia or marginalised Quaker-pacifist Pennsylvania: the Anglican model, which had come closest to realisation in the southern colonies, was not merely displaced but erased and forgotten as a possible pattern for a future America. Until at least the First World War, Americans from all backgrounds acknowledged that the values, stereotypes and aspirations of what the nineteenth century understood as the Puritan legacy were built into the minds of the rapidly multiplying citizens of the new Republic.[2] Within the United Kingdom, the Anglican heartland of the south east of England retained its overwhelming cultural hegemony until 1832 and considerable (if less than hegemonic) power thereafter.

Gradually, Americans' understandings of the essence of their Great Experiment were modified. The separation of Church and State soon entailed that the new Republic's sense of its crusading mission to reform the old world was summed up not in Deism or Arianism but in the inclusive and seemingly secular term 'democracy'. Democracy was now held to be the essence of the American experiment; other states were divided into 'democracies' and the objects of reform. Yet whatever the diverse and often helpful meanings of the term, it is clear that democracy – in the sense of debates over the franchise, the distribution of seats, or the representative machinery in general – was not central to the conflicts which rent the English-speaking world in the early-modern period, and was not at the heart of the self-image of any of the societies which made up that world. Its key term had been not 'democracy' but 'liberty', and liberty was a term which had its ramifications chiefly in the vast intellectual territories then occupied by law and religion.

As a result of the genesis of the Revolution in these bodies of thought, the new Republic was built 'centrally on utopian millennial expectations'.[3] Britain, avoiding revolution, crucially prolonged certain features of her public ideology until the millenarian challenge of the French Revolution had receded. In the last three decades of the eighteenth century America acquired a national myth of origins, built up from component sectarian myths; Britain in the same period turned her myths of origins into a saga of survival. America, having repudiated the homogenising Anglican-aristocratic mores integral to British rule, built its sense

[2] Winthrop S. Hudson (ed.), *Nationalism and Religion in America: Concepts of American Identity and Mission* (New York, 1970), pp. 2–3.
[3] Robert N. Bellah, *The Broken Covenant: American Civil Religion in Time of Trial* (New York, 1975), p. ix.

of national identity in part through the elaboration of the myth of the 'melting pot', a natural and beneficent process which would assimilate residents and immigrants in a rational modernity: beneath this myth, religion and ethnicity survived in a dynamic relationship and eventually experienced an explosive recrudescence.[4] Unreformed Britain remained set on a path towards a profoundly secular society with relatively little ethnic consciousness.

Where Britons began to dwell on (indeed sometimes to invent) immense continuities in their historic experience, and British ideals increasingly praised the stoic understatement of catastrophe, the American republic, freed from historical stabilities, embarked on a pattern of moral alternation: phases of moral endeavour which strengthened the persecutory and inquisitorial elements in society, succeeded by phases of broken covenants, corruption and despair.[5] In Britain the sacred trappings of the state were profoundly redefined but not wholly abandoned in 1832; British society found ways of sustaining its existing programmes of meliorative reform within the framework of the old moral order. In America a new and programmatic civil religion provided an evangelical impetus for a society unlike any the world had seen before: at once more ethical and more materialistic, more libertarian and more deferential to the sovereignty of collective opinion. With the passing of the old intellectual nexus of Church and State, British public life quickly lost its old preoccupations with tests and oaths; in America these formal affirmations of group integrity took on new life.[6] British formulations of liberty remained stubbornly specific, resisting incorporation into the generalised natural rights rhetoric of 1789;[7] they consequently proved far more open to augmentation and expansion than those of the new Republic. Where the Republic's inbuilt crusading ideology led to a second and equally devastating civil war, Britain's

---

[4] Scholars 'usually treat the religious institutions, cultural forms, and ideologies of immigrant Protestants, Jews, Catholics, and Eastern Orthodox Christians as backward-looking, dysfunctional, or arcane'. For the recent academic reaction against the older assumption (explicit in the sociology of Max Weber and Talcott Parsons) that religion and ethnicity would be submerged in the consumer culture of modern societies, see Timothy L. Smith, 'Religion and Ethnicity in America', *AHR* 83 (1978), 1155–85; idem, 'Congregation, State, and Denomination: The Forming of the American Religious Structure', *WMQ* 25 (1968), 155–76.

[5] Bellah, *Broken Covenant*, p. 2 and passim.

[6] Harold M. Hyman, *To Try Men's Souls: Loyalty Tests in American History* (Berkeley, 1959). Liberty of religion, once secured, had to be elaborately defended. For a 'harassment code' of 1783 at the Baptist college, later Brown University, see Reuben Aldridge Guild, *Life, Times and Correspondence of James Manning, and the Early History of Brown University* (Boston, 1864), pp. 304–7, article 8.

[7] G. R. Elton, 'Human Rights and the Liberties of Englishmen', *University of Illinois Law Review* (1990), 329–46.

led anticlimactically to a series of Acts extending the franchise in parliamentary elections.

If the colonies' misconceptions about and grievances against British rule were fossilised in the Constitution of the United States, Britain's constitution was more stridently defended also. The independence of so many of her European-populated colonies allowed the public structures of law and religion in Britain to survive with little change, at least until 1828–32 and in many ways thereafter. The common-law doctrine of sovereignty was left untouched in successive waves of domestic reform, in the 1780s, 1830s, 1860s and later decades. Responses to political challenges remained pragmatic, aimed at the efficiency of the bureaucratic machinery ('economical reform'), the armed forces or the electoral system; but the Anglican, common-law drive to uniformity remained, and the Irish rebellion against it of 1798 was met in classic fashion by the Union. The passage of that Act in 1800 marks the high point of state formation in the British Isles within that idiom.

The unified, absolute sovereign of the Anglican ascendancy meant that Britain's future after 1832 was to be one of sweeping, centrally-directed reform in all areas of national life; America, rationalised into the modernity of the 1780s, thereafter found it intensely difficult to restructure its machinery of government. The British constitution was a collection of contingencies: its contradictions were therefore seldom important. The American constitution, notionally a set of harmonious ideas, was equally the product of tactical imperatives; as such, it was involved in damaging internal contradictions from the outset. Rejection of a monarchical polity compelled the adoption of a republican democracy, despite the familiar colonial warnings that democracy entailed majoritarian tyranny. Montesquieu had observed that 'It is in the nature of a republic to have only a small territory; otherwise, it can scarcely continue to exist',[8] but it was necessary to argue after independence that a republic was, uniquely in the case of America, a formula for stable government in a large state. The English euphemism of a checked and balanced constitution was developed by Americans to the point where the rejection of monarchy required a division of sovereignty among the institutions of Federal and State governments; but the rejection of monarchy also entailed the vesting of sovereignty in a new and different abstraction, 'the people', and this unitary conception threatened the confederal ideal of avoiding tyranny by dividing and sharing authority.

The impact of seven years of fighting on American society was pro-

[8] Montesquieu, *The Spirit of the Laws*, ed. and trans. Anne M. Cohler et al. (Cambridge, 1989), p. 124.

found. Where British society was progressively disciplined by the demands of war overseas into a more austere, more hierarchical, more evangelical mode,[9] America's experience of violence, disease, betrayal, impoverishment, deceit and insecurity were destructive of that polite and commercial culture, at once patrician and transatlantic, into which the colonists had sought to integrate. One contemporary of the Revolution expressed an insight into the impact of war and the devastating inflation which chiefly financed it in an idiom different from that of the clerical jeremiad:

> Truth, honor, and justice were swept away by the overflowing deluge of legal iniquity, nor have they yet assumed their ancient and accustomed seats. Time and industry have already, in a great degree, repaired the losses of property, which the citizens sustained during the war, but both have hitherto failed in effacing the taint which was then communicated to their principles, nor can its total ablution be expected till a new generation arises, unpracticed in the iniquities of their fathers.[10]

Colonists seldom derived from the Revolution exactly what it was that they had sought; rather, the realities of rebellion and war created a profoundly different society, different in ways hardly foreseen or sought in 1776. Episcopalians had sought to perpetuate the social order of which they were part by resisting its subversion by 'popery and arbitrary power'; they inherited a polity in which the Anglican model had been wholly effaced as an option for future American society. Presbyterians and Congregationalists were the most numerous sects in the America of 1776; by 1800 the Baptists, closely followed by the Methodists,[11] had outstripped them all. Revolutionary intellectuals like Benjamin Franklin and Tom Paine had looked forward to a Deistic republic; by 1800 Deism had been swamped in many states by a massive evangelical revival. Even New England did not secure the sort of society for which its sons had fought, for Calvinist Congregationalism was soon profoundly modified by the proliferating Unitarianism of the early nineteenth century.

It was the Baptists, ironically the most lukewarm of the denominations about joining the Revolution, who profited most from its success. Yet

[9] Ford K. Brown, *Fathers of the Victorians: The Age of Wilberforce* (Cambridge, 1961); Richard A. Soloway, 'Reform or Ruin: English Moral Thought During the First French Republic', *Review of Politics* 25 (1963), 110–28.

[10] David Ramsay, *History of the American Revolution* (2 vols., Philadelphia, 1789; ed. Lester H. Cohen, Indianapolis, 1990), vol. 2, p. 462. Ramsay was over-optimistic about the material impact of the war: it dealt the American economy a devastating blow from which it took many years to recover.

[11] The 'brilliant success' of Methodism in America after the Revolution has been ascribed to the 'opportunity it afforded the English to affirm their ethnic origin on an anti-Anglican basis': W. R. Ward, *The Protestant Evangelical Awakening* (Cambridge, 1992), p. 351.

even the Baptists were not unambiguous about the outcome, for the war had its consequences also for the moral and religious ideals which had driven it forward to a Pyrrhic victory. For the Baptist Isaac Backus the Revolution quickly meant that 'the great men of the earth crouded in their fine wares upon us, which all ranks of people in America were fond of buying, to our unspeakable damage, in the sinking of public credit, and the most extravagant gratification of pride, intemperance, fraud, and cruel oppression. Rev[elations] 18. 23'.[12] The President of the Baptist college at Providence, James Manning, lamented the 'desolating devastation' that spread along the American coast with the war; 'language would fail to paint in proper colors the horrors of these days'. Formal religion collapsed; religious entrepreneurs flourished, like the preacher of universal salvation John Murray,[13] 'supposed to be a fugitive from justice in Great Britain'. Manning continued:

> Soon after this, two women, who pretended to a participation of Deity, set up new kinds of superstition. One of them pretended to be Jesus Christ in the form of a woman. In her preaching and praying she considered herself as the Mediator. The other pretended to pardon sins . . . She interdicted all intercourse between the sexes, so that separations between man and wife became common, among those who would attain to a state of absolute perfection . . . She, with her attendants, came to America from Liverpool, or its vicinity, about the commencement of the war . . . great multitudes are ensnared by these delusions, and follow their pernicious ways.[14]

In the imagery of the state, too, a secular Trinity replaced the Christian one. The Paineite Joel Barlow (1754–1812), member of the Society for Constitutional Information while in London, rescuer of the manuscript and responsible for the publication of Paine's *Age of Reason*, translator of the French Deist C.F. Volney's *Ruins of Empires* in 1802, published in 1807 *The Columbiad*, an immense philosophical poem celebrating American state formation: it praised 'EQUALITY', 'FREE ELECTION' and 'your FEDERAL BAND': 'This holy Triad should forever shine/The great

[12] William G. McLoughlin (ed.), *The Diary of Isaac Backus* (3 vols., Providence, 1979), 28 Dec. 1783.

[13] John Murray claimed to be one of George Whitefield's preachers, but 'on his Passage from England . . . used to mix with the common Sailors on Board of the Ship, drink & sing vain Songs with them . . . He used to say to them sometimes, on such occasions, that He had not determined what to turn his Hand to when He got to this country, but that He had a great Mind to turn Preacher – which the Seamen considered at the Time as a Jest . . .': John Rodgers to unnamed, 30 Apr. 1773, in Charles A. Anderson (ed.), 'Letters of John Rodgers, Preacher and Patriot', *Journal of the Presbyterian Historical Society* 27 (1949), 195–205, at 202.

[14] James Manning to Benjamin Wallin, 23 May 1783, in Guild, *Manning*, p. 293. Manning referred to Jemima Wilkinson and secondly to Ann Lee, founder of the Shakers, who emigrated to America in 1774. Both recommended, or demanded, celibacy.

compendium of all rights divine'[15] (his friend the former Bishop of Blois denounced the poem as an attack on Christianity).[16] Secular texts came to take the place of the covenants of colonial sects. The Constitution as a document itself became the centre of a 'popular cult'; it was widely regarded as 'fraught with supernal wisdom'; scepticism of its powers became 'the mark of political atheism'; it generated a 'ritual of the worship of the Constitution' as a system of law,[17] endorsed in time by Woodrow Wilson as 'an indiscriminate and almost blind worship of its principles . . . The divine right of kings never ran a more prosperous course than did this unquestioned prerogative of the Constitution to receive universal homage.' As Judge Addison of the Pennsylvania court of common pleas had put it in 1791, 'Man must have an idol. And our political idol ought to be our Constitution and laws. They, like the ark of the covenant among the Jews, ought to be sacred from all profane touch.'[18] His wish was granted: the Declaration of Independence and the Constitution, as one political scientist observes, became 'sacraments'; Congress assumed a 'theocratic' role; the Supreme Court became 'a kind of secular papacy'.[19] Irreverent nineteenth-century Britons increasingly pictured politics as a game. Since their religion was still not generally covenantal, even mass democracy did not transform British social relations into contractual ones.

Once the Old World sources of authority – elite social status or royal commission – were unavailable, new sources had to be sought in the fervour of nationalist zeal. The Founding Fathers, and especially their military leaders, became the objects of a strange reverence: one military historian has observed that the 'rhetoric surrounding Washington suggests that Americans did not want a new king or benevolent ruler so much as a high priest of the revolution, an exemplar of the qualities that

[15] Joel Barlow, *The Columbiad* (Philadelphia, 1807), p. 301.

[16] *DAB.*

[17] The Constitution is today exhibited to the people on the high altar of a secular church built for the reception of the sacred relic, the National Archives in Washington, D.C., with the Declaration of Independence displayed in an elaborate monstrance placed on the altar; a copy of Magna Carta resides in an obscure showcase of an ordinary gallery in the British Museum. The National Archives is a popular place of pilgrimage; Runnymede meadow, the reputed site of the signing of Magna Carta, is marked chiefly with a memorial erected by the American Bar Association.

[18] Frank I. Schechter, 'The Early History of the Tradition of the Constitution', *American Political Science Review* 9 (1915), 707–34, at 709, 715–16, 719, 733; H. von Holst, *The Constitutional and Political History of the United States* (8 vols, Chicago, 1889–92), vol. 1, pp. 64–79, 'The Worship of the Constitution and its Real Character'.

[19] Catherine L. Albanese, *Sons of the Fathers: The Civil Religion of the American Revolution* (Philadelphia, 1976), pp. 182–220. This important study traces the emergence of an undifferentiated 'civil religion' and does not explore the denominational contrasts and conflicts which have been emphasised here.

would achieve the continent's promised future';[20] an historian of American religion has found the appropriate analogy between Washington's reassuring role and the ability of the revivalist George Whitefield to convince his hearers that they indeed enjoyed divine grace.[21] In Britain, Wellington and Nelson symbolised stoic imperturbability and professional brilliance, but their private lives were widely discussed and they performed no function as moral icons during their own lifetimes.

Once the Revolution had been firmly identified as the first crusade of the American civil religion, it became necessary to canonise the zealots who had brought it about. The Founding Fathers, where possible, were turned from political opportunists, propagandists or self-seekers of tepid or heterodox religious belief into the Luthers and Calvins, the Melanchthons and Zwinglis of the *Novus ordo seclorum*. With some exceptions, like the now-notorious Tom Paine, each became the subject of a secular epiphany. Especially was this true of the unlikely figure of George Washington, a stolid man of limited imagination and still more limited religious faith, but now repeatedly hailed (without irony) as the Moses or the Joshua of a redeemed people.[22] On his election to the Presidency in 1789, the Presbyterian General Assembly presented him with a congratulatory address, professing to draw particular comfort from Washington's personal piety:

> Public virtue is the most certain means of public felicity, and religion is the surest basis of virtue. We therefore esteem it a peculiar happiness to behold in our chief Magistrate, a steady, uniform, avowed friend of the christian religion, who has commenced his administration in rational and exalted sentiments of Piety, and who in his private conduct adorns the doctrines of the Gospel of Christ, and on the most public and solemn occasions devoutly acknowledges the government of divine Providence.[23]

Washington's reply was all they could expect. He championed religious toleration, acknowledged their prayers, and coupled an ecumenical Deity with a lively regard for the value of religion as a social cement:

> While I reiterate the possession of my dependence upon Heaven as the source of all public and private blessings; I will observe that the general prevalence of piety, philanthropy, honesty, industry and oeconomy seems,

[20] Charles Royster, *A Revolutionary People at War: The Continental Army and American Character, 1775–1783* (Chapel Hill, 1979), p. 256.

[21] Alan Heimert, *Religion and the American Mind: From the Great Awakening to the Revolution* (Cambridge, Mass., 1966), pp. 147–8.

[22] For the canonisation of Washington, see Albanese, *Sons of the Fathers*, pp. 143–81; William A. Bryan, *George Washington in American Literature, 1775–1865* (New York, 1952); Barry Schwartz, *George Washington: The Making of an American Symbol* (New York, 1987).

[23] W. W. Abbot (et al., eds.), *The Papers of George Washington* (Charlottesville, 1983–), *Presidential Series*, vol. 2, p. 421.

in the ordinary course of human affairs are particularly necessary for advancing and confirming the happiness of our country.[24]

By the first centennial, the image of the Revolution as a holy war had expanded within the folk memories of the American sects to the point where the divisions and ambiguities within those denominations were forgotten. Presbyterians pictured the war as a Presbyterian crusade which sanctified martial heroism, turned the heterodox rhetoric of the Founding Fathers into the idiom of revivalist preaching, traced in the 'apparent chaos' of armed rebellion 'the will of God . . . working toward order and organisation', and found the culmination of order, reason and organisation in a constitution depicted in terms reminiscent of the millennium. A Presbyterian minister quoted the words of a centennial oration at Concord: 'The government was felt to be but a hand of protection and blessing.' He interpreted this fact: the Founding Fathers were 'under the aspiration of principles derived from God's holy word'; in the Revolution they 'crossed the Jordan from colonial bondage to national freedom'.[25] Yet, paradoxically, this retrospective homogenisation of the positions of colonial denominations acted to secularise the historical interpretation of the Revolution and to drain the role of the sects of its immense significance: if most men, regardless of denomination, eventually seemed to have endorsed the Revolution, then the Revolution's values and causes must by definition have been irrelevant to religious differences.

This trick of perspective did not eliminate the problem, but obscured it. Thanks to the historical episodes explored in this book, a modern American scholar could observe the paradox that despite the high level of formal religious observance in the United States, 'practically every species of traditional orthodoxy in Christendom is intellectually at war with the basic premises upon which the constitutional and legal structures of the Republic rest'.[26] Heterodoxy, revivalist enthusiasm and millenarianism were marginalised in mainstream historiography and became the study of specialists; American ideals of liberty and moral regeneration took shape within this framework of ideas nevertheless. It ensured that the dynamic given to the idea of liberty before and during the Revolution

---

[24] Ibid., p. 420.

[25] W. P. Breed, *Presbyterians and the Revolution* (Philadelphia, 1876), pp. 5–12.

[26] Sidney E. Mead, *The Old Religion in the Brave New World: Reflections on the Relation between Christendom and the Republic* (Berkeley, 1977), p. 2. For an argument that modern America suffered an 'identity crisis' as the result of a dissociation between the historically-integrated realms of law and religion, see Harold J. Berman, *The Interaction of Law and Religion* (London, 1974). This dissociation might more accurately be traced to 1776.

would not be lost thereafter, despite its secular translation.[27] Many were persuaded. John Adams wrote from Amsterdam to his wife on 18 December 1781:

> the great designs of Providence must be accomplished. Great indeed! The progress of society will be accelerated by centuries by this Revolution. The Emperor of Germany is adopting, as fast as he can, American ideas of toleration and religious liberty, and it will become the fashionable system of all Europe very soon. Light spreads from the dayspring in the west, and may it shine more and more until the perfect day![28]

Others interpreted the shared transatlantic inheritance differently, and deplored its division. Witnessing the fighting for New York, Lord Howe's secretary Ambrose Serle, moved to despair by the zeal of republican preachers, was driven to echo the harsh indictment of Lucretius: 'Such conduct in such persons affords too much Room for the Taunts of Infidels: Tantum Religio potuit suadere malorum'.[29]

---

[27] For the consequences in the nineteenth and twentieth centuries, see Conrad Cherry, *God's New Israel: Religious Interpretations of American Destiny* (Englewood Cliffs, N.J., 1971); George Armstrong Kelly, *Politics and Religious Consciousness in America* (New Brunswick, N.J., 1984); Nathan O. Hatch, *The Democratisation of American Christianity* (New Haven, 1989).

[28] Charles Francis Adams (ed.), *Familiar Letters of John Adams and His Wife Abigail Adams, during the Revolution* (Boston, 1875), p. 402.

[29] Ambrose Serle to Earl of Dartmouth, 25 July 1776, in Stevens (ed.), *Facsimiles*, vol. 24, no. 2040.

Index

Abercromby, James, MP, 93
Abernethy, John, Dissenter, 323, 324n
Achaean league, 90, 134
Acts of Parliament: 'Poyning's law' (1495),
74; Appeals (1533), 78, 157, 172–3;
Supremacy (1534), 67, 173; Union
(1536, 1543), 69; Sacrament (1547), 177;
Supremacy (1558), 73, 177; Uniformity
(1558), 73, 177–8; Assurance (5 Eliz. I,
c. 1, 1562), 176–7; Obedience (23 Eliz.
I, c. 1, 1581), 178; Recusants (1605),
178; Treason (17 Car. II, c. 2, 1666),
176; Conventicles (1671), 178;
Corporation (1661) and Test (1673), 92,
144, 160, 165–6, 178, 201, 334;
Uniformity (1662), 142, 153, 191, 226,
308, 323; Supremacy (Scots) (1669),
232; Heresy (1678), 177; 'Bill' of Rights
(1689), 1, 94, 97; Toleration (1689), 6,
84, 153, 160, 162–3, 169, 176, 178, 319,
323–4, 326, 332, 352, 353; Navigation
(1696), 250; Blasphemy (1698), 176–7,
179, 324; Regency (1707), 118;
Declaratory (1720), 74, 87; Colonial
Naturalisation (1740), 53; Heritable
Jurisdictions (1747), 72; Jewish
Naturalisation (1753), 283; Sugar
(1764), 98; Stamp (1765), 95–8, 103,
116–7, 168, 261, 266, 277, 298, 327–8,
356, 360, 365, 366–8, 376; Declaratory
(1766), 7, 93, 169, 356; Quebec (1774),
261, 273; Coercive (1774), 96; Boston
Port (1774), 269, 371; Catholic Relief
(1778), 285; Renunciation (1783), 74;
Defamation (1787), 170; Trinity (1813),
179; Catholic Emancipation (1829), 92,
144, 201; Ecclesiastical Courts (1843),
175; Aliens (1844), 53

Adams, John, and law, 12, 16n, 100, 109,
170, 281; and religion, 27, 30, 37–8, 273,
304, 329, 337, 369–71, 376; *Dissertation on
the Canon and Feudal Law*, 108, 167–9;
and revolution, 336–7, 391
Adams, Samuel, 105, 118, 371, 376
Addison, Judge, 388
Aird's Moss, battle of (1680), 230
Alamance, battle of (1771), 266, 269
Alberoni, Cardinal, 27n
Alfred, King, 18
Alison, Francis, Presbyterian minister, 33,
123, 357, 361
allegiance, 12, 49–62, 103, 105, 146, 164,
191, 304–5, 341, 357
Allen, Ethan, Deist, 244, 258n, 280
Allen, John, Baptist minister, 380
Allen, Robert, atheist, 290
Allestree, Rev. Richard, 34
Almon, John, publisher, 327
Amphyctionic Council, 133–4
ancien regime, in Britain, 23n, 141,
142n
ancient constitution, 16–17, 20, 56, 81–2,
112, 124n, 233, 276–7
Andrews, Jedediah, Presbyterian minister,
355n
Andros, Sir Edmund, governor, 7, 241,
245–6
Angell, John, 319, 354n
Anglicanism, see Church of England
Anglo-Saxons, 17–18, 43n, 108, 138
Anne, Queen, 32
Anson, Sir William, jurist, 63
anti-Catholicism, 19, 28, 32–3, 50–1, 82,
91, 103, 108, 118, 120, 129, 131, 136,
139, 147, 168, 181, 211–14, 224, 229,
234–5, 237–52, 254–6, 262, 263n, 264,

270, 272–3, 275, 282, 285, 287–9, 308, 328, 331, 344, 360, 365, 377
anticlericalism, 16, 19, 26–7, 180, 190–203, 342, 347
Antifederalists, 128, 130, 134, 136–7, 139n, 280
Anti-Jacobin, 334–5, 337
Apostles' Creed, 347, 350
Apollinaris, bishop, 350n
Apthorpe, Rev. East, 306
arbitrary power, 19, 24, 54, 64, 75, 78, 81, 86n, 99, 115, 224, 233, 239, 244, 247–8, 272–3, 275, 282, 304, 338, 360, 386
Argyll, Archibald Campbell, 9th earl of, and rebellion (1685), 230, 235, 237
Arians, Arianism, 28n, 32, 37–9, 115–6, 124, 166–8, 198, 289–90, 304, 309, 313–6, 318, 320–8, 330–1, 333, 336–7, 343, 350–1, 354, 364, 366, 370, 375, 380n, 383
Aristotle, 92, 95
Arminianism, 55, 114, 115n, 149n, 151, 160, 199, 308–9, 318, 320, 321n, 324, 330, 352, 355, 364–5, 370, 373n, 375
Arnall, William, 172n
Arnold, Benedict, loyalist, 298
Arnold, Thomas, 145
Articles of Confederation (1778), 103, 126–7, 131
Ashworth, Caleb, Dissenting teacher, 342
Athanasian Creed, 38, 161, 314, 318–20, 322–3, 328, 330, 343, 350
Atterbury plot (1720–2), 256
Augustulus, emperor, 81
Austin, John, jurist, 86n, 91
Austrian succession, war of (1739–48), 311
Aylmer, John, bishop, 49, 67

Backus, Isaac, Baptist minister, 115n, 373, 375–8, 387
Bacon, Nathaniel, and Bacon's rebellion (1676), 95, 240n, 242–4, 353
Bailey, Jacob, Congregational minister, 211
Bailey, Nathan, dictionary writer, 54n
Baltimore, Charles Calvert, 3rd lord, 241, 249
Bangorian Controversy, 26, 315
Baptist College (Brown University), 378, 384n, 387
Baptists, 31, 57, 115n, 139n, 160, 162, 183, 191, 199, 204, 207–11, 213, 216, 227, 253, 263, 284, 307, 318, 321–2, 334, 338, 339n, 342, 345, 372–81, 386–7
Barbeyrac, Jean, jurist, 100, 112, 128
Barlow, Joel, Paineite, 387–8

Barlow, William, bishop, 69
Barrow, Rev. Isaac, 34
Bartlett, Josiah, 337
Beach, Rev. John, 151n, 255, 368
Beatty, Charles, Presbyterian missionary, 216
Beccaria-Bonesana, Cesare, marchese de, criminologist, 116n
Belcher, Jonathan, governor, 364
Bellarmine, Roberto, cardinal, 155, 224
Belsham, Thomas, Socinian, 37n, 329
Belsham, William, 152–3
Bennet, Rev. Thomas, 346
Benson, George, Arian, 324
Bentham, Jeremy, 90–2, 110, 126, 133–5, 139, 382
Bermuda, 244
Berkeley, Sir William, governor, 244n
Bernard, Francis, governor, 280, 334
Bever, Thomas, jurist, 3, 82, 84
Beveridge, William, bishop, 185, 377
Beza, Theodore, Calvinist, 112
Biddle, John, 308
Bird, Benjamin, 28n
Blackburne, archdeacon Francis, 327, 343, 365
Blackstone, Sir William, jurist, 2–3, 5–6, 11, 18n, 75, 83–93, 97–100, 102, 105, 109, 111, 115–7, 118n, 119, 121–5, 126–30, 135, 138–40, 172, 176–9, 280, 315, 360
Blair, Samuel, Dissenting minister, 120
Bland, Col. Richard, 93, 103, 344–5
Blount, Charles, Deist, 346
Bodin, Jean, jurist, 65, 77, 82, 92
Bolingbroke, Viscount, 17, 54, 60, 346, 369
Bonham's Case (1609), 100
Boston, Mass., 12–13, 26, 105, 118, 207, 210, 241, 280, 323, 365–71, 376, 380
Boston massacre (1770), 371–2
Bothwell Brig, battle of (1679), 150, 228–9, 237
Boucher, Rev. Jonathan, 9, 92, 334, 341
bourgeois radicalism, 145
Boyne, battle of the (1690), 32
Bracton, Henry, jurist, 3, 76–7, 138
Brehon law, 73
Bridgen, Edward, Socinian, 329
Bright, Timothy, abridger, 47–8
Britain's Remembrancer, 31–2, 56n
Brougham, Henry, 290
Brown, Simon, Dissenter, 324n
Bryce, Lord, historian, 2
Buchanan, George, 27n, 51
Bunyan, John, 209

Burgh, James, Presbyterian propagandist, 31–3, 56n, 119, 184, 329

Burke, Edmund, MP, 11, 84, 222, 278–9, 304

Burlamaqui, Jean Jacques, jurist, 95, 97, 100, 109–10, 113

Burn, Rev. Richard, ecclesiastical lawyer, 170, 172–3

Burnaby, Rev. Andrew, 306

Burnet, Gilbert, bishop, 185, 315

Bute, John Stuart, 3rd earl of, 297, 328

Butler, Joseph, bishop, 326

Butler, Michael, mutineer, 286–7

Butler, Thomas, manufacturer, 186

cahiers des doléances, 60

Calamy, Edmund, sr., Presbyterian minister, 51

Calamy, Edmund, jr., Presbyterian minister, 34, 160–1, 319, 326

Caldwell, David, Presbyterian minister, 266

Calvin, Jean, and Calvinism, 39, 44n, 48, 55, 96, 112–16, 149n, 154–5, 160, 199, 204–5, 224, 231, 250, 252, 263, 293, 308, 313, 318–21, 324, 329, 332–4, 352, 355, 364–5, 370, 375, 386

Calvin's Case (1608), 50–3, 55, 71

Cambridge University, 244, 314, 317

Cambuslang, religious revival at, 43n, 264

Camden, Charles Pratt, 1st earl of, 103

Cameron, Richard, Presbyterian minister, 229–30

Cameronians, 230–3, 265

Caner, Rev. Henry, 207, 211, 368–9

canon law, 11, 79, 82–3, 108, 167–80

capitalism, history of term, 144

Care, Henry, 27n

Cargill, Donald, Presbyterian minister, 230

Carleton, Guy, general, 297

Cartwright, Major John, Deist, 124–5

Cary, Thomas, rebel (1709–11), 241

Cashel, Co. Tipperary, 289

Cato's Letters, 27, 116n

Caulfield, Dr., bishop of Wexford, 288

Cavendish, Lord Frederick, general, 296

Chalmers, George, 89

Chambers, Sir Robert, jurist, 89n, 110

Chandler, Samuel, Presbyterian minister, 320, 323–4

Chandler, Rev. Thomas Bradbury, 34, 216, 361n

Chandler, William, Quaker, 28n

Charles I, King, 56, 352; and America, 10, 225, 372; and constitution, 78n, 245–6; and Scotland, 71, 265

Charles II, King, 56, 227, 236; and Scotland, 71, 228–9, 265

Charles Edward Stuart (1720–88), Prince of Wales, King Charles III in the Stuart succession from 1766: restoration feared (1774), 9; cause of (1764), 118; (1776), 377; invasion attempt (1744), 256; rebellion of 1745, 256; Elibank plot, 257

Charles V, emperor, 67

Chartism, 43, 221

Chatham, John Pitt, 2nd earl of, 297

Chatham, William Pitt, 1st earl of, 123, 297, 315

Chauncy, Charles, Congregational minister, 153n, 323n, 369

Chillingworth, William, theologian, 120

Christology, 304, 308–10, 312–20, 330n, 347n, 353

Chubb, Thomas, Deist, 331

church courts, 11, 104, 106, 169–80

Church of England: in American colonies, 162–3, 203–17, 246, 255, 259, 261, 266, 293, 306, 338–51, 362–4, 377, 383, 386; Christology of, 313; Dissent, rivalry with, 4, 12, 30, 34, 88, 146, 149–53, 181–2, 190–203, 210, 213, 215, 266–7, 308, 354–5, 358–9, 368–9, 374; divisions, internal, 5, 142, 149, 339–41; ecclesiology, 308, 312; and national identity, 46–62; and political theory, 77–93, 146, 315; social teaching of, 28, 34–5, 141; and state formation, 62–75, 145, 153–67

Cicero, 95, 97, 116

civic humanism, *see* Commonwealthmen

civil law, see *see* Roman law

civil war, American Revolution as, 23, 132, 296–303

Claim of Right (Scots), 230–2

Clap, Thomas, 365n

Clarendon, Edward Hyde, 1st earl of, 56

Clarke, Rev. Samuel, Arian, 32, 37, 289–90, 321n, 325, 331, 346, 351, 355n, 365

class consciousness, absence of, 15

Clayton, John, Dissenting minister, 333n

Cleaver, William, bishop, 34n

Clinton, Sir Henry, 300

Coke, Sir Edward, jurist, 2–3, 12, 53, 80, 83, 86–7, 93, 97, 100, 104–5, 117, 129, 139, 173, 179

Cole, Nathan, Baptist, 373

Cole, Rev. William, 191n, 195, 198–9

Coleridge, Rev. John, 306

College of New Jersey (Princeton), 122, 264, 339, 355–7, 364

Colleton, John, governor, 241
Colman, Benjamin, Dissenting minister,
114
common law: and imperial relations, 2,
11–12, 27n, 88–93, 344; and natural law,
2–5, 18, 91–110; adapted in American
republic, 138–9; and Bentham, 18; and
state formation, 50–2, 62–75, 86–8, 131;
and political theory, 79–93; and canon
law, 171–80
Common Sense, 30, 38, 297, 329, 338, 341
Commonwealthmen, and Commonwealth
ideas: political idiom of, 20–33, 327; and
Deism, 38; and explanation of rebellion,
42, 221, 267, 271; term used, 213, 215,
328; ineffective, 282–3
comprehension, 321n, 326, 334
Compton, Henry, bishop, 232
Concord, Mass., 57, 371, 390
confederalism, see federalism
confessional state, 141
Congregationalism, Congregationalists, 26,
30, 34, 43, 57–8, 88, 95–6, 118–21, 124,
151, 162, 168, 183, 191, 200, 204, 210–
11, 216, 226, 249, 262–3, 266, 275, 277,
284, 307, 318, 323n, 325–6, 338, 339n,
352–3, 363–76, 378n, 379, 386
Congress, Continental, 8n, 11, 59, 109,
121, 126, 131, 134, 136, 270, 296, 302,
359–60, 362, 376
Congress, Stamp Act, 12, 95–6, 99
Connecticut, 33, 43, 280, 340, 379
conservative, -ism, history of term, 144–5
conspiracy theory, 9, 24, 39, 261–2, 283,
285, 328, 364–6
Constitution, American (1787), 60, 103,
125–40, 348, 388
contract theory, 122–3, 129, 234, 256, 268,
276, 315
Convocation(s), 8, 79, 159, 171–2, 316n
Conway, Henry Seymour, general, 296
Coode, Rev. John, rebel (1689), 240n, 241,
244, 248–9, 280
Cooke, Samuel, Dissenting minister, 114
Coombe, Rev. Thomas, 341
Cooper, Rev. Myles, 156, 306, 358
Cornbury, lord, Edward Hyde, later 3rd
earl of Clarendon, governor, 6
Cornbury plot (1731–5), 256
Cosin, John, bishop, 169, 226
Council in the Marches of Wales, 68
County Clare election (1828), 289
Covenanters, 234–5, 264–6, 330
covenantal religion, 44, 71, 149, 208, 213,
227–30, 233, 265, 275, 364, 388
Coxe, Tench, 138

Craighead, Alexander, Presbyterian
minister, 264–6
Crèvecoeur, J. Hector St. John de, 302
Cromwell, Oliver, 10, 56, 260–1, 265
Cromwell, Thomas, 67–8, 72, 74, 79, 99
Crosse, John, 323n
Cruden, Alexander, 144
Culpeper, John, rebel (1677–8), 241
Cumberland, William Augustus, duke of,
257
Cumberland, Richard, bishop, 26
Curwen, Samuel, émigré 11
custom, and constitutional law, 6, 18, 76–
7, 79–80, 94, 98, 116, 221
Cuthbertson, John, Presbyterian minister,
208–9

Danvers, Henry, and plot (1665), 227
Dartmouth, William Legge, 2nd earl of,
301
David, Rees, Dissenting minister, 329
Davidson, Robert, Presbyterian minister,
123, 361
Davies, Richard, bishop, 70
Davies, Samuel, Presbyterian minister,
114, 206, 355–6
Davyes, William, rebel (1676), 241
Dawson, Dr Benjamin, Socinian, 343–4
Deane, Silas, 33
Declaration of Independence (1776), 105,
121, 253, 269, 283–4, 296, 337, 339, 388
Declaration of Rights (English), 230–1
Deists, Deism, 15, 38, 123, 138, 167, 176,
179–80, 199–200, 284, 307, 309, 314,
320, 321n, 324, 328, 336, 338, 341, 344,
346, 355, 368, 369, 374, 383, 386
De Laune, Thomas, Dissenter, 368
Delaware, 132, 350
Democrats, political inclinations of, 186n
Denmark, 17
Dent, Abraham, 185n
de Retz, Cardinal, 65
Derham, Rev. William, 185
Dicey, Albert V., jurist, 63
Dickinson, John, 33, 58, 96–8, 101–2, 109,
121, 132, 137, 220
Dickinson, Jonathan, Dissenting minister,
113n, 115n
Dickinson, Moses, Dissenting minister, 114
Dincklage, lieutenant colonel von, 302–3
Disney, John, Socinian, 316, 329, 349, 351,
370
Disraeli, Benjamin, 145
Dissent, Dissenters: conflicts between
denominations of, 4, 162, 209–10, 215,
321–2, 362, 374–6, 378, 384; and

Dissent, Dissenters (*cont.*)
  Anglicanism, 4–5, 54, 63, 83, 142, 149–
    50, 160–7, 178, 203–17, 255, 275, 277,
    308, 319, 354–5, 359, 374; principles of,
    6, 18, 20, 25, 28, 30–3, 36, 39, 150, 194,
    208, 212, 259, 278, 297, 308–11, 317–35,
    337, 363, 371; and political discourse, 9,
    11, 42–3, 84, 99, 283; numbers, 13, 160,
    181–2, 191, 196, 203, 205, 211, 258, 274;
    and the Enlightenment, 15; not
    necessarily republicans, 37, 276, 338;
    and sovereignty, 111–25; transatlantic
    alliance, 277, 279, 283–4, 309, 312, 327–
    8, 331; social teaching, 151–2; and war,
    301–2; political mobilisation, 304, 307,
    310, 311n, 318, 322, 335, 337, 352–3,
    356, 359–67, 370–2, 374–5, 378–81
Dobbs, governor, 265
Dobel, Daniel, 185
Doctors Commons, 170, 174–5
Doddridge, Philip, Dissenter, 323, 326n
Domat, Jean, jurist, 100, 128
Dongan, Thomas, governor, 247
Drayton, William, 215
Drelincourt, Charles, 185
Drumclog, battle of (1679), 228
Drummond, Henry, 167
Duane, James, 109
Duchal, James, Dissenter, 323, 324n
Duché, Rev. Jacob, 341
Duffield, George, Presbyterian minister,
    123, 361
Dulany, Daniel, sr., 3
Dulany, Daniel, jr., 96
Dummer, Jeremiah, colonial agent, 33
Dundee, John Graham of Claverhouse,
    viscount, rebellion (1689), 230, 256
Dunkeld, siege of (1689), 230
Dunmore, lord, governor, 253, 346
Dwight, Timothy, 280
Dyer, George, 332

ecclesiastical polity, 6, 30, 84, 95–6, 120–1,
    141n, 142, 165, 168, 208, 224–8, 241n,
    259, 263, 285, 291, 304, 307–10, 312–3,
    316–9, 321n, 322, 324–5, 334–6, 342,
    348–58, 364, 368, 371, 373
Edict of Nantes (1598), 224, 254
Edinburgh Review, 290
Edmonds, Rev. John, 182
Edward VI, King, 172
Edwards, Rev. John, 181
Edwards, Jonathan, Congregational
    minister, 36, 40, 147–9, 263, 364–5
Edwards, Morgan, Baptist minister, 374–5
Effingham, Thomas Howard, 3rd earl of,
    297

Eldon, John Scott, 1st earl of, 74–5, 180
Elibank plot (1749–53), 256
Eliot, Andrew, Congregational minister,
    365–6
Elizabeth I, Queen, 48–9
Ellesmere, Thomas Egerton, 1st baron,
    lord chancellor, 50–1
Ely, Samuel, Congregational minister, 244,
    280
Emerson, William, Congregational
    minister, 372
Emlyn, Thomas, Socinian, 28n, 365n
empire, meaning of term, 79n, 157
Enlightenment, the, 14–20, 290
episcopacy: in colonies, 33–4, 215–6, 262,
    277–8, 328, 337, 340–6, 349–51, 363,
    365, 369, 371, 374; in Scotland, 71–2,
    227–33; in England, 312, 316, 327–8
Erskine May, Sir Thomas, 63
Escobar y Mendoza, Antonio, Jesuit, 155
Evans, Caleb, Baptist minister, 115, 329,
    333–4
exceptionalism, American, 13, 125, 138,
    303, 307, 382
Excise crisis (1733), 282
Exclusion crisis, 56n, 227, 233–6, 271–2

Faber, Rev. George Stanley, 55
Farmer, Hugh, Socinian, 329
Farmer's Letters, 97–102
Federalist, The, 134–6, 139
Federalists, 128, 130, 137, 140, 280
federalism, 62, 65–6, 72, 74, 87, 91–3, 100–
    3, 121–2, 126–40
Fendall, Josias, rebel (1660, 1680–1), 240–
    1
feudalism, feudal law, 16, 19, 68–9, 107–8,
    168
Fifth Monarchists, rebellions of, 225, 227,
    237
Filmer, Sir Robert, 10, 99, 118
Firmin, Giles, Socinian, 28n
Fisher, Edward, 264n
Fleming, Caleb, Socinian, 328
Fletcher, Andrew, 26
Fletcher, Rev. John, 306, 333–3
Forster, Rev. Nathaniel, 167n, 343n
Fortescue, Sir John, jurist, 3n, 67, 76
Foster, James, Dissenter, 323, 324n, 355n
Foster, Michael, judge, 128, 171
Fothergill, John, 327
Foxe, John, martyrologist, 47–8, 254, 287
France, 2, 14, 16–17; and nationalism, 20,
    46, 52, 60, 311; role in American
    Revolution, 22–3, 299; and Roman law,
    3n, 64–6; and Henry VIII, 70; and
    monarchy, 76–7, 81; English analogy,

193–4, 201; and revolution, 222, 287; and hereditary principle, 234; persecution of Protestants, 254–5; and invasion, 257; loyalists of 1776, 298; and Revolutionary war, 361
franchise, 97–9, 103, 235, 268, 271, 314, 338, 383
Francis I, King of France, 67
Franklin, Benjamin, Deist, 18, 58–9, 103–4, 111, 169, 259, 329, 337–8, 348, 355, 386
Frederick, Prince of Wales, 257
Frederick the Great, of Prussia, 255–6
Freewill Baptists, 263, 281
Fries, John, rebellion of (1799), 258, 279–81
Fry, John, 308
fundamental law, 18, 81, 87–8, 92, 94–6, 112–3, 115, 123, 125, 136, 231, 276
Furneaux, Philip, 84

Gabriel (Prosser)'s rebellion (1800), 253
Gadsden, Christopher, 33
Galloway, Joseph, loyalist, 29, 109, 111n, 133, 361
Garbett, Cyril, archbishop, 156
Garrett, John, Quaker, 261
General Convention of the Protestant Episcopal Church (1785), 349–51
Georg Ludwig (1660–1727), duke of Braunschweig-Lüneburg, Electoral Prince (from 1692), and Elector (from 1698) of Hanover, from 1714 also styled King George I of Great Britain, 17, 56, 189, 191, 250, 265, 272, 318
Georg August (1683–1760), duke of Braunschweig-Lüneberg, Elector of Hanover, from 1714 styled Prince of Wales and from 1727 King George II of Great Britain, 189, 250, 257, 265, 272, 282, 305, 318, 353, 355, 356
George William Frederick (1738–1820), from 1751 Prince of Wales and from 1760 King George III of Great Britain in the Hanoverian succession: and sovereignty, 6; and Pretender, 9, 212; and allegiance, 105, 113, 215, 296–7, 355, 377; public support, 186–7, 257, 260, 297, 318, 331, 333, 372, 374; and American Revolution, 253, 271, 281, 283
Georgia, 252, 299, 308
Germany, Germans, 17–18, 43n, 66, 84, 134, 208, 212, 253, 281, 299, 307, 391
Gerry, Elbridge, Antifederalist, 137
Gibbon, Edward, historian, 201
Gibson, Edmund, bishop, 17, 28n, 128n, 163–5, 170–2, 185, 306, 319n

Giles, William, 347
Gill, John, Baptist, 321, 375
Glanvil, Ranulf de, jurist, 3
God, is English, 49
Gooch, William, governor, 353
Gooch, Sir Thomas, bishop, 321
Gordon, Thomas, 26–7, 54, 366n
Gordon, William, Congregationalist minister, 124, 151
Goths, 16–17, 43n
Gough, Richard, 195n
Gove, Edward, rebel (1683), 241
Grafton, Augustus Henry Fitzroy, 3rd duke of, Socinian, 314–5, 331
Gray, Robert, colonel, 300
Great Awakening: term coined, 22; and intolerance, 26n; and American independence, 36; and recent historiography, 40–1; and challenge to ecclesiastical authority, 120–1, 262–3; and Jonathan Edwards, 148–9; and 'politeness', 209; and political implications, 250, 262–3, 277, 310, 336; and slave revolts, 252
Greene, Nathanael, general, 300
Green Mountain Boys (1770s), 258
Grenville, George, MP, 98, 261–2, 328
Gridley, Jeremiah, Boston lawyer, 12
Griffith, Rev. David, 123
Grotius, Hugo, jurist, 84, 95, 97, 100, 110, 113
Grove, Henry, Dissenter, 323
Gunpowder Plot (1605), 1, 32, 238
Gwatkin, Rev. Thomas, 342–6

Hale, Sir Matthew, LCJ, 2, 127–8, 173, 179
Hall, Robert, Baptist minister, 379
Hallet, Joseph, Dissenter, 323
Hamilton, Alexander, 102, 108n, 110, 131, 133, 341
Hamilton, Andrew, governor, 241
Hampden, John, MP, 219
Hancock, John, 33
Hanover, electorate of, 50, 104
Hanover, house of, 1, 44, 85, 166, 264, 319, 334, 352–3, 359, 361, 363
Harding, Thomas, Catholic convert, 50
Hardwicke, Philip Yorke, 1st earl of, 172
Harrington, James, 21, 26, 117, 364; for 'neo-Harringtonians', see Commonwealthmen
Harvard University, 364–5
Harwood, Edward, Socinian, 314, 319n
Hawley, Joseph, 280
Heineccius, Johann Gottlieb, jurist, 100, 128

Heinrichs, Johann, captain, 362
Hemphill, Samuel, Presbyterian minister, 355
Henley, Rev. Samuel, 342–6
Henri IV, King of France, 224
Henry II, King, 73, 87
Henry VI, King, 97, 103
Henry VIII, King, 67, 70, 72–3, 79–80
Henry, Mathew, Dissenter, 323
Henry, Patrick, 25, 59
Herring, Thomas, archbishop, 182, 186, 321
Hervey, James, 185, 206
Hervey, John, baron, 282
heterodoxy, see Arianism, Deism, Socinianism
Heylyn, Rev. Peter, 352
Hickes, Rev. George, Nonjuror, 344
Hiley, Rev. Haviland, 182
Hillsborough, Wills Hill, 2nd viscount, 374
Hinchliffe, John, bishop, 332
Hoadly, Benjamin, bishop, 27, 31, 34, 97, 161, 171, 196–7, 315, 345–6, 349, 366
Hobbes, Thomas, 80–1, 83n, 86n, 90n, 91, 95
Holland, Rev. William, 187, 189, 195, 198, 202
Holland House, 290
Hollis, Thomas, propagandist, 25, 168n, 318n, 327–9, 365
Hollis, Thomas Brand, Socinian, 329, 365
Holt, Sir John, LCJ, 173
Holy Roman Empire, 65–6, 90, 103, 135, 265
Hooker, Rev. Richard, 34, 69, 79–80, 85, 152, 157–61, 164, 175–6
Hopkins, Stephen, governor, 10, 337
Horne, George, bishop, 166n, 188, 306
Horneck, Anthony, 185
Horrocks, Rev. James, 342
Horsley, Samuel, bishop, 146, 165, 321n
Hotman, François, 17, 97
Huguenots, 112, 208, 212, 224, 253, 307, 362
Hunt, Rev. Thomas, 182
Hunter, Henry, Dissenting minister, 333
Huntington, Joseph, Dissenting minister, 114
Hurd, Richard, bishop, 306
Husband, Hermon, Regulator, 31, 267–8
Hutcheson, Francis, 290
Hutchinson, Thomas, governor, 53n, 90, 98, 105–8, 280, 334, 367

Independent Whig, The, 26–7, 273, 366n
Independents, *see* Congregationalists

individualism, 12, 99, 188–90, 193–4, 259, 384; history of term, 144
Industrial Revolution, absence of concept of, 14; history of term, 144
industry, history of term, 144
Inglis, Rev. Charles, 9, 341, 357–9, 361
Ireland, 28, 30, 48, 52n, 56, 66, 69–70, 72–5, 86–9, 104–5, 141, 154, 220, 255, 258, 269, 285–7, 298, 352, 354
Irish rebellion (1798), 288–9, 292
itinerancy, 208–10, 215

Jacobites, Jacobitism: in America, 10, 28–9, 212, 247, 255–6, 344, 356, 366, 368n; in Britain, 32, 56, 85, 87, 128, 139n, 156, 172, 230, 232, 255–6, 282, 284n, 289, 294, 328, 331
Jacobins, Jacobinism, 223, 256–7, 284n, 286–8
Jamaica, 88, 251
James I, King, 49–50, 70, 352
James II, King, 7, 71, 74, 112, 155, 160, 169, 227, 230–1, 239–41, 245–9, 269, 360, 372, 377
James Francis Edward Stuart (1688–1766), from 1701 King James III in the Stuart succession: attachment to (1762), 128; invasion of 1708, 256; restoration feared (1766), 368n
Jarratt, Rev. Devereux, 206–7, 263
Jay, John, 109, 134
Jebb, John, Socinian, 314, 316, 329, 342, 345
Jefferson, Thomas, Deist, xii, 33, 108, 121, 131, 138–9, 163, 170, 180, 270, 274, 279, 337–8, 341, 346–8, 350, 369, 374, 379, 382
Jesuits, 9, 214, 248n, 371
Jewel, John, bishop, 50n, 79n
Johnson, Rev. John, 170n
Johnson, Sir John, 298
Johnson, Marmaduke, printer, 26
Johnson, Samuel, 10
Johnson, Samuel, 115n
Johnston, Rev. Gideon, Commissary, 35, 162, 212–4, 260–1
Jones, Rev. William, 189, 202
Jones, Rev. William, of Nayland, 357
Jortin, John, historian, 317
Josselin, Rev. Ralph, 192n
Julius Caesar, 81
Justinian, Emperor, 3, 64, 75–7, 82, 100, 119, 138, 172

Kant, Immanuel, 38
Keith, Rev. George, 154, 216

Ken, Thomas, bishop, 28n
Keppel, Augustus, viscount, admiral, 296
Keteltas, Abraham, Dissenting minister, 115n
Kettlewell, John, nonjuror, 155n
Killiecrankie, battle of (1689), 230
King in Council, 2, 104; in Parliament, 4–5, 78–9, 83, 86, 89, 92–3, 99, 115, 117–8, 124, 169
King, John, bishop, 77
King, Peter, lord, 33, 312
King, Rufus, 132
Kingswood, religious revival at, 43n
Kippis, Andrew, Socinian, 277n, 329
Knox, John, Calvinist, 51, 155
Knox, William, undersecretary, 6–7, 205

Lafayette, marquis de, 38n
Landon, John, 323n
Lardner, Nathaniel, Arian, 37n, 323–4, 327
Laud, William, archbishop, and Laudianism, 71, 172, 272, 365
Lauderdale, John Maitland, 1st duke of, 228
Lavington, George, bishop, 28n, 147, 149
Law, Edmund, bishop, 26, 342–3, 349
Law, Rev. William, Nonjuror, 34
Lawrence, Richard, rebel, 243
Le Bret, Cardin, jurist, 65, 224
Lee, Ann, 387n
Lee, Arthur, 10, 97, 104, 107, 109, 219
Lee, Rowland, bishop, 68
Leechman, William, Arian, 290
Leeds, 188
Leisler, Jacob, rebel (1689), 241, 244, 246–8, 280
Le Jau, Rev. Francis, 212
Leland, John, Dissenter, 323
Leslie, Rev. Charles, Nonjuror, 28n, 344
L'Estrange, Sir Roger, 234n
Levellers, 227
Lexington, battle of, 57, 376, 378
liberal, -ism, history of term, 143
Limerick, treaty of, 298
Lindsey, Theophilus, Socinian, 37n, 316, 329
Lincoln, *Report from the Clergy*, 149, 182–3
Liturgy, Anglican, 349–50
Livingston, William, 109
Locke, John, Arian, 20, 21n, 32, 41, 92, 97, 113, 117, 133, 159, 305, 348n; American interest in, 25–6, 45; and natural allegiance, 54n; and Providence, 55–6; and nationalism, 57; denied by Blackstone, 86, 129; and natural law, 95,

110, 129; and liberalism, 145; and revolution, 224, 226, 268; and democracy, 235; theology of 236, 314
Louis XI, King of France, 17
Louis XIV, King of France, 17, 224
Lowman, Moses, Dissenter, 323, 324n, 327
loyalists (American), 9, 36, 128, 156, 296, 298–303, 306, 340–1, 379, 382
Lucretius, 391
Ludlow, Edmund, 26
Luther, Martin, and Lutheranism, 206, 250, 320
luxury, 24, 32, 184n, 209–10, 274, 372

MacGill, William, Arian, 290
MacGowan, John, 29n
Machiavelli, 19n, 220
Macintosh, Sir James, historian, 290
Macpherson, James, 28n
Madison, James, 31, 126, 132, 134, 138, 210, 337, 339, 373
Magna Carta, 1, 18, 83, 94, 97, 108, 124n, 360, 388
Maine, present state (1820), 211, 240, 280
Mainwaring, Roger, bishop, 10, 118
Maitland, Frederic William, historian, 63
Makemie, Francis, Presbyterian missionary, 6
Manchester, 185n
manifest destiny, American, 61n
Manning, James, Baptist, 378, 380, 387
Mansfield, William Murray, 1st earl of, 139
Mar, John Erskine, 6th earl of, 72
Mariana, Juan de, Jesuit, 155
Markham, William, archbishop, 306, 315
Martin, Josiah, governor, 269
Martin, Luther, 133
Martin, John, Dissenting minister, 333
Marvell, Andrew, 26
Mary, Queen, 47, 50n, 238
Maryland, 133, 240–1, 244–5, 248–9, 251, 353
Mason, George, 130, 337
Mason, Rev. John, 348
Massachusetts, 53, 89, 98, 105–8, 119, 121, 124, 132, 211, 241, 244–5, 249, 280, 334, 371, 379
material world: and colonial consciousness, 13, 44, 61–2, 151, 203, 213, 291, 293n; and British consciousness, 61–2, 141–2, 183–90, 282, 289, 291, 304, 317–8, 327
Mather, Cotton, Congregational minister, 246
Mather, Increase, Congregational minister, 246, 273n

Mather, Moses, Dissenting minister, 115n
Mathew, Thomas, 244n
Matthews v. Burdett (1701), 83
Mauduit, Israel, 323, 333
Maury, Rev. James, 163
Mayhew, Jonathan, Arian,
   Congregationalist minister, 9, 31, 116,
   168–9, 327, 336, 364–70
Mecklenburg county, North Carolina, and
   its Declaration of Independence, 264–5,
   269–71
Methodists, 139n, 147, 149, 151, 183, 198,
   252–3, 263, 312, 386
Micklejohn, Rev. George, 268
Middle Octorara, Pennsylvania, 265
Middleton, Conyers, Deist, 346
Middleton v. Croft (1736), 83, 172
Milborne, Jacob, rebel (1689), 247
militia, 299–303
Mill, James, 290
millenarianism (millennialism), 35, 39–41,
   56, 130, 220, 225, 227, 233, 238, 250,
   253, 267–8, 274–7, 280, 284, 288, 311,
   336, 383, 390
Miller, John, 144
Milton, John, 21, 25–6
Moir, John, 190n
Molesworth, Robert, viscount, 17, 25–6
Molyneux, William, 26
Monmouth, James Scott, 1st duke of, and
   rebellion (1685), 220, 228, 234, 236–8,
   244–5
Montesquieu, Charles de Secondat, baron,
   17, 78, 83, 95, 110, 116n, 131, 385
Moody, Samuel, Congregationalist, 364n
Moore, Clement Clarke, 348n
Morgan, Thomas, Deist, 370
Morgan, William, 69
Morris, Daniel, 261
Morris, Gouverneur, 131
Morse, Jedediah, historian, 371n
Morton, Rev. Andrew, 266
Mosheim, Johann Lorenz von, historian,
   317
Moyle, Walter, 25–6
Murray, James, Dissenting minister, 31,
   124–5, 267, 283, 329–31
Murray, John, itinerant Dissenter, 377n,
   387

nationalism, 19–20, 23, 40n, 44n, 46–62,
   67n, 250, 280, 289, 311, 388–91
nationality law, 2, 12, 46–62
natural law, natural rights, 2–6, 12, 18, 39,
   44n, 45, 51n, 61, 76–7, 80, 83–6, 89, 91–
   110, 384; and American Republic, 129–
   40; and Anglican doctrine, 158–9, 165,

175–6; and Dissent, 111–25, 190; and
   Parliament, 231; in America, 276
Neal, Daniel, Dissenter, 162
Neau, Elias, 254n
Nedham, Marchamont, 26
Nelson, Robert, Nonjuror, 34, 185
The Netherlands, 50
Neville, Henry, 25–6
Neville, Sylas, 328
Newcastle, Thomas Pelham Holles, 1st
   duke of, 85
Newcastle upon Tyne, 330
New England, 33, 40, 43–5, 47, 58–9, 67,
   95–6, 114–5, 151, 170, 205, 210, 212,
   216, 225, 240, 245, 253, 255, 259, 262–4,
   272–3, 277, 298n, 299, 307, 339 350,
   353, 363–72, 374–80, 383, 386
New Hampshire, 211, 241, 244, 280, 379
New Jersey, 133, 241–2, 251, 277, 299,
   302, 313, 340, 350, 364
New Lights, 36, 114, 120, 151–2, 198–9,
   207, 209–10, 259, 262–4, 266, 268, 288,
   372, 375
New Londonderry, 120
Newton, Rev. Benjamin, 189, 195, 200
Newton, Sir Isaac, Arian, xii, 32
New York, 6, 10, 13, 59, 97, 101, 131, 134,
   241, 244–7, 249, 251–3, 262, 277, 298–9,
   340–1, 348, 350, 356, 358–9, 361, 368,
   391
Nicene Creed, 350
Nichols, John, 314
Niles, Hezekiah, historian, 304
Nonjurors, 156, 158, 191, 226, 233, 256,
   309n, 344, 349
Nore mutinies (1797), 286–7
Norman Yoke, theory of, 17–18
North, Frederick, lord, MP, 271, 305, 318,
   360
North Carolina, 31, 123, 207, 241–2, 258,
   265–71, 299, 353, 356, 360–1
Nottingham, 197
Nowell, Rev. Thomas, 306n

O'Connell, Daniel, 74, 289
Old Lights, 36, 120, 210, 262, 263n, 372
Ollyffe, Rev. John, 160–1
Otis, James, lawyer, 88–9, 93, 100, 116–8,
   368
Overall, John, bishop, 158–60
Owen, Charles, 28n, 254, 320

Page, John, of Rosewell, 345, 350
Paine, Robert Treat, 127, 337, 376
Paine, Tom, Deist, 15, 30, 38, 244, 297,
   329, 336, 338, 341, 347, 386–7, 389
Paley, William, archdeacon, 84, 315

Palmer, Samuel, Congregationalist
minister, 37n, 162, 166n, 174n, 194, 329,
331–2
Pargeter, Rev. Robert, 181
Paris, 64, 279, 284, 348
Parkman, Ebenezer, Congregationalist
minister, 210–11
Parliament (Westminster), 79, 83, 87, 94,
99, 103–5, 111, 127, 158, 231
Parsons, Jonathan, Presbyterian minister,
205
Parsons, Talcott, 384n
Parsons' Cause, 163, 342
passive obedience, 9, 27, 79, 124, 155–6,
188–9
Pate, John, rebel (1676), 241
Paterson, William, 133
Patrick, Simon, bishop, 33
patriotism, term coined, 54–5; 60
Paxton Boys (1764), 258–60
Pearson, John, bishop, 33, 369
Peel, Sir Robert, 145
Pendleton, Edmund, 138
Pennamites (1770–1), 258
Pennsylvania, 59, 96, 121, 131–2, 208–10,
212, 216, 258–61, 267, 281, 293, 299,
350, 353, 360, 363, 373, 383, 388
Penry, John, Puritan, 51
Pentland Rising (1666), 228
Peter, Hugh, Puritan, 225
Peterhouse, Cambridge, 343, 348
Peters, L.L., Dissenting minister, 333
Petyt, George, 27n
Philadelphia, 26, 31–2, 109, 123, 128, 211,
258, 259–61, 341, 347, 349, 353–5, 356,
360, 373, 374–5
Pickard, Edward, Dissenting minister,
333n
Philadelphia Convention (1787), 8, 131–4
Pierce, Thomas, Dissenter, 323
Pilmore, Joseph, Methodist itinerant, 10,
263
Pinckney, Charles, 132
Player, Sir Thomas, MP, 235
Political Disquisitions, 31–3
Polwhele, Rev. Richard, 149, 191
Pontiac's war (1763), 259
popery, see anti-Catholicism
Popish Plot (1678), 227, 238, 245, 252
Porter, Rev. Thomas, 184
Potter, John, archbishop, 211, 306
Powers, Peter, Dissenting minister, 113n–
114
Pownall, Thomas, 44–5, 102–3, 107
Potter, John, archbishop, 33–4
Presbyterians, Presbyterianism, 6, 30–33,
57, 71, 73, 96, 109, 114, 119–23, 129,

142, 150–2, 161–2, 191, 198, 200, 204,
206, 208–16, 226–33, 237, 255, 259–64,
266, 268, 270, 275, 281–2, 284–8, 293,
307, 312, 318, 321, 325–7, 334, 338,
339n, 343, 349, 351–64, 374, 378n, 386,
389–90
Pretender, *see* Charles Edward Stuart,
James Francis Edward Stuart
Price, Rev. Joseph, 313–4
Price, Richard, Arian, 54, 124, 184, 274,
279, 318n, 329, 335, 337–8
Priestley, Joseph, Socinian, 45, 84, 133,
139, 166n, 277n, 283, 329, 332–5, 346,
347n
Prince, Thomas, Dissenting minister, 115,
255
primogeniture, 138
Prisot, judge, 179n, 180n
private judgement, right of, 5, 123, 190,
194, 262, 267, 314, 326, 332, 344
Protestant Dissenting Deputies, 284
Providence, 31, 38–40, 48–9, 52, 55–6, 66–
7, 89, 97, 117, 119, 144, 158, 187, 238,
252, 275, 302, 311, 336, 347, 389–91
Provoost, Samuel, bishop, 341, 348–9, 351
Pufendorf, Baron, jurist, 6, 83n, 84, 95–6,
97, 100, 110, 112–3, 116n, 128
Pym, John, MP, 219

Quakers, 53n, 58, 183, 191, 200, 204, 208,
210–11, 216, 226, 230, 242, 260–1, 293,
307, 318, 339n, 353, 383
Quarterly Review, 144
Quincey, Thomas de, 314–5

radical, -ism, history of term, 143, 304, 335
Ramsay, Allan, artist, 89–90
Ramsay, David, historian, 59, 362
Randolph, Edmund, 132, 341
Randolph, John, bishop, 149
Raymond, Robert, LCJ, 179
Raynolds, Peter, Dissenting minister, 114
rebellion of 1715, 31, 87, 254
rebellion of 1745, 31, 72, 87, 240, 254
Redesdale, John Freeman-Mitford, 1st
baron, 74–5
Reformation, 5, 18–19, 66–7, 69–70, 108,
168, 171, 174, 178, 223, 308
Regulator movement, 31, 215, 258, 266–9,
280, 356–7
republicanism, 21, 44, 47, 52–3, 63–4, 125–
40, 219, 256, 277–8, 333, 341, 352, 358,
362, 385
resistance theory: colonial, 41, 224, 268,
274, 278–9, 291, 336–7, 365–6; Calvinist,
44n, 154, 224n; Locke's, 236, 268;
Roman law, 78; Roman Catholic, 154;

resistance theory (*cont.*)
Scots, 27; Whig, 239, 291
Restoration (1660), 14, 17, 56, 74, 78, 80–1, 99, 107, 142, 154, 227, 294
revealed law, 3, 39, 83–4, 95, 176
Revolution of 1688–9, 5, 6, 17, 31, 95, 168, 219–20; 'principles of', 9, 18, 97, 100, 106, 118, 166, 249, 256, 305, 314, 316, 359; and ancient constitution, 18; undermined by Hale, 128; and Church, 155–6, 238; and Scotland, 230–3; in America, 241, 245–50, 265, 294
Rhode Island, 10, 204
Richmond, Rev. Leigh, 201–2
rights, of Englishmen, 1, 19, 40n, 94–6, 104, 112, 118, 219, 243, 248–9, 260, 360
riots: Gordon (1780), 285, 287, 297; 'bread or blood' (1816), 203; 'Captain Swing' (1830–1), 203, 221
Rippon, John, Baptist minister, 380
Rivers, David, Dissenting minister, 333n
Robe, James, 264n
Robertson, William, historian, 116n
Robinson, Robert, Baptist minister, 321–2, 324, 329, 332–3
Robinson, Rev. William, 340n
Robinson, William, Presbyterian minister, 206
Rodgers, John, Presbyterian minister, 387n
Roman law, 2–3, 11–12, 49, 52, 64–7, 71, 75–93, 103, 136, 172
Rose, Alexander, bishop, 232
Rotheram, Caleb, Dissenting teacher, 343
Rousseau, Jean-Jacques, 108
Rush, Benjamin, 33, 337
Russell, Lord William, 219
Russell, Lord John, Whig, 63
Rutherforth, Thomas, jurist, 113, 133
Rutherglen, rebellion (1679), 228
Rye House plot, 226, 237
Ryland, John, Baptist minister, 379

Sabellianism, 37, 320, 326n, 332–3
Sacheverell, Rev. Dr. Henry, 10, 283
St Bartholomew, massacre of, 112, 238, 252
St German, Christopher, lawyer, 79
Sallust, 116n
Salters' Hall conference (1719), 325–6
Sancroft, William, archbishop, 158–60, 272
Sanderson, Robert, bishop, 175
Sanquhar Declaration (1680), 229–31, 266
Schlatter, Michael, Swiss missionary, 13, 211
Schlözer, August Ludwig, professor, 362
Scotland, Scots, 30, 43, 48, 50, 52n, 56, 66,

70–2, 78n, 86–9, 104, 126, 208, 214, 220, 227–33, 253, 256, 260–1, 264–5, 269, 285, 289–90, 292, 294–5, 297–8, 307, 344, 349, 352–4, 357, 362
Scots Irish, 208, 212, 215, 253, 259, 261, 265, 267, 286, 288, 290, 292–3, 307, 353–4, 357, 362–3
Scougal, Henry, 28n
Seabury, Samuel, bishop, 9, 110, 341, 349–51
Secker, Thomas, archbishop, 181–2, 277, 326, 344
secularisation, 14–16, 39–40, 143, 223
Sellar, Abednego, Nonjuror, 156
Semple, Robert B., historian, 209, 374
separation of powers, 63, 78, 127, 351
Separatists, New England, 26, 210, 263, 372–3, 375
Serle, Ambrose, English administrator, 39, 203–4, 215–6, 301, 391
Settle, Elkanah, 234n
Seven Years' War (1756–63), 61, 95, 207, 211, 250, 255, 261, 264, 272, 294, 311
Shaftesbury, Anthony Ashley Cooper, 3rd earl of, 26, 54, 227–8, 235–7, 273, 331, 369
Shakers, 263, 281, 387
Sharp, Granville, 3, 6, 20, 37, 55, 119
Sharp, James, archbishop, 37, 185
Sharp, John, archbishop, 37, 185
Shays' rebellion (1786–7), 258, 279–80
Shelburne, William Petty, 2nd earl of, 277
Sheldon, Gilbert, archbishop, 160, 272
Shepard, Thomas, 365
Shepard, Samuel, Baptist minister, 379
Sherlock, Thomas, bishop, 28n, 164–5, 185, 306, 321, 358
Sherlock, William, dean, 156, 161, 185, 331, 346
Sherman, Roger, 109
Shipley, Jonathan, bishop, 315
Sibthorp, Rev. Robert, 118
Sidney, Algernon, 26, 92, 219, 226
Simancas, Eiclerus (Jacobus), 51
Simson, John, professor, 289–90, 331, 354n
Skinner, Rev. John, 189, 195, 199, 201–3
Slater, John, 33
slave rebellions, 251–3
Smith, Hezekiah, Baptist, 379
Smith, Robert, Dissenting minister, 114
Smith, Thomas, Congregational minister, 240
Smith, Rev. William (American), 341, 350n
Smith, Rev. William, 188
Smith, William, jr., historian, 101

socialist, -ism, history of term, 144
Society for Constitutional Information, 387
Society for the Propagation of the Gospel,
169, 173, 207, 211–2, 215–6, 265, 268,
313, 315, 339–41, 357, 361, 368–9
Socinians, Socinianism, 15, 28n, 37, 115,
166, 176, 236, 304, 309, 313–6, 320–1,
323, 326–30, 332–5, 337, 345, 350, 364,
368, 375, 380n, 386
Solemn League and Covenant (1643), 213,
227–8, 265–6, 270, 371
Somers, John, 1st baron, 27n, 133, 236
Somerset, 237
Sothel, Seth, governor, 241
South, Rev. Robert, 34, 154–5, 331, 346
South Carolina, 35, 132, 173, 212, 214–5,
242, 251, 253, 258, 260, 266, 299–300,
350, 353, 374
sovereignty: in law, 5–7, 236, 385; and
ancient constitution, 18; and statehood,
5, 44n, 50–1, 53, 62–75, 111; in political
theory, 75–93, 98–9; in imperial
relations, 100–10, 243, 294; and
American constitution, 125–40, 280, 385;
of God, 29, 117–9, 309, 352; and
heterodoxy, 315; and Dissent, 111–25,
274
Spanish invasion attempt (1719), 256
Spithead mutinies (1797), 286–7
Spotswood, governor, 252
Sprout, James, Presbyterian minister, 123,
361
Squire, Rev. Francis, 27n
States General, French, 60
Stevens, William, 188, 314n, 334
Stiles, Ezra, Congregational minister,
153n, 204, 364, 374, 376n, 378
Stillingfleet, Edward, bishop, 34, 147, 161,
312n
Stoddard, Solomon, 365
Stono rebellion (1739), 251
Suarez, Franciscus, Jesuit, 224
Swedish Plot (1717), 256
Sykes, Arthur Ashley, 370

Tacitus, 17, 81, 97
Tamworth Manifesto (1834), 145
Taylor, Ebenezer, Presbyterian, 260–1
Taylor, Jeremy, bishop, 34
Taylor, John, Dissenting tutor, 318–9, 323
Temple, Sir John, historian, 287
Temple, Sir William, 17
Tennent, Gilbert, Presbyterian minister,
268
Tennent, William, sr., Presbyterian
minister, 354–5

Tennent, William, jr., Presbyterian
minister, 115n, 215, 262, 374
Terrick, Robert, bishop, 342
Thackeray, Rev. Francis, 200–1
Thirty-Nine Articles, 123, 161, 200n, 270,
277, 313, 316, 319–20, 322–3, 330n, 332,
343, 346, 350
Thomas, John, bishop, 306
Thomas, David, Baptist minister, 373–4
Thompson, Benjamin, loyalist, 298
Thompson, Rev. Thomas, 313
Thornton, Matthew, 337
Tillotson, John, archbishop, 34, 120, 185,
349, 365
Tindal, Matthew, Deist, 346
Tocqueville, Alexis de, 60, 193
Toland, John, Deist, 318n, 346
Tong, Thomas, and Tong Plot (1662), 227
Tories, Toryism: in America, 10, 139, 299–
300, 341, 378; in England, 85, 87, 144–5,
188–9, 199, 239, 271–2, 305–6, 331
Toulmin, Joshua, 325, 332–3
Towers, Joseph, Socinian, 283, 329
Towgood, Micaiah, Congregational
minister, 28n, 206, 211, 313, 315–6,
322–3
Townshend duties, 97
Trenchard, John, MP, 235, 237
Trenchard, John, 25–7, 54, 366n
Trinity, doctrine of, 37–9, 45, 141, 161,
176, 308–9, 313, 320, 323–4, 332, 337,
343–7, 350, 353, 366, 373, 375, 379,
387
Trott, Nicholas, CJ, 173
Trout, Joab, Dissenting minister, 119
Trumbull, Benjamin, 26n
Trumbull, Benjamin, Dissenting minister,
114
Trumbull, John, 347
Trusler, Rev. John, 195–6
Tryon, William, governor, 207, 269
Tucker, Josiah, dean, 333
Tucker, St George, Deist, 138
Turner, Nat, rebellion of (1831), 253
Turner, Thomas, shopkeeper, 184–5
Tyler, Rev. John, 377n
typology, 146
Tyrrell, James, 26

Union with Ireland (1801), 63, 74, 88, 385
Unions with Scotland (1603, 1707), 8, 50,
63, 70–2, 87–9, 103, 107, 136, 233
Union with Wales (1536), 63, 67–70
Unitarian, *see* Socinian
United Irishmen, 286–8
Universalists, 263, 281, 387

Vane, Sir Henry, 225
Vattel, Emmerich de, jurist, 2, 100, 113, 133
Vaughan, Benjamin and William, Socinians, 329
Venn, Henry, Evangelical, 34
Venner, Colonel, 237
Venner, Thomas, Fifth Monarchist, 10, 225–6, 244, 292
Vermont, 280
Vesey, Denmark, rebellion of (1822), 253
Virgil, 97
Virginia, 31, 59, 66, 103, 114, 123, 132, 138, 151–2, 180–1, 206, 210, 213, 241–4, 251–3, 259, 263, 299, 307, 340–8, 350, 353, 355, 359, 373, 377–9, 383
Virginia, University of, 139
virtual representation, 79–80, 83n, 98–9, 103, 124, 333
Volney, C.F., Deist, 387
Volunteer movement, 285

Wade, John, 188n
Wake, William, archbishop, 185
Wakefield, Gilbert, Socinian, 15, 38, 315–7
Walder, James, 185
Wales, Welsh, 48, 52n, 66–70, 86–7, 278n
Walker, John, 357n
Wallin, Benjamin, Dissenting minister, 329
Wallis, John, 346
Walpole, Sir Robert, 21
war of religion: an aspect of 1776, 25, 33, 41, 45, 57, 139, 148, 204, 301–2, 307, 309–11, 336–9, 345, 357–9, 361–3, 372, 378–80, 390–1; an aspect of Irish rebellion of 1798, 288–9
Warburton, William, bishop, 152, 275, 312, 330n
Warren, Robert, 185
Washington, George, 32, 60, 121, 296, 299, 337, 357, 358–61, 378–81, 388–9
Waterland, Rev. Daniel, 37, 309n, 346
Watson, Richard, bishop, 188, 314–5
Watts, Isaac, Congregationalist minister, 37n, 323
Weber, Max, 384n
Webster, Alexander, 264n
Webster, Noah, dictionary writer, 52n, 143n
Welles, Noah, 151
Wellington, Arthur Wellesley, 1st duke of, 289
Wesley, Rev. Charles, 197–8
Wesley, Rev. John, 10, 206, 297, 309, 312, 333–4
Westminster Confession of Faith (1646), 270, 308–9, 320, 352, 356, 375n

Whately, Thomas, 98–9
Whiskey rebellion (1794), 258, 268, 279–82
Whiston, Rev. William, Arian, 325, 331
White, John, Congregationalist, 364n
White, Rev. John, 323n
White, William, bishop, 349, 350n
Whitefield, Rev. George, 28n, 43, 147n, 206, 210, 252, 262–3, 268, 308–9, 365, 372, 387n, 389
Whitney, Peter, Congregationalist minister, 9
Whole Duty of Man, 34, 150, 185
Wigglesworth, Edward, Dissenting minister, 114
Wilkes, John, Deist, 277, 283–4, 328n, 330, 380
Wilkinson, Jemima, 387n
William I, King, 17–18, 108
William of Orange, styled King William III from 1689, 17, 50, 56, 71, 74, 231–2, 239–40, 245, 249–50, 282, 353, 377
William and Mary, College of, 341–2, 350
Williams, David, Dissenting minister and Deist, 18–19
Williams, David, ecclesiastical lawyer, 172n
Williams, Elisha, Dissenting minister, 121
Williams, Rev. Peter, 167n, 200n
Williams, Roger, Baptist, 378
Williams, Solomon, Dissenting minister, 116n
Wilson, James, jurist, 33, 60, 82, 104–5, 108n, 109, 122n, 126–30, 133
Wilson, Woodrow, president, 388
Wilton, Samuel, Dissenting minister, 329
Wise, John, Congregationalist minister, 95–6, 241
Withers, John, 28n
Witherspoon, John, Presbyterian minister, 30, 115n, 122, 264, 357
Wodrow, Robert, Presbyterian historian, 228–30
Wolseley, Cardinal, 67
Wooddeson, Richard, jurist, 3n, 85
Woodforde, Rev. James, 189, 195
Woodmason, Rev. Charles, 209, 211–15
Woolston, Thomas, Deist, 28n, 179–80
Wythe, George, 337

Yale University, 26, 33, 364–5
York Minster, 201
Yorktown, symbolic significance of, 23, 375n

Zubley, John Joachim, 33, 101n